2-
2001

Storage Area Network Essentials

Storage Networking Essentials is both useful and readable, a rarity for a treatise on a subject as broad and dynamic as storage networking. Paul and Richard add just the right amount of historical perspective to show why the Storage and Networking communities were destined to meet. Going beyond succinct discussions of technology and implementation, the focus on compelling business motivations make this book an essential introduction approachable by a much wider audience than technical professionals.

Mike Dutch, Director–Strategic Business Development
TROIKA Networks, Inc.

Storage Area Network Essentials

A Complete Guide to Understanding and Implementing SANs

Richard Barker
Paul Massiglia

Wiley Computer Publishing

John Wiley & Sons, Inc.

NEW YORK • CHICHESTER • WEINHEIM • BRISBANE • SINGAPORE • TORONTO

Publisher: Robert Ipsen
Editor: Carol A. Long
Assistant Editor: Adaobi Obi
Managing Editor: Micheline Frederick
Text Design & Composition: North Market Street Graphics

Designations used by companies to distinguish their products are often claimed as trademarks. In all instances where John Wiley & Sons, Inc., is aware of a claim, the product names appear in initial capital or ALL CAPITAL LETTERS. Readers, however, should contact the appropriate companies for more complete information regarding trademarks and registration.

This book is printed on acid-free paper.♾

Published by John Wiley & Sons, Inc., New York

Published simultaneously in Canada.

This publication is designed to provide accurate and authoritative information in regard to the subject matter covered. It is sold with the understanding that the publisher is not engaged in professional services. If professional advice or other expert assistance is required, the services of a competent professional person should be sought.

Library of Congress Cataloging-in-Publication Data:

Barker, Richard, 1946–
    Storage area network essentials : a complete guide to understanding and
  implementing SANS / Richard Barker, Paul Massiglia.
      p. cm.
    ISBN 0-471-03445-2 (cloth : alk. paper)
    1. Computer networks.   2. Information storage and retrieval systems.
  3. Computer storage devices.   I. Massiglia, Paul.

  TK5105.5 .B347 2001
  004.6—dc21

                                                              2001044410

Printed in the United States of America.

10 9 8 7 6 5 4 3 2 1

The authors wish to dedicate this work to their respective families, always the unsung heroes of all-consuming projects like this. Not only did they support us throughout, but Barbara Barker spent countless hours in the early stages of the project editing Richard's prose and trying to make the manuscript *look* like a manuscript. For her part, Judy Massiglia spent hours driving across boundless tracts of the American southwest one summer so her husband could write while they rode. Now *that's* dedication.

In a very real sense, it wouldn't have happened without you both.

Thanks.

About the Authors

Richard Barker is a Senior Vice President of VERITAS Software Corporation, where he takes a particular interest in storage area networks and network-attached storage devices, especially as they relate to the deployment of highly scalable and usable storage solutions in the global enterprise market. He is a well-known author on CASE topics having written three best selling books in the Oracle CASE (computer-aided systems engineering) Method series. Before joining VERITAS, he served as Senior Vice President of the Consulting and Technical Services Division of OpenVision International, Ltd. and later as Senior Vice President, Product Division. From 1984 through 1994, he was a Senior Vice President of Oracle, responsible for worldwide development and marketing of Oracle's Development Methodology and CASE product set. Prior to that, he managed the development center for the IDMSX mainframe database product for International Computers Limited (ICL) and developed a distributed database system for the U.K. health service. Mr. Barker is also a former board member of the Storage Networking Industry Association (SNIA), the premiere international organization for development and promotion of storage networking technology.

Paul Massiglia is a Technical Director at VERITAS Software Corporation. He represents VERITAS at several standards and industry marketing associations, and writes and lectures extensively. His 21 years in the data storage industry segment have included marketing, engineering, and engineering management positions with the former Digital Equipment Corporation, Adaptec Inc., and Quantum Corporation.

Mr. Massiglia is the former Vice Chairman of the RAID Advisory Board and is currently a member of the Board of Directors of the SNIA.

CONTENTS

ACKNOWLEDGMENTS

M
y thanks to the board members of the Storage Networking Industry Association, who have contributed ideas and comments and have also reviewed early drafts.

My thanks also to Bill North, Guy Bunker, Paul Scammell, and Fred van den Bosch of VERITAS for their input and support.

Several suppliers of SAN software and hardware products offered assistance in the form of images to help illustrate this book. Their inclusion does not suggest that the particular supplier is any better or worse than any other—simply that the picture fit very well. We thank them all for their assistance.

–Richard Barker

I joined this project, which was originated by my manager and coauthor Richard Barker, in June 2000. Richard often jokes (at least, I *hope* he's joking) that I infiltrated his short project to produce a 100-page overview of SANs and turned it into a 500-page tome. Well, right he is about that! As I began to write, I discovered that there was a lot to be said about SANs and particularly about the systems and capabilities they enable that I felt hadn't been adequately covered in the existing literature. So the more we wrote, the more I felt there was to write. Even as we go to press, I can think of additional topics I'd like to cover, such as the role of a putative storage administrator, as well as more I'd like to say on several topics that are covered, like the emerging SAN technologies, whose descriptions are likely to be obsolete before this book reaches the shelves.

But I couldn't have come close to doing my part of this book alone. I wish to take this opportunity to thank the countless VERITAS colleagues and friends who contributed, sometimes unknowingly, to the constantly changing kaleidoscope through which I perceive SAN technology and the enterprise computer systems based on it. Some people who contributed in ways clearly above and beyond the call deserve to be singled out for special thanks:

To Andrea Westerinen, former Technical Director of the Storage Networking Industry Association, who provided the material for Appendix A on standards organizations and industry associations.

To the entire SNIA Technical Council for allowing me to participate in the discussions that led to Chapter 5 on storage network system architectures and particularly to David Black of EMC who kept my interpretation at least somewhat aligned with the

SNIA model. Also thanks to Bruce Naegel of VERITAS for several helpful suggestions on how to describe storage network architectures.

To Steve Macfarlane, Peter Grimmond, and Alan Randolph of the VERITAS Software Corporation consulting organization for providing real-world expertise on which Chapter 11 on SAN adoption processes is based. Particular thanks to Alan Randolph for his exhaustive review of the chapter and for enlightening me about the current state of SAN component interoperability as seen through the eyes of an implementer.

To Brett Cooper of the VERITAS SANPoint Control team for suggesting how to deal with the sprawling topic of SAN management and for reviewing and redirecting my interpretation of the topic.

I thank all these people for their contributions to this project and hasten to add that any remaining errors and omissions are to be laid solely at my door.

Last, I reiterate my thanks to my coauthor, Richard Barker, who managed to seam-lessly merge me into a going project and who remained unruffled each time he discov-ered that his words had been morphed into something else. Richard proves over and over again that less management is more.

—Paul Massiglia

*S*torage Networking Essentials: A Systems Approach, by Richard Barker and Paul Massiglia, is one of the most complete works addressing storage networking available today. Richard and Paul's thoroughly refreshing approach addresses storage networking from the data center. This is the first work I have had the opportunity to review that focuses on the complete solution from the enterprise application viewpoint. This unique approach to the highly complex topic of storage networking addresses the relevant topics required by systems administrators, implementers, and users of storage networking.

In order to understand my enthusiasm, I would like to take you on a short history of recent trends in storage networking.

> Storage networking has been maturing since the introduction of Fibre Channel in the early 1990s. At first, Fibre Channel interfaces to storage devices were basically server-attached storage (SAS)—a faster, fatter pipe that would allow storage to be located at a greater distance from the server, but it was still a point-to-point connection. All of the storage was dedicated to a single server, and the data was locked to the server. If there was a failure of the system, the data could not be recovered until the system was operational again.

> The introduction of Fibre Channel Arbitrated Loop (FCAL) for the first time allowed multiple servers and storage devices to exist on the same connection. FCAL marked the early demonstrations of storage networking, but it was not a very robust server connection. As a bus, it had shared bandwidth connection, it was cumbersome to implement, and it was wrought with early product failures and numerous compatibility issues. FCAL enjoyed limited deployment as a server to storage interconnection. Today it appears mainly as back-end disks to intelligent controller interconnect.

> The full, modern-day SAN potential was not realized until the introduction of the first cost-effective Fibre Channel switch, resulting in a switched fabric (FCSW). For the first time, multiple servers as well as data storage devices could exist on a single storage network. Multiple servers could now effectively share large storage devices, allowing open systems the advantage of options previously available only to data center configurations. For the first time data protection, high availability, disaster recovery, and data center wide backup are now available to open system environments.

Bringing us back to the present. Today, a physical interconnection has been defined. What does the future hold? Two discernable directions are emerging.

The first is the quest for a better interconnection scheme. Advancements continue in the Fibre Channel arena—technology that is faster, cheaper, smaller, and cooler, with more intelligence, will be emerging. New interconnection technologies also continue to emerge. SANs over IP and Infiniband are just two of these emerging technologies that will be competing with Fibre Channel in the future.

These new technologies will enable new functionality within the SAN. Interprocessor communications for data sharing and mobility, increased performance that allows more data to move more freely in the networks, longer and more reliable lines of communications, and much more.

The second development is the exciting new area of storage networking software, embracing the promise of technological breakthroughs. Storage networking has successfully demonstrated that a fundamental, interoperable interconnection infrastructure is alive and healthy, and is well on its way down the deployment path. We can now focus our attention on the real benefits of storage networking, software services, management, and automated policy-based operations. These areas will become the dominant focus of storage networking, propelling storage networking beyond mere interconnection strategies and into the realm of intelligent storage networking. . . . But I am getting ahead of myself.

Richard Barker and Paul Massiglia have assembled the essentials of the state of the art in storage networking with a focus on systems and software. Abundant high-quality illustrations, explanations, and definitions make this a must-read for anyone contemplating storage networking. "How This Book Is Organized" will give you some insight into the overall approach and recommendations for which section is best suited to your background.

I would also highly recommend this book for even the most battle-scarred veteran of storage networking.

It's in my library.

> **–Larry Krantz**
> **Chairman, Storage Networking Industry Association (www.snia.org)**

Welcome to *Storage Area Network Essentials: A Complete Guide to Understanding and Implementing SANs*, the book that cuts through jargon, simplifies storage networking concepts, and helps you determine how your organization's information services department can exploit this exciting new technology to meet evolving information processing needs.

Why is this book necessary? High-speed interconnect technology has made *storage area networks*[1] (SANs) based on both Fibre Channel and Gigabit Ethernet a reality. Every major storage and server vendor offers *SAN-enabled* products that use these advanced interconnects. We predict that essentially every enterprise will eventually employ storage networking, simply because it will be the only alternative. The question for information services departments is whether they will be able to manage SAN deployment or whether it will just happen to them. The successful information services administrators and executives will be those who understand storage networking and become its master.

Storage area networks enable new ways of moving, storing, and accessing data that promote more reliable and cost-effective enterprisewide information processing. SANs simplify data processing and management by off-loading many resource-hungry routine functions to intelligent devices and networks dedicated to and optimized for storage I/O traffic.

It's a safe bet that your competitors are considering storage networking if they are not already using it. As with most compelling new technologies, you either adapt and adopt or you're left in the competitive dust.

About This Book

This book is designed to help the reader understand storage area networks—the properties, benefits, architectural concepts, technologies, and, most important, the pitfalls of storage networking. You won't find detailed descriptions of Fibre Channel protocols or RAID subsystems; other books cover those and, in the authors' opinion, they aren't of primary interest to our intended audience. What you will find that we believe is unique is a description of how the new capabilities enabled by storage networking are implemented in products you can buy. How do they work? Which ones are easy?

---

[1] If it's *storage networking*, why isn't it just *storage networks?* Where did the *area* come from? We give our view of how storage area networks got their name in Chapter 1.

Which ones are hard? Which ones should be implemented early and which should be delayed until you have some SAN experience under your belt? These are the questions that we think other books on storage networking *don't* cover.

We've spent relatively little time on the emerging interconnects iSCSI, FCIP, iFCP, and Infiniband, which are undergoing development and standardization as this book goes to press. We have concentrated instead on things you can buy today, because those are the products that create the issues you will have to grapple with for the next couple of years.

Who Are You?

So who is our intended audience? In writing this book, we have made some assumptions about our readership. First and foremost, you are up-to-date enterprise information processing technology professionals and are familiar with distributed client/server computing. Your concerns are not so much with the details of any one technology as with acquiring an overall grasp of what technologies can do for you and what they're going to cost you in new skills and ways of doing things. In addition . . .

Networking

You use networks and understand how they have revolutionized enterprise information usage. Your daily professional life includes electronic mail and other client/server applications. The more adventurous among you may operate home networks to share resources among your personal computers. We've spent little time selling the benefits of interconnected enterprises.

Storage

Likewise, we anticipate that you are familiar with the principles of enterprise data storage and management. You know about formatting and partitioning hard disks. On a larger scale, you are familiar with *enterprise RAID subsystems* that provide storage for several servers and employ advanced techniques such as mirroring to improve data reliability and availability. You understand why backups and archives of important data are business necessities and you're familiar with techniques for creating and managing them and what a pain in the neck they are for the people who have to keep applications running.

Strategy

We assume that you are either undecided about introducing storage networking into your organization or that your organization has made the decision to introduce a storage network and *now what?* We believe you want to learn how a SAN can improve your organization's ability to exploit its information assets before you make significant capital and human investments in the technology.

And Last . . .

We believe that you're a professional who fashions the constantly changing mix of computer and network system products on the market into solutions to your organization's information handling problems. Our goal with this book is to make your job easier by giving you a comprehensive introduction to a radically new enterprise data processing paradigm that's sweeping the information services community: *storage networking*.

How This Book Is Organized

There are three parts to this book.

Part One: Understanding Storage Networking

In this part, we present an overview of the SAN concept. We describe what SANs are, how they evolved, what they do, and why enterprises should be using them. We expect this part to be of interest to executives and managers whose responsibilities include enterprise budgeting and planning. The SAN overview and benefits description contained in this part should give budgeters some ideas about the value of SANs to their organizations.

Part Two: The Parts: What's in a SAN

In this part, we drill down into the architectural, storage, networking, and software components that constitute SAN technology, with particular emphasis on the software components. Because other books have covered storage and networking concepts extensively, we've concentrated more on what we perceived to be the white space—architecture and software. We expect this part to be of interest to SAN-based application developers and managers. The technology descriptions should be of assistance when designing application topologies and data center operational procedures.

Part Three: SAN Implementation Strategies

In this part, we describe strategies for moving an enterprise from *server-centric* computing with local storage to a *storage-centric* information processing environment in which the central resource is universally accessible data. We have also included an extensive chapter (Chapter 12) on taming the beast—managing a storage network once you have one. We expect this part to be of interest to IT planners and technical strategists whose responsibilities include planning and leading SAN adoption for their organizations, as well as to IT administrators who will have to keep storage networks up, running, and servicing the organization's information needs.

Other Stuff

There's a lot of churning going on in the data storage and networking industries as we write this book. New interconnects, new management paradigms, and components with new functional splits are starting to appear. We've included an afterword in which we speculate a bit about the future and what it might bring in the way of changes to enterprise data processing and management.

The appendixes contain handy reference information, including a list of standards organizations and other industry groups that concern themselves with storage networking and a glossary of the terminology likely to be encountered during further study of storage networking.

Some Conventions: Terminology to Start With

We define terms that we believe may be unfamiliar to some readers in place as they are introduced. Our usage corresponds to the Storage Networking Industry Association's *Dictionary of Storage Networking Terminology*,[2] which is reproduced in part in Appendix 2. In addition, here are a few terms to get you started.

In this book, we mention *enterprises* frequently. We have chosen this as a blanket term to represent corporations, academic and research institutions, government organizations, and other institutions that use computers to support their business. The focus of this book is on larger enterprises that have multiple servers.

We use the term *data center* to refer to a room or set of adjacent or nearby rooms whose primary purpose is to house computing, networking, and storage equipment. Larger enterprises typically operate several data centers.

It is remarkable that in an industry as mature as data storage, consistent terminology for very fundamental concepts has not been widely adopted. Through its online dictionary, the Storage Networking Industry Association is attempting to standardize storage networking terminology. In general, we have tried to be consistent with the SNIA's usage. There a few key terms whose definitions will be especially helpful. These include:

- The term *disk drive* is used to represent the familiar rotating magnetic media random access nonvolatile data storage device.

- The term *disk* is used to denote either a disk drive (as above) or a virtual disk (sometimes called a logical unit number, or LUN) presented by a RAID controller. This book does not deal with removable disk media such as diskettes or other cartridge devices.

- The term *tape* is used to denote the linear magnetic recording media on which data is stored and accessed sequentially.

- The term *tape drive* is used to denote the transport mechanism in which tapes (as above) may be mounted in order to record and read data. In some cases, the term

[2] The Storage Networking Industry Association's Dictionary of Storage Networking Terminology can be found at www.snia.org/dictionary.

tape drive denotes both the mechanism and the media installed in it (e.g., *data is written to the tape drive . . .*).

- The term *media* is used to refer to objects on whose surfaces data can be permanently stored. Although the term *media* describes the circular platters on which a disk drive stores data, in practice, it is encountered more often when referring to storage objects like tapes and optical disks that can be separated from the mechanisms used to record data on them.

- The terms *library*, *media library*, and *robotic media library* are all used interchangeably to denote a machine that includes removable media storage, one or more tape drives, and a robotic mechanism to move individual tapes between storage and tape drives.

- The term *RAID subsystem* is used to denote a collection of one or more intelligent disk controllers that coordinate the operation of a common set of disk drives. Where the distinction is significant, the terms *embedded RAID controller* and *external RAID controller* are used to distinguish controllers mounted in server enclosures from those packaged separately from the servers they support. Large-scale RAID subsystems, which typically interconnect between dozens of disk drives and two or more computer access ports, are referred to as *enterprise RAID subsystems*.

- The term *storage device* is used to denote either a disk drive, a tape drive, a RAID subsystem, or a tape library containing both tape drives and a robotic media handler.

PART ONE

Understanding Storage Networking

In this part we present an overview of storage networking, defining what it is, what it does, how it evolved, and how an enterprise can benefit from a SAN-based information processing strategy.

CHAPTER 1

What Storage Networking Is and What It Can Mean to You

In this chapter we'll learn more about:

- What a storage area network is
- What properties a storage area network must have, should have, and may have
- The importance of software to storage area networks
- Why information services professionals should be interested in storage networking
- Information processing capabilities enabled by storage area networks
- Some quirks in the vocabulary of storage networking

What Is a Storage Area Network?

According to the Storage Networking Industry Association (and who should know better?):

A storage area network (SAN) is any high-performance network whose primary purpose is to enable storage devices to communicate with computer systems and with each other.

We think that the most interesting things about this definition are what it *doesn't* say:

- *It doesn't say that a SAN's only purpose is communication between computers and storage.* Many organizations operate perfectly viable SANs that carry occasional administrative and other application traffic.
- *It doesn't say that a SAN uses Fibre Channel or Ethernet or any other specific interconnect technology.* A growing number of network technologies have architectural and physical properties that make them suitable for use in SANs.

■ *It doesn't say what kind of storage devices are interconnected.* Disk and tape drives, RAID subsystems, robotic libraries, and file servers are all being used productively in SAN environments today. One of the exciting aspects of SAN technology is that it is encouraging the development of new kinds of storage devices that provide new benefits to users. Some of these will undoubtedly fail in the market, but those that succeed will make lasting improvements in the way digital information is stored and processed.

Let's dig a little deeper into this definition.

What Makes a SAN Different?

Anyone in the information technology field knows very well that computers are already connected to storage devices. If that's all a SAN does, what's new or different about it? The answer is a simple phrase that we'll keep coming back to over and over throughout this book:

Universal Storage Connectivity.

Computers are indeed connected to storage today, but are *all* of an installation's computers connected to *all* of its storage? That's the key point about SANs—they connect lots of computers to lots of storage devices, enabling the computers to negotiate device ownership among themselves and, ideally, to share data. If there is one defining characteristic of a SAN, it's universal connectivity of storage devices and computers.

To appreciate the value of universal storage connectivity, consider the conventional client/server computer system depicted in Figure 1.1.

From this business-as-usual picture of client/server computing, it's immediately apparent that by deploying multiple servers, an organization automatically creates unconnected *islands* of information. Each island is accessible by one computer but not the others. If Computer B needs to use data that was produced by Computer A, that data has to be copied to Computer B.

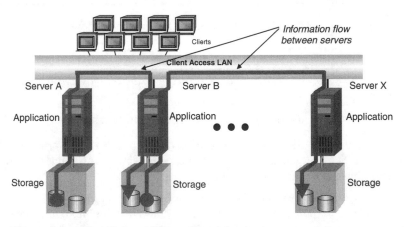

Figure 1.1   Client/server information islands.

There are several techniques for moving data between computers: backup, file transfer, and interprocess communication, to name a few. But the real issue is that the information services organization has to acquire and manage the extra resources required both to *copy* data from Computer A to Computer B and to *store* it at both sites. There's no business reason for this duplication of effort, other than that a computer needs data that was produced by another computer.

There's a more serious implication of an information processing strategy that relies on regular copying of data from computer to computer. Computers that receive data copies are often forced to work with data that is out of date simply because it's physically impossible to make copies in a timely fashion. Moreover, the extra operational complexity introduced by having to copy data between servers creates additional opportunity for costly errors.

Contrast this with the SAN-based distributed system architecture illustrated in Figure 1.2.

With a SAN, the concept of a single host computer that owns data or storage isn't meaningful. All of the servers in Figure 1.2 are physically connected to all of the storage devices. If Server F needs data that was produced by Server E, there's no need to copy it, because Server F can access the devices on which Server E stored the data. All that's required is a logical change of storage device ownership from Server E to Server F or, better yet, an agreement by Server E to stay out of the way while Server F is actively using the data.

Universal storage connectivity has some pretty powerful implications for information services departments:

■ There's no need to devise and schedule data transfers between pairs of servers.

■ There's no need to purchase and maintain extra storage for temporarily staging one server's data at another server.

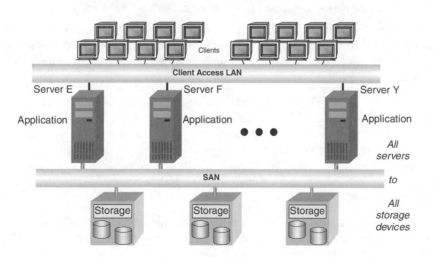

Figure 1.2   A SAN eliminates islands of information.

■ There's no need to worry about whether copies of data being used by two computers running different applications are synchronized (i.e., have exactly the same contents), *because the two computers are working from the same copy of data.*

Indeed, at this simplistic level, it's hard to see how any organization responsible for electronic information processing could *not* want a SAN. Let's drill still deeper and see how true that is.

What Makes a Good SAN?

The completely interconnected SAN architecture shown on the right side of Figure 1.2 is intuitively attractive, but if it's going to be the I/O backbone of an information services operation, it needs to have couple of qualities:

A SAN must be highly available. A single SAN connecting all computers to all storage puts a lot of enterprise information accessibility eggs into one basket. The SAN had better be pretty indestructible or the enterprise could literally be out of business. A good SAN implementation will have built-in protection against just about any kind of failure imaginable. As we will see in later chapters, this means that not only must the links and switches composing the SAN infrastructure be able to survive component failures, but the storage devices, their interfaces to the SAN, and the computers themselves must all have built-in strategies for surviving and recovering from failures as well.

The I/O performance of a SAN must grow or scale as the number of interconnected devices grows. If a SAN interconnects a lot of computers and a lot of storage, it had better be able to deliver the performance they all need to do their respective jobs simultaneously. A good SAN delivers both high data transfer rates and low I/O request *latency*. Moreover, the SAN's performance must be able to grow as the organization's information storage and processing needs grow. As with other enterprise networks, it just isn't practical to replace a SAN very often.

On the positive side, a SAN that *does* scale provides an extra application performance boost by separating high-volume I/O traffic from client/server message traffic, giving each a path that is optimal for its characteristics and eliminating cross talk between them.

The investment required to implement a SAN is high, both in terms of direct capital cost and in terms of the time and energy required to learn the technology and to design, deploy, tune, and manage the SAN. Any well-managed enterprise will do a cost-benefit analysis before deciding to implement storage networking. The results of such an analysis will almost certainly indicate that the biggest payback comes from using a SAN to connect the enterprise's most important data to the computers that run its most critical applications.

But its most critical data is the data an enterprise can least afford to be without. Together, the natural desire for maximum return on investment and the criticality of operational data lead to Rule 1 of storage networking:

When designing a SAN to access critical enterprise data, make sure the SAN is highly available (i.e., can survive failures of both components in it and components attached to it) and make sure it can grow well beyond anticipated peak performance needs without disruption.

What Makes a Great SAN?

So the fundamental feature of SANs is universal data storage connectivity. Universal connectivity enables a host of important benefits that we enumerate in Chapter 2. Depending on the particular SAN hardware and software components chosen, *additional* benefits may accrue from advanced functions being built into today's SAN devices. Again, we describe some specific features and benefits later on, but for now we assert Rule 2 of storage networking:

When evaluating SAN implementation options, once the basic capacity, availability, and performance requirements can be met, look for advanced functionality available in the chosen architecture and consider how it might be used to further reduce cost or enhance the information services delivered to users.

Why Connect Storage to a Network?

Throughout the journey into storage networking, it's important to keep sight of the benefits being sought. Throughout this book we try hard to distinguish between the *features* of storage networking, such as universal connectivity, high availability, high performance, and advanced function, and the *benefits* of storage networking that support larger organizational goals, such as reduced cost and improved quality of service.

The specific benefits that storage networking delivers are different in every situation, but with storage networking, as with any other aspect of information technology, benefits can be broadly classified as either:

- *reducing the cost* of providing today's information services or *providing or enabling new services* that contribute positively to overall enterprise goals.

Storage networking offers ample opportunity for an information services department to deliver both types of benefits. For example, in the realm of cost savings:

- If all online storage is accessible by all computers, then no extra temporary storage is required to stage data that is produced by one computer and used by others. This can represent a substantial capital cost saving.

- Similarly, if tape drives and robotic media handlers can be accessed directly by all computers, fewer of these expensive and infrequently used devices are needed throughout the enterprise. This, too, reduces total enterprise capital cost for information processing without diminishing the quality of service delivered.

- Probably most important, however, are the administrative and operational savings in not having to implement and manage procedures for copying data from place to place. This can greatly reduce the cost of people—the one component cost of providing information services that doesn't go down every year!

Similarly, consolidating storage on a network may enable information services departments to provide services that just aren't possible with storage attached directly to each computer. For example:

- SAN connectivity enables the grouping of computers into cooperative *clusters* that can recover quickly from equipment or application failures and allow data processing to continue 24 hours a day, every day of the year.

- With *long-distance* storage networking, 24 × 7 access to important data can be extended across metropolitan areas and indeed, with some implementations, around the world. Not only does this help protect access to information against disasters; it can also keep primary data close to where it's used on a round-the-clock basis.

- SANs remove high-intensity I/O traffic from the LAN used to service clients. This can sharply reduce the occurrence of unpredictable, long application response times, enabling new applications to be implemented or allowing existing distributed applications to evolve in ways that would not be possible if the LAN were also carrying I/O traffic.

- A dedicated backup server on a SAN can make more frequent backups possible because it reduces the impact of backup on application servers to almost nothing. More frequent backups means more up-to-date restores that require less time to execute.

Figure 1.3 illustrates the role a SAN occupies in a distributed client/server computing network.

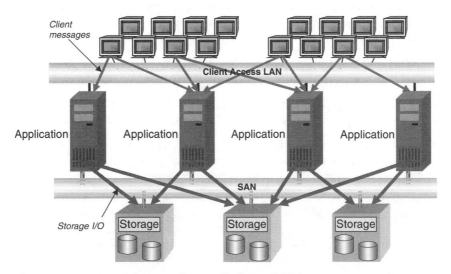

Figure 1.3 A SAN separates client traffic from disk I/O.

The Secret to SANs' Success: Software

Today, most of the public attention given to SANs is focused on the interconnects (such as Fibre Channel) that allow universal storage connectivity and the storage devices and computers that connect to them. But interconnects by themselves don't add any functionality to information processing, they only *enable* functionality to be added. To realize the benefits promised by SANs, not only must the hardware connectivity, performance, availability, and function be in place to enable them, system and application software must take advantage of the hardware to deliver them. Thus we have Rule 3 of storage networking:

Hardware makes SANs possible; software makes SANs happen.

SAN Software Capability

When evaluating SAN technology, the hardware components deserve close scrutiny, to be sure. More important, however, one must also scrutinize the software capabilities carefully to ensure that the implementation will deliver the functionality enabled by the hardware. The following sections give some examples of how software can make a SAN sing.

Sharing Tape Drives

It's very reasonable to expect to share a SAN-attached tape drive among several servers because tape drives are expensive and they're only actually in use while backups are occurring. If a tape drive is connected to computers through a SAN, different computers could use it at different times. All the computers get backed up. The tape drive investment is used efficiently, and capital expenditure stays low.

There's just one tiny problem. What is to keep a computer from (accidentally) writing to a tape while another computer is doing a backup? For two or three computers, an administrator can personally schedule tape drive usage so that this doesn't happen (unless something malfunctions, of course). As the number of computers and tape drives grows or as the applications running on them change, manual scheduling becomes increasingly difficult. What's really needed is a foolproof way for computers to negotiate for exclusive ownership of tape drives for the duration of a backup. When one computer wins a negotiation and is using a tape drive, others must be fenced off and kept from using the drive, even if an errant application or faulty backup schedule tries to do so.

Sharing Online Storage Devices

Sharing online storage, as shown in Figure 1.4, that's housed in an enterprise RAID subsystem is similar to sharing tape drives, except that more of it goes on and requirements for configuration changes are more dynamic. As Chapter 6 describes, a typical enterprise RAID subsystem makes the online storage capacity of one or more *arrays* of disks appear to be one or more very large, very fast, or very reliable disks. For now, accept that a RAID subsystem can look like several *virtual disks* from the viewpoint of host servers. It is quite reasonable that different servers be able to access those virtual disks at different times. For example, one server might collect a business day's transaction records on disk and hand them off to another server at the end of the day for summarization, analysis, or backup.

The problem here is similar to the problem of sharing SAN-attached tape drives among several servers: A server cannot be permitted to write data to a disk that another server owns at the moment. Some foolproof way of fencing off, or preventing other servers from accessing an allocated virtual disk, is needed. Moreover, a distributed system needs to remember *which* virtual disks have been allocated to (are *owned* by) which servers, even when one or more of the servers is shut down and rebooted.

Again, it's software to the rescue. Some SAN infrastructure implementations help by subdividing a SAN into disjoint zones, and some RAID subsystems allow virtual disks to be reserved as the private property of a single computer (masked from other servers). It takes management software to exploit all these features, or to simulate them in SAN implementations whose components don't offer the features. Effective management of the storage and I/O resources composing a SAN is covered in more detail in Chapter 12.

Application Failover

Since SANs connect all of an organization's storage devices to all of its servers, it should be possible to create *highly available* computing environments, in which a substitute computer can take over from a failing one, restart its applications, and resume processing its data. This configuration is shown in Figure 1.5. These things are computers after all, so they should be able to recognize the symptoms of failure and *fail over* automatically. Ideally, this would all happen transparently to applications, since it's not really practical to rewrite all of the world's applications overnight to take advantage of highly available computing environments.

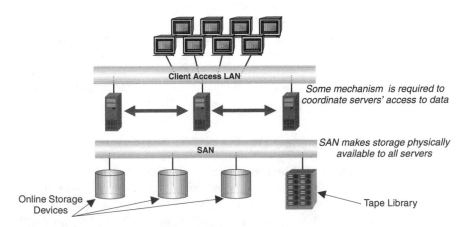

Figure 1.4 Coordinating shared devices in a SAN.

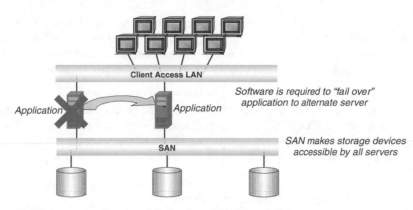

Figure 1.5 Application failover in a SAN-based cluster.

Although the concept sounds simple, the *clustering* of two or more computers to enhance application availability is actually one of the most complex operating system problems there is. Even recognizing and isolating failures is nontrivial. Once an application failure is recognized, ownership of exactly the resources it requires to run (and no others) has to be transferred to a failover server immediately, completely, and unambiguously. The application must be restarted and its state at the time of the failure recreated as nearly as possible. Again, it's software in the form of a *cluster server* or *cluster manager* that does all this.

Sharing Data

More advanced forms of computer clustering, as illustrated in Figure 1.6, allow for the concurrent sharing of data among different applications running on different servers. This can be extraordinarily useful, for example, for *incremental application growth* or *scaling*. Simply stated, if an application outgrows the server on which it is running, don't replace the server with a bigger one. Instead, simply connect another server with the necessary incremental power to the SAN, leaving the original system in place. Both servers can run separate copies, or *instances*, of the application, processing the same copy of data. More servers can be added as application capacity requirements grow.

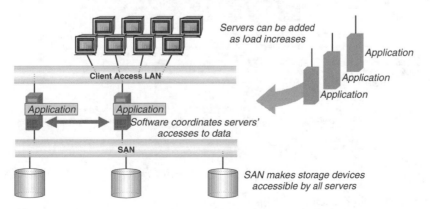

Figure 1.6 Shared data clusters enable applications to scale.

Applications configured this way are inherently highly available. If one of several servers running instances of the same application processing the same data fails, the remaining servers just take up the slack. Overall performance may decrease, but at least the application keeps running. That's *much* better than the alternative.

Data sharing can take any of several forms, from concurrent read-only access to different files in the same file system, all the way to the sharing of a single database by multiple instances of a single application. In all cases, however, the mechanisms for orderly sharing—keeping different applications from overwriting each others' updates to data—are provided by . . . *you guessed it* . . . software.

Direct Data Movement between Devices

Earlier, we mentioned the emergence of more intelligent storage devices with new functionality that is accompanying SAN deployment. One of the key functions being built into intelligent storage devices is the ability to exchange data directly with other intelligent devices in response to commands from a third party (e.g., a computer). Figure 1.7 illustrates such a set up. This capability promises to revolutionize backup, for example, by halving the amount of data movement required to create any kind of backup copy. Less obvious, but potentially at least equally useful, are the possibilities of mirroring or replicating data directly from one device to others.

Direct movement of data between devices needs two kinds of software. First, it needs software or firmware that implements the capability within the devices themselves. Second, host computer applications like backup and replication management that *use* the capability are required.

Summarizing SANs and Software

So, while high-performance, highly available, fully interconnected SANs are *necessary* to realize the benefits we have discussed, they are hardly *sufficient*. It takes system

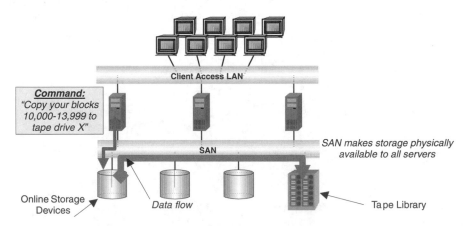

Figure 1.7 Direct copy of data between SAN devices.

software on a massive scale to bring to life the benefits that are promised by the underlying properties of SANs. The software required to make the most of SANs takes two forms:

- *System applications.* These applications build upon the basic SAN properties to provide a functionally enhanced execution environment for business applications. System applications include clustering, data replication, direct data copy between devices and the utility functions that use it, and so forth. Chapter 8 discusses system applications for storage networks.

- *Management applications.* These applications manage the inherently more complex distributed system environment created by the presence of SANs. Zoning, device discovery, allocation, and RAID subsystem configuration are examples of applications that fall into this category. Chapter 12 discusses software for SAN management.

Both of these types of application are necessary for the success of SANs and, ultimately, for their utility as a tool for reducing cost and improving the quality of enterprise information services. While this book discusses the hardware components that constitute SANs, a good portion of it is also given over to a discussion of the software capabilities that make SANs into such extraordinarily useful business data processing tools.

The Best Is Yet to Come: Radical Changes in Information Storage and Processing

Storage area networks are being deployed in large numbers today and are being used to solve real business problems. But, compared to their ultimate potential, the surface is just being scratched. This section touches on some of the more radical changes in distributed information storage and processing enabled by SANs.

Best-in-Class Computer Systems

SANs enable the interconnection of many servers to many storage devices of different types, including disk arrays and robotically controlled tape drives. Who is it that makes these devices and how is it that they all work correctly together?

Both of the market-leading SAN interconnect technologies, Fibre Channel and Ethernet, as well as the emerging *Infiniband,* are *standards-based*—that is, their specifications are defined by voluntary associations of (sometimes competing) companies and are easily available to the general public, rather than being the private property of one company.

Since the same interconnect specifications are available to anyone, in principle, any company should be able to build devices that interoperate with any other company's complementary devices, creating *heterogeneous* storage area networks. This, in fact, is a stated goal of the storage networking vendor community.

This goal has only partly been realized today. No vendor has developed all the components required to build a complete SAN, but most vendors are engaged in partnerships to qualify and offer complete SANs consisting of the partners' products. Today, consumers are well advised to make SAN purchases from a single vendor or, at a minimum, to choose a primary vendor for major components such as RAID subsystems and accept that vendor's recommendations for other SAN components. The industry is working toward a mode of operation similar to that of the LAN industry, where component interactions are sufficiently well understood that users feel relatively comfortable making purchases at the component level. Much energy is being devoted to interoperability, both in terms of making standards more precise and in terms of validating components against standard test suites rather than against individual complementary implementations.

Smarter Storage and Appliances

While the cost and performance of online storage have improved pretty dramatically over the last decade, its functionality has remained pretty much the same. While other major computer system subassemblies, such as network interface cards and video controllers, have become more intelligent and increasingly autonomous, a disk has pretty much remained a disk and a tape has remained a tape for the last decade.

It's only partly coincidental that with SANs becoming popular, storage device functionality is changing as well. Today, intelligent storage devices that can transfer data among themselves without passing it through a server are starting to be delivered. *Peer-to-peer I/O* improves quality of service by halving the bandwidth required to do bulk data transfers such as backup or replication of large file systems and databases. This will ultimately enable application designs that rely more on bulk data transfers, for example, to create more frequent backups or data replicas.

With intelligent storage devices, other advanced functions are also possible. For example, server-based hierarchical storage management software that compresses infrequently used data is available today. Implementing this capability in an enterprise RAID subsystem is technically feasible.

For other examples of how storage device intelligence might be exploited in the future, one need look no further than the storage middleware segment. Backup within the storage subsystem, clusters of storage subsystems, and autonomous global data replication are all possible. Some vendors have introduced these capabilities in *storage appliances* that are nothing more than computers dedicated to managing large amounts of storage and I/O capacity. With these storage appliances, the distinction between a computer and an enterprise storage subsystem essentially comes down to whether or not the box runs applications.

Heterogeneous Computer Systems

Today, it is quite common for users to *partition* the storage in large RAID subsystems and allocate the partitions to different computers made by different vendors and running different operating systems. The computers share the RAID subsystems' common resources (power, cooling, processors, internal bandwidth, cache, etc.), but each has its own private online storage capacity.

With a SAN, however, it should also be possible to *share* storage and data across computers. In principle, computers from Sun, Hewlett-Packard, IBM, and others should all be able to access data stored in one big enterprise storage subsystem made by EMC, Hitachi Data Systems, Compaq StorageWorks, or any other enterprise storage subsystem vendor.

Today, data sharing among heterogeneous computers is possible with *network-attached storage* or *NAS* devices. With other network storage devices, most notably enterprise RAID subsystems, it is not generally possible to share data among computers of different types (although some clustering technologies support data sharing among computers of the same type).

Many difficult technical problems must be solved before different types of computers can share data. By far the greatest of these is that each operating system and file system uses its own unique disk format, simply because there has never been any motivation to do otherwise. SANs provide this motivation because they interconnect the storage of different types of computers running different operating systems. Today, therefore, both academic and industrial researchers and developers are busily working toward the goal of universally accessible online data files.

Data Storage as a Service

Online information storage has traditionally been something that enterprises have implemented and managed for themselves. Whether so inclined or not, information services professionals have been forced to develop storage expertise, as it is they who are responsible for safeguarding the organization's information assets and keeping them accessible.

SANs are enabling a new generation of *storage service providers*, companies whose business consists of storing and managing the data from other enterprises. These companies take on the hard problems of providing secure data access at contractually defined *quality-of-service* levels. In the not-too-distant future, many enterprises may literally get their data storage from a plug in the wall, much as they get their voice and data communications services from external providers today.

Similarly, the long-distance connectivity of SANs will someday enable the secure interconnection of storage networks belonging to enterprises that do business together or that share a specific market. *Storage intranets* will allow partnering enterprises to replicate or even share information without risk of its being divulged to (possibly hostile) outside parties.

Widespread adoption of these new modes of operation would clearly require significant technological development security, as well as changes in user attitudes. They may or may not become prevalent. The point to be made here, however, is that SANs are enabling developers, entrepreneurs, and users to break out of the box as they design enterprise information storage and processing infrastructures. There are all kinds of possibilities. We probably haven't even envisioned the ones that will be the success stories of five years from now.

Back to Earth. . . .

But the information technology professionals in most organizations are responsible for keeping their enterprises' data secure and accessible while they await the brave new world of information processing. Even from this short-term vantage point, SANs have tremendous potential. Used optimally, SANs can improve applications' access to data, dramatically reduce unnecessary redundancy, eliminate bandwidth contention between client messages and data access, and off-load resource-intensive tasks like backup to intelligent storage devices on I/O-optimized interconnects. Information technology professionals cannot afford to ignore the near-term benefits of SAN technology.

A Couple of Closing Clarifications

This section touches upon a couple of aspects of terminology that in the authors' experience tend to be sources of confusion rather than clarification in discussions of storage networking. We hope it dispels some of the very basic uncertainty around SAN terminology for readers and lets them get on to the serious stuff.

Is a SAN Storage or a Network?

Strictly speaking, a SAN is a storage area *network*. Much energy is expended uselessly on silly arguments about whether the term *SAN* should include storage and computers or only the interconnects and other components that link the storage and computers together. Since it's difficult to imagine talking about a SAN without talking about the storage and computers it interconnects, we adopt the more inclusive usage in this book:

> *A storage area network (SAN) is a network of interconnected computers and data storage devices. As we use it in this book, the term SAN specifically includes both the interconnection infrastructure and the computers and storage that it links together.*

Of course, we frequently have occasion to refer specifically to the storage devices attached to a SAN, as distinguished from the more inclusive concept. We use the terms *SAN-attached storage* and *SAN-attached storage device* for this purpose.

What Is This Area Thing, Anyway?

One might wonder what the *area* in a storage area network is, and rightly so. From what we've described so far, the term *storage network* would seem to apply equally well if not better. What is this area thing, anyway?

There's a strong relationship between the SAN concept and the popular I/O interconnect technology called *Fibre Channel*. In fact, it's fair to say that Fibre Channel technology is what got the whole SAN movement started.

In the mid-1990s, the companies committed to developing Fibre Channel were in the doldrums. Five years or more had been spent on development, and the products and market weren't emerging as fast as investors would have preferred. Something was needed to generate excitement among consumers and jump-start growth.

Members of the Fibre Channel Loop Community and the Fibre Channel Association, the two trade groups promoting the technology at that time, hit upon the idea of capitalizing on the similarities between Fibre Channel and local area networking:

Universal connectivity. With Fibre Channel, lots of storage devices can be connected directly to lots of computers.

Campuswide separation. With Fibre Channel, storage devices don't have to be in the computer room. They can be anywhere on a fairly sizable campus.

Bandwidth multiplication. With *switches* (Chapter 7 describes switch capabilities), many high-performance links can be aggregated into a *fabric* with even higher aggregate performance.

Dynamic reconfiguration. Fibre Channel allows devices and computers to be connected to and disconnected from the network while it is operating.

Enabling of new storage usage styles. Just as local area networks enabled client/server computing, Fibre Channel connectivity enables new ways of using storage to achieve business goals. Sharing access to disk and tape subsystems and direct copying of data between devices are two examples.

Noticing the networking industry's success in creating a strong identity for itself through the use of the *LAN* acronym, the Fibre Channel community set out to achieve something similar by introducing the term *storage area network*, or *SAN*, to describe networks of intelligent storage devices and servers. White papers were written, lectures were given, and articles were published, all pointing out similarities between the local area network that connects all the computers in a building or campus and a storage area network, with the potential to likewise connect all the storage within a similar area. The SAN acronym, with its implicit analogy to LANs, was repeated over and over again.

Although the SAN concept was largely a so-called "marketecture" when first introduced, the aforementioned promises have essentially been delivered upon in the intervening years. The perception created by early Fibre Channel industry marketers has become reality. Products and capabilities are being delivered and the term *SAN* has become thoroughly embedded in the public consciousness.

Besides, storage networking makes a lousy acronym.

Is NAS Just SAN Spelled Backward?

One often hears discussions of network-attached storage, or NAS, usually in contexts that leave unclear whether NAS is a kind of SAN, a competitor to SAN technology, or something else entirely.

The term *network-attached storage* (NAS) is used pretty consistently throughout the industry to denote intelligent storage devices that connect to networks and provide *file access* to clients, which may range from desktop computers to enterprise-class application and database servers. From the time of their introduction, NAS devices have almost universally used Ethernet interconnects and TCP/IP-based protocols to connect to and communicate with their clients.

As we mentioned earlier, the term *SAN* is typically understood as including the storage attached to the network. What we didn't say earlier is that today the term *SAN* is also closely identified with *block-access* storage devices—that is, disk drives and devices such as RAID subsystems that behave as disk drives from the client's viewpoint.

Thus, as the terms are commonly used today:

A NAS device provides file access to clients to which it connects using file access protocols (primarily CIFS and NFS) transported on Ethernet and TCP/IP.

A SAN device (or, as we promised to call it, a *SAN-attached storage device*) is a block-access (i.e., it is a disk or it emulates one or more disks) that connects to its clients using Fibre Channel and a block data access protocol such as SCSI.

Figure 1.8 illustrates these two storage paradigms.

A glance at Figure 1.8 clarifies the major architectural difference between NAS and SAN storage as the terms are commonly used today. In the NAS paradigm, the *file system* that organizes blocks of storage into objects that are convenient for applications to deal with resides in the storage device. The NAS storage device is responsible for allocating storage space and for keeping clients from stepping on each others' toes as they make (possibly conflicting) file access requests. On the host side of the interconnect, a *file access client* translates applications' file I/O requests into network messages and sends them to the NAS device for execution.

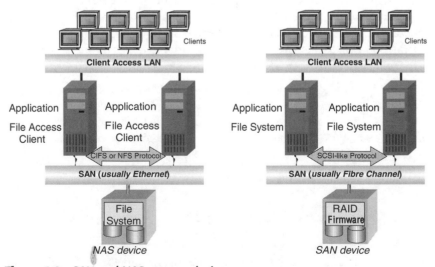

Figure 1.8 SAN and NAS storage devices.

By contrast, in today's SAN paradigm, the file system is on the computer side of the interconnect. Systemwide storage capacity management and conflicts among client data access requests are resolved by cooperation among the SAN-attached servers. This makes host-side software much more complex than with NAS devices.

By absorbing the file system (and hence the on-disk data format) into the storage device, the NAS model makes concurrent data access by different types of computers easy. In fact, today, NAS is the *only* widely available way to make the same data accessible to computers of different types.

That doesn't quite tell the whole story. NAS file access protocols are very general and functionally rich. Moreover, they usually connect to TCP/IP-based networks, which are designed to support very general interconnection topologies. Because of their functional richness and generality, these protocols are predominantly implemented in software, which executes slowly compared to the device-level firmware and hardware typically used to implement SAN protocols. Raw data access performance of NAS devices, therefore, tends to be lower than that of otherwise comparable SAN devices, and both client and server processor utilization for accessing data tends to be higher. In simple terms, the trade-off today is, therefore, as follows:

- *Choose NAS* for simplicity of data sharing, particularly among computers and operating systems of different types.

- *Choose SAN* for the highest raw I/O performance between data client and data server. Be prepared to do some additional design and operational management to make servers cooperate (or at least not interfere) with each other.

Vendors and users of NAS devices often assert that the networks connecting their devices to host computers are SANs, and *they are right*. According to the SNIA, a storage area network is any network that is predominantly used to transfer data between storage devices and computers or other storage devices. NAS devices are certainly storage devices and the mix of traffic on the networks that connect them to their clients is certainly dominated by storage I/O in any reasonably busy information processing operation. We mention this only to nip in the bud any possible confusion around this use of the term *SAN*. One can only hope that over time the vendor and user communities will evolve to a broader and more descriptive common understanding of the term *SAN*.

Of course, it's reasonable to ask, What about the other possibilities—block-access devices that use Ethernet to attach to clients and file servers that use Fibre Channel? Both of these are possible and, in fact, development is occurring within the storage industry that may result in both types of devices being brought to market. Today, however, almost all NAS devices are Ethernet-attached file servers and almost all SAN devices are Fibre Channel–attached block-access devices. Table 1.1 summarizes the state of affairs in SAN and NAS devices today.

Summary

- A storage area network (SAN) is any network whose primary purpose is to enable storage devices to communicate with computer systems and with each other.

Table 1.1   SAN and NAS Storage Device Taxonomy

		INTERCONNECT AND PROTOCOL	
		Ethernet and TCP/IP	**Fibre Channel**
FILE SYSTEM LOCATION	**File System in the Client**	"IP SCSI" protocol being standardized; products being developed but not yet widely available	Today's SAN devices
	File System in the Storage Device	Today's NAS devices	Hardware and software components exist, but products not widely available

- The key feature that defines a SAN is *any-to-any connectivity of computers and storage devices*. SANs reduce or eliminate the incidence of unconnected islands of information.

- SANs can reduce the cost of providing information services. In some cases, they can enable new services that it was not previously practical to provide.

- At the current state of this new industry segment, SANs' potential has barely been touched. Ultimately, SANs may lead to heterogeneous distributed systems in which applications running on different operating systems and hardware platforms can meaningfully access the same data.

- Already today, SANs are enabling new ways of providing information services, including an entire new industry segment called *storage solution providers*, who make quality of service-based access to storage available to their clients as a service.

- Strictly speaking, NAS devices connect to SANs, although the two acronyms are most often used with mutually exclusive meanings. The key unique feature of NAS devices is that they place the file system on the storage device side of the network. Today, the only widespread incidence of heterogeneous data sharing is with NAS devices.

CHAPTER 2

Benefits: What to Expect from SANs

I n this chapter we'll learn more about:

- The primary and secondary information processing *paradigm shifts* enabled by SANs

- New information processing capabilities that are enabled by these SAN paradigm shifts

- Ten ways in which information processing can be changed for the better by exploiting the primary and secondary SAN paradigm shifts

The SAN Paradigm Shift

Storage and network vendors are fond of saying that SANs represent a *paradigm shift* in information processing. A paradigm is nothing more than an abstract model for an object or a process and a shift is . . . *well* . . . a shift. In other words, the claim is that SANs enable fundamentally different ways of building computer systems and processing data. If that is in fact true, SANs should enable information technology users to:

- Do the things they have been doing in new and innovative ways—faster, more reliably, with better control, or less expensively.

- Do beneficial things that they may previously have wanted to do, but were prevented from doing by technology limitations.

Let's examine this supposed paradigm shift more closely and see if it's as radical as some would claim.

Properties of SANs

In Chapter 1, we learned that the fundamental properties of SANs are:

- Any-to-any connection between storage and computers
- High I/O performance over campus-type distances
- Physical separation of I/O to storage devices from client messaging traffic

In addition to these fundamental properties, a good SAN provides the failure tolerance and performance scalability expected of an enterprise networking solution. Beyond this, a *really* good SAN provides some advanced functions such as direct data copying as part of the network or it promises to evolve to provide such functionality nondisruptively in the foreseeable future.

So What's the Paradigm Shift?

The paradigm shift, however, comes from the fundamental SAN properties, not from the fancy stuff. It is a shift from conventional *server-centric* to *storage-centric* information processing. Let's discover more about this paradigm shift.

Conventional Information Processing

In a conventional enterprise information processing operation (i.e., one without a SAN), such as is illustrated in Figure 2.1, *servers* provide application and data access services to *clients*. Each server consists of a computer, one or more applications, and local storage for the data on which these applications operate. Each client is a computer that communicates with applications running on the servers.

The advantage of this *client/server* architecture is that clients hold little or no important and difficult-to-recreate enterprise data. The data used to run the enterprise is kept on a smaller number of (*one hopes!*) professionally managed servers with clearly

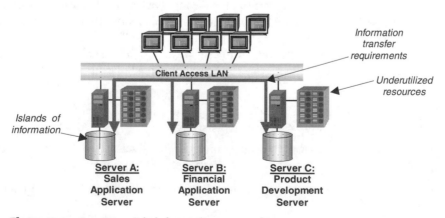

Figure 2.1 Server-centric information processing.

defined missions, rather than spread across unsecured, loosely managed desktop or departmental computers scattered throughout the organization.

In the conventional client/server computing paradigm (Figure 2.1), storage is *local* to each server. Each storage device is connected to only one server, called its *host* or *host computer*. Only the server to which a storage device is directly attached can open files, read and write data, create backup tapes, and perform administrative functions on data stored on the device. If other servers need access to a server's local data, some type of remote data access software is required.

Referring to Figure 2.1, if the Financial Application running on Server B needs access to sales records maintained by the Sales Application on Server A, the choices are as follows:

- Server A can be configured to run a remote file access protocol, such as Network File System (NFS), allowing the Financial Application on Server B to act as a client and request file access from Server A.

- A custom distributed application can be developed, with a *requester* component on Server B making data access requests and a *responder* component on Server A accessing the sales records and responding to the requests.

- If the Sales Application uses a relational database, Server B can send queries to Server A (using the Structured Query Language, SQL, for example), where the database management system can access data and return the required responses.

It is clear from Figure 2.1 that when storage is directly attached to servers, information processing architectures are necessarily designed around servers—they are *server-centric*.

Looking at Figure 2.1, it is easy to see that a server-centric information processing architecture with local storage results in unconnected islands of storage devices. What is worse from a business standpoint, these storage devices hold unconnected islands of data. Increasingly, this type of strategy is unworkable for enterprises, especially as they undertake to conduct business on the Internet, where the business day is 24 hours long and competition is a click away. Again referring to Figure 2.1, a typical electronic business requirement might be for data generated by the online sales application to be instantly accessible by the financial and product development applications,[1] and so forth.

With a server-centric information processing architecture, it is certainly possible for servers to communicate their actions to each other by sending messages on the client access LAN. This can create as many problems as it solves, however. Sales maintains *its* database of items sold. Finance maintains *its* database of items shipped, billed for, and paid for. Product development maintains *its* engineering bill of materials records.

---

[1] As the reader experienced in information services management will readily discern, a typical enterprise actually has many more requirements (opportunities?) for interaction among applications. In this description, we limit the numbers to keep the examples tractable.

- *Someone* has to get sales data to the Financial Application, to Product Development, and so forth.

- *Someone* has to reconcile all of these separate databases with each other periodically to make sure data is consistent across them.

- *Someone* has to keep all of the applications that manipulate these databases synchronized with each other, so that, for example, the data formats that finance expects are what sales actually sends.

The underlying point here is that with a server-centric information processing paradigm that uses local storage, a lot of work is required just to keep the servers in step with each other. The sole purpose of this work is to keep local copies of data managed by different servers synchronized (consistent) with each other. Except for untangling things that never should have gotten tangled in the first place, it contributes nothing to the organization's bottom line.

The Primary SAN Paradigm Shift

Imagine instead that all of the servers on a campus could directly access all enterprise data. This is the *storage-centric* information processing paradigm enabled by SANs and illustrated in Figure 2.2.

The key difference between the storage-centric information processing strategy illustrated in Figure 2.2 and the server-centric strategy of Figure 2.1 is that in the former, *all* of the servers are physically connected to *all* of the storage devices. There is no need to maintain multiple copies of data just because multiple servers need to access them. If a server needs access to a data object, it can access the object directly because it is physically connected to the storage device that holds it.

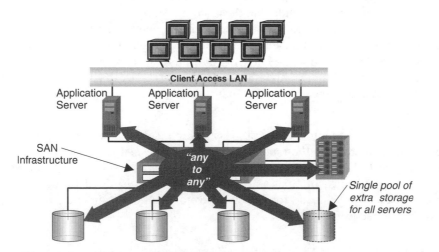

Figure 2.2 Storage-centric information processing.

New Ways of Doing Things

A SAN enables all of an enterprise's applications to rely upon and take advantage of having access to the same up-to-date data at the same time. Users have realized that SANs enable new ways of handling data that can improve their business, such as sharing data among widely distributed systems at speeds previously possible only with local data access.

The shift from server-centric to storage-centric enterprise information processing is reminiscent of the explosion in Internet use and the resulting rapid development of electronic commerce that happened in the late 1990s. Prior to the widespread availability of low-cost, high-performance communications, extensive market adoption of the Internet was not practical. Once high-speed, reliable, low-cost communications were universally available, however, e-commerce applications developed to use it, changing the way that both companies and individuals do business.

A similar phenomenon is occurring with SANs. Beginning in 1999 (or 1998, for the very brave), it became possible to buy high-performance SAN components and create data center–wide and campuswide storage area networks. For the most part, these SANs were initially deployed as alternatives to locally attached storage, a sort of SCSI on steroids. Many such SANs are now in place and their users have developed a level of comfort with them that makes them willing to experiment with the SANs' advanced capabilities. For example:

- Users are buying fewer tape drives and robotic media libraries per server, moving instead to SAN-attached backup devices that can be shared by several servers. Backup is evolving to become more enterprisewide, with globally managed pools of tape drives used to optimize backup for the enterprise as a whole.

- Similarly, users are increasingly willing to purchase multi-terabyte SAN-attached disk array subsystems and subdivide their capacity among several servers, in many cases running unrelated applications. This achieves economy of scale in both capital expenditure and management and, in addition, makes it relatively easy to redeploy disk storage capacity among servers as business needs change.

- Users are taking advantage of high-performance, long-distance networking technologies such as Asynchronous Transfer Mode (ATM) and wave division multiplexing (WDM) to mirror or replicate data across long distances (tens, hundreds, or even thousands of miles). The obvious application for long-distance replication is disaster recovery. Less obvious, but increasingly popular applications are data publication and consolidation and transporting data for round-the-clock *global computing* in organizations with round-the-clock global businesses.

The Secondary SAN Paradigm Shift

The SAN concept changes information processing in another way as well. Conceptually, a storage area network is an additional network added to an existing distributed information system infrastructure, as Figure 2.3 illustrates. Creating a separate path for I/O between storage devices and servers alters distributed system performance characteristics in several ways:

- *Load on the enterprise network decreases significantly.* With a separate SAN carrying data between servers and storage devices, the capacity of the enterprise network to carry application messages is dramatically extended. Network capacity increases, but, perhaps more important, the wide variations in application performance, as, for example, when a network backup starts or finishes, disappear.

- *Absolute I/O performance improves.* We have already mentioned that SAN interconnects offer high levels of performance—two leading technologies transfer data at 1 gigabit per second. There's an additional benefit, however, because SAN protocols are optimized for high-volume I/O traffic (i.e., optimized for bulk data movement rather than, like a LAN, for transient connections, short messages, and complex topologies). When there's a lot of data to be moved, moving it efficiently is important, no matter how great the bandwidth of the interconnect hardware.

- Finally and perhaps most dramatically, *a SAN simply eliminates a lot of the data movement that an organization previously required to process its information.* This reduces overall resource requirements and allows the organization to devote a larger share of its information services budget to solving problems related to the conduct of business.

This secondary paradigm shift has to do with dramatic increases in available I/O capacity. These increases come about both because SANs themselves are high-performance interconnects and because the new ways of doing things enabled by SANs simply eliminate a lot of the overhead I/O traffic inherent in distributed client/server computing with locally attached storage.

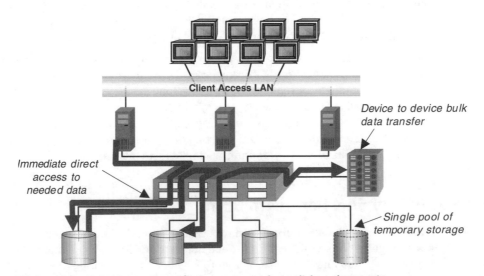

Figure 2.3 A SAN separates client messages from disk and tape I/O.

More New Ways of Doing Things

More I/O performance on tap allows application designers and operations managers to think in terms of new ways of doing things:

- With more available I/O bandwidth, it becomes practical to mine more data to discover trends that affect the enterprise.

- More complex transactions that service the customer better can be designed. For example, a customer relationship management (CRM) application can make a customer's historical data available to a service representative in real time, on the assumption that the representative *might* need it. If historical data is, in fact, needed, the customer's perception is one of personal attention and great service.

- Scheduling becomes simpler if it is no longer necessary to avoid certain operations or curtail normal business activity because backup is running.

- Conversely, more frequent backups become possible, leading to lower-impact, more up-to-date backups and, hence, faster restores when restoration of online data from a backup becomes necessary.

- In very I/O-intensive applications, a higher level of raw performance may make advanced capabilities like the mirroring of more than two copies of data or server-based RAID practical from a performance standpoint.

A Model for Enterprise Information Processing

To explain why the changes in enterprise information processing enabled by the primary and secondary SAN paradigm shifts are beneficial, we use as a model the medium-size enterprise, illustrated in Figure 2.4. The medium size of the modeled operation is chosen for representational simplicity. The model scales to larger information processing operations. Much of the discussion pertains to operations within a single data center, so the model would apply to smaller, single-data-center enterprises as well.

Figure 2.4 illustrates the essential components of a medium-size distributed enterprise client/server information services operation from a data storage and I/O perspective. The hypothetical enterprise illustrated in Figure 2.4 is neither very large nor very small. Its information processing is done in four separate locations, all of which are connected by a wide area network (WAN). Local area networks (LANs) provide client/server communications at each of the locations. The characteristics of each location's LAN that interest us are as follows:

Financial LAN. This LAN includes servers that run applications, each with its own local storage, as well as a financial database server with its own storage for corporate financial databases. Some of the data held on this LAN is *mission critical*—the enterprise couldn't function without it. The database server is equipped with tape and possibly robotic library resources for backup. This LAN provides access to corporate financial data to a relatively large number of knowledge workers using desktop computers.

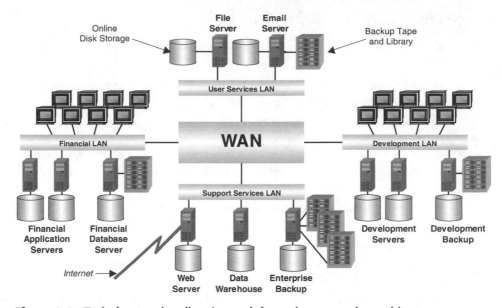

Figure 2.4 Typical enterprise client/server information processing architecture.

Development LAN. Developers use this LAN for product or application system development. Its characteristics are similar to those of the Financial LAN. Each server manages its own data, serving a relatively large number of developers' workstations. While the cost of losing data on this LAN would be high (development work would have to be recreated), it wouldn't affect the enterprise's ability to function in the short term. The backup server on this LAN would be used to back up development work done on the LAN itself. The backup server's local disk storage would be used for staging and for tape media catalog management.

User Services LAN. This LAN provides services such as electronic mail to users throughout the enterprise. It services relatively few local clients, providing the bulk of its services to corporate users on other LAN segments. This LAN might also contain data of sufficient, but not mission-critical, value (e.g., electronic mail) that local backup resources would be justified.

Support Services LAN. This LAN provides additional internal services, as well as network access to the outside world (Internet). One important enterprisewide support service is central backup for servers throughout the enterprise that are not equipped to back up their data locally. Another is the data warehouse that is *mined* to develop trends from historical information. The data warehouse server has an inherent need to communicate with the enterprise's other servers. Like the User Services LAN, the Support Services LAN services relatively few local clients, but provides its services to desktop computers and servers on other LAN segments.

Ten Ways the SAN Paradigm Shift Changes Information Processing for the Better

Let's examine ten important information processing changes enabled by SANs and how these changes could benefit the enterprise.

Change 1: More Storage for Less Money

A common problem with production applications is running out of online storage space:

- *In a database,* all of the space allocated for tables and indexes is full and a table has to be extended.
- *In a file system,* all of the file system's space has been allocated to files and a new file must be created.
- *In a disk, disk array,* or *server-based volume,* all of the raw storage capacity has been allocated to file systems and a new file system must be allocated.

If any of these conditions occurs, applications fail. This is unacceptable for an enterprise that needs continuous access to its information to operate.

Occasionally, space runs low because an application over allocates space or doesn't free temporary storage when finished with it. A SAN doesn't help much with this type of problem. When it occurs, system administrators have to find and remedy the underlying cause and then resume normal operations. Isolating and fixing this type of problem can be difficult and time consuming, but, fortunately, it is infrequent. Most such problems are caught before applications go live. If they aren't, it's a good argument for more comprehensive preproduction testing.

More typically, online data simply grows faster than planned because the enterprise and its information processing needs are growing faster than planned. When this happens, the remedy is simple: Someone has to allocate additional storage, format it as required, and incorporate it into the application's file systems or databases. These are all fairly run-of-the-mill system administration procedures. The biggest challenge for system administrators is *noticing* impending storage shortages before they occur so that storage can be added to the system and prepared for use before a shortage becomes critical and applications start to fail.

Well-run data centers use system management software tools to monitor database and file system space utilization. Many of these tools allow a user to define *policies* that automate storage management, for example, to detect an impending space shortage and run a corrective script before the problem becomes critical.

For example, a data center might define a policy of extending a file system's capacity by 20 percent when the monitoring tool signals that 80 percent of existing capacity is allocated. If the disk or volume on which the file system is allocated has sufficient free capacity, it is usually straightforward to extend the file system's size.[2] If, however, the underlying storage device were full, it would first have to be made larger before the file system could be extended.

Both of these actions can be automated in a *script* of operating system commands that is executed automatically by the system management tool that detects the file system capacity threshold event. The details of what the event is (file system 80 percent full) and what happens when the event occurs (allocate 20 percent more storage to the file system; extend the underlying volume if necessary) are collectively called a storage management *policy*. Policy-driven system management tools monitor for such events and automatically take remedial action when they occur.

For this example, we have assumed that disk capacity is available if required to extend the volume. Experienced system administrators often maintain a pool of unused disk storage connected to a server and ready for instant deployment in case such needs arise. Unfortunately, experienced system administrators who manage many systems must maintain *many* such pools—one for each server that is running a critical application. Figure 2.5 illustrates this, zooming in on the development LAN segment from the enterprise model of Figure 2.4.

The main reason to maintain extra storage on every critical application server is time. When available storage runs dangerously low, it's important to take steps quickly to avert outright application failure. There's no time to take disks off the shelf and install them where they are needed while critical applications are running at the danger level, much less to order more disks and wait for delivery. Maintaining extra

---

[2] There are a few file systems that cannot be extended while in operation, but their use in enterprise data centers is decreasing.

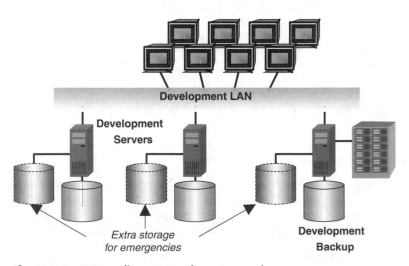

Figure 2.5 Extra online storage for emergencies.

online storage capacity that can be deployed in an emergency buys the system administration team time to configure still more storage devices before the next emergency.

There are two disadvantages to maintaining a separate online storage capacity pool for each application server:

■ *It's expensive.* Storage assets that are sitting idle waiting for an emergency to occur are costing money and not delivering any value to the enterprise (until a storage emergency occurs, of course).

■ *It's inflexible.* Alas, it is not always the server with the biggest storage reserve that has the biggest unexpected capacity demand. System administrators can find themselves in the awkward situation of having extra storage on some servers, while a critical application on another server fails because of a storage shortage.

Using a SAN to connect all of a data center's storage to all of its servers mitigates both of these problems. A single data center-wide pool of storage can be connected to the SAN, and capacity from it can be allocated to any server as it is needed. Figure 2.6 illustrates this usage.

If an application's need for additional storage is permanent, time to acquire and install additional physical storage has been gained without risk to applications. If the need is temporary, the storage can be returned to the pool when the emergency is over and used by other servers as required.

With a SAN, storage is preinstalled, but it's preinstalled on the SAN rather than on any particular server. When a server needs more storage, a simple system management operation allocates additional storage to the servers that need it.

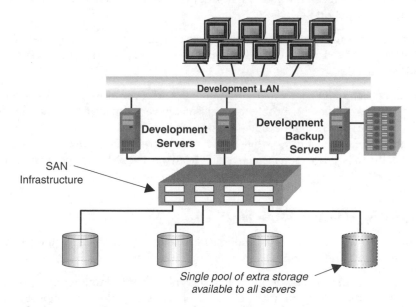

Figure 2.6   Using a SAN to pool extra online storage.

Connecting a data center-wide storage pool to a SAN and making it available to all the servers in the data center solves the two aforementioned problems:

- *It reduces capital outlay.* It would be highly unlikely for all of a data center's servers to experience storage emergencies at the same time. With a little experience, system administrators can plan capacity for realistic data center worst-case scenarios. Such scenarios probably require much less pooled storage than would a pool-per-server strategy.

- *It is flexible.* There is no need to plan for storage emergencies on a per-server basis. Since the extra storage resources can be allocated to whichever server needs them, system administration only has to plan for the worst expected case on a data center-wide basis and not for all of the worst cases that can happen with all of the servers. Moreover, in this scenario, the same storage can be used with different operating system platforms. There's no need to plan for a Windows pool and a Unix pool. The SAN-connected storage is initialized for a particular operating system when it is allocated.

So the storage-centric information processing paradigm enabled by SANs effectively provides more available storage to the data center with less capital expenditure and lower management cost than a per-server storage approach. But the advantages of SAN-enabled capacity pooling go beyond that. Capacity pooling also makes it possible to rotate temporary storage among several servers. For example, many applications have cyclic needs for additional storage—monthly or quarterly closings, periodic data analyses, and so forth—that can require large amounts of storage for relatively brief periods. This is different from a storage emergency in that the periodic needs of applications are known in advance. Without a SAN, each server must be configured with enough storage to meet its worst-case needs, even though much of the storage may be used only for very short periods.

Again, with a SAN to pool storage, capital costs can be reduced. A single set of devices can be dedicated for data center-wide temporary use and passed from server to server according to need.

The net effect is that SAN-attached storage solves one of the most bothersome enterprise information processing problems—a mismatch between available extra storage capacity and the servers that need it—and does so in a way that reduces overall data center storage requirements. So while it's not quite *infinite free storage for all*, SANs do enable significant storage management simplifications and reduce capital costs at the same time.

Change 2: More I/O for Less Money

Most information processing organizations like the one illustrated in Figure 2.4 spend most of their time and computing resources on the following:

- *Processing transactions,* during which servers exchange large numbers of relatively short messages with many clients over constantly changing logical connections and make large numbers of I/O requests for relatively little data. We call applications that process transactions *I/O intensive.*

- *Moving data in bulk*, during which large amounts of (usually sequential) data move between two points in response to a small number of commands. We call applications that move data in bulk *data intensive*.

The communication needs of these two application types are very different. To process transactions efficiently, a communications infrastructure needs:

- The ability to manage large numbers of short-lived logical connections between clients and servers

- The ability to handle complex network topologies, with data possibly moving via different routes between the same two points and arriving out of order

For transaction processing, efficient high-volume data movement is usually a secondary consideration. This is quite different from the requirements of bulk data transfer, for applications such as backup, data mining, or catalog distribution, for which the following are true:

Connections are long-lived. Once communication is established between source and target, the best possible scenario is an unobstructed path between them until they have exchanged an entire bulk data object.

Data throughput is paramount. The most important thing in backup is to keep tapes streaming. The most important thing in data mining is to keep the processors supplied with data to scan and analyze. The most important thing about catalog distribution is to get it done with so that new catalogs can be used.

But while the requirements of transaction processing and bulk data transfer are quite different, the two have shared network capacity since the advent of client/server computing. This has primarily been an artifact of the available technology rather than the result of conscious design. With SANs, it is now possible to separate these two kinds of communication traffic onto separate networks that are optimized for each, as Figure 2.7 illustrates.

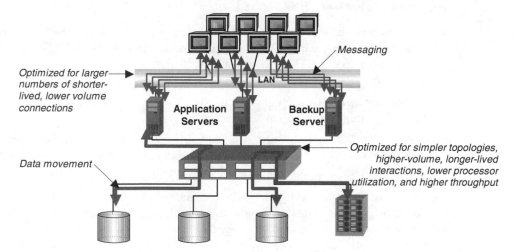

Figure 2.7   A SAN separates I/O from client messaging.

With SANs, the I/O performance potential of a distributed client/server computing operation increases in three ways:

- The addition of a network infrastructure increases the capacity of components within the data center to intercommunicate.

- Both the messaging networks and the storage networks are optimized for the types of traffic that predominate, so each performs its task more efficiently.

- Utilizing the device-to-device data transfer, discussed in Chapter 1, significantly reduces the amount of data that must be moved to accomplish data-intensive tasks such as periodic backups.

Thus, adding a SAN tends to increase the overall performance of a system beyond what would be expected from the bandwidth of the SAN alone. Now we grant that this isn't exactly *less* money; there's the small matter of paying for the SAN infrastructure itself and all the SAN-enabled devices. But we do assert that those funds can often be justified based on the benefits of the primary paradigm shift that comes from any-to-any connectivity. In many cases, improved application performance is an extra benefit.

The more efficient I/O that comes with SANs has three main effects:

- Transaction throughput improves, because the I/O that supports the transactions uses more optimized SAN facilities.

- The predictability of transaction response time improves, because bulk data movements no longer interfere with transaction traffic.

- Backups and data mining improve, because they use optimized data movement facilities.

Thus, the question becomes: How can information processing organizations take advantage of this increased I/O capacity to do things in new and different ways? While the answer is specific to each situation, there are three broad categories in which improvements are highly likely for any data center:

- Since transaction messages no longer share the wire, it may be possible to process more transactions, accommodating more business growth, while deferring growth of the client access network infrastructure.

- Alternatively, it may be possible to enrich client interactions, for example, by embedding images or animations in the data flow, where, without a SAN, network bandwidth might have precluded doing so.

- Since higher I/O performance means that data gets mined faster, it may become affordable to drill down deeper, doing more extensive and detailed analyses than would be possible with less efficient I/O facilities.

Perhaps most important, with more efficient channels for making backup copies, it may become possible to integrate more frequent backups into the data center workload, leading to a better quality of service due to lower impact on operations and faster, more up-to-date restores.

Change 3: Better Data Protection for Less Money

The principle of pooling SAN-connected storage devices to reduce capital outlay can also be applied to tape drives and robotic media libraries. Buying and owning tape drives and media handling devices has always been frustrating for information services providers. On the one hand, they are more expensive than disk drives, both because they are mechanically more complex and because they are produced in lower volume. On the other hand, they are only used while backups are actually being made, so for most of the time, these expensive assets sit idle.

Again, SANs come to the rescue, as Figure 2.8 illustrates, using the development LAN segment from Figure 2.4. As Figure 2.8 suggests, it makes sense to connect tape drives to a SAN, where they can be time-shared, rather than to dedicate them to individual servers.

Unlike disk drives, tape drives are inherently single-stream devices, owned by one backup job at any instant. A server cannot be permitted to write blocks of unrelated data in the middle of another server's long stream of backup data. For the configuration illustrated in Figure 2.8 to succeed, therefore, it must be possible to guarantee exclusive control of a tape drive for the duration of a backup job. For two or three servers managed by a single administrator, tape drive allocation can probably be administered manually. Before long, however, backup schedules start to conflict and questions of which server should own which tape drive become too complex to deal with without automation. Effective SAN utilization requires an arbitrator that grants control of each tape drive to one and only one backup server at any instant.

As with online storage pooling, the SAN advantage is better service for less money. The less money part is self-evident. If each tape drive can be switched from server to

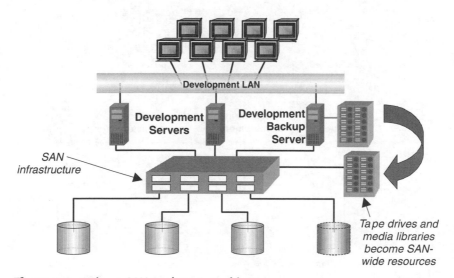

Figure 2.8   Using a SAN to share tape drives.

server, fewer tape drives are required. Better service is provided because when a tape drive in a pool fails, it doesn't mean that any particular server can't be backed up. Since any tape drive can be allocated to any server, the requirement is that there be enough functioning drives in the SAN to meet the SAN's requirements, not that each server's individual requirements be met.

Change 4: Global Access to Global Data

As we say many times in this book, the most important benefit of a SAN is that data is potentially accessible by every computer (and therefore to every user) connected to the SAN. But *every* can have different meanings in different contexts, as we illustrate starting with the example in Figure 2.9.

To illustrate our point, assume that a new financial application needs access to engineering data, perhaps to factor product cost into pricing or profitability models. In the pre-SAN era (Figure 2.5), the financial system developers would have had two choices:

Copy the required engineering test data in bulk from the Engineering Development server to the Financial Development server. This could be accomplished by creating a tape backup or by a direct disk-to-disk copy over the LAN. This approach is simple to implement, but it has the inherent problems of high resource consumption and stale data—the financial application developers run the risk of working with slightly out-of-date engineering data. Moreover, if the copied data is updated on the Financial Development server, those updates may have to be reflected back into the real data attached to the Engineering Development server.

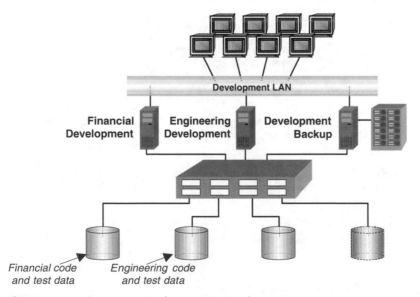

Financial code and test data   *Engineering code and test data*

Figure 2.9 Using a SAN to share access to data.

Create a special distributed program to access the data. The client side of this program would run on the Financial Development server, making requests for engineering data. The server side would run on the Engineering Development server, responding to those requests by accessing data and delivering it to the Financial Development server. Updates to engineering data could be handled in the same way. The disadvantage to this approach is the cost of developing and maintaining the special program for cross-accessing data.

With a SAN, however, as Figure 2.9 illustrates, there is a physical connection between the Financial Development server and engineering test data. Even with the simplest of SANs, it is possible to transfer ownership of the required engineering data to the Financial Development server for periods of time. No data movement is required and the Financial Development server is guaranteed up-to-date data. With more sophisticated SAN-aware file systems, the engineering data can even be shared between the two servers.

The example of Figure 2.9 represents a relatively simple SAN that's implemented entirely within one data center. In a medium-size data center with only a few storage subsystems and servers, this SAN might consist of a single Fibre Channel switch.[3] In larger data centers, switches would be connected to provide greater storage and server connectivity. In still larger centers, networks of enterprise-class *directors* with greater connectivity and built-in failure tolerance would be employed to provide data center-wide connectivity.

The point here is that the any-to-any connectivity, common storage access, and data sharing discussed here are within the confines of a data center. It's also possible to design or evolve to SANs with larger scope, as the next section will discuss.

Change 5: Less Duplication, More Consistency

There's an adage that a person with one watch knows what time it is, while a person with two watches is never quite sure. This principle applies equally well to information processing.

In a typical conventional (i.e., pre-SAN) data center there is enormous duplication of online data. Duplication of online data costs money in three ways:

- *It uses capital resources that must be purchased and maintained.* Every copy of a database means both another set of disks to store the copy and enough network bandwidth to make the copy without disrupting real work.

- *It inherently forces part of the organization to work with out-of-date data.* Making copies of data takes time. Making copies of a lot of data takes a lot of time. But life has to go on while data is being copied, so users of data must sometimes work with what they have, even though it's out of date.

---

[3] Although that's a bit risky from an availability standpoint—review Chapter 1 for the criteria for a good SAN.

- *It's error prone.* Elaborate procedures must be set up to make sure that weekly financial results are computed using the most current sales data. *Elaborate* is a code word for "prone to failure." Every procedural error costs precious time and people to repair. The worst are the errors that aren't caught until too late or that aren't caught at all. These can result in expensive mistakes, because decision makers don't have timely data upon which to base decisions.

The basic SAN architecture inherently solves this problem beautifully. A company with several information processing sites can unify its storage in a single SAN and share online data among the sites. Departmental systems can be consolidated into a divisional or enterprise computing facility. An organization that *really* wants to consolidate can require that desktop computers and workstations store even local data in the SAN. With the right storage management policies, this can eliminate duplication all the way to the desktop. (Some enterprises have effectively adopted this strategy by using powerful NAS devices connected to *thin clients*—desktop computers that have little or no storage capacity of their own.)

Change 6: Taking It to the Streets: Really Global Access to Really Global Data

SANs come in different sizes. In many cases, SAN deployment starts with the installation of a network *hub* or *switch* within a computer room. This is the kind of SAN that Figure 2.9 illustrates. In this case, "all storage" amounts to the storage devices connected to the switch and "all servers" is the servers connected to the switch.

Early deployments of SAN technology were mostly of this "in the computer room" type, partly because the technology wasn't ready for anything bigger, but mainly because users weren't ready to trust anything more ambitious to new, unproven technology.

The result is illustrated in Figure 2.10, where the financial and development locations have been upgraded to SANs. The enterprise's financial information is accessible by all of the financial servers and its development information is accessible by all of the development servers. However, if a financial application needs development information to budget, for example, the path is through the servers and across the enterprise network. So while the local SANs have improved things, there's still room for improvement if technology permits.

And technology does permit, as Figure 2.11 illustrates.

Today, wide area network interfaces to SAN infrastructures are available from SAN infrastructure vendors. These interfaces connect to any of several communication technologies, ranging from T1 and T3 links to ATM-based networks. More modern wave division multiplexing technology is used to link SANs directly to each other across large campuses and cities at speeds of gigabits per second, creating *metropolitan area networks*, or MANs. The result is a more global version of Change 4—data

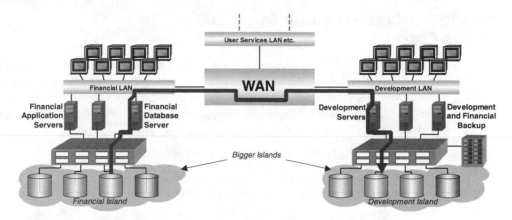

Figure 2.10   Bigger islands of information.

becomes universally accessible across the enterprise, even if the enterprise processes its information at widely separated locations.

There's a tiny caveat to global data accessibility. Not even SANs can suspend the laws of physics. The particular law we have in mind here is the speed of light. It takes time to move data across distance. Moreover, in a trip around the world, data will be relayed several times, with each relay introducing a slight delay in the transmission. It's probably not a good idea for bank tellers in Hong Kong to depend on accessing data stored in, say, New York, to satisfy impatient customers. In situations like this, the laws of good sense supersede the laws of physics. As we will learn in Chapter 8, however, SAN-optimized software techniques that include long-distance data replication and global clustering can make something very like this a practical reality for many applications. *Keep reading.*

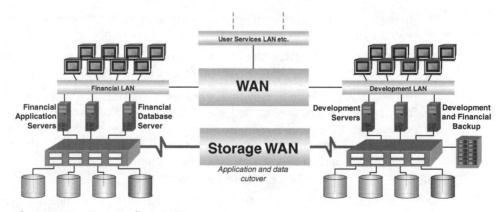

Figure 2.11   Metropolitan SAN.

Change 7: Clusters Come Out
of the Closet

Clustering has been a well-understood enterprise computing concept for some time. A *cluster* is a set of independent computers interconnected to the same storage and clients, and managed to provide a single, coordinated computing service. Proprietary clusters, built exclusively from components supplied by a single vendor, have been available since at least the mid-1980s.

On the surface, the clustering concept only has advantages:

■ Configuring servers so that if one fails another can automatically restart its applications and continue servicing clients improves application availability.

■ Configuring servers so that client requests can be routed to any of several servers running identical applications enables incremental application scaling.

■ Interconnecting several servers that run related applications reduces overall management cost.

■ Building clusters out of mainstream computer system components means that the cost of highly available, scalable computing tracks the cost of mainstream computing.

From a practical standpoint, however, there has been one giant limitation to the development of clusters of open systems. If an application is to fail over to a backup server or if several instances of an application are to process the same data, the servers need to be connected to the data. To be sure, *dual-initiator* SCSI-based systems, in which two servers and several storage devices are connected to each SCSI bus, are quite feasible. Indeed, this is the basis of the limited form of clustering implemented by the original Microsoft Cluster Server (MSCS or Wolfpack I). This solves some availability problems, but does little to abet application scaling, since it's difficult for two servers to access a single SCSI storage device concurrently.

By now, the answer should be obvious. By enabling lots of servers to connect to lots of storage devices, SANs enable:

■ More general forms of clustering for availability, in which one server can cover for several others

■ *Scaling* clusters in which multiple servers process the same data concurrently (with more than a little help from software, as we will describe in Chapter 8).

In Chapter 4, we drill down into clusters. For now, Figure 2.12 gives a basic idea of the benefits of SAN-based clustering. Notice that Figure 2.12 is almost identical to Figure 2.9. In fact, from a hardware standpoint, it *is* identical. The difference is our good friend, software. Clustering is a software technology that makes servers aware of applications running on other servers and enables them to take over and restart the applications if the servers on which they are running fail.

Thus, for example, in Figure 2.12, the organization appears to have decided that engineering development is the most important function of the development site. The clus-

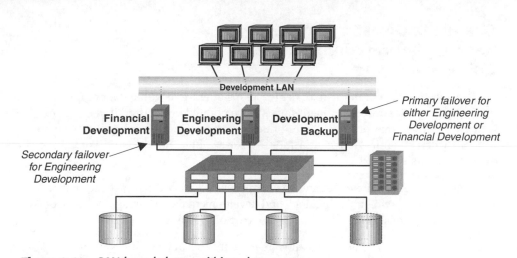

Figure 2.12   SAN-based cluster within a data center.

ter of computers is set up so that if the Engineering Development server fails, its applications are restarted on the Development Backup server. This would impact backups negatively, but the organization has apparently decided to accept this impact rather than add another standby server.

This much could be accomplished with a two-node cluster without a SAN. What's new with SANs is the ability to set a policy that declares the following:

- Financial Development applications can also be restarted on the Development Backup server if their own server should fail.

- Engineering Development is *really* important. If its server fails and the Development Backup server fails at the same time, development applications are restarted on the Financial Development server (albeit with some impact on that server's normal activity).

The SAN has enabled two important capabilities that weren't possible with two-node clusters:

- *N-to-1 failover.* In Figure 2.12, either Engineering Development or Financial Development can restart on the Development Backup server if their own servers fail. Two application servers have been protected for the price of one standby server.

- *Cascading failover.* It is possible to declare an application to be so important that it will restart and run as long as a single server in the cluster is functional.

Yet again, the any-server-to-any-storage-device connectivity provided by SANs enables important new functionality that reduces capital cost and improves quality of data processing service.

Change 8: Disaster Recovery— Keeping Information Processing Going and Going . . .

Clustering within the data center keeps operations going if a computer or other critical application component fails. As we pointed out earlier, it is even possible to configure so that processing continues if *several* computers fail. But what happens when an entire data center fails, as, for example, if a disaster like a fire or flood befalls it?

Again, SANs make a strong answer possible. Figure 2.13 illustrates a *metropolitan cluster*, in which the financial and development departments operate from different, widely separated locations, but are part of the same cluster.

The organizational policy appears to be that it's of highest importance to keep its financial applications operational, even if a disaster incapacitates the entire financial data center.

As with the example of Figure 2.12, primary failover is done within the data center. Because of personnel and other logistical considerations, local failover is always the best policy for handling local failures. If local failover isn't possible because, for example, the financial data center is under water, the cluster configuration allows the financial database and applications to fail over to servers at the development site. Of course, the story's not quite *that* simple. Not only do the servers at the development site have to be designated as secondary failover servers for the financial applications, the data storage strategy has to ensure that there is always an up-to-date replica of the financial applications' data at the development site. In Chapters 6 and 8, we'll discuss storage management strategies that make this happen.

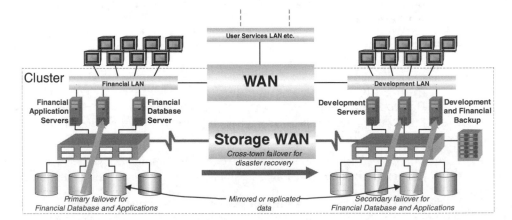

Figure 2.13   SAN-based metropolitan cluster.

Change 9: Cutting Down—More Is Not Always Better

A little study of Figure 2.4 makes it obvious that the User Services and Support Services data centers have similar characteristics:

- Both manage data that is critical to the enterprise and therefore both require significant backup resources and high-quality professional management.

- Both service clients that are predominantly on other LAN segments at remote locations. There is probably little or no client physical access required at either data center.

Since neither of these data centers needs to be physically close to its clients and both require high-grade professional management, an obvious question arises as to whether it would make economic sense to consolidate them into one larger data center. Figure 2.14 illustrates the consolidation of these two data centers.

Disaster recoverability considerations aside, it almost always makes sense to consolidate data centers into fewer, larger centers when physical proximity to clients is not a consideration. The savings from data center consolidation come in three forms:

- *Less supporting infrastructure.* In an equivalent real estate market, it is typically less expensive to maintain one larger business location than two smaller ones, because fixed costs need to be paid only once.

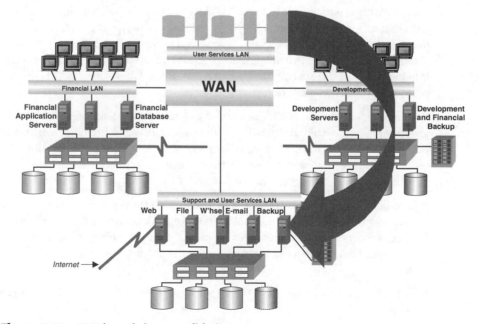

Figure 2.14   SAN-based site consolidation.

- *Lower personnel cost.* As with supporting infrastructure, the cost of people is usually less with fewer locations than with more. Fixed costs such as building security, maintenance, and operations are lower with fewer locations.

- *Lower capital cost.* As suggested earlier, the ratio of required extra storage to total online storage is often reduced when storage is consolidated at one location.

More important than the cost savings, however, is the improved quality of storage and application service that can be delivered because having fewer sites means that there are fewer things to fail.

Change 10: Global Computing for Global Enterprises

More and more enterprises are going global—selling their products or providing their services in Europe, Asia, and Australia, manufacturing offshore, or buying from foreign suppliers. Whatever they're doing, global enterprises need global information services.

It's one thing to have data centers around the world. It's quite another to have them present a coordinated view of the organization that's based on data that's consistent worldwide.

SAN technology's ability to connect servers to distant storage devices (Changes 6 and 8) provides the underpinnings for a consistent view of data across an entire global enterprise. But there's one tiny problem: global response time. SANs are unfortunately subject to the speed of light. That's the limit on how fast data can move across distance. Within a data center the time it takes to move data is negligible. Transmitting data halfway around the earth however can take as much as a tenth of a second, depending on the path. Moreover, most global communications are relayed several times on their path, with a small delay introduced at each step. This would be very visible in application response times, which are usually predicated on I/O operations that complete in a few milliseconds.

So reaching around the world for data to execute a transaction probably isn't the greatest system design. But what about organizations like financial institutions or support providers that have to provide their services on a 24-hour basis? How does the teller in Singapore access the New York customer's funds transfer records or the service technician in Sydney get at the history of the customer in Frankfurt?

It should be no surprise by now that SANs provide the answer . . . but with a twist. Not only does successful global computing require the communications technology to connect computers and storage around the world, it also requires the software in SANs. Two types of SAN software in particular lay the groundwork for computing around the world:

- *Clustering*, as we discussed in Change 7, with the addition of global clustering capability

- *Data replication*, a technology similar to mirroring, but which is able to work successfully over long distances on links that are less than completely reliable

Together, these software technologies combine to enable enterprises to cre... grated information processing operations that literally operate around the cl... around the world. Figure 2.15 illustrates global information services.

Figure 2.15 illustrates information processing sites distributed across the eart... connected to two distinct networks, one for client messaging and one for bulk data transfer between storage devices and servers. While these are shown as two different networks, in actual practice they would often share the same technology and, indeed, even the same facilities. The networks would typically be at least logically separate, however, so that bulk data transfers interfered minimally or not at all with enterprise messaging.

To make global information processing work requires not only these interconnections, but also the software to make the widely separated data centers operate as a coordinated whole. That clustering would be in use at each data center goes without saying. But what if a disaster incapacitates an entire site?

We'd like, for example, New York to be able to take over for San Francisco or Sydney to take over for Singapore, if something really bad happened. For that to be possible, New York and Sydney need both:

- *Up-to-date state information* about the systems at San Francisco and Singapore, respectively

- *Up-to-date copies of the data* those sites are processing and the applications they're using to process it

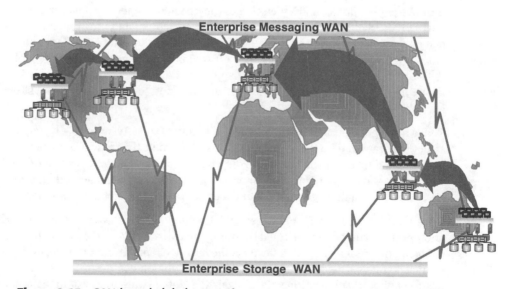

Figure 2.15   SAN-based global computing.

In an operation of the scale illustrated in Figure 2.15, all networks would obviously be replicated on separate physical facilities at a distance from each other for disaster protection. To keep the diagram simple, we have not illustrated these.

- *The red button,* the signal that tells New York or Sydney that its companion data center is indeed down and it should take over and start being the real processing site

The need for up-to-date state information and data is obvious. The red button is needed because shifting an application from one site to another distant site is a complex decision that involves logistical and human considerations as well as factors that are discernable by the computer systems. Global clustering is different from clustering within the computer room or metropolitan clustering in that fully automatic failover is generally not desirable. What is required instead is that the computer systems at the two sites be able to prepare for instant transfer of responsibility at a signal that is given by an administrator at one of the sites.

Getting up-to-date data to the failover sites in a global cluster is also a challenge. As we have already mentioned, the speed of light is not negligible across global distances. If we were to simply mirror data between, say, San Francisco and New York, the *propagation delay* (time to transmit data across the country and receive a response) for every I/O would be part of the response time for every transaction. For most global applications, this is simply not tolerable.

What is typically done instead is to *replicate* updates to data made in San Francisco at the New York data center. Data replication is one of those technologies that's deceptively simple to describe and devilishly complex to implement. We start with identical images of data at both sites (in Chapter 8 we'll talk about how we get these identical images). San Francisco processes its data as if it were a completely local data center. Each time it updates a database, the replication software remembers the update and sends it to New York, where it is applied to the corresponding database there.

If things get hectic in San Francisco and the updates happen too fast for New York to keep up, the San Francisco data center just queues them and they reach New York as fast as network bandwidth allows. That, of course, means that New York can be out of date by a few updates. That's the trade-off we make to be able to compute globally. If the stars line up badly and a disaster happens in San Francisco during a particularly busy time, a few updates may be lost as we transition the main processing site over to New York.

That's not a good situation, but compare it to any of the alternatives—trying to reconstruct the state of data from backup tapes and journals that may or may not be available, depending on the nature of the disaster in San Francisco. We can shorten the window by buying more bandwidth between sites that protect each other, but timeliness versus local throughput is a fundamental trade-off in global computing.

Once we're replicating data between widely separated sites, we have set the stage for another powerful benefit enabled by storage networks: *follow-the-sun* computing. Global applications are global because they serve clients around the world. When San Francisco hits stride, New York is packing up to go home and Europe is finishing a leisurely dinner. Transaction volume against a global computer system, whether it's transferring money, providing customer service, or delivering Web pages and processing transactions, is likely to be heaviest during the business day in any given time zone.

In an ideal world, the primary processing site for a global application would be in Frankfurt during the European business day, shift to New York as Europe left for the day, move to San Francisco as New Yorkers packed it in, and migrate to Sydney or Singapore at the end of the California business day.

By replicating data for disaster recovery, we are setting ourselves up for just such a scenario. If we replicate a customer service database that's being processed in Frankfurt at a data center in New York, then we're within a few seconds of having the global data we need on site when the Germans go home for the night and we want to switch the primary processing site to New York, where it's just time for lunch. That's what the shaded arrows in Figure 2.15 indicate. By *cascading* data around the world, replicating it from Frankfurt to New York to San Francisco and to Sydney, we are setting the stage to move the processing site for the data right along with it.

Global computing is in its infancy today. It is a pretty expensive proposition practiced primarily by the largest enterprises. With storage networking technology, however, global computing is *possible* for the first time. The entire history of computing is one of expensive technology entering the market and providing benefits so compelling that it drives further development, higher volumes, and sharply declining prices. Eventually, the new technology creates an entire new market in which it is mainstream. Microprocessors, personal computers, storage, video display technology, local networking, and high-speed wide area networking have all followed this pattern. Why should we expect global storage networking and global computing to be any different?

Summary

- SANs enable any-to-any connectivity between servers and storage devices and improve the ability of organizations to move their data. These capabilities enable the primary and secondary SAN paradigm shifts.

- SANs can lower information processing capital costs through increased device and capacity sharing, as well as through more efficient communications (Change 1, Change 2, Change 3).

- SAN technology enables universal data access, even across widely distributed enterprises (Change 4, Change 5, Change 6).

- SAN technology enables servers to be organized into clusters for highly available application access and disaster recovery (Change 7, Change 8).

- SANs enable the consolidation of data centers with similar characteristics for increased economies of data processing scale (Change 9).

- SANs lay the groundwork for truly global computing—the ability to process the same information around the clock from any data center around the world, with both the data and primary application execution site migrating to optimal locations as requirements dictate (Change 10).

CHAPTER 3

Leading Up to SANs: One View of Data Center Evolution

I n this chapter we'll learn more about:

- How the processing of digital information has continually evolved to become increasingly flexible and approachable

- How the technologies have enabled users who require access to digital information to get ever closer to it—to have faster, more reliable, more flexible access

- How the repeated leapfrogging of technology and the applications and usage modes it enabled have almost inevitably led down the path to storage networking

A Bit of History

Practically since its inception, digital information processing has been a story of great performance improvements and equally sharp cost reduction curves, overlaid with increases in reliability. The (somewhat wishful, we think) adage is that if automobiles had followed the same performance and cost curves as computers, a car would cost a few dollars, last a lifetime, and go several times around the world on a single tank of gas.

While all have improved greatly, the different computing technologies, processors, memories, online storage, display technology, and communications have progressed at different rates and in different directions. Over the years, this progress had motivated changes in the *architecture* of computer systems—in the way vendors put the parts together, as well as in the way users buy and configure the parts to make systems that solve *their* problems.

Since this is a book about storage networking, in this chapter we discuss the history of enterprise information processing architectures, concentrating on three technology aspects:

- Where data is stored
- Where data is processed
- How data gets from the storage site to the processing site

and three usability aspects:

- *Interactivity*. How users of information interact with the computers that produce it.
- *Responsiveness*. How quickly planned requests for information are satisfied.
- *Adaptability*. Ability to respond to unplanned requests.

We examine each generation of computing architectures from the standpoint of the problems they solved, as well as problems they did *not* solve and new problems they introduced. Our goal is to understand how digital data has continually gotten closer to its users, becoming more accessible and timely and therefore more usable in the conduct of business. We will examine barriers that have sprung up along this path and how technology has evolved to overcome them.

Mainframe Generation I: The Rise of the Data Center

We begin our look at computing architectures with the batch processing generation of the 1960s, the time during which computers came into general commercial use. This was the generation of computers from the BUNCH—Burroughs, Univac, NCR, Control Data Corporation, and Honeywell, and, of course, IBM Corporation. The computers of this era were physically very large and consumed lots of electrical power. They had to be cooled extensively (which consumed even more power) and were very susceptible to humidity and dust. In short, they needed to be kept in carefully controlled environments.

The environmental requirements of these computers, coupled with their cost and the novelty of the electronic computing phenomenon, dictated that these computers be kept in special *data centers* and administered by trained professionals. One of the tasks of these professionals was to interact with other members of the organization who programmed the computers to support the organization's business. In the early years, there was little distinction between *administration* (keeping the computers running) and *usage* (using the computers to solve business problems). Over time, these two professions diverged and they have developed in different ways, as we describe in the paragraphs that follow.

The way these computers were used was dictated partly by the technology of the time—physically large and power-hungry components—but also, we think, partly by the fact that there was no prior history to build on. There was no precedent to say that computers should be big or small or central or distributed, so the industry and profession naturally gravitated to what was convenient for the technology: specially constructed data centers located in or near the main organizational premises.

The information processing architecture built around these early computers was partly dictated by and partly fed back into the design of the computers themselves. Since the computer was located centrally, it made sense for the data it processed to be located centrally as well. Moving data between computer and storage was the province of elaborate *I/O channels*, custom-designed interface electronics packages that moved data between a computer and a storage device over distances of a few yards at blinding speeds of hundreds of kilobytes per second.

Early I/O channels were very expensive. Moreover, computers needed more information than could be contained on a single storage device, so designers conceived the idea of the *shared I/O channel* that would connect several storage devices to a computer. From a very early age, computer systems and software were designed around the idea of *one computer, many storage devices*. This simple but powerful concept of increasing storage capacity by adding more storage devices has been developed and refined in the intervening years, but it's still one of the fundamental building blocks of today's storage networks.

For our purposes, the most significant aspect of these early I/O channels is that each was specific to a single computer system type. It took a long time for two ideas that we take for granted today to become commonplace principles of computer system architecture:

- *Layered design.* I/O channel design should be strictly segregated from computer system design so that one set of storage and other peripheral devices can be used with different types of computer systems.

- *Standardization.* I/O channel design should be standardized, so that different vendors' computers and storage devices can be connected to each other, because history has shown that no one vendor can be best at everything.

This latter idea was especially difficult for vendors to accept. Huge legal and market battles were fought over vendors' right to control their I/O channel architectures and what was connected to their channels by whom. While the industry has evolved significantly in terms of its acceptance of standards (to the great benefit of users!), the truce between computer suppliers and storage device suppliers, and nowadays between both of them and the suppliers of the storage networking infrastructure, is still uneasy at times.

There was very much a priesthood/laity aspect to the organizational culture that grew up around these early computers, fostered partly by the small number of people who understood the machines, but also by the usage characteristics. The characteristics of this era's computing were the following:

Interactivity. With first-generation computers, interactivity meant people interacting with people. People who needed access to information made formal or informal requests to other people whose job it was to keep the computers running and produce the requested information.

Responsiveness. The style of data processing in this era was the scheduled *job*. Predefined computing tasks were performed at set times. Ad hoc tasks would generally be handled on a best-efforts basis. In this environment, overnight response, even for recurring requests, was commonplace.

Adaptability. The computers of this era were difficult to use and not well understood. Small cadres of skilled people would be charged with both understanding users' requests and fulfilling them. Fulfillment usually meant writing custom programs. Because of the expense of writing and maintaining programs, users had to justify their requests extensively before information services departments would work on them. This tended to encourage careful analysis before requests were made to the information services department. Response time for ad hoc requests tended to be measured in weeks or months.

Thus, while this generation of mainframe batch computers represented tremendous progress over the manual record-keeping methods that preceded them, the machines were essentially very efficient, reliable electronic file clerks. They seldom erred, but they did require significant tending from skilled professional staffs. The era of using computers to aid decision making and simplify business practices had not yet arrived.

Mainframe Generation II: Timesharing

While business practices for using computers to process batches of information were solidifying in the 1960s, the research community was proceeding in another direction altogether. Researchers had noticed that there was an imbalance in computing. Computers could execute the electronic instructions that process information *much* faster than information could be fed to them. Much of the computers' time was spent idly waiting for data to arrive from storage or to be put back into storage. And, of course, if the computer had to wait for a human to do something, such as feed some cards into a hopper or mount a disk pack or reel of tape, it could practically take a vacation.

Researchers asked themselves whether all this wasted (and expensive!) computing power could be put to use. Could the computer manage its own time and use those idle moments, perhaps to work on another job? The answer, of course, was a resounding yes, and thus was born the multiprogramming operating system and its near descendant, the timesharing system.

The principle of multiprogramming is simple.[1] When the computer notices that it will have to wait for some external event over which it has no control, such as a disk seeking or spinning, it carefully files away a complete description of the job it is working on in its memory, retrieves the description of another job from its memory, and begins working on that job. It works away on that other job until *it* needs something that isn't immediately available (usually data from a disk or tape), files it away, and begins working on a third. Eventually, it gets back around to the original job and makes more progress on it, and so it goes.

Multiprogramming increased the utility of computers, particularly their ability to use their spare computing power to do ad hoc jobs, but it didn't fundamentally change the characteristics of organizations' computing architectures. The computer was still kept

---

[1] As with most things in computing, the devil is in the details. Today's multiprogramming operating systems are among the most complex bodies of software in existence.

in the glass house and tended by the priesthood. Mere mortals approached gingerly, with the proper degree of respect.

Researchers were working on something else, however, that was to change the face of commercial computing profoundly and forever: *timesharing*. Noting that computers did the simple things they did a million or more times faster than human beings, researchers conceived the idea that computers could process and assemble information that was keyed in by people using the teletype machines that were common in the communications industry at the time. The assembled information could be interpreted as commands to the computer and these commands could be executed using the multiprogramming technique previously described. The net effect was that a person would perceive that he had his own private computer, while the computer was actually acting on behalf of several humans simultaneously. Each person would have a *share* of the computer's *time*; hence, the name *timesharing*.

As Figure 3.1 illustrates, timesharing did not change computer hardware architecture profoundly. The whole idea was to share a large computer among many users, and the more powerful the computer, the more users who could share it. There was a widespread belief at this time that computing could be delivered more efficiently in larger packages—a computer that executes 10 million instructions per second needs roughly the same amount of packaging, floor space, power, administration, and other overhead as does a computer that executes 1 million instructions per second. Thus, the more users a computer could accommodate, the less expensively computing could be delivered to the organization.

Thus, the physical computing architecture went largely unchanged—the large computer in its environmentally controlled glass house cared for by an army of experts and processing data that was stored on disk drives in the same room connected to it by I/O channels.

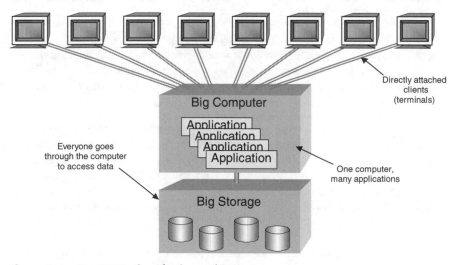

Figure 3.1   Pre-1980: timesharing architecture.

Timesharing did begin the introduction of two profound changes in computing, however, that are still with us today:

The concept of using a network to access the computer was born. The users who operated these teletype terminals[2] usually found it more convenient or congenial to work elsewhere; thus, wiring had to be run to connect them to the computer. It became commonplace for data centers to include network wiring technicians in their staffs.

Computers started to become more approachable by the general populace. The notion that instead of one console for interacting with the computer, there could be a hundred or more terminals from which anyone could access information from various locations was a powerful one. While a tremendous amount of language and tool development still had to occur so that lay users could get some utility out of their access to the computer, the fact that anyone in the organization could have direct access to data started an evolution of the role of the computer priesthood from *controllers of all access to corporate information* to *providers of a service enabling users to access corporate information directly.*

So the state of enterprise information processing during the 1970s and early 1980s was the glass house in which a large central computer with many local disk drives attached to it was connected to terminals outside the glass house from which users were able to access information without the intervention of a professional operations staff. The stage was set for four concurrent streams of innovation that changed computing into what we know today: online transaction processing, minicomputers, local area networks, and the standardization of software.

Online Transaction Processing: Instant Gratification for Users

Timesharing put access to computing and data at the fingertips of many users. But, of course, giving many users access to important data creates a gigantic security problem. Larcenous, disgruntled, malicious, and even incompetent users all had the potential to alter or destroy important business records. The question became how to preserve the undeniable benefits of instant access to information, while protecting the organization against purposeful or unwitting threats to its data.

The software industry's answer to this dilemma was *online transaction processing* (OLTP). An OLTP system is a software framework within which interactive applications can be built and in which users are prevented from performing all but a prescribed set of business functions and from accessing all but a defined set of data. Users of an online transaction processing system may be able to add, change, and delete customer records, for example, but they may not open and browse files, move

---

[2] Which were rapidly supplanted by glass teletypes, or character cell video terminals.

data between directories, execute arbitrary programs, or perform other system utility functions.

OLTP further divided the user community into two distinct roles. A small number of users concentrated increasingly on administering the systems and on developing and maintaining applications, using timesharing as their tool. A much larger segment began to treat the computer as a means to accomplishing their business goals. While the administrative and development-oriented user remained skilled in computer operations and software techniques, the new breed of OLTP user was uninterested in becoming a computer expert. For him or her, simpler was better. Developers of OLTP systems concentrated hard on ease of use to minimize training and familiarization time, as well as to minimize the possibility of error. The result has been an increasing familiarity with computers among the general population. Today, most people can be classified as computer users, in the sense that they are generally familiar with concepts such as visual feedback from keystrokes and mouse clicks, start buttons, enter keys, and so forth.

OLTP systems have a secondary benefit that was of great importance on the path to storage networking. Because they provide limited operating context for users, OLTP systems are very efficient in their use of hardware resources. Because they operate within strict rules, OLTP systems can bypass much of the checking and searching common in more general-purpose timesharing systems. Since they are limited to a small set of predefined operations, OLTP systems can *prestage* many of their activities, reducing setup time to execute user commands. This architecture generally enables OLTP systems to support many more users on a given hardware configuration than general-purpose timesharing would support. As OLTP made it less expensive to put access to computers in the hands of users, enterprises increasingly automated their day-to-day business. Today, it is a rare business that doesn't process its orders, manage its inventory, control its shipping and billing, and service its customers using computers that run OLTP-based applications.

Minicomputers and Beyond: Diseconomies of Scale

While the large computer companies of the BUNCH were adjusting to the timesharing phenomenon and the requirement it created for them to deal with hundreds of users rather than with professionally trained information services departments, another force was building in the world of digital computing. A group of small startup companies, led by Digital Equipment Corporation in Massachusetts, was asserting stridently that computing could be delivered more economically and flexibly by *smaller* computers rather than larger ones.

These minicomputer companies had lots of technology arguments on their side, but their basic premise was that the very economies of scale of large computers had engendered huge overhead infrastructures of equipment, premises, and, most of all, people, all of which actually stood in the way of getting things done, rather than facilitating progress. Users, these minicomputer advocates argued, should take things into their own hands. Install a small computer, manage it within the user department, dedicate it to running the lab or tracking inventory or whatever the department does, thereby avoiding the complexity that makes it so hard to get things done in the main data center. Users should control their own information processing destinies.

The argument was very attractive, particularly to departments like laboratories, shipping, warehousing, and process control, which were just discovering the benefits that computerization might offer them, but which were frustrated by their requests for information processing being prioritized behind more traditional financial and accounting applications.

In part because their machines were inexpensive and flew under the radar of corporate purchasing authorities, these emerging computer users prevailed, and the minicomputer age was upon us. Minicomputer companies became the great success stories of the 1970s and 1980s, with Digital, Data General, and Hewlett-Packard leading the charge, followed closely by the more traditional companies which realized that they had better adapt and adopt or else they would be cut out of this new growth segment of the computer market.

Viewed in the context of the road to storage networking, the minicomputer revolution continued the trend of user empowerment that was begun by timesharing. Increasingly, computers were used directly by people whose jobs were not computing; they were doing the engineering or manufacturing or selling or order processing or inventory control or other work of the organization. They viewed their computers as tools, as they viewed their machine tools or forklifts—as things that helped them get their jobs done, the less obtrusively, the better.

The minicomputer made one profound change on enterprise information processing architecture that has led directly to the need for storage networks. It spread computers and information all around the enterprise. As computer use increased during the 1970s, it slowly became apparent that information was an increasingly vital commodity in the conduct of business. Protecting it from loss or destruction, securing it against unauthorized access, and maintaining its integrity became an integral part of being in business.

Prior to minicomputers, enterprises' valuable digital information was located in one or at most a few well-protected, environmentally controlled data centers, specially built for the purpose. Security, availability, and access problems could be approached from a data center viewpoint. For example, if the problem was security, it could be solved by installing fortress-like doors and walls around the computer room and tightly controlling who got in and when. If the problem was data protection, a backup schedule that involved computers, tape and disk drives, and operators in the computer room itself was what was required.

Minicomputers changed all that. Suddenly, enterprises found themselves with computers everywhere. There was little centralized knowledge of even what computers they owned, let alone what information of what value was stored on any of them. The realization of their exposure was slow to dawn on most enterprises,[3] but when it did, there was mass information panic.

Local Area Networks

Using a network to connect distant computers to each other or to sources of input had been commonplace since the early 1970s. Typically, circuits designed to provide voice telephone service were adapted to carry digital data through the use of modems. Because information can be successfully conveyed between humans with little bandwidth, circuits designed for voice traffic are typically capable of only 3 to 5 kilohertz of bandwidth.

Narrow bandwidth works for voice traffic because the rate at which information is conveyed (speech) is low, and because the receiver is highly intuitive and has a lot of contextual information on which to base error correction. Computers have neither of these properties. They can receive information very rapidly compared to human speech, but they accept all information at face value—they process data exactly as it is received, applying no judgment. Telephone signals and modems, therefore, are most suitable for digital communications between humans and computers or for conveying relatively small packets of information that are thoroughly error-checked upon receipt.

Observing that many of the desirable interactions between computers were between computers within a few hundred yards of each other, researchers in the late 1970s proposed that a technology that allowed much higher data transfer rates would be useful, even if data was to be transferred over short distances. As is usual with good ideas, several vendors entered the fray with similar (but incompatible) technologies. After protracted struggles between baseband and broadband transmission and between party-line and ring topologies, the *Ethernet* technology developed jointly by Xerox Corporation, Digital Equipment Corporation, and Intel ultimately emerged as the market winner.

The road to ubiquity has been a long and winding one for Ethernet, but the basic technology is essentially ubiquitous today. It would probably be impossible to find a data center whose computers are not interconnected by Ethernet. Computers routinely exchange information with each other at speeds that support both transaction processing (low latency) and network backup (high bandwidth). New buildings are wired for Ethernet just as they are wired for telephone service.

The interconnection of computers using Ethernet has arguably led to the most significant changes in the way computers are built and used that has occurred since the

---

[3] With a few exceptions, such as finance and banking, where the business *is* information. These organizations were quick to realize not only the impact that minicomputers could have on their operations, but also the importance of the information they housed. Banking and finance provided much of the market impetus that drove minicomputers and the client/server computing wave that followed them to such a rapid maturity.

computer itself was introduced. Networked computers can exchange information in real time. Data can be moved from where it is produced to where it is consumed. Users can access information that is miles away from them. The trend toward smaller, simpler single-application computers that began with the minicomputer received a giant boost from computer networking. If computers can be networked, then the isolated bits of information produced and managed by departmental computers can be accessible across the enterprise.

Widespread availability of computer networking got the creative juices flowing in enterprise information processing departments. These departments began to design information processing architectures predicated on communication of data between computers. Of course, such architectures required continuously available networks, as well as sufficient bandwidth to make transferring large amounts of data between computers with very low latency practical.

From a storage networking standpoint, local area networks and the metropolitan and wide area networks into which they have more recently matured had a profound effect on computing: For the first time, application designers and system administrators were able to design applications assuming that data can be managed at one computer and delivered to another computer on request. New applications (and there seems to be an endless supply of those) could be implemented without negotiating for a share of the large central computer. Data that existed elsewhere in the organization could be accessed over the network for use by the new application. The network quickly moved from advanced feature to business necessity.

The Standardization of Software

While minicomputers and local area networking were developing, an equally interesting evolution was occurring in software. The earliest computer applications were custom-developed by the enterprises that used them. They reflected organizational business practices and, as those practices evolved, the applications had to evolve to keep pace with them.

Not only were the business policies and practices reflected in these early applications unique to the organization and the types of computers it used, the data they stored and the formats in which they stored it were also unique. Organizations using similar or even identical accounting or inventory management practices would implement and maintain very different software suites for these applications. Moreover, as organizations added more applications, certain key data was inevitably required by more than one application. It became common practice to maintain separate copies of customer lists, sales records, and so forth, for each application requiring them.

Slowly and painfully it dawned on users that reinventing and maintaining unique applications and data management tools for common business functions were wasteful in the extreme. Not only was there the ongoing direct expense for development and maintenance, there was also a competitive dimension. An enterprise implementing a customer application to perform some business function for which its competitor has bought a ready-made package is still incurring development expense while the competitor is reaping benefit.

As a result of this realization, a data management and application software industry began to emerge. While packages for virtually all common business functions are available today, nowhere is standardization more apparent than in the area of relational database management systems. It was apparent from the early days of computing that in almost every business application, records would have to be located, collated, sorted, and otherwise kept in order. Database management systems do all of this in a standard way. Moreover, they separate the management of data from applications and provide applications with common mechanisms for accessing highly structured data. By doing this, they make it practical for many applications to use the same data, eliminating multiple data copies and the expense and propensity for error that they bring along with them. Database management systems have proven their worth over and over again in commercial computing. Analysts' estimates vary, but it is safe to assume that today between 50 and 80 percent of all online business data is managed by relational database management systems.

A Pause to Take a Breath

So we have reached the late 1980s in our whirlwind tour of enterprise computing. The original mainframe computers are, by and large, still in place, executing enterprises' "bread-and-butter" applications, most of which have gone online using OLTP techniques to serve users directly. Minicomputers are appearing everywhere and most new application development is being done for them. Local area networks are common, and distributed enterprises have linked their LANs with wide area networking facilities. Most enterprise computers intercommunicate using standard transport protocols, although there is little standardization of application protocols as yet, except with databases. In short, digital information processing has never been so inexpensive, so widely deployable, and so quick to implement as it is with networks of low-cost minicomputers distributed across the enterprise.

Of course, there are a few nagging concerns. As distributed minicomputers become more important to the conduct of business, the data they manage becomes correspondingly more important. And this dataw is physically scattered throughout the enterprise in sites that are not nearly as well protected, environmentally controlled, or professionally managed as corporate data centers. Slowly and belatedly recognizing the value of their distributed information assets, businesses are beginning to charge their information services departments with gaining control of their proliferating data.

And then the tornado strikes . . .

The PC and Client/Server Computing

Over their lifetime, minicomputers have developed in several different directions (indeed, one seldom hears the term *minicomputer* anymore), including enterprise and departmental servers, high-powered workstations, and, perhaps most important, the personal computer (PC).

Almost as soon as technology enabled the development of economical but functionally complete computer systems that would fit comfortably on a desktop, users recognized their value and began to deploy them. Initially purchased for personal applications like word processing and spreadsheets, personal computers quickly took the place of glass teletypes and other types of user terminals connected to timesharing computers and OLTP systems. The early rationale for desktop computers was simple. While individually not very powerful, these PCs were quite fast compared to human thought processes and reaction times. They were easily able to take over many of the tiny tasks of timesharing and online transaction processing, such as screen formatting and input validation, from the main computer.

For one user, these simple tasks don't amount to much, but when multiplied by hundreds or thousands of users, the savings in central compute power can be quite substantial. Relieved of these simple but onerous tasks, the central computer becomes better able to do the big data access and analysis jobs it's really good at.

These tiny desktop computers were of limited usefulness by themselves. They didn't have the storage capacity for large amounts of data, nor did they have the processing capacity to analyze it. They needed to obtain these data access and processing services from the large central computers. They became *clients* and the central computers with lots of storage and processing capacity became *servers* that did the hard stuff for them.

Early client/server computing might be thought of as timesharing or online transaction processing with *very* intelligent terminals. It differs in one important respect, however. Since the client is a full-fledged computer with full-fledged network access, it can connect to any server on the network. No longer were users tethered to a single computer; their desktop computers could connect to any server on the network with a few keystrokes.

The ability of client computers at the desktop to connect to multiple servers accelerated the move toward distributed enterprise computing. If a new application implemented on a server could be accessed from anywhere in the organization, why not implement each new application on a new server . . . creating an island of data for that application as Figure 3.2 illustrates.

As the trend toward client/server computing became clear, application architectures adjusted to respond to it. The most visible adjustment was in the relational database area, where a standard means of communicating requests for data emerged in the form of Structured Query Language (SQL). As it gained popularity, SQL enabled more and more applications to be developed separately from the data they operated on. With SQL, it was possible for client computers to encapsulate requests for data and send them to a remote database management system running on . . . *you guessed it* . . . a server.

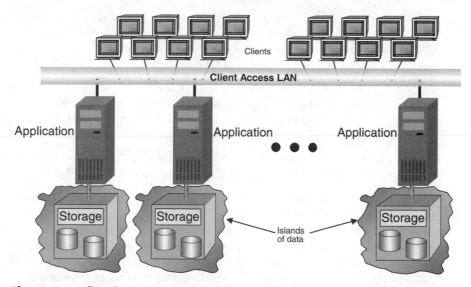

Figure 3.2   Client/server computing architecture.

Specialized Servers

The standardization of data access languages and protocols led to attempts to produce specialized computers optimized for storing and accessing databases. As with many other cases of special-purpose computers, the theory was that a machine built specially for a single purpose could be optimized to achieve that purpose more economically than a general-purpose computer that relied on software to customize it for its task.

With the notable exception of embedded processors, this theory has not proven very successful, perhaps due to the speed with which basic computer technology has progressed. A specialized machine designed to incorporate the base technology that is available at the time of its design is out of date by the time it is introduced because base technology has improved in the meantime. Moreover, because specialized machines are built in smaller volumes than general-purpose computers, they never achieve the production economies of scale of higher-volume general-purpose computers, which translate into lower cost in the market. A few of these special-purpose database machines persist, but, for the most part, users have found it more effective to create their own database servers using general-purpose computers with widely available database management packages.

As acceptance of client/server computing grew, organizations finally seemed to realize the value of the information assets that were scattered around their enterprises. A generation of storage management software developed to care for the increasingly valuable data stored on servers spread throughout organizations. This software includes:

RAID and mirroring software. This is found both in *firmware* that runs in RAID controllers and in server-based *volume managers*. RAID and mirroring technology *virtualize* physical storage, insulating applications from physical device characteristics, and protecting against data loss due to disk failures. We discuss RAID and mirroring technology in Chapter 6.

Journaling file systems. These provide both high performance and data integrity through the use of *logs* or *journals* of important activity that enable them to recover quickly after system crashes. We discuss file systems in Chapter 8.

Client/server backup. This copies up valuable data assets over the network to a secure, managed backup server. We discuss backup in Chapters 4 and 8.

With client/server computing also came the development of specialized servers for generic functions such as printing, faxing, electronic mail, backup, file access, and database access. The last two are of particular interest in the development of storage networking. Just as client/server computing enabled a single desktop computer to access any number of applications, specialized file and database servers enable any number of applications running on different servers to access the same data.

With dedicated file and database servers, not only does data consistency improve due to the reduction or elimination of redundant copies, but enterprises also improve their ability to access and manage their data assets:

- Data concentrated in one place can be properly safeguarded, both environmentally and against malicious damage.

- Data concentrated in one place can be accessed, protected, and backed up professionally, using advanced hardware techniques such as large cache, RAID, and robotic media libraries, as well as trained staff familiar with complex but repetitive procedures and able to handle exception conditions as necessary.

Limitations of Specialized Servers

Concentrating data on specialized data servers accessed by multiple application servers is a long stride toward the concept of storage networking. In fact, a NAS device is essentially a file server. According to our definition (in Chapter 1), if the network that connects a NAS device to its clients is used predominantly for storage traffic, this is, in fact, a storage network.

Simply dedicating servers to file or database access was an important step toward enterprisewide access to consistent data, but certain limitations remained:

- Too much data continued to be duplicated, consuming both storage and network resources, as well as the development and operational resources required to create and manage the duplication procedures.

- Working with duplicates of operational data inherently limited the timeliness of the data used to make important business decisions.

- Too much bulk data transfer continued to be done using networks optimized for many short-lived connections rather than few, high-volume connections. This was especially true of backup.

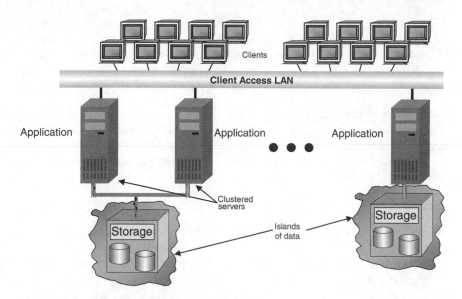

Figure 3.3 Clustering servers for failure tolerance.

- Failure tolerance, the ability to survive disk, server, and other component failures, had to be provided on an ad hoc basis for each dedicated file or database server. Figure 3.3 illustrates server failure tolerance provided by clustered servers.

- Scaling, or the ability to accommodate more data online, was limited in several dimensions, including how many storage devices and client interfaces could be connected to a dedicated data server. Each storage device belonged to one dedicated file or database server; any data shared had to be accessed through that server. Thus, while application servers were able to share data through network connections, ironically, database servers themselves were not. Ability to process file or database access requests was limited by the computing power of the largest affordable server.

- With limited scaling, each time storage requirements grow beyond the practical limits for existing data servers, an additional server is required. This creates a barrier to load balancing, an additional starting point for data searches, and another box to manage. Thus, management cost grows stepwise with data storage growth.

Global Enterprises and the Need for Global Data

Local area networks enabled client/server computing to grow quickly to the size of a *campus* or cluster of computer rooms. In a distributed enterprise, each campus would typically become an information island within which data might be consistent and widely accessible. With only LAN technology available, however, there was little chance of systematic coordination among the islands. LANs and client/server computing enlarged the scope of enterprise data consistency, but did not make it universal. Consistent data across global enterprises had to await the development of high-bandwidth, long-distance network links and data replication techniques.

These technologies and techniques have evolved and today it is possible (albeit somewhat expensive) for widely separated interconnected storage subsystems to maintain near-real-time data consistency. It is possible (although not normally recommended) for a transaction processing application to reach halfway around the world for data to satisfy a client request.

Today, storage wide area networks (*SWANs?*) are used for two main purposes:

- *Disaster recovery.* By maintaining an (almost) up-to-date replica of operational data at a distant alternate data center, an organization can resume data processing relatively quickly after a disaster. More precisely, availability of operational data and the means to process are not the limiting factors in getting back into operation.

- *Publication and consolidation.* Centrally produced data can be replicated at remote sites to improve responsiveness and reduce network latency and bandwidth requirements. Similarly, data generated at widely separated locations, such as regional sales offices, can be collected for coordinated enterprisewide analysis.

Wide area networks that are dedicated to transferring data between servers and storage devices or between pairs of storage devices can legitimately be called storage area networks by our definition in Chapter 1. (See Figure 3.4.)

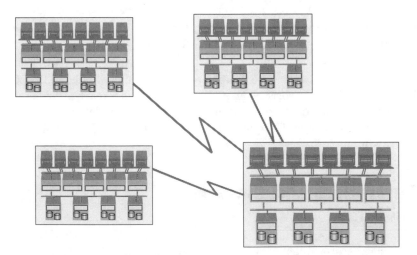

Figure 3.4 A WAN of SANs.

External Storage Subsystems

The final historical development to be discussed on the long and winding road from centralized batch computing to globally interconnected enterprisewide online information processing is one that is still going on today: the trend away from storage devices within the server cabinet to independently housed, powered, cooled, and managed *intelligent storage subsystems*. Moving storage devices out of the computer enclosure has two important implications:

- It puts storage devices into a different *failure domain* from any single server. With server-mounted storage devices, a power failure in the server or, indeed, even an operating system crash or hang makes the storage devices inaccessible. With independently housed storage devices, as long as a storage device itself is working, it can be accessed over its interconnect by *some* server.

- It makes storage devices accessible by multiple servers. Mounting storage devices in their own enclosure inherently requires that they connect to their host computers using an external interconnect. Excepting proprietary interconnects, the first widely deployed external storage interconnect was parallel SCSI. While limited in both connectivity and distance compared to today's Fibre Channel and Gigabit Ethernet interconnects, parallel SCSI does allow a storage device in a separate enclosure to be connected to two or more servers. Multihost access laid the groundwork for clusters of computers connected to the same storage devices and coordinating their accesses to data.

With increasing market acceptance of separately enclosed external storage subsystems, the stage was set for storage networking to develop:

- Local area networks connected each desktop computer user to any number of applications, possibly running on separate servers.

- External storage subsystems provided consolidated packaging, power, cooling, and failure protection for large amounts of storage with multiple host computer connections.

- Increasingly, designated servers were dedicated specifically to file or database serving, creating a need to scale beyond the capacity of the largest such server.

- LANs became popular beyond anyone's expectations, creating chronic traffic overloads that limited organizations' ability to share data across servers, even though the servers had connections to the data.

- Inevitably, different servers running different applications needed to share data.

What was needed now was interconnect technologies that would provide efficient universal access to storage devices (external storage subsystems, file servers, or database servers) at performance levels appropriate to the enterprise and with the ability to scale performance with enterprise and/or data growth. In short, the stage was set for storage area networks.

Summary

- Commercial computing started as a human-intensive batch-oriented process, with inherently long response times and inherent inflexibility.

- Timesharing began the process of accustoming users to instant response and established the concept of a network connecting users to computing resources.

- Minicomputers established the principle of a computer per application, resulting in distribution of important data throughout the enterprise.

- Local area networks and personal computers connected each user to an arbitrary number of applications running on different computers, making it possible for any user to access any of the enterprise's data within a campus. This was the concept of *client-server computing*.

- Specialized servers developed for several generic applications, such as printing, faxing, (more recently) Web access, electronic mail, and, of particular interest in the development of storage area networks, files and databases.

- Specialized file and database servers were the first manifestation of storage networking. They made data available to multiple application servers, as well as directly to desktop users.

- In parallel with the evolution of client/server computing, storage devices evolved from private attachment to one server to separately packaged, powered, and cooled subsystems that could be attached to multiple servers simultaneously, limited only by the capabilities of their interconnects.

- As enterprises grew increasingly global, it became desirable to link their local area networks and share consistent data across the entire enterprise. Implementing wide area storage networks had to await the development of affordable high-performance communications facilities, such as ATM-based networks and software-based replication techniques to keep data nearly synchronized across long distances while still providing adequate local response times.

- Maturing client/server computing created the need for storage area networks. Failure-tolerant external storage subsystems made it possible to share access to storage devices. With both a requirement and the key enabling technology in place, storage networking needed only a suitable interconnect technology to become a reality. This technology first emerged when Ethernet was used to access file and database servers. More recently, Fibre Channel technology has enabled storage networks of block-oriented storage subsystems.

Killer Apps for SANs

I n this chapter we'll learn more about:

- The important applications that provide the motivation for developers to develop SAN products and for users to purchase and use them

- The nature of backup, the application that users love to hate

- How SANs have made it easier for information processing departments to provide their user organizations with highly available data

- How mirroring can be used to make it possible to recover important data and resume processing operations after a site disaster

- How a SAN can complement clustering technology, increasing flexibility, while at the same time potentially reducing the cost of high availability

- Using replication technology to abet disaster recoverability and to perform several functions of great utility in distributed production computing

Killer App 1: Backup—The Application Everyone Loves to Hate

Not long after users started storing valuable data on disks, they discovered that disks can't be trusted. They fail at the worst times and take all the data stored on them with them when they go. Thus was born the concept of making *backups*—copies of online data on separate recording media from which operating data can be recovered if the disk holding it fails.

When business computing was new, getting clerical jobs done in minutes rather than weeks was a magical concept. A computer could whip through a week's worth of filing or account updating in a few minutes. Doing a day's work in eight hours wasn't particularly taxing. During evenings, the computer would often be used by programmers developing new application software. In this environment, data could be backed up during the late-night hours, inconveniencing no one except the computer operators who had to be awake and on duty.

Shrinking Backup Windows

As time went on, however, electronic information became increasingly popular and enterprises depended on it more and more to operate. When timesharing and online transaction processing became the norm, they tended to occupy computers during business hours. This resulted in clerical tasks (*batch updates*) being deferred to the evenings. Software developers suffered, losing some of their access to the computer. What access they still had occurred at less desirable times of the day. The amount of time left to do backup was inevitably squeezed to make room for more important functions—more important, that is, until something went wrong and data had to be recovered from nonexistent backups. Then backup was suddenly perceived as *exceedingly* important, but, of course, nothing could be done to recover lost data.

Time intervals during which a computer is unoccupied by other tasks and therefore available for making backup copies of important online data are called *backup windows*. The basic problem created by enterprises' increasing reliance on computing to operate is that backup windows have been shrinking. With round-the-clock transaction processing (*so you can use your MasterCard at all-night diners*), the windows essentially shrank to nothing. Since the computer has to be available for processing transactions all the time, there is no time available for doing backups. The awful reality seems to be that the more an enterprise relies on its online information to operate, the less opportunity there is to protect that information against loss due to disk or other failures.

Why a Backup Window Anyway?

If applications can't be halted so that a backup can be performed, why not just use some of that excess computing power and I/O bandwidth and copy the data while it's being used? This is a legitimate question and, in fact, most backup programs are capable of operating in modes that approximate this.

For applications that operate on many small, unrelated files, such as office automation, this mode of operation works pretty well. For the more fundamental business applications, however, such as accounting, sales, shipping, and shop floor control, it is important that each backup copy of operational data be *consistent;* that is, it should represent the state of the business at a point in time when no incomplete transactions are in progress.

The simple example of Figure 4.1 will make the need for online data consistency clear. Consider a retail bank's demand deposit accounting (DDA, or checking account) application. Each time a customer makes a withdrawal, his or her account balance must be debited and the cash-on-hand balance for the cash drawer from which money is disbursed must also be reduced.

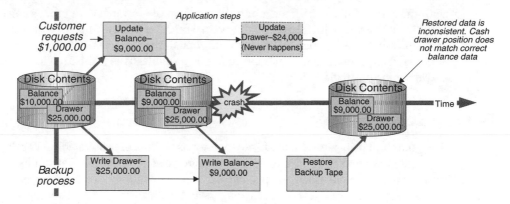

Figure 4.1   Data corruption due to inconsistent backup.

If a backup of DDA data is made while transactions are being processed, then it is possible (likely, even) that a customer record will be backed up after a cash withdrawal has been recorded in it but before the corresponding cash drawer balance is updated. If some kind of failure were to necessitate that the backup copy be restored, it could be troublesome for the teller, because the bank would find cash apparently missing from the cash drawer (cash gone from the drawer, with no corresponding computer record to reflect any disbursement).

A similar scenario can occur if the backup operation copies the cash drawer record after the disbursement is reflected in it, but copies the customer's account record before it is debited. If this backup copy is ever restored, the customer gets free money in the sense that cash has been disbursed to him or her, but after the restore there is no record of a withdrawal from the account. After the backup is restored, the customer could withdraw the same money from the account again.

The point here is not to analyze all possible scenarios that could occur with inconsistent backups. These two simple examples illustrate that consistent backups of operational data are a *must* for any application that is important to an enterprise.

Consistent Backups

The most obvious way to keep data consistent while it is being backed up is not to use it during the backup. If an application is stopped in an orderly fashion, no transactions are being processed during backup. There is no reason for data to change, so consistency is automatic. But inability to use data while it is being backed up takes us back to the problem of the incredible shrinking backup window. For many applications, there isn't a backup window. Particularly with the prevalence of Internet-based commerce today, there is simply no time at which applications can be shut down so that a backup can be made. Other techniques for protecting data must be identified and implemented.

Some very innovative software techniques (which we will discuss in Chapter 8) have been developed to enable consistent backups to be made while data is in use. But even with these techniques, the impact of backup I/O on operational data processing can be significant. Backups are inherently *I/O intensive*. After all, the objective of backup is to get as much operational data as possible copied from the disks on which it is processed to other disks or tapes as quickly as possible. This is the area in which SANs can be particularly helpful.

Backup Schizophrenia

The goals and priorities of backup technology, as well as of system administrators' implementations of backup procedures, often result from conflicted attitudes on the part of users. From a user's perspective, backup costs money (for tape drives, media, and backup software), resources (managers and operators to administer backup procedures), and time (required to execute backups, during which operations are impacted somehow). And the biggest reason for all this cost is that the computers and storage devices sold to them by the same vendors can't be trusted. From the user's standpoint, therefore, an ideal backup would be:

Cheap. It consumes minimal resources.

Unobtrusive. It has minimal effect on operations.

Automatic. It requires minimal attention from operators and managers.

Instantly accessible. It can be restored quickly and reliably when necessary.

In other words, computer users' attitude toward backup is similar to the public's attitude toward police: When everything is going fine, they should be invisible; but when they're needed, they should be on the spot instantly, execute flawlessly, and disappear into the background when their work is done.

Different Uses, Different Backups 1

Backup serves a wide range of purposes, but thinking about it in terms of three basic threats against which it can protect provides good background for understanding why backup technologies have evolved as they have and why SANs are especially suitable for enhancing backup. Backup copies of data are useful in the following situations:

Hardware failures. These can range from the failure of a single disk to the destruction of an entire data center, making some or all of an enterprise's operational data unrecoverable. Data objects are destroyed if they are stored on the failed devices. Destroyed objects may or may not be related to each other.

Software failures. These are procedural errors in an application that corrupt operational data. Data objects that are corrupted are generally related to each other, but there is no fixed relationship between corrupted objects and the devices on which they are stored.

User errors. These include errors such as inadvertent deletion or overwriting of files that are later required. In these cases, the set of destroyed objects generally impacts the ability of a user or set of users to function, rather than an application and all the users attached to it.

If we were trying to protect against any one of these failure modes, the choice of a backup strategy would be relatively straightforward. For example, if the goal is to protect against hardware failures, one appropriate strategy would seem to be maintaining a bit-for-bit replica of the contents of all the devices we are trying to protect on a separate set of devices. This is, in fact, a useful strategy and, in the form of mirroring and replication technology, has almost taken over from backup as the preferred means of protecting operational data against hardware failures.

Unfortunately, system administrators seldom have the luxury of protecting data against only one type of failure. Their mandates tend to be more in the form of, "*Keep our operational data accessible, no matter what!*" So while variations of mirroring and replication technology can be configured to provide almost arbitrarily good protection against device and data center failures, they will also:

■ Write data corrupted by application errors every bit as reliably as they write correct data.

■ Faithfully record the file system or database metadata updates that result from a user's mistaken deletion of an important file on all mirrors or replicas of the file system.

Because they are optimized to serve different purposes, mirroring and replication technologies have different goals than backup:

■ Mirroring and replication attempt to preserve the bit-for-bit state of storage devices or files as they change.[1]

■ Backup attempts to preserve the state of a set of data objects as of some past point in time at which they were known to be consistent.

The ideal mirror or replica keeps the contents of all replicated devices or files identical to each other. The ideal backup does something quite different: It captures an image of data at an instant in the past, so that if need be, everything that has happened to the data since that instant can be forgotten, and the state of operations (as reflected in the data) can be restored to that instant.

The distinction between the broad swath of destruction cut by an application bug and the (usually) limited impact of a user error is a more subtle one. In both cases, we want desperately to return data to its state before the error—before the buggy application was installed or before the user hit that fatal enter key. In the former case, it is likely that a point-in-time image of a rather large mass of data will have to be recreated. The common technique starts with restoring all of an application's files to their start at some point before the error occurred. From that point, a log of transactions can be played against the old (error-free) version of the application to create a correct current state of operations to the extent possible. From a backup standpoint, the focus

---

[1] In this case, *physical storage devices* is a long-winded way of saying disk drives. *Virtual storage devices* are the virtual disks emulated by enterprise RAID controllers.

is on moving a large amount of data quickly from backup storage media to the disks on which operations will resume.

Recovering from user errors has somewhat different requirements. It is likely that data destroyed by a user has relatively little effect on other parts of the information processing operation. Therefore, a restore operation that pinpoints the destroyed objects and restores only them is the preferred technique. The ideal backup for this type of recovery is one that can pick a few objects out of a (possibly) much larger backup set and restore them quickly, without regard to other aspects of the operation. Many enterprise backup software suites allow the restoration of individual data objects to be delegated directly to the users to whom the objects belong.

So we have three different requirements for backup copies of data:

- *Protection against storage device failure*, best served by bit-for-bit copies of device contents made in real time or as close to real time as possible.

- *Protection against destruction of a large amount of related data* (as might be caused by application error), best served by backup techniques optimized for fast, high-volume restores.

- *Protection against destruction of individual files* that are unrelated to other parts of the information processing operation, best served by backup techniques optimized for quickly locating and restoring individual objects within a larger backup set.

As we will see, SAN technology enables significant improvements in all three of these data protection techniques.

Different Uses, Different Backups 2

With backup techniques, the user can pay now or pay later, but he or she will pay. Backup copies of data may be either:

- *Full*, meaning that all of the objects in the backup file set are copied, regardless of how recently they have been modified or whether a previous backup copy exists; or

- *Incremental*, meaning that only objects in the backup set that have changed since some previous event (usually a prior backup) are copied

For almost all applications, incremental backup is preferable at backup time, since, in most cases, the number of objects that changes between backups is very small compared to the entire set of objects in the backup set. If backups are done daily or even more frequently, it is not uncommon for less than 1 percent of objects to change between backups. An incremental backup in this case moves 1 percent of the data that a full backup would move and uses 1 percent of the I/O resources. Incremental backup seems like a clear win.

And so it is, until a full restore of all data is required. A full restore from incremental backups entails starting with a restore of the newest full backup copy, followed by restores of all newer incremental backups. That can mean a lot of media handling—

time consuming if done by an automated robotic handler; time consuming *and* error prone if done by a human. Thus, restore from full backups is generally simpler and more reliable than restore from combinations of full and incremental backups.

For recovering from individual user errors, the situation is just the opposite. The argument runs like this. Users tend to work with one set of files for a period of days or weeks and then set them aside and work with another set. There is thus a high probability that a file destroyed by a user will have been used recently and therefore will be copied in incremental backup operations. Since incremental backups contain a small fraction of the data in a full backup, they can usually be searched much faster if a restore is required. The ideal from the individual user's standpoint is therefore lots of small incremental backups.

Some enterprise backup software suites offer a compromise: the ability to consolidate a baseline full backup and several incremental backups into a new, more up-to-date full backup, which becomes the baseline for further incremental backups. While costly in terms of resources (tapes, tape drives, and bandwidth) and time, these *synthetic full* backups simplify restoration, so the capability is very popular with users.

With this as background, we embark on a tour of the physics of backup in various system topologies, leading up to the distributed enterprise information processing system, where SAN technology enables new techniques that result in higher-quality, more frequent backups at less impact on online operations. Chapter 8 has more to say about the software aspects of enterprise backup.

Backup on a Single Computer

Figure 4.2 illustrates perhaps the simplest case of backup: one computer with one I/O bus to which both online storage (the disk drive) and backup media (the tape drive)[2] are attached.

Figure 4.2 is representative of both small servers and desktop computers. Although far removed from the distributed enterprise systems for which SANs are most applicable, the figure illustrates two key points about backup that are equally true for these distributed systems and that, in fact, are two of the reasons why backup is a killer app for SANs:

- *Backup costs twice as much as it seems to.* Cost, in this case, refers to I/O bandwidth required to move data from its source (the disk containing online operational data) to its target (the tape drive). With conventional backup architectures, disks and tapes are peripheral devices, capable only of responding to host commands to transfer data between themselves and computer memory. Thus, in Figure 4.2, every byte of data to be backed up would be read from the disk into the computer's memory and written from memory to the tape, passing across the I/O bus twice in the process.

[2] Throughout our discussions of backup, we will use the tape drive as the archetype of a backup device. While we recognize that other types of backup devices are used, notably optical and magnetic disks, tape is by far the most prevalent backup media today. Moreover, tape presents certain challenges uniquely suited to SANs.

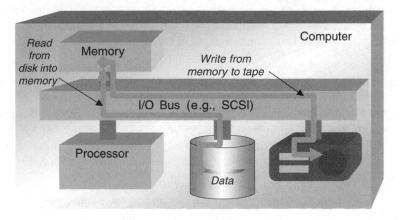

Figure 4.2 Backup within a single small computer.

- *Backup is inherently resource contentious.* Given that we have to move backup data twice, the least we'd like to be able to do is to buffer the transfers, so that the disk could be sending the next block of data to the computer memory while the tape was absorbing the current block. In the example of Figure 4.2, however, the disk and tape drives both use the single I/O bus for data transfers. Now all popular shared I/O bus architectures allow only one device to transfer data at any one instant. Thus, when the disk is busy sending data to the computer's memory, the tape has to wait. There goes the chance of overlapping reads and writes for better performance!

In actual fact, this contention isn't quite as bad as it sounds, because today's buses are much faster than today's devices and the devices simply buffer data until the bus is free and then send it out. But the situation is not ideal. With the simple architecture illustrated in Figure 4.2, often the disk or tape drive has to stall, waiting for a chance to transfer data.

Stalling is bad enough for disks; if the bus isn't ready when the disk needs it, a revolution can be lost waiting for data to spin around past the read head. For tapes, it's disastrous. Today, all tapes use *streaming* technology to avoid the need for ultra fast acceleration and deceleration of fragile media. In essence, when starting to write, the tape drive backs the media up and gives it a running start so that by the time it's positioned to write, tape is moving at full speed. Disks don't have the acceleration problem because they're spinning all the time.

Once a tape is in motion, the drive can *stream* data to it, writing consecutive blocks at full speed for as long as it has data to write. If the data supply fails, however, the drive has to slow the tape down and stop it. Before more data can be written, the tape must be backed up and another running start made. As one might imagine, these *repositioning cycles* are deadly to throughput, each requiring tenths of a second.

What could make a tape drive starve for data? Why, bus contention, of course. By I/O bus standards, tape drives transfer data slowly—10 megabytes per second is common.

But they need a steady supply of data to keep the tape moving. If a disk drive's activity prevents a tape drive from getting its little bit of data when it needs it, the dreaded repositioning cycle occurs. For this reason, the backup architecture illustrated in Figure 4.2 is useful only in the smallest systems or in those with fairly relaxed backup window constraints.

A Little Relief: Multiple I/O Buses

Figure 4.3 illustrates how a slightly larger server might be configured with two or more I/O buses for backup. In this configuration, the disk drive(s) to be backed up are connected to separate I/O buses from the tape drive that will receive the data. Connecting disk and tape drives to separate buses means that the two no longer contend for the same I/O bus bandwidth. In principle, there is still contention for access to the computer's memory, but computer memory bandwidth is typically quite high compared to I/O; moreover, memory access is highly interleaved, so neither the processor nor any I/O bus is starved for data.

The configuration shown in Figure 4.3 eliminates bus bandwidth contention between disk and tape drives. Larger servers can usually be configured with multiple I/O buses; these can often be paired so that several backup operations can take place at once. For situations in which tape drives can absorb and write data faster than disks can deliver it, some backup software suites support the multiplexing of data streams from several concurrent disk backups onto a single tape in order to keep the tape drive streaming.

To move data from disk to tape within a single computer, configuring the computer with enough I/O buses and connecting disk (or RAID array subsystems) and tape drives on separate buses is a pretty good solution. In Chapter 8, we discuss software techniques that reduce the amount of data that must be moved for a consistent

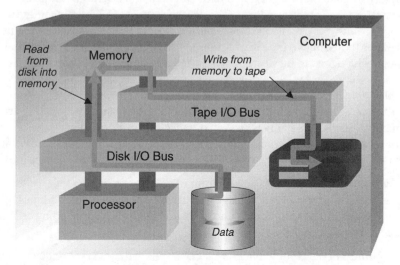

Figure 4.3   Backup within a slightly larger single computer.

backup. Whether little or much data must be copied, however, moving it faster is always preferable.

Backup in Client/Server Environments

Within the confines of a single computer, a SAN is hardly necessary. As we pointed out in Chapter 3, client/server computing is pretty much the way enterprise information is processed these days. Client/server computing means lots of servers managing important data that must be backed up. Thus, in a large enterprise, the configuration illustrated in Figure 4.3 could be replicated hundreds or even thousands of times. This is undesirable for several reasons:

Tape equipment is expensive. Not only are tape drives expensive to buy and own, they are idle for most of their lives. An enterprise with tape drives connected to all of its servers has a lot of hardware assets sitting around doing nothing for a lot of the time.

The cost of managing distributed backups is high. If every server does its own backups, the administrative staff must understand both backup procedures and the nature of the data managed by each server. In many cases, employees with other day jobs are drafted as part-time administrators. While this may present the illusion of lower cost, an employee responsible for system administration is not doing his or her day job while administering computers. Moreover, since part-time system administration is just that—part time—there is little incentive or opportunity for the employee to become really proficient. This can mean high frequency of errors and low quality of service.

It creates barriers to improving quality of storage service. There are several reasons for this, largely having to do with economies of scale. Quality issues with part-time system administrators are noted in the preceding paragraph. A full-time system administrator who is measured on his or her work has both better incentive and more opportunity for excellence than a part-time one. If an organization requires hundreds or thousands of tape drives, there is a strong temptation to select inexpensive units, which tend to be slower and less reliable than more costly ones. The result is backups that take longer and fail more frequently. Perhaps the most important factor in backup quality is robotic media libraries. These devices are expensive and therefore difficult to justify, but their value in reducing media handling errors is inestimable. Finally, it is unlikely that an organization with hundreds of servers will construct hundreds of environmentally controlled, physically secure media vaults. Media reliability and longevity are likely to vary from location to location.

From the very early days of client/server computing, users and developers alike realized that making every server responsible for its own backups would ultimately be untenable. Users demanded solutions and software vendors responded by creating *distributed backup managers*.

The basic premise of distributed backup management is that it is more cost-effective to concentrate the *execution* of backup in a few locations that can be equipped with the best hardware resources and physical facilities. Figure 4.4 illustrates distributed backup management architecture.

In Figure 4.4, backup hardware resources have been concentrated at the server labeled *Backup Server*. *Backup Server* and each of the application servers cooperate to make backups on a schedule that avoids contention among application servers for backup resources. All the tape and media resources are concentrated at *Backup Server*. Since the same resources work on behalf of all the application servers, they are used more efficiently. Since the enterprise of Figure 4.4 has only one backup site, it can afford to create an environmentally optimized, physically secure facility, better protecting both its data and its media. With all tape drives and media concentrated in one place, robotic media handlers may very well be able to justify reducing media handling and therefore errors. Tapes can be pooled for lower overall cost and minimization of failed jobs due to lack of media. Since operations personnel at the *Backup Server* site manage backups for a living, they tend to get pretty good at it, improving the quality of storage service. All in all, distributed backup management seems to be an answer to client/server computing's prayer.

In the backup architecture illustrated in Figure 4.4, data reaches *Backup Server* over an enterprise network that interconnects all of the organization's electronic data processing equipment, including clients, application servers, and special-purpose devices such as print, mail, and fax servers. This, in a nutshell, has been the perennial weakness of distributed backup because:

- It uses the enterprise network to move large amounts of data between application servers and backup servers. This interferes with the application messaging traffic for which the enterprise network was installed in the first place.

- Until recently, the most widely deployed messaging networks had limited bandwidth (100 megabits per second per link) relative to the large and growing amounts of data requiring backup. Application servers were able to supply and multi-tape backup servers were able to absorb backup data streams faster than the network could carry them.

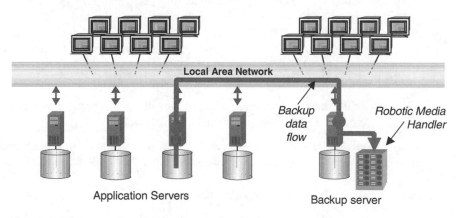

Figure 4.4 Conventional client/server backup.

- The TCP/IP network protocols used in messaging networks are optimized for very large numbers of connections over complex network topologies rather than the topologically simpler data transfer-intensive connections required for backup. The protocols are designed for arbitrarily large networks with complex routing and therefore incur a lot of software overhead that makes them suboptimal for carrying storage traffic.

- The backup data path is long. Data must be read from disks by the application server, sent over the network to the backup server, transferred from the network into backup server buffers, and written to the backup device.

In recent years, organizations have learned the trick of dedicating separate network segments to backup. This gets backup traffic off the enterprise messaging network and, in fact, makes the segments into storage area networks according to our definition in Chapter 1, but it does not increase bandwidth or improve protocol efficiency. Using gigabit Ethernet in these segments increases bandwidth, but does nothing for protocol efficiency or data path length.

In summary, managed distributed backup is generally recognized as the preferred technique for protecting data in multiserver data centers. Concentrating backup resources and skills in one place creates economies of scale and improves quality of storage service. Higher-speed networks have improved backup performance and shortened backup windows. The major issue remaining is the impact of backup data movement on the enterprise messaging network.

As we have argued earlier, SANs can both improve the quality and reduce the impact of backups on operations in a variety of ways. The following sections discuss ways in which SAN technology can be used to improve backup in general and enterprise client/server backup in particular.

Improvement 1: LAN-free Backup

The frequently heard *SCSI on steroids* metaphor might imply any of several things about a SAN, all in the general vein of improving SCSI capabilities. As a simple example of this, consider the length of a communication path. Different variations of parallel SCSI support different maximum bus lengths, but the longest is the 25-meter separation enabled by any of the *differential* SCSI variations.[3] With Fibre Channel (the most popular SAN interconnect today), optical cabling enables two interconnected devices to be separated by as much as 10 kilometers. Various vendors have developed proprietary technologies that support even greater separations.

Long-distance links between devices enable modes of operation not possible with short-distance parallel SCSI links, as Figure 4.5 illustrates.

In Figure 4.5, an application server is connected to a SAN that is nothing more than a point-to-point Fibre Channel link to its tape drives and robotic media handler. Most tape

---

[3] Appendix 1 contains pointers to Web sites where you can find the official stories about all of the major I/O interconnects.

drives are available only with parallel SCSI interfaces, making it impossible to connect them to Fibre Channel or other SAN technologies. An active industry segment has sprung up to provide *protocol bridges* and *storage routers* that convert between parallel SCSI and Fibre Channel serial SCSI protocols. These devices have served two basic purposes:

1. They enable the connection of legacy storage devices to Fibre Channel SANs, thus enabling users to adopt SAN technology while preserving major storage device investments.

2. By enabling the connection of tape drives to SANs, they have enabled the number one killer app for SANs: backup.

Most enterprise RAID subsystems and a few tape drives are now available with Fibre Channel host interfaces, obviating the need for protocol bridges and routers with newly purchased storage. Their usefulness will persist as long as legacy parallel SCSI storage is in use. Today, vendors of these devices are developing bridging capability between Fibre Channel and other emerging SAN technologies (about which we say more in Chapter 7), so users can expect that protocol bridges and routers will be a part of the SAN scene for a long time.

Figure 4.5 also shows the enterprise LAN being used as the control path over which the application server directs the media handler to load and store tape media. Robotic media handler vendors are moving toward in-band robot control, using the SAN as the control as well as the data path. This simplifies cabling and path management.

Separating an application server from its tape drives may be desirable for any of several reasons. Perhaps the most common is a requirement to locate the media handler and tape drives in a physically secure, environmentally controlled, professionally man-

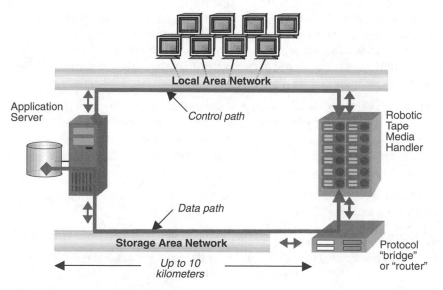

Figure 4.5   Long-distance backup.

aged vault for the safety of the data on the tapes. The application server, on the other hand, may need to be located elsewhere, for network interconnect reasons, reasons of human accessibility, and so forth.

The configuration delivers two of the SAN benefits:

- High-volume data transfers are removed from the enterprise LAN and performed over the SAN, which is dedicated to this purpose.
- Storage devices (tape drives in Figure 4.5) are widely separated from the application server that processes the data they hold.

It is also instructive to consider two potential SAN benefits that are *not* delivered with this simple configuration:

- With only one application server and one group of tape drives, the broad interconnectivity potential of SANs is not being exploited.
- Data to be backed up still traverses a somewhat lengthy path. In Figure 4.5, data is read from online storage into application server memory and sent over the SAN through a buffer in the bridge or router to a tape drive.

Broad interconnectivity is not of interest to an enterprise with only one application server. To interconnect a lot of devices, an enterprise needs to have a lot of devices to interconnect. Shortening a highly utilized backup data path, however, would be universally beneficial. We shall return to this aspect of SAN-based backup shortly.

Improvement 2: Tape Drive Sharing

We have already observed that the any-to-any connectivity property of SANs enables multiple servers to share the same storage devices. *Enables* is the key word here. Figure 4.6 illustrates a SAN configuration in which two application servers with data to back up share a robotic media library. The SAN connects both servers directly to the tape drives that are mounted in the media handler (through a bridge or router if necessary), but it does not arbitrate between them for ownership of the drive. That's where software comes in.

Unlike disk drives, tape drives are by nature single-stream devices. When an application (e.g., backup) job writes data to a tape drive, it generally assumes that its stream of data is the only thing being written to the tape. From start to finish, a backup job must own the tape(s) it's writing exclusively. No other job can be permitted to intermix data with the backup stream.

In a situation such as we illustrate in Figure 4.6, it is important that jobs running on application servers:

- Be able to negotiate for temporary ownership of the tape drives they need.
- Be guaranteed exclusive ownership of the tape drives for the duration of a backup job so that other servers cannot write to them.
- Be able to relinquish ownership of tape drives when finished using them and inform waiting jobs so that they can negotiate for the drives.

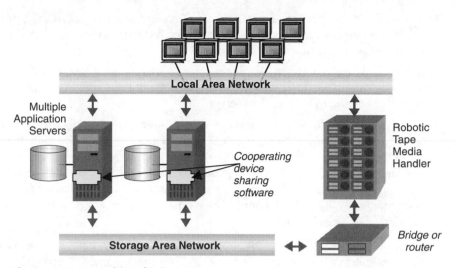

Figure 4.6 Tape drive sharing.

■ Have tape drive ownership taken from them if they or the servers on which they are running fail so that tape drives are not locked up by jobs that are no longer running.

The technology required to implement tape drive sharing goes by several names—*shared storage*, *LAN-free backup*, *tape pooling*, and so forth. Its essential capabilities are:

■ It must be distributed; that is, cooperating instances (copies) of it must run simultaneously on all servers eligible to share tape drives and intercommunicate with each other to negotiate tape drive ownership.

■ It must control the SAN I/O path over which commands and data move between servers and tape drives.

■ It must be able to detect failure of application jobs that own tape drives or of the servers on which they are running, so that it can seize ownership of those drives and make them eligible for reallocation.

One way to look at tape drive sharing is that it creates a pool of tape drives available to all servers connected to the SAN. Pooling tape drives among several servers has several beneficial effects:

Fewer tape drives are required. Because tape drives are typically used only during backup, a typical server needs tape drive access for relatively brief intervals. If backup schedules are staggered so that all the servers connected to a SAN perform their backups at different times, ownership of tape drives can be passed from server to server as needed. Four or five tape drives might adequately serve the needs of 20 or more servers.

Tape drives are utilized more efficiently. Tape drives are expensive to buy and own. An enterprise can maximize the value derived from its backup hardware assets by increasing tape drive *duty cycle*.

Failure tolerance increases. When tape drives are SAN-attached, failure of a tape drive does not mean that a server cannot back its data up. Any SAN-attached tape drive can be used to back up any server.

Robotic media handlers become more affordable. Because they provide a cleaner tape environment and virtually eliminate human handling, robotic media handlers are perhaps the best way to improve enterprise backup reliability. They are expensive and are therefore cost-justifiable only for the largest servers. If the media needs of several servers can be aggregated, however, a shared media handler may be justified more easily. By making a pool of tape drives and media accessible to several servers, a SAN enables this.

Tape sharing is a SAN killer app for another reason. It is a low-risk, low-impact way for an information services operation to test-drive SAN technology. The investment required to explore SAN technology by sharing tapes consists of:

- The *SAN infrastructure* to interconnect servers to tape drives. This consists of a small Fibre Channel switch and a host bus adapter for each of the servers to be connected to the SAN.

- *Bridges* or *routers* to connect legacy tape drives to the SAN. If an organization's existing drives can be bridged to the SAN, new drives are not required.

- *Tape pooling software* required to ensure dedicated ownership of tape drives.

Each server's backup is usually independent of other backups, so it is often possible to try modest experiments, sharing the tape drives of only a few of a data center's servers and adding to that number as experience is gained and confidence grows. The first server added to the SAN without its own tape drives represents savings. As more servers (and tape drives) are added, human management (e.g., console monitoring and media handling) is consolidated and savings increase. Ultimately, a robotic media handler may be justified, improving quality of storage service while reducing cost still further.

Improvement 3: The Designated Backup Server

The next obvious step in exploiting SAN capabilities for backup can be taken when disk storage is connected to the SAN, as illustrated in Figure 4.7, where one server has been made responsible for running all backups. When an application server requires backup, it sends a request to the backup server (in practice, the backup server is more likely to have a predefined backup schedule for each server). The backup server takes control of the disk drives containing the data to be backed up and performs the operation.

Dedicating a server to backup eliminates the CPU and I/O overhead of backup from all application servers. Of course, if an application server must relinquish control of its data for backup, the applications that process that data can't run during the backup. Applications that operate on other data *can* run, however, and will experience no degradation from the backup job, because it is running elsewhere.

A dedicated backup server can be configured especially for the purpose. CPU requirements for backup are not great, but a large memory for buffering and multiple I/O buses and adapters for moving data are generally appropriate. Organizations deploying SAN technology can sometimes add memory and I/O bus adapters to obsolete servers and employ them as dedicated backup servers.

Ideally, a dedicated backup server would be able to share an application's online storage devices with the application and perform the backup while the application continued to run. This is, in fact, possible, using some advanced software techniques discussed in Chapter 8.

Improvement 4: Serverless Backup

According to our definition in Chapter 1, a SAN's primary purpose is to connect storage devices to computers *and to each other*. The "and to each other" part of this definition anticipates a technology development that is only now beginning to emerge from the laboratory: direct transfer of data between storage devices without passing it through a server.

As noted earlier in this chapter, the simplest improvement a SAN can make in a data center is the removal of storage I/O traffic from the enterprise LAN. This is of particular value with data transfer-intensive applications like backup, whose goal is to move data from application server to backup server in the shortest possible time. Conventional client/server network backup loads the enterprise network, resulting in sluggish

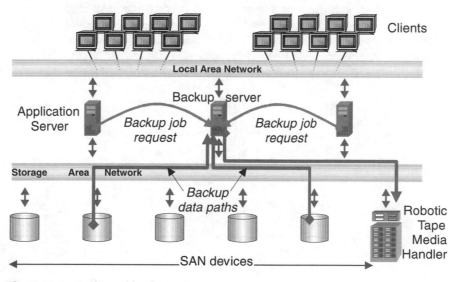

Figure 4.7   Dedicated backup server.

response to clients, even from servers that have nothing to do with the backup in progress.

With *LAN-free backup*, bulk data travels over a SAN. LAN-free backup removes backup data transfers from the LAN, with the result that backup no longer affects the performance of uninvolved clients and servers.

LAN-free backup does not shorten the path that data must travel from disk to tape. In the model of Figure 4.7, backup data is transferred from a disk over the SAN to the backup server's memory, transferred again over the SAN to a tape drive buffer, and finally written to tape. Some robotic media handlers contain embedded servers that *stage* data for writing to tape. In these devices, the data path is even longer.

If both disk and tape drives are connected to the SAN, it should be possible to transfer data directly between them, without using server buffers to hold it while in transit. Figure 4.8 depicts this scenario, which is commonly known as *serverless backup*.

In Figure 4.8, both disk and tape drives are connected to the SAN. A server backing up its data issues special commands whose general form is "read a designated range of data blocks and send them directly to the designated tape drive."[4] Copying data in this way is referred to as *serverless* backup, because the data being copied does not pass through the server. While not in the path of bulk data transfer, a server controlling a serverless backup is very much involved, as it issues the *SCSI remote copy* commands to the disk, tape drive, or bridge that does perform the data movement.

---

[4] In the SCSI command protocol, additional commands whose general form is "issue a read command to a designated disk drive and write the data returned to tape" enable the tape drive or bridge to which it is connected to control copying.

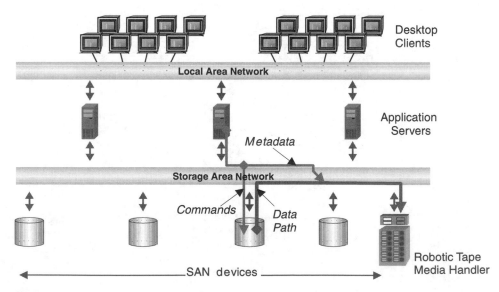

Figure 4.8 Using a SAN for serverless backup.

Serverless backup is something rarely seen in computing: It saves resources by eliminating work. With both conventional and LAN-free backup, data is read from disk into server buffers and written to a tape drive buffer. Thus, all data being backed up is transmitted twice. Moreover, the data consumes buffer space and memory bandwidth in the server. With serverless backup, data is transferred directly from disk to tape buffers, eliminating half the data movement. No server buffers are required, nor is server memory bandwidth consumed. For organizations with hundreds of gigabytes or terabytes of online data, the time and I/O resource savings can be substantial.

It is also sometimes argued that backup processing time is reduced by serverless backup, since each SCSI extended copy command both reads and writes, so only half as many I/O commands are issued and processed by the server. Since extended copy commands are more complex to formulate, this effect should be small.

While not exactly trivial, SCSI extended copy commands would be relatively simple to implement if all that was required was to copy sequences of data blocks from disk to tape. To support restoring individual files, backups must contain not only data, but also *metadata* that describes file structures. Conventional backups inject this metadata into the data stream as it passes through the server on which the backup program is running. With serverless backup, however, data does not pass through the server, so this opportunity does not exist. SCSI remote copy technology therefore allows a host to insert metadata that it supplies into a stream of data being transferred from a disk to a tape.

Serverless backup enhances the value of the dedicated backup servers discussed in the preceding section. When the SAN backup architecture is LAN-free (i.e., transferring backup data into and back out of the backup server), the SAN itself can become a bottleneck. By halving the amount of data transferred during backup, serverless backup can extend the saturation load level for a given SAN hardware configuration.

Serverless backup is not yet widely deployed, as this book is being written. Like most of SAN technology, serverless backup requires both *enabling technology*, in the form of storage or network devices that can execute SCSI extended copy commands, and *exploiting software*, in the form of backup engines that issue the commands and supply metadata to create structured backup tapes. All signs point to general availability of both hardware and software required for serverless backup solutions by the time this book goes to press.

Improvement 5: Off-Host NAS Backup

Thus far, we have discussed improvements in the necessary evil of backup from the point of view of block-oriented SAN devices as we defined them in Chapter 1. The use of SAN architecture with NAS devices (also defined in Chapter 1) is also beneficial to backup of data stored in these devices.

Backing up data stored in NAS devices is a bit different from backing up data stored on SAN devices. SAN devices (as defined in Chapter 1) are block-access devices. Information about which blocks belong to which files resides in the host computer that controls the devices. Thus, a host computer running a backup program can query the

SAN device about which blocks constitute a given file and use the response to set up a SCSI remote copy command.

With NAS devices, on the other hand, the interface to the device is a file interface. There is no way for a server to ask which blocks constitute the contents of a file. The concept does not exist, since NAS devices do not export a raw device abstraction. Thus, for an application server to back up data stored on a NAS device, it must open files on the NAS device, read the data in them, and send that data to the (local or SAN-attached) backup device. There is no way to implement the serverless backup concept.

NAS developers have created a backup capability that is functionally similar to serverless backup, however. Figure 4.9 illustrates two NAS devices attached to a storage area network. (Today, this SAN would probably be implemented using Ethernet technology.) One of the NAS devices is configured with a locally attached robotic media library. The other is configured without a local library; however, there is a robotic media library attached directly to the SAN. (Today, the library would probably have an embedded server for staging backup jobs to an embedded disk drive before they are written to tape.)

As Figure 4.9 suggests, it is possible for NAS devices to provide the equivalent of serverless backup, as well as an in-the-box backup. Both of these are achieved through the use of a protocol called *Network Data Management Protocol* (NDMP), controlled by the *Internet Engineering Task Force* (IETF). The IETF is responsible for a variety of network-related standards.[5] The NDMP enables a backup program to send commands to a NAS device with local backup devices.

---

[5] Appendix 1 contains a list of organizations responsible for the major storage networking–related standards and the standards for which each is responsible.

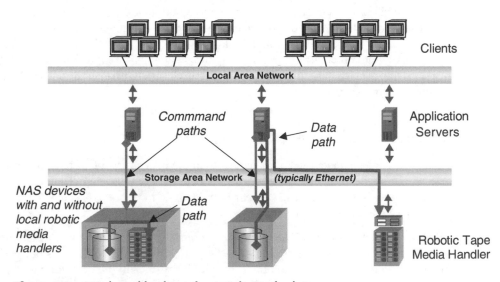

Figure 4.9 SAN-based backup of network-attached storage.

One form of NDMP command causes the NAS device to read file metadata and/or data and write it to a local tape without ever sending it to the server that issued the NDMP command. This is illustrated on the left side of Figure 4.9. In this case, the NAS processor plays the same role as an application server or dedicated backup server backing up data stored on SAN devices (Figures 4.7 and 4.8). This type of backup is serverless in the sense that data is never sent over the SAN, so there is little or no impact on SAN performance.

The limitations of this configuration are, of course, our three SAN friends, sharing, scaling, and availability.

- Tape drives and media robots attached directly to a NAS device are owned by the device and cannot be addressed by other NAS devices.

- Each NAS device requires its own backup hardware resources. It is less likely that a robotic media handler can be justified.

- When a backup hardware resource connected to a NAS device fails, the NAS device cannot back its data up.

When an organization's data is spread across multiple NAS devices, tape drives and media robots connected to each device are not the optimal answer for backup.

The right side of Figure 4.9 illustrates an alternative use of a SAN to back up data stored in multiple NAS devices. In this configuration, a backup program running in the application server reads data from the NAS device and writes it to the backup device (a tape drive with a network interface), usually through a bridge.

This backup configuration, of course, suffers from the principal disadvantage of conventional distributed client/server backup—the data path is long. Data being backed up is read from the NAS device into the server on which the backup program is running and written back over the SAN to the backup device. The backup devices are typically front-ended by a bridge or server that provides buffering and protocol conversion, making the path even longer. Figure 4.10 illustrates an interconnect configuration that is starting to appear in NAS products. This configuration minimizes the backup data path and also has further-reaching consequences for availability and scaling of NAS-based storage.

In Figure 4.10, a second SAN (the device SAN) connects storage devices to multiple NAS devices. NAS devices configured this way (without local storage) are often called *NAS heads*.

Fibre Channel is the obvious technology for this second SAN. In this configuration, the NAS heads play a role similar to that of the application servers in Figure 4.9, effectively becoming file servers with SAN-attached shared physical storage. Since storage devices are connected to a SAN, any of the NAS heads can address any storage device directly. A NAS head needing to back up its data can therefore take control of the tape drives it needs for the duration of a backup. With intelligent devices or SAN infrastructure, the serverless backup illustrated in Figure 4.8 is also possible. Thus, SANs make shortened data paths and server off-loading (in this case, the NAS heads are the servers) possible for NAS-based data centers.

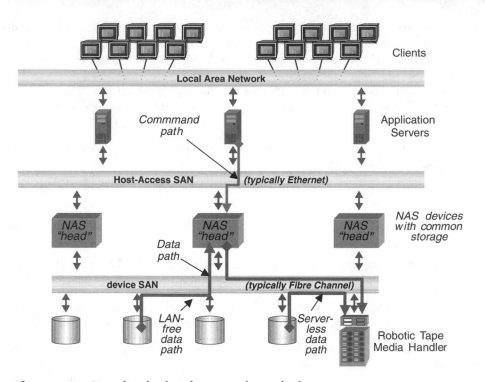

Figure 4.10 Serverless backup for network-attached storage.

As we discuss later in this chapter, this type of configuration has broader implications because the NAS heads' online storage is also connected to the device SAN. Each storage device is directly addressable by all of the NAS heads. In effect, it becomes possible to create clustered NAS devices that enhance availability and scaling.

At first glance, it might appear that the application data access path has been elongated by the configuration of Figure 4.10, because data must traverse two networks between application and storage device. If we consider that in conventional NAS devices the actual disk drives are connected to the NAS processors and memory subsystem using local SCSI buses, it is clear that as long as the disk drive access time on the device SAN of Figure 4.9 is comparable to that of local storage, both configurations have roughly equivalent data access times.

Killer App 2: Highly Available Data

As we have observed more than once, one key architectural benefit of SAN technology is that it enables a group of interconnected servers to share the same copy of any online data. This is good because it reduces storage cost and improves data consistency. It is also dangerous because if that one copy of data is destroyed or becomes inaccessible, *all* of the enterprise's servers are incapacitated. The single copy of data had better be virtually indestructible.

It's a long-established fact of information processing life that any component in a system can fail. Over the years, vendors and users have evolved various techniques for insulating storage and processing against these failures. In general, these techniques consist of installing redundant system components and switching operations to them when primary components fail. Switching can be:

- *Manual,* as with a substitute network hub or switch into which network cables are plugged if the primary one fails

- *Logical,* as with a substitute network interface card (NIC) to which an administrator reassigns an IP address if the primary card fails

- *Automatic,* as with a cluster of servers, one of which automatically restarts applications if the server on which they have been running fails

Disk drives also fail, of course, and a substantial body of RAID technology has evolved to protect against data loss when a disk drive fails. Chapter 6 goes into detail about RAID technology.

Disk drives differ from network cards, switches, and even processors because they hold the persistent record of enterprise state in the form of data. If a disk drive fails, not only must it be replaced, but the data on it must also be recreated and made available to applications, preferably without delay. Thus, disk drive failure protection mechanisms have three problems to solve:

- Get the failed disk drive replaced by another one.
- Get the data that the failed disk drive held onto the replacement drive.
- Provide continuous access to data while all this is happening.

There is one further complication: Disk drives aren't the only system component whose failure can make data inaccessible. The host bus adapters that connect disks to servers can fail or cables can break or be disconnected inadvertently. If a RAID controller sits between the disk drives and servers, it, too, can fail. Highly available access to critical enterprise data means covering all these eventualities. SAN technology improves the quality of storage service that an information services organization can provide to users by increasing both the *number* and *kinds* of survivable failures.

Mirroring 101

Mirroring, or keeping two or more identical copies of data online, is the deceptively simple concept that lies behind much of highly available data. Figure 4.11 illustrates the basic concept of online data mirroring.

Figure 4.11 is deceptively simple. Expressed in words, it seems to say:

> *Write all data to two separate disks at the same time. When both disks are functioning, data can be read back from either, because the contents of both are identical. If one should fail, data can still be read from the other one. This keeps applications running, buying time to replace the failed disk and get operational data copied onto it.*

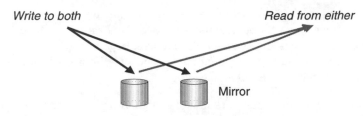

Figure 4.11 Basic concept of mirroring online data.

Of course, as with most aspects of electronic data processing, the deceptively simple description masks enormous complexity. Developers who implement mirroring concepts must consider:

Performance. Writing data to twice the number of disks requires twice the bandwidth.

Data integrity. Writes to different disks seldom if ever happen at precisely the same time. This complicates recovery from failures that occur during writes.

Data availability. Not only disks but also cables, interfaces, and the mirroring software itself can fail.

We discuss technologies for dealing with these problems in Chapters 6 and 8. For now, we want to concentrate on how mirroring technology works and the options opened up by SAN-attached storage.

Drilling Down into Mirroring: Who's Doing What to Whom

Mirroring is enabled by hardware and implemented in software. The hardware consists of disk drives and the cables, controllers, host bus adapters, and memory buses that connect them to one or more servers. Mirroring software intercepts each application I/O request, converting each write into a pair of writes to different devices and choosing a single target to satisfy each read.

Figure 4.12 illustrates the places at which commands and data are transformed as they traverse the long and winding hardware and software path between applications and disk storage:

- *The file system* converts application requests to read or write streams of bytes in a file to requests to read or write strings of consecutively numbered blocks on a server-based volume or a virtual disk presented by a RAID controller.

- *The volume manager* converts requests to read or write volume blocks into requests to read or write blocks on one or more physical or virtual disks.

- *The driver* converts requests from the I/O request protocol used within the host operating system to the SCSI or Fibre Channel Protocol used by the storage interconnect.

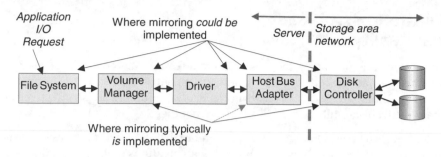

Figure 4.12   The path of mirrored data.

- *The host bus adapter* converts commands and data between computer memory format and the physical signaling protocol of the interconnect.

- *The disk controller,*[6] if present, converts SCSI or Fibre Channel requests made to virtual disks into one or more requests to physical disks.

As Figure 4.12 suggests, mirroring could be implemented at any point on this path, each having its own advantages and disadvantages. At some point in history, probably every type of mirroring implementation has been done; today, however, there are basically three locations in systems at which mirroring is implemented:

- *The volume manager,* a server software component that forms a layer between file systems and host bus adapter drivers. The main purpose of volume managers is to *virtualize* whatever the server perceives as physical disk drives, presenting it in a form more convenient for file system use. Chapter 8 has more to say about volume managers.

- *The disk controller.* Today's disk controllers contain powerful general-purpose processors, in addition to special-purpose elements for moving, copying, and computing against blocks of data. They are the most frequent location for RAID and mirroring implementations in larger servers.

- *The host bus adapter.* Several vendors have developed host bus adapters on steroids—devices that fulfill the format conversion role of traditional host bus adapters, but which also interface to multiple I/O buses and implement RAID and mirroring algorithms. These devices are popular in smaller departmental servers because of their low cost and high performance. They are of limited usefulness in enterprise servers because it is difficult for them to provide multihost access to data.

Each of these implementation sites for mirroring has different interactions with and implications for SANs. The first key distinction we need to explore is the difference between server-based mirroring and mirroring based within the host bus adapter or external disk controller.

---

[6] In this book, when we speak of *disk controllers,* we generally mean aggregating disk controllers to which several disk drives can be attached, rather than the integrated circuit within a disk drive that controls the drive's operation.

RAID Controllers: A Lesson in Virtual Reality

For system administrators, the most important feature of modern RAID controllers, whether they are embedded within a server enclosure or external to it in their own cabinets, is that the best ones are invisible. RAID controllers are so effective because they are so successful at acting like they are not there!

The ideal RAID controller emulates one or more disk drives as far as reading and writing data are concerned.[7] Whatever internal manipulations it performs to protect against disk drive failure or to enhance I/O performance are transparent to the computers using it to store and access data. External RAID controllers that use I/O buses or storage area networks to connect to servers are also completely transparent to operating system I/O drivers.

Thus, a RAID controller may mirror the same data on two or three or more disk drives, but these are presented to the I/O bus as if they were a single drive. Similarly, the RAID controller may use RAID algorithms to protect data on 4 or 5 or 10 drives against the failure of any one of them, but, again, the entire set appears as a single drive from the computer's point of view. Figure 4.13 illustrates this concept of storage device *virtualization*.

Figure 4.13 illustrates two sets of disk drives managed by RAID controllers. On the left of the figure, the contents of two drives are mirrored. From the standpoint of computers using this array, there is one *virtual disk drive* whose capacity is the same as that of one physical drive. The RAID controller makes sure that all host computer writes are

---

[7] The *management* interface used to configure and manage disk drives connected to a RAID controller is another matter that we will take up in Chapter 12.

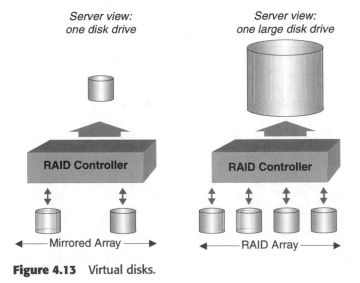

Server view: one disk drive

Server view: one large disk drive

RAID Controller

RAID Controller

◄——— Mirrored Array ———►

◄——— RAID Array ———►

Figure 4.13 Virtual disks.

written to both disk drives and selects a drive to execute each host computer read request.

Similarly, on the right side of Figure 4.13, a RAID controller is using RAID algorithms to manage four disk drives and present them to host computers as one virtual disk drive with three times the capacity of one of the physical drives.

For purposes of reading and writing data, a virtual disk drive is identical to a physical disk drive. It has a fixed number of blocks, any consecutive range of which can be written or read with a single command. Compared to a physical disk drive, a virtual drive may be extremely reliable or may perform extremely well, but functionally it doesn't do any more or less than the physical disk drive.

Volume Managers: The Other Disk Virtualizer

Because RAID controller designers succeed so well at disk drive virtualization, the virtual drives presented by their RAID controllers can be used just as if they were actual disk drives. Disk drives are used by:

- *File systems*, which impose a structure on disk drive block spaces in which opaque file objects can be created and destroyed, grow and shrink

- *Database management systems*, which impose a much more rigid structure on disk drive block spaces, in which a variety of highly structured data objects can be stored

- *Volume managers*, which virtualize disk drive storage in a way similar to that of RAID controllers

- The occasional *application*, although these have all but disappeared

It is the volume manager that is of interest to us here. Volume managers were conceived during roughly the same period as RAID controllers. Originally, volume managers were targeted to provide RAID controller functionality in situations where it was not possible or desirable to use RAID controllers. They became increasingly popular in a broader range of applications, once it was realized that they could manage virtual disks as well as physical ones. Thus, it is possible, for example, to mirror the contents of two virtual disk drives, each of which is actually a RAID array managed and presented by a RAID controller. Figure 4.14 illustrates this scenario.

In Figure 4.14, each RAID controller is presenting its I/O bus with a single virtual disk that is based on a RAID array managed by the controller. Two large virtual disks are visible to the server's disk drive over its I/O bus or SAN. The volume manager software in the server *aggregates* these two virtual disks by mirroring the data on them. The volume manager presents a single *volume* whose capacity is that of one of the RAID controller virtual disks. File systems and database managers use the volume. The host interconnect and the interconnect between RAID controller and disk drives might be either I/O buses or storage area networks. And this is where SAN technology comes into the highly available online data picture.

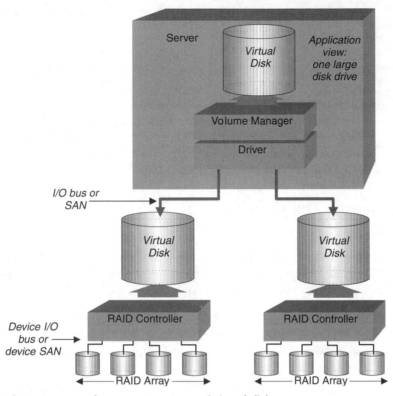

Figure 4.14 Volume management of virtual disks.

The SAN Difference

The entire configuration illustrated in Figure 4.14 can be implemented without SAN technology. Disk drives with parallel SCSI interfaces can be connected to RAID controllers with total bus length of 12 meters or less. RAID controllers can be connected to computers using similar SCSI buses. To increase maximum separation between RAID controllers and computers (to 25 meters), *differential* SCSI buses can be used. While this is a perfectly viable configuration and, indeed, is widely deployed today, it has some limitations:

- The number of devices that can be interconnected is limited. A parallel SCSI bus can interconnect no more than 16 devices, including computers, RAID controllers, disks, and tape drives.

- The maximum distance between interconnected devices is limited to 25 meters or less, because that is the maximum total length of a parallel SCSI bus.

- The number of computers it is practical to connect to a single SCSI bus is limited by inherently unfair SCSI bus arbitration algorithms. In principle, any device connected to a parallel SCSI bus can be either an initiator of I/O requests (i.e., a computer) or a target of I/O requests (e.g., a disk drive). In practice, a device's priority is determined by its bus address. More than three or four computers on a single bus creates the potential for starvation of the computers with lower bus priorities.

SAN technology relieves all three of these limitations and thereby opens new possibilities for highly available data. Even the simplest SAN topology, the Fibre Channel arbitrated loop, can accommodate as many as 126 interconnected devices, compared to parallel SCSI's 16. If one considers that today's largest clusters support 32 interconnected computers, this leaves plenty of connectivity for online storage devices (RAID subsystems). While an arbitrated loop provides good connectivity, its bandwidth doesn't scale as computers and storage devices are added to the SAN. Arbitrated loop is also not the optimal interconnect availability solution, as we discuss in Chapter 7. For all applications except disk drive interconnection, a SAN fabric based on one or more Fibre Channel switches is generally a preferable alternative.

A fabric-based Fibre Channel SAN can expand to accommodate hundreds of interconnected devices. Switching technology multiplies available bandwidth by carrying multiple simultaneous transmissions between pairs of interconnected devices at rated link speed. Thus, for a Fibre Channel interconnect with a link speed of 100 megabytes per second in each direction, a switch with eight ports could potentially move as much as 800 megabytes per second as long as four of the devices were communicating with four other devices, as Figure 4.15 illustrates.

Figure 4.15 represents four storage devices (probably RAID controllers) and four servers connected to the eight ports of a switch. For illustrative purposes, each switch port is represented twice. The vertical column represents the port that initiates a connection; the horizontal row represents the port receiving the connection. Thus, the server connected to port 8 has initiated a connection with the RAID controller connected to port 1, and so forth. Once a port is busy with a connection, it cannot accept additional connections. Thus, if the four servers initiate four connections with four

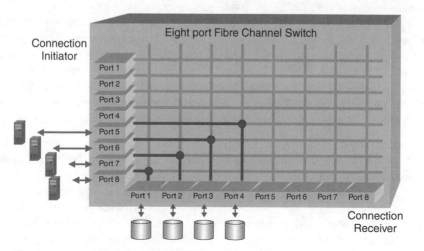

Figure 4.15   Switch-based Fibre Channel SAN fabric.

separate storage devices, the switch is operating at capacity, with no ports free either to initiate or to receive additional connection requests.

Figure 4.15 represents an idealized situation, in that the four servers request connections to four different storage devices. If the server connected to port 7 requested a connection to the storage device connected to port 1, for example, the request would not be honored and the server connected to port 7 would have to wait for the port to become available. The worst case would occur if all four servers requested connections to the storage device connected to port 1. Three of the four would be forced to wait and the aggregate data transfer rate would be 200 megabytes or less.

Fibre Channel switches that are functionally equivalent to that illustrated in Figure 4.15 are available with as many as 64 ports. Considering that one port can connect to a RAID subsystem with storage capacity of 10 terabytes or more, it is clear that some sizable storage area networks can be constructed with switched Fibre Channel fabric.

SANs and Available Data

Having understood how storage area network switching works, we turn now to the question of how SANs can improve data availability by protecting against disk and other I/O component failures. The first thing to realize about highly available data in SANs is that any of the storage device icons in Figure 4.15 could represent a RAID subsystem. Thus, each box in a SAN built using the switch represented in Figure 4.15 could be highly available in its own right. And as we describe in Chapter 6, today's enterprise RAID subsystems protect against loss of data due to disk, power supply, cooling device, controller module, and even bus failure. Thus, a high degree of failure tolerance comes from simply buying the right RAID subsystem and configuring it properly. What does the SAN bring to this party?

Answering this question requires a look inside a SAN-based enterprise I/O subsystem. Figure 4.16 illustrates the characteristics of such a system that are important for our purposes. As we have mentioned, enterprise RAID subsystems are typically engineered to be completely failure tolerant. In most cases, they provide controller failure tolerance by duplicating RAID controller modules. In normal operating circumstances, when all components are functioning, the two RAID controllers can divide up the disk drives, each managing some of them. Thus, for example, the two disk drives at the lower the left of Figure 4.16 are managed by the controller on the left, which mirrors all host computer writes to both of them. In this scenario, data written by an application typically traverses the SAN once. The two writes to the mirrored disks are handled by the RAID controller, which sends the same data twice from its internal buffer.

Data can also be mirrored by a server-based volume manager, as discussed earlier in this chapter. This scenario is illustrated by the two topmost disk drives in Figure 4.16 (the assumption is that each drive is presented directly to hosts by a RAID controller). Such a configuration has both advantages and disadvantages. The major disadvantage is that all data written by applications traverses the SAN twice, since mirroring is performed on the host-computer side of the SAN. The advantages are that I/O load can be spread across controllers and switches and that a RAID controller failure does not require failover of the mirrored disk drives to an alternate RAID controller.

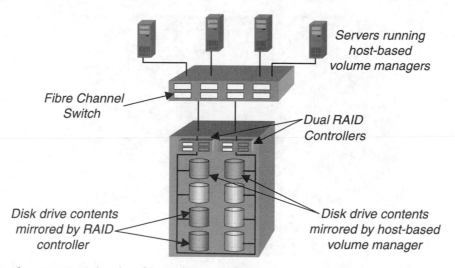

Servers running
host-based
volume managers

Fibre Channel
Switch

Dual RAID
Controllers

Disk drive contents
mirrored by RAID
controller

Disk drive contents
mirrored by host-based
volume manager

Figure 4.16 Mirroring data within a single RAID subsystem.

Volume manager mirroring of disks within a parallel SCSI-attached RAID subsystem can be limited by a scarcity of ports (bus addresses). With a SAN, however, ports are abundant, so configurations of the sort shown in Figure 4.16 are practical.

The advantage of volume manager-based mirroring in a SAN becomes more apparent with two or more RAID subsystems. Figure 4.17 illustrates this.

In Figure 4.17, one controller in each RAID subsystem manages an array of disks. The arrays may be mirrored or part of a RAID array, but each is failure tolerant in its own right. Each array is presented to the SAN as a single virtual disk.

Because these virtual disks are functionally identical to disk drives, they can be managed by server-based volume managers, which can mirror data across them and present file systems with a volume that is very reliable indeed. Not only can such a volume sustain a failure of a disk drive in one of the arrays; it can also sustain an event that incapacitates an entire RAID subsystem. If the two RAID subsystems are located at a distance of several kilometers from each other (which is possible with optical Fibre Channel), data can even continue to be accessible after a *site disaster*.

Moreover, when all system components are functioning properly, I/O load can be spread across two RAID controllers, as well as two SAN connections, for better performance.

The configuration illustrated in Figure 4.17 exploits SAN connectivity and link distance to separate failure recovery mechanisms from disaster recovery mechanisms. If a disk drive or RAID controller fails, recovery can be entirely local, within the confines of the RAID subsystem. If an entire location fails, however—as, for example, when a fire, flood, or massive power outage occurs—the server-based volume manager provides continued access to data and restores full data redundancy at the disaster site when equipment and facilities are again available.

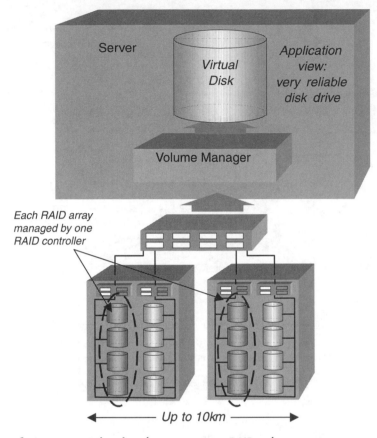

Figure 4.17   Mirroring data across two RAID subsystems.

The disaster recoverability and failure tolerance of this configuration are enabled by the two fundamental SAN properties:

1. The large number of interconnections available in a SAN makes possible the interconnection of very large amounts of storage.

2. The large intercomponent separations available in a Fibre Channel SAN, coupled with volume manager mirroring, enable the placement of mirrored copies of data at distances that can survive many common physical disasters.

Killer App 3: Disaster Recoverability

Mirroring technology can be combined with the distance and connectivity properties of SANs to enable new and different ways of recovering from disasters.

The Third Mirror Theme

The most obvious causes of data unavailability are component failure and site disaster. But other factors can make data inaccessible as well. Chief among these is backup. Backup can force applications to shut down because their data must be frozen, or remain unchanged during the course of the backup, so that a consistent image is obtained. *Copy-on-write* software techniques, which we discuss in Chapter 8, can reduce backup windows to almost nothing. With these techniques, however, applications contend with backup for I/O resources, potentially overtaxing device and interconnect bandwidth. Most enterprise backup suites allow backup I/O to be *throttled*, limiting the resources consumed, but this leaves administrators with a Hobson's choice between poor application response and very long backup times. Again, SAN technology solves this problem, through configuration such as that illustrated in Figure 4.18.

In the configuration illustrated in Figure 4.18, a server-based volume manager mirrors operational data to *three* different failure-tolerant disk arrays. Two of the mirrors are full time; that is, they always reflect the current state of operational data. The third is frozen periodically and separated, or split, from the others so that consistent backups can be made while applications are running.

Split Mirrors for Backup

The procedure for backup using a split mirror is:

1. The administrator *quiesces* or pauses all applications using the data that is to be backed up. This is an application-dependent action that may involve stopping applications and databases and even unmounting disks. Its purpose is to cause a consistent image of operational data, with no partially complete transactions in progress, to appear on all disks.

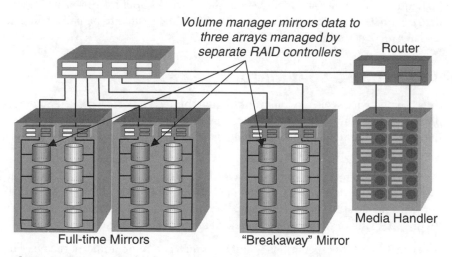

Figure 4.18   Using a third mirror for impact-free backup.

2. The administrator splits one mirror from the volume, leaving two full-time mirrors.

3. The administrator restarts applications, using the same volume, which now (invisibly to applications) consist of one less mirror.

4. The split mirror is mounted as a separate volume or device containing an image of application data frozen at the instant when applications were quiesced.

5. A backup is made from the *frozen image* of application data on the split mirror.

6. When the backup is complete, the split mirror is merged back into the live volume. With most volume managers, this merger does not interrupt applications, although performance may be affected.

The purpose of this split mirror backup procedure is to enable backups to be performed while operational data is in use. The backup represents the state of operational data as of one single instant at which no transactions were outstanding, so it is consistent. Consistent data is a preferable starting point for backup-based recovery, because transaction logs can be played against a data image restored from such a backup without fear of perpetuating (and therefore magnifying) data inconsistencies.

Copy-on-write checkpoints, discussed in Chapter 8, also freeze images of operational data. When these checkpoints are used for backup, both applications and backup access the same storage devices simultaneously. Since backup is inherently I/O-intensive, this can make application performance unacceptable. When a split mirror is used as a backup data source, backup I/O is directed to separate devices and SAN links. As long as the SAN has adequate overall bandwidth, backup need have very little impact on application I/O performance. In a large data center, the backup program can even execute on a separate server, eliminating its computational impact on applications as well.

Using a split mirror for impact-free backup does not inherently require a SAN. The same steps can be performed and a similar effect achieved with locally attached storage. As we have already discovered in several examples the two key SAN properties—high interconnectivity and long-distance links—make split mirror-based impact-free backup practical for large data centers and flexible enough to be part of an enterprise disaster recovery strategy.

Other Ways to Use Split Mirrors

SAN connectivity scales to hundreds of interconnected ports, so the configuration illustrated in Figure 4.18 can potentially be replicated for dozens of RAID subsystems. Long-distance optical links allow split mirrors of operational data to be placed at a distance from the main processing site.

Figure 4.19 illustrates a disaster recovery configuration in which a recovery site is located up to 10 kilometers from the main data center. Data processed by applications at the primary data center is mirrored on three different RAID arrays, as illustrated in Figure 4.18. One of these arrays is located at the disaster recovery site.

A key feature of this scenario is that it separates component failure recovery from disaster recovery. As Figure 4.19 suggests, the mirrored data at the primary data center enables recovery from any storage subsystem failures without recourse to the recov-

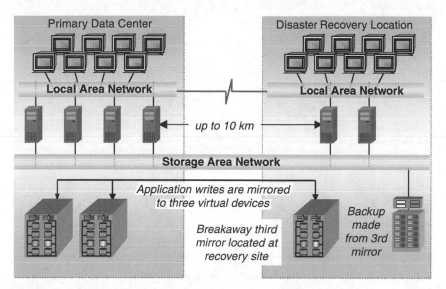

Figure 4.19 Disaster recovery using long-distance SAN.

ery site. Servers at the primary data center can also be *clustered*, protecting against server, operating system, and application failure, again without involving the recovery site.

If, on the other hand, the primary data center does experience a bona fide disaster, the mirror at the recovery location contains up-to-date data. Applications can be restarted at the recovery site and processing can continue.

The distinction between local component failure recovery and disaster recovery is important because moving a data center has much broader implications than data availability or even substitute computers. Recovering from a disaster requires rerouting network connections (easier today with the Internet so widely used for business), getting people to the recovery location, and, depending on the nature of the disaster, dealing with physical security and habitability issues.

Another way to view the architecture illustrated in Figure 4.19 is as enabling impact-free backup. The figure shows backup devices collocated with the split mirror at the recovery site. The recovery site may, in fact, be a secure vault in which backups are stored.

The same basic architecture can be adapted for more efficient resource utilization by designating pairs of sites to serve as disaster recovery sites for each other. Figure 4.20 illustrates a *symmetric disaster recovery* architecture.

In Figure 4.20, data centers A and B both use server-based volume management to maintain remote copies of their respective data. With sufficient server capacity at each site to run the other site's critical applications, each site can serve as the disaster recovery site for the other. This architecture, of course, assumes that one site will survive a disaster.

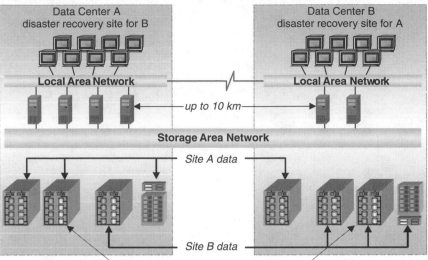

Figure 4.20 Symmetric disaster recovery architecture.

Unlike Figure 4.19, the split mirrors in Figure 4.20 are located at the data centers where data is processed. The remote mirror in Figure 4.20 is synchronized with operational data at all times and so protects against both storage failure at the primary data center and site disaster.

It goes without saying that an extended SAN such as Figure 4.20 illustrates requires redundant paths connecting the two data centers. Users who adopt architectures such as this often route optical links on two different geographic paths to protect against environmental events that can interrupt both paths at the same time.

Killer App 4: Clusters—Continuous Computing

Today, continuously available data is a must for any large enterprise. But in some ways, continuous data availability is only the tip of the enterprise survival iceberg. Data that survives disasters is crucial to survival; the ability to access and process it continuously is crucial to success. Again, SAN technology is a powerful enabler because—*is this a surprise?*—it makes a lot of data accessible to a lot of servers over long distances. Clustering technology is the layer of software that makes meaningful use of SAN connectivity to automate highly available and scalable computing.

Requirements for Highly Available Computing

Highly available computing is conceptually similar to highly available data—an organization's ability to process data survives failures of applications, operating systems, and servers. The techniques are similar as well—systems are built with redundant inter-connected elements that can substitute for each other if necessary. It is only the tech-nology details that are different. Because application functionality is so much more complex and varied than storage functionality, recovery from a failed application is necessarily more application-specific than, for example, recovery from a failed disk drive in a RAID subsystem.

When a disk drive fails or is unable to read data, the failure is instantly and unambigu-ously visible. Depending on the nature of the failure, a disk drive does one of the fol-lowing:

- Indicates its inability to function
- Responds to commands in a nonsensical way
- Fails to respond at all

All of these possibilities are readily discernable by applications. Commands return error status, return incomprehensible status, or simply return no status at all (time out). Over the years, disk drive and software driver technologies have matured to the point that what to do in each of these circumstances is relatively well under-stood.[8]

Compare this with an application or server failure. Most applications are completely contained within a single server. The only way to know that an application or the server on which it is running has failed is lack of response to clients. But how long should a client wait for response before concluding that a server or application has failed? Can a client tell whether an application has failed or whether it's just very busy? How can a client tell whether it's the server or the application (or something in between) that has failed? Can a client assume that because it's getting no response, other clients are getting no response as well?

All of these questions have the same answer, "*It depends on the application.*" When an application is subject to high peak loads, even very simple transactions may take a long time to execute. A network segment could experience momentary congestion, causing some clients to be starved for response. A seemingly simple query might entail extensive data analysis. Every situation is different.

Similarly, once it's clear there has been a failure, what to do to recover also depends on the application. When a storage device fails, recovery is pretty straightforward. For a mirrored device, an alternate copy of data is read. For RAID devices, RAID algo-rithms enable data to be reconstructed. If the failed device is not failure tolerant, a backup copy of data must be restored. With luck, a transaction log will be available to bring the state of data close to the point of failure.

With applications, the situation is potentially much more complex. Most transaction processing applications can be restarted without much loss of work, because their work consists of many concurrent tasks of short duration. The consistency of their data, however, is another story. If an application fails with many parallel threads of

---

[8] Although, as volume manager, file system, and application developers will point out, there is much room for improvement in the specificity of driver error reporting.

activity in progress, its data files are likely to be left in a messy state, with several partly complete transactions reflected in them. For example, any accounting transaction consists of updating at least two accounts so that an overall balance is maintained.

- A point-of-sale transaction must deduct from inventory and add to cash on hand or account debit.

- A funds transfer must debit the sending account and credit the receiving account.

- A change of a hotel, car, or airline reservation must add to one inventory and deduct from another.

All of these transactions require multiple updates to data. If an application fails with some of the updates done and some not yet done, data is out of balance. If the application is restarted and allowed to execute more transactions against its out-of-balance data, things only get worse. This can't be allowed to happen.

To prevent this situation, applications and the database management systems on which most of them rely create *journals*, or files in which they record what they are going to do before actually doing it. An application or database manager typically writes a journal entry that describes its intent to update data with a transaction before performing the update and another entry when the update is complete. If a failure occurs, application or database restart procedures scan the journal for transactions started but never finished and finish them before accepting any new transactions. This is called *playing back* the journal.

Thus, for a highly available computing environment in which data processing as well as data can survive or quickly recover from component failures, three fundamentals are required:

1. The environment must include extra resources that can take on the functions of failed resources. This typically means either a standby server or excess capacity within a separate server that normally performs other tasks.

2. Data must be restorable to a consistent state from which applications can be restarted without fear of further corruption. (In transaction processing applications, some loss of work in progress may be acceptable).

3. Applications must be restartable on the standby servers and must be able to reconnect to clients and restore or recreate shared state in such a way that clients recognize how much (if any) work in progress was lost due to the failure.

These are the fundamental attributes of cluster technology. A cluster of servers is a set of interconnected servers that are connected to the same storage devices and the same clients. In principle, any server in a cluster is able to perform any task that involves applications and data access. Thus, any server in a cluster should be able to serve as a substitute for any other, either because of a failure or because an application's requirements have expanded beyond what can be handled by a single server.

Positioning Clusters: Degrees of Availability

The three aforementioned requirements for high application availability do not automatically imply clustering. One could, in principle, recover from a failure by restoring the latest consistent data backup to alternate storage devices connected to an alternate server, replaying a series of journals to bring data up-to-date, and restarting applications on the alternate server. Reconnecting clients to the right applications and restoring their state would be an application-specific aspect of recovery.

For many of today's critical applications, this procedure is simply too slow to be viable. These applications, which are rapidly becoming commonplace, must be available constantly—24 hours a day, 365 days a year. An outage of several hours can have severe financial impact, as Table 11.1 suggests. According to Table 11.1, even a brief outage can be cripplingly expensive.

Various design techniques, enumerated in Figure 4.21, are available to reduce out-of-service time due to a hardware or software failure. The overall point of Figure 4.21 is that data processing time lost to unplanned system outages can be made very small—for a price. At the very top of the cost scale are custom-designed failure-tolerant systems. These systems are typically designed to run two or more identical processes in parallel on separate computers, with frequent cross-checking. They are usually found in life-or-death applications such as aircraft or power plant control, where the consequence of even momentary failure cannot reasonably be measured monetarily. For most business applications though, the cost of unavailability *can* be measured financially. For these, Figure 4.21 suggests a range of techniques of varying cost that can be employed to provide different degrees of data and application availability. For any business application, a cost point can be chosen at which enough availability is delivered.

Figure 4.21 is discussed further in Chapter 11. The part of the figure that is of interest here is the band labeled "High Application Availability." The three solutions listed in this band provide progressively higher application availability by protecting against more types of failure:

- *Two-node clusters* consist of two servers connected to the same storage devices and clients. These clusters protect against failure of one server by restarting the failed server's applications on the alternate server.

- *Multinode clusters* consist of more than two servers. With SAN connectivity, multinode clusters can be configured so that any application can fail over to any server. Multinode clusters can protect against more than one server failure and also against a failure of a server while another is being serviced.

- *Data replication* allows updates to critical data to be copied in (almost) real time across distances too long for mirroring. When coupled with clustering techniques adapted to function over long distances, data replication enables an organization to survive disasters that incapacitate entire data centers or geographic areas.

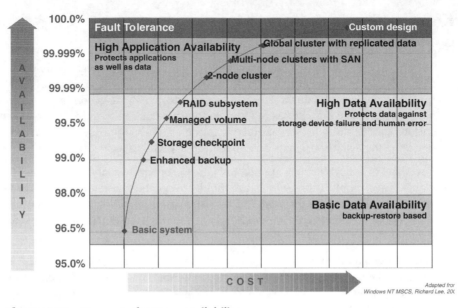

Figure 4.21 Degrees of system availability.

These three availability solutions are progressively more expensive to implement; however, all are significantly less expensive than completely failure-tolerant custom hardware and software designs.

Tiers of Clusters

Servers are typically clustered to achieve one or both of two goals: improved application availability and application scaling. While these two goals overlap, they do have some distinct attributes. Developers of clustering technology have generally concentrated on one of the two goals and, as a result, cluster technology appears in several specialized forms in a typical enterprise data center:

- *Client load balancing*, using either cooperating network routers or cooperating application server software to distribute incoming client requests across server resources.

- *Application scaling*, using multiple servers running identical application instances across which incoming client load is distributed by the load balancing function.

- *Application availability*, using multiple servers, one of which can run an instance of an application, coupled with mechanisms that enable the instance to restart on another server if the one on which it is running fails.

- *Data access scaling and availability*, using servers that communicate with each other to provide multiserver access to databases or files.

Figure 4.22 illustrates multi-tier data center clustering.

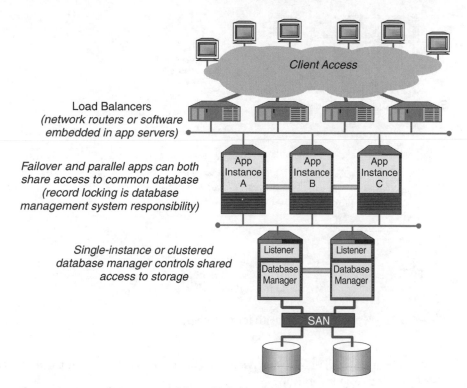

Figure 4.22   A data center with multiple tiers of clusters.

The multi-tier data center architecture illustrated in Figure 4.22 emphasizes the differences in clustering for incremental scaling and clustering for high availability. The former emphasizes application-specific communications among the servers constituting the cluster for the purposes of load balancing.

The servers in this cluster contain relatively little data state. Restarting after a failure, therefore, consists mostly of reestablishing client connections with copies of the application. The assumption at this tier of the cluster is that the impact of an imperfect reconstruction of client state is relatively small. It is generally regarded as acceptable for a user to restart the transaction being worked on at the time of a failure.

This contrasts with the availability tier of the cluster, whose responsibility is managing the integrity of data. When something fails at this tier, necessitating a redistribution of work among the surviving servers, considerable effort is expended on making sure that data is consistent. This might include playback of database logs and checking file system metadata for integrity.

The separation of function in this two-tier model is not absolute. Some level of recoverability is required at the application level and some amount of load balancing occurs at the database level.

The SAP R/3 accounting and financial application is a well-known example of this architecture. SAP R/3 is often configured with a back-end database server and one or

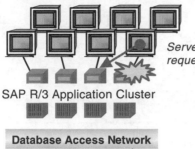

Server failure causes client requests to be rerouted

SAP R/3 Application Cluster

Database Access Network

Database cluster

Database server failure causes failover to alternate database cluster node

Storage devices accessible by both database servers

Figure 4.23   A two-tier cluster with local storage.

more application servers to which users are connected. Figure 4.23 illustrates a typical SAP R/3 two-tier configuration.

When applications are configured in this way, an application server failure causes client transactions to be rerouted to an alternate server according to an algorithm that is determined by the application itself. This is particularly useful with read-mostly Web server applications, for which there is little or no transaction context held at the Web service application level.

Because there is little transaction context at the application server level, the mechanics of failover are simple. In essence, the surviving servers negotiate to redistribute client load among themselves and subsequent client requests are routed to an application server from the survivor set.

Dealing with failure at the data server tier is somewhat more complex because the transaction context that matters (i.e., that is required for data integrity) is maintained there. When a database server believes that another database server has failed, it must:

■ Block transactions running locally from making further progress.

■ Determine for certain that the suspect server has failed. All surviving servers must negotiate to a common view of which data servers are operational.

■ Fence off the failed server as quickly as possible so that it is blocked from executing any more I/O requests to the application's data.

■ Force the release of any data locks held by the failed server.

■ Replay logs and perform other data manager–specific actions required to obliterate the effects of any partially completed transactions from the failed server.

- Reassign network addresses as required for the remaining data server(s) to take over the client load of the failed server.

- Allow transactions in progress to complete and allow new client transactions to be accepted for execution.

Different clustering implementations use different techniques to achieve these goals. Yet, all of them must detect the failure of a server, unwind the effects of any tasks in progress on the failed server at the time it failed, and restore the application's data to a known consistent state before the remaining servers in the cluster can be allowed to proceed.

Detecting and Reacting to Failures

Detecting the failure of a server in a cluster can be a nontrivial problem, simply because applications are not generally instrumented to report on their health. Failure detection in clusters, therefore, consists of detecting the absence of events. In effect, an application or server has failed if it does not respond properly to a request about its health.

One of the functions of a cluster manager software component is thus the emission of periodic heartbeat messages directed to cluster managers running on other servers in the cluster. In typical implementations, the absence of one or more heartbeat messages triggers a cluster manager to undertake a more exhaustive determination about whether a server is still running. Typical cluster management software products require two or more separate communications paths between clustered servers to reduce the incidence of misinterpreting a communications failure as a server failure.

If the cluster manager determines that failover is required, a predesignated secondary server restarts each of the application's resources in the correct order, after making sure that they have been stopped on the original server.

One critical piece of failover is the network addresses used by the application instance on the failed server. In some implementations, applications address a clusterwide *alias* and the cluster's servers route client requests among themselves in order to balance load. In other instances, another surviving server must begin responding to the failed server's network addresses.

Failover Trade-offs in Clusters

A server taking over load for a failed server connects to the same storage devices as the failed server and runs as many of the failed server's applications as are required for continued operation of the business. In some instances, older, less powerful servers are paired with newer, more powerful ones. When the more powerful server fails, failing all of its applications over might result in overload and unacceptably poor performance. Therefore, only the most critical applications are restarted. The decision as to how much cost an organization is prepared to bear in order to have continuously available applications and how many applications can be made available after a failure and at what performance levels is one of the classic trade-offs of cluster technology.

Clusters allow another kind of trade-off to be made. Many organizations have numerous routine information processing tasks to perform, such as reporting, database and file system reorganization, data mining, and software development and maintenance. These tasks are important, but they are not generally time critical and they are not critical to the continued operation of the organization.

The servers that run these noncritical tasks can often be paired with servers that run critical applications. When a critical application server fails, noncritical tasks can be suspended and their computing resources taken over to run critical applications. Thus, the computing assets required for highly available computing can be utilized during the large percentage of the time when everything is functioning properly. It is only when they are needed that noncritical tasks are suspended and their resources pressed into service to keep the organization in operation.

Clusters and SANs

So far, this discussion of clustering has had little to do with storage area networks. If, however, as Figure 4.24 illustrates, we imagine the system architecture of Figure 4.23 projected onto the number of applications that even a modest-sized enterprise is likely to have in operation, weaknesses become apparent.

In an enterprise with several separate applications, keeping critical applications highly available can quickly become expensive in several dimensions:

- Significant extra computing resources are required, not all of which may be usable for noncritical application tasks.

- A certain amount of configuration inflexibility exists—resources may be available in one cluster when they are required in another.

- A certain amount of data inflexibility is also inevitable—data required by one application may be managed by another application running on another cluster.

By increasing the number of storage devices and number of servers that can be interconnected, storage area networks address all of these problems, as Figure 4.25 illustrates.

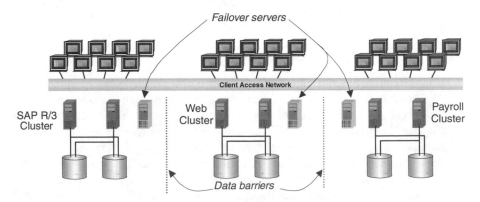

Figure 4.24 Cluster partitioning with locally attached storage.

In Figure 4.25, all of the storage has been interconnected on a storage area network. Not only can the storage itself be allocated more flexibly, but server costs can also be dramatically reduced as well. As the figure suggests, considerable cost savings can result from consolidating all applications into a single cluster.

With a single cluster, there is no need to dedicate a failover server for each application. A single failover server can protect against the failure of any one of the application servers. Thus, if the SAP R/3 application or the Payroll application compute load does not require a second server, the total number of application servers can be reduced.

As with RAID, a large cluster offers the option of trading cost against failure protection. For example, if in the cluster illustrated in Figure 4.25 a single failover server for all three applications is deemed too risky, additional failover servers can be added to the cluster. The system administrator can configure as many or as few servers into the cluster as are felt to be required for adequate protection. As described earlier, it is entirely possible to run routine backup, data mining, reporting, or development jobs on these failover servers when all equipment is functioning and they are not required to keep operations going.

The concept of combining several single-application clusters into one larger cluster works because of SANs—all of the combined cluster's servers have access to all of the data storage and therefore any of the servers can fulfill any of the application roles.[9] This same concept opens up similar possibilities for storage savings—as with computing resources, if all unallocated storage is accessible everywhere in the cluster, there is no need to dedicate spare devices or to form smaller mirrored volumes to meet individual application needs when larger ones might be more appropriate.

With large SANs, consisting of multiple interconnected switches or directors, the loosely coupled cluster concept described previously can be extended to enterprise

---

[9] Of course, all of the servers in the cluster must have the same architecture and be running the same operating system and cluster manager.

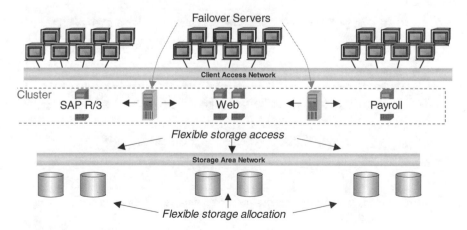

Figure 4.25   A SAN increases large cluster flexibility.

scale. Cluster managers typically offer facilities for assigning applications to preferred servers and designating a sequence of servers to which a given application may be failed over. When servers are connected in a large enterprise cluster, as illustrated in Figure 4.26, they can be organized in subsets dedicated to particular applications. The number of servers in a subset can be dictated by application scaling needs or other considerations. Since the SAN connects all of the servers to all of the storage, the number of failover servers required is determined solely on business grounds. Similarly, the consideration of whether a failover server may be used for a noncritical purpose such as development when it is not in operational service becomes an administrative decision. Furthermore, application coexistence rules (e.g., test versions of applications must shut down when the servers they are running on are required for production applications) can be much more flexible. The basic principle of large clusters whose storage devices are SAN-attached is that no rules about what applications can run on which servers are a result of hardware connectivity. With SAN-attached storage, such rules become administrative and can be set by administrators for purely business purposes.

When many servers running different applications are interconnected in a loosely coupled enterprise cluster with SAN-attached storage, several further management simplifications become possible:

- Ad hoc jobs become simpler to schedule. When unplanned processing requirements arise, compromises must often be made, either in terms of scheduling the unplanned work or accepting lower performance while unplanned work shares a server with normal day-to-day processing. Since a SAN connects all storage to all servers in the cluster, all that is needed to accommodate an unplanned requirement is available processing resource *somewhere* in the cluster.

- Similarly, planned maintenance becomes simpler to schedule. When a server needs a hardware or software upgrade or other maintenance operation that requires shutdown and restart, the applications it is running can be moved to

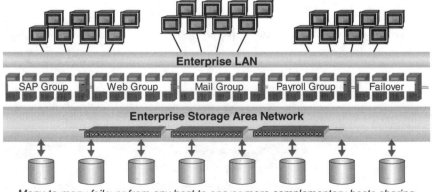

Many-to-many failover from any host to one or more complementary hosts sharing same storage via the SAN

Figure 4.26 Large (enterprise) cluster using a SAN.

other servers and run from there while the maintenance operation is performed. Again, all that is needed is available processing resource somewhere in the cluster. The larger the cluster, the greater the likelihood that available processing resource can be found.

- For applications that grow beyond the capacity of a single server, load can be spread across multiple servers, with one server bearing the bulk of the load and others handling short-term overloads. This feature can be used to defer the purchase of additional capital assets or to handle overloads that are periodic, as, for example, holiday seasons in a retail application.

- As more servers are added to a cluster, the probability of unused processing resources increases. These resources can be used to provide high availability for applications for which it might not otherwise be justified, thus increasing the number of applications that an organization can protect against failure.

The net result of these benefits of clustering is threefold. First, the equipment cost of high availability diminishes to the point where it is possible to consider it for many or most of an organization's applications. Second, administrative cost is reduced because a cluster with many interchangeable resources is easier to manage. Fewer ad hoc policy decisions need be made, which reduces the probability of a potentially costly wrong policy decision. Third, quality of service improves, simply because the pool of resources that can be deployed to solve a problem is larger.

Heterogeneous Clusters

Today, the state of clustering technology supports homogeneous clusters—clusters whose servers all run the same operating system. A key challenge for the future is the concept of heterogeneous clusters, in which servers of different architectures cooperate to achieve clustering goals. While heterogeneous clustering is generally perceived to be a worthwhile goal, developers must face formidable challenges in making it a reality. Chapter 9 discusses some of these challenges. New technologies, such as Java and other platform-independent programming languages, are a step toward heterogeneous clustering. A second important step would be standardization of the format of data stored on disks. Finally, standardized platform-independent mechanisms for communication among servers and among applications running on different servers would be required for truly heterogeneous clusters.

The industry is just beginning to perceive that heterogeneous clustering might be possible, and users are beginning to perceive that heterogeneity may be a reasonable demand to place on their suppliers. While they are not to be expected in the near future, it is not beyond the realm of possibility that clusters of heterogeneous servers will one day be possible.

Killer App 5: Data Replication

Our final killer app for SAN technology is the replication of data over long distances. Using SAN (e.g., Fibre Channel) technology, data may be replicated across distances of a few kilometers simply by mirroring it to widely separated devices. For replication over longer distances, other networking technologies (e.g., ATM, WDM) may be employed, along with alternative software techniques that take into account the time required to propagate data through a complex network and the inherent unreliability of long-distance links.

From an application standpoint, however it is achieved, replication of data across long distances offers several benefits:

Disaster recoverability. Up-to-date replicas of critical data that survives a site disaster (e.g., a fire, flood, power grid outage, civil insurrection) can enable an organization to get back on the air quickly after such a disaster. While far from a complete disaster recoverability solution, a replica of online data is a necessary component of such a solution.

Data publication. Many organizations create online data, in the form of catalogs, price lists, experimental results, climatological records, and so forth, at one site and publish it to several sites. Data replication technology can be used to publish such data automatically on demand or on a timed schedule.

Data consolidation. By the same token, many organizations create data at many sites and periodically roll it up for analysis, processing, and record keeping at a central site. Data created at several sites may be replicated to storage resources at one or more central data centers.

Data movement. Organizations occasionally need to move data from one location to another, as when a data center moves, or from one SAN to another, as when wholesale replacement of a server, storage plant, or data center is required. Replicating data from the old site to the new one can make such events significantly less disruptive.

Each of these applications of data replication has slightly different requirements that we will discuss in the following sections.

Replication for Disaster Recoverability

As we enter the third millennium, more and more organizations are simply unable to function without being able to process their electronically stored data. Without the ability to recover from a disaster that incapacitates their data centers, such organizations would simply cease to function. For them, disaster recoverability is becoming a necessity.

The data requirements for recovering from a disaster are simple: The more up-to-date the data at the recovery site, the easier it is to restore operations and continue to process data. The ideal mechanism for recovering from a physical disaster that destroys a data center would be real-time mirroring of all updates to critical data from the main data center to the disaster recovery site. While Fibre Channel makes this possible up to a separation of 10 kilometers, many organizations do not see this as adequate. Some disasters, such as the World Trade Center bombing in 1993, are tightly contained, and backup data and processing resources that were 10 kilometers away would protect against them. Others, such as the San Francisco earthquake of 1989 or the Mississippi River flood of 1993, have a much wider radius of destruction, and recovering from them would require data at a distance of hundreds of kilometers. For these applications, replication software techniques rather than simple mirroring are required.

The second dimension of making data recoverable after a disaster is currency. Again, in an ideal scenario, every single update to operational data would be reflected instantaneously at the recovery site. While disaster could occur while replicated data is in transit, the loss would be minimal and organizations could elect to either bear the loss or use journal playback techniques to restore the recovery site data to the state of the main data at the instant of the disaster.

While keeping data at the recovery site as current as possible is desirable, it is not always affordable. There are two dimensions to affordability in this context:

1. Communication links of high enough performance to support real-time transmission of the main database update load to the recovery site may be very expensive.

2. Even with the best possible physical communications connecting main data center and recovery site, the time required to transmit and record every update to data may lead to unacceptably long response time for client requests.

For either of these reasons—or, more likely, both—it is not always possible to keep data at the recovery site in perfect synchronization with operational data at the main data center. The ability to store main data center updates in a journal and transmit them to the recovery site on a resource-available basis is the foundation of the data replication technologies that are most often used to maintain copies of an organization's operational data at a disaster recovery site.

Replication for Data Publication and Consolidation

The needs of data publication and consolidation are somewhat different from those of disaster recovery. Publication and consolidation are usually not time critical. For example, when a catalog or price list is published from a headquarters to several field offices, it is typically transmitted in its entirety while an old version of the document is in use at all sites. Only when the new document is complete and error free at all target sites do all sites switch simultaneously from using the old document to using the new one. If the new document is a few minutes late or early, there is no impact on the business. Figure 4.27 illustrates replication for the publication of data.

Consolidation is the inverse of publication, but has essentially the same requirements. Data is typically sent to a consolidation site after an event. For example, each of a company's field offices might send a day's transactions to a headquarters site for consolidation, posting, sales analysis, inventory management, and a variety of other purposes at the end of each business day. The process for this would typically be to close out a transaction file at each field office (and immediately open another one if opera-

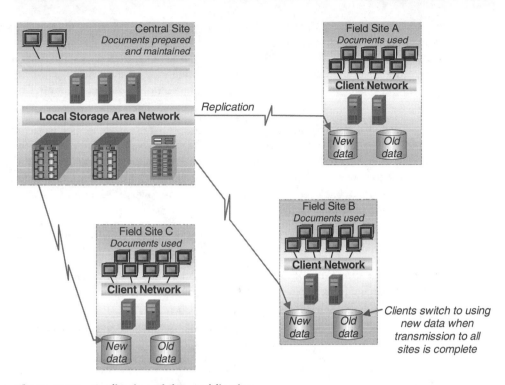

Figure 4.27   Replication of data publication.

tion is 24×7, of course) and send the closed file to the headquarters. Again, there is not much impact on the business if files arrive a few minutes earlier or later. Thus real-time replication requirements are not nearly as stringent as in the case of disaster recovery.

If not real-time performance, what *are* the requirements for replication for publication and consolidation? As Figure 4.27 makes apparent, one vital requirement is the ability to replicate data from one source to multiple targets or, in the case of replication for consolidation, from several sources to one target. Replication products that do not support multiple targets are not useful for publication.

A second requirement, less obvious from the figure, is flexibility in describing the data to be replicated. Ideally, it should be possible to replicate an arbitrary set of files on the source system to an arbitrary path on each target, as Figure 4.28 illustrates. In Figure 4.28, each field office stores its daily data on a different disk and replicates.

A third requirement for replication used to support publication or consolidation of data is that it be schedulable. A primary objective in enterprise information processing operations is reduction of management cost. One important way to reduce management costs is to automate as many routine operations as possible. Thus, the replication operations illustrated in Figures 4.27 and 4.28 would ideally be executed on perhaps a daily schedule. Once the schedule was set up, there would be no need for administrator action thereafter, unless some kind of exceptional condition occurred.

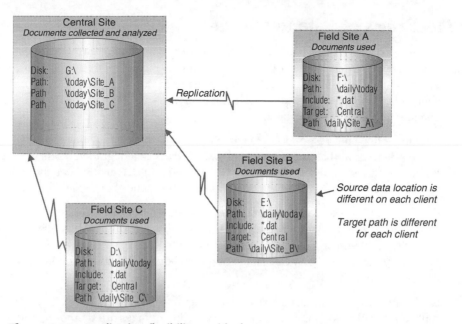

Figure 4.28   Replication flexibility: an ideal.

Data replication for publication and consolidation almost always occurs on networks that use TCP/IP protocols and is almost always defined in terms of file objects. This distinguishes it from replication for disaster recovery, which today is most often done using volume objects.

Because it operates on file objects, data replication for publication and consolidation must be situated above the file system in the I/O protocol stack. Most implementations of this type of data replication are server-based, although in principle it is possible to implement it in a network-attached storage device.

Replication for Data Movement

Another use for data replication occurs when data must be moved from the purview of one system or storage area network to that of another. Moving data may be required because, for example, a data center site is being moved. Even within a data center, replication may be the easiest way to move a large amount of data from one server to another, as, for example, when growth requires that a server be replaced with a larger one or an application is migrated from one server architecture to another.

Replication for the purpose of moving data typically has much the same requirements as replication for publication or consolidation. It is typically not time critical, but it usually requires that data be replicated selectively and may require that data be accepted from several sources (as, for example, when two or more smaller servers are replaced by one larger one). A replication facility that can handle publication and consolidation is usually suitable for moving data as well.

The Mechanics of Data Replication

The characteristic that distinguishes data replication from mirroring is its tolerance for propagation delay and for link outages. Volume managers that support mirroring are typically designed to treat all mirrors equally, in the sense that all are considered equally fast and equally reliable.[10] In most implementations of mirroring, there is no concept of a master and a slave.

If a mirror does not respond to I/O commands from the volume manager, the typical strategy is to treat that mirror as failed and fall back to a degraded mode of operation. When the mirror (or a substitute) is returned to service, it must be caught up by having its contents overwritten with the contents of the remainder of the mirror set.

Replication technology treats storage devices quite differently. Replication technology recognizes the concept of a master or primary volume upon which applications are operating, and one or more slave or secondary volumes to which data is being replicated. In most implementations, it is not possible for applications to use data while it is being replicated.

Replication technology also treats the inability to reach a disk quite differently. With replication technology, the assumption is that link outages are temporary and will be repaired. Updates to primary volumes are therefore logged at the primary site, for later delivery to temporarily unreachable secondary sites. When secondary site links are restored, updates recorded in the log are sent to them.

To implement these capabilities, the algorithms for replication are necessarily much more complex than those for mirroring. Replication managers must handle situations in which some secondary sites are reachable and some are not, log-full situations, and other conditions that just don't arise with mirroring.

The second complicating assumption behind replication technology is that I/O to primary volumes is faster than I/O to secondary volumes. Given the configurations typical of replication, this is almost trivially true. To be reflected at a secondary site, an update must first be transmitted over a network and then traverse the I/O stack at the secondary site. In other words, a secondary site update must go through the same operations as the primary one, *plus a trip across the network*. The trip across the network (which is bidirectional, since the update must be acknowledged) would be added to application response time for every single update, as Figure 4.29 illustrates. For many applications, this is regarded as unacceptable.

The same mechanism used to ride through link outages is used to keep application response times at acceptable levels while data is being replicated. The replication manager appends each application update to a log as well as writing it to the actual primary volume. A separate thread of the replication manager reads the log from the front (it is important that updates at secondary sites occur in the same order as at the primary) and sends updates to secondary sites. The replication manager is therefore much more complex than a mirroring volume manager, since it must manage transmis-

---

[10] In Chapter 6, we will discuss volume managers that allow one mirror to be designated as preferred.

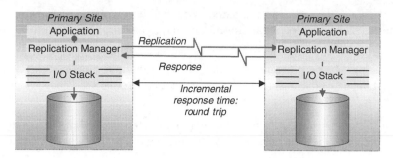

Figure 4.29   Primary and secondary response time.

sion and acknowledgment of each update to each secondary site and reflect current status in its log.

If an application begins to update its data very rapidly, links to remote sites may not be able to keep up. When this occurs, the replication log starts to fill. When the rate of application updates slows, the log empties and replication is in near real time.

Allowing the replication log to fill rather than holding up application progress until secondary updates have been written is referred to as *asynchronous replication.* When replication is asynchronous, secondary locations can fall behind in the sense that updates that have been written and acknowledged at the primary site may not be reflected at the secondary site for some time. (Most replication managers allow *throt-tling* to limit the amount by which secondary sites can be out of date.) This compli-cates recovery from primary site disasters, since applications may have acted on updates that are not reflected at the secondary site. By using asynchronous data repli-cation as a disaster recovery mechanism, an organization is accepting the risk of a small amount of data loss, balancing it against better application response time in everyday operations.

The Bottom Line: Continuous Global Access to Timely Information

By now it's clear that the new applications enabled by SAN technology are actually new ways of organizing, accessing, and managing data. It's not that SAN technology introduces new accounting, transaction processing, Web server, electronic business, or other techniques. It's that it enables managers to exploit technology more effec-tively to provide better quality of service to the users of these applications.

For example, removing backup from the application availability timeline enables infor-mation processing departments to offer 24×7 application access. Today, this can be a survival issue. Of course, it goes without saying that failure-tolerant, highly available data is a must for continuous computing. SAN technology can be used to protect against a wider variety of threats to data integrity. RAID subsystem-based protection against hardware failure can be augmented by server-based volume management to create snapshots of operational data for mining and impact-free backup purposes.

Similarly, the any-to-any connectivity of SAN technology makes clustering dramatically more useful—larger clusters make failover more flexible, enable applications to scale beyond the capacity of a single server, and actually reduce the cost of making applications highly available.

Replication technology introduces a global component to this, making it possible for organizations to consider the possibility of conducting their data processing on a global scale.

Summary

- Electronic business has essentially eliminated computer system idle time and sent developers on a search for less obtrusive solutions to "the backup problem."

- An important complication for backup designers is that to be truly useful, a backup copy must represent the state of a set of data at a single point in time. With today's technology, applications and database management systems must usually be made quiescent for an instant in order to get a backup started. This is an area for future development.

- Backups protect against hardware failures, software malfunctions, and user errors. Volume managers and RAID subsystems are tending to assume more of a role in protecting against hardware failures. The role of backup in creating point-in-time images of enterprise data remains, however.

- Today's backup technology allows administrators to choose from a spectrum of options that simplify restores (full backups) or make backing up data faster and less obtrusive to applications (incremental backups).

- SANs enable several improvements in the way client server backup is done. These range from the sharing of expensive, low-duty-cycle tape drives and libraries to LAN-free backups that move data on the SAN from source to target, to the future potential for serverless backups in which data moves directly from source device to target device without passing through a server at all.

- Online data can be made highly available through the use of RAID controller or server-based volume management technology. Often, these two technologies can be combined advantageously, resulting in higher capacity, higher availability, and higher performance than can be achieved by either alone.

- Clustering technology organizes the resources required to run an application and manages failover from one server to another. Failover may be automatic, as when a server fails and its applications are restarted on an alternate server, or manual, in which an administrator forces an application to migrate from one server to another for maintenance purposes.

- Data replication technology can be used to enable recovery from site disasters, for publication or consolidation of data in a distributed enterprise, or for moving data from one server to another. Variations of replication technology are used to replicate volumes, files and directories, and databases.

- Replication technology differs from mirroring in that it is designed to work with unreliable connections between primary and secondary sites and designed for situations in which the time required to propagate updates to secondary sites cannot be part of application response time.

PART TWO

The Parts: What's in a SAN

The beauty of SANs is that they connect a lot of storage devices to a lot of servers and place in the administrator's hands the choice of which server gets to access which storage devices. This is a great idea; it would have made information processing a lot easier if we'd thought of it years ago. The not-so-simple fact is that a lot of technology had to fall into place for SANs to become possible.

This Part describes the four major categories of storage networking technology: architecture, storage, networking and software. Some of this technology (for example, optical data transmission) predated SANs; most of it has been developed as part of the SAN wave over the last few years; some of it is still developing. In any case, it's an impressive array of capabilities that has had to come together in a relatively short time to bring SANs to fruition.

CHAPTER 5

Storage Networking Architecture

I n this chapter we'll learn more about:

- The software and hardware elements that make up the path between stored data and applications that need it

- Different subsets of these elements that are used to create different application data access models

- The architectural components that constitute a storage area network-based system

- Different ways in which developers implement these essential elements in different storage area network components together to build storage area network-based systems

The Path from Data to Application

For online data to be useful in the conduct of business, it has to be accessible to applications. Applications need to be able to perform the following:

- *Add* new records to online databases—for example, to record events such as sales or deliveries.

- *Update* existing records, as, for example, to record a transfer of funds from one account to another.

- *Delete* obsolete records, as, for example, when orders, deliveries, customers, partners, employees, and so forth pass from current to former status.

- *Analyze* records, as when a transaction database is mined for demographic or sales information.

Applications deal with data as *records* organized for business convenience. For example, an order record might contain a customer identification number, a list of items and quantities ordered, and pricing information. The customer identification number might provide linkage to a customer record containing customer name, address, and credit information.

This contrasts, of course, with the way in which data is stored on disk and tape storage devices—as strings of encoded binary digits. These strings of data must be moved between storage media and application memory, with several transformations along the way in order to be used by applications. These movements and transformations are fairly universal—just about any online data used by applications passes through some sequence of them. What distinguishes different storage networking system configurations from each other is the point in the network at which the transformations occur.

From Bits to Records

The gray shapes in Figure 5.1 represent the four principal system components that transform online data on its path between application and physical storage.

From bottom to top (i.e., from more physical or less abstract to more application-oriented or more abstract), the four data transforms represented in Figure 5.1 are:

The disk. While they are often thought of as physical entities because they are packaged as physical boxes or bricks, modern disks as seen through ATA, SCSI, or Fibre Channel Protocol (FCP) interfaces[1] are already abstracted. Firmware in disk drives

[1] Chapter 7 discusses these and other interfaces in more detail.

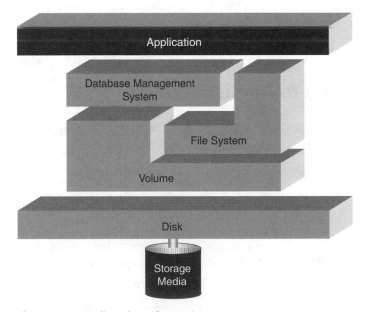

Figure 5.1 Online data abstractions.

transforms on-media representations of data so that all three of these interfaces, and indeed all disk I/O interfaces in use or under serious consideration today, present numbered blocks of data into magnetic, optical, or other representations that are stored *correctly* (i.e., the device does not introduce errors in the data) and *persistently* (i.e., once written, a block of data *stays* written until overwritten, even if the device is powered off and on again before reading). A key architectural property of disks is that their storage capacity is fixed—they always make the same number of blocks available to their clients for storing data.

The volume. Disks are often logically combined by software that uses mirroring, RAID, and striping techniques to improve their net storage capacity, reliability, or I/O performance characteristics. Software that combines disks in this way presents disk-like storage entities to its clients. These disk-like entities are commonly known as *volumes*, *logical units* (abbreviated *LUNs*, for the numbers by which logical units are identified in popular I/O protocols), or *virtual disks*. Architecturally, volumes are like disks, in that they present their clients with numbered blocks of storage where data can be stored persistently or retrieved. They are unlike disks in that their storage capacity (the number of blocks they present) can be increased or decreased by administrative action.

The file system. Disks and volumes are too inflexible for applications to use directly. Applications often need larger data objects whose contents can be completely or partially read or written. For practical application use, many thousands of these objects must be available. The objects must be easily created, easily eliminated when no longer required, and able to grow and shrink during their lifetimes. Finally, it must be possible to name them symbolically and organize them into a hierarchy for application convenience. This is the description of a file system—software that transforms the set of numbered blocks presented by a disk or volume into a hierarchy of named objects (files) of different sizes, each of which is an ordered stream of blocks, any subset of which can be read or overwritten. Files can be created and destroyed by applications, as well as extended, truncated, and moved around within a directory hierarchy.

The database management system. The meaning of data within a file (which bytes are to be interpreted as names and addresses, whether numbers are represented as bit character strings, and so forth) depends on applications that create and use the data. In the earlier days of computing, it was common for each application designer to create a unique organization for the data in files used by his or her application. One application might represent names and addresses as fixed-length strings, while another chose variable-length strings with commas as delimiters. This made data sharing among applications difficult, as well as making each application difficult to maintain in its own right. As the value of data sharing became apparent, *database management systems* evolved to provide application-independent means of organizing data so that multiple applications could use the same data and so that the data itself could evolve independently from applications. Database management systems transform the numbered blocks presented by disks, volumes, or file systems into more business-oriented data items, such as character strings, Boolean values, binary and floating point numbers, and arrays of these objects. The most popular form of database is the *relational* database, which organizes related data items into *records* and orders sets of like records into *tables*. Relational database management systems also maintain relationships between records of different types (for example, using customer identification number to relate an order record to a customer record) and enforce data consistency rules and transactional constraints. To accomplish this, database management systems maintain their own internal data objects, such as *indexes* by which records can be located quickly and *logs* in which transactional activity is recorded in case recovery is required.

Data Transformation Paths

Different application and system architectures use different combinations of these four transformations. Figure 5.2 illustrates five different data transformation paths that are commonly found in application systems.[2]

Path 1: Files on Disks

This path, on which the application uses files in a file system that is organized directly on disk storage, might be thought of as a traditional application architecture. It was certainly the first application data access architecture to gain widespread acceptance

---

[2] Other paths exist, such as applications that write and read data directly to and from physical disks. These are both highly specialized and increasingly rare, so they are not covered in detail here. The five transformation paths illustrated in Figure 5.2 constitute the vast majority of application architectures in use today.

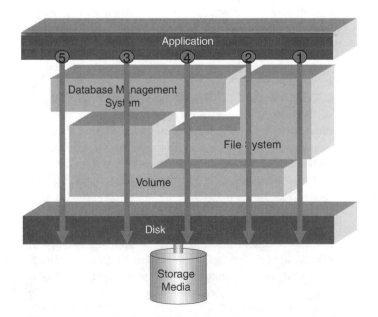

Figure 5.2   Application usage of data abstractions.

in modern computing and is still the most common architecture found in personal computer applications, such as word processors, spreadsheets, and electronic mail clients. This architecture has two major limitations for client/server applications, however:

- Since the file system uses physical disks directly, without an intervening volume manager, none of the capacity aggregation, data availability, or I/O performance advantages of volumes are possible.

- Since the storage capacity presented by disks is not expandable, running out of storage capacity has a high impact on applications. When available disk storage is exhausted, data must be backed up, a larger disk installed in place of the full one, and data restored to it. While all this is happening, data is unavailable. For this reason, file-based application systems designs increasingly use the architecture represented by Path 2.

Path 2: Files on Volumes

This path is used by applications that organize their own data. Volumes provide these applications with capacity expansion, enhanced data availability, and greater I/O performance. Improved data availability and I/O performance are transparent to applications and file systems. Online capacity expansion is not transparent, however—at least to file systems. For a file system to take advantage of volume expansion, it must be specifically designed to do so. Older file systems designed for physical disks often use internal data structures that are related to disk capacity. If the capacity of the disk changes, these structures become invalid. Newer file systems are generally designed to be volume aware and so are more suitable for applications whose data needs can change rapidly and without warning.

Path 3: Databases on Volumes

Today, most enterprise applications are designed to use one or more of a small number of popular database management systems. Chapter 3 enumerates the advantages of database management systems. While they are very good at organizing data and preserving its integrity, databases work best when stored on very reliable storage devices, such as volumes. From the database management system's perspective, it is organizing raw blocks of storage such as would be presented by a disk. In actual fact, the volume manager uses mirroring, RAID, and striping techniques to provide high-performance, highly available disks to the database management system. Thus both ideals are attained:

- The volume manager provides the reliable, high-performing storage substrate.

- The database management system organizes data for application convenience and enforces integrity and transactional constraints.

Recalling that the principal architectural difference between disks and volumes is the latter's ability to expand and contract, database management systems that store their data on volumes should make use of the latter's ability to change size.

This combination of advantages would appear to make databases using volumes as their underlying storage the ideal data access path for modern client-server applications. The world of applications, alas, is not an ideal world. Frequently, applications that use databases for primary data storage also use files for ancillary data such as control information, utility scripts, reports, and logs. If the database is stored directly on volumes, the application needs two different sets of storage devices with different management techniques. For this reason, most database management systems have been designed so that they can also use files as underlying storage.

Path 4: Databases on Files

To a database management system, a file and a volume are essentially identical. Each provides a set of blocks in which the database management system can store records organized in its own format. Each can be expanded when the database requires more storage capacity. Both can be moved among storage devices, should I/O load balancing be required (although moving a file is usually somewhat simpler).

A database management system uses a file as a sort of container whose space it organizes into tables, indexes, logs, or other control information. These container files can be stored in a file system along with other application files or files that the database management system itself requires, and manipulated using file system utilities. Thus, for example, a database stored in files can be backed up together with other application files using a file system backup utility program.

The ability to manipulate database container files is a powerful argument in favor of using file systems as underlying database storage. Indeed, file system internal locking and caching functions are sometimes specially adapted for use with database management systems as described in Chapter 8. Most database management systems today are able to store data in container files. There are a few important exceptions, however. Some databases must be stored directly on disks due to database management system design. One important example of this is distributed database management systems that allow an entire cluster of servers to access a single database image concurrently.

Path 5: Databases on Disks

Much of storage networking development has occurred concurrently in different parts of the network, computer, and software industries. Some features required to fully exploit SAN capabilities are either very recent or still remaining to be done. One example of this is *distributed database management systems* that allow a single database image to be accessed concurrently by multiple applications running on different servers. Oracle Corporation's *Oracle Parallel Server* is such a distributed database manager.[3]

Distributed database management systems were generally developed before SAN capabilities were really mature. There was relatively little collaboration with the stor-

---

[3] There is another type of distributed database management system in which each instance of the database manager manages a partition, or slice, of the database. The instances cooperate with each other to execute transactions that affect data in multiple slices. From the SAN point of view, such database managers are simply applications (database manager instances), each of which has its own private storage (database slices).

age and I/O industry. One legacy of development in isolation is a common requirement that distributed databases be stored directly on disks, rather than on volumes or file systems. In large part, this requirement results from the fact that, until recently, server-based volumes that function in clusters have not been available. To get disk-like behavior as seen from all servers running the distributed database management system, it was necessary to store the database on a disk. Volumes managed by RAID controller software (usually called *virtual disks*) could be used as distributed database storage, while server-based volumes could not. Recently, cluster-aware server-based volume managers have become available, so this situation is changing.

Network Storage Systems

The preceding section describes the transformations that occur in the movement of data between application and storage media:

- On-media representation to disk blocks
- Disks to volumes
- Volumes to file systems
- Files, volumes, or disks to databases

This section discusses the computer system components in which the transformations may be implemented. Figure 5.3 illustrates the components used to construct SAN-based client-server systems. The following sections use these generic components along with the transformations described in preceding sections to illustrate functional partitioning in various popular storage network system configurations.

In contrast to the rest of the figures in this book, the icons in Figure 5.3 represent physical disks that perform the media representation-to-disk transformation. In systems that include SANs, disks are connected to RAID controllers (❶, ❷), to storage servers (❸), and occasionally directly to the storage area network fabric (❹).

External RAID controllers organize disks into *arrays* and present *volumes* to their clients.[4] External RAID controllers may connect to SANs, to storage servers, or directly to application or database servers. External RAID controllers that connect to SANs are separately powered and enclosed in specially designed disk subsystem cabinets. Most include multiple SAN connections or *ports*. They may be contrasted with *embedded* RAID controllers that plug into mainboard or I/O backplane expansion slots within the server enclosure. The latter are inherently bound to the servers that house them and are not network storage devices in their own right.

Storage servers, as the term implies, are servers dedicated to performing storage functions. Network-attached storage devices are storage servers, as are a new class of devices known as *storage appliances*.

---

[4] When presented by RAID controllers, volumes are usually called *virtual disks*, *LUNs* (logical units), or *logical disks*. Since this chapter discusses aggregation and virtualization at application server (host), storage server, and RAID controller levels, we use the term *volume* throughout for simplicity.

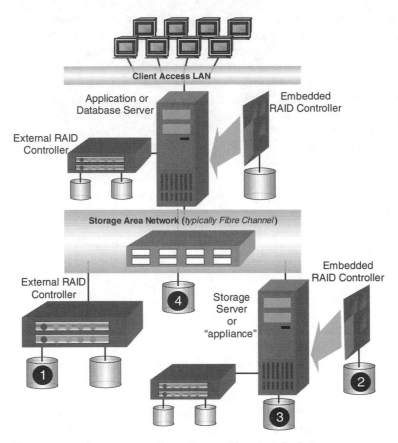

Figure 5.3 Components of a system with networked storage.

Storage area network infrastructure components include switches, hubs, routers, and bridges. Their basic function is to route data through the storage area network. Routers and bridges additionally perform protocol transformations (but not data transformations of the kind discussed in the preceding section). Switches multiply overall SAN bandwidth by connecting pairs of components for the transmission of data between them. Like other infrastructure components, they do not transform data as it passes through them.

Storage Network System Configurations

The following sections describe SANs from two perspectives:

- Software components that transform data as it moves between storage media and application memory

- Hardware components that move the data

Different SAN system topologies combine these components in different ways. This section describes the more popular topologies constructed from these components.

Figure 5.4 describes data access in a simple system consisting of an application server with locally attached storage (i.e., without a storage area network). In this system, volumes are provided by RAID controllers (external and embedded) augmented by a server-based volume manager. The file system resides in the application server.

A RAID controller aggregates and virtualizes disks attached to it, but has no control over other RAID controllers' disks. To aggregate and virtualize disks attached to multiple RAID controllers, a server-based volume manager is used. A server-based volume manager can be very useful for aggregating the storage capacity or I/O performance of two or more RAID controllers. The technique can also be used to increase failure tolerance.

Basic SAN Model

Chapter 1 discussed the difference between NAS and SAN as the terms are commonly used. The model of hardware components and data transformations helps with understanding this difference. Figure 5.5 illustrates the data access model for a simple system with a SAN. In this system, the file system runs in the application server. Volume functionality would typically be provided by external RAID controllers attached to the SAN, possibly augmented by a server-based volume manager.

As first mentioned in Chapter 1, the major distinction between NAS and SAN storage is that, with SAN-attached storage, the storage subsystem presents volumes or virtual disks to application servers, which provide file system and/or database management functionality. With NAS devices, file system functionality resides in the storage subsystem, as the following example illustrates.

NAS Appliance

Figure 5.6 represents a system in which the online storage is provided by a NAS device. NAS devices may include special-purpose hardware optimized for accessing

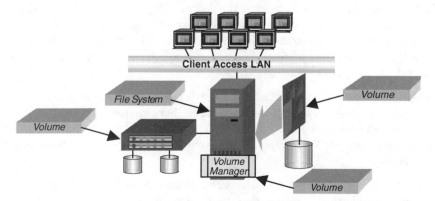

Figure 5.4   Data access model for a simple system.

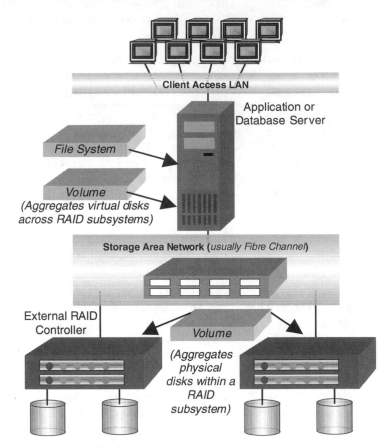

Client Access LAN

Application or
Database Server

File System

Volume
(Aggregates virtual disks
across RAID subsystems)

Storage Area Network (*usually Fibre Channel*)

External RAID
Controller

Volume

(Aggregates
physical
disks within a
RAID
subsystem)

Figure 5.5   A basic SAN system.

data on disks or they may be conventional servers dedicated to providing file services to clients. Their physical storage may consist of directly attached disks (❶) or of volumes presented by embedded (❷) or external (❸) RAID controllers.

Whatever their internal construction, the distinguishing feature of NAS devices is that they provide file system functionality. In other words, application servers make file access requests over the storage area network (which today is usually based on Ethernet technology and IP protocols). The NAS device interprets and executes these requests and receives or delivers data.

Since they handle file access requests, NAS devices clearly require different I/O protocols than SAN-attached storage devices. Today, there are two such protocols in widespread use: the Network File System (NFS) protocol used widely in Unix systems and the Common Internet File System (CIFS) commonly used between Windows clients and servers.

Moreover, since the vast majority of applications are designed to access local files, NAS devices require a little help from the application server to make their file systems

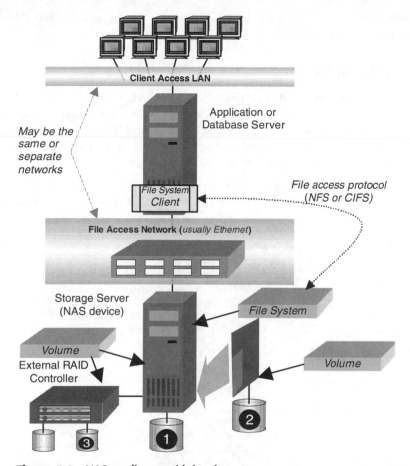

Figure 5.6 NAS appliance with local storage.

appear identical to local ones. The server software component that does this is typically called a *network file system client* or *redirector*. Its function is to intercept file access requests directed to NAS devices, encapsulate them in a network file access protocol, and send them to the NAS device for execution.

Some NAS devices house both storage server and disks in self-contained enclosures. In these devices, which are often positioned as *appliances* by their makers to connote simplicity, the storage server typically implements volume management, although NAS appliances with embedded RAID controllers are possible. In many cases, the hardware in a NAS device is the same as that of the simple application server illustrated in Figure 5.4. The only property that makes such a server a NAS device is the *absence* of applications.

There are also *enterprise NAS devices* that use external RAID subsystems to house and manage their disks. In these devices, the RAID controllers provide volumes, sometimes augmented by volume management software in the storage server. An enterprise NAS device may connect to an enterprise SAN and control some of the storage devices on it. Enterprise NAS devices with their own private SANs are also available. The next example illustrates an Enterprise NAS configuration.

Enterprise NAS Device

The configuration represented in Figure 5.7 differs from that of Figure 5.6 in that the storage devices (disks and RAID subsystem virtual disks) in the enterprise configuration are not permanently dedicated to a single NAS device. The device access SAN makes it possible to transfer ownership of devices from one NAS device to another, for example, in the event of failure or to rebalance I/O load.

Enterprise NAS devices often have the same requirements as any other enterprise server: They must be highly available and scalable to meet changing enterprise needs.

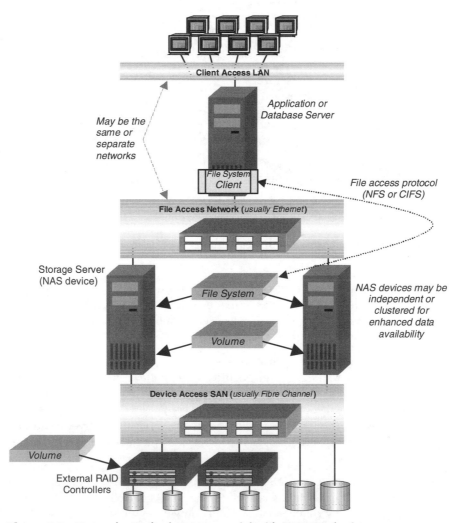

Figure 5.7   Network-attached storage model with SAN-attached storage.

Figure 5.7 can also represent an enterprise NAS configuration in which the two NAS devices cooperate to control the same physical storage devices. The storage devices may be disks or external RAID controllers, the latter providing one level of volume functionality.

In this configuration, two NAS devices cooperate as a cluster (as described in Chapter 2). Since both have access to the same data, they coordinate to present consistent file system images to application clients. If clustered NAS devices augment RAID controller volumes with their own volume managers, these must cooperate as well, so that all NAS devices in the cluster have the same picture of volume state at all times.

A file system in which multiple instances running on different servers cooperate to present the same picture of files to all servers is called a *cluster* file system. Later examples illustrate SAN-attached storage with such file systems.

In-Band SAN Appliance

A SAN appliance[5] is a variation of the configuration shown in Figure 5.7 that presents volumes rather than files. SAN appliances aggregate and virtualize disks and RAID controller volumes and present volumes to database or application servers. Figure 5.8 illustrates a configuration that includes a SAN appliance. We call these devices *in-band SAN appliances*, because the appliance is in the path taken by data on its way between host and storage media.

In-band SAN appliances are typically constructed using conventional computers with host bus adapters and storage devices. One can imagine that as this storage genre becomes popular, vendors will develop special-purpose hardware optimized for storage service, much in the way that specialized RAID controller hardware has developed. SAN appliances deliver three unique benefits:

- *Fanout.* A SAN appliance can connect enormous amounts of online storage to a SAN. Using enterprise RAID controllers for physical storage, a SAN appliance can connect literally dozens of terabytes to a SAN.

- *Investment protection.* Because it is essentially a server, a SAN appliance supports the storage devices that the server supports. In many cases, this enables the connection of legacy storage devices to the SAN.

- *Advanced function.* Because they are based on server operating systems, SAN appliances can (in principle) support volume management, clustering, embedded backup, and other advanced storage access and management features that are typically available only with servers. Since these functions are performed inside the box, they consume no bandwidth on the enterprise SAN.

The SAN appliances represented in Figure 5.8 use a back-end SAN to connect to storage devices. The storage devices may either be directly attached disks (❶) or they may be volumes presented by external RAID controllers (❷). Two or more SAN appliances may be clustered together to improve data availability.

[5] SAN appliance is a term coined by the authors and at the time of printing is not yet in general use with a commonly understood definition.

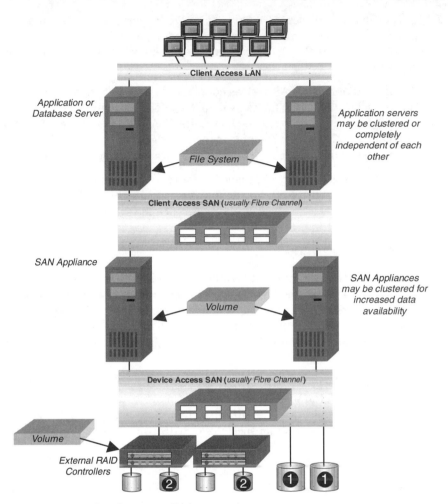

Figure 5.8 In-band SAN appliance.

In-band SAN appliances can be deployed using Fibre Channel both as the back-end connection to storage devices and as the client SAN for connecting to application servers. A SAN appliance is typically configured with multiple host bus adapters, some of which connect to storage devices and others of which connect to application servers.

Because of their relatively rich software execution environment, SAN appliances' forte is flexibility. For example, they can easily restrict access to volumes on a server-by-server basis. Thus, clients of a SAN appliance could be either completely unrelated servers or cooperating clusters of servers that share common data. As Figure 5.8 indicates, SAN appliances provide no file system functionality; in systems that use this model, the file system runs in the application server.

Out-of-Band SAN Appliance

Another class of SAN appliances provides volume services through cooperation between the appliance itself and a software *virtualization client* running in the host. Figure 5.9 illustrates an out-of-band SAN appliance configuration.

In Figure 5.9, a single SAN connects storage devices directly to application servers. A SAN appliance is also connected to the SAN, but it is not in the data path between applications and data (hence the name *out-of-band*).

In this configuration, the role of the SAN appliance is to be aware of all the storage devices and servers connected to the SAN and to maintain a global information repository that describes which storage devices have been combined as arrays and which servers have the right to access them. When an application, database manager, file system, or volume manager running in a server accesses a disk on the SAN, the server's virtualization client communicates with the SAN appliance to determine which devices represent the disk. The SAN appliance returns mapping information indicating which storage device or devices are used to realize the requested disk.

Once a connection between a server and a virtualized device has been made, data access is directly between the server and the physical storage device. Any block mapping required at this level (as, for example, for mirrored devices) is performed by the virtualization client.

Like their in-band cousins, out-of-band SAN appliances make large amounts of storage directly to sets of servers, which may be either unrelated to each other or cooperating as a cluster. Large collections of consolidated storage devices can be managed in a wide variety of cooperating and noncooperating server environments.

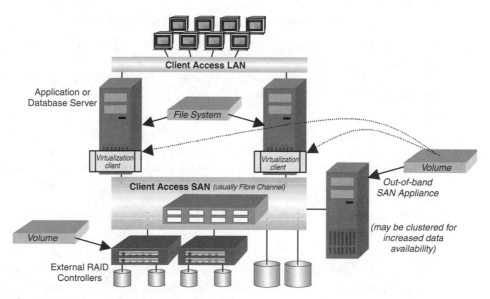

Figure 5.9   Out-of-band SAN appliance.

The advantage of the out-of-band SAN model is that once a connection between a virtualized storage device and a server is made, data access occurs on a direct path between application server and device. There is no extra step in the data path as with in-band SAN appliances.

With today's SAN protocols, out-of-band SAN appliances carry a certain level of risk. All of the servers in a configuration such as that shown in Figure 5.9 must be trustworthy. When given mapping information by the SAN appliance, they must stay strictly within the bounds of that mapping information. This trustworthiness is enforced by the virtualization client software, which is typically supplied by the SAN appliance vendor. If a malicious user infiltrates a server however, or if a pathological failure causes a server to write data to random SAN addresses, data could be destroyed. In-band solutions like the SAN appliance described in the foregoing section, RAID subsystems, and NAS devices use the same path for obtaining access rights and accessing data and so do not have this risk associated with them.

Cluster File System with Central Metadata

Some file systems take advantage of SANs' connectivity to shorten the path between applications and data using techniques similar to that illustrated in Figure 5.9.

A file system organizes the blocks presented by a disk or volume into *metadata*, user data, and free space. While a file system stores several types of metadata, the one of interest here is the map that describes which disk or volume blocks contain the user data for each file. When an application opens a file, the file system locates and reads the file's metadata into a cache. When an application reads or writes file data, the file system consults its cached metadata to translate file data addresses specified by the application into disk or volume block addresses used in I/O requests.

Since a file does not normally move from one disk or volume location to another while it is being used, any server with access to the file's metadata could, in principle, read and write its data directly from disks or volumes. This is the premise of cluster file systems such as Figure 5.10 illustrates.

Figure 5.10 represents a cluster of application, database, or file servers connected to a SAN. Each server runs an instance of a cluster file system through which its applications access data. Figure 5.10 represents a cluster file system with a central metadata server. One of the servers (the one on the left) has been designated the *metadata server*. It handles all application requests that require reading or writing of file system metadata. All other servers are *data servers*. They may access user data, but may not directly read or modify metadata. Data servers do not create, delete, extend, truncate, or move files.

The role of a data server is similar to the role of the virtualization client in the example of Figure 5.9. A virtualization client converts volume block addresses into device and block addresses on the SAN and issues I/O commands. A cluster file system instance in a data server converts file addresses specified by applications into device and block

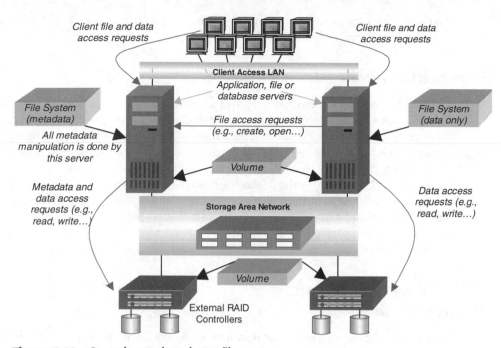

Figure 5.10   Central metadata cluster file system.

addresses on the commands and issues I/O commands. The difference between the two lies only in the degree of integration with the server-based file system.

If an application request to open a file is received by the server on the right of Figure 5.10, its file system instance requests that the server on the left provide the file's metadata, particularly the map for translating between file block addresses and disk or volume block addresses. Armed with this map, the server on the right can translate applications' file read and write requests into disk or volume addresses and issue disk or volume I/O commands. These commands cause data to move directly between server and storage device, without involving the metadata server.

Of course, cluster file systems are much more complex than this simple description suggests. For example, application requests to extend or truncate open files must be coordinated with the metadata server to make sure no application on another server is accessing a file while its state is changing. The metadata server itself must be robust—its function must migrate to one of the data servers if the metadata server fails. The benefits of data sharing are sufficiently compelling that cluster file systems are beginning to appear in the market.

The benefit of direct access to data from multiple servers is particularly compelling in Web-related applications, where both system load and growth can be extremely difficult to predict. In these applications, files typically are essentially always open, so metadata server load is light and accesses to data can be distributed across the cluster's servers. Cluster file system architecture can also be used as a foundation for NAS clusters as illustrated in Figure 5.7.

Symmetric Cluster File System

Figure 5.11 represents another type of cluster file system. In this implementation, all application servers on which file system instances are running act both as metadata servers and as data access servers. This *symmetric cluster file system* model offers management simplicity, reduced failover time, and, for some applications, more flexible scaling; however, it is much more complex to implement than the single metadata server model described in the preceding example. While vendors to the open system market are moving in this direction, examples of this model today are found primarily in proprietary products. These products are delivered by system companies such as IBM and Compaq, which control all of the system and SAN components during the development cycle.

RAID Subsystem-Based Volume Replication

Data can be replicated over long distances as described in Chapter 2. Replication can be done at the volume, file, or database level, with each requiring slightly different

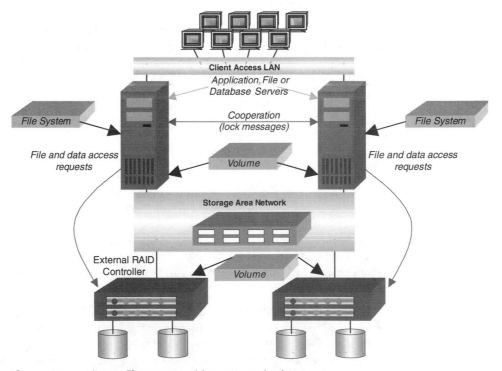

Figure 5.11 Cluster file system with SAN-attached storage.

techniques. As Chapter 8 describes, application response requirements usually dictate that data replication over long distances be asynchronous; that is, application data writes at the primary site may be delayed for a short time if the network is congested or a server is overloaded. This behavior requires logging techniques, also described in Chapter 8, that distinguish replication from mirroring.

Figure 5.12 illustrates volume replication using RAID subsystems equipped with network access. One of the RAID subsystems sends data updates directly to the other with no server involvement.

In Figure 5.12, applications run at the primary data center (on the left side of the figure). Each application write request to a replicated volume is trapped by the RAID controller and transmitted with its data to a corresponding RAID controller at the secondary or target site. The RAID controller at the secondary site writes the data to a corresponding volume. Between them, the source and target RAID controllers manage data flow completely. Coordination at the server level is only required to start and stop replication and to establish application quiet points so that, for example, a mirror can be split from a target volume to create a backup.

Since RAID controllers present volumes to application servers, they have no information about file system or database state. Without server assistance, a RAID controller cannot know when the data on its volumes is consistent (e.g., when no updates are partially complete). For this reason, it is difficult for applications at a secondary site to use data on replicated volumes while replication is occurring.

With file system or database management system cooperation, it is possible to freeze replication at instants when data on replicated volumes is consistent. If a secondary replicated volume is mirrored, this would provide an opportunity to split a consistent mirror at the target site for use by backup, analysis, or other applications.

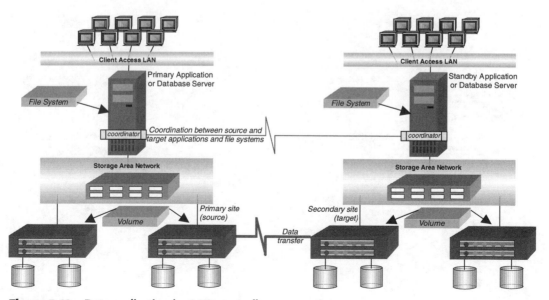

Figure 5.12   Data replication by RAID controller cooperation.

If replication stops at an instant when file system consistency cannot be guaranteed (e.g., because of a crash or disaster at the primary site), the target site must usually treat the replicated volumes as having experienced a system crash and perform an integrity check before mounting them for use. Thus, part of a disaster recovery procedure must be to run file system integrity checks and play back database logs against secondary replicated volumes.

Because it is awkward to use replicas while replication is occurring, volume replication is employed primarily for situations in which data replicas are to be used after replication stops. Disaster recovery is one obvious application of this type. With server-level coordination, volume replication can also be used to create remote snapshots of data for reporting, mining, or backup purposes.

Server-Based Volume Replication

Volume replication is also found at the server software level. Its properties are similar to those described in the preceding example. Figure 5.13 illustrates server-based volume replication.

In Figure 5.13, *volume replicators* in two widely separated servers cooperate to replicate data on groups of server-based volumes. The volumes may be made up of disks or, more likely, they may be aggregates of volumes presented by SAN-attached external RAID subsystems, as the figure illustrates.

In this model, the server-based replicator at the primary site intercepts application write requests to replicated volumes and transmits them with their data to the secondary site, where the server-based replicator writes data to equivalent volumes. As with RAID subsystem-based volume replication, server-based volume replicators have

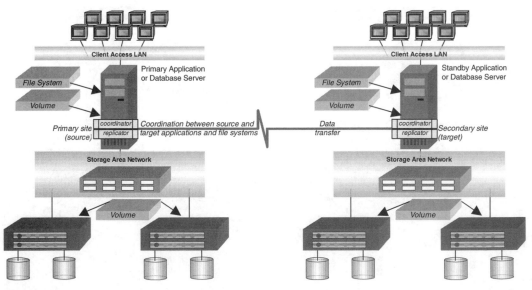

Figure 5.13   Server-based volume replication.

no information about file or database management system on-disk state. Server-level coordination is required if applications at the secondary site are to use data from replicated volumes while replication is occurring.

Server-based volume replication typically uses TCP/IP protocols. It is often employed to *publish* data to multiple secondary sites. Like RAID subsystem-based volume replication, server-based volume replication can be used for disaster recoverability or, with server-level coordination, for creating snapshots of data for reporting, mining, or backup.

File-Based Data Replication

Figure 5.14 illustrates another common form of long-distance data replication: file replication. In this model, updates to selected files at the primary site are trapped and transmitted to secondary sites, where they are written through its file system. The replicated objects are groups of files rather than volumes as in the preceding examples. With file replication, file-level context information is available to replicators. With some restrictions, replicated data at secondary sites can be used while replication is in progress. File replication does not require coordination between primary and secondary site volume managers.

File replication can be used for disaster recovery by making up-to-date copies of critical data available at a remote site. Because of its more comprehensive coverage and lower overhead, however, volume replication is usually chosen for this purpose. File replication is more popular for publishing online data (e.g., catalogs, price lists, Web pages) and for consolidating data created at several sites to a single location for centralized analysis, reporting, or backup. File replication generally has higher overhead

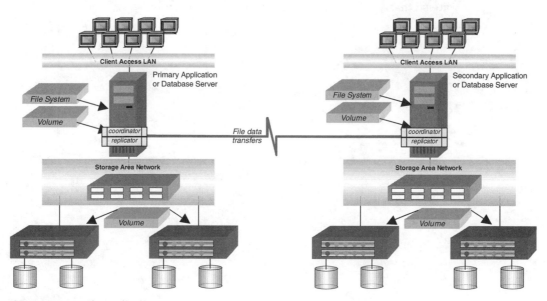

Figure 5.14 File replication.

than volume replication because replicated data traverses a longer software path at the secondary site. The offsetting advantages are the flexibility of selective replication and the ability to make some use of replicated data while replication is occurring.

Summary

- The four basic transformations undergone by data as it moves from storage device to application are: (1) signals to blocks (the *disk* abstraction), (2) disk blocks to aggregated and virtualized blocks (the *volume* abstraction), (3) blocks to files (the *file system* abstraction), and (4) files to records (the *database* abstraction). In a system incorporating a storage area network, these abstractions may be provided by different physical system elements.

- There are five different ways in which applications commonly use subsets of these data transformations.

- The only practical implementation site for the disk transformation is the physical disk drive.

- The volume abstraction may be implemented in an embedded or external RAID controller, in an in-band or out-of-band SAN appliance, or by a volume manager running in an application or database server.

- The file system abstraction is found both in storage servers (NAS devices) and in application or database servers.

- Both NAS devices—storage servers and application servers—may be clustered to improve application availability and scaling. When servers are clustered, volume management and file system capabilities implemented in them must be cluster-aware so that access to data can be coordinated properly.

CHAPTER 6

The *Storage* in Storage Networking

I n this chapter we'll learn more about:

- The building blocks that make up the storage devices used in storage networking configurations

- Why disk and tape drives by themselves aren't enough

- Techniques for combining disks into arrays to increase storage capacity, I/O performance, and data availability

- Component faults that can result in data availability loss and how RAID subsystem engineers have designed to protect against them

- How buyers of network storage products can navigate among the sometimes bewildering array of choices available to them

Challenges for Network Storage

Sometimes it seems as though the network side of storage networking gets all the attention. For the first time in the history of computing, it is possible to connect all of a data center's storage to all of its servers and therefore to all of its electronic information users. But universal connectivity creates challenges for storage devices as well. Can today's storage devices adjust to this new way of doing things?

Fortunately, storage is a relatively simple area for a prospective purchaser to evaluate. There are only three questions that are worth asking:

- How much does it cost to store a gigabyte of data?

- How well does the storage perform when servers are accessing it?

- How often does the device break and how long does it take to fix?

As usual, there's a lot lurking behind these simple questions. We begin by attacking the question of cost. And because most enterprises have more disk drives than any other component, we shall consider them first.

The Cost of Online Storage

People tend to think about disk storage cost in pennies per megabyte. As this book is written, personal computer disk storage costs less than a half cent per megabyte. So why do personal computer disks cost $200 or more, just like they did last year? The answer is simple: Disk drive capacity is increasing at something like 60 percent per year.

NOTE
Disk drive price tends to stay constant; disk capacity increases over time.

Increasing disk capacity for a constant price is handy for personal computer users—it enables new computer uses such as downloading music and video clips, playing games, internet conferencing and long-term investment tracking. For enterprises, the returns are even greater. Low cost storage enables enterprises to deal with complex data types, keep historical data online for ready access, and conduct their business electronically.

Disk Economics

The sub-penny-per-megabyte disks are the low-performance disks used in personal computers. Server disk storage is somewhat more expensive—from $0.02 to $0.05 per megabyte for high-capacity, high-performance disks. The same disk capacity that costs the personal computer user $200 is going to cost the industrial buyer $800 to $1500.[1] What's going on here? Aren't things supposed to be cheaper in larger quantities?

Disk economics are at work. Disk companies make about 10 times as many personal computer disks (the kind that have the 40-pin interface called EIDE, ATA, or UDMA) as server disks (the kind that have SCSI or Fibre Channel interfaces). The personal computer disk market is simple. More capacity is better. Performance isn't a high priority, because one user can hardly keep a disk busy.

Because so many personal computer disks are made and because performance is a secondary consideration, disk companies have squeezed the last possible bit of cost out of them. Customers who buy disks for the data center, on the other hand, typically demand high performance and capacity *and* are willing to pay for it. So disk companies build what they ask for—disks with fast rotational speeds, high-performance

---

[1] Because disk prices change rapidly, it's impossible for this book to be current. The reader should pay attention instead to trends and relationships in this section and use current market data when evaluating disks.

interfaces, and large cache memories—and amortize the engineering cost over a smaller number of units, driving unit price up.

NOTE

Disk capacity is cheap; high performance is expensive.

Enclosure Cost

The cost of disks is only the beginning of data center online storage cost. For $1,000 or so, the buyer gets something that looks a little like a black brick. To be useful, this brick must be mounted in an enclosure that will keep it dust-free and cool, supply clean power to it, and provide a plug for its I/O interface. The cost of enclosures varies widely, depending on capacity, redundancy, and interface type. A fair estimate, however, is that an enclosure adds between 5 and 25 percent to the cost of a disk, depending on its features. A CIO or administrator whose job is taking good care of enterprise data would normally be well advised to opt for higher-quality, higher-cost enclosures.

NOTE

Even though the advanced technology is in the disks, a substantial portion of online storage cost lies in power and packaging.

The Cost of *Usable* Data Center Storage

The most significant component of online storage cost is that of connecting the storage devices to computers. As with disks, the smaller the system, the lower is the cost of connecting it to its storage. For personal computers, disk connection cost is negligible—the cable that connects one or two storage devices to an ATA interface is usually included in the cost of the computer. Small servers that use directly attached SCSI disk and other storage devices generally include a SCSI *host bus adapter* (HBA) or *application-specific integrated circuit* (ASIC) that can connect up to 15 devices. Additional adapters can usually be configured for $100 to $200,[2] for a per-port connection cost of under $10.

All but the smallest servers are usually configured with their disks connected to intelligent RAID controllers. RAID controllers protect against disk failure, increase storage connectivity, and usually enhance I/O performance.

Single-server data centers or data centers with many small, unrelated servers often configure *embedded* RAID controllers that plug directly into a server's I/O bus (e.g., its PCI bus). Larger servers or groups of servers are typically configured with *external RAID subsystems* that connect a pool of storage devices to several servers through separate host ports.

[2] Like all cost estimates in this book, this one is time specific and is given more to suggest an economic order of magnitude than for its absolute value.

In general, the bigger it is (measured in maximum disk capacity, I/O performance, or host connectivity), the more a RAID subsystem adds to online storage cost. A failure-tolerant enclosure, large cache, redundant RAID controllers, and supporting hardware can add up to several times the cost of the disks in it. For SAN-attached storage, the infrastructure cost (SAN ports to connect to storage device ports) is also not negligible. The dominant components of intelligent SAN storage subsystem cost are the intelligence and connectivity.

Finally, in recent years, the software to control and manage storage subsystems has become an increasing part of the systems' value. RAID, zone and path management, disk reconstruction, split mirrors, replication, off-host backup, and other software capabilities are becoming an increasing part of the storage budget.

NOTE
Storage subsystem vendors have figured out that they are actually software vendors, too.

Some RAID subsystem capabilities are also available as software. Mirroring, RAID, data replication, and other storage subsystem functions are all available both for servers and for *storage appliances*. In many cases, the choice is between:

- Hardware solutions, which are actually software that runs in a RAID controller. These solutions are server-independent, but are specific to the storage devices for which they are engineered.

- Server- or appliance-based solutions, which are independent of storage device type, but run only on server and operating system platforms for which they are designed.

It is often possible to combine both of these capabilities advantageously.

The Bottom Line: Paying for Online Storage

The biggest component of SAN storage cost is that of enterprise RAID subsystems. Enterprise RAID subsystems are designed to deliver available, high-performing SAN-attached storage to multiple servers. Moreover, in this relatively mature industry segment, support organizations are in place to keep them running all the time.

As with most good things, this high quality of storage service (QoSS) comes at a cost. A fully configured enterprise RAID subsystem (i.e., one with the maximum number of the largest possible disks installed) has a high cost per gigabyte; a partially configured one is even more expensive, because the subsystem's shared resources are amortized over less storage capacity. This suggests that it may be most cost effective to add enterprise RAID subsystems at times when projected storage growth will intercept the enterprise subsystem's maximum capacity relatively soon after installation. Server-based volume management can be a helpful adjunct during enterprise RAID subsystem transitions. Server-based software provides much of enterprise RAID subsystem functionality using lower-cost hardware. It can make enterprise RAID subsystem transitions smoother, as well as prolonging the lifetimes of the storage assets they replace.

SAN-attached storage tends to be more costly than even enterprise-class locally attached storage. The higher capital cost is one of the factors that prospective purchasers must balance against the benefits of SAN-based storage-centric information processing strategies described in Chapters 2 and 4.

Making SAN Storage Perform

RAID controllers and server-based volume managers aggregate disks and present their storage capacity to file systems, database managers, and applications as disk-like entities that are usually called disk arrays or volumes. Aggregating disks increases:

Capacity. If a file system or database is larger than the largest available disk, a volume manager or RAID subsystem can concatenate the capacity of several disks and present the result as a single, larger disk that will hold the object.

Availability. Two or more disks can be mirrored or made into a RAID array, thereby protecting against loss of data or data availability due to disk failure.

Performance. Aggregated disks divide and conquer to improve I/O performance. Large I/O requests can be subdivided, with pieces executed concurrently by several disks. Streams of small I/O requests can be subdivided and directed to different disks for parallel execution.

Significant research and development have gone into storage device aggregation, and developers have come up with some pretty innovative solutions. Fortunately, most aggregating techniques for improving storage performance are actually configuration options—by configuring enough of the right kind of components in the right way, an administrator can provide very high levels of I/O performance. The administrator's challenge lies more in being aware of impending I/O performance needs and reconfiguring to meet them before they arise.

Part 1 has extolled the benefits of SANs' universal connectivity amply. There's a corresponding caution, however: Servers contending for access to data can easily create more demand than a single storage device or RAID subsystem can satisfy. The system administrator who installs a SAN must be prepared to configure for data center-wide optimal performance and to monitor usage so that changing requirements can be met without disruption.

Disk Aggregation and Virtualization

RAID controllers and volume managers emulate disks. They present larger, faster, more reliable disk-like entities to file systems, database managers, and applications. This ingenious concept has led to rapid and complete user acceptance of disk aggregation. Any software that uses disks can also use aggregated volumes. No file system or database modifications are required to take advantage of larger capacities, higher performance, and greater data availability.

Disks are aggregated with software. The software may run in a RAID controller, in an application server, or in a server acting as a storage appliance. Sets of disks aggregated by RAID controllers are typically called *arrays*. The storage devices presented to file systems are called *LUNs* (for logical unit numbers) *or virtual disks*. In servers and appliances, *volume managers* aggregate disks. The aggregated storage devices presented to file systems are called *volumes*.

Disk Aggregation by Striping

For applications to run as fast as possible, I/O requests should execute as quickly as possible. The most important disk aggregation technique for improving performance is the *striping* of data across several disks. Striping makes the performance of several disks available to applications almost as if they were one.

In order for volume managers and RAID controllers to make several disks look like one, they must combine the separately numbered blocks of each disk into a single sequence of volume block addresses. Software maintains a correspondence between disk block addresses and volume block addresses.

Striping is one such correspondence. When data is striped across an array of disks, sequences of volume blocks correspond to sequences of disk blocks, as Figure 6.1 illustrates.

As can be seen from Figure 6.1:

- Volume blocks 0–3 correspond to Disk A blocks 0–3.

- Volume blocks 4–7 correspond to Disk B blocks 0–3.

- Volume blocks 8–11 correspond to Disk C blocks 0–3.

Volume blocks 12–15 "wrap around" corresponding to Disk A Blocks 4–7. Volume blocks 16–19 correspond to Disk B blocks 4–7, and so forth. The resulting volume

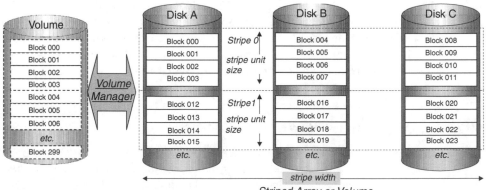

Figure 6.1 Striping data blocks across several disks.

block space is distributed across Disks A, B, and C in a geometrically regular sequence.

To understand how striping makes a volume outperform a disk, it helps to realize that almost all applications use storage in one of two different ways:

- They make lots of I/O requests, but don't ask for a lot of data in each request (imagine a Web page server or transaction processor).

- They make relatively few requests, but ask for a huge amount of data in each one (imagine a video server).

In this book, we call applications that make lots of I/O requests *I/O intensive* and applications that move a lot of data with each request *data intensive*.

Striping and Data-Intensive Applications

It's easy to see how striping data across several disks benefits data-intensive applications. Imagine that an application requested the first 12 blocks of data from the volume illustrated in Figure 6.2. The volume manager would analyze the application's volume request and convert it into three disk requests, one each to Disks A, B, and C. Since the disks are independent and execute requests concurrently, data is delivered in about a third of the time.[3]

Striping and I/O-Intensive Applications

The benefit of striping data across a volume for I/O-intensive applications is a little less obvious. To appreciate it, we need one more piece of information about I/O-intensive applications: Unlike data-intensive applications, they don't request data in

---

[3] The examples in this chapter use artificially small numbers for clarity of illustration. In real volumes, data addresses are usually striped across disks in units of 32 to 256 blocks.

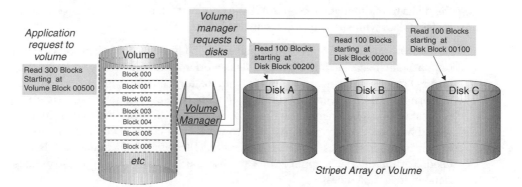

Figure 6.2   How striping improves I/O performance for data-intensive applications.

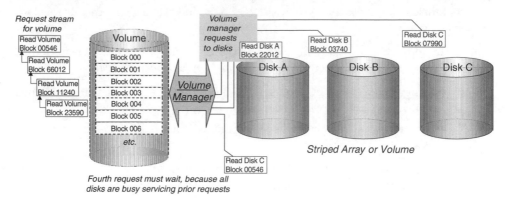

Fourth request must wait, because all
disks are busy servicing prior requests

Figure 6.3 How striping improves I/O performance for I/O-intensive applications.

sequence. In most cases, their requests are distributed randomly across the blocks of a disk or volume. (See Figure 6.3.)

A disk can execute only one I/O request at a time, so if an application makes I/O requests faster than a disk can execute them, an *I/O queue* builds up. Requests at the end of the queue take longer to complete, because they don't get started immediately.

Suppose that an I/O-intensive application uses a striped volume instead of a disk. If requests for data are randomly distributed across the volume's blocks, there's as good a chance that they will be routed to one disk as to another. So if Disk A is busy executing a request when the application makes a second request, there's a two-out-of-three chance that the request will be routed to Disk B or Disk C. In other words, if an application makes I/O requests too rapidly for one disk to handle, spreading data across several disks in a volume can effectively multiply disk speed by as much as the number of disks in the volume.

The beauty of striping data across several disks is that it scales. If an application needs more I/O requests per second or more data transfer speed, more disks can be added to its volume. (Of course, each time a disk is added, data must be *restriped* across all of the disks to maintain the balance.) Some volume managers and RAID controllers can restripe data while a volume is being used by applications.

Striped volumes make both I/O-intensive and data-intensive applications perform better, basically because they get more disks working simultaneously to satisfy application I/O requests. There are a few applications for which striping doesn't improve I/O performance. For example, imagine an I/O-intensive application that waits for each request to finish before making the next. Since this application's volume manager would have only one request at a time to work on, it could keep only one disk busy. Performance in this case would be essentially the same as if a single disk had been used. Fortunately, such applications are few and far between, so data striping is beneficial in most instances.

One seldom sees disk striping software or disk striping controllers for sale. Disk striping is only part of comprehensive volume management. Volume managers and RAID controllers have many capabilities, of which striping data across disks with or without failure protection is one. The ability to stripe data across a volume, and to restripe it when the volume expands, is an important feature to check for when evaluating volume managers, RAID controllers, or storage appliances.

Server-Based and Controller-Based Striping

Both server-based volume managers and RAID controllers implement disk striping. It's reasonable to ask whether one is preferable to the other. As with so many aspects of computing technology, the answer is, "It depends." When striping is implemented in a RAID controller:

- It executes without using any server processing power or memory (and therefore detracting from resources available for applications).

- It executes in a processor (the RAID controller's microprocessor) that is more closely coupled to disks than the typical server, allowing for better control.

- It doesn't have to be upgraded (or at least reinstalled) every time there is a server or operating system upgrade.

On the other hand, a server-based volume manager also has advantages:

- It does not require special hardware, so it is a low-cost way to get started.

- It accesses disks through operating system drivers and so generally supports more flexible configurations (for example, striping data across two different kinds of disks).

- It can stripe data across virtual disks presented by RAID controllers, aggregating the I/O performance of two or more RAID subsystems.

The strong points of volume managers are complementary to the strong points of striping RAID controllers. This suggests that administrators should explore possibilities for combining both technologies.

Data striping is only half of the volume management story, however. The complete picture requires looking at how volume managers (and RAID controller software) protect enterprise data in a SAN from disk and other component failures.

Keeping SAN Storage Up and Working

The conundrum in putting enterprise storage on a SAN is that, while it enables all servers to access all data, when data becomes unavailable no servers can function. Connecting vital storage to a SAN so that all servers can get at it requires a plan for delivering continuous data availability.

Storage can fail in several ways:

- Disks can fail.

- The connection between disks and servers, the SAN itself, can fail.

- RAID controllers can fail.
- Power can fail while updates are in progress, leaving data in an unknown state.
- Server software, including operating systems, file systems, database managers, and applications can fail.

Fortunately, volume managers and RAID controllers protect against data loss due to most of these failures and offer at least some help with all of them.

RAID: Protection Against Disk Failures

One of the earliest areas of focus for RAID subsystem and volume manager designers was protecting against data loss due to disk failure. Much of this work began in the 1980s, when disks were a much different proposition than they are today:

- They cost 1,000 times more per megabyte.
- They failed 50 times as frequently on the average.

In any enterprise storage strategy, therefore, economical protection against data loss due to disk failure figured prominently.

The standard data protection technique of the 1980s was backup. Periodically, sets of related data would be copied verbatim from online disks to tapes and stored. If a disk failed (or if an application went haywire and corrupted data), the newest tapes would be retrieved from the vault and the data on them *restored* to new disks. Applications would restart using the restored data.

A well-managed enterprise backup is a necessary last line of defense against major failures, such as application-induced data corruption or site disasters, but it has some shortcomings as protection against less catastrophic events such as disk failures.

- *If a disk fails, applications can't run until data is restored onto a new disk.* A new disk could be preinstalled and ready, but restoring the backup takes time, during which applications are unavailable.
- *Restored data is as stale as the newest backup.* All updates between the time of the backup and the time of the disk failure are lost when the backup is restored. In the best case, a journal can be read and applied to the restored data—more application downtime. In the worst case, updates are just lost and have to be recreated or worked around.

Research on this problem in the late 1980s resulted in fundamental changes to the storage industry and arguably, data processing itself. The research showed that data can be protected against loss due to disk failure. RAID controllers and volume managers were born and the software content of storage devices increased markedly. It became realistic to design application systems for continuous operation. A generation of 24×7 applications, starting with online transaction processing (e.g., automatic teller machines) and culminating in today's World Wide Web and ebusiness, was enabled.

As with performance enhancement, data is protected against disk failures by *aggregating* the capacity of two or more disks. In this case, however, instead of using all of the aggregated capacity to store user data, some of it holds *check data* that can be used to rebuild user data if a disk fails. Since ordinary disks are aggregated into arrays for data protection and since part of their capacity is used to store redundant check data, the term RAID (redundant array of inexpensive disks) is used to denote a group of disks aggregated to improve data availability.

Several RAID techniques have been implemented over the last decade. From today's standpoint, the important ones boil down to two:

Mirroring. Two or more copies of every block of data are kept on separate disks.

Parity RAID. Also called *RAID 5*. One disk in an array holds a checksum of data in the corresponding blocks on the array's other disks. The checksum plus the remaining blocks enables the contents of any block from any disk to be reconstructed if necessary.

Mirroring is sometimes called RAID 1, because it was the first of several data protection techniques described in a particularly famous research paper.[4] It was well known among storage developers even before the research that led to RAID began. Conceptually, mirroring is simple. Every time a file system, database manager, or application writes to a volume, the volume manager copies the data to all of the volume's disks. The drawback to mirroring that led researchers to search for lower-cost alternatives was the cost of disks in 1988. Today, with disk storage cost in the pennies per megabyte range, mirroring looks very attractive for a lot of enterprise data, especially online databases that are updated frequently in the course of business.

When it was introduced, parity RAID was attractive to buyers because the hardware cost of protection is low. However many disks constitute an array, only the equivalent of one disk is required for holding check data. In the late 1980s, with disk storage costing $10 per megabyte, the difference between one disk of overhead to protect four disks of data and four disks of overhead for the same purpose was substantial. Today, with disk storage costing a few pennies per megabyte, the advantage of parity RAID over mirroring is much less clear, especially when one considers the performance side effects of parity RAID.

To understand the performance side effects of parity RAID, it helps to have an idea of how the technology works. Figure 6.4 gives a simplified view of the parity RAID concept.

Figure 6.4 illustrates the Nth data block on each of the volume's disks. Disks A, B, C, and D hold user data. The parity disk holds check data, which in this example is the sum of the contents of the data blocks. If a disk fails (for example, Data Disk B), its contents can be reconstructed by subtracting the contents of Block N on each of the remaining data disks from the contents of Block N of the parity disk ($33 - 10 - 2 - 6 = 15$).

[4] A Case for Redundant Arrays of Inexpensive Disks, ACM SIGMOD, 1988.

Figure 6.4 Parity RAID.

In real life, parity RAID uses a bit-by-bit XOR (exclusive OR) computation rather than the decimal sum illustrated in Figure 6.4. The details of that need not concern us here—only the fact that as long as all but one of the disks can be read, data from the missing one can be reconstructed and delivered to applications.

For parity RAID to work, the parity in the Nth block has to represent the sum of the contents of the Nth blocks of all the data disks. In Figure 6.4, for example, if the 2 in the Nth block of Data Disk C were overwritten with a 5, then the contents of the Nth block of the parity disk would have to be changed to 36. Volume managers and RAID controllers maintain this correspondence. The easiest way for a volume manager to synchronize parity when data is updated is for it to:

■ *Read* the contents of the data block to be updated.

■ *Read* the contents of the corresponding block on the parity disk.

■ *Subtract* the former from the latter.

■ *Add* the new data supplied by the application to the sum.

■ Re*write* the updated parity block.

■ *Write* the application's data to the data disk.

Since volume managers are transparent to applications, all this work happens behind the scenes. An application makes one write request to a volume; at least four disk I/O requests have to be executed to satisfy it. It doesn't take long for I/O resources to be saturated at this rate.

This hidden overhead occurs only when applications write data. Parity RAID volumes perform like striped volumes when data is being read. Thus, in terms of I/O performance, parity RAID is pretty good for read-mostly applications (e.g., Web services) and not so good for applications that update a lot (e.g., transaction processing).

Mirroring versus RAID versus Data Striping

Both mirroring and parity RAID data protection can be combined with data striping to improve I/O performance. Volumes outperform individual disks *and* protect against data loss. The only drawback is incremental hardware cost—a little in the case of parity RAID, more in the case of mirrored volumes—at least for applications that read more than they write.

There are other considerations, however, that affect a decision to use a mirrored or a RAID volume for a particular file system or database. Perhaps the most important is that a mirrored volume contains two or more complete copies of data that can be split and used separately. For example, a database may need to be both continuously available and backed up periodically. A mirrored volume can be split into two parts, each containing a complete copy of the database. One of the copies can be backed up while applications continue to process the other. When the backup is complete, the copies are resynchronized in preparation for the next backup cycle.

Interconnect Failures

Mirroring and RAID protect against disk failures, but disks aren't the only things that fail. The I/O bus or SAN link that connects storage device to servers can also fail, making data inaccessible. Do failure-tolerant volumes protect data against these failures? Conceptually, the answer to this is simple. An interconnect failure is equivalent to a disk failure . . . *if* the mirrored or RAID volume is configured properly.

A RAID volume can survive the failure of *one* of its disks. Thus, if an interconnect (consisting of integrated circuits and firmware as well as wires or optical conductors) failure incapacitates only one disk, a RAID volume survives. Figure 6.5 illustrates RAID volume configured to survive and not survive an interconnect failure.

The RAID volume on the left in Figure 6.5 has a separate interconnect between each disk and the server or RAID controller. If an interconnect fails, only one disk is inaccessible and the volume can continue to function by reconstructing data, as outlined in the preceding section.

The volume on the right in Figure 6.5, on the other hand, shares an interconnect among several disks (two would be enough). If the interconnect fails, access to more than one disk is lost and RAID reconstruction no longer works. The conclusion is that care is required in configuring volumes for maximum failure tolerance.

Smaller RAID controllers and servers may not have enough separate I/O interconnects to support configurations such as that illustrated on the left in Figure 6.5. Many embedded RAID controllers include three channels, for example. An administrator is forced to compromise. Either RAID volumes must be limited to three disks (less storage-efficient than the five-disk volume illustrated in the figure) or the risk of a failed channel resulting in volume inaccessibility must be accepted. Larger servers and RAID controllers do not have this limitation.

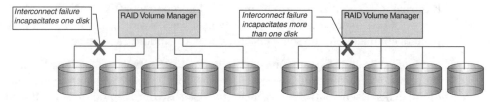

Figure 6.5   Individual interconnects increase failure tolerance.

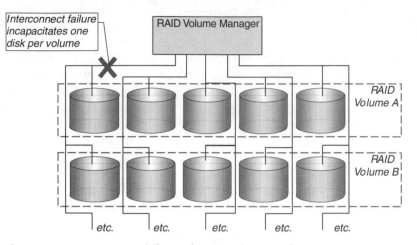

Figure 6.6 Interconnect failure tolerance of RAID volumes.

The limitation isn't quite as bad as it seems. While one RAID volume can sustain the loss of only one of its disks, any number of RAID volumes can sustain the loss of a single disk each. Thus, configurations like that illustrated in Figure 6.6 are popular.

In Figure 6.6, a total of five interconnects are available, but each interconnect can connect several disks (this is the case for SCSI or Fibre Channel Arbitrated Loop). As long as no more than one disk of each volume is configured on each interconnect, any number of five-disk RAID volumes can be configured. If a channel fails, one disk from each volume is lost and all volumes must use reconstruction to read and write data. That's better than losing access to data because someone jiggled a cable loose, however. Experienced administrators take care to configure RAID and mirrored volumes so that a single interconnect failure won't put them out of business.

RAID Controller Failures

The next type of failure to consider is failure of a RAID controller. RAID controllers are supposed to *protect* against failures. When the RAID controller itself fails the impact on data availability can be huge. RAID controller designers are keenly aware of data availability and design their products accordingly. External RAID controllers and embedded RAID controllers impact data availability in different ways.

External RAID controllers use external I/O interconnects (like SANs!) to connect to servers. Controller failure tolerance is typically achieved by pairing two or more controllers connected to the same disks and host computers, as Figure 6.7 illustrates.

In Figure 6.7, all disks are connected to two external RAID controllers. When everything is working, the controllers usually partition I/O load, with each controlling half of the disks. Each controller organizes its disks as volumes and presents them to servers. The two controllers also communicate with each other, using either the SAN or a private interconnect of some kind.

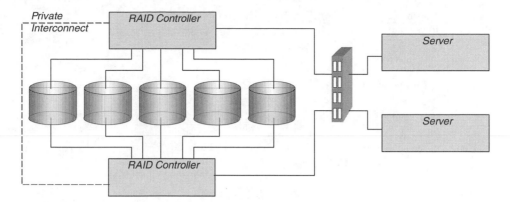

Figure 6.7   Failure-tolerant external RAID controllers.

At a minimum, the two controllers exchange *heartbeats*. A heartbeat is a message whose purpose is to assure the recipient that the sender is functioning. A controller uses the absence of heartbeats to determine that another controller has failed.

Transparent and Nontransparent Failure Tolerance

Since both of the RAID controllers in Figure 6.7 use the same interconnect to connect to host computers, the volumes they present necessarily have different addresses (for example, Fibre Channel LUNs). When one controller fails, the other takes control of its disks and presents its volumes at the same addresses used by the failed controller. With the exception of possible minor glitches during the transition, the change in control is transparent to applications. The same volumes are addressed at the same addresses, even though another controller is managing them.

This is an elegant solution, but it does have a drawback: If the SAN infrastructure fails, then all access to data is lost. One solution to this problem is to connect each RAID controller to a separate SAN segment, as illustrated in Figure 6.8.

With an I/O subsystem configured this way, all data is still accessible if a SAN segment fails, because control of all disks can be taken over by the controller whose host connection is still working.

Some subsystems take this even further, by equipping each RAID controller with two or more host interconnects as Figure 6.9 illustrates, so that not only servers but also RAID controllers can be connected to two SAN segments. This configuration eliminates the necessity to shift all disks to one controller if a SAN segment fails.

What all of these solutions have in common is that servers must participate in recovery from failures. Since a controller failure means that volumes suddenly show up at different addresses, possibly on different segments (different host bus adapters),

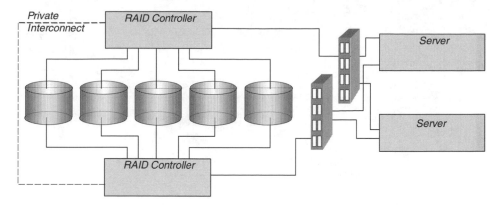

Figure 6.8 Nontransparent failure-tolerant RAID controller configuration.

servers must be aware of which volumes are the same and which are different. Today, the standards for how operating systems should deal with *dynamic multipathing* are still evolving and each platform deals with it in its own way.

Atomic Operations and Data Integrity

RAID and mirrored volume updates are *nonatomic* operations. In other words, they consist of multiple steps that *all* have to complete for correct behavior. If a RAID controller loses electrical power with an update half done (for example, one copy of mirrored data written and the other one not written), the volume could return corrupt data at some time in the future. For example, if power fails with one copy of a mirrored data block written and the other not, then future reads of that block can return different results depending on which mirrored disk is selected to satisfy the read.

Many RAID controllers use write-back cache to enhance I/O performance. A write-back cache holds data or parity that needs to be written to disk, but may not yet have

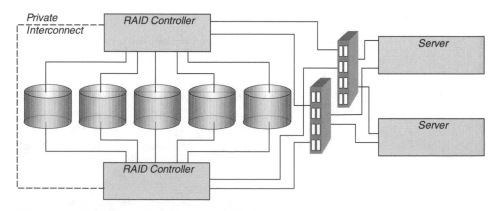

Figure 6.9 Fully redundant RAID controller interconnects.

been written. If a controller fails with unwritten data in a write-back cache, the integrity of the controller's volumes is suspect. For example, a data update may have been written, but the updated parity may still be in cache. If data is ever reconstructed from the on-disk (out-of-date) parity, it will be corrupt.

If a RAID controller is to be truly failure tolerant, it must protect against loss of state and cache contents when power fails (or when the controller fails). The most common solution to this problem is for interconnected RAID controllers to communicate state changes and changes in their respective write-back cache contents to each other. Dual port cache memory, the I/O interconnect, and private interconnects have all been used for this purpose. Whatever the implementation technology, the important thing for RAID controller users is that operation state and cached data be preserved in case of controller failure so that data is not lost.

Really Big RAID Controllers

Over the last 15 years, storage has gradually been declaring its independence from the rest of the computing industry. Most major RAID subsystem players are companies or divisions that weren't even in the business 15 years ago. Today, many large users devote the same level of attention to enterprise storage vendor selection and purchase that they devote to computer systems. In effect, storage vendors have maneuvered themselves on a par with computer system, network, and data management software vendors.

In parallel with this shift in the way computer systems are purchased, there has been a shift in data center architecture. Fifteen years ago, the role of storage was as a peripheral to a single computer system. Today, several vendors offer *enterprise storage subsystems* that can connect a single pool of failure-tolerant storage to many servers—subsystems that connect 32 hosts to as much as 10 terabytes are readily available. Administrators are able to manage a consolidated pool of storage, shifting capacity from computer to computer as requirements indicate, even without a SAN.

The many-to-many connectivity of SANs is accelerating this trend toward storage consolidation. RAID subsystem vendors are already using SANs to establish cooperation among multiple RAID subsystems, forming, in effect, storage clusters.

Enterprise storage subsystem vendors tend to position their products as *black boxes* with lots of computer connections to lots of RAID-protected storage. They tend not to emphasize the internal architecture of their products. Users may wonder whether these enterprise boxes deliver the same level of failure protection as smaller subsystems in which dual redundant RAID controllers are clearly identifiable.

Users need not be concerned. Enterprise storage subsystems are every bit as failure tolerant as smaller subsystems. If one looked inside these large subsystems (which, admittedly, their vendors discourage) one would find the same or a greater level of redundancy as in smaller subsystems with redundant RAID controllers. Host interfaces, cache, power and cooling, disk interfaces, and the paths between them are all redundant and protected against individual failures. Enterprise storage subsystems go one step further, actually diagnosing their own problems and calling home to request service if they detect an actual or impending failure. Enterprise storage subsystem vendors are extremely conscious of their position as the keystone of IT and, if anything, overengineer their products for continuous data availability.

Embedded RAID Controller Failure Tolerance

At the other end of the server price spectrum, less attention is paid to surviving embedded RAID controller failures. This is because an embedded RAID controller is effectively an integral part of its host computer. It relies on the host for power and cooling. Its host connection is an internal I/O bus like PCI, rather than an external I/O bus like Fibre Channel or SCSI. The intimate relationship between computer and embedded RAID controller makes it difficult to treat failures of either separately. For the most part, embedded RAID controllers are used in single-host applications where it is appropriate to regard most controller failures as equivalent to host failures.

There are two important cases where embedded RAID controller failures and host failures should be isolated and treated separately:

- In an embedded controller with a write-back cache, cache contents should be preserved for a period of time if power or the host system fails. This allows a recovering controller to write data cached prior to the failure to disk, restoring volume consistency. Most embedded RAID controllers use rechargeable batteries that maintain cache contents when power is off and allow them to survive power failures of hours or even days without data loss.

- If a computer in a *cluster* (Chapter 8) fails, another computer must be able to restart its applications and process its data. If the data is stored by an external RAID controller, this is not a problem, because computer failure has no effect on the storage subsystem, so the failed computer's data is available to the computer taking over its work. A computer failure takes an embedded RAID controller down with it, however, possibly with state information (e.g., about partly complete updates) and data in its cache. If another computer in the cluster takes over the failed computer's disks, data on them could be in an inconsistent state. Data corruption would inevitably result.

Recognizing the appeal of low-cost embedded RAID controllers, some vendors have developed mechanisms by an embedded RAID controller can exchange state information with and update the cache contents of a RAID controller embedded in another system. Generally, these mechanisms involve using one or more of the controllers' device interconnects to exchange information.

Volume Manager Failure Tolerance

As discussed earlier, it's perfectly feasible to do RAID without RAID controllers. Server-based volume managers implement RAID and mirroring functionality in the operating system I/O stack. From an availability standpoint, server-based volume managers have similarities to embedded RAID controllers, because they rely completely on a working host environment. If server power fails or an operating system crashes, the volume manager fails with it.

Like RAID controllers, server-based volume managers must leave persistent tracks so that operations in progress at the time of a failure can be recovered. Since they run on servers, options such as cache battery backup are not generally available to them. Instead, server-based volume managers rely on disk logs. Before they start an update, they write a log entry indicating their intent. When the operation completes, another log entry is made. Volume manager logs are read during recovery, and partially complete updates are completed or backed out as appropriate.

Logging makes it possible for server-based volumes to be mounted on several clustered servers as long as one volume manager instance controls each volume. If a server fails and its workload and data shift to an alternate server, the alternate server recovers the volume as if from a failure. Any operations in progress at the time of failure are completed or backed out. Cluster-aware server-based volume managers are available today. Such volume managers take advantage of SAN connectivity to make volumes simultaneously available on an entire cluster. The primary use of cluster volume managers is to support *cluster file systems* that allow more than one computer to open files in the same file system simultaneously. Cluster volume managers and file systems are discussed in Chapter 8.

Choosing among Storage Options

The technology in storage subsystems is interesting—fascinating, even. But administrators tasked with providing enterprise storage need help making decisions. How does one interpret vendor claims and make intelligent decisions?

Fortunately, it's not as difficult as it may sound. The storage subsystem industry has matured to the point where RAID and mirroring subsystems can generally be trusted to do the right thing. Users can make decisions based primarily on the traditional storage metrics of cost of capacity, I/O performance, and availability.

When planning storage for a SAN, the decision tree takes a sharp fork rather early. In today's world, one either connects file servers to application servers (probably using fast or gigabit Ethernet as the interconnect) or connects enterprise RAID subsystems to application and file servers (probably using Fibre Channel as the interconnect). There are a few extant examples of other options, but today, this is the mainstream.

With both options, a little due diligence on candidate storage products is in order. Prudent administrators ask questions such as the following:

- Does the subsystem use mirroring and RAID to protect against data loss due to disk failure?

- Can RAID and mirrored volumes be configured to protect against interconnect, power supply, and cooling failures as well as disk failures?

- Does the subsystem protect against controller or main processor failure, including making disks controlled by a failed controller available through a substitute one?

- Does the subsystem use write-back cache to enhance application performance, particularly update performance?

- If the subsystem uses write-back cache, are the contents of the cache safe when the subsystem itself fails (e.g., due to power failure or software crash)?

- Does the subsystem connect to multiple host computers simultaneously?

- If the subsystem is cluster-capable, does all the host support required for clean application failover exist? Can a server import and do I/O to volumes on alternate paths?

- Does the subsystem support hot swapping of disks and other components (including controllers) that may fail so that protection can be restored without downtime?

- Does the subsystem preserve the state of operations, by logging or by using a non-volatile cache so that failures that happen while updates are in progress don't leave corrupt data behind after recovery?

- Is the subsystem supported by all servers in the SAN and expected to be connected to the SAN?

- Does the vendor have a policy of regularly qualifying new components so that, for example, online storage capacity can be increased when higher-capacity disks are introduced, without having to swap out the entire subsystem?

- Does the subsystem support enough disks on enough interconnects to meet the capacity and performance needs anticipated over its expected lifetime?

- Does the subsystem offer comprehensive management tools that are easy to learn and straightforward to use in the relevant host environments?

- Does the subsystem anticipate component failures and respond proactively (e.g., by sending alerts to system administrators or help desks or by calling the vendor so that repair can be initiated)?

It's easy to present this list of questions to a hardware RAID subsystem vendor. It's a little more difficult to find a single point of contact to answer questions if server-based software volume management and RAID subsystems are to be combined.

Software volume management may require digging a little deeper into the details to get a complete capabilities picture, but it does have some distinct advantages:

- Software volume management supports modest beginnings. All that's required are a few disks and host bus adapters. Software does the mirroring, RAID, failover, sparing, resynchronization, monitoring, and so forth.

- Software volume management supports more heterogeneous configurations, with different kinds of disks and host bus adapters. This can be important if legacy hardware must be intermixed with new hardware.

- Software volume managers can manage RAID controller-based volumes, as Figure 6.10 illustrates. Software based volumes whose "disks" are virtual can aggregate the performance of two or more RAID controllers by striping data across them or increase failure tolerance by mirroring data across two or more RAID controllers.

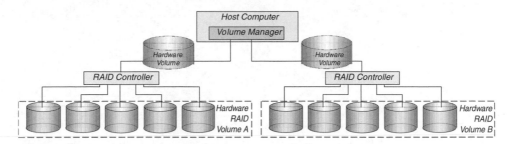

Figure 6.10   Combining hardware and software volumes.

It is wise to consider software volume management as part of an overall SAN storage strategy, possibly as an alternative to RAID subsystems, but much more likely as a complement to them.

Summary

- The three major metrics for evaluating online storage are cost of capacity, I/O performance, and data availability.

- A surprisingly large portion of enterprise online storage cost is in the subsystem (enclosure, power, packaging, host interconnect) rather than the disks.

- The chief technique for increasing online storage I/O performance is data striping. Data striping enhances performance of both streaming and transaction processing applications, provided that I/O requests are made properly.

- Mirroring and RAID are the chief techniques for enhancing the availability of data stored online. Mirroring is more expensive, but offers both superior protection against more failures and additional functionality, such as split mirrors for backup or analysis of frozen images of operational data.

- Striping, mirroring, and RAID are implemented in servers, RAID controllers, and *storage appliances* that present either volumes or files.

- RAID controllers are *external* to their hosts, connected by SCSI or Fibre Channel, or they are embedded in their host's enclosures, connected to an internal I/O bus such as PCI. Embedded RAID controllers fail along with their hosting computers. Some vendors implement disk failover for embedded RAID controllers to enable two-server clusters.

- Most advanced storage functionality is delivered by most of the products on the market today in some form. Users' decision trees should include not only basic properties (cost, performance, and availability), but also second-order features enumerated in the body of this chapter.

CHAPTER 7

The *Network* in Storage Networking

I n this chapter we'll learn more about:

- The standards, components, interconnects, and protocols that constitute Fibre Channel, the dominant SAN interconnect technology in use today

- The development process that led to Fibre Channel

- The different topologies that compose Fibre Channel SANs, their properties, and the infrastructure components required to implement them

- How very large Fibre Channel SANs can be constructed by aggregating the connectivity and bandwidth of multiple switches

- Emerging physical interconnect technologies that may complement or challenge Fibre Channel

- Other developments in storage networking that may change the way storage networks and data center computer systems are purchased and deployed

Fibre Channel: The 800-Pound Gorilla of SANs

Perhaps the most important enabler for SANs is Fibre Channel. Arguably, it can fairly be said, Fibre Channel is an interconnect technology whose properties, are the catalyst that has made SANs happen.

- Connectivity

- Distance and cost options

- Bandwidth (interconnect and protocol efficiency)

- Failure tolerance and recoverability

Fibre Channel is interesting to study, not just from a technology standpoint, but also for the process by which it was developed. Unlike previous I/O architectures developed by one company and presented to the industry and market as a fait accompli, Fibre Channel development was *standards-based* almost from its inception. Starting with a group of companies called the Fibre Channel Systems Initiative (FCSI) and moving over the years into the X3T11 Committee of the American National Standards Institute, practically the entire development process for Fibre Channel standards has been open for anyone to observe and participate in. As the technology moved from specifications to components and from there to products, standards activities were augmented by plugfests, in which developers brought prototypes together to test their interoperability.

An open development process is good for a lot of reasons, but it's a slow process. Added to the normal technical challenges is the challenge of achieving consensus among companies with different interests and perspectives. Open development takes time.

Fibre Channel: The Standards

There's a lot to Fibre Channel. First and foremost, it's a family of interconnect standards. Fibre Channel standards specify the properties of the following:

- *Optical and electrical transmission media* of several types
- *Signaling conventions*, such as how bits are represented, how sequences of bits are assembled into words, which bit patterns make up valid words, and what happens on the interconnect when no bits are being transmitted
- *Transmission protocol conventions*, such as how words are assembled into frames for transmission and how frames are assembled into messages
- *Functional protocol conventions*, such as the formatting and sequencing of command messages and data messages and error handling and recovery

Fibre Channel began life among a group of companies devoted to producing a standard for next-generation I/O technology. Even in the intensely competitive computer and networking industries, companies realized that nobody was dominant enough to go it alone—that in order for an interconnect technology to succeed it would have to have the support of many companies with many different core competencies. The process of developing Fibre Channel has become the blueprint for computer and communications industry new technology initiatives.

Fibre Channel: The Chips

Standards enable devices made by different vendors to intercommunicate, but they are of little use unless vendors actually build useful devices that implement them. The second step toward a useful Fibre Channel, therefore, is application specific integrated circuits (ASICs) that implement the standards. The true faithful in the early days of Fibre Channel were the ASIC companies. It was they who had to make the enormous investments in special-purpose chips for which there was no existing market. Without them, Fibre Channel simply would not have happened.

Fibre Channel: The Devices

Once there are ASICs, the next requirement is devices that use the ASICs. Devices include disk and tape drives and host bus adapters that move data in and out of computer memory.

Some disk drive vendors, notably Seagate Technology, were quick to embrace Fibre Channel. Seagate was a leader in the development of the low-cost *arbitrated loop* topology variation that made it practical to use Fibre Channel as a disk and tape drive interconnect.

Tape drive vendors were slower to adopt Fibre Channel as a direct interconnect for their devices (although they are now appearing). The reasons for this are partly economic and partly technical. On the economic front, tapes are sold in much lower volume than disks. A tape drive vendor therefore amortizes development cost over a smaller number of units. Moreover, tapes tend to have longer service lives than disks. This occurs partly because tapes tend to operate at lower *duty cycles* (they're working less of the time) than disks and partly because users develop large collections of tape media and are loath to change devices out of fear that new devices won't be able to read old tapes.

The slowness with which Fibre Channel–attached tapes have developed has spawned an entire subindustry—the bridge and router industry—that we discuss shortly.

Fibre Channel: The Infrastructure

To realize the many-to-many connectivity promise of Fibre Channel, another class of devices is also necessary: central connection points that fulfill a role similar to that of a telephone switching system. As with other networks, all Fibre Channel SAN-attached computers and devices plug into these central connection points and the connection points route data between pairs of devices that need to communicate.

There are two basic types of Fibre Channel central connection points:

Hubs. Hubs are used with arbitrated loop topology. Hubs pass signals arriving from one port to the next port in the loop. It is up to the devices to intercept and process signals addressed to them.

Switches. Switches are used with fabric topology. Switches establish temporary logical connections between pairs of devices, allowing the devices to intercommunicate directly. Unlike a hub, a switch connects multiple pairs of devices at the same time, resulting in greater overall system bandwidth.

One more type of Fibre Channel connection point deserves mention: the *bridge* or *router*. A bridge is a specialized switch that converts between two different interconnects—for example, Fibre Channel and parallel SCSI. Thus, for example, a Fibre Channel host bus adapter connected to a Fibre Channel-to-SCSI bridge could communicate with SCSI disks, tapes, and RAID subsystems.

Bridges and routers are particularly useful when a data center is making a transition to Fibre Channel from an older technology such as parallel SCSI. With literally millions of parallel SCSI devices in use in data centers, managers don't want to hear:

I have great new I/O technology that will deliver all kinds of benefits to you. All you need to do to use it is to scrap all your existing storage devices and install devices that use my new technology to do the same thing you're doing with your existing devices.

A much more convincing argument would be:

Install my new I/O infrastructure and you can bridge between it and your existing SCSI storage and computers. You can phase the bridges out during your normal storage and server replacement cycles as you phase in native Fibre Channel devices.

Routers bridge between protocols and also translate device addresses so that, for example, one Fibre Channel port can connect to an entire string of parallel SCSI devices.

Fibre Channel Variations:
Coping with Complexity

The extensive connectivity, long distance, high performance, and robustness of Fibre Channel make it ideal for all kinds of storage I/O applications. In fact, there's something in Fibre Channel for everyone:

Cost. Fibre Channel is attractive for connecting disks to server and RAID controllers because it enables each server or controller port to accommodate lots of disks. But to be practical the per disk connection cost must also be low. Fibre Channel Arbitrated Loop topology minimizes the costs of connecting large numbers of disks to servers and RAID controllers.

Performance. Fibre Channel is an ideal RAID subsystem-to-server interconnect, because it enables cross-connection of servers and RAID subsystems for increased performance as well as path failure tolerance. But for a Fibre Channel fabric to be practical for this purpose, overall fabric I/O performance must be very high. Since there are few RAID subsystem and host connections in a typical data center (relative to disk connections), cost is a secondary consideration for this application.

Distance. Fibre Channel is ideal for connecting tape drives mounted in robotic media handlers to computers, because the interconnect distances it supports allow backup tapes for several widely dispersed application servers to be placed in safe, environmentally controlled, professionally staffed facilities. Again, the number of tape connections in a typical data center is relatively small, so cost is a secondary consideration for this application.

Overhead. It seems that Fibre Channel would also be ideal for connecting file servers to application servers because the efficient protocol designs and largely hardware implementations enable high I/O performance with low server and storage device processing overhead. For that to be practical, Fibre Channel would have to support file access protocols as well as the block access *Fibre Channel Protocol* (FCP) with which it was initially designed.

So the promise of Fibre Channel, universal storage interconnection at high performance over long distances, is challenging to realize because there are so many conflicting application requirements. The Fibre Channel answer to this challenge is a family of standards accommodating:

- Several types of *transmission media* that support increasing maximum interconnect distances at increasing levels of cost

- Three *topologies*, or shapes, in which Fibre Channel SANs can be configured, again with increasing levels of connectivity and performance at increasing cost

- A structure that accommodates *multiple upper-layer protocols* to enable file access and other protocols to be layered upon a base Fibre Channel message transmission network

Fibre Channel Transmission Media

Network *transmission media* are the cables or electromagnetic carrier waves over which messages travel. Different network applications have different transmission media requirements. For example:

- A string of disk drives is unlikely to need a long-distance interconnect, but does need a low-cost one so that interconnect cost doesn't overwhelm the cost of the disks themselves.

- Tape drives, on the other hand, need long-distance interconnects so they can be put into vaults that physically protect data. There aren't many tape drives in a typical data center (relative to the number of disks), so cost isn't as much of a factor as it is with disk interconnection.

Fibre Channel standards specify 26 different kinds of transmission media as this book is written! A lot of them are simply historical—artifacts of a lengthy standards-based development process. For example, there are standards for quarter-speed (25 megabytes per second) and half-speed copper media, because systems using these speeds were developed and shipped before higher-speed electronics supporting 100-megabyte-per-second transmission were available. At the other end of the spectrum, standards also specify new types of media suitable for 200- and 400-megabyte-per-second data transfer. Media and electronic components capable of transferring data at 200 megabytes per second are being delivered as this book is written. Higher-speed components are in development as next-generation, even higher-performing solutions. Broadly speaking, the Fibre Channel transmission media that are readily available today are these:

- *Electrical* (often called *copper* because that's what they're made of) wires that are inexpensive to manufacture and integrate into electronic equipment. Electrical Fibre Channel standards specify a maximum transmission distance of 30 meters.

- *Low-cost optical* (*multimode fiber*) that costs significantly more than copper, but that can carry data transmissions for up to 2 kilometers at acceptably low error rates.

■ *High-cost optical* (*single-mode fiber*) that can support data transmission over distances of up to 10 kilometers, but that costs significantly more than multimode fiber to manufacture.

There's a pretty obvious match between these different classes of Fibre Channel media and I/O applications. For example, an enclosure designed to fit in an equipment rack and hold 10 disks needs a copper interconnect, because that's the least expensive alternative. Moreover, cable runs inside a disk enclosure are only a few tens of centimeters, so maximum distance is not a problem.

On the other hand, for an office building or campus with servers distributed around it, longer-distance interconnection to a central storage pool is a must. A central backup vault for an extended campus full of data centers may well require higher-cost optical media, because the distances between data centers and the central vault are so great. Moreover, the importance of reliable backup copies of critical enterprise data in a safe place makes interconnect cost a secondary consideration.

Initially, the number of Fibre Channel media types caused a problem for component manufacturers and system integrators. It is prohibitively expensive for them to carry three different kinds of every Fibre Channel device in inventory to allow each application's needs to be met optimally. To solve this problem, Fibre Channel vendors have developed *media converters* that convert between on-module electrical signals and either copper or optical signals. Media converters are small, low-cost devices with optical connectors at one end and standard electronic connectors at the other. Media converters enable Fibre Channel device manufacturers to build one type of port with a standard electronic input and output. When a device is configured for use, the appropriate converter adapts it for an electrical or optical application.

The first Fibre Channel media converters developed were called *gigabit link modules* (GLM). A GLM is a printed circuit module with a standard electrical pin interface to a Fibre Channel circuit module and one of the three transmission media type connectors as an output. Fibre Channel interfaces such as host bus adapters would contain standard sockets into which GLMs would plug, giving the interface an electrical or optical *personality*.

GLMs solve an inventory problem for vendors and integrators, but for field reconfiguration of installed equipment, they require that cabinets be accessed by trained service people. This makes a Fibre Channel expensive to own, if not to purchase. To deal with this problem and reduce device cost still further, developers came up with a second generation of Fibre Channel transmission media converter, the *gigabit interface converter* (GBIC).

A GBIC plugs into the electrical port of a Fibre Channel module and converts between electrical Fibre Channel signals and one of the optical standards. GBICs can be installed by anyone. There is no need to open a storage device or server enclosure to install or remove a GBIC; it simply plugs in to the device's electrical signal outlet.

GBICs allow vendors and integrators to build and stock one model of each component and, at the same time, make user serviceability of Fibre Channel SANs possible. Low component cost and easy maintenance have been keys to broad adoption of Fibre Channel in data centers.

Fibre Channel Protocols:
One Size Does Not Fit All

Protocols are the rules that govern the meaning of frames of information transmitted between two devices. A data communications protocol specifies the following:

- The format and meaning of messages and what kind of messages can be sent at what times

- How control messages and user blocks of data are distinguished from each other, aggregated or subdivided into units for transmission and disassembled, recognized, and processed when received

- How transmission and protocol errors are recognized and recovered

Describing data communications protocols in terms of these three tasks makes them sound simple, but in reality modern protocol design is a hugely complex task. But the data storage and I/O industries have been designing protocols for a long time. The protocols that are vital for communicating between storage devices and servers in a data center are mature and well developed, and lots of different devices implement them. SCSI-based storage devices have been shipping for over 15 years; Fibre Channel (FCP) storage devices for almost half that time. During that time, vendors have learned a lot about how to specify I/O commands and data transfers, about interoperability, and about cooperative error recovery.

I/O protocols belong to one of the three following families:

- Protocols used to communicate between servers and disk drives or RAID subsystems

- Protocols used to communicate between application servers and file servers

- Protocols used to communicate between application servers and database servers (which are of minor concern for us here)

The Fibre Channel designers understood very well that all computer system I/O could not be reduced to using a single protocol. In the first place, Fibre Channel was intended for both bulk storage I/O and other purposes, such as intercomputer communication. Even in the storage arena, users perceive benefits in both file and block access storage device models. Fibre Channel protocols were therefore designed with data transportation protocol functions carefully segregated from upper-layer protocols (ULPs) that are used to impart meaning to transported messages and data.

Recent events seem to have validated this philosophy, as additional protocols gain momentum. In particular, the *Virtual Interface Architecture* (VIA) protocol, which enables direct communication between "applications" such as file systems and database managers and very intelligent storage devices, is being prototyped by several hardware and software vendors. A closely related *Direct Access File System* (DAFS) protocol that uses VIA to reduce file access latency is also beginning to emerge as a competitor to the mature Common Internet File System (CIFS) and Network File System (NFS) protocols for file server access.

The reality today is that any I/O interconnect will have to support multiple data access protocols for the foreseeable future. Adopting a physical interconnect requires the purchase of cable, infrastructure components, and endpoint components. It requires that buildings and campuses be wired and that installation, maintenance and reconfiguration skills be developed or contracted. It requires certain commitments to the configuration of premises and the topology of computer systems and data centers.

In short, adoption of a network interconnect is a major decision with large and long-term capital and personnel implications. Nobody wants to rewire an office building or campus with a new network infrastructure until technology change makes it absolutely necessary.

On the other hand, messaging protocols are continually evolving. HTTP, HTML, SMTP, and other protocols that essentially drive the Internet today were either nonexistent or in a germinal stage when the Ethernet infrastructures that carry a good bit of their traffic today were installed. To some extent, the same is true with I/O protocols. SCSI has evolved through three generations of implementations and Fibre Channel's management protocol, Generic Services (GS), was as yet undeveloped when Fibre Channel networks were first deployed.

The obvious solution to the asynchronous evolution of physical interconnects and functional protocols is to design layered protocol schemes so that one primitive (lower-level) protocol set can host several upper-layer protocols simultaneously. This separation is nowhere more apparent than with the Internet Protocol (IP) and its predominant upper-layer protocols, TCP and UDP, which are designed for strict isolation between layers as well as strict isolation from physical transmission media. Arguably, the durability of the Internet is due in some large part to this strictly adhered-to layered design, which has endured over nearly two decades of evolution.

Fibre Channel Protocol Layers

Isolation of functional protocols from the transmission protocol is exactly what the designers of Fibre Channel did. Fibre Channel's *protocol stack* is carefully designed as a series of layers that separate the meaning of messages and data from the packetization, framing, sequencing, and transmission error recovery aspects.

The first upper-layer protocol to be supported by vendors of Fibre Channel storage devices was a packetized version of the SCSI I/O command set called simply Fibre Channel Protocol, or FCP. Over time, additional upper-layer protocols have been developed. Today, it is possible to use FCP, IP, and VIA simultaneously on the same

Fibre Channel physical link. There are host bus adapters that can support multiple upper-layer protocols simultaneously for maximum exploitation of the tremendous communication infrastructure resource represented by a Fibre Channel SAN.

Topology: The Shape of a Fibre Channel SAN

The *topology* of a network defines how many of what kinds of objects can be connected in what ways, without regard for the location of individual objects, the distance between them, or the performance of links. Network topologies are dictated by a combination of application requirements and technology availability. For example:

- Because there so many disks connected to a typical SAN, the priorities for disk interconnection are high density and low cost. Generally, there's no need for long-distance interconnects and, relative to the average disk, the performance of even a single Fibre Channel link is pretty high.

- Because it's the I/O access point for many disks, a RAID subsystem needs very high I/O performance, especially if it's an enterprise RAID subsystem serving several computers. There are far fewer RAID subsystems than disks connected to the typical SAN, so interconnect cost is a secondary priority. Furthermore, physical configuration considerations may require longer distances between a RAID subsystem and the computers for which it holds data than are required for disk interconnection.

- For backup applications, connectivity and performance demands aren't especially high (there typically aren't many tapes connected to a SAN and, compared to Fibre Channel data transfer rates, tapes are slow). Long distance can be very valuable for backup however, enabling tape libraries to be located in physically secure and environmentally protected vaults.

Fibre Channel supports all of these requirements, in part because it specifies three different topologies or network shapes:

- *Point to point*, in which two devices are directly connected to each other by a Fibre Channel cable.

- *Arbitrated loop*, in which a number of devices time-share a single transmission path. A Fibre Channel arbitrated loop can connect up to 126 devices. In practice, arbitrated loops are most often used to connect strings of disks to host bus adapters or RAID controller ports and are typically configured with 20 or fewer devices.

- *Switched or fabric*, in which each device is directly connected to a central connecting point called a *switch*. The switch makes and breaks momentary connections between pairs of devices that need to communicate with each other. Like Ethernet switches, Fibre Channel switches are high-performance devices that are capable of intermediating several simultaneous communications between pairs of devices at the same time. Thus, while the total bandwidth between any two devices is the speed of one Fibre Channel link (today, 100 megabytes per second in each direction), with a switched topology, the total systemwide bandwidth can be an order of magnitude or more greater because multiple communications between pairs of devices can occur concurrently.

Point-to-point topology, illustrated in Figure 7.1, is the simplest Fibre Channel interconnection alternative, but it hardly qualifies as a storage network. It did enable basic Fibre Channel technology to get started before the infrastructure pieces were all in place. It is primarily used to connect RAID subsystems and tape drives to servers in server-centric systems. Its advantage over the then-incumbent parallel SCSI technology was that it allowed longer-distance interconnects to be supported. Today, point-to-point Fibre Channel is rarely deployed.

Point-to-point Fibre Channel interconnection delivered on the promises of higher I/O performance and greater separation between servers and their storage devices. More complex topologies were required to deliver on the connectivity promise. In order to connect many servers to many storage devices, common connection points are required. Fibre Channel common connectivity is provided by hubs and switches, which, while appearing similar physically and in block diagrams, differ substantially in their internal construction and capabilities.

Both switches and hubs are central cabling points to which servers and storage devices connect. Their interconnect topologies are radically different, however. A Fibre Channel hub implements the arbitrated loop topology. It effectively routes a single transmission path through a string of computers and storage devices (collectively called *nodes*). Figure 7.2 illustrates Fibre Channel hub connectivity.

A Fibre Channel hub is effectively a box full of loop ports, or *L-Ports*, interconnected in a loop topology. Each port routes its incoming signal carrier to the outgoing carrier of the adjacent port. The last (leftmost in Figure 7.2) port in the hub routes its incoming signal to the outgoing signal of the first (rightmost in Figure 7.2) port, forming a continuous loop. A Fibre Channel hub performs no *arbitration* or control of access to the loop. Responsibility for arbitration in a Fibre Channel loop is distributed among the devices connected to the loop's ports.

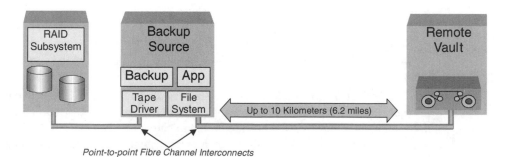

Point-to-point Fibre Channel Interconnects

Figure 7.1   Point-to-point Fibre Channel network.

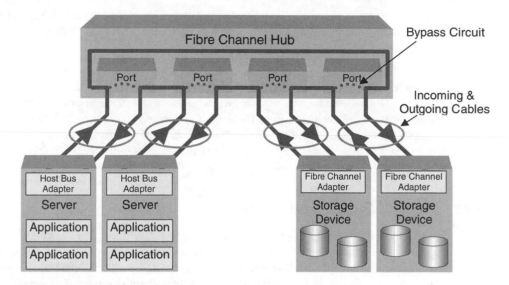

Figure 7.2   Fibre Channel loop interconnectivity.

Appearances to the contrary, only two devices on a Fibre Channel arbitrated loop can communicate at any one time. Which two devices communicate is determined by arbitration. Every time a loop is free, an *arbitration phase* begins. The arbitration determines which device gets to transmit commands or data next. Unlike parallel SCSI, Fibre Channel arbitration rules guarantee that over time, every device has equal access to the loop. This ensures that no devices are starved for I/O because higher-priority devices are monopolizing access to the loop. Fairness notwithstanding, the key property of Fibre Channel arbitrated loop topology, is that the total bandwidth available on a single loop is the bandwidth of a single device's access port (100 megabytes per second with today's loop technology).

Fibre Channel arbitrated loop protocol requires that data *frames* propagate entirely around the loop. For this reason, as Figure 7.2 suggests, a break in the loop caused by a failed device would effectively block all data transfer on the loop. Fibre Channel hubs therefore have one other very useful function: They provide *bypass circuits* that prevent the loop from breaking if one device fails or is removed. If a device is removed from a loop (for example, by pulling its interconnect plug), the hub's bypass circuit detects the absence of signal and immediately begins to route incoming data directly to the loop's next port, bypassing the missing device entirely. This gives loops at least a measure of resiliency—failure of one device in a loop doesn't cause the entire loop to become inoperable.

The virtue of the arbitrated loop topology is low interconnection cost. A hub port ASIC performs no data buffering, routing, or protocol translation. The only intelligence it contains is the ability to recognize the absence of a carrier signal incoming from a device and reroute data to bypass the device. Hub ports are therefore relatively low-cost parts to manufacture. Similarly, the hub itself contains no buffering or logic; it is little more than power, packaging, and interconnection for port ASICs.[1]

Early in the life of Fibre Channel, the arbitrated loop topology was used to connect disk drives, RAID subsystems, and tape drives (through bridges and routers) to servers. As Fibre Channel technology has matured, and more advanced infrastructure components have been developed, the role of arbitrated loop topology has been increasingly relegated to connecting disk drives to RAID controller ports or to host bus adapters. Today, many Fibre Channel arbitrated loop hubs are integrated into RAID subsystem or disk enclosures and are invisible to the casual observer.

Fibre Channel Fabric Topology

Externally, a Fibre Channel switch looks similar to a hub. It is an enclosure with a panel containing several (8 to 16 is common) sockets used to connect cables to the switch's internal port logic. A switch performs quite differently from a hub, however. Figure 7.3 depicts the key characteristics of a Fibre Channel switch. For simplicity, a four-port switch is depicted. Actual switches contain more ports.

[1] Although some hubs, called *managed* hubs, contain logic that enables monitoring of and control over individual ports.

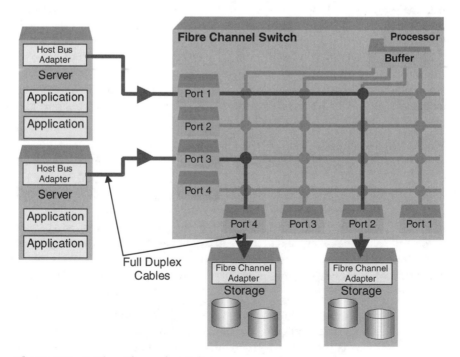

Figure 7.3 A Fibre Channel switch.

Each of the ports represented in Figure 7.3, called fabric ports or *F-Ports*, is full-duplex (able to send and receive data at the same time). Figure 7.3 represents this by depicting the port twice—vertically on the left edge and horizontally on the lower edge. The vertical row represents the ports' transmitters and the horizontal row represents receivers. In the example of Figure 7.3, the servers attached to switched Ports 1 and 3 are sending data to the storage devices attached to Ports 2 and 4, respectively. Any of the four ports' transmitters can send data to any of the four ports' receivers. A port receiver can receive only one transmission at a time; but all port receivers can be in operation concurrently. Thus, while any individual transmission is limited to the speed of one path (100 or 200 megabytes per second with technology available as this book is written), multiple concurrent transmissions through the switch are possible.

Figure 7.3 also represents two key features that are unique to switches: control processors and buffering. Since they are considerably more complex than hubs, Fibre Channel switches require management. Connections between pairs of devices are continually being set up and deleted. Subsets of ports are organized into zones, failed devices are detected, and so forth. Switches contain processors that provide this management functionality, as well as a management interface to the external environment so that administrators can set SAN policies.

Management of Fibre Channel fabrics is done by a management server software component in the switch, communicating with external SAN management tools either in band (using the Fibre Channel itself) or out of band, using an Ethernet or serial connection.

Buffering within the switch provides elasticity, resolving small instantaneous differences between device transmission and reception rates, but, more important, it enables devices of different technology levels to intercommunicate. As this book is written, the Fibre Channel industry is in the midst of a transition from first-generation *1-gigabit* (100-megabyte-per-second) devices to second-generation *2-gigabit* (200-megabyte-per-second) devices. Many users have large installed bases of first-generation technology devices and a desire to make the SAN technology transition over a long period of time. With switches that support both 1-gigabit and 2-gigabit port interfaces, this is possible. The switch buffers transmissions from the transmitting device at its native speed and retransmits them to the receiving device at *its* native speed. The Fibre Channel transmission protocols are designed so that switch ports and the devices attached to them negotiate to determine the highest possible speed that both devices support.

With the hypothetical switch shown in Figure 7.3, as many as four simultaneous transmissions could occur, for an aggregate system bandwidth of 400 or 800 megabytes per second. Figure 7.3 shows a four-port switch for illustrative convenience. In actual practice, there are two general classes of switches:

- *Local* SAN switches, typically with 8 or 16 ports. Larger networks can be constructed by interconnecting local SAN switches. When local switches are used, SAN failure tolerance is typically achieved through the use of independent parallel fabrics connecting the same sets of storage devices and servers.

- *Enterprise* switches, sometimes called *directors*, with 64 or more ports and advanced availability features such as internally redundant components and the ability to download firmware updates while the switch is operating.

Both local SAN switches and enterprise directors can be interconnected to each other, to construct larger SANs than can be supported by a single switch or director. In principle, hundreds of computers and storage devices can be interconnected on a single SAN. When Fibre Channel switches are interconnected, data must sometimes be routed through two or more switches on its path from source to target. Figure 7.4 illustrates the interconnection of multiple switches into a larger integrated fabric.

Switches are interconnected to each other using the same ports used to connect nodes to the switches. Thus, every additional switch in a fabric could mean one less device interconnection on every switch in the fabric. If two 8-port switches are used to make a fabric, one port on each switch connects to the other switch and the remaining 14 ports can be used to connect devices. If three switches are interconnected, 2 ports on each switch connect to other switches and the remaining 18 ports connect to devices. If four such switches are interconnected, 3 ports on each switch connect to other switches and the remaining 20 ports connect devices. At five switches, 4 ports per switch are required for fabric interconnection, leaving 20 ports for device connection. There is no gain in device connectivity when the fabric expands from four to five switches.

To minimize this problem of diminishing connectivity, Fibre Channel switches are usually *cascaded*, as Figure 7.4 illustrates. In Figure 7.4, one switch, called the level 2 switch, is dedicated to connecting only to other switches. Each of the remaining switches in the fabric connects to the level 2 switch and to devices. This topology can interconnect a total of 9 switches, with 56 devices attached, as Figure 7.5 illustrates. Three- and four-level cascaded SANs are also possible; however, for availability and manageability reasons, it is usually advisable to build very large SANs using enterprise directors as building blocks.

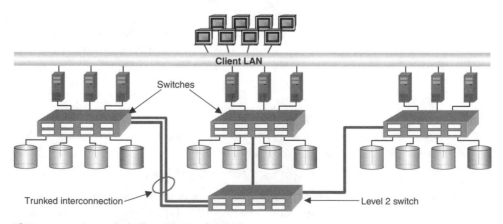

Figure 7.4 Cascaded Fibre Channel switches.

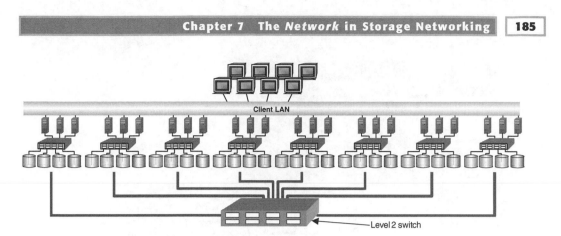

Figure 7.5   Two-level cascaded SAN using eight-port switches.

Of course, with the topology illustrated in Figure 7.5, data sent between a source connected to one switch and a target to another must be routed through the level 2 switch. This increases latency through the SAN (the time required for data to get from source to target) and it makes the level 2 switch a potential bottleneck for the entire SAN. With larger, more complex topologies, both of these potential problems are amplified.

Fibre Channel switches implement a standard network routing algorithm called *find shortest path first* (FSPF) to route data through the SAN. Networks with up to seven levels of routing (e.g., two interconnected four-tier networks) are certified by vendors at the time this book is written. The potential for a level 2 (or level 3 or level 4) switch to become a SAN bottleneck is minimized by interconnecting multiple ports on two switches, as Figure 7.4 illustrates. Switch vendors implement *trunking* technology to balance traffic among multiple links used to connect a pair of switches, making the use of these links transparent to applications and management tools. Designing a large SAN using this multilevel cascading technique requires balancing connectivity against throughput requirements.

It is through switched fabric topology that the connectivity of Fibre Channel SANs is truly achieved. With the availability of switches, Fibre Channel SANs truly became a reality. Because switches are more complex than hubs (Figure 7.3), the port cost of connecting to a switch is necessarily higher. This is not problematical for servers or RAID subsystems, for which SAN port cost can be amortized over a large computing capability or a large amount of storage. For disks, however, high port cost creates a problem. In some instances, the cost of connecting a disk to a switched fabric can exceed the cost of the disk itself. A lower-cost solution is needed.

Connecting Disks to a Fibre Channel Fabric

Fibre Channel arbitrated loop topology has a low connection cost that is suitable for connecting disk drives to a SAN. Switched fabric topology is good for solving intercon-

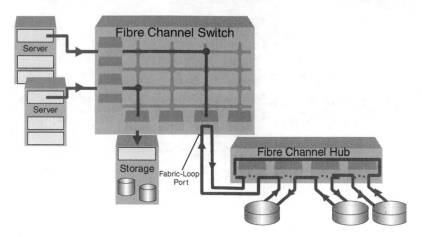

Figure 7.6 Combining Fibre Channel fabric and loop.

nection problems of greater complexity. It is easy to imagine circumstances in which connecting a string of disks to a switched fabric would be useful. Systems that use server-based volume management to provide disk performance and availability are one example. Figure 7.6 illustrates a mixed topology in which a loop of disks is connected to a single port on a Fibre Channel switch.

Fibre Channel designers designed carefully in order to reconcile the fundamentally different protocols used on low-cost loops and high-performance switches. The result is a special type of port that connects an entire loop of devices to a single port on a switch. With this port, called a Fabric (to) Loop Port or *FL-Port*, strings of disks that use the low-cost arbitrated loop interconnect can be connected to ports on switches. FL-Ports are useful both for connecting large numbers of disk drives directly to a SAN fabric and also for extending the lives of legacy Fibre Channel components built to support arbitrated loop topology.

Emerging SAN Interconnect Technologies

Fibre Channel is clearly the dominant SAN interconnect as this book is written. With the emergence of viable Fibre Channel fabric topology components, it became obvious that there had been pent-up demand in the market for the benefits that SANs promise:

- Interconnectivity of all the storage devices and servers in a data center

- More scalable I/O performance delivered over longer distances than is possible with parallel SCSI

- Ability to switch ownership of storage devices from one server to another or to share concurrent ownership of a storage device among several cooperating servers

And so forth

Even though functionality was incomplete, management tools were lacking, and interoperability among different vendors' products was less than perfect, Fibre Channel SANs were deployed in large numbers. Today, these shortcomings have either been remedied entirely or work is well under way to remedy them. Fibre Channel SANs are clearly past the early adopter stage and are moving into the market mainstream. Analysts' surveys consistently indicate that virtually all enterprise data centers have at least a SAN strategy, if indeed they have not already deployed SANs.

New Wires for Storage Networks

Fibre Channel has not been without its shortcomings. In particular:

- Fibre Channel interconnect components remain at relatively high cost levels that inhibit the technology's adoption in smaller systems.

- While the promise of SANs includes wide area separation of storage and servers and very complex network topologies, Fibre Channel has been slow to develop wide area capabilities.

The combination of these perceived shortcomings and the attractiveness of the data storage and networks has spurred development of alternative storage networking technologies aimed at overcoming these shortcomings of Fibre Channel. While no alternative technologies have come to market in volume as this book is written, there is considerable industry momentum behind two of them:

ipStorage (use of TCP/IP as a storage interconnect). Several vendors and vendor coalitions have been exploring ways to use TCP/IP as a storage networking protocol. These efforts are converging on an Internet Engineering Task Force (IETF) working group that is developing a set of proposed standards that are collectively called *iSCSI* (for Internet SCSI). iSCSI primarily attacks the problems of very long distances and complex storage network topologies, but there is reason to expect that it will reduce interconnect cost as well, because it uses hardware components that are already produced in high volumes for general networking application.

The major functional attraction of iSCSI is that it uses as an underlying transport the most mature and tested protocol suite in existence (TCP/IP). Layered on top of TCP/IP, iSCSI would instantly have access to essentially all transmission media and topologies in use today, allowing very general storage networks to be constructed. The challenge for iSCSI is its very generality. Historically, TCP/IP and protocols based on it have been implemented in server-based software, unlike Fibre Channel, whose protocols were specifically designed to be silicon-based so that message and data transfer processing overhead would be low. Today, for a given link speed and processor, it takes considerably more processing power to handle TCP/IP messages and data transfers than Fibre Channel ones. This could make iSCSI untenable for applications within the data center, which in turn would tend to marginalize the technology. Several vendors have announced that they are developing silicon to perform large parts of TCP/IP processing. If these developments succeed to the point where iSCSI processor overhead was comparable to that of Fibre Channel for a given I/O load, then the other advantages of iSCSI (mature, well-established underlying network infrastructure, presumable low cost due to high component volumes, and lower management cost due to streamlining of required skill sets) should make it attractive to users and a powerful competitor to Fibre Channel.

Infiniband. This is a new standard, developed by a new standards and marketing organization (the Infiniband Trade Association) that is aimed primarily at enabling more general server system topologies by reducing the cost of high-performance, low-latency interconnection of I/O to servers. Infiniband is heavily backed by Intel Corporation, whose announced intent is to integrate Infiniband interfaces into its processor support ASICs. This would effectively make Infiniband the free choice for storage networking, as the interface would be native to many servers. With close ties to the Virtual Interface Architecture (VIA), Infiniband promises to reduce the cost and improve the performance of storage networking within the data center. For longer distances, Infiniband specifications anticipate the use of routers to bridge between Infiniband and longer-distance networking technologies (including Fibre Channel).

Because it is so closely identified with Intel Corporation, Infiniband is likely to enter the market as an interconnect for Intel (Windows and Linux) servers, increasing the applicability of those systems to complex data center problems that require clusters, multihosted enterprise RAID subsystems, and so forth. Because of its close relationship with VIA, the technology (coupled with emerging file access technologies discussed in the following section) may also enable a generation of NAS devices with very low data access latency compared to today's devices. This could alter today's balance in which SANs used to connect block access storage devices to application servers dominate NAS devices in the data center market. As discussed earlier, the attraction of NAS devices, which eliminate much of low-level storage management from the administrator's workload and enable different application server platforms to share access to data, is a powerful one. The primary drawback to the NAS approach to date has been protocol overhead and the high data access latency it engenders. If a combination of Infiniband, VIA, and DAFS (described in the following section) could enable NAS devices with access latencies and throughput comparable to today's Fibre Channel SANs, consumers might well shift buying patterns in favor of NAS.

Changing a physical I/O infrastructure is a complex undertaking, both for the industry and for users. For an I/O technology to be marketable to the broad majority of users, the industry must develop standards to a reasonable state of stability; design and build electronic interface components; integrate components into host bus adapters, switches, RAID controllers, and other devices; develop software drivers for a variety of operating system platforms; develop component management tools; and integrate them into frameworks. The users must be educated in the benefits of the new technology and, when convinced, must formulate plans for phasing it into their operations in ways that are nondisruptive and that conserve capital and human investments. Both components of this change take time.

Fibre Channel, for example, began serious development in the late 1980s. In the mid-1990s, enough components were available on the market to permit users to adopt the technology for enterprise applications. Not until 1999 did Fibre Channel SANs become attractive to mainstream data center users.

Both iSCSI and Infiniband are in the late standards stage. Specifications are complete enough that product development can occur and is occurring as this book is written. Product introduction on a mass scale should occur during 2002 for both technologies. If the technologies are successful in delivering their anticipated benefits, a more rapid adoption cycle than Fibre Channel is to be anticipated, simply because Fibre Channel technology has already convinced users of the benefits of consolidating storage in a SAN and making it accessible to all servers in a data center and beyond. Nevertheless, it will probably be two to four years before either iSCSI or Infiniband achieves anything like the prominence of Fibre Channel as a SAN interconnect.

Other Storage Networking Developments

It is not only in the physical interconnect area that storage networking is undergoing evolution. New developments with the potential for changing the shape of SANs are also occurring in file access protocols and in the repartitioning of the functions of file systems and volume managers.

In the file access protocol area, developers are reacting to the emergence of Virtual Interface Architecture-capable hardware components. VIA is a midlayer protocol specification that enables an application to intercommunicate directly with applications running on other servers, bypassing virtually all of the software protocol stacks of both servers. Conceptually, VIA relies on message and data buffer pools that are dedicated when two remote applications establish a connection. For as long as the connection lasts, the applications can exchange messages and data directly with each other using these pools without fear of corrupting other applications or the operating environment. VIA basically trades setup time and complexity for simplicity during operation. With hardware assistance (for example, to signal an application that a message has arrived or to move data directly from host bus adapter buffers to application memory), VIA promises to dramatically reduce the latency and overhead of remote application intercommunication.

Two of the most attractive applications for VIA are NAS devices and database managers. In both cases, application servers make requests for data access that pass through a software protocol stack both before and after delivery. Similarly, data transfers almost always result in one or more bulk data movements at least on the receiving end of a communication. The ability for an application to formulate a request and have it directly transmitted to a file server and for the file server to place data directly into application buffers should dramatically improve the performance of file servers.

Two efforts are under way to exploit VIA (or VIA-like) transport protocol capabilities to improve file server performance. The Direct Access File System Collaborative is developing a completely new file access protocol based on a combination of NFS and

CIFS properties and relying on VIA-like transport protocol characteristics. The developers of NFS are also actively pursuing extensions to the NFS protocol that would allow it to take advantage of similar transport protocol capabilities.

Repartitioning Storage Functions

More radically, other vendors and organizations are proposing various repartitionings of file system and volume manager functionality, primarily to take advantage of the increased intelligence that is available in storage devices. One of these activities is a standards project for so-called object-based storage (OBS) being conducted within the ANSI T10 SCSI standards organization. OBS is a proposed standard for disk-like storage devices that are capable of managing their capacity and presenting file-like *storage objects* to their hosts. These storage objects are like files in that they are byte vectors that can be created and destroyed and can grow and shrink during their lifetimes. Like a file, any consecutive stream of the bytes constituting a storage object can be read or written with a single command.

Storage objects are known by identifiers and located through an external storage manager, which effectively functions as a file lookup service.

The premise of OBS is that by off-loading part of the functionality of a file system into storage devices, SANs can be made to scale more effectively, because every time storage is added, processing capacity dedicated to performing storage functions is added as well. Convincing demonstrations of the OBS concept have been conducted in the academic arena. The barrier to commercial adoption is the amount of existing computer infrastructure that would have to change to enable OBS adoption—everything from file systems to volume managers to RAID subsystems to management tools. It is likely that this technology will initially be adopted in specialty segments for which its benefits are overwhelming. Whether it spreads into general use depends on success in those areas.

OBS is essentially an out-of-band virtualization technique as described in Chapter 5. Similar, but less radical, developments have been proposed to enhance the viability of out-of-band virtualization of storage using more conventional server-based volume management techniques.

Out-of-band storage virtualization is attractive because it shortens the path between application server and data. Once the location of a file or volume is ascertained, the application server makes its I/O requests directly to the storage device containing the data. The Achilles heel of out-of-band virtualization, as well as shared file systems and databases, has always been that data integrity is completely dependent on all servers sharing access to the data obeying access rules at all times. A malfunctioning server can destroy data by writing in the wrong place at the wrong time.

This shortcoming represents a risk inherent in data sharing among cooperating servers and completely eliminates the possibility of sharing storage among noncooperating servers connected to a SAN. To improve the reliability of shared data solutions among cooperating servers, as well as to enable storage sharing among noncooperating servers, developers have proposed secure protocols for communication between servers and storage devices. Functionally, these protocols do not differ markedly from today's SCSI protocol and its derivatives. The difference lies in the security aspect. Various approaches have been discussed, but all reduce to providing servers with keys when their access rights to storage are established. These keys have encoded in them what storage the server is allowed to access. If a server is ejected from a cluster, its key is invalidated and its I/O requests are not accepted by the device.

Secure access to storage devices is a feature of the academic work on which object-based storage is based. The latter development applies the principle to a more conventional host-based volume storage architecture, which could be implemented with relatively little change in the functionality of today's storage devices.

Both of these concepts are exactly that—concepts. While they are intuitively attractive, widespread adoption would require significant change throughout the data access and management functions of today's data center computer systems. It is likely that adoption of either of these technologies would occur over a period of several years in the future.

Summary

- Fibre Channel is the dominant SAN interconnect in use today. Fibre Channel technology consists of standards, base ASIC components, system components constructed using the base ASICs, infrastructure components, and protocols.

- The three Fibre Channel topologies are point-to-point, arbitrated loop, and switched fabric. Both low-cost, short-distance electrical and higher-cost optical transmission media are specified.

- Arbitrated loop was the first Fibre Channel topology to be developed for use as a SAN. Its primary benefit is low port cost. An arbitrated loop does not multiply bandwidth. All devices connected to a loop share 100 megabytes per second of available bandwidth. Today, arbitrated loop topology is used primarily to connect disk drives and legacy Fibre Channel devices.

- Switched fabrics are the real enablers for SANs. Switches multiply bandwidth by supporting simultaneous transmission of data between multiple pairs of devices.

- Arbitrated loops can be connected to switched fabrics using FL-Ports. This enables disk drives to be connected directly to a switched fabric SAN, for example, for use by host-based volume managers.

- iSCSI is the name for a converging set of developments aimed at using TCP/IP as a storage interconnect. The attractions of iSCSI are that complex topology, security, and long-distance connection problems have all been solved by the base networking technology and that the volumes in which network components are sold should make iSCSI a relatively inexpensive interconnect. The challenge is to reduce the processor overhead of processing iSCSI packets to be comparable with that of Fibre Channel.

- Infiniband is another emerging interconnect that may challenge Fibre Channel within the data center on a cost basis. Over time, Infiniband interfaces are expected to be built into all Intel servers, making it a low-cost alternative for low-end SANs. Infiniband is squarely targeted at the data center. The specifications discuss bridging to other technologies as required for long-distance applications.

- In addition to new interconnects, upper-layer protocols are evolving as well. Two file access protocols, DAFS and NFS, are actively working on the use of VIA to reduce access latency for file servers. Other activities include the standardization of a protocol for object-based storage and research and development on secure protocols that would allow access to host-based volumes from noncooperating servers.

CHAPTER 8

Basic Software for Storage Networking

I n this chapter we'll learn more about:

- How operating in a SAN environment changes some of the fundamental properties of operating systems

- Software components that solve basic operating systems in a SAN environment

- How server-based and RAID subsystem-based volume manager software has been enhanced to provide failure-tolerant storage in the SAN environment

- How file systems can affect application performance, availability, and manageability, and how file systems have been enhanced to complement SAN-based systems

Software for SANs

As we've already observed more than once, hardware makes SANs possible, but it's through software that they realize their promise. It takes several kinds of software to make a SAN fully effective, including:

- Operating system components, such as *I/O drivers*, that not only fulfill the conventional driver role, but that also have unique SAN-related capabilities

- Storage middleware components, such as *volume managers* and *file systems* that are enhanced to exploit SAN capabilities

- Application middleware components such as *cluster managers* and *tape-sharing software* that implement the availability and scaling functionality enabled by SANs

- *Applications and database managers*, which can be made SAN-aware so that they can exploit SAN-enabled capabilities like load balancing

- *Enterprise backup managers*, that are able to make consistent backups of data with minimal overhead *while the data are in use* by applications

- New types of software such as *SAN managers*, that exist specifically to manage the SAN environment

Sections that follow discuss each of these software components, but first we discuss some unique situations that arise when a computer system is expanded "outside the box," to become distributed, making the communication paths among its software components long and sometimes circuitous.

The Data Center I/O Stack

The software that makes a modern commercial computer system function is a carefully architected *stack* of components, each providing specific services to layers above it and each depending upon specific services from layers below it.

Figure 8.1 illustrates a typical software stack for a server system with emphasis on the data access and management components. The major interfaces in the data storage access stack are numbered. Virtually any path between application and storage that can be traced in Figure 8.1 can be found in some system in practice. The most common ones are these:

Almost all applications use either a file system or a database manager to organize their data (interfaces ❶ and ❷). While applications can be found that access storage devices directly, the advantages of robust, highly functional file systems and database man-

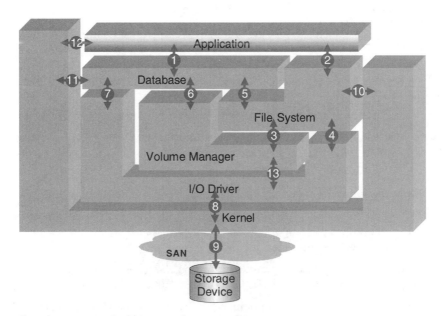

Figure 8.1 A typical server software environment.

agers are so overwhelming that applications that do not use them are rare and becoming rarer.

File systems either access storage devices directly (interface ❹) or access virtual disks presented by a volume manager (interface ❸).

Database management systems typically store data either in container files (interface ❺), in managed volumes (interface ❻) that they perceive as disks, or directly on disks or disk partitions (interface ❼).

Ultimately, physical disks or virtual disks presented by RAID subsystems are accessed through a driver that controls a hardware I/O interface or controller (interfaces ❹, ❼, and ⓭, followed by interface ❽). The controller communicates with real or virtual storage devices (interface ❾).

In addition, certain I/O-related control and management functions such as memory allocation and timer services, are typically performed by the kernel operating system. These services are required by applications, database managers, and file systems (interfaces ❿, ⓫, and ⓬).

Our discussion of the software required to realize the full potential of SANs is predicated on application execution environments similar to that depicted in Figure 8.1. The environment depicted in Figure 8.1 is broadly representative of any of the operating system platforms in general use today.

Special Considerations for SAN Software

Modern operating systems and data managers do an outstanding job of coordinating access to data by multiple applications in a single server. When a storage area network is used to connect multiple servers to multiple storage devices, some aspects of this coordination take on special significance.

- *Discovering devices and reacting to state changes.* When a server starts up or when another server or a storage device joins or leaves the SAN that information must be made known to other server storage devices. In single-server systems, not only are configurations more static, but there are never other servers to consider.

- *Controlling access to storage devices* by servers, including resolving different servers' views of the same SAN and ownership disputes. In a single-server system, the owner of the storage devices is always clear.

- *Controlling access to data objects* (files and records) by servers, including coordinating access to data from multiple applications on different servers. In a single-server system, the (one) file system or database manager is a chokepoint through which all I/O requests flow. It is easy to block access to files or records if other applications have them in use. In a SAN-based system, different servers must exchange messages to negotiate for ownership of data objects.

The following sections explain why these functions are more complicated in a SAN than in a single-server computing environment.

Discovering Devices

For system administrators familiar with parallel SCSI I/O subsystems, separating the concepts of storage device and infrastructure may be somewhat unfamiliar. A parallel SCSI bus can be no more than 25 meters long and connects a maximum of 16 or fewer *nodes*—storage devices or servers (actually, host bus adapters). Compare this to Fibre Channel SAN with its theoretical limit of 2^{24} interconnected devices (and practical limits in the hundreds or thousands of devices).

To discover what devices are connected to a parallel SCSI bus, drivers typically issue INQUIRY commands to each of the 7 or 15 possible bus addresses (the 8th or 16th address is that of the server issuing the commands). If a device is present and functional, it responds to the INQUIRY command addressed to it; if no device is present at an address, the INQUIRY command times out.

This discovery system for parallel SCSI is crude, but effective. In the worst case, on a bus connecting one server to one device, 14 INQUIRY commands corresponding to 14 unused bus addresses time out during discovery. This causes a delay of a few seconds, but an entire parallel SCSI bus scan still completes in under half a minute.

Compare this with a Fibre Channel arbitrated loop, to which a maximum of 126 devices can be attached. A SCSI-style scan of all valid bus addresses with a 2-second command time-out would take about 5 minutes to complete. Since I/O bus scanning must precede disk mounting and data manager and application startup, this 5-minute period would be added on to system startup time. Worse yet, if a device were added to or removed from a loop, issuing inquiry commands to discover the new or removed device would cause a 5-minute pause in all I/O to the loop. Instead of this, Fibre Channel arbitrated loop protocol specifies an ultrafast loop initialization protocol (LIP) by which device addresses are reassigned and reaffirmed each time there is a change in the membership of the loop. Loop initialization consists entirely of low-level protocol messages that are handled by the Fibre Channel ASICs, for the most part. LIP completes in under a second and leaves all devices in a loop with valid addresses and aware of other devices with which they may need to communicate.

Discovery would be even more problematic with a Fibre Channel switched fabric, for which there are 2^{24} valid device addresses. Scanning all 2^{24} valid addresses to discover which correspond to storage devices or server host bus adapters connected to the fabric is simply not an option.

To enable servers and storage devices connected to a fabric to discover each other efficiently, storage networking technology has borrowed the concept of a *name service* from peer networking. Fabric-based SANs include *name servers*, computers with *well-known* network addresses (the name server is found at the same addresses on all Fibre Channel fabrics). The responsibility of these computers is to record the names, device characteristics, and port addresses of all devices that have announced that they are connected to the SAN and to divulge them on request.

A storage device or server "joins" a SAN (connects to it logically) by executing a *fabric login* (FLOGI) operation. The device registers itself by exchanging messages with the name server at its well-known address. The name server records the address of the server or device and some information about its characteristics, including an invariant worldwide name by which it is known, no matter what port it is on.

When a server wishes to discover what storage devices are connected to a fabric, it queries the name server, which returns a list of addresses and device characteristics. The server can then connect to each storage device and issue inquiry commands to verify that the device is connected to the SAN at the registered address, that it is in fact the type of device represented by the name server and to determine additional device characteristics, such as storage capacity.

Controlling Access to Storage Devices

A legacy of past computer system design that is still reflected in most of today's operating systems is the presumption of one computer at the center, with peripheral devices being owned by it, in the sense that only the computer can physically access the devices. Early disk controllers connected to computer backplane buses, where they controlled the operation of disks as directed by instructions from the computer and contended for access to memory with the computer and with other peripheral device controllers.

While this model is no longer reflective of the intelligent network storage devices available today, it is still reflected in many operating system assumptions. A significant amount of contemporary storage subsystem, SAN fabric, and SAN management tool development is directed at adapting operating systems to the more peer-like model that storage area networks represent.

Important differences between computer-centric and storage-centric system architecture arise when a computer's operating system first starts up or when a disk is first recognized. Computers take control of disks by mounting the file systems on them. Mounting a file system includes (among other actions) writing on the disk a notation that it is in use. With a computer-centric architecture, it is appropriate for the computer to take control of every storage device it "sees"; otherwise, the device goes unused. With a storage-centric architecture, if two or more computers are to mount a SAN-connected disk simultaneously, they must be aware of each other and their respective file systems must be able to recognize and accommodate each others' actions.

If a file system instance is not equipped to coordinate its accesses to storage with other instances (and most are not), the server on which it is running must be able to guarantee exclusive access to its (physical or virtual) storage devices. There are three basic techniques for limiting storage device access to one server (or to a specific set of servers) in a SAN with universal physical interconnectivity.

- *Server-based access control.* Cluster managers often use operating system and I/O device services to reserve a device for exclusive access by one server. While this is undoubtedly the most flexible means of making device access exclusive, it requires cooperation among all servers connected to a SAN, whether they are part of the cluster or not. When multiple clusters share access to a SAN, the clusters must cooperate with each other to guarantee SAN-wide exclusive device access.

- *Fabric-based access control (zoning).* Fibre Channel switches are able to divide a fabric into either disjoint or overlapping *zones* and limit communications to devices within a zone. Fabric-based zoning is independent of both host and storage device technology, but must be integrated with server-based SAN managers (discussed in Chapter 12) to be useful. The more popular SAN managers support major fabric-based zoning facilities to enable the use of zoning.

- *Storage device-based access control (LUN masking).* Similarly, many RAID subsystems can be configured to restrict their virtual disks (LUNs) to communicating with designated SAN addresses. Storage device-based access control can be used to restrict access to storage devices—for example, to the servers in a cluster—but it does not restrict servers from communicating with other servers as does fabric-based zoning.

Controlling Access to Data Objects

Exclusive access to SAN storage devices is appropriate for independent servers and for *shared nothing* clusters. Clusters that can share access to data objects (files and database records) have far wider applicability, however. Sharing access to data objects means different things at different levels in the I/O software stack.

Device sharing. The ability of two or more servers to access a storage device is a fundamental prerequisite to any kind of data sharing. Shared device access is integral to storage networking; typically, it must be limited (by cooperation, zoning, or LUN masking as previously described) rather than enabled. The ability to share access to devices does not automatically enable data object sharing, because it provides no coordination among the sharing servers.

Volume sharing. Volumes are nothing more than sets of disks under common management. Volume managers keep track of volume state by writing descriptive metadata on the disks themselves. If two or more servers are to *share* access to a volume, coordination is required, because metadata updates must (1) be coordinated so that updates from two servers do not overwrite each other and (2) appear simultaneously to all servers sharing a volume.

File system sharing. Common access to a storage device makes it possible for two or more servers to share access to a file system on the device, even if they do not concurrently access data within an individual file. As with shared volumes, accesses to file system metadata must be coordinated to avoid corruption of file system structures. In addition, sharing a file system among two or more servers introduces the complication of *cache coherency.*

Because file system metadata are typically updated much more frequently than volume metadata, they are often kept in cache to improve system performance. If two or more servers are caching the same file system metadata items, those items must be *coherent;* that is, all servers must see the same values for the same metadata items at all times. Different file systems have different cache coherency techniques, but all reduce to making all servers mutually aware of all metadata updates. One common technique is to *lock* metadata items before they are updated. In a cluster, this means that a server wishing to update metadata must secure exclusive access rights to that metadata through the services of a *distributed lock manager*.

File sharing. Shared access to a file system provides the administrative convenience of managing one pool of files that can be processed by applications running on any of a cluster's servers. A further level of flexibility is provided if applications can share access to the *same file*. File sharing enables, for example, distributed database managers that share data access to use container files as their underlying storage. It also enables file-based applications to share access to a single file. Sharing access to a file requires the ability to lock access to ranges of file data so that each application write appears to be executed atomically. It also requires that the applications themselves be aware that they are sharing data and share data in ways that make business sense.

Database sharing. Perhaps the archetype application for data sharing is the relational database. It is common for two or more instances of a database manager running on separate servers to access the same database for availability and performance reasons. For data integrity such a configuration must include in a lock manager to reserve exclusive access to individual blocks and records for one database manager instance at a time.

Shared Access Data Managers

Virtually all commercially significant applications use either database managers or file systems to access data. Besides organizing data for application convenience, these data managers provide an important function that is especially germane in SAN environments: They coordinate applications' data accesses so that each application perceives itself as the sole accessor of file system or database objects.

File systems and database managers achieve this effect by *locking* access to the data objects they control. For example, when a file is created, a typical file system allocates storage space for data structures that describe the file and perhaps some space for file data. The data structures that describe file system free space and data objects are stored on the volume containing the file system. To update these structures correctly, a file system must *serialize* access to them so that, for example, two concurrent updates do not interfere with each other, leading to incorrect results.

Suppose, for example, that a hypothetical file system has 1,000 consecutive free blocks of storage starting at block 1,000 and that these are described by an {address, length} descriptor in a chain of such descriptors. The row labeled "before" in Figure 8.2 illustrates this scenario using a single-link chain structure for simplicity.

To allocate space for a 500-block file, this hypothetical file system might scan its chain of free space descriptors looking for the first one with at least enough space to meet its requirement. In Figure 8.2, this would be the first descriptor. To allocate 500 blocks, the file system removes them from the free space pool by modifying the descriptor and rewriting it as illustrated in the "after" section of the figure. (The allocated storage

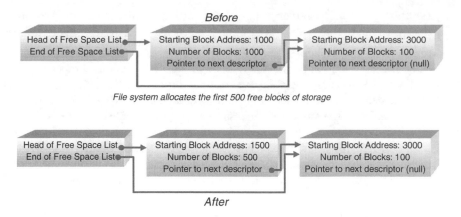

Figure 8.2 The need for serializing access to critical data structures.

addresses are recorded elsewhere in data structures that describe the file.) Thus, in order to allocate storage, this file system must read a free space descriptor, modify its contents, and rewrite it.

Suppose now that two applications make nearly simultaneous file allocation requests and that these are processed by two concurrent file system execution threads (most file systems support some level of parallel thread execution). If both threads traverse the free space descriptor chain at approximately the same time, they might both see that there are 1,000 free blocks starting at block 1,000. If both threads are allocating less than 1,000 blocks, they might both decide to use the 1,000-block free space extent starting at block 1,000. Both threads would deduct the space they allocated from the free space descriptor and rewrite the descriptor. The result would be that both of them would have allocated the same blocks to different files, which would certainly cause data corruption. Not only that, the file system's free space descriptor chain is likely to be corrupt as well. If the two threads allocate different numbers of blocks, either some space will be lost (if the application requesting more blocks writes last) or, worse, some space may appear to be eligible for allocation, *even though it is already allocated to two files!* Obviously, this cannot be allowed to occur.

File systems and database managers guard against this type of scenario by serializing access to critical data structures and user data while they are being read and updated. In the scenario just described, if one thread were granted exclusive access to the file system's free space chain until it had completely allocated its required storage, the second thread would not see the space as available and the error scenario described would not occur. Access to critical data and structures is usually by *locking* them, using software components called *lock managers*.

Lock Managers

A lock manager limits concurrent access to data objects by different execution threads by granting or denying the threads' requests for control of the objects. For example, if an execution thread requests access to our hypothetical file system's free space chain and the chain is not currently being accessed by another thread, a lock manager would grant the request and record the fact that it had done so. If another thread were to request access to the same resource, the lock manager would deny that request, either by failing it explicitly or by blocking the requesting thread from executing until the resource was available.

A key feature of software locks is that they are a kind of gentlemen's agreement among software components. Resource locking works only if all components that access resources use locks correctly. There is no protection against faulty system software that neglects to lock resources before using them. Applications are prevented from abusing resource locks because they access critical resources and data through file systems or database managers. These system components are expected to lock resources before using them. Only a file system or database manager bug would cause concurrent access to data or metadata structures that should be serialized. Developers of these software components go to great lengths to test their products against such eventualities.

How Lock Managers Work

A lock manager is a fundamental component of any multithreaded operating system, file system, or database manager. Designs differ widely and a treatise on lock management is outside the scope of this book. For our purposes, a lock manager may be thought of as representing each resource by a unique name. Locks themselves are memory data structures that include the name of the locked resource, an identifier for the locking application or system process, and an indicator of the nature of the lock. For example, to lock a range of blocks in a file, lock manager might create a data structure similar to that illustrated in Figure 8.3.

Figure 8.3 illustrates a hypothetical data structure that might be used to lock ranges of blocks in files. The resource identifier consisting of {file path name, starting block number, ending block number} identifies any given range of blocks in any file uniquely. A lock manager could maintain a list of all block ranges for which applications or sys-

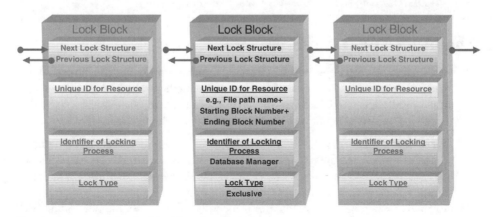

Figure 8.3   Hypothetical locking data structure.

tem processes had been granted locks. Each application lock request would be compared with the list to determine whether it conflicted with any existing lock. A conflict might cause the lock manager to reject the request or to place it in a queue waiting for conflicting locks to be released by their applications.

Lock Management in Distributed Systems

The objective of the foregoing discussion was not to provide an exhaustive description of lock management, but to illustrate that lock managers work by manipulating data structures in memory. In a cluster, servers have no access to other servers' memories. If access to data objects is to be shared, lock information must be distributed throughout the servers' memories. Instead of executing a few instructions to access a lock data structure, a server must exchange messages with other servers in the cluster to manipulate lock structures. Thus, determining whether a data object is locked is not a matter of a few instructions (microseconds), but rather a message exchange (hundreds of microseconds or even milliseconds).

Computer System I/O Performance

Many client/server applications make a lot of I/O requests per second, for a few kilobytes of data each. Such applications are called *I/O intensive*. Request order is unpredictable, particularly when many clients are being served, so data is accessed in *random* order. The combination of random access and small I/O requests means that *locating* data (getting disk read/write heads to the right spot on the right disk platter) has more to do with I/O performance than *transferring* data. Faster access to data on disks translates directly into better application performance. There are two main techniques for improving disk access speed for I/O-intensive applications:

- *Caching* data in solid-state memory (thereby eliminating disk access entirely)
- *Distributing* the I/O access load across more disks

Cache and I/O Performance

Cache can be very effective at increasing application read performance. Data read from disk into cache once can be delivered to applications over and over again. Even if it is modified, cached data can still be delivered directly from cache and written to disk lazily at the scheduling convenience of the cache manager.

When an application writes data, a cache manager either *writes* the data *through* to disk before completing the application's request or *writes* data *back* to disk at some later time (*lazily*). With *write-through* cache, data is safely stored on disk before the application's write is considered complete. Write-through cache does not improve performance when data is written, but if recently written data blocks that are still in cache are reread, they are delivered directly from cache.

By contrast, an application write is considered complete as soon as the data is delivered to a *write-back* cache. Writing data to disk occurs later, at a time that optimizes cache manager performance. Write-back cache improves write-intensive application performance markedly because applications need not wait for I/O to complete before proceeding. Write-back cache introduces a data integrity risk, however, if the cache is *volatile* (i.e., if the validity of its contents depends on continuous system operation). If a system failure causes cache contents to be obliterated before they have been written to disk, applications may behave incorrectly. For example, an automated teller application might write a debit record to a customer account and then trigger cash disbursement. If the system crashes with the debit record still in cache, cash may have been disbursed with no record of the disbursement.

Database management systems' strong transactional semantics limit their ability to make use of write-back cache, preserve data integrity through strong transactional semantics. Database managers typically *log* applications' update requests safely on a disk before regarding transactions as committed. The reason is simple. If the data updates that constitute a committed transaction exist only in cache, a system failure could eradicate all trace of the transaction, possibly resulting in business actions that are inconsistent with electronic records.

Database vendors generally discourage the use of volatile write-back cache in operating systems, disk drives, and RAID subsystems. They argue with write-back cache, a database manager may think that data has been safely stored on disk and act accordingly, when in fact the data is still susceptible to crashes. Database managers, therefore, often make no use of one of the most significant I/O performance enhancements available.

I/O Load Balancing

The second technique for improving I/O-intensive application performance is to distribute data across more disks, thereby increasing the number of I/O requests that can be executed simultaneously. In principle, this should improve performance by reducing that average time an I/O request must wait for other requests to finish executing. Unfortunately, most applications have I/O hot spots—a few files or tables that are accessed much more frequently than the rest of the application's data. Some hot spots, like root blocks and control files, are inevitable. Others change over time. For example, early in the American business day, blocks that contain east coast customer records might be hot spots in a customer database. As the day progresses, I/O activity would probably shift to blocks containing west coast customer records.

If a file is stored on a single disk, that disk's performance limits the rate at which the file can be accessed. It is not uncommon for one or two of an application's storage devices to be completely busy (*saturated*) with I/O requests, while the remainder are nearly idle. This suggests that one might improve application performance by rearranging data so that frequently accessed blocks are on separate devices and paths. While this works in principle, it is often ineffective for three reasons:

- *It is time and resource consuming.* To improve performance by rearranging data, an administrator must monitor access rates, analyze data, and move data objects from busy devices to idle ones. The last thing most administrators need is more repetitive work. The last thing most online data files need is more background I/O while they are in use.

■ *It is not guaranteed to be accurate.* Using analysis of past activity as a basis for relocating data assumes that future access patterns will be the same as the past patterns on which the analysis is based. If different data are accessed on Tuesday than were accessed on Monday, tuning based on Monday's access patterns is not likely to improve performance.

■ *It may not be possible.* It may be impossible to subdivide a busy file or table in such a way that accesses to it can be evenly distributed. For example, if a file is subdivided by record key range, frequent access to a single key range (as, for example, from a sorted batch of transactions), would cause the device containing the busy file subdivision to be accessed, while devices containing other segments would be idle.

By contrast, *striping* data across several storage devices balances almost any I/O load across physical I/O resources. Data striping spreads each file or database table across multiple storage devices in a way that is orthogonal to application data organizations such as record keys. With data striping, it doesn't matter which data objects get hot; each object is automatically distributed across several disks, so access load tends to distribute uniformly across hardware resources.

Volumes: Resilience, Performance, and Flexibility

Enterprise data centers are expected to keep data continuously available, even though disks, I/O interconnects, and even computers may fail. A volume manager is an important data availability tool. A volume manager combines disks into failure-tolerant *volumes* that can survive disk and I/O interconnect failures. To file systems, database managers, and applications, volumes are functionally equivalent to disks. Volumes can survive physical disk failures using *RAID* or *mirroring* techniques. Volumes can also stripe data across several storage devices to improve I/O performance by distributing I/O load across physical resources, as previously described.

Volume managers are found in RAID subsystems, in server-based software, and in *storage appliances* (servers dedicated to providing file access or block device access to clients). While all are roughly equivalent from a functional standpoint, server-based mirrored and RAID volumes differ in two key respects:

■ *Flexibility.* RAID subsystems tend to be highly integrated, and support a limited variety of physical disk types that have been qualified by the system vendor. Server- and appliance-based volume managers are invariably based on relatively conventional operating systems, which means that they support any physical storage devices that those operating systems support. This property is often useful when a variety of storage devices that have been acquired over a period of time are repurposed. A storage appliance or server-based volume manager can combine different types of devices into volumes with desirable properties.

■ *Server-based volumes complement RAID subsystems.* For terabytes of data, hardware RAID subsystems are advisable, for several reasons, including packaging convenience, performance optimization, and serviceability. While RAID subsystems present volumes of their own (LUNs), server-based volume managers can aggregate these for greater capacity, availability, or performance (for example, by mirroring or striping data across LUNs presented by two or more RAID subsystems).

Technical Properties of Volumes

Both RAID subsystem-based and server-based volumes are disk-like storage abstractions whose aggregate behavior comes from volume managers that present disk-like entities to file systems, database managers, and applications. Volume managers organize disk storage capacity into concatenated, striped, mirrored, or RAID volumes.

Volumes must be *persistent;* that is, each time a computer or RAID subsystem starts up, its volume manager must be able to determine which blocks on which disks should be presented as which type of volume. Volume managers typically provide this persistence by dividing disk storage capacity into:

■ *Private* or *hidden regions*, in which *metadata* (information about volumes' makeup) are stored

■ *User data areas*, which are available for creating volumes and storing data

Volume manager metadata is vital to user data integrity. If volume metadata is not available, a volume manager cannot determine which blocks on which disks to present to which devices. Metadata must therefore be redundant, so that as long as enough disks to meaningfully present a volume are functioning, the volume manager can determine how to present it.

Volume managers typically organize disks into *groups* and replicate the metadata for an entire group on several of its disks. With replicated metadata, volume membership can be determined and volumes started at system startup time, even if not all of the disks in a group are operating.

Failure-Tolerant Volumes: What Kind of Protection?

Volume managers typically support both *mirrored* and *parity RAID* failure-tolerant volumes, as well as non-failure-tolerant ones. Table 8.1 summarizes the data availability characteristics of various popular volume types.

As Table 8.1 indicates, mirrored volumes offer the best protection against disk failures, simply because, with more disks holding redundant data, certain multiple disk failures are survivable. Moreover, when a disk in a mirrored volume *does* fail, the performance impact is lower than with parity RAID. Typical volume managers can mirror data on:

Table 8.1 Volume Availability Characteristics

VOLUME TYPE	DATA AVAILABILITY	COMMENTS
Mirrored (2x) (sometimes called RAID 1)	Very high	Useful for critical data objects smaller than a disk or LUN.
Mirrored (3x or more)	Ultrahigh	Useful for critical data objects that must be frozen and backed up or mined while online.
Striped and mirrored (2x or more)	Very high	Useful for critical data objects larger than a disk or LUN.
Striped with parity (RAID 5)	High	Useful for important read-mostly data Protects against only one disk failure.
Striped without parity (sometimes called RAID 0)	Lower than for a single disk	Useful for easily replaced or low-grade data.
Concatenated (capacity aggregated)	Lower than for a single disk	Useful for easily replaced or low-grade data where performance is secondary.

- Portions of two or more disks
- Two or more entire disks
- Two or more sets of disks with data striped across them

Some volume managers allow storage capacity to be added to a volume while it is in use, enabling storage to expand as needed. Some also support movement of data from one disk or LUN to another while the data is in use by applications. Volume managers that can mirror three copies of data are useful for capturing *frozen images* of data for backup, mining, or application testing. One mirror can usually be "split" from a volume, allowing applications to continue processing (still failure-tolerant) data while the frozen image is backed up or mined. (See Figure 8.4.)

High-Performance Volumes: Balancing I/O Load

Volume managers can *stripe* data across several disks or LUNs. Striping improves I/O performance by balancing an I/O load more or less uniformly across several disks. Data can be striped across disks in the following ways:

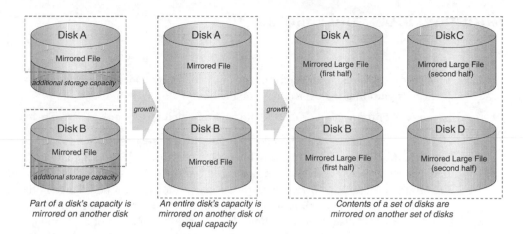

Figure 8.4 Volume manager mirroring configurations.

With no failure protection. This configuration, sometimes called *RAID 0*, balances I/O load across disk resources, but does not protect against disk failure. Because of its low cost and good performance characteristics, it is useful for temporary data that can easily be reproduced if a failure occurs. Striping with no failure protection is not ideal for critical or difficult-to-reproduce data.

With parity protection. This configuration is often called *RAID 5*.[1] It protects against disk failure at lower hardware cost than mirroring, because one extra disk protects an arbitrary number of data disks against a single failure. RAID arrays are complex to update, which makes them unsuitable for frequently updated data. RAID arrays are best suited for data that is infrequently updated, so that write performance is not a major issue. Web pages and warehoused data are typically suitable for RAID storage.

With data mirrored on two or more disks. This configuration is sometimes called *RAID 1+0* or *RAID 0+1*. It combines failure tolerance and load balancing. While the hardware cost is high, striping with mirroring is the ideal combination of failure tolerance, performance, and flexibility for critical online data. With the low cost of disk hardware today, striping with mirroring should be used for all enterprise-critical information, such as sales and financial records, as well as for frequently updated data, such as inventory, manufacturing, or shipping records.

---

[1] RAID 5 is one of a family of data protection techniques in which redundant *check data* is used to reconstruct user data if a disk containing it fails. The best-known of these techniques are called RAID 3, RAID 4, and RAID 5. RAID 3 relies on rotationally synchronized disks. RAID 4 uses conventional disks, with all check data information concentrated on one disk. RAID 5 also uses conventional disks, but distributes parity information across them. Collectively, these techniques are called *parity RAID* because all use the same check data mechanism.

Mirroring, RAID, and Failures

Two kinds of failures affect the availability of failure-tolerant volumes:

1. *A failure* of a disk that is part of the mirrored or RAID volume, or a failure of an access path that makes a disk unreachable.

2. *A crash* of the system or RAID controller in which the volume manager is executing.

When one disk in a mirrored volume fails, application requests can be satisfied simply by accessing the remaining mirrors. If a disk in a parity RAID volume fails, the volume manager must *regenerate* any data requested by applications by reading from the remaining disks and performing computations on the data it reads. Thus, both mirrored and RAID volumes can tolerate any single disk failure as Figure 8.5 suggests. Rapid recovery is also important, however, to avoid the chance of a second disk failure causing data loss. Recovery from a disk failure includes:

- Physically configuring a working substitute for the failed disk
- *Rebuilding* the contents of the failed disk on the substitute disk, inclusive of any updates made during the outage

Volume managers typically support *hot spares*, predesignated replacement disks. When a disk fails, the volume manager automatically allocates a predesignated spare and begins to rebuild the failed disk's contents. (See Figure 8.6.) This eliminates the need for human intervention and minimizes the time required to restore data protection.

Volume managers rebuild failed disk contents transparently while applications are using the affected volume. Rebuilding is I/O intensive, however, and can interfere with application execution. Some volume managers allow rebuilding I/O to be *throttled* to minimize the impact on application performance.

System Crash Safeguards

Even though they entail multiple I/O operations on different disks, application writes to mirrored and RAID volumes must appear to be *atomic;* that is, each write must

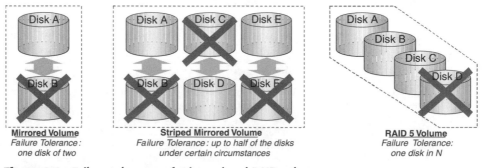

Mirrored Volume
*Failure Tolerance :
one disk of two*

Striped Mirrored Volume
*Failure Tolerance : up to half of the disks
under certain circumstances*

RAID 5 Volume
*Failure Tolerance:
one disk in N*

Figure 8.5   Failure tolerance of mirrored and RAID volumes.

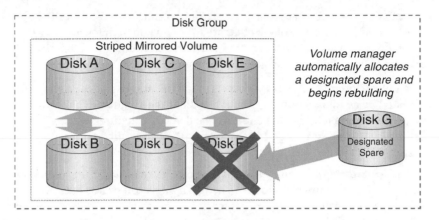

Figure 8.6   Hot spare minimizes exposure to a second failure.

occur either in its entirety or not at all. For example, an application write to a mirrored volume must be reflected on *all* of the volume's disks. Similarly, every application write to a RAID volume must result in both parity and user data being updated.

Guaranteeing atomic updates is one of the most difficult volume management problems, because the systems in which the volume managers are running can crash with updates partially complete. If this occurs, data can be corrupted in ways that may not be discovered until long after the crash is recovered from. For example:

- If a system crash occurs before all mirrors of a mirrored volume are written, subsequent application read requests return different data depending on which of the volume's disks executes a particular read command.

- If a system crash occurs after data on a RAID volume is written but before the corresponding parity is updated, the corruption remains latent after the system restarts. Only when *another* disk fails and data from it is rebuilt using the out-of-date parity does the corruption appear.

Guaranteeing that situations like this do not occur or, in other words, that failure-tolerant volume updates are atomic requires:

- Detecting that a system crash may have left a volume in an inconsistent state

- Restoring the volume's internal consistency (e.g., making all of a mirrored volume's mirrors identical or making parity correspond to user data for all blocks in a RAID volume) as quickly as possible after crash recovery

One simple solution is to assume that any volume contents may be inconsistent after a system crash, and rebuilding the entire volume. This would require recomputing *all* of a RAID volume's parity blocks. For mirrored volumes, one would be chosen as a master, and its entire contents would be copied to the others. Neither of these is practical. Assuming that an entire volume is untrustworthy after a system crash results in long recovery time, since the entire volume must be rebuilt before file systems, databases, and applications can be restarted.

A preferable strategy for detecting and restoring volume consistency after system crashes is to log a record of blocks that are in play while updates are in progress. Such a log can be read when restarting after a crash to determine which blocks *might* be inconsistent. Only these blocks need be recovered.

■ A simple solution for *RAID volumes* is to log the number of each *stripe* of data updated by an application request. When all of the commands that constitute the update are complete, the log entry can be deleted. When recovering from a system failure, only stripes recorded in the log need to be rebuilt because only they can possibly be at risk.

■ For *mirrored volumes*, one efficient type of log is a bitmap with each bit representing a fixed number of blocks. When an application writes data, bits corresponding to updated blocks are set in the log. When the writes are complete, the bits are reset. When recovering from a crash, only blocks that correspond to bits set in the log need be recovered.

Figure 8.7 illustrates these logging techniques.

Before executing an application write request to a RAID volume, the volume manager logs the numbers of stripes being updated. Request completions are also logged. When recovering from a crash, the volume manager regenerates parity only for stripes whose numbers are in the log. Since only a very small fraction of a volume's stripes are likely to be undergoing update at any instant, this minimizes recovery time and, therefore, the time until file systems, databases, and applications can restart.

Similarly, before executing an application request to a mirrored volume, a volume manager updates the volume's log to indicate the range of blocks being updated.

To minimize logging overhead, write completions can be logged lazily with low-priority I/O. This could result in some needless recovery, but that is a small price to pay for minimizing logging overhead.

I/O Performance with Volumes

In addition to enhancing data availability, volumes can be configured to outperform individual storage devices. Each type of volume has slightly different I/O performance

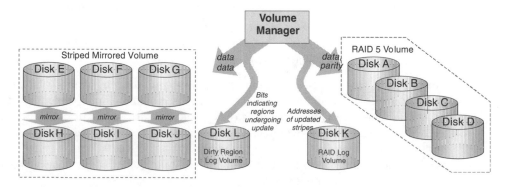

Figure 8.7   Volume manager logging.

characteristics. Awareness of volume performance characteristics is helpful when placing data on storage. Table 8.2 summarizes performance characteristics for the most popular volume types.

As Table 8.2 indicates, a mirrored volume outperforms a disk when reading data because a volume manager can minimize wait times by choosing the volume's least busy disk to satisfy each read request. Requests don't *execute* any faster, but average completion time is lower because less time is spent waiting for service.

Write performance of a two-mirror volume is slightly lower than, but comparable to, that of a single disk. Each application write request must be mirrored on each of the volume's disks; however, the disk writes are independent (unlike RAID writes) and can execute concurrently. Application write execution time is essentially the execution time for the slowest individual disk write. In addition, a small overhead is incurred each time the blocks affected by an application write are logged.

Application writes to RAID volumes perform poorly relative to disk writes because each application write requires a series of disk reads and writes, as well as a log entry. RAID volumes are therefore not ideal for storing frequently updated data.

Striped Volumes

Volume managers *stripe* data across disks, transparently distributing files and database tables across I/O resources. Figure 8.8 illustrates the effect of data striping on application data location.

Table 8.2   Volume Performance Characteristics

RAID VOLUME	PERFORMANCE	COMMENTS
Mirrored (2x) (sometimes called RAID 1)	High read performance Slightly below average write performance	Mirrored disk writes are independent, so effect on application response is minimal.
Mirrored (3x or more)	High read performance Below average write performance	Need to mirror every application write can affect performance of write-intensive applications.
Striped and mirrored (2x or more)	Very high read performance High write performance	Striping mitigates performance penalty of multiple disk writes.
Striped with parity (RAID 5)	High read performance Low write performance	Write performance can be hidden by write-back cache.
Striped without parity (sometimes called RAID 0)	High read and write performance	Highest performance of all listed volume types.
Concatenated (capacity aggregated)	Average read and write performance	Single file access performance similar to a single disk.

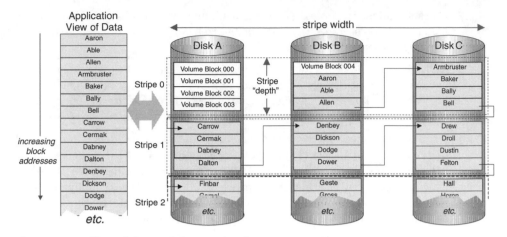

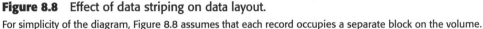

Figure 8.8 Effect of data striping on data layout.

For simplicity of the diagram, Figure 8.8 assumes that each record occupies a separate block on the volume.

The left side of Figure 8.8 illustrates a file that contains a sequence of records sorted by name. A volume manager maps volume blocks to disk blocks in (conceptually) horizontal *stripes*. In Figure 8.8, volume blocks 0–3 correspond to blocks 0–3 on Disk A; volume blocks 4–7 correspond to blocks 0–3 on Disk B, volume blocks 8–11 correspond to blocks 0–3 on disk C, and so forth.

When discussing striping, each disk is sometimes called a *column*. The number of consecutive volume blocks that correspond to consecutive blocks on one disk is called the *stripe depth* (four blocks in Figure 8.8). One stripe depth of blocks on all of a volume's disks is called a *stripe* (e.g., Stripe 0, Stripe 1, and Stripe 2 in Figure 8.8).

As Figure 8.8 illustrates, striping spreads an ordered sequence of data items across a volume's disks. This improves I/O-intensive applications performance for most distributions of requests.

- If application I/O requests are uniformly distributed, disk I/O requests tend to be uniformly distributed across the volume's disks. This maximizes the number of concurrently active disks when requests overlap in time.

- Even if application I/O requests "cluster," as, for example, if an application accesses several records corresponding to names beginning with the letter D in Figure 8.8, striping still causes disk I/O requests to be distributed.

Since striping is independent of data's application meaning, I/O tends to distribute uniformly across disks (be balanced) for almost any pattern of application requests.

Volume managers can stripe data across both mirrored volumes and RAID volumes. Striping improves read performance for all of these. For mirrored volumes, data striping further mitigates the already small write penalty by spreading a write load across multiple disks. For RAID volumes, the overhead I/O required to execute application writes dominates write performance, even with striping. For this reason, RAID volumes are most suitable for read-mostly data.

Management Flexibility

By *virtualizing* disk storage, some volume managers introduce a level of flexibility that is not available with disks. Volume managers enable a system administrator to:

- *Expand* or contract a volume's capacity.
- *Move* block ranges of data to alternate physical locations.

Both expansion and data movement can typically occur while volumes are in use; however, both are I/O intensive. For example, when addition of a disk (a column) expands a volume, data must be restriped so that I/O remains balanced.

Similarly, moving a column entails copying its entire contents. Both operations can affect applications' I/O performance adversely. In most cases, reduced application performance is preferable to the alternative of stopping applications entirely to move or restripe data.

Expanding a volume is useful when storage requirements grow, especially unexpectedly. Expanding a volume's capacity is much simpler than the alternative of spreading data across two or more disks, modifying applications and control files and updating scripts to reflect the change.

Moving a column from one disk to another can avert outage due to a gradually failing disk. Also when two volumes share a disk, moving a column of one can rebalance I/O by relocating a busy volume to less heavily utilized disks.

File Systems and Application Performance

Volumes provide robust, high-performing block storage. For applications to use this storage effectively, it must be organized by a file system. A file system can contribute substantially to application performance, as well as its flexibility and manageability, especially in a highly connected SAN environment. A well-engineered file system can improve application performance in several ways:

- Data allocation techniques
- I/O efficiency
- Recovery from system crashes
- Dynamic utility functions
- Frozen image techniques

File System Space Allocation

Conventional Unix file systems manage online storage space in fixed-size *allocation units* or *file system blocks*, each consisting of a sequence of disk or volume blocks.

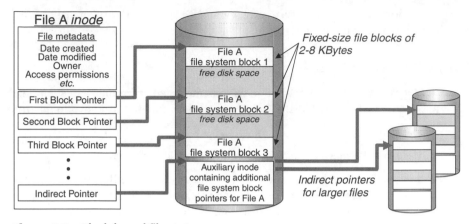

Figure 8.9 Block-based file system.

They use on-disk data structures called *inodes* allocated from the file system's space pool to describe files. An inode contains metadata about its file, as well as *file system block pointers* that indicate the location of the file's data. Figure 8.9 illustrates a block-based file system's description of a file.

As Figure 8.9 suggests, each block pointer corresponds to a file system block. A file system block typically consists of between 4 and 16 storage device blocks. When an application reads or writes file data, the file system uses these block pointers to convert the file data address into a volume or disk address, to which it addresses its I/O request.

Since inodes have limited space for pointers, large files that require many pointers store additional pointers in *indirect* inodes, as shown in Figure 8.9. Reading and writing such files requires occasional extra file system I/O to retrieve auxiliary inodes so that data can be located. A second level of indirection exists for *really* large files.

Application I/O requests for consecutive file system blocks are most efficiently executed if the corresponding storage device blocks are also consecutive. This allows the file system blocks to be transferred with one device I/O request. Block-based file systems examine their inode mappings to determine whether a sequence of application requests can be satisfied with one device I/O request or whether they must be broken up into several device requests.

Thus, block-based file systems can impose I/O overhead on an application because they may have to issue multiple device requests to satisfy a single application request. Moreover, since the units in which storage is allocated are small, there is a high likelihood that files will be allocated or extended noncontiguously, resulting in even more overhead I/O.

Extent-Based File Systems

Some file systems use *extent-based* space allocation to reduce or eliminate this overhead. As illustrated in Figure 8.10, such file systems allocate storage space in variable-length *extents* of one or more file system blocks, rather than in fixed-length allocation units. An extent is an arbitrary number of consecutive file system blocks that can be concisely described by a starting block number and a block count. Because an extent can be very large, a single inode can contain a large file's entire block map. This reduces overhead I/O, resulting in better application I/O performance.

The key advantage of an extent-based file system is that it enables larger contiguous areas of storage to be mapped with minimal overhead. Large contiguous storage areas are beneficial for the following reasons:

Data descriptors are more compact. Because each extent descriptor can map many blocks, fewer descriptors are needed to map a file. Translation between applications' file data addresses and device block addresses is faster.

File scans are more efficient. Larger contiguous storage areas enable most large file I/O requests to be satisfied with a single device I/O request. This reduces both the number of I/O requests required to do a given job and rotational latency (time lost waiting for disks to rotate to a data transfer starting point).

Device fragmentation is reduced. Larger areas of contiguous storage reduce *disk fragmentation*, a condition in which logically contiguous file data are stored in non-contiguous blocks. Fragmentation reduces I/O efficiency because it increases the chance that an application's file I/O request must be split into two or more device I/O requests for execution.

Sequential I/O policies can be more aggressive. Contiguously located data can be *read ahead* of application requests. This increases the speed with which a file can be scanned sequentially.

Larger files can be supported. Extent-based storage allocation makes it easy to describe very large files. Extent-based file systems do not suffer many of the maximum file size and maximum file system size restrictions of conventional file systems.

If a file is extended many times during its life, the number of its extents may exceed the capacity of an inode, even with an extent-based file system. When this happens, it

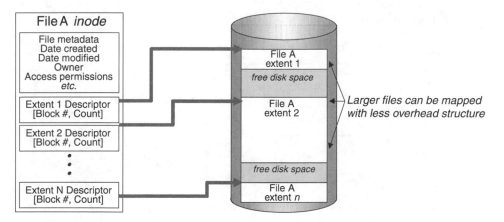

Figure 8.10 Extent-based file system.

is common for a file system to completely reformat the file's main inode as an *indirect inode*. All descriptors are replaced by pointers to *indirect* inodes (the first of which is a copy of the original inode). Figure 8.11 illustrates the use of indirect inodes to describe a very large file in an extent-based file system.

Preallocation and Alignment

Some applications create, extend, and delete files frequently. Others, particularly database applications, have relatively static file structures. Database *container files* are seldom created, extended, or deleted, although their contents may change frequently. Some file systems take advantage of this property to improve I/O performance by allowing storage space to be preallocated when files are created (before any data are written). Preallocation of storage has two advantages:

- *Optimal data layout.* If data requirements are known a priori, as is common with databases, an administrator can optimize space utilization and balance I/O load by preselecting the storage devices on which key files will reside.

- *Minimal space allocation failures.* If permanent files are preallocated, then the need to extend them is infrequent. Ad hoc jobs that create and delete temporary files frequently are therefore less likely to cause space allocation failures for permanent files.

Some file systems and database managers use preallocation to align files on boundaries that are optimal for the underlying storage devices. For example, a file system that uses a striped volume could size and align file system blocks or pages with volume stripes. Alignment minimizes split file system blocks or database pages that cross volume boundaries, necessitating the splitting of some application I/O requests into multiple device I/O requests.

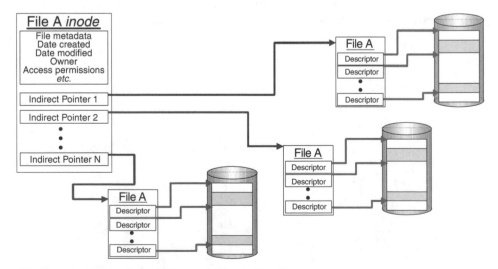

Figure 8.11 Extent-based file system large file allocation.

Back Doors for Database I/O

From a manageability standpoint, files are ideal containers for database management systems' data. Files are easy to extend and move. Multistream backup jobs can be structured around files, making backup more parallel. This management convenience comes at a cost, however. File-based I/O exacts a performance penalty because of the many inter- and intrafile protections provided by file systems—protections that are of little use to database managers. The largest of these penalties are the movement of data from database buffers to system cache before writing, and the serialization of write requests to every file. Some file systems are able to approach raw storage device database I/O performance with files by enabling database managers to bypass both of these protections.

Figure 8.12 illustrates the conventional I/O for a database that stores its data in container files. Each database write is first processed by the file system. Typically, the file system moves data from application (database manager) space to a system *buffer cache* to which the application has no access. Then, to preserve proper file semantics, the file system locks the file before writing. While it entails significant CPU overhead and serializes write requests to a file, this behavior is appropriate for most applications because it stops them from inadvertently modifying data between making a write request and having it completed.

For database managers, this is unnecessary, since they coordinate their own I/O and control their own buffer contents very carefully. Some file systems enable database managers to make I/O requests directly to the file systems' storage devices, bypassing both the movement of data to the system buffer cache and file access locking and the serialization it entails, as Figure 8.13 illustrates.

File systems that provide this fast path I/O capability also allow the affected files to be accessed conventionally. This allows the database manager the high-performance back-door access it requires without sacrificing the manageability advantages of data-

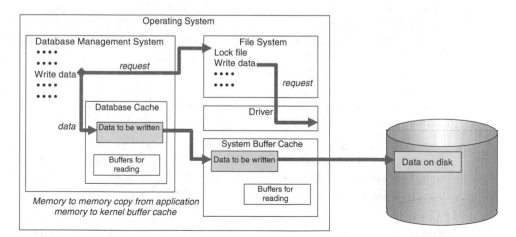

Figure 8.12 Conventional file-based database I/O path.

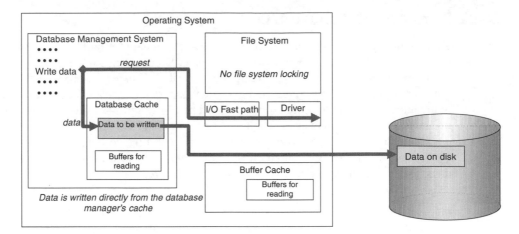

Figure 8.13 Fast path I/O for file-based databases.

base container files. Fast path I/O provides database access performance equivalent to that of raw device I/O for two reasons:

- *Lower-overhead I/O.* Data moves directly from database cache to disk, with no CPU-intensive intermediate copy. This eliminates processing overhead and also reduces memory requirements, since data is cached once instead of twice.

- *More concurrent I/O.* Bypassing file locks enables a database manager to make many concurrent I/O requests. This increases database I/O parallelism and also gives host bus adapter drivers, RAID controllers, and disks larger I/O request queues on which to base performance optimizations.

Using Large Memory Effectively

Enterprise-class servers have evolved to use 64-bit operating systems that can address physical memories larger than 4 gigabytes. But, many databases and applications have not made this transition. A 32-bit application or database manager can only address up to 4 gigabytes of memory. Very large or especially active databases could make good use of the much larger physical memories in enterprise servers to cache data if they could somehow address it. In other cases, enterprise servers host several databases, each with a private cache sized for worst-case requirements. Server memory must be sized for combined worst-case requirements, even though much of the memory may not be required most of the time.

There are file systems that solve both of these problems. They enable 32-bit database managers to utilize large memory, and at the same time decrease total cache requirements for multiple databases in a server. They do this by intercepting database I/O requests and caching data in a private cache, as Figure 8.14 illustrates.

As Figure 8.14 suggests, such file systems write data directly from database cache to storage devices. While writes are occurring, data are also copied to a large cache managed by the file system in cooperation with the operating system. Subsequent reads

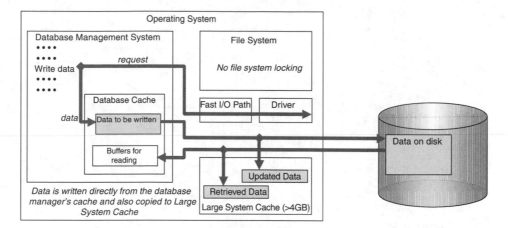

Figure 8.14   File system support for large cache.

are satisfied from this cache, at access speeds much higher than storage device I/O speed. Similarly, data read by applications is copied to the large cache as it is delivered. If requested again, this cached data is delivered immediately with no device latency.

Copying data between database cache and large system cache incurs some overhead. Until applications and databases can be converted to 64 bit versions, however, it at least improves scaling by enabling the use of large physical memories.

In systems that run multiple database instances, this architecture provides another important advantage: reduction of overall cache requirements. Cache allocated to a database manager instance is available only to that instance. A database instance may be lightly loaded, but its unused cache is not available to other, busier, instances. A large system cache managed by a file system allows each database instance to run with a smaller private cache, because the large system cache is available to all database instances and uses global *least recently used* (LRU) management. Figure 8.15 gives an example of dynamic cache utilization made possible by this technique.

Fast Recovery from System Crashes

Critical enterprise applications must be designed assuming that their systems will crash. A recovery strategy that gets applications back in operation quickly after system crashes is a vital component of any enterprise data center strategy.

File system recovery—verifying the structural integrity of file systems and repairing any inconsistencies caused by the crash—is an unavoidable step in crash recovery. File system integrity must be verified before databases and applications can be allowed to use data.

Whenever files are created, extended, truncated, or deleted, the file system updates inodes and other *metadata* that makes the file system's disk image *self-describing*. Most file system operations entail multiple metadata changes. For example, when a

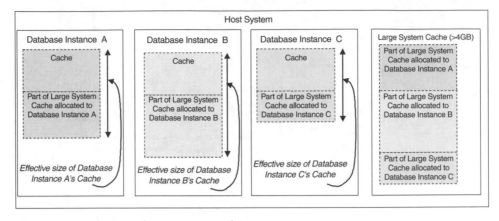

Figure 8.15 Sharing a large system cache.

file is extended, its inode must be updated to reflect the extension, and the storage space into which it is extended must be moved from the file system's free space pool. Most file systems cache metadata changes and write them lazily to improve day-to-day I/O performance.

When a system crashes, the possibility that cached metadata updates may have been lost makes file system integrity suspect. Even if operations appear complete from an application viewpoint, metadata may not yet have been written. A crash can result in lost files or disk blocks or, worse, disk blocks allocated to two or more files.

The usual means of verifying file system structural integrity after a crash is to run a program that validates file system metadata and repairs it if necessary before the file system is mounted. In Unix systems, this program is called *fsck* (file system check). Windows operating systems include an equivalent program called *CHKDSK*.

The fsck and CHKDSK programs validate file system structures, making sure that no disk blocks are "lost" (i.e., neither allocated to files nor free for allocation) or multiply allocated. They may undo partially complete updates, causing recent application actions to "disappear", but they leave file systems structurally intact. These programs can take a long time to run (2 to 5 minutes per gigabyte of data, by one estimate). Since file systems cannot be mounted until checking is complete, applications and database managers cannot begin executing. Recovery times can run to minutes or hours, reducing system availability.

Journaling file systems use an alternative recovery technique based on logging their *intent* to update metadata before actually updating it. A file system log is conceptually similar to the volume manager logs discussed previously. Each time file system metadata changes (e.g., when a file or directory is created, extended, or deleted), the file system logs a description of the updates that constitute the change before performing them. File system logs are typically small, designed to hold only the number of metadata updates likely to be in progress concurrently.

When recovering from a system failure, a journaling file system reads its log and verifies that all metadata updates described in it are reflected on storage devices. At any instant, the number of updates described in a log is a very small fraction of the total amount of metadata in a large file system. Replaying logs is normally orders of magnitude faster than running a full *fsck*. Log-based recovery enables file systems to recover from a system crash more quickly. This in turn enables database and application recovery to start sooner, increasing system availability.

Online File System Administration

In most enterprises, information processing systems grow and change over time. Growth and change inevitably require data storage *reorganization*. For example:

- As applications use a file system, the storage space they occupy becomes *fragmented*, leading to inefficient allocation, wasted space, and poor performance.

- File systems and databases outgrow their storage device capacity and need to be moved to larger devices.

- Files and database tables must be relocated to different devices to balance I/O load, to avoid device failures, or for other administrative reasons.

- Files and databases must be moved from one server or geographic location to another for business reasons.

Most of data storage administration amounts to moving data objects from one storage device to another. Moving data is counter to the fundamental enterprise data center requirement of maximizing application and data availability. Some file systems are designed so that administrative functions can be performed while data is being used by applications. These include defragmentation, relocation, file system expansion, and frozen image creation.

File System Defragmentation

As applications run, file system storage space is continually allocated and deallocated. Over time, files, directories, and file system free space all become *fragmented*. In a fragmented file system, as the right side of Figure 8.16 illustrates, file extents and free space are highly intermixed. Space available for allocating new files is distributed among many small block ranges. Requests to create large contiguous files may fail, even though the file system has enough free space. Other requests succeed by allocating many small extents, but the overhead of accessing fragmented files leads to suboptimal file I/O performance.

Most file systems are able to *defragment* the storage space they occupy to remedy this condition, using either integrated components or separate defragmentation utilities. Defragmentation consists of moving files or directories from one storage device location to another to consolidate free space, and updating metadata to reflect new file locations. Ideally, file movement is transparent to applications, which access files identically before, during, and after the move. When files and directories are contiguous, as on the left side of Figure 8.16, the file system is said to be *defragmented*. In this state, free space is consolidated and large extents can be allocated.

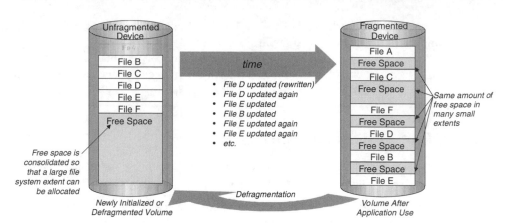

Figure 8.16 Storage fragmentation and defragmentation.

Moving a file that is not in use is easy—the file is copied and the original is deleted. Moving a file while it is being accessed by applications is more challenging. Figure 8.17 illustrates one technique for moving a file while it is in use.

To move a file using the technique illustrated in Figure 8.17, a file system first allocates space for the entire file. File extents are then locked and copied one by one. As each extent is moved, file system metadata is updated to reflect its new location and the extent is unlocked to allow application access. If an application attempts to access an extent that is being moved, its I/O request stalls until the move is complete. Similarly, if the file system attempts to move an extent that is in use by an application, *its* I/O stalls until the application releases the blocks.

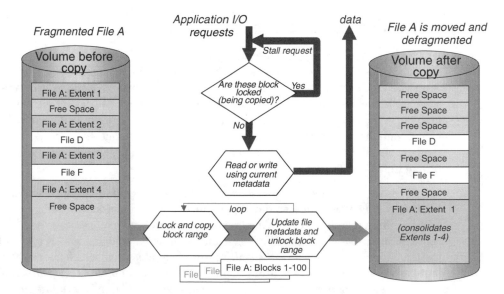

Figure 8.17 Moving an open file.

The ability to move a file while it is in use is one key element of file system defragmentation. The other is an algorithm for continuously making optimal file placement decisions until the file system is defragmented (i.e., most files are contiguous and located adjacent to each other, and free space extents are consolidated). This is challenging because applications may be creating, extending, deleting, and truncating files while the file system is being defragmented.

Moving Active Files

Defragmentation is a constant concern with file systems whose rate of file creation and deletion is high. This is not generally the case with databases, whose container files are typically few in number and relatively static. There are other reasons, however, for moving database tables and files while they are in use. In fact, this ability is one major reason why files make ideal containers for database data. For example:

- Policy changes, such as moving a file or database whose importance has increased from a simple volume to a mirrored volume, can be implemented while the data is in use.

- Entire file systems that grow uncomfortably close to the capacity of the devices holding them can be moved to larger devices, thus averting application failures due to out-of-space conditions.

- Files and databases can be moved from storage devices identified by predictive failure analysis as in danger of failing to other devices.

The same underlying online file movement technique use to defragment a file system can be used to implement all of these capabilities.

Online File System Expansion

Perhaps the most frequent reason to relocate files or database tables while they are in use is *online storage capacity expansion*. As applications evolve:

- They deal with more data.
- They gain more users.
- The amount of their historical data grows.
- They are functionally enhanced.

All of these tend to increase storage requirements. The ability to expand a file system's capacity makes it possible to meet demands for increased storage capacity without downtime. Most database managers support storage expansion, either automatically or by administrative action. For databases based on container files, expansion is easy—up to the capacity of the file system. Volume managers typically support online volume expansion. Some file systems also integrate with these capabilities and are capable of discovering expanded volumes and expand themselves to use the newly available space. Applications that use file systems and database managers with these capabilities are well insulated from out-of-space conditions—up to the limit of *physical* storage capacity.

Backup and Continuous Data Access

The need for continuous data availability that is increasingly characteristic of enterprise data centers conflicts with other data usage requirements such as:

- Making regular, consistent backups of critical data
- Mining operational data, conducting analyses to discern business trends

Requirements like these generally do not modify the data they process. They interfere with applications because, ideally, the data they process does not change while they are processing it. If online applications are changing data during a backup, the result is likely to be inconsistent, reflecting partially complete transactions, mismatching account balances, and so forth. Similarly, if data changes during analysis, the analysis is inaccurate at best and may be completely useless.

A backup is most valuable when it represents a *transactionally consistent* view of business state as reflected in its data. Data restored from such a backup does not reflect any incomplete transactions. For backups to have this property, they should be made when no application updates are occurring.

One way to ensure transactionally consistent backup is not to run applications while backing up their data. Backups made while data is not in use are called *cold* backups. Since no application updates occur during a cold backup, transactional consistency is automatic.

Cold backup is the fastest backup technique, because there is no application I/O to interfere with backup I/O. Unfortunately, cold backup requires a *backup window*, a time interval sufficient to make the backup during which data is unavailable to applications. Backup windows typically occur during late-night hours or on weekends when little business is being transacted. With electronic business, however, data must be available to applications all day, every day. Cold backup does not meet online business data availability requirements.

Moreover, over time, online data typically grows, causing backup times to grow correspondingly. But if backup windows even exist, they either remain the same or shrink; cold backup becomes an even less viable option.

Frozen image techniques have been developed to help reconcile conflicting data access requirements like these.

Frozen Images

A frozen image is a usable image of the records in a database, the data in a file system, or the blocks of a volume, as they existed at a known instant. Database managers, file systems, RAID subsystems, and server-based volume managers all incorporate *frozen image* technologies. The making of a frozen image is transparent to applications— almost. Frozen image creation requires a point in time at which the data whose image is to be frozen is known to be transactionally consistent.

Some database managers are designed to be frozen image aware. They are able to suspend operation, completing transactions in progress and flushing cached data to storage devices without completely shutting down. Applications that use such database managers for *all* their data are automatically frozen image capable. Most applications are not frozen image aware and must be stopped completely in order to guarantee that their on-disk data is transactionally consistent.

There are two basic techniques for creating frozen images:

■ *Split mirrors.* If one mirror is separated, or split, from a mirrored volume, it represents the volume's state at the instant of splitting. The split mirror can be used for backup or data mining while the volume's other mirrors continue to service applications. Data must be transactionally consistent when a mirror is split from its volume.

■ *Copy-on-write checkpoints (also called snapshots).* A database manager, file system, or volume manager can transparently save "before images" of all data written after a given instant. This data can be returned when backup requests data from the frozen image, for example. Data must be transactionally consistent at the instant of frozen image creation.

Both of these techniques result in two data images:

■ *The original* database, file system, or volume, which can be read and written by applications as soon as the frozen image is created.

■ *The frozen image,* which can be backed up or mined. Some frozen image techniques allow a frozen image to be modified; others create read-only images.

Split Mirror Frozen Images

Mirroring is almost always done at the volume, rather than at the file system or database level. Splitting one mirror from a volume containing a file system or database is an often-used technique for freezing the file or database image for backup. For 2-mirror volumes, splitting leaves both the primary volume and the split mirror vulnerable to disk failure. For this reason, some users create 3-mirror volumes. Splitting a mirror from such a volume leaves the primary volume protected against disk failure.

When a mirror is split from its volume and mounted as a separate file system, it becomes an independent data image, with no ongoing relationship to its source volume. Application updates to the source volume are not reflected on the split mirror. For backup and other uses of the frozen image, this is precisely the desired behavior. After the frozen image has been used, however, it is desirable that the split mirror reflects these application updates as quickly as possible.

When a backup made from a split mirror is complete, the split mirror must rejoin its volume and be resynchronized so that future backups can use the same technique. With no way to identify changes made to the volume while a mirror was split and no way of knowing whether the split mirror itself was updated, the split mirror must be treated as though it were a new disk with completely unknown contents.

Adding a disk to a mirrored volume requires copying the volume's entire contents to the new mirror because a volume manager has no information about which blocks of storage represent data and which are unused space. Copying is time and I/O resource consuming. Thus, if a split mirror is used for periodic frozen image backup, time must be allotted for a complete resynchronization each time a backup completes.

If the changes made to a volume with a split mirror are logged, however, and if no data is written to the mirror while it is split from its volume, a significant optimization is possible. Newer forms of split mirror technology log changes to the main volume starting at the moment of splitting. As long as the split mirror's contents do not change, it can be resynchronized by copying blocks from the change log. For brief separations, such as for backup, only a small percentage of the main volume's data is likely to change while a mirror is split from its volume. So called *fast mirror resynchronization* by log playback resynchronizes much faster than copying the volume's entire contents.

While they consume a lot of disk storage, split mirrors have two properties that make them the preferable frozen image technology in many circumstances:

Completeness. A split mirror is a complete image of the data to be backed up or mined. If the main volume should fail, the mirror represents a consistent, nearly up-to-date data image from which to launch recovery.

Performance. Since a split mirror and its main volume occupy different storage devices, applications using the main volume do not compete with backup or data mining for I/O access. With a SAN, the split mirror can even be moved into a separate zone and backed up or mined by a separate server, completely eliminating interference with applications.

Copy-on-Write Frozen Images

The other popular frozen image technology is called *copy-on-write*. Frozen images created with this technique are called *checkpoints* or *snapshots*. File systems for which checkpoints exist are called checkpointed file systems. To applications, a checkpoint appears to be a separate database, file system, or volume whose contents are an image of data frozen at the instant of checkpoint creation. Data and checkpointed file systems can be updated by applications, while checkpoints themselves are usually read-only.

A checkpoint is initiated by:

- Pausing the database or file system to be checkpointed to make its contents transactionally consistent

- Creating a *changed data list* data structure in which to record the addresses of changed data.

- Allocating space for a *changed data area* in which to record *before images* of data as application updates occur

Once the changed data list and changed data area exist, both checkpointed file system and the checkpoint can be made available to applications.

Checkpoints *copy* data *on write*, creating *before images* of data changed by applications. The first update to a data block after checkpoint creation causes the data's

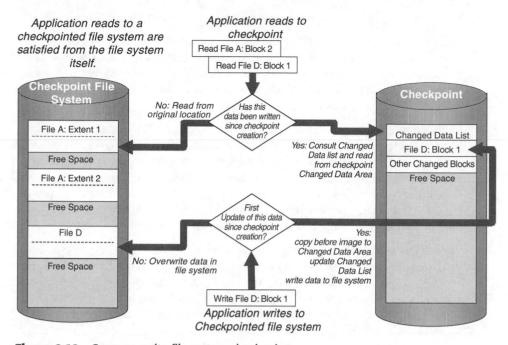

Figure 8.18   Copy-on-write file system checkpoint.

prechange value (its before image) to be copied to the changed data area before it is overwritten. The changed data list is updated to indicate the location of the before image. Figure 8.18 illustrates I/O to a file system checkpoint and to the checkpointed file system.

When a backup or other program reads data from a checkpoint, the checkpoint manager determines from the changed data list whether the requested data has been updated since checkpoint creation. If it has not, the read is satisfied from the original data location in the checkpointed file system. If the data *has* been overwritten, its before image is read from the changed data area.

The storage space consumed by a checkpoint is equal to the number of distinct data blocks updated while the checkpoint is active plus a small amount for the changed data list. Unless they run for a very long time, or unless a large percentage of data is updated, checkpoints require much less physical storage than split mirrors.

Properties of Consistency

Like split mirrors, checkpoints are made transactionally consistent by pausing access to data while they are created. For a checkpoint to be transactionally consistent, it must represent data with:

- No partially complete transactions in progress
- All completed transactions reflected on storage devices (not just in cache)

A database, file system, or volume in this state is said to be *quiescent*.

To a volume manager, all data blocks are equivalent. It has no way of ascertaining the consistency of a file system using it for storage. Similarly, a file system can stall I/O requests and flush (write to disk) any cached data to make *its* disk image consistent, but it cannot easily ascertain whether a database for which it is providing storage has transactions in progress.[2]

This limitation is sometimes overcome by integrating file system and database administration tools. A file system can direct a database manager to complete outstanding transactions, flush its cache, and stall any new transactions so that a consistent checkpoint can be created. Once the database is quiescent, the file system creates a checkpoint and re-enables database operation. This technique minimizes the time during which data is unavailable, while guaranteeing that checkpoints represent consistent database states. Figure 8.19 illustrates database checkpoint creation.

Once created, a checkpoint appears as a read-only database, file system, or volume. Backup programs can use it as a source. Data read from the checkpoint is identical to what would have been read from the source at the moment of checkpoint creation. A database or file system backup made from a checkpoint is thus equivalent to a cold backup. The difference is that a live copy of data may be read and written by applications while its checkpoint is being backed up.

While checkpoints reduce application downtime for backup from hours to the seconds required for their creation, they exact a cost in application performance. The first time after checkpoint creation that a data item is written, the item's before image must be copied and the changed block list updated. Thus, application writes can perform errat-

---

[2] A database might have transactions in progress with no I/O requests outstanding. For example, transactions involving human interaction often have one or more think times during execution. Typically, no database I/O occurs during these periods because the human is considering the next action.

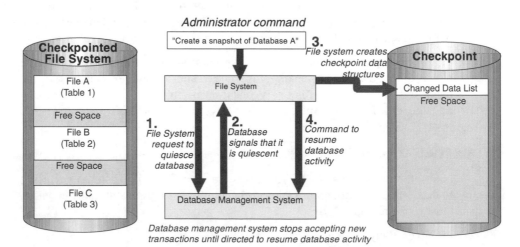

Figure 8.19 Creating a file system checkpoint of a database.

ically while checkpoints are in effect. This is a relatively small price to pay, however, for consistent backups with nearly continuous data availability.

Other Types of Checkpoints

The basic copy-on-write checkpoint capability just described has been developed into highly sophisticated data recovery tools. Two specialized checkpoint capabilities deserve particular mention:

Multiple checkpoints. Some file systems can accommodate multiple checkpoints concurrently, with each capturing the file system's image at a different instant. The before images in these checkpoints can be used to restore or *roll back*, the file system (and, hence, a database that uses it for storage) to its state at any time for which a checkpoint exists. This capability is useful when a file system or database becomes unrecoverably corrupted, for example, by an application bug or administrative error. The file system can be rolled back to a time prior to the corruption or occurrence of the procedural error.

Data-less checkpoints. In one alternate form of checkpoint, only identifiers of changed data items are kept and not the before images. These so called *data-less* checkpoints can be used to perform highly efficient changed block incremental database backups. The use of data-less checkpoints for enterprise backup is described in Chapter 10.

Summary

- A *data access stack*, consisting of driver, volume manager, file system, and database manager is required to deliver data to applications in a useful and convenient form. In SAN environments, instances of these components running in different servers must often interact with each other to enable device ownership transfers or data sharing.

- One key capability for any data access stack is lock management, which enables cooperating system components to coordinate access to system objects. Lock management is sometimes provided as an operating system service. In other instances, file systems and database managers provide their own lock managers for their own objects. Within a single server, locks can be managed as internal data structures. Among multiple servers in a SAN, lock management entails passing messages among cooperating servers, at much higher overhead than locking within the server.

- It is almost always beneficial for servers to use one or more volume managers to organize storage for presentation to file systems and database managers. Volume management is implemented primarily in RAID subsystems and in server-based software components, although there is an emerging class of volume managers that occupy a position in the SAN infrastructure itself. Volume managers coordinate access to multiple disks or LUNs, providing improved I/O performance and data availability.

- File systems can contribute to application availability and performance in a variety of ways. Space allocation by variable size extent uses storage space efficiently and tends to improve I/O performance by reducing the overhead of accessing file data and enabling large application I/O requests to translate directly to large I/O requests to devices.

- Part of recovering from system crashes is verification of the integrity of data on storage devices and in file systems before applications and databases can restart and begin to use the data. Volume managers keep logs of which volume blocks are in play to enable recovery. Journaling file systems log their intent to perform meta-data updates before actually performing them. Replaying the logs after crash recovery enables file systems to ascertain the integrity of their metadata structures much more rapidly than verifying the entire structures.

- Database managers are an increasingly important means for applications to organize their data for business purposes. File systems have been designed to optimize database managers' access path to data without sacrificing the manageability that comes from using container files to store database data. The features of such file systems include the ability to do I/O directly from database cache, bypassing file system write locking, and making use of very large cache to improve database performance and to enable several databases to time-share a large cache memory.

- A key manageability feature of enterprise file systems is the ability to move data objects while they are in use. This enables management operations like defragmentation to be performed without taking data offline.

- Frozen image technology enables backups and analyses of unchanging images of data while the data itself is in use. The two principal frozen image technologies are split mirrors and copy-on-write. Split mirrors are complete copies of data and offer flexibility and performance independence of backup from applications. Copy-on-write images are efficient to create, but have some application performance impact. Some file systems are able to maintain multiple copy-on-write frozen images, enabling file system contents to be rolled back to any of several points in time.

CHAPTER 9

Advanced Software for Storage Networking

In this chapter we'll learn more about:

- Why and how data is replicated across long distances, and why replication is different from mirroring

- Different forms of data replication and the advantages of each

- How SAN-attached servers can be combined into cooperative clusters for enhanced application availability and higher performance

- The special capabilities needed by volume managers and file systems in order to enable data to be shared by the servers in a cluster

- How clustering and replication technologies can be combined to provide the ability for applications to recover after a disaster that incapacitates an entire data center

Data Replication

Large enterprises nearly always have multiple data centers because customer, supply chain, and internal user response requirements make it most efficient to store online data close to where it is used. Inevitably, this means that the same data must be available at several widely separated locations. Price lists, product specifications, Web pages, and similar data must often be *replicated* at several of an enterprise's operating locations. Obviously, it is important that such data be identical throughout an enterprise. If data is to be identical throughout an enterprise, it must be *replicated* or periodically published from the location at which it is processed to remote locations where it is used. Changes to all data replicas must be *synchronized* so that they appear at all locations at approximately the same time.

Data may also be replicated for *mining*. Enterprises have discovered that historical data can be stored inexpensively in *warehouses* and analyzed for trends that help determine business strategies. While data mining is extraordinarily useful, it is also extremely I/O intensive. Operational data cannot be mined without severely impacting application performance. To avoid adverse impact, online data is sometimes replicated to a data warehouse. The replica can then be mined while applications continue to process the live data.

The third and perhaps most important reason for data replication is *disaster recovery*. For most enterprises, the economic consequences of a data center-disabling event are a survival issue. Enterprises need strategies for recovering their ability to process data soon after fire, flood, vandalism, power grid failure, software failure, or other events that incapacitate an entire data center or the data in it. An up-to-date replica of operational data at a remote location unaffected by the disaster can mean the difference between rapid recovery and total enterprise failure.

Types of Data Replication

Whether the purpose is publication, mining, or disaster recovery, the nature of data replication is the same. Up-to-date copies of data are maintained by systems at one or more locations far from the primary data center. These copies are kept identical (*synchronized*) with the data processed by the enterprise's information systems.

Data replication is implemented both in server-based software and in RAID subsystems. Wherever it is implemented, data replication synchronizes one or more *secondary* copies of data with a master or *primary* copy that is being processed by applications. Data can be replicated at different levels of abstraction:

Database. Some database managers are able to transmit database updates to remote servers that maintain running copies of a primary database. The remote servers apply the updates to their database copies, keeping them synchronized with the primary one. Database replication can minimize network bandwidth requirements, because concise transaction descriptors can be transmitted rather than individual data updates. Moreover, databases are usually replicated on a transactional basis, so remote database replicas only ever contain complete transactions. Database replication is not capable of replicating any data not part of a database.

File. Updates to files in a *primary file system* can be replicated to one or more *secondary file systems* on different servers. File system replication keeps primary and secondary file and directory contents in synchronization. Integrity of secondary file system structures is never at issue, because all updates to replicas are applied through file systems at the secondary locations. File system replicas keep data identical from a file system standpoint, not from the standpoint of the underlying volumes or storage devices.

Volume. Updates to a *primary storage device* or *volume* can be replicated to one or more *secondary devices* connected to different servers. Volume replication keeps corresponding blocks of replicated devices in synchronization, but has no awareness of the meaning of the blocks it replicates.

All of these forms of data replication can be implemented in server-based software. RAID subsystems can only replicate storage device contents, because they have no intrinsic awareness of the meaning of the data blocks they replicate. A storage device may be completely occupied by a file system or database, in which case replicating the device effectively replicates the file system or database. Without file system or database awareness, however, secondary locations cannot distinguish database transaction commitments or file system metadata updates from data writes, so it is impossible for software at a secondary location to determine the state of replicated data while replication is in progress. In general, it is impossible to make use of volume replicas at secondary locations while replication is occurring. Moreover, if replication stops unexpectedly, as, for example, if a primary location disaster occurred, the file systems or databases at secondary locations must undergo recovery before they can safely be used by applications.

The Nature of Data Replication

Figure 9.1 illustrates data replication implemented at the server level. In the figure, applications or database managers running on the primary server update databases, files, or volumes. Replicas are maintained on secondary servers. This diagram illustrates three key points about server-based replication:

- *Databases, file systems, and volumes can all be replicated using (separate) server-based technologies.* Database and file replication are typically integrated with database managers and file systems, respectively. Volume replication is often loosely coupled with file systems or database managers to provide a level of synchronization between replication actions and points of file system or database internal consistency.

- *Replication is one-to-many.* There is a single source (the primary location) and one or more targets (secondary locations) for each replicated database, file sys-

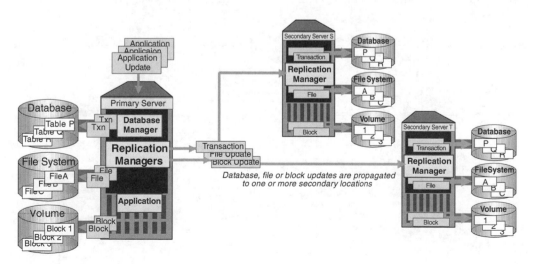

Figure 9.1   Data replication.

tem, or volume. Applications running at the primary location read and write data. Applications at secondary locations may have limited access to database or file system replicas while replication is occurring, but volume or storage device replicas cannot be used until replication stops.

■ *Server-based replication uses conventional storage devices and network connections, so configurations are flexible.* No special hardware is required, nor are dedicated communication links architecturally necessary (they may be advisable for performance reasons). Primary and secondary data replicas need not be stored on identical disks or volumes.

Data Replication versus Mirroring

Ideally, mirroring would fulfill the business needs met by data replication technologies. Two facts of distributed data center life make mirroring inadequate, however:

■ Distances between primary and secondary data centers, routing hops, and momentary network overloads can make data update transmission time intolerably long in terms of its effect on application response.

■ Brief network outages can occur frequently enough to make the frequent mirror resynchronization they would imply unacceptable.

Replication technologies are designed to have minimal effect on application performance and to restore replica integrity transparently after brief network or secondary location outages. They typically do this by logging every update to the replicated data at the primary location before transmitting to secondary locations.

Since data is logged at the primary location, applications need not wait for it to be written at secondary locations. This immunizes application performance from network overloads and the inherent latency of writing data remotely.

When a network or secondary location fails, the primary location continues to log updates to replicated data, as Figure 9.2 illustrates. After recovery, updates logged dur-

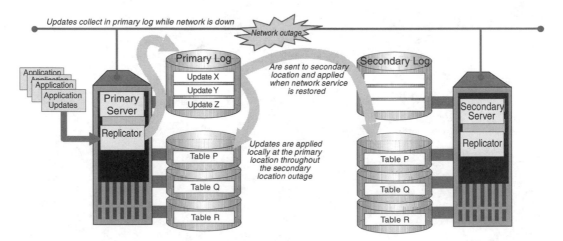

Figure 9.2 Replication and system outages.

ing the outage are sent to affected secondary locations. Thus, recovery from brief outages is transparent to applications, both functionally and from a performance standpoint.

Replicators typically send periodic *heartbeat* signals between the primary server and each secondary server. Heartbeat signals ensure that both parties are aware of the connection state at all times, whether or not there are application updates to replicate. Communication failures are therefore discovered proactively, rather than reactively when applications attempt to update replicated data.

Different Types of Data Replication

While all three forms of replication accomplish the same basic goal—maintaining identical data on widely separated servers—there *are* differences that stem primarily from the nature of the replicated objects. These differences determine the type of replication best suited to each application.

Database Replication

Database replication maintains replicas of database objects—either individual tables or entire databases. It is typical for database replication to be done on a transaction basis—only complete transactions are applied to secondary database replicas. Because of the highly structured and transactional nature of databases, database replication often has other unique properties as well:

Delayed updates. One important reason for replicating data is to recover from disasters at the primary data center. Recovery from physical disasters is intuitively obvious—application processing resumes using the most up-to-date database replica available at a secondary location. Less obvious, is recovery from another type of disaster—a faulty application or operational error. These can corrupt data beyond repair before the corruption is detected. To protect against this, some database replicators are able to delay the application of updates to secondary database replicas. Updates are typically transmitted to secondary locations and held there in queues until the time to apply them has come. In effect, a secondary database replica becomes a series of frozen images of the primary database.

Bidirectional (multimaster) replication. Some database replication facilities support the updating of replicated data at both primary and secondary locations. This feature can be useful, for example, in maintaining identical copies of an enterprise database at multiple locations, each of which predominantly updates data that pertains to it. This technology is inherently susceptible to conflicting updates—the same database object updated simultaneously at two different locations. Database managers that implement bidirectional replication must include facilities for resolving such conflicts. One common technique is to report conflicting updates to applications for ad hoc resolution.

Concise updates. The nature of database replication objects makes replication of certain kinds of updates much less communication intensive than is the case with file system or volume replication. For example, a transaction that changes a field in every record of a large table can be expressed in a single concise SQL statement, which can be transmitted to secondary replication locations. A file system or volume replicator would be forced to transmit every file or volume block update resulting from such a transaction, because they lack the context to express the updates in more concise form.

Programmability. Unlike file system and volume replication, which are purely administrative in nature, database replication typically has more of a programmatic nature. The complexity of database replication, including the number and kind of replicated objects, the sources and targets of replication, the possibility of delayed updates and the potential for conflicting updates when bidirectional replication is used, requires a degree of specification complexity that is more amenable to a procedural programming language than to an administrative one. Individuals responsible for implementing database replication are typically application developers rather than administrators.

Database replication is suitable for all three of the primary uses of replicated data. Bidirectional replication can provide a symmetric disaster recovery solution (i.e., an enterprise can recover its data from a disaster that incapacitates any one of its data centers). Snapshots of tables can be replicated to remote locations at designated times for mining. Similarly, a single snapshot of a set of tables can be published to any number of secondary locations, for example, to provide consistent inventory or price information at all of an enterprise's locations.

File System Replication

File system replication replicates updates to files without regard for the location of updated data on a storage device. The contents of files in a replicated file system are identical to those at the primary location, but there is no guarantee that primary and secondary location files are stored at corresponding storage device block addresses.

Because file system replicators have contextual information about replicated files, they can implement functions that are not possible for storage device replicators:

Selective replication. File system replication managers can restrict replication to designated lists of files and directories. This can be useful for publishing data portions of which are location specific. Common data can be replicated to all secondary locations, while data specific to individual secondary locations can be replicated to those locations alone.

Nonidentical destination paths. Because file system replicators have access to directory information, each secondary location can specify a unique target path for storing replicated data.

Use of data at secondary locations. File system replicators replicate file open and close functionality at secondary locations. Since secondary locations have awareness of which replicated files are in use, applications at secondary locations can be allowed limited access to replicated file systems.

Storage Device Replication

With storage device replication, all blocks written to storage devices at the primary location are replicated to devices of equal capacity at each secondary location, without regard to the meaning of the data blocks being replicated. Device replication cannot distinguish between application updates to data, database journal updates, file system metadata updates, free space map updates, and so forth.

Since no file system or application context is associated with device replication, it is not generally possible to use device replicas at secondary locations while replication is occurring. This makes storage device replication most suitable for two general types of applications:

Data publication. Some organizations maintain data at a central (primary) location and publish it for use at multiple secondary locations. Web pages, price lists, product specifications, and other documents used at multiple business locations are prime examples of this kind of replication. A similar application is *data consolidation*, as when an enterprise's field offices send locally generated information to headquarters at the end of a business day or week.

Disaster recovery. A *disaster recovery site* is a secondary data center located far enough from the primary data center to continue operating if the primary data center experiences an unrecoverable disaster. Primary location storage device contents are replicated to devices at the disaster recovery site. If a disaster strikes the primary location, applications can be restarted quickly at the disaster recovery site, resuming processing using the (up-to-date) data replica.

Both of these application classes use secondary location data replicas *after* replication ceases rather than while it is occurring. This makes them well suited to storage device replication, which has low processing overhead at the primary site.

Replication Policies

Data replication is *policy based.* Its normal mode of operation is for administrators to define replication tasks that run either continuously or periodically. Replication implementations typically allow system administrators to define policies, including:

- The primary location files or devices to be replicated
- The secondary location file system or device targets
- The closeness of synchronization between primary and secondary locations
- Rules for handling brief network and secondary location outages

Once policies have been set, replication is typically automatic, requiring no intervention unless an exceptional event such as a network outage or site disaster occurs.

Synchronous and Asynchronous Replication

Most replication technologies permit a system administrator to choose between one of two options:

- *Synchronous replication,* with every application update at the primary location written and acknowledged by all secondary locations before it is regarded as complete.

- *Asynchronous replication,* with secondary location updates permitted to lag behind primary location application writes by a limited amount.

Synchronous replication simplifies the conversion of data at a secondary location into primary data after a disaster, because very little data is ever in the pipeline. But synchronous replication affects application performance adversely, because waiting for secondary location updates to complete results in longer response times. Asynchronous replication essentially eliminates network and secondary location performance (but not update logging) from application response time, but makes recovering data after a disaster more complex because secondary replicas can be slightly out of date.

Synchronous Replication

Replicated data at a secondary location is said to be *up to date* if it is identical to its primary location counterpart. For data to be up to date at every instant, all application updates must be replicated synchronously to all secondary locations. This means that each application update must be written both at the primary location and at all secondary locations before an application's write is considered complete.

If network links are busy or if the number of secondary locations is large, synchronous replication can result in unacceptably long application response times. One compromise that reduces application response time without sacrificing data integrity is to regard an application's write to a synchronously replicated object as complete when it has been:

- *Logged* at the primary site
- *Transmitted* to all secondary sites and acknowledged

Figure 9.3 shows a timeline for this optimization, indicating actions that may occur concurrently. With this strategy, an application write to a synchronously replicated device takes longer than a write to a nonreplicated device by:

- Local logging time (primarily disk I/O time)
- Data transmission to the most distant (in time) secondary location
- Time to receive an acknowledgment from the most distant location

As Figure 9.3 indicates, applications need not wait for disk I/O at the secondary location. The algorithm illustrated in Figure 9.3 secures data against two causes of replication failure.

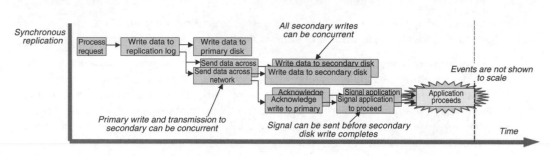

Figure 9.3   Optimized synchronous replication timeline.

- *Unrecoverable primary location disaster*, because a replica of every application update always exists at each secondary location.

- *Secondary location system or communications link failure*, because all updates are logged at the primary location and can be applied when the network or secondary location fault has been repaired.

Asynchronous Replication

Even when synchronous replication is optimized as previously described, peaks in application I/O rate, momentary network overloads, or simply a large number of secondary locations can make synchronous replication impractical from an application performance standpoint. *Asynchronous* replication is useful for these conditions.

With asynchronous replication, application write requests are considered complete as soon as the replicator at the primary location has logged them. Transmission to secondary locations occurs *asynchronously*, usually after application execution has continued. Figure 9.4 contrasts timelines for synchronous and asynchronous replication.

As Figure 9.4 illustrates, asynchronous replication reduces the total start-to-finish time for application write requests. Equally important, brief network overloads or outages

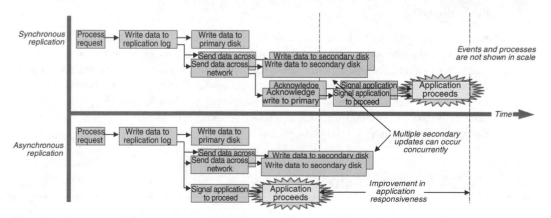

Figure 9.4   Comparison of synchronous and asynchronous replication.

do not *stall* application execution. Application execution continues as soon as updates are logged locally, independent of communication link and secondary location activity.

Asynchronously replicated updates are sent from the primary replication log to secondary locations as rapidly as network and secondary location loading permit. Transient network overloads eventually clear, allowing the primary location log to drain as secondary locations catch up. *Chronic* network overload results in unbounded primary log growth, however, and applications will eventually stall. Asynchronous replication insulates against short-term overloads and outages, but is not a substitute for inadequate steady-state network bandwidth.

The advantages of asynchronous replication are:

- *Better application response* (compared to synchronous replication)
- *Overload tolerance* from short-term network congestion
- *Fast recovery* after secondary location crashes or network outages

The disadvantage of asynchronous replication is that there are times when secondary location data is not completely up to date. If a secondary server or a communication link fails when replicated data is in this state, updates are transmitted from the primary log and written after the failure is repaired. If a primary location experiences an unrecoverable disaster, its replication log may not be retrievable; recovery at the secondary location starts with slightly out-of-date data.

To limit this exposure, asynchronous replicators typically limit the number of writes or maximum amount of time by which secondary locations may be out of date. When this limit is reached, application writes stall (i.e., no completion signal is given) until the amount of unsent data in the log falls below a permissible threshold.

Even though complete data consistency is not guaranteed, performance considerations usually make asynchronous replication an operational necessity, especially over long distances. Either momentary update overload or heavy network loading from other sources can increase application response times unacceptably with synchronous replication. Asynchronous replication eliminates network and secondary location delays from application response time, making replication practical where it otherwise might not be.

An outage thought to be temporary may become permanent, necessitating the transformation of a secondary location into the primary data center. If this occurs, some updates logged at the original primary location may be lost, because they had not yet been transmitted. It is therefore important that replication performs secondary location updates in the order in which data is written by applications at the primary location. This avoids the potential problem of an older update overwriting a newer one because the latter arrived later at a secondary location due to network congestion.

Using Data Replication

The characteristics of long distance data replication make it a very flexible failure and disaster recovery tool. Fully exploiting its benefits however, requires planning and design on the part of the administrator. The following sections describe some of the considerations that should enter into data center recovery planning.

Hybrid Data Recovery

If a primary location disaster occurs during asynchronous replication, secondary location data may be slightly out of date. At the instant of disaster, some updates that have been processed to completion at the primary location (possibly having resulted in consequent application or user actions) may have been in transit or logged for later delivery. Such updates are not reflected in the secondary location data used for disaster recovery. For example, if an electronic retail application has sent a message to a warehouse ordering shipment of goods, but the customer billing record is still in a replication queue when disaster strikes, a purchaser could receive goods without ever being billed for them.

Hybrid replication techniques using database or file system journals can sometimes assist with recovery under these circumstances. For example, Figure 9.5 illustrates database tables stored in replicated container files. These files are replicated asynchronously for performance reasons. The database *journals*, however, are replicated synchronously to different storage devices. A primary location disaster could result in loss of some database table updates. But, the replica of the database journal used to recover the database replica would be up to date, because it is replicated synchronously. The secondary location database replica can therefore be recovered to current status by reading the journal and applying the updates in it.

Disasters and Failures

With an up-to-date remote replica of vital data, an enterprise can resume processing data relatively soon after a site disaster. Up-to-date data outside the radius of disaster is a vital part of continued operation, but it is only a part. Other considerations, such as operating procedures, staff, communications, and transportation generally make it undesirable to move operations from a primary data center to a disaster recovery site

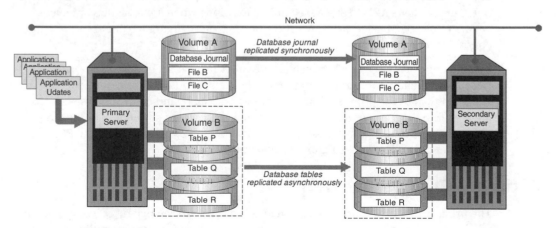

Figure 9.5   Hybrid replication strategy for a database.

unless there is a bona fide disaster. In general, it is preferable to treat system crashes and component failures as local problems if possible.

- *Mirroring* or RAID with automatic sparing is generally a more appropriate solution for local storage device failures.

- *Clustering* with automatic application failover (discussed in the following section) is generally a more appropriate solution for system crashes that leave a data center basically intact and able to function.

An important part of any disaster recovery strategy must be objective criteria for distinguishing among:

- *Local failures* of devices and systems that can be repaired locally.

- *Short-term failures* of communications or secondary location systems that may interrupt replication temporarily, but are ultimately recoverable.

- *More permanent disasters* of a duration that necessitate a secondary data center taking over the data processing workload.

Appropriate procedures for each of these scenarios should be outlined in a disaster recovery plan and tested.

Replication and Data Consistency

A database or file system's on-disk image is *transactionally consistent* when:

- No transactions are in progress.

- There is no unwritten data in cache.

Transactionally consistent file systems and databases are the most suitable source for both backups and disaster recovery replicas. Some applications have additional unique data consistency criteria that are impossible for a replicator to meet. Because data consistency can be application specific, some replicators incorporate application programming interfaces (APIs) that allow applications to send *in-band control* messages to secondary locations at specific points in a replicated data stream. An application can use these APIs to signal secondary locations when some significant event occurs (close of a business day, overflow of a log, etc.). Figure 9.6 illustrates in-band control of replication.

In-band control messages effectively freeze replication at secondary locations. Because replication preserves write order, data at secondary locations is frozen in a state identical to the primary location state when the in-band control message was injected into the data stream. A designated application at each secondary location receives the in-band control message, processes it, and uses a companion API to recommence replication, as Figure 9.6 illustrates.

Reciprocal Disaster Recovery

The primary and secondary replication location roles are relative to a given replication job. It is quite feasible for a server to be the primary location for one replica and a sec-

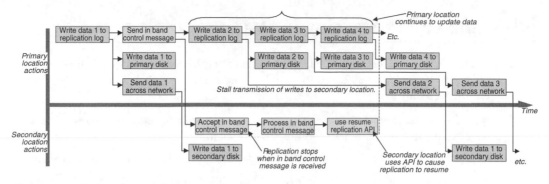

Figure 9.6 In-band control message timeline.

ondary location for another. Figure 9.7 illustrates how this can be exploited for *reciprocal disaster recoverability*.

The two servers illustrated in Figure 9.7 run applications A and B, respectively. Application A's data is replicated to storage devices connected to application B's server, and conversely. If either location is incapacitated, its application can be restarted on the server at the surviving location and work with up-to-date data.

As an enterprise deploys more application servers in different locations, it becomes increasingly prudent to consider a reciprocal disaster recovery strategy based on replication technology. Using data replication an enterprise can position itself for rapid resumption of operations when a disaster incapacitates an entire data center. The principle cost for this protection is an investment in the following hardware:

- Storage devices required for data replicas
- Incremental server processing and memory capacity to handle replication and provide adequate application performance in the event of failover
- Sufficient network and I/O bandwidth to accommodate replication traffic in addition to normal application traffic

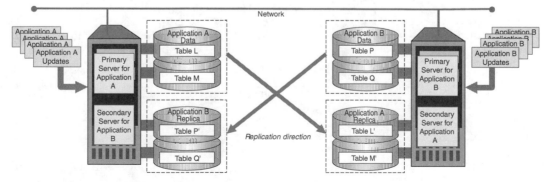

Figure 9.7 Reciprocal disaster recoverability.

Clusters: The Processing in Data Processing

In today's enterprises, highly available online data often isn't enough. Applications must also be highly available. Data centers must meet three challenging needs of the enterprises they serve:

■ *Continuous application service* to customers, partners, and employees, even if systems fail or entire data centers are incapacitated

■ *Application performance growth* as demand grows, with minimal service disruption

■ *Control over the quality of application service* through coordinated management of widely distributed data centers

Clustering technology can solve these modern enterprise-computing problems. Clustering coordinates the operation of several computers to enhance availability, scalability, or both, for applications and database managers. Figure 9.8 shows the principal architectural features that define an application or database cluster.

Data Center Clusters

For our purposes, a cluster is any set of interconnected servers whose operation is coordinated to achieve a beneficial effect. Figure 9.8 illustrates the basic features of an application or database cluster: a set of servers connected to common storage devices and accessible to all clients. Clusters are most often deployed to enhance application or database availability and to enable application and database performance to scale beyond the capacity of a single server. A given cluster technology may be designed primarily to enhance availability or to support application scaling, but, in fact, most clusters provide both benefits in some measure.

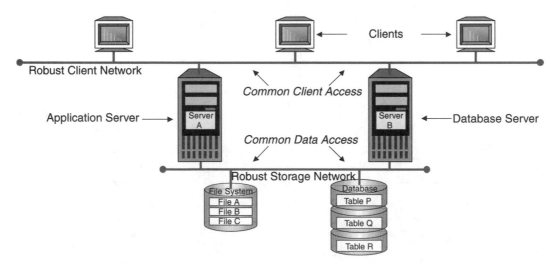

Figure 9.8   Basic data center cluster model.

As the number of servers in a typical data center proliferates, a third reason for deploying clustering begins to emerge. Some cluster implementations allow multiple servers to be managed from a single console. Especially in larger data centers, lower management cost can be a significant benefit.

Data Center Clusters in Perspective

Data processing availability and scaling requirements have motivated the development of a broad range of failure-tolerant, scalable clustering technologies at different levels in the data center. Most enterprise data centers could benefit from the application of clustering techniques throughout. Figure 9.9 illustrates a data center system that employs clustering technology at least at three different levels.

Client requests entering the system represented in Figure 9.9 are received by a set of cooperating network routers that use load balancing technology to distribute them across a number of application servers. While the routers' primary function is to distribute incoming load evenly across application resources, this technology is also failure tolerant. If a router fails, the other routers redistribute the load among them.

The network routers depicted in Figure 9.9 distribute client requests among a cluster of application servers that access a common set of data. This technology allows an

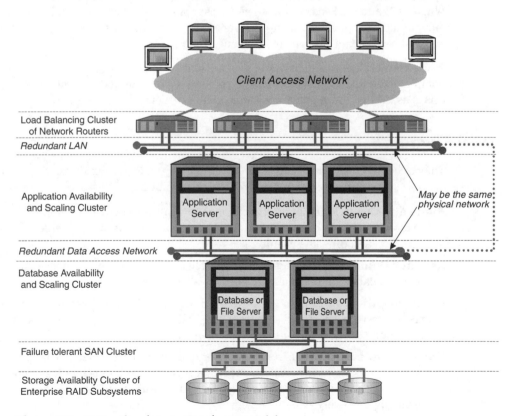

Figure 9.9   Enterprise data center cluster model.

application to service load levels that are beyond the capacity of a single server. In addition, if an application server fails, it stops responding to the network routers, which redistribute the workload among the remaining application servers.

In the model depicted in Figure 9.9, shared data access is provided by the third tier in the server hierarchy—a cluster of database or file servers. Different file servers and database managers use different mechanisms to cooperate with each other, but the net effect is that data manager instances running in the servers at this tier cooperate to form a cluster that coordinates data access requests, ensuring data consistency. Again, at this level, failure of one of the data access servers typically results in application data access load being redistributed across the remaining servers.

The data access servers in Figure 9.9 access their storage through a SAN. In this case, a failure-tolerant SAN is represented, providing redundant switches or directors and redundant paths to all devices. Of course, as switches or directors are added to the network, the overall performance of the SAN also increases. Thus, access to storage also offers both enhanced availability and scaling.

Finally, in systems of this scale and complexity, failure-tolerant scalable RAID subsystems are generally regarded as a requirement. Features such as disk and path failure tolerance, mirrored write-back cache, hardware performance assists, and controller failover that are typical of these subsystems would justify the name *storage clusters*. When SAN-attached and combined with host-controlled clusterwide volume management and data replication, failure-tolerant storage subsystems provide a robust, scalable enterprise data storage environment.

While systems like that depicted in Figure 9.9 are complex, they provide the kind of completely scalable, highly available client/server computing that is vital to enterprises as they go electronic and become global in their business scope.

Why Clusters?

The concept of clustering is attractive to computer users because it has the potential to solve some of the long-standing problems in computing:

Application continuity. If a server fails or an application crashes, another server in the cluster can take over its workload, because all servers are connected to the same data and the same clients.

Network failure ride-through. If network links fail, clients can use alternate paths to access data and continue to operate.

Accommodation of growth. If the demands of an application become too great for existing servers, additional servers can be added and the workload can be redistributed among the new, larger server complement.

Management cost control. As the number of clustered servers in a data center grows, much of system management remains centralized, thus helping to control the cost of the one information services resource whose price-performance ratio doesn't double every year—people.

Disaster recoverability. If an entire data center is incapacitated, remote computers coupled to the cluster can take over its workload and network names and resume processing using a replica of online data.

Clustering technology has solutions for all of these problems. Clusters of up to 32 interconnected servers that protect each other from failure and are managed as a unit are not uncommon. Coupled with data sharing technology, clustering enables several instances of an application running on different servers to cooperate, increasing overall throughput well beyond that of a single server. Long-distance clusters enable enterprises to recover the ability to process data after a data center disaster.

Applications and Clusters

Since clustering essentially enhances application properties, a reasonable starting point is to understand an application as a typical cluster manager sees it—as a *service* provided by a *group* of interrelated system *resources*.[1] For example, a Web application service group might consist of:

- *Disks* on which the served Web pages are stored

- *Volumes* built from the disks

- A *file system* that adds structure to the volume

- A *database* whose tables are files in the file system and whose rows contain pointers to Web page files

- The *network interface cards* (NICs) used to export the Web service to clients

- One or more *IP addresses* associated with the Web service

- The Web server *application program* and associated code libraries

Cluster managers make use of two significant aspects of this service group view of an application:

- For a service to run on a particular server, all the resources it requires must be available to that server. The service group is a convenient mechanism for a cluster manager to determine the set of required resources.

- The resources constituting a service have *interdependencies*. Some resources (e.g., volumes) must be operational before others (e.g., file systems) can become operational. Similarly, when shutting down, some resources (e.g., file systems) must be stopped before others (e.g., volumes) can be stopped cleanly.

It is convenient to visualize a service group as a graph in which nodes represent resources and edges represent dependencies. Figure 9.10 shows a resource dependency graph for the Web application service group just described.

---

[1] While the descriptions of clustering in this book are meant to be universal, clustering technology does not yet have a widely accepted common body of terminology. The authors have adopted terminology that is in use and that seems to fit the concepts being described, with due apologies to technology developers who feel that their terminology is more representative.

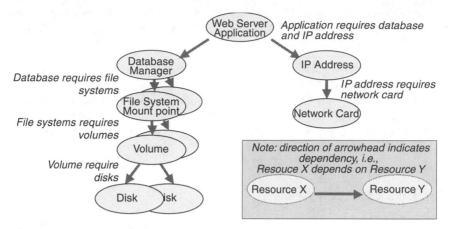

Figure 9.10   Resource dependency graph.

In Figure 9.10, arrowheads point to *child nodes* that represent resources required for other resources (*parent nodes*) to function. Volume resources require that disk resources be online, file system resources require volumes, and so forth.

The resource dependency graph in Figure 9.10 has two independent subtrees, rooted in the database manager and IP address, respectively. The Web application requires both database manager and IP address to function; but the database manager and IP address are independent of each other. Resource dependencies are important when a service group is starting or stopping, because independent resources can be started and stopped concurrently, whereas dependent ones must be started and stopped in sequence. Referring to Figure 9.10, the disk and network card resources can be started concurrently, as can their respective parent resources. The Web server application cannot start until both database manager and IP address have started, however. The more independent resources a service group has, the faster it can start and stop.

Kinds of Resources

There are two types of cluster resources: *movable resources* that move when the application moves to another server and *permanent resources* instantiated on each server eligible to run the application. For example, an application's data and the SAN-attached storage devices on which it is stored are movable resources. If the application starts on an alternate server, that server would take control of the storage devices. By contrast, network cards are permanently installed in servers. For an application to start on an alternate server, that server must have a network card designated as a resource in the application's group. As a third example, an IP address used by clients to communicate with an application would migrate to an alternate server with the application.

Starting and Stopping Resources

Cluster managers monitor application resources (discovered from graphs such as that depicted in Figure 9.10) and execute administrator-defined policies when events requiring action occur. For example, a service group may start up automatically when the cluster itself starts. A cluster manager uses resource graphs such as that to determine resource start order.

A cluster manager starts a service by activating resources represented by leaf nodes in its resource dependency graph. Referring to Figure 9.10, for example, a cluster manager would activate the disks and network card concurrently because they do not depend on each other. As soon as the disks were online, the cluster manager would activate the volume; as soon as the network card was online, the cluster manager would activate the IP address that depends on it, and so forth. The Web application would not start until both the database and IP address resources were active.

Similarly, when deactivating a service, a cluster manager begins at the top of the graph. In the example of Figure 9.10, a cluster manager would stop the Web application first, followed by the database and IP address (concurrently), and so forth.

Dependencies among Services

Some cluster managers recognize interdependencies between entire service groups. For example, it may be inappropriate for two services to run at the same time, as with test and production versions of an application. Alternatively, an application service might require another, as, for example, a shipping application that sends messages to an invoicing application when items are shipped. Relationships like these are expressed in *service group* graphs similar to that of Figure 9.10, but specifying interdependencies among services. Cluster managers enforce these dependencies. For example, a cluster manager may be configured to prevent both test and production versions of an application from running at the same time or to require that an invoicing application be running before allowing a shipping application to start.

Failover Services

The most frequent reason for encapsulating an application in a cluster service group is to support *failover* (restart on an alternate server) if the server running the application fails. All of a cluster's servers have access to resource dependency graphs. When an application fails, the server designated as its *failover server* (i.e., the server on which it is to be restarted) detects the failure because it is monitoring the service group. When a failure is detected, the failover server refers to the application's resource dependency graph to determine the order in which resources must be started.

Some cluster managers support *cascading* application failover from server to server in sequence. To configure an application for cascading failover, an administrator designates an ordered list of servers eligible to run the service. Referring to Figure 9.11, an application might be configured to run on Servers A, B, and C, in that order. If Server A is operational, the cluster manager would start the application on it. If Server A were to fail, the cluster manager would restart the application on Server B. If Server B were to fail while Server A was still down, the cluster manager would restart the application on Server C. Since the application is not eligible to run on Server D, it does not run unless at least one of Servers A, B, and C is operating.

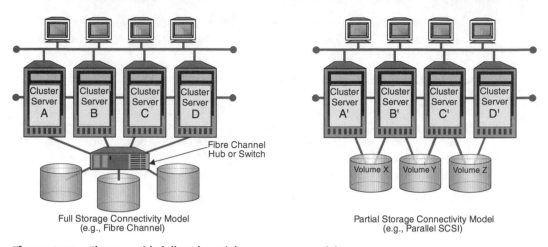

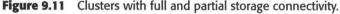

Full Storage Connectivity Model
(e.g., Fibre Channel)

Partial Storage Connectivity Model
(e.g., Parallel SCSI)

Figure 9.11 Clusters with full and partial storage connectivity.

For a server to run an application, all of the required resources must be accessible. Limited access to storage can limit the selection of servers on which an application can run. Figure 9.11 illustrates *partial storage connectivity* with local storage and contrasts it with the full connectivity of SAN-attached storage.

- With *full storage connectivity*, every server in the cluster has a direct physical connection to all storage devices in the cluster.

- With *partial storage connectivity*, not all servers are directly accessible by all storage devices.

With full storage connectivity, any server in a cluster can be a failover server for any application. Thus, in the cluster on the left of Figure 9.11, an application service that normally runs on Server A could fail over to Server B, Server C, or Server D. In the cluster represented on the right of Figure 9.11, however, an application that normally runs on Server A' could fail over to Server B', but not to the other servers, because they have no access to its data.

Similarly, an application service that normally runs on Server B' could fail over to Server A' if it depends only on Volume X, or to Server C' if it depends only on Volume Y. If the application uses both Volume X and Volume Y, it cannot fail over at all in this configuration.

This example illustrates the SAN connectivity advantage. In a SAN with full storage connectivity, such considerations do not arise. Application configuration is much simpler and the range of failures against which protection can be offered is greater.

Parallel Application Service Groups

To support application growth beyond the capacity of a single server, some cluster managers implement *parallel* application service groups. Multiple instances of a paral-

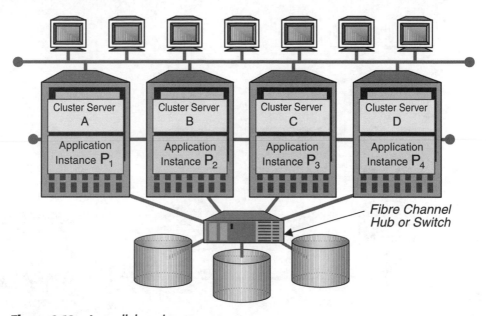

Figure 9.12   A parallel service group.

lel service group can run on different servers at the same time. Figure 9.12 illustrates a cluster configured to run a parallel application service on four servers.

Figure 9.12 represents a cluster running an instance of application service P on each of its four servers. Since applications essentially process data, this scenario immediately raises the question of how multiple application instances running on different servers coordinate their accesses to a common data pool.

Some parallel applications operate on separate copies of what is nominally the same data. As each instance of the application updates data, the copies inevitably drift out of synchronization. Such applications require periodic data resynchronization. Figure 9.13 illustrates parallel applications processing separate copies of data with periodic reconciliation.

Cluster applications such as that illustrated in Figure 9.13 are obviously best suited to applications in which there is little interaction between individual data updates or no updating at all. Web servers often have this characteristic. An online retail sales application that processes and records sales records might run as a parallel application service. If the retail application were to update a common inventory file, however, and provide customers with shipping schedules based on current inventory, this configuration would not be suitable, because all servers would need read-write access to the same inventory information.

Increasingly, parallel applications require concurrent read-write access to shared file systems or databases. There are three basic techniques for sharing data among the instances of a parallel application in a cluster:

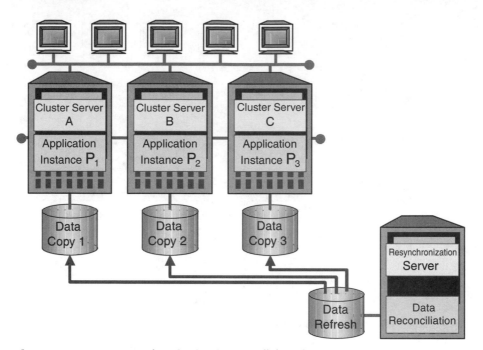

Figure 9.13 Data resynchronization in a parallel application.

- *The application* itself may take responsibility for coordinating concurrent accesses to shared data. In this case, the data access semantics are completely application dependent.

- *A shared file system* (described later in this chapter) may be used to coordinate access to files. Well-understood file system access rules (for example, whether multiple concurrent writers are acceptable) govern application file accesses across the clusters. In this scenario, coordination of accesses to data *within* files remains the responsibility of the application instances.

- *A shared database manager* may be used to coordinate access to data stored in a cluster database. Instances of a database manager operating on different servers cooperate with each other to coordinate accesses to database data and preserve typical database access semantics (for example, locking records that are read with the intention of updating).

There are two types of shared databases, using *partitioned* and *common* data, respectively. A partitioned shared database makes each database instance responsible for accesses to a slice of the database. For example, the cluster illustrated in Figure 9.13 might equally run a partitioned shared database, with Server A responsible for the first 1,000,000 records, Server B responsible for records 1,000,001 to 2,000,000, and Server C for records 2,000,001 to 9,999,999. Application requests would be fielded by the database instance on the server on which the request was made and transmitted to the responsible server for execution. For example, a request for database record 1,250,909 made by an application instance on Server A would be transmitted to Server B for execution, with the results being returned to Server A for relaying to the requesting application.

A common data shared database is one in which all instances of the database manager operate on the same physical copy of the database. Such database managers must coordinate among themselves to avoid situations in which two or more instances are updating the same data records at the same time. This is typically done using high-speed interconnects to pass locking information back and forth among the instances. A common data shared database requires a SAN for common data access.

Partitioned data shared databases do not inherently require SANs; Indeed, their development may derive largely from application needs for database scaling that preceded the widespread availability of universal storage interconnection. They have the further advantage of minimizing network traffic among different database manager instances, and they scale well as long as database accesses remain balanced across the instances. High availability is a challenge with the partitioned data shared database model. In most instances it is achieved by database manager slice-by-slice replication of the database to other database instances running on different servers.

Common data shared databases do require SANs because all database manager instances process the same copy of the data. The common data model balances the load more flexibly, because all database manager instances are capable of accessing all data. On the other hand, it is easier for common data shared databases to saturate their I/O resources, and for record-locking traffic to overwhelm the interconnect between servers. High availability is easy with common data shared databases because failure of an instance can be worked around by redirecting requests made to that instance to a surviving database instance.

Managing Cluster Resources

A cluster manager needs three controls over cluster resources:

- *Start*. The cluster manager must be able to make the resource available for use by parent resources in its application service group.

- *Stop*. Similarly, the cluster manager must be able to stop a resource from operating in the course of stopping its service group.

- *Monitor*. The cluster manager must be able to determine whether a resource is operating properly, so that the operational status of service groups can be determined and failover decisions made.

Obviously, the actions required to start, stop, and monitor different types of resources differ significantly. Activating a disk, for example, might require issuing a spin-up command, whereas activating a database would require running the database manager main process and issuing the appropriate start command(s). From a cluster manager's point of view, the same result is achieved: A cluster resource becomes available. However, the actions performed to achieve the result are quite different.

Cluster managers typically handle the functional disparity among resources by supporting resource-specific *agents*—software modules with entry points that can be invoked by the cluster manager to start, stop, and monitor the resources they control. When invoked, each agent performs whatever actions are necessary to control its particular type of resource.

A cluster manager invokes these resource agent entry points in the appropriate sequence to start and stop application services, to perform application service *failover* (essentially a stop followed by a start on another server), and to monitor resource state.

A well-defined cluster resource agent architecture decouples agent development from that of the cluster manager itself. To support a particular type of resource, a developer develops an agent for the resource independently of the cluster manager. This structure makes it possible for multiple developers to integrate capabilities into cluster frameworks. This is particularly important for commercial application software, which often has unique requirements for startup (particularly after a dirty shutdown caused by a system crash) that could not easily be incorporated into an application-independent cluster framework.

Cluster Interconnects

Cluster functionality requires intercommunication among cluster manager instances. Clusters are typically interconnected in three ways:

- *Client.* In order to serve the same applications to clients, the servers constituting a cluster must be connected to the clients. Increasingly, client interconnection uses either the enterprise network or the Web.

- *Storage.* Similarly, if servers are to be alternate execution sites for an application, or are to run an instance of a parallel application processing shared data, they must have a common connection to the application's data.

- *Cluster.* The servers in a cluster must be able to intercommunicate in order to exchange state information and initiate failovers when required.

While some clustering technologies support different physical interconnects for each of these purposes, it is equally common to find cluster interconnection sharing a physical interconnect with client connections (typically Ethernet) or the storage interconnect (typically a Fibre Channel SAN).

Because one of the main reasons for installing a cluster is to enhance application availability, all cluster interconnects should ideally be redundant. A highly available application that is unable to deliver its services because it can't communicate with clients or that can't start because it can't access its data is of little use.

A redundant cluster interconnect also mitigates a generic clustering problem sometimes called the *split brain*. This problem arises because it is impossible for a server in a cluster to distinguish between failure of another server with which it is communicating and failure of the interconnect between the two.

Without a means of distinguishing server failure from interconnect failure, a cluster manager cannot safely initiate application failover. If it does, there is a risk that two servers that cannot intercommunicate will both be running the same application processing the same data with no coordination between them. This circumstance, if allowed to occur, would almost certainly result in data corruption. Redundant interconnects for cluster intercommunication reduce the probability of split brain, although they do not entirely eliminate it.

Client and Storage Interconnects for Clusters

For management simplicity, the servers in a cluster should be connected to the same clients and should be able to access the same storage. Clusters with parallel SCSI-attached storage are normally limited to four or fewer servers, because parallel SCSI's fixed-priority bus arbitration tends to result in *starvation* if more than four I/O initiators (servers) share a bus. Moreover, a parallel SCSI bus can interconnect a maximum of 16 devices (computers, disks, tapes, or RAID subsystems). Adding more servers to a SCSI-based cluster reduces the number of storage devices that can be connected— exactly the opposite of scaling. Storage area networks essentially eliminate storage connectivity limitations. A switched Fibre Channel *fabric* allows a theoretical maximum of 2^{24} devices to be interconnected.

Storage Devices for Clusters

In principle, any type of multihosted storage device, including directly attached disks, can be used for cluster data storage. But the main purpose of clustering is robust, scalable data processing so highly available storage devices with multiple access paths are most appropriate. Many clusters are configured using failure-tolerant external RAID subsystems for storage. In some cases, these subsystems must be integrated with clustering software so that failover of storage devices is done properly. Even though RAID subsystems nominally emulate SCSI or Fibre Channel disks, switching control of logical units from one server to another often requires device-specific actions. Where this is the case, the cluster agent construct can be used to provide the necessary functionality.

Cluster Data Models

Only the server running a single-instance application needs access to the application's data. When failover to another server occurs, control of the data moves to the failover server, but there is never a time when two or more servers are accessing the application's data concurrently. In fact, some clustering technologies do not even support concurrent data access. The term *shared-nothing cluster* is often used to describe clusters that do not support concurrent access to data from multiple servers.

Shared-nothing clusters are adequate for single-instance applications, as well as for multi-instance applications that have no need to share data (e.g., read-only Web servers). Shared-nothing clusters also make suitable platforms for partitioned shared databases.

Most business applications essentially maintain records by updating files or databases. For these applications to scale using clustering technology, it is vital that every instance read and write the same data image so that all updates are instantly visible throughout the cluster. For these applications, a cluster must enable multiple servers to mount a single file system or open a single database at the same time. Moreover, application instances must be able to read and write data in the shared file system or database without fear of incorrect results due to other instances' actions.

Uncoordinated access by application instances running on different servers can cause data corruption in a variety of ways. Suppose, for example, that an online sales application updates a running total of daily sales volume. Each time a sale is made, the current daily sales total is read from storage, the amount of the new sale is added to it, and the result is written back to the same storage location. Figure 9.14 illustrates one way in which two instances of this application running on different servers might result in an incorrect daily sales total.

The data corruption problem illustrated in Figure 9.14 can occur because the application instances running on the two servers are unaware of each other. When instance P_2 reads the daily sales total, it is unaware that instance P_1 has already read and *cached* the total with the intent of updating it. For correct operation, both instances' read-modify-rewrite sequences must be *atomic;* that is, each sequence must occur in its entirety without any intervening operations on the daily sales total record.

Distributed Lock Management

If the application instances performing these updates were running in the same computer, a file system or database manager with support for *multiple simultaneous writers* would provide for correct operation. Such data managers *lock* or temporarily reserve access to, blocks in a file or records in a database to prevent simultaneous updates by two or more processes.

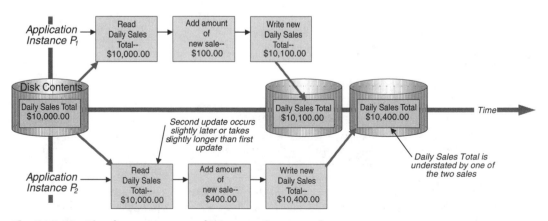

Figure 9.14 Simultaneous access data corruption scenario.

If the processes represented in Figure 9.14 are running in different computers, *distributed* lock management is required. While a local lock manager maintains information about locked data items in memory data structures, distributed lock manager instances in each cooperating server exchange messages to signal the locking and unlocking of data items. File system instances in separate servers that cooperate using distributed lock management are collectively called a *cluster file system*. Most database managers support similar functionality with built-in distributed lock managers designed specifically for database objects.

Server-Based Volume Management and Clusters

As Chapter 8 describes, a *volume* is a collection of disks presented to file systems and databases as one or more disk-like entities with more desirable I/O performance and availability properties. The role of a volume manager is twofold:

- Convert each read or write request to the volume into one or more storage device I/O commands, issue those commands, and manage the resulting data flow.

- Implement striping, mirroring, or RAID algorithms that improve performance and protect against data loss due to storage device failure.

Unlike a file system, a volume manager does not restrict access to data. Any application or data manager that can secure the right to access a volume from its operating system is permitted to read or write any block in the volume's user data area. What a server-based volume manager *does* do is:

- Ensure that every write to the volume is converted to the I/O commands necessary to maintain the volume's failure tolerance (e.g., every write to a mirrored volume results in write commands to all of the volume's disks).

- Maintain a consistent view of volume state—which disks or parts of disks make up a volume, their operational status, and how data is organized on them.

Within a single server, a volume manager is in the path of every I/O request and management operation. This enables it to reproduce disk-like semantics, for example, by ensuring that read and write requests to overlapping block ranges are processed atomically. Similarly, when an administrator issues a command to extend a volume's capacity, a volume manager allocates additional storage and updates the persistent data structures that describe the volume. The volume manager does this in a manner that (1) is recoverable from system crashes and (2) presents a consistent external view of the volume throughout execution of the command.

Volume Management in Clusters

For a volume to be cluster-accessible, a consistent view of its contents and state must be presented to all of the cluster's servers. Thus, for example, if two applications issue uncoordinated writes to overlapping volume block ranges, either write may occur first, as would be the case with a disk, but the volume must always reflect the results

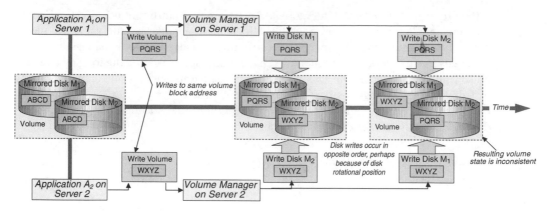

Figure 9.15 Cluster volume data corruption scenario.

of complete writes as would a disk. Figure 9.15 illustrates an example of unacceptable behavior—a mirrored volume that becomes internally inconsistent because writes to its two disks execute in different order.

Figure 9.15 illustrates two nearly simultaneous writes to the same block range of a mirrored volume from different servers. The volume manager instance on each server converts the volume writes into pairs of disk writes. Unless the two volume manager instances coordinate their activities, the order in which disk write commands are executed can result in inconsistent contents on the volume's two disks.

Similarly, if volume manager instances running on two servers in a cluster attempt to reconfigure a volume, for example, by extending its capacity, updates to the volume's on-disk metadata must be carefully coordinated so that scenarios similar to those illustrated in Figures 9.14 and 9.15 do not occur.

There are two basic cluster volume manager architectures: *master/slave* and *symmetric*. In a master/slave architecture, the *master* server performs all metadata changes to a volume. Other *slave* servers in the cluster request any metadata changes they require from the master server. Typically, a master server blocks access during metadata updates, so that changes appear simultaneously to all servers. Thus, all servers have the same view of a volume at all times. Figure 9.16 illustrates master/slave cluster volume manager architecture.

With master/slave cluster volume manager architecture, failure of a volume's master server could make metadata updates impossible. Practically speaking, therefore, *any* instance of a cluster volume manager with master/slave architecture must be able to become a master in case of a failure. In typical implementations, surviving volume manager instances negotiate among themselves to determine which will become the master when an established master fails.

The alternative to master/slave cluster volume manager architecture is a *symmetric* model, in which any volume manager instance in the cluster can update volume meta-

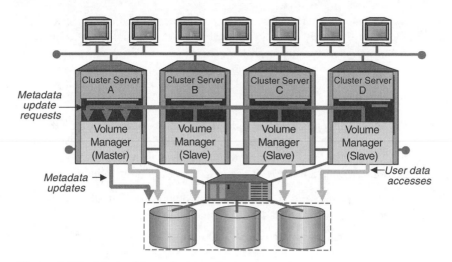

Figure 9.16 Master/slave cluster volume manager.

data directly. As with the master/slave model, all servers must see the same view of a volume at all times, so any server updating metadata would have to block access to its volume during the update, just as with the master/slave model. Figure 9.17 illustrates symmetric cluster volume manager architecture.

As Figure 9.17 suggests, a symmetric cluster volume manager instance must lock access to a volume before updating its metadata in order to present a consistent vol-

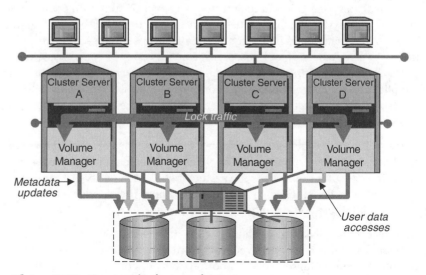

Figure 9.17 Symmetric cluster volume manager.

ume view to all servers in the cluster. Since volume metadata changes are relatively infrequent, the complexity of the symmetric architecture is difficult to justify, and so symmetric cluster volume managers are seldom encountered, although they do exist.

Cluster File Systems

For parallel cluster applications (or indeed, for any set of applications that run in a cluster and access related data) to share access to a file system without risk of data corruption, a *cluster file system* is required. The issues in clusterwide access to a single file system are quite similar to those of cluster volume management:

- File system metadata updates must be coordinated so that all servers in the cluster have a consistent view of the file system at all times.

- File read and write semantics must be the same as those of a single-instance file system.

As with volume managers, cluster file systems are implemented using both master/slave and symmetric architectures to coordinate updates and provide a consistent view of files across a cluster.

Typically, applications and users create, extend, and delete files and directories much more frequently than they change volume configurations. File system metadata therefore changes much more frequently than volume metadata. A symmetric architecture in which all servers access storage devices directly would seem to be advantageous. Not only is each server's path to metadata shorter (there is no intermediate server to be contacted as illustrated in Figure 9.16), but the processing and I/O load of file system metadata updates is distributed across all of the cluster's servers.

This analysis ignores the effect of lock traffic, however. Just as with a volume manager, a cluster file system instance must lock access to metadata before updating it. Applications that manipulate files frequently can cause a symmetric cluster file system to generate large numbers of lock messages. Not only do these messages flood the cluster interconnect, waiting for file system operations to complete but they can also block application execution. So the trade-off between master/slave and symmetric cluster file system architectures is much less clear than the corresponding volume manager trade-off. Both file system models have been implemented.

In a master/slave cluster file system, the master instance performs all metadata updates. Slave instances communicate applications' metadata update requests to the master, which executes them. Thus file system metadata integrity is guaranteed because all updates flow through a single point without the extensive locking traffic a symmetric architecture could imply.

File systems provide disk-like semantics when data is written. This means, for example, that when simultaneous write requests from two applications modify overlapping file block ranges, the result when both writes are complete may reflect either request, but does not reflect parts of both. This effectively means that when an application writes data to a range of file blocks, other applications must be restricted from accessing those blocks for the duration of the write. Cluster file systems must lock access to block ranges during updates in order to reproduce this behavior. This is especially important with applications that were not developed with awareness of cluster properties (which today includes virtually all applications). Virtually all applications depend on single-server file system semantics. If they are to execute correctly in clusters, the cluster file system must reproduce single-server behavior.

One important way in which file systems differ from volume managers is that the former derive part of their I/O performance from caching data in server memory, either in anticipation of future requests (*read caching*) or to optimize write scheduling and application responsiveness (*write-back caching*). In a cluster, data cached by each file system instance must be *coherent*—an application read request should return the same data no matter which server in the cluster executes it. For example, if Server A holds a block of data in its cache and Server B updates the same block of data on disk, the contents of Server A's cache are no longer valid. Server A must be made to recognize that if an application requests that block of data, the block's new contents must be read from disk, because the image in cache is no longer current.

Cluster file systems typically use the cluster interconnect to keep file system cache coherent. When a server broadcasts its intent to update a data block, other servers in the cluster with cached copies of that block *invalidate* their cached copies. If the block is subsequently requested by an application, it is read from disk.

The Significance of Shared Data Clusters

Cluster-aware volume managers and file systems broaden the applicability of cluster technology. Without clusterwide access to data, parallel applications are limited to those that do not require clusterwide updating of data (e.g., read-only Web servers) or those designed so that each instance updates its own copy of data, with periodic reconciliation. Read-only applications obviously solve only a limited class of problems; applications that must pause to reconcile data periodically are inherently not continuously available.

Cluster volume managers and file systems make it possible for application instances to access the same data concurrently, enabling the transaction processing applications that constitute the majority of commercial data processing to operate as parallel cluster applications, scaling beyond the capacity of any single server.

A cluster that supports application scaling is automatically highly available as well. Instances of a parallel application do not typically restart when a server fails. Continued client access is provided by rerouting requests to a surviving application instance. Often, client requests to parallel applications are dynamically routed by load balancing routers or cluster software. With a load balancer, failure of an application server causes client requests to be redistributed among the remaining servers.

Disaster Recovery and Global Clusters

Today, data processing operations tend to become global in scope much more quickly than in the past. As an enterprise globalizes, continuous availability becomes even more of a challenge:

- The high application availability provided by clusters is no longer enough—the cost of a sitewide disaster that incapacitates an entire data center for a long period may be outright failure of the enterprise.

- If a global enterprise conducts data processing operations from one data center, some of its users will necessarily be far from applications in terms of message transit time, resulting in poor response time and susceptibility to local competition.

- Management of global data processing operations can become prohibitively expensive and in a rapidly changing environment, downright impossible. Procedural consistency can be difficult to attain with wide geographic separation.

Some vendors are combining clustering technology with storage replication and specialized management capabilities as a means of addressing these problems. While they are sometimes positioned as global cluster technologies, these packages have unique capabilities that are required by the problems they are designed to solve.

Coordinating application execution and data replication over long distances introduces functionality and performance issues that are not present with clusters within a data center.

Failover triggers. Within a data center, failing an application over from one server to another usually happens either because the server failed or because an administrator forced the failover to perform maintenance. In an integrated global computing facility, other reasons for failover are possible. For example, an application might run at one location during business hours at that location and move to another location for the next shift. Worldwide integration requires the ability to define a wide variety of events and mechanisms for reacting to them.

Heartbeating. One function of cluster manager instances is to continually monitor each others' status by watching for periodic *heartbeat* messages at regular intervals. Absence of one or more heartbeat messages starts the process of determining whether a server has failed. Within a data center, guaranteed regular heartbeats are relatively straightforward, because distances between servers are short, links are very reliable, and dedicated links are affordable. On a global scale, regular heartbeats cannot generally be guaranteed except at prohibitive cost (e.g., by using a dedicated satellite link for heartbeat messages). To support cluster-like capability on a global scale, a more flexible heartbeating mechanism is required. Not only must more variation in timing be tolerable, but the very facility used to signal between widely separated sites must be flexible.

Application access. Applications typically export their services over virtual network links identified with IP addresses. Clients locate these addresses by querying a

Domain Name Service (DNS) server using a symbolic name (e.g., accounting. bigcompany.com). The DNS server responds with an IP address of the service. If an application fails over in a cluster within a data center, the IP address of the failed server can be taken over by the failover server. Existing clients renew their connections to the service at the same IP address and resume operating. In a global system, this is usually not possible. If an application moves between two widely separated locations, it is almost certain that the application's IP address will have to change, making DNS entries that point to the old address obsolete. It is necessary, therefore, to update DNS servers to point to an application's new location (expressed in its IP address) when a wide-area location change occurs. Global high-availability system software must provide for DNS servers to be updated as part of moving an application from one location to another.

Failover impact. In a well-designed data center, failover only impacts resources within the center. Clustered servers are close to each other, with SAN connections to data. Clients, even if connected to redundant routed networks, are usually accessible from network switches or routers that are under control of the data center. In most cases, the same operations personnel, offline storage media, and supplies serve the failover server. Moving an application's execution site across a wide area has none of these properties and therefore cannot be done casually. In many instances, human judgment is a requirement in the failover decision path. Global high-availability system software must allow for human interaction at all stages of failover or application migration for whatever purpose.

Heterogeneity. Today's information technology buying patterns make it highly likely for an enterprise with global operations to be operating servers made by different manufacturers, running different operating systems and, indeed, even different clustering technologies. Integrating these into a global computing facility, even if only for management purposes, requires management tools that can bring diverse management capabilities together into a single global management console with universal paradigms that map to different systems' capabilities.

Figure 9.18 illustrates a hypothetical model for a global computing facility.

Figure 9.18 depicts two sites, Site I and Site II, located at a distance from each other. The distance is assumed to be such as to require:

- Wide area, possibly routed networking
- Different operations staffs
- Data replication rather than real-time mirroring for maintaining common data images

Figure 9.18 illustrates the usefulness of the concept of a *site* (a physically proximate collection of possibly clustered computing resources) as distinguished from a cluster of cooperating computers with common attachment to clients and storage. The figure also postulates a site master, a server or cluster that is:

- Connected to other sites in the global computing facility
- Connected to all systems at the site that are part of the global computing facility

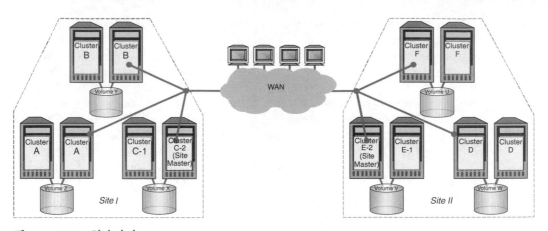

Figure 9.18   Global cluster.

The site master concept simplifies the global awareness requirements on all other servers and clusters at a site. In Figure 9.18, Server C-2 of Cluster C is the site master for Site I and Server E-2 of Cluster E is the site master for Site II. The site master is the conduit through which information about a site's clusters is communicated throughout the global system.

In an integrated global computing facility, someone has to be in charge. Available architectures typically task one site master as a *global master*. The global master server is typically the only server to issue commands that affect the global facility. This philosophy prevents redundant commands from being issued, largely due to the variable latencies inherent in global networks. Obviously, if a global master server fails, an alternate must be designated. One possibility is for the remaining site master servers to negotiate an alternate global master. Another is for a sequence of global masters to be predesignated by installation policy.

Each cluster in an integrated global computing facility typically operates according to its normal policies as defined by local administrators. Superimposed on local policies, however, are facilities that allow for the following global management techniques to be employed:

- *Remote cluster management*, so that a worldwide collection of interconnected heterogeneous systems and clusters can be managed from a single console.

- *Heartbeats between sites*, possibly using user-defined mechanisms appropriate to network facilities or applications, so that failure of entire sites can be detected.

- *Automated event-driven policies* that allow application service groups to migrate between clusters or between sites to support both disaster recovery and time-based or ad hoc migration of applications.

In general, integrated global computing facilities automate and support the management of worldwide networks of heterogeneous systems and clusters from a single console.

Global Computing and Disaster Recovery

When combined with long-distance data replication as described earlier in this chapter, integrated global data processing facilities can automatically recover from site disasters. Figure 9.19 illustrates a hypothetical disaster recovery scenario using a combination of volume-level data replication and *global clustering*.

In Figure 9.19, Clusters P and Q are widely separated. Data from Cluster P's Volume X is replicated to Cluster Q's Volume Y across a wide area network. The I/O latency implied by the long distance requires that replication be asynchronous, so as not to affect application response time adversely. Application P_1 can run on any of Cluster P's servers and fail over within the cluster using cluster mechanisms.

Similarly, Application Q_1 is eligible to run on any of Cluster Q's servers and fail over within Cluster Q using cluster mechanisms. Application Q_1 might consist of:

- A script to stop replication, disengage Volume Y as a secondary replica, and remount it as a local read/write volume for Application Q_1's use

- A script or program to perform any necessary application-dependent data recovery (e.g., log playback) before Application P_1 is restarted

- Execution of the program image(s) for Application Service P_1

With global clustering technology, these two clusters can form an integrated global computing system. The servers within each cluster exchange local cluster heartbeats. In addition to this, designated *site master* servers at each site exchange global heartbeats. Global failover policies come into play when a global heartbeat fails. Global heartbeat failure may indicate a site disaster, or it may be caused by a more benign condition such as failure of the heartbeat mechanism. Whatever the reason, global clustering technology makes it possible to predefine a policy for dealing with the failure. One policy might be to start executing Application Q_1 automatically. This may be risky if the heartbeat loss is the result of a communications failure. A more conservative policy might be to notify a system administrator of the condition, allowing human intelligence to be applied to the decision process.

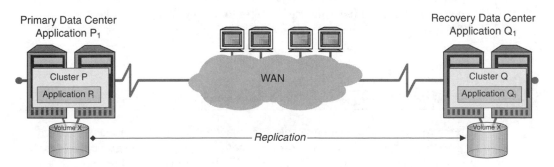

Figure 9.19 Combining cluster and replication technologies.

Wide area application failover introduces further complication. Whereas all the servers within a local cluster would normally be part of the same network domain, this is not generally true for widely separated systems. Transferring a failed cluster's IP addresses to a distant cluster is not normally effective. Clients must use Internet domain names to establish connections to applications that are to be clustered globally. Part of the global failover process requires that the site at which an application is restarting reregister the application under its domain name. Global cluster managers include *DNS agents* of some form to perform this registration. In the example of Figure 9.19, a site failover procedure would communicate with the network's DNS server to reassign the application's domain name to IP addresses in the Internet domain of which Cluster Q is a part.

To maximize resource utilization, *reciprocal failover* configurations similar to that described earlier in this chapter are often employed. Under normal circumstances, both sites run separate applications and replicate data to each other. If one of the sites should fail, the other reassigns its network addresses and restarts its applications.

"Following the Sun"

In a global enterprise, online computing activity peaks tend to migrate around the world in a diurnal cycle that corresponds to business hours. When the business day ends in New York, it's early afternoon in California. When Californians go home from work, early risers in Asia are just getting started for the next day, and so forth.

On the other hand, enterprises have discovered that efficiency is optimal when information is processed close to the consumer, in terms of network transit time. Thus, the online information processing challenge for global enterprises is to maintain a single consistent worldwide information store while keeping processing that is closest to those who need it most—throughout the 24-hour day.

An integrated global computing facility based on long-distance clustering technology combined with data replication can meet both of these needs. The same mechanisms that implement the automated disaster recovery previously described can be policy-controlled to occur on a timed basis. An application's primary processing site can migrate around the world during the course of a day, "following the sun," as it were. As a site becomes the current application processing site, it establishes itself as the primary location for data replication. While the site is primary, data updates are sent from it to secondary sites. Thus, with brief outages for application and replication reconfiguration, a global enterprise's data processing applications can migrate around the world during the course of a day.

Clusters and Storage Area Networks

Clusters are most flexible and most easily managed when their storage is connected to a *storage area network* (SAN) that provides complete direct connectivity among all storage devices and servers. By connecting all of the servers in a cluster to all of the storage devices, SANs increase flexibility, make parallel service group scaling possible

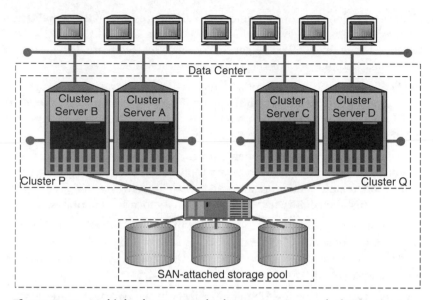

Figure 9.20   Multiple clusters attached to a common pool of SAN storage.

for a wider range of applications, and enable application failover to cascade from server to server for ultrahigh availability.

In many enterprise data centers today, SANs have evolved to encompass all of the storage. In such data centers, several clusters of application or database servers may be connected to a common pool of storage devices. Figure 9.20 illustrates a data center in which Cluster P and Cluster Q, each consisting of two servers, are connected to a common pool of SAN-attached storage devices.

Data center-wide storage connectivity allows storage capacity to be deployed wherever and whenever it is needed with only management operations. When all storage devices have physical connections to all of the servers in a data center, excess storage capacity on one server or cluster can be reallocated to another server or cluster without physical reinstallation. Today, most operating systems support device reallocation while the respective servers are online, so that reboots are not required in order to use newly allocated storage capacity. Instead of an overflow storage pool to meet the emergency needs of each server, a single pool can meet the needs of an entire data center. The larger the data center, the greater the potential savings.

Summary

- Although both technologies have the objective of maintaining identical copies of data on separate storage devices, mirroring and replication implementations differ in the mechanisms they use to achieve their objectives because of the environments in which they are intended to be used.

- Mirroring implementations assume that path failures are unlikely, and that the latency cost of writing data to all mirrored devices is equal. Replication implementations assume that it takes longer to write data to secondary devices than to primary ones, and that periodic network outages are to be expected.

- Replication can occur at the volume, file, or database level. Each form of replication has slightly different semantics and different performance characteristics. RAID subsystems are only able to replicate at the volume level, because they lack file and database state awareness.

- Data can be replicated synchronously or asynchronously. With synchronous replication, applications wait for secondary replicas to be written. With asynchronous replication, update queues are allowed to build up at the primary location as a buffer against momentary network or secondary location overloads.

- Asynchronous replication generally results in better application performance, but creates a risk of some data loss if a disaster occurs while data are in flight" between primary and secondary locations. Disaster recovery procedures must take this risk into account.

- Data replication can be used symmetrically between two data centers, with each center replicating the data it processes to the other for safekeeping. In this scenario, each center can serve as the recovery location for the other's applications.

- Clustering technology enables readily available mass-produced computer system components to be configured to provide high application availability and, in some instances, scaling of application capacity beyond that of a single server.

- Cluster managers typically organize the program, network, and data resources that constitute an application into *service groups* for purposes of starting and stopping and monitoring. Service groups are classified as failover groups or parallel groups. One instance of a failover service group runs in a cluster at any instant. Multiple instances of a parallel group may be active. The application instances of a parallel service group may or may not share data. Those that do share data must either coordinate their own data accesses or access data through a cluster file system or database manager.

- Shared-nothing clusters do not enable multiple servers to access the same data simultaneously. These clusters, which do not inherently require SANs because they do not share data are mainly useful for single-instance failover applications and for partitioned shared databases.

- *Shared data* clusters enable multiple instances of a parallel service group to share the same data. A shared data cluster augments the cluster manager with either a cluster file system or database manager. These data managers coordinate application instances' accesses to data so that application behavior is as it would be on a single server.

- Cluster file systems and volume managers may use either master/slave or symmetric architecture. In a master/slave architecture, one server makes all metadata updates, whereas in a symmetric architecture, each server can lock metadata and access it directly.

- Clustering techniques can be extended over a wide area with relatively little modification. Coupled with data replication, *global clusters* can partially or completely automate recovery from a site disaster.

- Two important differences between local and long-distance clustering are the reliability and latency of the heartbeat mechanism and the reassignment of network addresses when a failover occurs. Heartbeat performance or reliability may make it desirable to involve humans in failover decisions. Network considerations dictate the use of Internet domain naming for client access. This in turn necessitates the reassignment of domain names when a global failover occurs.

- Global clustering can also be used to migrate a worldwide application's primary processing location around the world over the course of a day by inducing failover of applications and reassigning replication mastership to different sites on a time basis.

CHAPTER 10

Enterprise Backup Software for Storage Area Networks

In this chapter we'll learn more about:

- The nature of enterprise backup, as distinguished from personal computer backup

- Typical architecture for enterprise backup managers and why managed backup scales to very large enterprises

- Different forms of backup, including full and incremental backup, and how the two can be combined to reduce the time required to back up online data

- How frozen image technology can be used to all but eliminate the backup window when data is unavailable for application use

- How LAN-free and serverless backup technologies can reduce the load imposed by backup on the enterprise LAN and SAN, respectively, and how these facilities change strategies for deploying backup software components

Backup Management for SANs

The hardware control and data movement aspects of backup in the SAN environment have been discussed in Chapters 2 and 4. This chapter discusses the capabilities and characteristics of enterprise backup management software, including new capabilities that are enabled when operating in the SAN environment.

Enterprise Data Protection

As an important enterprise asset, online data must be protected against loss or destruction, *no matter what happens.* Enterprises protect their data so that:

- Processing can resume as quickly as possible after a server, application, storage device, software or site failure or operational error

- Data can be copied or moved to where it is needed, when it is needed by the business

- Regulatory and business policy record retention requirements can be met

With electronic business, a primary goal of information services departments is keeping data available for access as continuous as possible. Backup must work around online processing, accomplishing its task with minimal disruption of application access.

Data protection basically consists of making electronic copies of data objects:

- *Periodic backups* of online files and databases that can be used to recover from application or human errors

- *Electronic archives* that can be removed from data centers to secure vaults

- *Running replicas* of data (discussed in Chapter 9) that can be used to recover after a site disaster

- *Transport copies* of data that can be used to move it from where it is used less to where it is used more

The seemingly simple action of copying data objects from source to target, contains significant technical challenges:

- Designing and implementing policies that allow data to get to where it is needed when it is needed, even if failures or procedural errors occur

- Keeping track of which data objects are at which location(s), for example, which backups are on which tapes and where those tapes are stored

- Maintaining the mutual consistency of sets of data objects as they are copied

- Minimizing *service outage time* during which data objects are unavailable to applications because they are being copied

- Determining when in backup policy changes would be beneficial, for example, when backups should be more frequent or when data should be replicated remotely to reduce network traffic

Backup

Backup, or the process of making separable copies of online data, is central to any data protection strategy. A *backup,* or copy of a set of data objects, ideally reflects the contents of all objects as they existed at a single instant.[1] Backups may be:

[1] There are fuzzy file and database backup techniques that create copies of changing data with limited currency and consistency guarantees. These can be combined with logs to restore databases after a failure, but they have limited use as durable business records.

- *Kept at the data center*, so that if a storage device, system or application failure, or an operational error destroys online data, a reasonably up-to-date copy can be restored to serve as the starting point for recovery.

- *Moved to alternate sites* to protect against environmental events that destroy an entire data center. If a recent backup of operational data survives a data center disaster, data processing can be resumed more quickly.

- *Made unalterable* (for example, copied to CD-ROM) to provide durable records for regulatory or business policy purposes when the data is no longer required to be online.

Conceptually, backup is simple. A system administrator decides which data is critical, determines a backup schedule that minimizes impact on online operations, and invokes a backup manager to copy data. As with so many of the subjects discussed in this book, however, the difficulty is in the details:

Weight of numbers. In large data centers, system administrators back up data from many servers of different types. The sheer volume of work becomes formidable. Moreover, it requires skills and experience unique to each platform.

Reliable execution. For a backup strategy to protect enterprise data, backups must actually be performed reliably and on schedule. In a busy data center, immediate demands can cause operators to neglect routine backups.

Media handling errors. Large data centers inevitably accumulate large collections of tapes or other backup media. When handled by humans, backup media can easily be damaged, destroyed, misplaced, or inadvertently overwritten.

Pressure to perform. When online data is actually lost and must be restored from a backup, the situation is typically tense. Seldom-practiced restore procedures must be performed under pressure to get applications back online. Under pressure, it is easy to misread instructions, load the wrong media, or override built-in procedural safeguards. The result can be long restore times, incorrect restores, or even failure to restore data at all.

A class of applications known as *enterprise backup managers* has evolved to overcome these difficulties. Typical enterprise backup managers automate backup schedules and manage media for many different client and server platforms, and safeguard against procedural errors that can reduce backup dependability.

Enterprise Backup Architecture

To understand the differences between an enterprise backup manager and a simple backup copy program that might run in a personal computer, it is helpful to consider the architectural elements of enterprise backup. Figure 10.1 illustrates an enterprise backup manager architecture.

Figure 10.1 illustrates four major elements of enterprise backup:

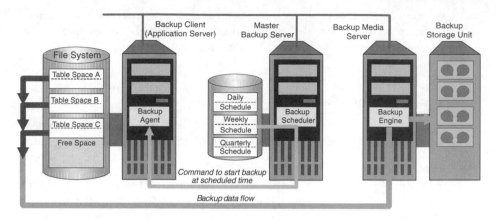

Figure 10.1 Enterprise backup manager architecture.

1. *Backup clients*[2] (sometimes simply called *clients*). The term *backup client* is used to denote both a computer with data to back up, and a software component that runs in such a computer, reading data from online storage devices and feeding it to a *backup server*. This use of the word *client* can be confusing, because the most important enterprise backup clients are application, database, and file *servers*.

2. *Backup servers* (sometimes simply called *servers*). Similarly, this term denotes either a computer or a software component that receives data from a backup client, writes it to backup media, and maintains a record of its actions. It is sometimes useful to distinguish between two types of backup server:

   ■ *Master backup servers* schedule backup jobs and maintain *catalogs* of backed-up data objects. The software component that performs these functions is sometimes called a *master server* or *backup manager*.

   ■ *Slave backup servers* (sometimes called *media servers*) copy data objects to and from backup media at the direction of a master server. The term *slave backup server* usually applies to a computer rather than a software component. Slave backup servers control *backup storage units*.

3. *Backup storage units* are magnetic tape or disk drives, optical disk drives, or robotic media handlers whose operation is controlled by a media server.

4. *Backup media* are the tapes and disks upon which backups are written. Unlike online storage, whose storage media is integral to the drive (at least for enterprise-class storage devices), backup media are *removable* from the drives that read and write them.[3]

---

[2] As with clustering, there is not a generally accepted common terminology for backup concepts. The authors have used what they feel to be descriptive terms that are also representative of industry practice.

[3] Although with the decreasing cost of online storage, disk drives and RAID subsystems are increasingly used to hold backup copies of operational data.

Backup Control and Data Flow

Enterprise backup is the result of a three-way cooperation among a master backup server, a backup client, and a media server:

- The master backup server initiates and monitors *backup jobs* according to a *backup schedule* that it maintains. In a large or distributed enterprise with multiple media servers, the master server would typically use both predefined policies and current load conditions to choose a media server for each job.

- A backup client runs the backup job, reading data from online storage and sending it to the designated media server.

- The designated media server typically assigns one or more backup storage units, selects and loads media from a pool, receives data from the client and writes it to the media. Media servers typically allocate backup storage units to jobs based on predefined policy criteria and current unit availability.

- At the end of a job, the media server sends a list of the data objects actually backed up to the master server for cataloging.

The hope is always that backups will never be restored, since restoring a backup means that a major error has occurred. But when restoring data *is* necessary, the steps are similar to those for backup:

- A backup client sends a message to a master server requesting that one or more backed-up objects be restored. Clients typically have read access to master server catalogs that list backed up objects so that they can make precise requests. They display the contents of these catalogs to users and administrators through graphical interfaces.

- The master backup server receiving the restore request identifies the location of the media that holds the requested objects and directs the media server to cooperate with the client to perform the restore.

- The media server locates and mounts the media containing the data objects to be restored and sends data to the requesting backup client.

- The backup client receives data from the media server and writes it to designated location in a local file system. It is not uncommon to restore data objects to different paths than those from which they were backed up.

Scaling Backup Operations

Although the terms are often used to refer to computers, the *backup client, master server*, and *media server* roles are fundamentally software component roles. In small systems, all three of these components typically run in the application server and execute backup procedures according to a preset schedule. Since they are defined architecturally and implemented modularly, however, any of the components can be moved to a dedicated server as enterprise data center growth requires, with minimal disruption of defined backup procedures. Figure 10.2 illustrates how enterprise backup can scale as the enterprise data center grows.

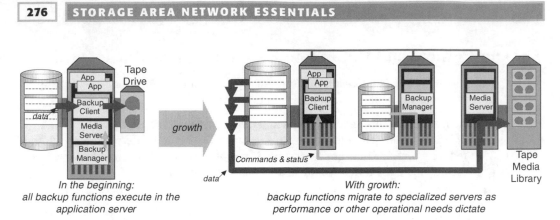

In the beginning:
all backup functions execute in the
application server

With growth:
backup functions migrate to specialized servers as
performance or other operational needs dictate

Figure 10.2 A scalable backup architecture.

The data center illustrated in Figure 10.2 starts with a single server in which both applications and backup run. Backup schedules, media pools, and job attributes are defined. As the enterprise grows, load on the application server increases and it can no longer support backup in addition to applications. Additional servers dedicated to managing backups and writing data to tape media are installed. The control paths between backup software components change from interprocess communications to network messages. Similarly, backup data flows across a LAN or SAN. The original backup procedures and schedule remain essentially intact, however. The same components intercommunicate the same commands and status information using different paths.

The advantages of a scalable enterprise backup architecture become even more apparent with further growth or as data processing becomes distributed. Figure 10.3 illustrates how this backup architecture expands to support distributed processing.

Figure 10.3 illustrates two major benefits of a scalable backup architecture:

1. *Central control.* An enterprise master server maintains backup schedules and data catalogs for many application servers (backup clients). One point of control allows a central administrative team to manage backup operations for a distributed enterprise with hundreds or thousands of application servers.

2. *Resource scaling and sharing.* Using this architecture, media servers can be added when and where they are required. Tape drives, especially in combination with robotic media handlers, are expensive resources with low duty cycles. Attaching them to one media server that is shared among several application servers is extremely attractive from an economic standpoint.

A distributed architecture such as Figure 10.3 illustrates minimizes administrative cost and makes optimal use of expensive hardware resources, but it comes at a cost in network traffic. Enterprise backup managers use techniques like data compression and bandwidth throttling to minimize the impact of backup on application network traffic, but, inevitably, large amounts of data must be transferred from backup client to media server at times that may be inopportune for other applications. An enterprise implementing a backup strategy for distributed data centers must evaluate the network traf-

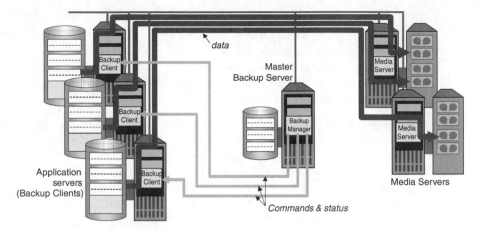

Figure 10.3   Backup architecture for large enterprises.

fic impact of distributed client/server backup, as illustrated in Figure 10.3 and decide among four basic ways of moving bulk backup data:

- Sharing the enterprise network between application and backup traffic.
- A private backup network for server-based backup (*LAN-free backup*).
- Using the storage area network for backup data transfers (*serverless backup*).
- Localized backup with media servers on some or all application servers.

The choice typically depends on a combination of enterprise network loading, application server loading, cost, and backup manager capability factors.

Enterprise Backup Policies

The large and growing amount of data required to operate any enterprise must be backed up on a schedule that meets enterprise needs for backup currency and consistency. Backup is very resource intensive, so there is a corollary requirement to minimize its impact on applications. System administrators express the trade-off between these two conflicting objectives in *backup policies*. A backup policy is a set of rules that specifies:

- *What* data objects are to be backed up
- *When* a set of data objects should be backed up
- *Where* the backup of a set if data objects should be made and stored

Which Data Objects to Back Up

Deciding *which* data to back up requires knowledge of both enterprise needs and business policies and data processing operations. Backup policies must be defined to produce adequately up-to-date backups of important data, but at the same time, they must not keep those objects out of service for intolerable periods.

Which data to back up in a particular job is typically specified as a list of files or directories. For applications that create and delete files frequently, specifying directories rather than files makes it unnecessary to modify the backup policy specification when files are created or deleted.

Negative backup data specifications are also useful. Unix file systems, for example, are often mounted subordinate to a root directory to enable all of a system's data to be described by a single tree. To back up the (usually infrequently changing) root directory on a different schedule than its subordinate file systems, the latter must be explicitly excluded from each backup specification that includes the root. Most enterprise backup managers support *exception lists* that exclude lists of files and directories from backup specifications.

When to Back Up

Determining *when* to run backup jobs also requires both business and data center operational knowledge. Backups must be frequent enough for the data to be useful if they are required, but seldom enough that application impact is tolerable. Enterprise backup managers allow the creation of multiple jobs that can be scheduled as appropriate for the nature of the objects. Armed with this capability and with knowledge of enterprise needs, administrators must balance between worst-case backup age (which represents the worst-case quantity of data updates that must be recreated by other means) and the impact of backup on both involved and uninvolved applications.

If resources were not a consideration, the obvious backup policy would be to back up all online data constantly—to make a copy of every file every time it changed. But, resources *are* a consideration. Constant backup would consume huge amounts of processing, I/O, and network capacity, as well as large amounts of storage and catalog space, adversely affecting both budgets and application performance. Backups are therefore specified and scheduled to minimize application impact. For enterprises with predictable busy and idle periods, it obviously makes sense to schedule backups during idle periods. As more business is conducted online, however, predictable idle periods no longer exist. Techniques that allow backup to coexist with applications are required. The effectiveness of its impact minimization techniques is a measure of the quality of an enterprise backup manager.

Where to Back Up Data

On the surface, *where* to back up data appears to be a simple question. The backup client is the data source. It must perforce read backup data from online storage devices. The destination is a media server. The particular media server to receive a backup is determined by business goals, equipment and media availability, and current network and server load.

Enterprise backup managers typically allow the master server to select a media server to execute each backup job. Similarly, it is typical to allow the media server to select the backup devices to be used for each job.

Finally, backup media (tapes and optical disks) are typically organized and managed in *pools*. Each scheduled backup job causes media to be allocated from a designated pool. The media server usually makes the specific media choice using algorithms that equalize usage (and therefore wear). Enterprise backup managers also typically *manage* media: For example, they maintain cleaning and retirement schedules and keep track of media's physical location and current usage.

Backup Automation

Enterprise backup managers typically bundle backup policy parameters including

- Backup client or clients
- File and directory lists
- Eligible media server or servers
- Media type and named pool
- Eligible backup device or devices
- Scheduling and priority information

into a single abstraction that is sometimes called a *backup class* or *backup job type*. Backup managers manage backup classes automatically, cooperating with clients and media servers to initiate, monitor, and log scheduled backups, manage media, and report exceptions. Once a workable backup class is defined, it is usually unnecessary for an administrator to be involved in backup operations. Operations staff are typically able to load and unload media following backup manager instructions. If a robotic media handler is present, even that is automated. Automating backup exploits what computers do best—repetitive operations whose very repetitiveness make them error prone when performed by humans.

Minimizing the Impact of Backup

This section discusses several techniques used by backup managers to minimize the impact of backup on applications. Techniques implemented by backup managers as well as techniques that integrate backup with other SAN software capabilities such as frozen image technologies and device sharing are both discussed.

Full and Incremental Backup

Typically, backups are scheduled to occur frequent enough that only a small percentage of files change between any two successive backups. The *incremental backup* technique exploits this fact to minimize backup resource requirements. An *incremental backup* of a file list is a copy of the files or directories named in the list that have changed since some *reference backup* was made. Backup clients use file system metadata to determine the time at which each file last changed, and compare this time to the time of the reference backup. Figure 10.4 illustrates the difference between full and incremental backups of the same data.

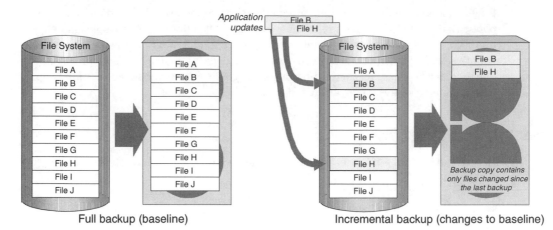

Figure 10.4 Full and incremental backup.

Incremental backup does not replace full backup of an entire file list; it reduces the frequency with which time-consuming full backups must be made. An incremental backup contains data that have changed since some earlier point in time for which a *baseline* backup exists. To restore an entire file list from an incremental backup, the baseline backup is first restored. The incremental backup is then restored, replacing changed files in the restored baseline.

If only a small percentage of the files in a backup file list have changed since the last backup, then only a small percentage of the files must be copied to make an incremental backup. An incremental backup typically completes much faster (orders of magnitude) than a full backup of the same set of data objects and consequently has significantly less impact on online applications.

The Impact of Incremental Backup

Enterprise backup managers that support the incremental backup technique maintain online catalogs containing the media location of each active version of each backed-up data object. Restoring an individual file from incremental backups is therefore roughly equivalent to restoring it from a full backup—the backup media containing the file is located and mounted and the file is copied from it to online storage.

Restoring an entire file list from incremental backups is more complicated. First, the newest *full* baseline backup is restored and then all incremental backups newer than it are restored in age order (oldest first). Enterprise backup managers control the order of incremental restores and guide the administrator through the correct sequence of media mounts. Figure 10.5 illustrates the restoration of an entire file system from a full backup and several incremental backups.

Data centers typically schedule relatively infrequent (e.g., daily or weekly) full backups at low-activity times (e.g., late nights or weekends), with more frequent (e.g., daily or hourly) incremental backups. This results in lower application impact than a com-

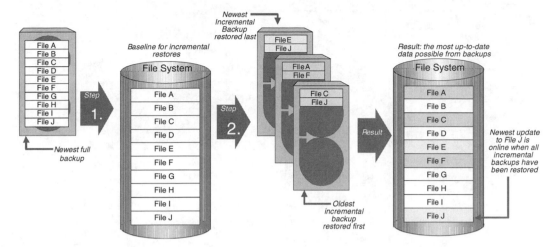

Figure 10.5   Restoring data from incremental backups.

plete full backup policy, because only a few data objects are copied during the incremental backups. File system restore times, however, are necessarily longer than with pure full backup and involve more media handling.

Different Types of Incremental Backup

Enterprise backup managers typically support two types of incremental backup, called *differential* and *cumulative*. A differential backup is a copy of all the files in a file list that have been modified since the last backup of any kind (full or incremental). Thus, with a policy of weekly full and daily differential backups, the most current file system restore possible results from restoring the newest full backup and then each of the newer differential backups in age order (the scenario illustrated in Figure 10.5). The later in the week, the more incremental restores would be required and the longer a full file system restore would take.

A *cumulative backup* is a copy of all files modified since the last *full* backup. Restoring a file system from cumulative backups requires only the newest full backup and the newest cumulative backup, as Figure 10.6 illustrates. Restoring file systems is simpler and faster, but at a cost of lengthening backup times as the time since the last full backup increases.

Combining Cumulative, Differential, and Full Backups

Full, cumulative, and differential backups can be combined to balance the impact of backup on applications against full file system or database restore time. Table 10.1 illustrates this using a weekly backup schedule in which full, differential, and cumulative backups combine to balance backup time and restore complexity.

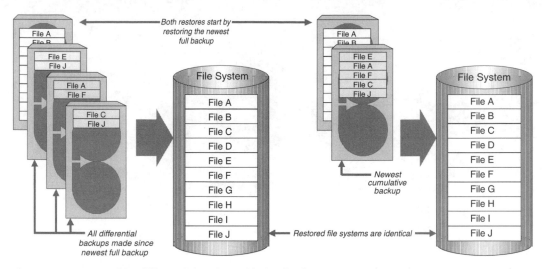

Figure 10.6 Restoring differential and cumulative backups.

Each Sunday, a full backup is made. On Monday and Tuesday, differential incremental backups are made. On Wednesday, a cumulative incremental backup is made and it is no longer necessary to use Monday's or Tuesday's backups in a full restore (they may still be useful, for example, to restore individual data objects or to restore the file system to a point in time other than the most current possible).

On Thursday, Friday, and Saturday, differential incremental backups are made. The full restore procedure for any of these days would be to restore Sunday's full backup to establish a baseline, followed by Wednesday's cumulative incremental backup, and Thursday's, Friday's, and Saturday's as appropriate. In this scenario, the largest number of backups required to do an up-to-date restore is five (for restores to the point in time at which the Saturday differential backup was made).

Enterprise backup managers typically enable administrators to define automatic backup schedules similar to that illustrated in Table 10.1. With robotic tape handlers, a backup schedule like this becomes completely automatic. No system administrator or computer operator action is required once a backup class has been defined and a schedule similar to that illustrated in Table 10.1 has been established. Backup managers automatically allocate media from a pool and recycle media whose retention period has elapsed.

Synthetic Full Backups

The appeal of incremental backup is obvious: Much less data to back space up means much less elapsed time, processing resource, and I/O bandwidth devoted to backup. On the other hand, the simplicity of restoring an entire file set directly from a full backup is equally attractive.

Some enterprise backup managers offer a compromise: the ability to merge a baseline full backup and several incremental backups into a new, more up-to-date full backup.

Table 10.1 A Sample Weekly Backup Strategy

	SUNDAY	MONDAY	TUESDAY	WEDNESDAY	THURSDAY	FRIDAY	SATURDAY
Type of backup	Full	Differential Incremental	Differential Incremental	Cumulative Incremental	Differential Incremental	Differential Incremental	Differential Incremental
Content of backup copy	Full database as it stood on Sunday.	Files changed since Sunday's full backup.	Files changed since Monday's differential backup.	Files changed since Sunday's full backup.	Files changed since Wednesday's cumulative backup.	Files changed since Thursday's differential backup.	Files changed since Friday's differential backup.
Full restore procedure	Restore Sunday's full backup.	Restore Sunday's full backup and Monday's differential backup.	Restore Sunday's backup, Monday's and Tuesday's differential backups.	Restore Sunday's backup and Wednesday's cumulative backup.	Restore Sunday's full backup, Wednesday's cumulative backup and Thursday's differential backup.	Restore Sunday's full backup, Wednesday's cumulative backup, Thursday's and Friday's differential backup.	Restore Sunday's full backup, Wednesday's cumulative backup, Thursday's, Friday's, and Saturday's differential backups.

This new *synthetic full* backup then becomes the baseline for future incremental backups. Synthetic full backups are made by merging the contents of full and incremental backup into a new backup written on different media. The master backup server's catalog of backed-up objects is used as a guide to which objects to keep and which to discard as the new backup is made.

While they are costly in terms of physical resources (tapes, tape drives, and bandwidth) and time, synthetic full backups simplify restoration, so the capability is popular with system administrators.

Copy-on-Write Technology and Backup

Copy-on-write technology (described in Chapter 8) is the technique of capturing *before images* of data as it is modified by applications. This technology has been adopted by some file systems to create *frozen images* or *checkpoints* of entire file systems, as Figure 10.7 illustrates. The primary purpose of these frozen images is to enable point-in-time backups of file systems and databases while they are in use.

Frozen file system or database images created for the purpose of backup should be initiated at instants when no I/O operations are in progress and all cached data is also reflected on storage devices. Enterprise file and database systems that support frozen images include either APIs or management commands that:

- Cause transactions in progress to be completed and drained from the system.
- Block new transactions from being initiated.
- Flush cache (write any as-yet unwritten data to storage devices) so that all cached data is also reflected on persistent storage.

These capabilities go under different names, such as putting a database in *backup mode*, initiating a checkpoint, or creating a snapshot, but all have the effect of

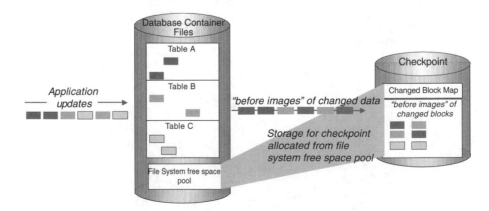

Figure 10.7 A file system checkpoint.

enabling a backup program to work with the image of a database or file system as it was at some point in the past, while applications continue to update the actual data.

When first created, copy-on-write frozen images occupy very little storage space—they require only an empty *changed block list*. As applications update data, space is allocated, *before images* of the data being updated are copied, and the changed block list is updated to indicate which data have changed.

Frozen images can nearly eliminate *backup windows*, the intervals of time during which data is unavailable to applications because it is being backed up. Either full or incremental backups can be made from frozen images of file systems or databases.

Some file systems are capable of maintaining multiple copy-on-write frozen images, as Figure 10.8 illustrates. While each frozen image uses storage capacity, this facility provides very flexible backup and restore choices. Referring to Figure 10.8, for example, if T1, T2, and T3 were points at which the disk image of application data were consistent, application data could be backed as of any or all of those times. Checkpoints can also be used to roll back an operational file system or database to its state at a previous point in time. This facility can be useful if an application error results in data corruption that is discovered only after the application has run for a period of time. If a checkpoint exists for a time at which data is known to have been correct (for example, before the erroneous application was installed), its before image can be written over the current data, returning it to a precorruption state upon which further recovery can be based.

Multiple checkpoints have substantial benefits, but they do consume resources. Application writes take longer on the average when checkpoints are in use. Checkpoints can also cause unexpected space allocation failures if they are allowed to accumulate indefinitely. To prevent this, file systems that support multiple checkpoints typically

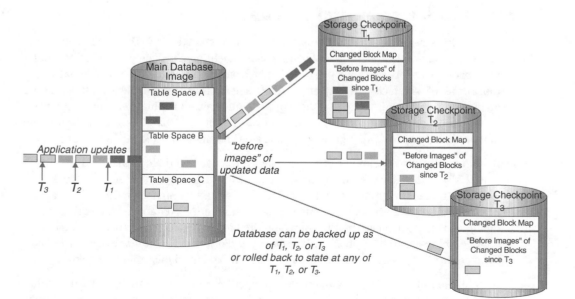

Figure 10.8 Multiple checkpoints for rollback.

allow them to be marked eligible for deletion when space is needed. Alternatively, an administrator can schedule a script to monitor file system free space and delete old checkpoints or take other corrective action when it drops below a prescribed level.

Backup and Databases

Major database managers include integrated point-in-time backup facilities, making the definition of an enterprise backup strategy even more complicated. While different databases' mechanisms differ in detail, the basic technique is similar to that used to create a volume or file system *copy-on-write* frozen image. Database activity is stopped momentarily to establish a point of transactional consistency, the backup thread is initiated, and database activity resumes. While the backup is running, each application modification to the database causes a copy of the object's prior contents to be saved. When the backup reads data, these *before images* are returned. When any other program reads data, current object contents are returned.

A backup made in this way represents the contents of the database at the point in time at which the backup was initiated. This technique, often called *hot database backup*, is well accepted and widely used. Some enterprise backup managers are able to manage hot database backups that are actually performed by the database management system. This allows database backups created by the database manager to share the enterprise backup media pool with other backup classes.

Hot database backup increases database I/O activity significantly, both due to I/O requests from the backup itself and due to extra I/O operations required to capture before images of data that are altered by applications while the backup is in progress.

Changed Block Incremental Backup

While it is extremely useful for file-based applications, particularly those that manipulate large numbers of files, incremental backup is less helpful in reducing the impact of database backup. Databases typically store data in a small number of large container files, most or all of which change frequently (albeit slightly) as the database is updated. Thus, an incremental backup technique that copies each changed file in its entirety is likely to include most or all of a database's container files, even if only a miniscule fraction of the data in them has changed. Figure 10.9 illustrates incremental backup of a database.

If a copy-on-write checkpoint is active, however, its changed block list identifies individual *blocks* that have changed, irrespective of whether they represent user data, database metadata, or file system metadata. For a file system used to hold database container files, a checkpoint's changed block list identifies database blocks that have changed, rather than just the files in which the blocks reside. The new contents of changed blocks can be used to make a *changed block incremental backup* of the database, in most cases, at far lower overhead than a file-based incremental backup.

If a checkpoint is made solely to enable changed block incremental backup, it is sufficient to record only the addresses of changed blocks; copying before images of data is unnecessary. The changed block addresses in a *data-less checkpoint* can be used to

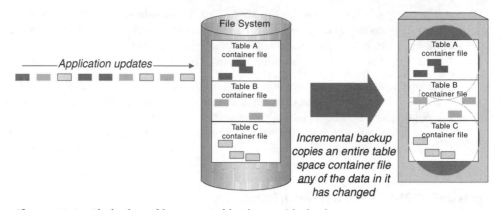

Figure 10.9   Limitation of incremental backups with databases.

create a backup that contains only blocks changed since the checkpoint was initiated. Figure 10.10 illustrates changed block incremental backup.

A changed block incremental backup contains the contents of only those database blocks modified since the time of checkpoint creation. If only a small percentage of data is updated in this interval, the changed block incremental backup image is correspondingly small. Compared to a full backup, changed block incremental backup typically takes very little time and uses very little storage and I/O bandwidth.

Like file-based incremental backups, changed block incremental backup does not eliminate the need for full backup; it only reduces the frequency with which full backup is required. Each changed block incremental backup is relative to the previous checkpoint, for which a backup must exist if restore is to be possible. Restoring data when this technique is used starts with restoration of a full backup followed by restoration of the complete sequence of changed block incremental backups up to the point in time to which data is being restored.

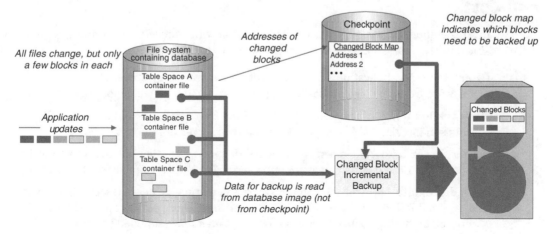

Figure 10.10   Changed block incremental backup.

By greatly reducing the impact of backup on applications, changed block incremental backup encourages administrators to schedule more frequent backups. More frequent backups not only reduce bandwidth and storage capacity requirements, they also enable data to be restored to points in time that are closer to instants of failure.

As with file-based incremental backups, the reduced resource requirements of changed block incremental backup increase restore complexity, since all changed block incremental backups must be restored in order of decreasing age. Enterprise backup managers that support changed block incremental backup track backup sequences and guide administrators through the incremental restore process.

Multistream Backup: Multiplexed and Parallel Backup Streams

Unfortunately, there is no inherent match between the I/O performance at the two ends of a backup data stream. At the source are high-performance disks or even higher performance disk aggregates. At the target are tape drives whose nominal data transfer speed is significantly lower, but which must be kept streaming to avoid time-consuming tape repositioning cycles. In the middle is an enterprise network or a SAN subject to congestion in its own right. The challenge in configuring resources is to meet the following requirements:

- Enough tape drive bandwidth at the target to get the job done on time

- Enough bandwidth at the source to feed the needs of allocated tape drives

- Enough network bandwidth between the two so that neither becomes a bottleneck

- Enough restraint so that backup network traffic does not intolerably affect the performance of applications

Factors Affecting Backup Speed and Cost

In a distributed information processing operation with many servers containing valuable data, several variables can affect the speed of backup jobs:

Client load. An application server busy with other work may prevent backup client software from reading data fast enough to keep the backup data path busy.

Network load. A network busy with application traffic may prevent a backup client from sending data fast enough to keep a media server or tape drive busy.

Media server load. A media server may be too busy with other backup jobs (or other types of work, if it is also an application server) to keep its tape drives busy.

Tape drive data transfer rate. A tape drive's performance degrades significantly if data is not fed to it fast enough to enable it to *stream* (i.e., tape continually in motion and writing data). A short gap in the data stream supplied to a tape drive can result in a much larger interruption of data flow as the drive repositions its tape to recommence writing.

Additionally, effective media utilization can be an important backup consideration. High-capacity tape cartridges typically have two to four times as much capacity as a disk. A policy of frequent incremental backups adopted for business reasons may result in many small backup files, each occupying only a small fraction of a tape's capacity. Not only are underutilized backup media costly, unnecessarily large libraries of media also increase the probability of media handling errors. Enterprise backup managers enable multiple backup files to be stored on one tape cartridge or other media.

Multiplexed Backups

Many enterprise backup suites *multiplex* or interleave data from several backup jobs on a single tape, to mitigate both the performance variation and effective media use problems. When multiple backup streams are interleaved, each stream's data blocks are tagged with a job identifier and written in order of arrival at the backup server. Tagging backup blocks allows a restore process to identify the blocks that must be searched when restoring data from a particular backup job. Figure 10.11 illustrates multiplexed backup.

With more data arriving at a media server, tape streaming increases, improving total backup throughput for the media server, but possibly increasing the elapsed time for any particular backup job. Since data from several jobs goes onto the same tape, media utilization increases. If a single file or file system must be restored from an interleaved backup, the media server filters the blocks read from backup media. Users are generally not aware that backups are interleaved.

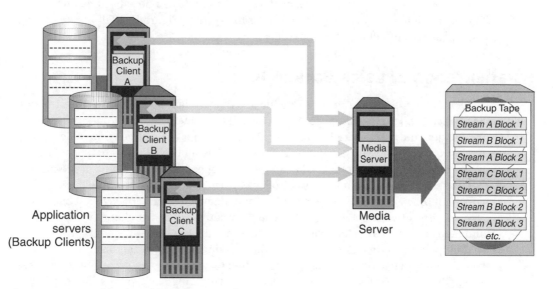

Figure 10.11 Multiplexed backup.

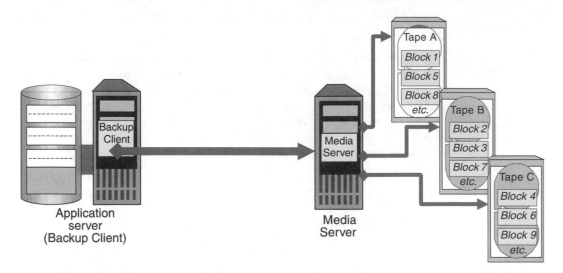

Figure 10.12 Parallel backup streams.

Parallel Backup Streams

In large systems, high-performance networks and storage devices or volumes can often supply data faster than a single tape drive can absorb it. To meet the needs of such systems, backup managers are able to speed up a backup job by writing its data to multiple tapes concurrently. *Parallel backup streams* can be especially effective in making a full backup of a large database or file system. Figure 10.12 illustrates a single backup source directed to three parallel backup streams.

Parallelization of Large Backup Jobs

A backup job typically processes one file at a time. A database that uses files for storage typically uses a few large container files. If container files are processed as one backup job, they are backed up serially, whether or not the source storage devices or target tape drives are capable of higher speeds. The multiplexing techniques described in the preceding paragraphs can be combined to speed up full backups of file-based databases. If each of a database's container files is defined as a separate backup job and all of the backup jobs are scheduled for concurrent execution, several backup streams are active at once. Depending on the relative speeds of client, network, server, and tape drive, it may be appropriate to direct parallel jobs to different tape drives or to multiplex them onto one tape. Thus, the speed with which a full backup of a file-based database can be accomplished is limited by hardware resources. In most cases, adding hardware or network resources and restructuring backup jobs can improve the speed of such backups.

Sharing Tapes

The use of a SAN to share a tape drive or robotic media library among multiple servers was discussed in Chapters 2 and 4. If a tape drive is connected to a SAN, either directly or through a bridge or router, then any media server connected to the same SAN can, in principle, use it as a backup target device.

Again, the adage, "hardware makes SANs possible, software makes them happen," applies. For tape sharing to be viable, it must be strictly controlled so that, for example, a media server does not try to take ownership of a tape drive and mount a tape while another media server is using the drive as one target of a multistream backup job. A media server must have a foolproof mechanism for allocating tape drives, including guarantees that, once allocated, a tape drive will stay allocated and not be usurped by another media server or application. On the other hand, if a media server fails with tape drives reserved, there must be a mechanism for discovering the failure so that the drives can be released for other usage.

Some enterprise backup managers incorporate facilities that allow tape drives to be shared in a SAN. In one implementation scheme, the master server has access to a systemwide inventory of tape drives, including information about which media servers and tape drives are connected to the same SAN. Media servers wishing to allocate tape drives make lease requests to the master server, which returns device identifiers that can be used to address tape drives in the SAN. Media servers must renew leases periodically; otherwise, the tape drives are returned to a pool for further allocation.

When a media server has a tape drive allocated to it by the master server, it issues a device reservation command to the drive to prevent other applications that may be unaware of the master backup server from attempting to use it.

LAN-free and Serverless Backup

If an application server is connected to a data center SAN, it can take ownership of a SAN-attached tape drive. A media server can direct the application server to read data from online storage devices and write it to the tape drive using an application protocol called the Network Data Management Protocol (NDMP). Figure 10.13 illustrates the operation of so-called LAN-free backup.

In the example of Figure 10.13, a master server sends a backup job to a media server. The media server determines that the backup client is NDMP aware, and that an eligible tape drive is or can be connected to it. After causing the backup client to reserve the tape drive, the media server uses the NDMP protocol to issue backup commands to the client. The NDMP server component executes the commands, which are of the general form, "read file data and write it to tape." The backup is accomplished entirely without transferring any data on the enterprise LAN. Data moves from source disks or volumes through the backup client's memory to the SAN-attached tape(s); hence, the name *LAN-free* backup.

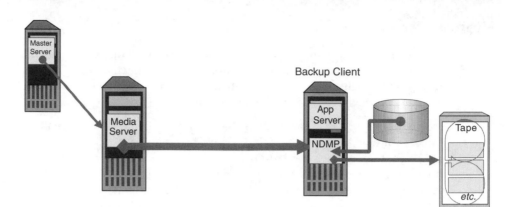

Figure 10.13   LAN-free backup.

LAN-free backup can also be employed between two local devices; it does not absolutely require a SAN to function. By allowing tape drives to be shared among different servers, however, a SAN makes it more economical to implement LAN-free backup in large data centers with multiple application servers that take on the role of backup clients. The primary benefit of LAN-free backup is the removal of backup data transfers from the enterprise LAN.

A more recent technique for accelerating backup—serverless backup—has evolved concurrently with SAN technology, and is often associated with it. Serverless backup is a technique for copying data directly from online storage to backup media without buffering it in a server. Serverless backup uses recently standardized SCSI *remote copy* commands that allow a server to issue a command to one device (e.g., a disk), directing it to transfer data directly to another device (e.g., a tape) without passing the data through a server's memory. An alternative version of remote copy enables a target device (a tape drive) to request data directly from a designated address on a source device (a disk or volume).

With conventional backup, data must be read from a source device into server memory and written to a tape. If both disk and tape are directly connected to the media server, each gigabyte of data backed up requires that 2 gigabytes be transferred on I/O buses. If the media server and backup client are different computers, an additional gigabyte of data is transferred on the enterprise LAN. If data can be transferred directly from online storage device to tape, the SAN bandwidth consumed is reduced by half.

Remote copy requires devices capable of executing the somewhat complex commands in order to function. Hardly any disk or tape devices have this capability today. The first devices to adopt this technology have been Fibre Channel bridges and routers. Using these devices, conventional disk and tape drives can be made to transfer data directly between each other. It is reasonable to expect that enterprise RAID subsystems will also be enhanced to support serverless backup in the future.

When a media server writes a stream of backup data onto a tape or other backup device, it injects metadata into the stream for error detection and correction, and to make data on the tape self-identifying. Since this metadata is generated by the media server, it cannot be supplied by a device that is pushing data directly to or pulling data directly from another device. Recognizing the necessity of injecting metadata into a data stream, the developers of the SCSI remote copy standard allowed for command data block formats in which metadata supplied by the server issuing a command could be transmitted to the master device for the remote copy. The commands have the general form, "insert the following n bytes into the directly copied data stream at offset p from the start of the stream." With this facility, enterprise backup managers can implement serverless backup without having to change their tape media formats.

Because it makes direct copy from disk to tape so attractive, serverless backup changes the parameters that typically define a backup strategy. Rather than concentrating backup for a large number of clients into a small number of media servers, it becomes more advantageous to make each application server a media server and use tape sharing to maximize the utilization of a pool of tape drives. Some backup managers also support the use of dedicated servers as targets of remote copy commands. These servers are programmed to appear as remote copy-aware tape drives on a SAN. Upon receiving remote copy commands, they read data from the designated SAN-attached disks and write it to tapes, injecting metadata into the stream as indicated by the command format.

Summary

- The three primary architectural roles in enterprise backup are the backup client, which controls the data to be backed up; the backup server or media server, which controls the backup target devices; and the master server, which manages backup job schedules and maintains a catalog of backed-up data objects and their locations on backup media.

- Separating enterprise backup into these three roles enables coordinated managed backup to scale across entire enterprises. Each of the roles can be replicated as dictated by geographic, performance, or other requirements.

- An enterprise backup manager automates the scheduling of backup jobs, including job timing, backup device selection and allocation, and cataloging of backed-up objects. With a robotic media library and well-designed procedures, an administrator should be able to set and forget backup schedules.

- Enterprise backup managers use several techniques to minimize the performance and availability impact of backup on applications. Chief among these is incremental backup, in which only data objects changed since the time of some baseline backup are copied. Incremental backup—of which there are two varieties, differential and cumulative—reduces backup time compared to full backup, but does so at the expense of restore complexity.

- Frozen images can be used as a source for backup while the data whose image was frozen continues to be processed by applications. Frozen images may be split mirrors or they may use copy-on-write technology. The latter are called *snapshots* or *checkpoints*.

- Some file systems can support multiple copy-on-write checkpoints representing images of a single file system frozen at different points in time. Using multiple checkpoints allows data to be backed up at a variety of points in time. It also enables rollback of a file system to its state at any of several known points in time. Rollback is useful when an unnoticed application or procedural error causes data corruption that is not detected until after the damage to data is done.

- Incremental backups are not optimal for databases, which consist of a small number of large container files, most or all of which change when a database is updated. To provide effective incremental backup of databases, some file systems enable changed block incremental backups, in which only file system blocks changed since some known point in time are recorded. Because their impact on resources is so small, changed block incremental backups enable databases to be backed up much more frequently than other techniques. This improves the quality of storage service by shortening restore times after database or system crashes.

- Enterprise backup managers support multiplexing of several data streams onto a single tape, as well as the distribution of a single high-speed data stream across several tape drives. Combinations of these two capabilities can be used to adjust between a variety of backup source, target, and network speeds.

- Sharing SAN-attached tapes is both cost effective and an easy way to introduce an organization to SAN technology. In order for media servers to share tape drives effectively, there must be a tamper-proof device reservation system. Enterprise backup managers provide these capabilities.

- LAN-free backup eliminates backup traffic from the enterprise LAN. LAN-free backup requires an NDMP server to transfer data from disk to tape, and an NDMP client in the media server to issue the data transfer commands.

- Serverless backup copies data directly from disk to tape without passing it through media server buffers. Serverless backup requires at least one storage device capable of executing SCSI remote copy commands. Today, this capability is most often provided by Fibre Channel to SCSI bridges.

PART THREE

SAN Implementation Strategies

In this part the discussion of SAN technologies and benefits shift to a how-to discussion for SAN implementation. Our hypothesis is that there's no such thing as a SAN deployment per se; instead, there are information processing strategies for solving business problems that may best be implemented using SAN technology.

We also include a discussion of managing a SAN, both from the point of view of the capabilities and underlying technologies required and from the point of view of what must be accomplished. Our hypothesis here is similar: SAN management in and of itself is uninteresting. What *is* interesting (and vital to success) is effective global management of the complex, interconnected enterprise and data center systems, and clusters that are enabled by SAN technology.

CHAPTER 11

Adopting Storage Networking

I n this chapter we'll learn more about:

- The business importance of data and application availability
- The difference between business benefits and technology benefits
- Common business reasons for adopting storage networking
- Steps in planning and implementing an enterprise information processing strategy that includes storage networking
- How to get maximum benefit from consultants
- Benefits, technical challenges, and contingency plans for implementing the most common data center facilities enabled by storage networking

Why Adopt Storage Networking?

Whether and how an organization adopts storage networking is ultimately a business decision. Business decisions to take action generally require justification in one of two general forms:

- If the action is taken, a product or service that the organization is already delivering can be delivered with higher quality or at lower cost.
- If the action is taken, the organization will be able to deliver a product or service that it *cannot* deliver at any price if the action is not taken.

In other words, information services departments justify changes in the way they work either because the changes make delivering their services better, faster, or cheaper or because the changes enable them to deliver new services.

Benefits and the Mechanisms for Delivering Them

A decision process to deploy, expand, or adapt a storage networking configuration should never lose sight of the premise that storage networking is a mechanism for delivering services of benefit to the enterprise. The deployment (or not) of storage networking should ultimately be justified in terms of the business benefits it delivers.

Determining whether information processing services will deliver business benefits should start with an analysis of business processes. Analyzing business processes can help avoid *technology seduction*—the adoption of technology because it seems modern or streamlined or otherwise desirable, without determining whether it delivers benefit to the business over and above the incumbent way of doing things.

Several business process analysis methodologies are available. From an information services standpoint, however, they all result in a set of requirements to collect, process, and store data. Knowledge of a business's data requirements is the starting point for rational assessment of the benefits of storage networking.

From Business to Storage

Viewed from an information services standpoint, a business process consists of a chart of actions that result in data being collected, processed, and stored. For example, a retail sales process might consist of the following actions:

- Capturing records of sales transactions as they occur and storing them in disk files
- Recording the fulfillment of the sales (shipments of goods)
- Periodically consolidating sales transactions and reconciling them with Independent data about cash received
- Periodically (less frequently, perhaps weekly or monthly) moving sales transaction records to a data warehouse for backup, mining, reporting, and other analysis

This listing is obviously incomplete. For example, bookkeeping and compensation applications would also rely on sales data, as well as data from other sources. In fact, interactions among different business processes *generally* require that data produced by one process be used by one or more others. This is the simple fact of business life that makes the universal interconnectivity of storage area networks so valuable.

Technology and Business Benefits of SANs

As we have said consistently throughout this book, *the most significant feature of a SAN is that it connects many servers to many storage devices.* Thus, an important outcome of business process analysis is a global determination of which processes need access to which data, because this determines SAN interconnection needs.

The need for multiple applications that support different business processes to access the same data is the key opportunity for SAN deployment to deliver business benefits. For example:

A SAN can reduce the capital cost of storage. Because all SAN-attached servers have direct access to all SAN-attached data, there is no business need to keep any more than one logical copy of a business data set online in a data center.[1] The information processing benefit is lower capital expenditure for physical storage. The business benefits include lower information services capital budgets, lower management cost, and greater data reliability (due to the superior physical environment of a central data center).

A SAN can reduce storage management cost. Eliminating redundant storage capacity and unneeded processing steps not only reduces capital and operational cost, it also reduces the number of objects the data center has to manage. Moreover, because SANs are fully interconnected, it becomes possible to consolidate management across the data center and around the world. The information processing benefits are lower operating cost and better quality of service. The business benefit is better quality more up-to-date information at lower cost to the business.

A SAN can reduce I/O bandwidth requirements. With only one logical copy of data, there is no need to copy data for other applications' use. This eliminates both I/O bandwidth and elapsed copying time from the data center work flow. The information processing benefits are lower capital cost (because less storage and I/O infrastructure is required) and improved work flow (because data copying is replaced either by switching device ownership or by sharing data). The resulting business benefit is lower information services cost.

A SAN can improve the accuracy and timeliness of business data. With a fully interconnected SAN, all applications process the real data, not out-of-date copies. Moreover, one less step in the data processing chain is one less opportunity for procedural error. Fewer steps—particularly fewer human-assisted steps—mean fewer errors in the long run, as well as fewer opportunities for data loss or theft. Fewer procedural errors ultimately mean less cost to the business, as well as better quality and more timely information with which to run the business.

A SAN can extend the useful life of capital equipment. SAN interconnectivity makes it easy to *repurpose* equipment—to move older disks or RAID subsystems to another system—when, for example, storage devices are upgraded. Not only does the standards-based nature of SANs make storage devices independent of servers, but repurposing is generally done via administrative actions performed at a console. Because everything is interconnected, expensive and disruptive physical reconfiguration is seldom necessary.

---

[1] There are definitely requirements to keep more than one *physical* copy, such as a mirror for failure tolerance or a mirror that can be split for low-impact backup.

An Important Additional SAN Benefit

Along with every business requirement to store and process data comes a corresponding requirement to protect the data from loss or destruction. From a business standpoint, backup is pure cost. Backup represents resources, time, and effort that must be expended as a consequence of a business decision to store a given set of data online. Resources expended on data protection effectively constitute an insurance policy for data and therefore for the business. Reducing the cost of data protection by deploying a SAN is tantamount to reducing the cost of this insurance. SANs can reduce the cost of data insurance by increasing the utilization of hardware assets.

Tape drives, for example, are used only while backups are actually being performed. In most cases, the advanced backup techniques described in Chapter 8 can be used to reduce time and bandwidth requirements of backup so that tape drives' duty cycles are even lower. If tape drives could be connected to several servers in sequence, one set of drives could be able to serve the needs of several servers. But connecting storage devices to multiple servers is exactly what SANs do.

In addition, SAN deployment can improve the quality of data protection. With more servers able to share a set of tape drives, cost justification of a robotic library becomes easier. Robotic libraries improve the quality of data backups principally by reducing human handling of storage media. Not only is contamination reduced, but misfiling and incorrect media loading are essentially eliminated.

The combination of increased automation and advance backup techniques such as block-level incremental backup and device-to-device data copying dramatically reduce backup times. Shortened backup times allow business to back up their data more frequently, thereby enabling more up-to-date restores. The net result is higher long-term average data availability for businesses.

SAN Benefits in a Larger Information Processing Context

The foregoing SAN benefit analysis considers only information accessibility strategies. A more accurate picture of the business benefits of SANs may be obtained by considering the overall business value of information accessibility and reconciling this view with the data availability enabled by SANs.

In electronic business, the ability to process information can mean enterprise survival because the competition is literally "a click away". Table 11.1 lists the cost of inability to process information for various periods for two businesses for which online data processing essentially *is* the business. A typical home shopping operation processes large numbers of relatively low-value transactions. With a stock brokerage, on the other hand, individual transaction values can be much greater, so the cost per minute of downtime is correspondingly higher.

The rows of Table 11.1 are extrapolated from the top row by multiplication. In reality, other factors, such as inability to meet financial obligations, would cause even larger consequences than the financial cost suggested by the table.

Table 11.1   Cost of Downtime: Some Examples

PERCENTAGE OF UPTIME	ANNUAL DOWNTIME	ANNUAL COST (HOME RETAIL)	ANNUAL COST (BROKERAGE)
99.9999%	30 seconds	$950	$53,750
99.999%	5 minutes	$9,417	$537,500
99.99%	52 minutes	$98,000	$5,590,000
99.9%	8.75 hours	$988,750	$56,000,000
99.5%	43.7 hours	$5,000,000	$280,000,000
99%	87.6 hours	$10,000,000	$560,000,000
98%	180+ hours	$20,000,000+	$1,000,000,000+
95%	450+ hours	$50,000,000+	$3,000,000,000+

The value of uptime may differ for different enterprises, but the overall message of Table 11.1—that downtime is cripplingly expensive—is a universal one. As Chapter 2 suggests, SAN technology enables new information processing techniques that can sharply reduce downtime, which, as can be seen from Table 11.1, can mean very significant cost savings or even survival for an enterprise.

How Much Downtime Is Too Much?

When lost opportunity cost due to computer system downtime is considered, SAN adoption appears in a different light. It may well be possible to justify accelerated SAN adoption not just with direct benefits, but with the reduced financial impact that comes from higher uptime. Considering storage networking as an enabling technology, there is a continuum of techniques that can elevate data and application accessibility to the very nearly continuous. Figure 11.1 illustrates several data and application availability techniques that increase accessibility at increasing cost.

The availability baseline illustrated in Figure 11.1 is an adequately managed but otherwise unremarkable computer system that is backed up on a reasonably frequent and regular basis (e.g., daily incremental and weekly full backups). For example, the system might serve the needs of a retail operation that does business only during the normal business day. The 96.5 percent uptime suggested in Figure 11.1 would amount to a total of about three days of annual downtime for a system with a duty cycle of five 8-hour days per week.

With basic data availability, backup is the only failure protection mechanism. The implicit assumption is that the duty cycle of the system allows for an adequate backup window. For any failure that affects data, including system crash, application fault, or disk storage subsystem failure, recovery consists of repairing the fault, restoring a backup, and restarting operation.

Basic data availability may be adequate for an 8×5 system. Such systems are a dying breed in the electronic business era, where 24×7 operations have become the norm.

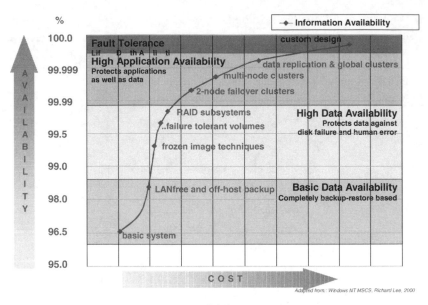

Figure 11.1 Degrees of system availability.

For a system that runs 24 hours per day and 7 days per week, 96.5 percent uptime would mean an average of about 12 days per year of downtime. This is clearly inconsistent with 24×7 operation. So the first lesson to draw from Figure 11.1 is that basic data availability, defined as periodic backup, is inconsistent with anything even *approaching* continuous operation.

Figure 11.1 suggests that LAN-free and off-host backup, both of which are enabled by SANs, increase uptime. Both of these techniques reduce backup impact on applications, which in turn enables more frequent backups. More frequent backups means shorter restore times and less journal playback or other forms of data reconstruction, which in turn means less time until applications are back in operation after a failure.

As Figure 11.1 also suggests, this improvement comes at a cost. The cost comes from a combination of incremental SAN hardware and software that enables tape drive sharing and, for off-host backup, the transfer of online data ownership between application server and backup media server.

LAN-free backup, whether off-host or not, still takes backup source data offline during the course of a backup. Moving further up the availability curve, frozen images, whether of the copy-on-write variety (Chapter 8) or of the split mirror variety (Chapter 4), enable applications to operate while backup uses the frozen image. The incremental cost of frozen image technology is primarily software, although some additional online storage may be required to hold frozen images.

Further along the availability curve, failure-tolerant volumes and RAID subsystems replace backup as the primary mechanism for keeping data available when disks and other I/O hardware components fail. Very rarely do device and I/O path failures in systems equipped with these technologies result in application downtime. Data availability improves because systems can ride through hardware failures and because there are fewer situations in which backups must be restored. With failure-tolerant volumes and RAID subsystems, the primary role of backup becomes recovering from application, data manager, and procedural errors.

The next group of major improvements in availability comes from enhancing application availability. The simplest of these is *failover clustering* described in Chapter 8. A failover cluster increases availability by automatically restarting applications on a secondary server when a failure of the primary server is detected. When clustering is combined with mirroring or RAID, applications continue to operate:

- If a storage device fails
- While backup copies are being made (except for a brief pause that allows the data image to be frozen with data in a consistent state)
- If a server or application fails (except for a brief interval while the application restarts on a backup server)

Of course, a shared I/O interconnect such as a SAN is required to enable a backup server or failover server to access a failed primary server's data.

Enterprise-class clusters support more than two servers and shared volumes and file systems. These features increase availability still further by allowing applications to survive more than one server failure. Using optical SAN interconnects, the servers that constitute such a cluster can be spread across campus distances, protecting against still more potential failures. Shared data reduces failover time by simplifying file system recovery in most instances. Of course, for cascading failover, the servers eligible to run an application must be connected to the storage devices that hold the application's data. SANs provide the robust universal connectivity that enables cascading failover.

Although Figure 11.1 shows increasing cost between two-node failover clusters and larger shared data clusters, Chapter 2 makes the point that multiserver clusters can actually reduce the cost of enhanced application availability by enabling a single failover server backstop several application servers.

The next major availability enhancement comes from replicating data over long distances. Replicated data, when augmented by global clustering for application failover, protects against disasters that incapacitate entire data centers. Typically, there is a substantial cost increment between clustering within the confines of a campus and global clustering with replicated data, due largely to the cost of high-performance long-distance networks.

All of these availability enhancements are achieved through the integration of mass-produced hardware and software components. While highly available systems include more storage and SAN infrastructure components than conventional systems of equivalent workload capacity, they do not generally require specialized components such as are custom-built for *failure-tolerant* systems. Truly failure-tolerant systems are typically custom-designed for a specific purpose and delivered in small volumes, making them very expensive.

The very high cost of failure-tolerant systems plus their failure to track the mainstream of hardware, software, and network evolution lead most managers to opt for clustering to enhance data and application availability.

Who Needs SANs?

Early adopters of SAN technology have tended to be enterprises whose business is, in one way or another, information. Internet service providers, the so-called dot-coms, and other companies, most or all of whose business is the management of online electronic information, have been early adopters for two reasons:

■ *Need.* Many of today's largest users of storage networking did not exist as enterprises 10 years ago. Their businesses have grown rapidly from the idea stage through early adoption to mainstream. Their information processing growth has been nothing short of phenomenal. Faced with constant growth, these enterprises have been forced to adopt unproven technology strategies that represent the only way to meet their growth needs.

■ *Low user expectations.* Because these enterprises were primarily in new businesses, their customers had no prior *quality-of-service* expectations. Internet access, home shopping, online libraries, and similar applications represented such huge improvements over the methods they replaced that early users were willing to tolerate occasional service outages. The tolerant attitude of their customers made it feasible for these enterprises to adopt technologies that had yet to prove themselves in widespread deployment. Of course, as enterprises mature and their markets broaden, user expectations rise, creating pressure for robust, continuous application and data access.

Today, these nontraditional enterprises have some of the most advanced information processing infrastructures on the planet. Driven by need, they have adopted new technologies as fast as they became available. More traditional enterprises have been slower to move. These *brick-and-mortar* businesses have massive legacies of data, applications, and users to service. For them to adopt new technology is a complex process of melding with existing information processing infrastructures without disrupting the flow of business.

The breath technology options for minimizing down time and their associated cost make it clear that executive management must concern itself with the issue if data availability. Executives in the electronic business era must assess the impact of downtime in their businesses and formulate their data availability strategies accordingly.

Developing a SAN Deployment Strategy

While it should be clear by now that the authors are very much in favor of storage networking, we do not recommend that enterprises adopt *SAN deployment strategies*. As the foregoing discussions indicate, a SAN is better regarded as a tool that can help achieve business goals. A preferable approach in our opinion is to merge the new capabilities enabled by SANs into enterprises' mainstream information technology planning processes. SANs are enabling data center operational improvements at the same time that electronic commerce is casting up new and greater challenges for the information services community. SAN capabilities help meet these challenges.

Thus, our preferred approach to SAN deployment would be an iterative sequence of steps.

1. Determine current business information requirements and estimate possible future requirements. Pay particular attention to the relative importance of different requirements. While it is always advisable for an enterprise to be expert in its own business processes, technology-aware business process consultants can help make users aware of possibilities enabled by technology and their cost.

2. Learn about the new information handling and processing capabilities enabled by SANs.[2] Learning is not a substitute for experience, but a necessary prerequisite.

3. Match current and projected information requirements with technology capabilities, some of which are enabled by SAN technology, but others of which are unrelated to SANs.

4. Devise an ideal enterprise information processing strategy that delivers needed business benefits unconstrained by cost.

5. Audit the enterprise's installed information processing base to determine the starting point for deployment. Auditing should include capital equipment, computer processes, and human assets.

6. Develop a cost-constrained plan for deployment of capabilities indicated by the new strategy. The plan should include clear business and technical objectives that executives can use to measure success against business objectives. Consultants can be useful at this stage because experience has shown that inexperienced users tend to over design SANs. The plan developed at this stage typically feeds the enterprise budgeting process. During this stage, planners must continually verify that the elements of the plan that survive the budgeting process continue to form a coherent strategy.

7. Choose a logical first step to implement and perform a detailed design. This is an appropriate stage to engage consultants with broad SAN expertise. At today's state of SAN maturity, prototyping to prove concepts is generally advisable. Prototyping can catch many problems before systems go into production.

8. Implement and roll out the first elements of the SAN strategy.

9. Analyze the rollout, both to determine what went well or badly and to verify that the problems being solved are still the right ones. Analysis rollout particularly with respect to whether business and technical objectives have been met. The analysis should determine what went well or badly and also verify that problems being solved are still the right ones. Feedback from this analysis may lead to modifications in future implementation stages.

---

[2] For example, buy copies of this book for your entire information services staff.

10. Iterate on this sequence of steps. Projects should be rolled out in succession; however, it is important to revisit the strategy periodically to make sure that a plan still makes business sense in light of things that have transpired in the environment since the plan was written down.

There's very little here that's unique to SANs, and properly so. SANs are a tool for solving business information problems or for enabling new business information handling capabilities. They don't change the fundamentals of good business information processing system design. The key to getting value from a SAN is to understand that it can enable new information capabilities (frequent, consistent frozen images for very current data mining, to name one) and to integrate those capabilities into the business information planning process as appropriate.

Nine Steps to Successful SAN Deployment

The following sections elaborate the steps of our preferred approach to SAN deployment enumerated in the preceding section.

Step 1: Determining Business Information Requirements

In some ways, determining business information requirements is the most challenging part of the planning process, because it inherently requires out-of-the-box thinking. Not only must IT planners try to see things through users' eyes, they must apply their knowledge of what is technically possible to users' perspective of what is necessary. Determining information requirements is partly an input gathering process, but also partly an educational one, with the IT planners doing the educating. It is sometimes helpful to engage business process consultants at this stage to help stimulate novel

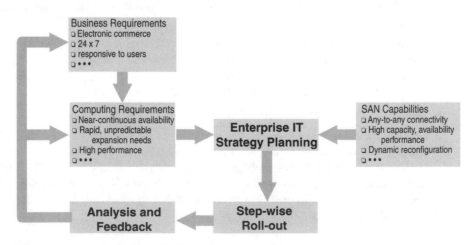

Figure 11.2 Information strategy planning.

perspectives. In addition to IT planners and business process consultants, business information requirements would ideally include representative of effected parts of the business and executive management.

This is also the process step during which the IT organization starts to build rapport with the rest of the enterprise. At this stage, planners must balance the need to learn about business processes and the need to instruct users about what is easy and what is hard, what is abundant and what is expensive. Information users are often highly attuned to their information needs, but blissfully unaware of implications on enterprise information processing. For example, they tend to be unaware of the importance of high availability (and of its cost!). Part of the planners' task during this step is to bring users to a realization of the larger implications of their wishes. The other part is to learn what it is about information processing that makes life difficult for users and to create proposals for improvement that might not occur to users with limited knowledge of information technology.

Finally, IT planners should recognize that periodic redefinition of information requirements spans the enterprise requiring a big picture view. Indeed, one of the factors that makes requirements determination so challenging is the need to devise a strategy that can accommodate all of an enterprise's information processing needs, some of which are unknown, some of which will change their goals or scope, and some of which will simply fall by the wayside.

Requirements determination is a good practice throughout a business, not just in information technology. It is not something new that is occasioned by storage networking. The main impact of storage networking at this stage is that it enables new capabilities (cross-campus data mirroring, frozen image backups, and so forth).

Step 2: Learning Technology's Capabilities

Electronic information processing technology has been undergoing rapid change practically since its inception half a century ago. Storage networking only continues this trend (or is it a tradition?). The goal of this step is not for IT planners to become Fibre Channel Ethernet experts, but for them to understand both the capabilities that are enabled by those and other emerging SAN technologies and the practical limitations of the technologies and their implementations.

This step is particularly important because the manifold promises of SAN technology require extensive supporting software to realize. For example, with SAN any-to-any connectivity, it is *possible* to share data among several applications running concurrently on different servers. But sharing data requires clustering software, as well as a cluster file system. In this case, the SAN is very much the enabler and the software delivers on the promise. As we observed in Chapter 1: *Hardware makes SANs possible; software makes SANs happen.*

It is particularly important for IT planners to understand the difference between potential and reality. While SANs enable the benefits described in Chapter 2 in principle, different computing platforms and software suites deliver them to different degrees. The role of the IT planner is to evaluate and understand the degree to which SAN benefits can be delivered on different computing platforms and by different software suites. Specialized education and consulting can be helpful at this stage. Since SAN component vendors have not been chosen, however, a vendor's training department is probably not the best choice for training or consultation. Fortunately, the SAN industry has spawned an active training segment and vendor-independent training and consulting are readily available.

Step 3: Matching Requirements with Technology

On the surface, this step is simple. Users supply a list of requirements. Vendors supply lists of capabilities (which the newly informed IT planner is sure to analyze critically). By matching the two against each other, requirements that are impossible to meet can be identified and one or more best fits can be found.

Of course, this analysis is a *little* more complicated than it sounds. Users may be blissfully unaware of the technology implications of what they perceive as business requirements. A perceived business need to analyze several weeks or months of sales or operations data, for example, might imply the following:

- Significant online storage to hold historical data
- Significant I/O bandwidth to scan historical data for analysis
- Even more significant I/O resources to move current data to the warehouse without impacting the availability or performance of online applications
- Development, operations, and management personnel to install, configure, and maintain the warehouse

The task of the IT planner is to use a knowledge of available technology and of local constraints and requirements to make users aware of the implications of what they perceive as requirements and to help them arrive at a balance between the desired and the possible.

Storage networking is something of a special case in IT requirements planning because it introduces so many new capabilities, of which users are not likely to be aware. A user is likely to realize that critical data must be backed up, but without prior experience, he or she is not likely to assume that off-host backup using a frozen image can reduce an application's backup window to almost (but not quite) nothing. Similarly, a database administrator may understand the need for frequent database backups, but without knowledge of changed block incremental backup technology, he or she is unlikely to assume that hourly incremental backups can be synthesized into full backups for faster and simpler restoring.

In no step of the planning process is trust between IT planners and users more crucial, because in this step, the user must often make decisions based on assertions that are not verifiable by direct experience. The user just has to have faith in the IT planner. The IT planner had better be right!

Step 4: Real Planning

Two factors distinguish this step from "matching requirements with technology," as described in the preceding section:

- *Integration.* During this step, IT planners consider the totality of an enterprise's data processing needs or at least the total needs of a data center or campus. For example, we have described several ways in which storage consolidation enabled by storage networking can save money. These boil down to storage device pooling or data sharing, either on a concurrent or on an interval ownership basis. During this step, planners get down to cases and determine what benefits would accrue from pooling which storage and which data can be shared among which applications.

- *Cost.* During this step, planning begins to get real, in a financial sense. To the synthesis of what is desired and what is possible is added the constraint of what is affordable. Again, it is important to conduct this step in the context of total enterprise data processing strategy, so that the enterprise does not find itself funding data processing projects whose purpose is to feed data to other projects that are not funded.

Since the planners' view at this stage is global as well as cost constrained, this is a good time to make a first estimate of the direct cost or saving that will result from implementing storage networking as planned. Without going into too much detail (somewhat futile in a world where data processing requirements can change literally overnight), planners should be able to assess the direct costs of adopting storage networking (infrastructure components, storage devices, host bus adapters, software, personnel, training, and so forth) and balance them against user estimations of business benefits.

Out of this analysis comes a first pass at an enterprise or data center *storage network architecture.* The architecture should include determinations of such criteria as:

What databases or file sets must be online with what type of failure protection and what level of access performance—the quality of storage service (QoSS). This information helps determine the overall shape of a storage network—the number and interconnection of switches, the number and type of storage devices, and the topology of paths between storage devices and hosts.

Which applications require access to which data and how they gain access (concurrent sharing or interval ownership). This information plays a role in server placement decisions and clustering requirements and constraints. Applications needing access to much of the same data are obvious candidates to run on the same servers or in the same cluster. Loosely coupled applications may be candidates for loosely coupled sharing techniques such as interval ownership of devices or data replication.

The relative criticality of different applications and data. This helps to determine several aspects of the plan, including the mix of host, infrastructure and storage-based storage and data virtualization, cluster design, failover and parallel application strategies, and backup strategies and techniques.

The data protection strategy for every major data set. Data protection, as we have defined it, is protection against the logical destruction of data by a malfunctioning (buggy) application or by procedural error. The universal protection strategy is backup, but that doesn't begin to tell the story. Related data objects that must be mutually consistent must be backed up together so that restores produce a consistent result. Backup frequency and type (full or incremental) must be balanced against application availability requirements and restore scenarios. Application procedures for establishing consistent frozen images must be designed. Data center operations policies must be formulated (What level of response should be given to what type of request to restore data from a backup? What should operators do if a backup fails?). And finally, archiving and vaulting strategies must be considered for long-term records retention and disaster protection, respectively.

Disaster recoverability needs. Disaster recoverability is expensive. The extra data center equipment and software it requires are only the tip of the cost iceberg. Premises, network facilities, and staff are likely to dwarf the IT capital cost of disaster recoverability. A larger disaster radius (as, for example, is faced by enterprises located in earthquake- or flood-prone areas) can dramatically increase telecommunications cost. The cost implications of disaster recoverability generally make it an enterprise decision rather than strictly an IT one. Once the enterprise decision has been made, however, it becomes an IT planning responsibility to design, implement, and operate the required networks, computing facilities, data, and applications. The planning should be comprehensive, including a conscious rationale for the disaster recoverability decisions made about each of the enterprise's major applications and data objects.

Growth. Any IT planning process must account for growth expectations. While electronic commerce has tended to increase data processing entropy, planning is still an enterprise necessity. Enterprise plans have information technology components, so the need for IT planning does not change. What *does* change with electronic commerce is the nature of IT planning. Any reasonable IT plan has a (large) component that deals with known entities—ongoing operations and well-defined developments, as well as a (smaller) component that might be thought of as a contingency allowance. With increased need for enterprises to react rapidly to change, the contingency portion of an IT becomes larger relative to the known portion. SANs play well here, because they increase the flexibility of storage resources, allowing them to be installed in advance and deployed anywhere as they are needed.

The storage network architecture provides an enterprise basis for setting the priorities of different information processing developments and deployments. It also provides constant awareness of relationships between components of data center operations. It can help avoid the trap of deploying technology while deferring deployment of services that make use of the technology.

Step 5: Auditing the Current Situation

Unless the enterprise is brand new, storage networking won't be deployed in a vacuum. As with any new technology, an important factor in storage networking adoption is making the transition from old to new with minimal disruption to the business. This is particularly important because enterprise storage is expensive. Enterprises typically have large investments in storage, amortized over relatively long periods of time—as much as five years in some cases. If it required wholesale replacement of enterprise storage, storage networking would be quite difficult to justify.

While native storage devices are the best way to maximize storage networking benefits, significant benefits can be derived using preexisting local storage devices. There are several options for incorporating local storage into a storage network. The two most important ones are:

- *Bridges and routers.* A thriving industry segment offers SAN *bridges* and *routers* that attach legacy parallel SCSI storage devices to Fibre Channel SANs. These devices connect parallel SCSI tape drives and RAID subsystems to a Fibre Channel SAN, making them shareable among the servers attached to the SAN. In most cases, bridges and routers add little or no overhead to the communication path, so native device performance is available.

- *Software storage appliances.* Another way of incorporating existing storage devices into a SAN is to use a *storage appliance.* Like the bridge and router solutions, a storage appliance is an intelligent device that connects tapes, RAID subsystems, and even disks to a SAN. Unlike the bridge and router, a storage appliance performs significant transformations on data. Storage appliances are essentially servers. They include volume managers that aggregate storage device capacity and performance and enhance data availability (for example, by mirroring virtual disks from two or more RAID subsystems). In addition, some storage appliances are capable of executing off-host, off-SAN backups.

Which (if either) of these investment preservation techniques can and should be adopted depends on specific capabilities required as well as the value of the storage devices to be preserved. A complete audit of existing storage assets is required to determine their residual value and balance that value plus the cost of bridging them into the SAN against the cost of replacement storage devices.

An audit of storage assets should extend beyond capital equipment. A transition from local storage to a SAN environment requires new management skills and possibly new ways of doing things. How best to develop these new skills and incorporate SAN capabilities into data center operations can only be determined with a complete understanding of current skills and practices.

Step 6: Merging IT Plans with Enterprise Plans

Armed with both a realistic, affordable plan for IT improvements that achieve business benefits and a knowledge of current assets and how they figure into a transition from legacy to new technology, IT planners can create a minimally disruptive transition plan and fold it into overall enterprise business planning.

The result of merging an IT evolution strategy into overall corporate plans is budgetary approval to proceed with some or all of the development steps laid out in the strategy. The strategy should thus include realistic rollout plans for new capabilities. Rollout plans must include capital, implementation, training, testing, cutover, and contingency plans, such as fallback strategies in the event of any conceivable failure. The overall evolution should carefully schedule individual projects so that human and financial resources are neither unduly strained by rapid-fire deployments nor wasted by nonoptimal phasing of individual projects.

An important, but often undervalued, aspect of new IT developments is the selling of the development to its customers, who are often uninvolved in the planning and implementation. Setting user expectations and keeping users apprised of progress and the implications of progress on their operations and daily lives can be an important factor in the success of a new IT implementations.

Step 7: Design and Vendor Selection

When an enterprise has committed resources to an IT strategy, the emphasis changes from planning to the design and execution of concrete projects. In the case of a SAN deployment, the general design of the SAN conceived during the planning stages should be validated by more detailed design at this stage. Detailed design of a SAN should include the standard five considerations of IT system design:

- *Function.* At a very basic level, the SAN must meet enterprise's requirements. If the planning stages indicated a requirement for campuswide mirroring, for example, with split mirrors used for backup, then the chosen SAN must support this in all respects. Maximum link distances must be within the capability of the chosen interconnect technology. Host-, infrastructure-, or RAID subsystem-based mirroring with an adequate number of mirrors must be available with the chosen technologies. Split mirrors must be supported. The management components of the SAN infrastructure must support the transfer of storage device ownership from one server to another. If SAN-based enterprise backup is part of the implementation strategy, all backup components must have complementary capabilities—for example, NDMP support or off-host backup support at both client and server ends of the connection.

- *Availability.* Similarly, a SAN must be designed to provide the level of availability required for each application and data object. Storage devices and access paths must be appropriately redundant. Redundant paths must be physically configurable and both storage devices and servers must support them. If server-based volume management is part of the solution, it, as well as base operating system drivers, must support multipath storage device access. As active components that can fail, switches and routers must be configured with redundancy in mind. Some switches are internally redundant; others are modular designs from which redundant multiswitch configurations can be constructed. For SAN-based backup strategies, the ability of the entire strategy to survive tape drive and library failures must be evaluated. This is not to suggest that all SAN components must be configured for redundancy, but that all redundancy decisions should be made consciously.

- *Performance.* Performance is probably the least likely aspect of a SAN design to be slighted, but it nonetheless deserves careful consideration, as it is not without subtleties. There must be adequate throughput between servers and their respective storage devices. Designs must accommodate possible interserver or interapplication interference or avoid them. For example, an enterprise RAID subsystem may have enough disks to meet the I/O request rate needs of several applications, but insufficient processing power to process all the requests. In a multitier Fibre Channel fabric, routed paths may increase I/O request latency, ultimately resulting in unacceptable application response times. The number of tape drives configured must have adequate throughput for the amount of data to be backed up within a window. Alternatively, the number of client backups streamed to a single tape drive must match the drive's performance so that tapes *stream* during backup.

- *Security.* Within the data center physical security can generally be assumed and therefore SAN design consideration are similar to those of conventional systems. As long physical connections are not exposed to untrusted environments great reliance can be placed on file system, database, application security. SANs with long distance interconnection almost inevitably pass through physically untrustworthy environments and must therefore be treated like any other enterprise network facility in terms of firewalling data encryption, authentication, and other network security practices.

- *Cost.* Cost is actually more of a constraint than a requirement. All of the functional, availability, performance, and security decisions made during SAN design are ultimately tempered by cost considerations. If planning (*Step 6*) has been accurate, there should be no cost surprises at this stage. Nonetheless, cost must be reviewed and refined at this stage, as it is at this stage that financial commitments are initiated.

A useful technique at the detail design stage is a modeling exercise that covers aspects of the SAN such as:

- *Exceptions.* What are the consequences of a link or hardware component failure.

- *Secondary failures and other worst-case scenarios.* (For example, what is the recovery strategy if the network fails during a restore.)

- *Capacity limits.* (For example, what happens if a network backup is schedule to use an already saturated link.)

- *Design assumptions.* (For example, what would be the effect if the actual network load was 20, 50, 100 percent greater than the design assumption.)

Modeling can answer questions like these and possibly avert expensive and disruptive events after the SAN is deployed.

In the earlier steps of SAN deployment, IT planners need good overall conceptual knowledge of SAN technology and capabilities. At the design stage, however, actual expertise is a must. In this step, planners may need highly technical training. Training is a precursor to experience rather than a substitute, so it is also highly advisable to engage experienced consultants, at least for initial deployments.

SAN consultants take different forms, including independent consulting companies, consulting divisions of SAN component vendor companies, and consultancy services available from system integrators as part of a system purchase. Prior to vendor selection, the former is probably the best choice. Whichever types of consultant are used, planners should clearly understand their motivations when evaluating their recommendations. For this reason, the best time to engage technical consulting services is after planning is complete, so that the enterprise has a clear idea of its goals and their affordability and before irrevocable commitments to technology approaches are made. As an enterprise gains experience with SANs, it may become increasingly self-reliant. In the beginning, however, without practical implementation experience, knowledgeable consultants can shorten the learning curve, avoid overdesign, and increase the probability of success considerably.

The state of SAN maturity as this book is written is another reason to engage highly experienced technology consultants in this and later steps of SAN deployment. The reality today is that SAN component interoperability is not as mature as LAN interoperability. SANs are more sensitive to hardware and firmware revision levels, software qualification, and so forth. Different vendors test interoperability using different revisions of complementary products. Sometimes, there *are* no right answers—for example, about whose qualification matrix to use. Consultants with extensive experience in SAN deployment can help planners and developers wend a way along this torturous path. It's usually a good idea for an enterprise to be self-sufficient, so every attempt should be made to treat consultant engagements as a learning experience. But this type of learning experience accelerates deployment rather than elongating it and has a solid experience base rather than being theoretical.

A design technique that is particularly appropriate in an enterprise's early experience with SAN is prototyping. Prototyping appears to be expensive, because it requires capital purchases, personnel, training, and premises, all with an unknown outcome. But it is far less expensive than a premature production-level commitment to an approach that won't work in a particular situation. Prototyping is particularly suitable when the deployment of unique features enabled by SANs is considered for the first time— serverless backup, changed block incremental backup, or clustering, for example. The impact of these modes of operation on existing applications is difficult to estimate in advance, in all four of the major dimensions—function, availability, performance, and cost. Will serverless backup really reduce backup time? Does it interfere with application performance? Can tapes be driven at speed? Are allowable backup times met? The answers to questions like these can be estimated analytically. But prototyping representative configurations before making major commitments to deployment can be an important confidence builder, especially when an enterprise has little hard experience on which to base informed judgments.

Prototyping in the form of benchmarking is obviously an effective way to validate performance adequacy, but it is also an excellent means of determining and evaluating failure tolerance and recoverability strategies. Application and database failover times, file system recovery and database journal playback, storage device replacement procedures, and dozens of other aspects of data availability should be tested before major commitments are made.

Design includes not only the SAN infrastructure and the components that connect to it, but also the operational procedures, system management tools and processes, skill development, and personnel required to operate the business systems in a SAN environment. Each of these must be assessed, planned for, scheduled, and integrated with the rest of the plan to devise a comprehensive deployment strategy.

Step 8: Rollout

Finally, with goals clear, planning and budgeting done, design complete, vendors chosen, and initial training accomplished, it's time to implement the first SAN-based solution. The two keys to success at this step are timely execution and cutover planning. An enterprise's first SAN is likely to have a significantly different system topology than its legacy data center systems. The learning curve can be significant, particularly for operations and system management staff. The biggest risk at this stage is leaving the enterprise unable to conduct a part of its business because some step in the rollout failed. Conservative, phased implementation strategies mitigate this risk, but even with them, solid plans for cutting over from legacy systems to SAN-based ones, including contingency plans at each stage, are an absolute necessity. The need to fall back to legacy systems in the event of a disaster often implies substantial periods of parallel operation during which legacy systems and the new SAN-based systems run side by side.

A failure at some point in SAN rollout without a viable fallback strategy can leave an enterprise unable to conduct a crucial part of its business, as well as destroy user confidence in their IT functions, with far-reaching effects on future deployments. This is a step at which it is prudent to sacrifice savings for security—to extend the lease on legacy RAID subsystems for an extra quarter, to authorize on-call overtime for operations personnel, to spend the time and resources to make extra backups, and so forth. It is also a stage at which user expectations must be carefully managed it is far better to promise less and deliver more than to promise too much and not deliver.

While not always possible, in general it is prudent not to treat a system rollout as complete before all of the business processing cycles (e.g., daily, weekly, monthly, quarterly, annual) it affects have elapsed. For example, if SAN-based backup is implemented, all backup cycles, including full and incremental backups, hourly, daily, weekly, and any others, should be experienced before the rollout is considered complete. Moreover, restore, full backup synthesis, and any other ancillary procedures should be tested extensively. It is probably impractical to test all possible scenarios, but a selection of the most important cases that exercise the broadest possible range of technology features should be chosen and tried.

Step 9: Iteration, Review, and Learning

An enterprise's first SAN implementation is undoubtedly the most difficult, because of unfamiliarity with the task and fear of failure. Once it succeeds, a SAN deployment team's confidence increases and other deployments can be tackled in sequence. It is important, however, to learn from each deployment. It's a well-known adage that we learn from our failures, but there are also lessons to be learned from our successes. The most obvious of these are schedule refinement and vendor choices. Actually deploying a SAN gives a much more accurate idea of how long it takes to run cables, install and configure infrastructure and storage components, install and configure software, and the many other tasks required. Only by deploying a SAN does one finally learn whether performance has been estimated correctly, whether operators and administrators can manage the distributed systems, whether applications share data properly and expeditiously, and so forth. The point here is threefold: It is important to take good notes during an implementation, to learn from them, and to adjust plans for later deployments to reflect the lessons learned in earlier ones.

Changing a plan based on past experience isn't admitting failure, either of the implementation process or of the plans. It's admitting both that reality can be fluid and that learning can, in fact, take place and be applied to improve future experience.

Not only are review and learning important for planning, design, and implementation teams, they are important for users as well. Clearly, users of any system must be trained whenever the system changes in a way discernable to them. Less obvious, but also important, is that users be made a party to the process as much as possible. Keeping them informed of both operational changes discernable to them, and what's being changed, why it's being changed from a business standpoint, what the technology challenges are, and how they are being met creates involvement and is likely to lead to a more proactive and ultimately a more satisfied user. But user involvement goes beyond a one-way information flow, users should be encouraged to participate in the process as equals whose reactions and suggestions should be heeded and acted upon by the implementation team. To the extent possible, the user should actually *become* a part of the implementation team.

Critical Success Factors

Throughout SAN adoption there are a few recurring themes that are key to success.

Success at each stage. It is always important to build on a solid foundation. In SAN deployment, this means that each stage of the implementation should be complete and successful before the next is undertaken. If SAN backup is experiencing mysterious dips in performance every so often, it's probably not a good idea to add routers and start moving legacy RAID subsystems onto the SAN. If cluster failover time for an application is minutes instead of the expected seconds, it's probably not a good idea to make an additional application into a cluster service. Especially when SAN technology and products are new to an enterprise and not well understood, it is important not to introduce any more variables than necessary into the changing environment.

Keeping user confidence. The user of IT services, particularly the in-house user, is the customer. It is important that the customer's needs be met. SAN technology primarily affects the back-end (servers and storage) of the data center. Changes in this part of a data center are often visible to users only as service disruptions. Some of the most important benefits of SAN deployment are even less visible—storage pooling, tape sharing, application clustering, and so forth. Thus, while SAN deployment improves things for the enterprise as a whole, the perception of users can easily be that the data center is becoming less reliable, that things are changing capriciously, or worse. To counter this, users should be kept informed as SAN implementation progresses. At each stage, users should be systematically told what has changed from a technology standpoint, what changes they are likely to observe, as well as the business and technical reasons for change and how it fits into the overall enterprise strategy. An informed user is more likely to be an understanding user when the inevitable problems that characterize any major transition occur.

Keep an eye on the ball. It is always important to remember that the ultimate goal is to provide benefits to the enterprise, not to build a SAN. As a SAN grows and more of the enterprise's IT functions come to depend upon it, it is easy to slip into viewing the SAN as an end in itself and to forget that the SAN is only one tool for delivering lower-cost, more effective data processing to the enterprise. It is entirely possible that some data processing functions will *not* benefit from being incorporated into the SAN. At each stage of the implementation, enterprise goals should be reassessed to make sure they still make sense in light of both changing enterprise business goals and actual results of prior SAN implementation stages.

SAN Adoption Alternatives

Because it is probably the most difficult, the first step of a phased strategic implementation of any new technology or business process should be approached most conservatively. Not only should the technical difficulty of the implementation step be modest, but the implementation procedure should be gradual, with procedural redundancy and contingency plans built in throughout. For example, a reasonable way for an enterprise to get its feet wet with SANs might be to implement a backup SAN, leaving its online systems in place and doing business as usual, but augmenting them with connections to SAN-attached tape drives. The legacy backup procedures, software, and hardware should be left in place. If something goes wrong with the SAN or with the shared tape backup procedures, a return can be made to the old procedures and at least the enterprise will not have lost any capability.

While some steps in the SAN adoption process (for example, installation of the initial infrastructure) are a physical necessity, others are matters of choice. This and the foregoing argument suggest that the sequence in which applications and data center functions are migrated to a SAN should be influenced by two other factors in addition to business benefits:

- *Technical challenge.* When a SAN is first deployed, the deployment team is necessarily at its least experienced. Even if the enterprise has taken the sensible steps of using consultants and employing IT specialists with prior SAN experience, these people will not have coalesced as a team, nor have an existing SAN as a pattern. This suggests that early SAN deployments should be less technically challenging, because becoming a team and gaining experience with the actual SAN as it grows is enough of a challenge in itself.

- *User challenge.* Human beings resist change. Even if a change is for the better an individual (user), tends to react by resisting it, just because it is different from the patterns to which he or she is accustomed. User resistance to change is an inevitable hurdle that must be overcome in any SAN implementation that effects data processing in a user visible way. This suggests that another criterion in choosing which functions or applications to implement first is the impact on users, thus for example backup procedures such tape sharing and LAN free backup are good candidates for early implementation because they are invisible to users and effect only operations staff. More obtrusive applications such as the installation of as distributed database are probably better candidates for later implementation.

- *Impact of failure.* When a SAN implementation team is new and inexperienced, the probability of failure or error is greatest. However good the intentions and thorough the planning, there is a chance that any given stage of a SAN deployment will fail in a way that impacts the enterprise's ability to operate. This suggests that the earlier stages of SAN adoption should be those applications and data center functions that least impact an enterprise's overall ability to operate. Thus, for example, an enterprise that can't run backup because something went wrong with its SAN-based backup installation is at risk of losing data, but is still fundamentally able to do business (process transactions, mine data, generate reports, and so forth). An enterprise whose point-of-sale application has failed because of a flawed attempt to make it a cluster service is not. Clearly, the shared tape backup is a better candidate for the first stage of SAN implementation.

Choosing a simple problem to solve with the first SAN deployment has another benefit as well: Nothing breeds success like success. If a modest first stage is defined and implemented successfully, management and user approval should make subsequent support easier to obtain. The following sections evaluate some of the more popular usages of SAN capabilities from the standpoint of technical challenge and impact on an enterprise's ability to operate its business.

LAN-free Backup: Easing One's Way In

LAN-free backup is perhaps the simplest application of SAN technology. In a SAN context, LAN-free backup refers to backups in which the target tape drive(s) are connected to the backup server via a SAN. The benefit of LAN-free backup is that backup data is not transferred across the enterprise LAN. There are no busy periods when it is difficult to process transactions or otherwise conduct business because a backup is using most of the enterprise LAN's available bandwidth.

With a SAN, tape drive ownership can be transferred from server to server. Backup schedules can be staggered to keep tape drives active. A secondary business benefit of LAN-free backup is, therefore, more effective tape and library resource utilization.

The technical challenge in adopting LAN-free backup is relatively low. A SAN infrastructure must be installed, including Fibre Channel switches and Fibre Channel host bus adapters for backup servers. Tape drives must be installed and configured. It may be possible to repurpose legacy tape drives by attaching them to bridges that convert their native SCSI protocol to Fibre Channel, although this may constrain the fallback strategy. A backup manager that supports tape sharing must be selected, installed, and configured. There must be a data asset transition plan that allows the affected parts of the enterprise's tape library to be read when the new system is in use.

As long as LAN-free backup adoption includes a fallback strategy that allows the enterprise to use its legacy backup data and methods, the business risk of failure is quite low. Depending upon the type of problems encountered, the worst impact on operations is probably from unanticipated backup window changes or unexpected server loading. In some instances, there may be supportability issues with host bus adapters or other infrastructure components, but once these are overcome or circumvented by adhering to vendor-qualified combinations of components, LAN-free backup should be stable.

Storage Pooling: Administrative Flexibility

One of the most obvious benefits of SANs is that they enable storage for many servers to be pooled so that incremental storage requirements can be met from a single pool rather than from a pool per server. Pooling storage also allows repurposing by shifting ownership from one server to another. The obvious benefits are reduced capital cost because less physical storage is required and greater ability to react to ad hoc demands because unanticipated demands can be met by assigning ownership of devices to the server that requires them.

Since no data access coordination is required, storage pooling is among the least technically challenging of SAN applications. All that is required is SAN management tools that are able to control storage device ownership and to fence off I/O requests to a device from all but the owning server. This can be accomplished with host bus adapter-based LUN mapping, infrastructure-based zoning, or storage device-based LUN masking or reservations, or simply by cooperation among the servers connected to the SAN. All of these are typically invoked through server-based management tools. Some management tools support multiple techniques and choose the appropriate one for the devices and infrastructure.

Storage pooling is the disk version of tape sharing. It has minor implications on application operations. With an obvious payback in capital savings and minimal risk of adverse effect on operations (few, if any, application or procedural changes are required), storage pooling is an excellent candidate for early SAN implementation.

Frozen Image Backup: Eliminating the Window

Another capability enabled by SANs is the near elimination of backup windows through the use of frozen image technology. Again, frozen images, using either split mirrors or copy-on-write techniques, do not inherently require SAN technology. But the server and storage device connectivity of a SAN make frozen images more practical in a wider variety of situations:

- With no practical limit to storage device connections, server-based mirrored volumes become more practical to implement.

- With no practical limit to server connections, it becomes more practical to designate a backup server and transfer ownership of the frozen image to it for the duration of a backup.

Frozen image backups enable nearly continuous application operation. An application need only pause for long enough to establish a consistent on-disk image of its data and to initiate a frozen data image, either by splitting mirrors or by creating copy-on-write frozen images. The application can then continue with read-write access to its data. In electronic business, continuous access can mean the difference between success and failure for critical applications.

Implementing frozen image backup with SAN-attached storage devices is primarily a matter of software support for SAN features. First and foremost is the frozen image technology itself. Frozen image technology is available in several forms, including both server-based and RAID subsystem-based implementations. Both split mirror and copy-on-write variations are available. The primary requirement is that image initiation be a management operation so that scripts can automatically create frozen images and start backup jobs. Some enterprise backup managers are integrated with frozen image technologies, easing the design task. Since frozen images are presented as virtual storage devices that appear and disappear during system operation, host environments must be able to discover new storage devices during operation, rather than just at boot time. This is not an issue with server-based volume managers, but RAID subsystem-based implementations require operating systems that can discover new devices while they are running.

Selecting a frozen image technology depends on factors related both to backup and to other aspects of application operation. For example, a split mirror necessarily occupies different storage devices from those containing the primary data. Backup I/O therefore has minimal effect on application performance because it is directed at different devices. Similarly this may not be true of copy-on-write frozen images. Similarly, when a backup made from a split mirror is complete, the split mirror must be merged with primary data volumes. In the worst case, this requires copying all data from primary volumes to the split mirror device(s). More sophisticated split mirror implementations track changes made while a mirror is split and remerge by copying only changed data. By contrast, copy-on-write frozen images are disposed of simply by reclaiming the space they occupy.

Finally, the cost of a split mirror is such that it is seldom practical to maintain more than one. Copy-on-write frozen images, on the other hand, are economical with space. Some implementations can maintain multiple frozen images, enabling backups to be made at frequent intervals. Some copy-on-write implementations also support rollback to any one of several points in time. With split mirrors, this is seldom practical.

Off-host backup complicates the picture somewhat. Off-host backup using split mirrors requires SAN functionality similar to tape sharing. It must be possible to transfer ownership of a split mirror from an application server to a backup server and back again when the backup is complete. This can be accomplished with SAN management tools that implement zoning or by coordination among clustered servers. Copy-on-write frozen images present still further complications because they only contain data that has changed since image initiation. Reading a copy-on-write frozen image requires access to primary data. If one server is to perform backup while applications running on another continue to use data, the file system or database must be mounted simultaneously on both. This requires cluster file system or database technology, which is among the most sophisticated of all SAN software.

Data Sharing: The NAS Way

Network-attached storage, in the form of file servers, is perhaps the easiest way to begin reaping the benefits of SAN technology in the online domain. Almost all file servers support the two common file access protocols—Common Internet File Services (CIFS) and the Network File System (NFS). Almost all operating systems include client *redirectors* that enable them to use one of these protocols to access files stored on a NAS device. Files stored on NAS devices can be processed by applications designed for local files with little or no modification. Even the network used to access NAS devices uses familiar enterprise LAN technology. In fact, the enterprise network itself is often used for data access. As utilization increases, it becomes increasingly desirable to install a private network for data access, which by our definition (Chapter 1) is a SAN, even though its protocol is TCP/IP.

The benefits of NAS are access to data from a variety of different application server platforms and ease of data management. Many NAS devices are packaged as appliances that are optimized to do only one thing: provide NFS and CIFS file access. NAS devices can consolidate storage for many of an enterprise's computing platforms, thereby achieving pooling benefits and reducing management cost. Most NAS implementations include backup facilities, either locally managed or managed by a server-based enterprise backup manager using the Network Data Management Protocol (NDMP) to send commands to the NAS device.

NAS devices are available both as tightly integrated packages that include their own disk drives and built-in RAID capabilities and as software packages that run on new or repurposed servers and use legacy disks or RAID subsystems as storage.

Moving from locally attached online storage to a NAS strategy is essentially a wholesale replacement of online storage. While it is possible to leave the local storage devices in place for a transition period, falling back to using them in the event of a problem with the NAS installation becomes difficult after the NAS storage has been in use for a period of time and applications have updated data stored on it. Thus, while it simplifies operations, particularly in heterogeneous data centers, NAS is one of those transitional steps that it is important to get right.

Application Availability: Clustering for Failover

Clustering is a relatively new data center capability that enables an application to resume operation quickly after a server failure or a failure of the application itself. The business benefit is obvious: continuity of data access in spite of server or application failures. Clustering is another data center facility that is not strictly dependent upon SANs, but as we observe in Chapter 8, SAN connectivity increases the applicability of clustering, makes larger clusters with more flexible failover strategies, and reduces the cost of clustering by enabling configurations in which one failover server backstops several different application servers. An important reason that SANs increase the applicability of clustering is that, with a SAN, a failed application's storage, and therefore its, data is accessible to any of several alternate servers.

Clustering is deceptively simple to describe: Two or more servers monitor each others' operation and when a failure is detected, the failed server's applications are restarted on other servers. From a developer's standpoint, however, clustering poses some complex challenges. Low-overhead heartbeat protocols, failover models that ensure that an application has the right resources to restart after a failure, and management tools that allow administrators to configure applications to use cluster facilities are among the engineering challenges of clustering. From a SAN standpoint, one of the key challenges of availability clustering is automating the transfer of storage device ownership to another server. Another, increasingly important as more critical applications are clustered, is blocking access to storage devices from servers that have been ejected from a cluster.

A decision to adopt clustering for higher application availability requires significant planning and design of application services, cluster topologies, and failover strategies. All of these challenges are in addition to the challenges of SAN technology itself. It therefore seems preferable to choose clustering as one of the later stages of SAN adoption. When a SAN is in place and has been shown to work and administrators have experience with managing it, the SAN can be treated as a known quantity during cluster adoption.

The adoption of clustering is a major step for an enterprise data center and one not to be taken lightly. If, however, a cluster is designed so that its normal configuration (in which all servers are performing their intended tasks) closely resembles the data center prior to cluster adoption, a reasonable fallback strategy in the event of problems is to simply suspend failover and run the cluster as so many separate servers. Thus, in most cases, the potential impact of failure of a clustering implementation on the enterprise's ability to process data should be small.

Shared Data and Parallel Clustering: Application Scaling

A parallel cluster is one in which several instances of an application or several related applications run concurrently in different servers and process the same data. A SAN is prerequisite to a parallel cluster, because servers can only process data to which they have access. The business benefit of parallel clustering is twofold: Applications can scale beyond the capacity of a single server, and application availability is even higher than with availability clusters because restart after a failure isn't required in a parallel cluster.

Web serving is a popular application for parallel clustering. Early Web servers would operate on independent copies of Web site data. Incoming client load would be balanced across them. If a server failed, incoming client load would be redistributed across the remaining servers. With each instance of the application having its own copy of data, data sharing was not an issue. For such read-only or read-mostly applications, a data replication source could update data for all instances periodically. For applications such as online sales, data updates made by different servers were generally independent of each other and periodic reconciliation was adequate.

To use parallel clustering with other types of application-notably transaction processing, for which all instances must have the same view of data at all times—*data sharing* is required. Data sharing means the ability to mount and read and write a file system or database on all of the servers running instances of the parallel application. Data sharing is implemented by *cluster file systems* and *distributed database management systems*, both of which require foundational clusters. Thus, incorporating data sharing into a data center strategy requires all of the following:

- A cluster
- The cluster file system or distributed DBMS itself
- Applications able to make cooperative use of the shared data

In other words, a substantial body of sophisticated environmental software is required for data sharing. None of this software is likely to be present in a data center that has not adopted shared data clustering, so the data center probably lacks skills in these areas. As with availability clustering, SANs expand the applicability of parallel clusters by connecting more applications to more data, so SAN adoption is likely to be a precursor of shared data cluster adoption. But facing the challenges of SAN adoption at the same time as those of an entire new application software infrastructure is a high-risk strategy. This suggests that parallel clustering should be adopted even later in a SAN implementation strategy than availability clustering.

Data Replication I: Publication and Decision Support

In Chapter 1, a SAN was defined as any network whose primary purpose is to move data between storage devices and servers or other storage devices. Data replication typically uses either the enterprise network or, for RAID subsystem-based implementations, a private network, to *publish* data from where it is created to where it is held or used. Chapter 8 describes several different replication technologies and usage modes. For publication, intermittent replication that has defined stopping points so that data replicas can be used is generally most appropriate.

In general, the benefit of data replication for publication is that it allows an enterprise to use its data more effectively without losing control over its integrity. For example, product or customer data maintained at one site can be replicated to many other sites for rapid response to customer inquiries in the field. Replicated data can be used to populate a data warehouse with near-current business data with minimal effect on the applications processing that data.

Replication is implemented either at the server level or within a RAID subsystem. The former generally allows more flexible specification of what gets replicated. The latter is less flexible, but has less performance impact on applications.

Since data replication uses either the enterprise network or a dedicated network, there are few SAN implications of adding data replication to an existing data center.

Application implications may be significant, however, and first among these is performance. After an initial synchronization phase, network load due to replication is proportional to the amount of write traffic at the primary server.

Replication poses no significant SAN-specific challenges, but it does require careful scheduling of the more I/O-intensive phases of replication. Asynchronous replication can decouple replication from application performance during application peaks. When designing replication for data publication into a data center operation, the network load imposed by initial synchronization must be carefully considered. For networks that are heavily loaded throughout the day, it may be preferable to perform initial synchronization by transporting removal media to secondary locations.

Most replicators support a limited number of concurrent replicas. Limits range from 1 or 2 (common with RAID subsystems) to 16 or more. Even when replication is asynchronous, a large number of replicas can result in heavy network traffic and primary location processing load.

Some replicators are able to *cascade*, replicating data from a primary location through secondary locations to a larger number of tertiary locations these are particularly useful for replication private web sites to large number of enterprise locations. The risk of a failed attempt to implement replication to enterprise data processing is low. Since it is transparent to applications, replication typically has little effect on them if it fails. Disabling replication can usually restore data center operations to what they were prior to the installation of replication.

Data Replication II:
Disaster Recoverability

It is a rare enterprise that can operate today without access to its data. While failure-tolerant volumes and RAID subsystems with dynamic multipathing protect against storage subsystem component failures and clusters protect against server and application failure, enterprises must also consider protecting their data against disasters, defined as events that render an entire data center inoperative.

To recover rapidly from such a disaster, an enterprise needs both a backup data center, located at a safe distance from the main data center and a means of stocking the backup data center with up-to-date data so it can take over operations if a disaster befalls the main data center. Data replication is the perfect technology for this purpose. After a startup phase in which data at primary and backup data centers is synchronized, replication transmits all updates made to live data over the network to the backup data center, where the updates are written to persistent storage.

While undeniably substantial, the business benefit of data replication is difficult to calculate. An enterprise IT planning team must ask how the enterprise would behave if a data center disaster were to occur. Could it survive without access to data for the length of time required to repair the data center and restore data from backups? In many cases, the answer is no. Thus, a backup data center with data replicated to it from the main data center may be an enterprise survival issue. Enterprises should also consider whether a single backup data center is a sufficient disaster recovery strategy in some cases it may be appropriate to replicate critical enterprise data to two or more recovery sites and to distribute primary data center applications to these sites in the even of a primary data center disaster.

Such a disaster recovery strategy is not inexpensive. In addition to the premises and capital equipment, there are operating costs for at least a skeleton staff, as well as communications facilities. There are training issues to be considered as well. The backup data center staff must be experienced in operating the enterprise's applications. In other words, a decision to adopt data replication for disaster recovery is really a decision to adopt an entire disaster recovery strategy of which data replication is a minor (although vital) part.

The SAN implications of adopting data replication for disaster recovery are minor (for example, because the enterprise network can usually be used for data transmission), but the overall complexity is significant. Replicating data is only the beginning of a data recovery strategy. In most cases, replication must be asynchronous for performance reasons. At the instant of a disaster, there may be data in transit—already updated at the main data center but not yet transmitted to the replication site. Disaster recovery must include a strategy for dealing with data in transit at the instant of disaster. The strategy might range from ignoring the lost data (possibly appropriate for low-value, high-volume transactions) to replicating database logs synchronously (so that recovery databases can be reconstructed from intact database logs), with other options in between.

Since replication is transparent to applications and does not require changes to application structure, the operational consequences of a failed implementation of disaster recovery replication are minor (with the exception that the enterprise loses the ability to recover its data and resume processing after a disaster).

Going Global: Wide Area Clustering

Wide area data replication sets the stage for integrated global data processing. Maintaining up-to-date data at a remote site enables recovery from disaster, but procedures for transferring data center operations to the backup site must still be defined. Global clustering automates the movement of application operations between widely separated sites. Global clustering can automate failover decisions and operational details, such as communicating with DNS servers to redirect network names.

Again, implementing global clustering has relatively little effect on a data center's SAN per se. But because it affects computing strategy at all of an enterprise's data centers, it has a ripple effect on each individual center. Policies must be set and decisions made to distinguish failover within a single cluster at a single data center from migration of an application and its data from one processing site to another. The circumstances under which this may occur and the sequence of steps to make it happen must be clearly defined and understood at both the sending and the receiving sites. If application migration is done for reasons of global responsiveness (Chapter 8) rather than disaster recovery, then the design must provide for clean transitions with no lost data in transit.

Global clustering generally relies on component technologies, such as local clustering and long-distance data replication, to achieve coordinated global computing and automated disaster recovery. To maximize the chances of success, an enterprise IT organization should have mastered the underlying technologies before linking its failure-tolerant data centers into a worldwide coordinated computing facility.

The Potential for Disaster: One Egg, One Basket (Also Known as the SAN Two-Edged Sword)

Today, Fibre Channel and gigabit Ethernet, both with high-speed switches, are the primary enablers for storage area networks. These low-latency, ultrafast interconnects enable orders-of-magnitude more data to be transmitted far faster than ever before, over longer distances, more reliably, and with lower access latency.

Prior to SANs, servers were only able to access data that was stored locally or that was accessible by the enterprise LAN. The result was data duplication, with inevitable inconsistency. Worse yet, data was available only to users with access to the servers on which the data was stored. Enterprises were forced to operate with stale, inaccurate, and incomplete information.

With a fully interconnected SAN, any of an organization's data can be accessed by any of its servers. The advantages of the any-to-any connectivity of a SAN are many:

- Anyone in an organization can (in principle) access any data at any time. Restrictions on access to data become a matter of policy and software capabilities rather than inability to connect. If the organization wants to enable access to data from a server, it can be done.

- The data seen by users is always up to date because logically there *is* only one copy. Enterprise decision making is based on the best data available.

- Data duplication is reduced or eliminated. (Physical duplication for failure protection and enterprise survivability-locally for failure tolerance and remotely for disaster recovery[3]—are still strongly recommended).

The Other Edge

Of course, if all of an organization's applications operate on the same copy of data, then a faulty application that corrupts data corrupts it for *all* applications. More rarely, but also more insidiously, a malicious user who corrupts or destroys data deliberately can easily have enterprisewide consequences. Even less frequently, a hardware or sys-

---

[3] *Local data redundancy* is the maintenance of two or more identical copies of each storage or data object. Local data redundancy protects against component failures, such as disks, channels, and media. Remote data redundancy is the maintenance of two or more identical copies of data at widely separated locations. *Remote data redundancy* protects against disasters that incapacitate an entire site, such as fire, flood, electrical grid failure, and civil insurrection. Remote data redundancy is one essential part of a disaster recovery strategy designed to enable a secondary IS site to resume processing in the event that an emergency incapacitates the primary site.

tem software component can fail destructively, writing random data at random locations. The potential for small faults to have large consequences suggests that when a SAN is deployed, extra attention should be given to what would be good application design practices in any case:

Data safeguards. The conventional means of protecting against application and operational faults that corrupt data as it is processed is to make frequent backups so that when corruption is discovered, a restore can be run to roll data back to a point in time that is known to predate the corrupting influence. From that point, logs can be played back selectively against the restored data to bring its state up to the moment of failure or at least close to it.

Procedural safeguards. While most data centers today are at least nominally secure against intrusion by outsiders, when a SAN is used to consolidate a large amount of data served to many applications running on different servers, the potential impact on the enterprise requires heightened security measures. Security must be provided against intrusion by unauthorized parties, against unauthorized actions by parties who are authorized to be present in the data center, and against users performing unauthorized actions.

Physical safeguards. Similarly, the potential for damage to the enterprise from lost data is typically great enough to justify both enhanced data center environments (e.g., with climate control and fire, water, and other environmental protection) and provision for disaster recovery at remote data centers.

System safeguards. While the ability for any server to read or write data to any storage device enables most of the advanced functionality discussed in this book, it creates the necessity of preventing servers from reading and writing data unless it is appropriate for them to do so. In designing a SAN that will connect multiple servers to multiple storage devices, multiple layers of protection against undesirable data access, whether from faulty or rogue applications or faulty system hardware or software, are required. These safeguards may take any of several forms, including storage (e.g., LUN masking), infrastructure (e.g., zoning), and host (e.g., host bus adapter mapping) access restriction technologies. In addition to these mechanisms that prevent unwanted physical data access, SAN-based consolidated systems require logical protections (e.g., exclusive ownership of tape drives during a backup, exclusive control of devices while volume metadata is updated, exclusive control of data files or records while they are being updated).

All of these safeguards offer protection from threats against which the most visible failure protection mechanisms-storage failure tolerance, and clustering-are powerless. The latter mechanisms protect against hardware faults and one-of-a-kind software failures. A RAID array or mirrored volume, however, will write corrupt data every bit as reliably as it writes correct data. A failover cluster will restart an application that is corrupting data just as faithfully as it restarts a well-behaved application.

While failure-tolerant storage and clustering are excellent techniques for keeping a data center on the air when failures happen, they are no substitute for the other types of failure protection mentioned in this section.

Summary

- Storage networking is a tool for improving an enterprise's data processing capabilities, not an end in itself.

- Storage networking should be adopted only as part of an overall IT improvement plan that has its roots in business requirements.

- An enterprise's storage network must be carefully planned to minimize the risk of failure. Contingency plans for falling back to old ways of doing things should exist at all stages.

- Consultants can be beneficial to SAN implementation in several ways. In the assessment stage, business process consultants aware of SAN capabilities can suggest new ways of doing things that might not occur to SAN-unaware users. Progressing to design, technology consultants can provide unbiased evaluation of alternative approaches and can help avoid overdesign. During prototyping, experienced consultants can accelerate the learning curve for new technology. And finally, during implementation, technically expert consultants are an insurance policy against technical failures. At all stages, IT planners should be aware of consultants' motivations and temper their advice with this understanding.

- The state of storage network component interoperability today makes prototyping a must for new storage network implementations. Vendor interoperability lists must be carefully adhered to if problems are to be avoided.

- Different capabilities enabled by storage networking have different degrees of difficulty, different impacts on the data center status quo and different paybacks. All of these factors should figure into a storage networking implementation plan, with the less difficult and less disruptive steps being executed first.

- Involving users at each step of the way is crucial. Not only is the user the ultimate judge of success or failure, but users are also an excellent source of input for adjusting plans in reaction to changing business situations.

CHAPTER 12

Managing SANs

I n this chapter we'll learn more about:

- Why SANs pose special management challenges for system administrators
- The administrative functions that constitute SAN management
- The SAN components that must be managed
- How SAN management differs from the management of locally attached storage
- A hypothetical ideal SAN management environment
- The state of SAN management today
- Management challenges for the SAN industry

SAN Management Defined

Throughout this book, we've been describing new information processing capabilities that SANs enable and the benefits of adopting them. Like all good things in life, however, the benefits come at a cost: SANs create an enterprise communications infrastructure that must be managed on an ongoing basis. *Management* may be the most overloaded information technology term of the decade. Worse yet, the industry segment that has sprung up around SANs has taken to using the term *SAN management* to include broad aspects of storage and system management that existed before anyone ever thought of a SAN. One way to think of a SAN is as providing network services that move data through space and storage services that move data through time. Not surprisingly, then, our definition of SAN management consists of two types of tasks: network management tasks and storage management tasks.

Network Management Tasks

In general, network management tasks are performed so that the enterprise can move its data optimally in the face of changing requirements and conditions. Network-related SAN management tasks include:

- *Configuration* of paths between storage devices and computers, including planning for recovery from path failures.

- *Control* of logical SAN connections so that exactly the right set of servers have access to exactly the right storage devices at exactly the right times.

- *Allocation* of bandwidth among SAN-attached storage devices and computing devices so that enterprise application performance needs are met.

- *Authentication* of clients so that only genuine clients are able to access exactly those data assets for which they have authorization.

- *Encryption* of data as it moves throughout the SAN so that erroneous or malicious behavior does not result in noncooperating servers connected to the SAN being exposed to data they are not authorized to see.

- *Monitoring* of network paths so that both soft (e.g., link overload) and hard (e.g., path failure) faults are detected as quickly as possible.

- *Event handling* so that network loading problems, faults, security breaches, and breach attempts are remedied promptly with minimal adverse impact on enterprise operations.

- *Inventorying* of network components so that the enterprise has an accurate picture of its storage network infrastructure, including the location and state of components and links, as well as hardware and firmware revision levels for intelligent devices.

- *Maintenance* of network components, particularly with regard to keeping hardware and firmware revision levels up to date within the limits imposed by the need for consistency among components from different suppliers.

Storage Management Tasks

Just as network management tasks are performed so that enterprises can move their critical data to where it needs to go, storage management tasks, as the name implies, are those concerned with storing data safely and accessing it rapidly. Storage management tasks include:

- *Configuration* of RAID subsystems, storage appliances, and file servers so that the right quantity of storage of the most appropriate type is available to meet application requirements and so that storage resources are used effectively.

- *Allocation* of storage devices and storage capacity to servers, applications, and users so that each storage client has the required private or shared access to storage devices or quantities of online storage of the most appropriate type.

- *Fault detection*, isolation, and recovery from storage device faults so that failures do not catch the administrator by surprise and result in service outages.

- *Tracking* of storage assets so that the enterprise knows what assets it has on hand and what state they are in, for purposes of capacity planning and resource accounting.

- *Monitoring* of storage devices so that both soft (e.g., I/O overload, mirror failure) and hard (e.g., device failure) faults are detected as quickly as possible.

- *Event handling* so that loading problems, device faults, security breaches, and breach attempts are remedied promptly with minimal adverse impact on enterprise operations.

- *Inventorying* of storage subsystems and devices so that the enterprise has an accurate picture of its storage capacity, including the location and state of subsystems and devices, as well as hardware and firmware revision levels for intelligent devices.

- *Maintenance* of storage components, particularly with regard to keeping hardware and firmware revision levels up to date within the limits imposed by the need for consistency among components from different suppliers.

What Gets Managed in a SAN?

The objects upon which the SAN management tasks just enumerated are carried out are the components that make up a SAN. These include:

Storage devices. As we have used the term throughout this book, *storage devices* consist of both disk drives and tape drives, as well as embedded, external, and enterprise RAID subsystems and tape libraries. For disk and tape drives, management consists of device discovery, establishing and maintaining secure logical connections with servers, fault detection and isolation, and asset tracking and maintenance. RAID subsystems add array configuration, spare and unused drive management, and soft failure recovery to this list. Tape libraries additionally require management of removable media and unused media.

SAN infrastructure components. These include hubs, switches, routers, bridges, and link components. Management of these components includes establishing and maintaining *zones* (sets of ports that are allowed to intercommunicate), provisioning (allocating capacity among clients), fault detection and recovery, and asset tracking and maintenance.

Servers. Servers interface to the SAN through *host bus adapters* (HBAs), also called *network interface cards* (NICs). HBA management consists of fault detection and recovery (e.g., by reconnecting to devices using an alternate path), controlling the server's end of the logical connection between server and storage device, and asset tracking and maintenance.

Environmental software. SANs are possible because of hardware components. SANs work because cooperating software components running in storage devices and subsystems, in SAN infrastructure components, and in servers interact to provide reliable, secure, high-performance paths between applications and data. Device firmware, drivers, volume managers, file systems, cluster managers, and so forth, must be kept at consistent revision levels and patched as necessary to keep them functioning properly in cooperation with each other.

Application software. One of the important data processing styles enabled by SANs is the creation of clusters of servers that cover for each other in the event of application or server failure. Applications and the resources they require to run must be logically grouped and the movement of an application from one server to another must be carefully sequenced. Running applications must be monitored (in an application-specific way) to determine whether failover would be appropriate.

Data. Another important benefit enabled by SANs is sharing of data by applications running on clusters of cooperating servers. Keeping shared data, whether at the block (volume) or file system and database level, consistent requires coordination among the clustered servers. Data management in a SAN-based cluster requires cooperation among file system or database management system instances so that structural (metadata) modifications are atomic, as well as cooperation with volume managers and RAID subsystems so that, for example, mirrors can be split (as described in Chapter 8) at moments when file systems or databases are consistent.

The Basics: What's Special about Managing a SAN

The fundamental goal of SAN management is to keep enterprise data flowing freely between the storage that holds it and the servers that process it. But this has been an administrative responsibility of information services departments long before SANs were conceived. It's legitimate to ask what has changed. What's so different about keeping data flowing in a SAN that it caused a new industry segment to spring up and users to bemoan the fact that system administrative life isn't what it used to be?

Discovery: "Hello, Who's Out There?"

The most obvious difference between managing a SAN and managing locally attached storage stems from a basic difference between networks and typical I/O buses—the number of things that can be connected. With the exception of a few proprietary technologies, the parallel SCSI I/O bus is nearly ubiquitous as a local storage attachment. Parallel SCSI protocol uses its 8 or 16 data signals for device addressing in a way that limits the number of devices that can be interconnected on a single bus to 8 or 16, respectively.

When a server needs to determine what storage devices are connected to a parallel SCSI bus, it is a relatively simple matter to send a command to each of the 8 or 16 possible addresses. The addresses that answer are devices; the ones that don't aren't. A simple command takes a few microseconds of bus time and perhaps as much as a few milliseconds of processing time. Waiting for time-outs from bus addresses that don't correspond to devices takes a second or so. Thus, in a matter of a few seconds, a server can figure out what local storage devices are connected to it.

This contrasts with the situation in a SAN. Even in the simplest SAN configuration—the Fibre Channel Arbitrated Loop (FC-AL)—it is possible to interconnect 126 devices.[1] Polling or sending messages to every possible bus address to see which addresses correspond to devices could take as much as eight times as long as on an I/O bus. Moreover, polling works just like you wouldn't want it to—the fewer devices connected, the more time-outs from addresses that don't correspond to devices and, therefore, the smaller a SAN, the longer it would take to get it started.

But the Fibre Channel Arbitrated Loop is a trivial problem compared to the switched fabrics that are much more prevalent in the world of SANs. A device that uses Fibre Channel's switched fabric protocols can have any of 16 million possible addresses. Clearly, trying to discover what's attached by polling every possible address would take days. Some other solution is needed.

There's another network-like characteristic of SANs that makes local storage device discovery methods inadequate as well: Devices can connect to or disconnect from an operating SAN. A server might go through its startup procedure, discovering devices connected to the SAN, but later when it tries to use a device, discover that it's not there anymore. Similarly, new devices might be connected to a working SAN. How is a server to discover that they are present so it can use them?

The SCSI bus and the operating systems that support it were not initially designed to allow devices to be added to or removed from an operating bus. Newer forms of SCSI combined with advanced packaging technology enable operating systems to support *dynamic reconfiguration*—the addition or removal of devices while a bus is operating. Operating systems whose storage is connected to SCSI buses solve this problem by *rescanning* buses that are reconfigured—freezing application I/O activity while they poll each of the 8 or 16 possible addresses. Again, for many applications, the few seconds of interrupted I/O is a tolerable price to pay for the ability to access a device that is added while the system is operating.

Again, rescanning is not a solution for SAN device discovery. Not only would it take too long to be viable, but when a device is removed from a SAN, (1) it may return to a different location or (2) another device may appear at its location.

But First, "Hello, I'm Here"

To solve the problem of discovering SAN-attached devices, SAN developers have adapted a well-understood and mature TCP/IP networking technique. The large number of devices that can be connected on a TCP/IP network and the transient nature of the connections have led the networking industry to the concept of registering devices with a central repository of information about what is connected.

As new devices are added to a network, they register themselves with a repository of information about the network called a *name server*. The name server is simply a persistent table with an entry for each device that has announced that it is connected to the network.

How does a device find the name server in a network? It's another networking technique that is simplicity itself. Recognizing that every network needs certain common

---

[1] In this context, a device is either a storage device or a host bus adapter port in a server.

functions, organizations that create network standards reserve a few network addresses and preassign functions to them. These addresses are called *well-known addresses* and are not used for any other purpose. For example, a Fibre Channel name server uses address xFFFFFC. Because this address is standard, every vendor who builds a component to attach to a Fibre Channel SAN can safely program that component to register itself with a name server at Fibre Channel address xFFFFFC, secure in the expectation that a name server will be found at that address.

In principle, a SAN name server could be located anywhere in the network. In fact, in TCP/IP-based networks (remember, these can also be SANs—see Chapter 1), name servers are often implemented as software components in servers. In Fibre Channel SANs, however, name service has become the province of the switches that constitute the SAN infrastructure.

Fibre Channel switch vendors have developed sophisticated protocols between switches to ensure that each SAN fabric (set of interconnected switches) presents one name service that is physically distributed for fault tolerance. This is a complete solution for single-SAN organizations in which all storage is literally connected to all servers. For organizations that operate multiple SANs, intelligence at another level that is aware of multiple SANs is required.

Next, "Who Else Is There?"

For storage devices, which respond to requests but do not initiate any of their own, registration with a name server so that they can be found is sufficient. Servers, however, must determine what else is connected to the SAN—storage devices, other servers with which they might need to communicate, and fabric infrastructure elements with which they might need to exchange management information.

To enable servers to determine what is on the network, name servers respond to requests whose general form is "tell me about all connected devices" or "tell me about the next device." Fibre Channel SAN name servers use the latter form of the request. A server desiring to learn what devices are connected to a SAN makes a request specifying a Fibre Channel port address. The name server returns information about the next higher numbered port for which a device has registered. This gives the server a starting point for its next request, allowing rapid traversal of a very large address space.

What's In a Name?

A name server provides information about ports to which devices are attached. In a Fibre Channel SAN, this information is limited to what variations of the transport protocols the device is able to use and a node name, useful with servers (nodes) in which multiple host bus adapters (ports) are configured or in RAID subsystems (nodes) that include multiple host interfaces (ports).

Once a device is known to a server, higher-level protocols are used to determine more about the device. Fibre Channel storage devices, for example, use Fibre Channel Protocol (FCP), which is based on SCSI to communicate with servers. FCP includes inquiry commands that can be used by a server to determine whether a device is a disk or tape drive or other type of device.

During the course of its life, a storage device can be disconnected from a SAN port and reconnected to a different port with a different port address. Worse yet, a completely different device can be connected to a port once occupied by a known device. The problem is worst in Fibre Channel Arbitrated Loop SANs, where addition or removal of a device can result in all devices on the SAN acquiring different network addresses.

Of course, this problem can also occur with locally attached storage. A disk can be moved between two enclosures and appear at a different address. Operating systems have traditionally solved this problem by writing *signatures* on disks. Signatures are nothing more than recognizable patterns in well-known locations that a disk driver can read to determine the identity and usage of a newly discovered disk. The form of these signatures, unfortunately, differs from operating system to operating system. With locally attached storage, this is not a problem, because the server that queries the disk is always the same, so the signature is always recognizable.

But SANs enable many-to-many connectivity, so the signature scheme doesn't work so well. A disk signature may be written by one operating system and read by another that doesn't recognize its format. Alternatively, a disk may have been part of a pool of unused storage and simply not have a signature written on it. How is a server to recognize the difference? Is a disk connected to a port available for use because it contains no signature, or has the disk had a signature written on it by an operating system that uses an unrecognizable format?

Storage devices designed for use in a SAN solve this problem with a device-invariant characteristic called a *worldwide name*. A worldwide name is associated with a device at the time of its creation and remains with it throughout its life. Servers can inquire about both, the port worldwide names and the node worldwide names of devices, to ascertain whether a disk appearing on a port is the same device that had previously appeared on a different port or is a different device.

The New Meaning of *Host*

As the preceding section hinted, SANs alter the relationship between storage devices and servers. With locally attached storage, the computer is a *host* environment for the storage devices. If storage is locally attached, the host can use it freely, because no other host will contend for it. In this situation, operating system-specific disk signatures work, because only one operating system will ever try to read any given disk. Polling bus addresses works, because there are so few of them. Even in clusters with locally attached storage, the hosts are homogeneous and there are typically only two of them to contend for storage devices. Clustering software includes elaborate mechanisms for determining device *ownership* (the right to write to a storage device without corrupting data or metadata) and for transferring ownership when things fail or administrative actions are required. With SANs, all this changes. The most fundamental change is that a storage device no longer has a single host. Any server connected to the SAN has the capability to read and write data to the device. In a SAN environment, significant administrative effort goes into determining just exactly which servers are allowed access to just exactly which storage devices and when and how device ownership can change.

With locally attached storage, the server is in charge. Thus, when the server bootstraps its operating system, it makes decisions about its storage devices, even to the extent of deciding which disk it will boot the operating system from. Some operating systems exercise restraint, mounting (i.e., establishing connections to and preparing for application use) only those storage devices indicated in configuration files. Others are less forgiving, assuming that if a storage device is addressable, it belongs to them.

In a SAN, this is obviously not a viable operating practice. Not all servers can bootstrap at precisely the same instant. In fact, in general, it's impossible to predict what sequence bootstrapping will take during a general startup and when a server will reboot while other servers on the SAN are running. Moreover, if storage is indeed to be pooled, as SAN architecture promises, and the pool deployed to different servers running different operating systems, these omnivorous platforms cannot be tolerated.

Zoning: Who Gets to Do What to Whom?

Obviously, in a SAN environment, at least some storage device assignments must be predesignated before servers can even bootstrap. It's worth thinking about the root cause of this limitation—the fact that today's server operating systems were designed from a perspective of server-centric computing. The server is in charge and storage is subordinate to it. As has happened with networks, a long period of evolution is to be expected until server operating systems become generally cognizant of other servers that are also attached to their storage devices and begin to negotiate for access rights rather than assuming them. Indeed, one can envision a day when different server operating systems will recognize each others' disk signatures and formats and will actually be able to share data with each other. In the even more distant future, one can imagine that operating systems will recognize a common universal on-disk data format, much as they recognize common communication message formats today.

Until that day comes, however, administrators of SAN-attached storage have to live with operating systems as they are. A way is needed to allow the connectivity and storage pooling benefits of SANs to be exploited without the chaos that could ensue from uncoordinated access to the storage by operating systems that are unaware of each other.

For Fibre Channel SANs, component vendors have taken the lead in solving this problem with a collection of capabilities that go under the general titles of *zoning*, *LUN masking*, and *LUN mapping*, depending upon whether the implementation is switch based, host bus adapter based, or RAID subsystem based. The goal of all three of these capabilities is to restrict the accessibility of storage devices to servers, in effect subdividing the SAN into a set of private subnetworks within each of which cooperative sharing of storage resources is possible. While the techniques used differ in detail, all of these technologies work by blocking access to ranges of Fibre Channel addresses.

In the case of zoning, a switch maintains tables of Fibre Channel port addresses that are permitted to intercommunicate. If a port attempts to establish communication with a port address not in its zone, the switch simply blocks that communication. As is the case with the name servers discussed previously, switches that are aggregated into larger SAN fabrics use clustering techniques to provide a distributed zoning service, so that all devices on the SAN see the same picture, both from within their own zones and across zones when a remote management interface is used.

Figure 12.1 illustrates how switch-based zoning works in a Fibre Channel SAN. Two switches cooperate to maintain two disparate sets of port addresses, allowing those in Zone A to intercommunicate, but blocking them from communicating with addresses in Zone B, and conversely.

Zone B in Figure 12.1 might be configured to run backup, since the tape drives are in its zone. This should make apparent the necessity for dynamic adjustment of zones. When the backup is complete, it would be desirable to move the tape drives from Zone B to Zone A so that other servers could back up their storage.

Switch-based SAN zoning is server independent. Zones are set up by management commands directed to switches. Thus, zones persist whether or not servers are up and running. Perhaps more important, zones persist even if servers fail in unpredictable ways that might otherwise corrupt data.

LUN (logical unit number) binding is implemented in host bus adapters in order to limit a server's visibility to logical units. Server-based software, assisted by firmware in the HBAs themselves, restricts the addresses from which messages are accepted. The scope of HBA-based zoning is the server in which the HBA is installed.

Some Fibre Channel–based RAID subsystems implement a form of restricted addressing called *LUN masking* that was originally developed for parallel SCSI-based subsystems. A LUN masking subsystem maintains a table of which Fibre Channel port

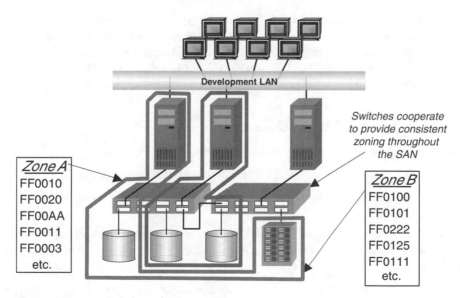

Figure 12.1 Switch-based SAN zoning.

addresses are permitted to send messages to which of its logical units (virtual disks). This differs slightly from the Fibre Channel address-based zoning done by switches, in that a single Fibre Channel port address may present multiple logical units to the SAN. Several servers may address the same RAID subsystem Fibre Channel port, but no conflict arises as long as the FCP commands are addressed to different logical units.

The scope of RAID subsystem–based LUN masking is the RAID subsystem in which the mapping is done. A RAID subsystem can protect against undesired access to any of the virtual disks or LUNs it presents, but has no control over any other RAID subsystems or other components connected to the SAN. Thus, if RAID subsystem–based LUN mapping is used to protect against undesired device access

- Each RAID subsystem in the SAN must be managed separately.
- Some other means must be used to control server access to other device types such as tapes and to other servers.

While each of these implementations has its strengths and weaknesses, it is clear that none of them is a complete solution to secure data access:

- Switch-based zoning is perhaps the most versatile of the three methods of device access control, but its scope is limited to the devices connected to a single SAN fabric (collection of interconnected switches). This is fine for organizations that have all of their storage connected to a single SAN; however, for those with multiple SANs, each SAN must be managed separately.
- HBA-based LUN binding can control accesses made to a server, but does not limit accesses to, for example, storage devices, from other servers.
- RAID subsystem–based LUN masking protects individual virtual disks against undesired access, but each RAID subsystem, as well as other types of interdevice communication, must be managed separately.

It is thus clear that none of the hardware components that constitute a SAN can offer a complete solution to data access security. What is needed is an entity with visibility to the entire scope of all of an enterprise's SANs and awareness of the capabilities offered by the switch, RAID subsystem, and HBA components. This global scope is one of the important roles played by SAN management software suites.

Routing: Accept What You Cannot Change

As we discussed in Chapter 7, Fibre Channel switches are of one of two types:

- *Directors*, high-performance, fault-tolerant devices which typically contain 64 or more ports.
- *Departmental switches*, typically with fewer ports than directors and without internal fault tolerance. Departmental switches are typically deployed in pairs to provide fault tolerance at the level of the entire switch.

As we discussed in Chapter 7, enterprises must choose between more costly but fault-tolerant and scalable directors and lower-cost less scalable departmental switches that make fault tolerance the system designer's responsibility. In either case, it is likely that, at some point, the enterprise will outgrow a single switch and will install a configuration similar to that illustrated in Figure 12.2.

In Figure 12.2, a storage device (physical or virtual disk) connected to Switch 3 transfers data directly to a tape drive connected to Switch 6, for example, to perform serverless backup. The two are connected to different switches, with no direct path between them. Likewise, Server B and Server D may need to intercommunicate, for example, if they are part of same cluster. Again, there is no direct path between Switch 1 and Switch 2.

In both cases, messages between the communicating parties must be routed through a third server. In both of these examples, Switch 5 is the intermediate step in the path.

Figure 12.2 illustrates a relatively simple multiswitch configuration; much more complex configurations are in use as this book is written. It should be apparent that decisions about which routes messages and data should take through a SAN can easily become very complex. When one considers that switches and links can fail, the complexity is multiplied manifold.

There is good news here. Routing problems such as that illustrated in Figure 12.2 were encountered in the early days of networking, and solution algorithms were developed. Fibre Channel switch developers have adopted these techniques and, by and large, have made routing data through their products transparent to users. Each vendor's switches, whether of the director or of the departmental class, cooperate among themselves to establish, monitor, and maintain optimal routing paths for data. These routing algorithms are generally transparent to users and automatically adjust to changes

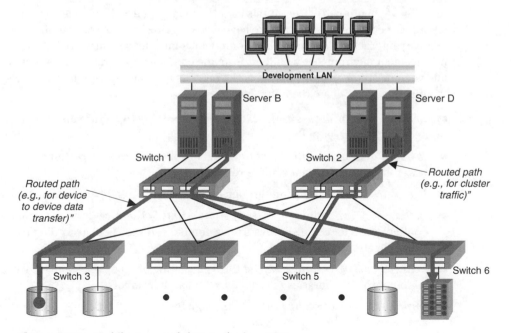

Figure 12.2 Multihop routed data paths in a SAN.

in configuration such as addition or removal of switches or links between them. Where additional bandwidth is required, switch vendors typically support multiple links between pairs of switches and automatically balance traffic across them.

This reduces the user's design problem to one of making sure that sufficient links exist between the switches combining a SAN fabric to (1) provide redundancy to protect against single points of failure and (2) provide the aggregate end-to-end bandwidth required between pairs of endpoints. The switches themselves cooperate to use the resources with which they are provided optimally.

An Ideal SAN Management Environment

A SAN consists of the following hardware and software components:

- Servers attached to the SAN infrastructure by host bus adapters
- RAID subsystems, storage appliances, and disk drives (typically mounted in enclosures and called JBODs)
- Tape drives and robotic media libraries
- Routers and bridges that connect legacy parallel SCSI devices to the SAN
- Switches and hubs that constitute the SAN infrastructure
- Software and firmware for controlling and managing each of the SAN components
- Applications that run in SAN-attached servers and process data stored on SAN-attached storage

As we have mentioned earlier in this chapter, managing a SAN includes operations on all of these components. But, as we have also described in the discussion of zoning, complex interactions between SAN components must also be managed. An ideal SAN management environment would perform the component operations and manage interactions automatically to provide the benefits normally expected from SANs which the reader will recall are the following:

- *Reduced storage acquisition cost* through the ability to acquire and manage storage in fewer, larger units
- *Reduced data availability cost* through consolidation of storage capacity into fewer, higher-performance, more resilient units
- *Better utilization of capital* through enterprisewide trend-based capacity planning
- *Better, more controllable quality of storage and I/O service* through the ability to configure and deploy resources from a common storage pool according to changing application requirements
- *Reduced backup cost and impact* through sharing of tape drives and easier justification of robotic libraries to reduce media handling errors
- *Improved application availability* through the clustering of several servers with access to the same storage devices

- *Reduced management cost* through the ability to manage enterprise resources centrally using advanced tools with global visibility

Realizing each of these benefits requires that SAN resources be manipulated to achieve enterprise goals. The ideal SAN management environment would translate policies expressed in terms of these enterprise objectives into automated event-based actions in support of these objectives. In such an ideal environment, the role of the human administrator would change from policy execution to responding to exceptional events and, more important, acting strategically to refine policies based on changing enterprise needs. The following sections discuss some of the manipulations that would be required to achieve each of these goals.

SAN Management and Online Storage Cost

The reduction of online storage cost through consolidation of capacity into fewer, larger devices is perhaps the most intuitively obvious benefit of deploying a SAN in a multi-server information processing environment. With locally attached storage, each server must host (be attached to) enough online storage capacity to meet its worst-case needs In information processing environments that have short-term peaks in their storage requirements, this can result in artificially high enterprisewide online storage needs.

Even without peaks in demand, savings from consolidating storage are possible. For example, the data center illustrated in Figure 12.3, contains 10 servers, each with 80 gigabytes of RAID storage. Fifty disks of 20-gigabyte capacity are required. The 20-gigabyte disk capacity point is probably optimal from a load balancing standpoint— each server's I/O load is spread among five disks.

If all of this storage is consolidated in a SAN, however, it is likely that fewer disks will be required. Four arrays of five 50-gigabyte disks provide the same capacity, in units of 200 gigabytes per array. If it is possible to subdivide the 200 gigabytes presented by one of these arrays and present 80-gigabyte volumes to each of the servers, the number of disks can be reduced from 50 to 20, as Figure 12.4 illustrates, with the attendant

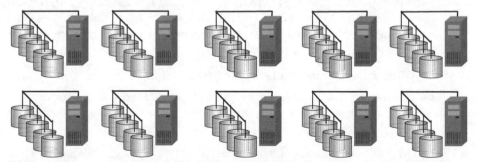

Each server is connected to a 5-disk RAID array of 20 gigabyte disks, for a usable storage capacity of 80 gigabytes per server

Figure 12.3   Cost of locally attached storage.

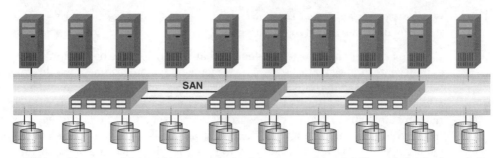

SAN enables use of fewer, higher-capacity disks for greater reliability and distribution of all servers' I/O load across all disks

Figure 12.4   Reducing storage cost by consolidating.

lower cost (recall that in Chapter 6 we asserted that, over time, disk drive cost remains roughly constant, but capacity increases) and higher reliability. (Statistically, a population of 20 components experiences a fault less often than a population of 50 similar components.)

Virtualization: Allocating Capacity Rather Than Disks

In order for consolidation to be effective, it must be possible to allocate storage *capacity* rather than storage devices to individual servers and clusters. In the preceding example, the consolidated storage consists of 4 five-disk arrays, each with 200 gigabytes of usable capacity. If each array is sliced into two volumes of 80-gigabyte capacity and one of 40 gigabytes and pairs of 40-gigabyte volumes can be consolidated and presented as single volumes, each server can be allocated 80 gigabytes of storage, just as in the local attachment case. Figure 12.5 illustrates this virtual disk configuration.

It is often argued that cost savings from consolidating storage are offset by the high infrastructure cost of a SAN. On a per-port basis, SANs can seem expensive compared to locally attached storage because the HBAs that attach servers to the SAN are more expensive than parallel SCSI HBAs, and also because each server HBA or storage host port is connected to a port on a switch. While it is true that today SAN infrastructure is considerably more expensive than the components required to attach storage directly to a single server, the following are also true:

- Often, when storage is consolidated, less total capacity is needed.
- Consolidated online storage is usually placed in a more secure, environmentally controlled location, reducing the chances of data loss due to malice and environmental factors such as overheating.

In addition, consolidation of storage results in flow-through benefits in performance, quality of storage, and I/O service and management cost that are enumerated in the sections that follow. Even if SAN component costs (which are falling as more enterprises deploy SANs, reducing component cost through higher volumes) are higher,

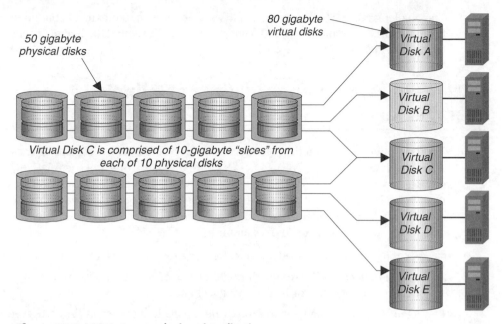

Figure 12.5   SAN storage device virtualization.

most multiserver enterprises should seriously consider SAN deployment as an information processing strategy with long-term payback.

In order to reduce the cost of online storage through consolidation, as in the example of Figure 12.5, certain SAN management capabilities are required:

- It must be possible to configure RAID subsystems to present fault-tolerant arrays similar to those illustrated in Figure 12.5.

- It must be possible to subdivide large fault-tolerant arrays into virtual disks or volumes, as illustrated in Figure 12.5.

- It must be possible to restrict the access of servers to virtual disks.

- If the fault-tolerant arrays and virtual disks are presented by server-based volume management software, it must be possible for volume manager software instances running in multiple servers to coordinate access to physical disks so that the volumes' structural metadata remains consistent. (If virtual disks are presented by a RAID subsystem's controller, the controller is a single point of coordination for them and metadata consistency is not an issue at the SAN level).

These management capabilities are typically available for RAID subsystems and volume management software. Each vendor, however, has developed a unique management style and so SAN users must learn different management techniques and set up different procedures for each type of RAID subsystem or volume manager deployed. This increases management cost both because administrators spend more time learning and less time doing and because procedures that are performed less frequently tend to take longer and be performed less reliably.

The challenge for SAN management software vendors is to create a common interface for configuring and managing RAID subsystems and directly attached disks controlled by volume management software.

SAN Management and Quality of Online Storage Service

There is much discussion today among developers and users of enterprise data storage about *quality of service* (QoS). In a SAN context, quality of service is relatively straightforward, because the measures of storage quality are straightforward—capacity, availability, and I/O performance. Ideally, online storage would have infinite capacity, never fail, and transfer data in no time. None of these ideals is realizable, but all can be approached at a cost. For example:

- *Capacity* can be increased by concatenating several disks into a large volume.
- *Availability* can be increased through the use of RAID, by mirroring data on two or more sets of disks, or by deploying a cluster.
- *I/O performance* can be increased by deploying higher-performing subsystems, by striping data across several disks, or by providing multiple access paths to data.

All of these have cost associated with them. Thus, online storage quality of service consists of balancing how well each of these fundamental online storage attributes is provided to clients against the cost of providing it.

Quality of service is obviously highly application specific. Life-and-death applications may justify nearly any expenditure to achieve adequate application response and ultra-high availability. Online historical data such as past transaction records, on the other hand, might be highly cost sensitive, both because there is so much of it and because the impact of losing it is relatively minor. Even within a single enterprise, different databases and file systems often have both differing degrees of importance and different application requirements and therefore require different quality-of-service levels. To make the equation more complex, quality of service must be measured in all three dimensions—capacity, availability, and I/O performance.

Storage Capacity

Capacity is the most straightforward of the quality-of-service metrics. Users and application managers contract with their information services operations for the quantity of storage required by their applications. In the past, this has been relatively simple. Managers have planned their application growth requirements on a quarterly or annual basis and communicated them to the information services department, which in turn would order the required amount of storage capacity and deploy it at the agreed-upon times.

More recently, the popularization of electronic business has made planning storage capacity requirements more difficult. So-called ebusiness is characterized by rapid, unpredictable changes in storage capacity requirements. Product announcements, promotions, and similar business events can create overnight requirements for large amounts of storage capacity, which may be permanent or which may evaporate just as quickly.

This has affected the way in which information services organizations provide and measure quality of service in the capacity dimension—how quickly capacity requirements can be met has become an important measure of the quality with which storage capacity is provided. To meet users' incremental storage demands with very short turnaround time, an information services department must purchase and configure extra storage capacity in anticipation of these needs. This costs money, which in most cases can justifiably be charged back to user departments that contract for their ad hoc demands for incremental storage capacity to be met with very short turnaround.

Data Availability

Availability is a somewhat less straightforward dimension of quality of service, principally because the spectrum of technology options is so broad. At the lower end of the online storage availability scale is disk storage with no provision for fault tolerance or recovery (e.g., by restoring a backup). In enterprise data centers, this level of availability is generally suitable only for temporary storage of easily reproduced intermediate processing results.

In a rough upward progression, other quality-of-service levels in the availability dimension are:

Non-fault-tolerant storage with backup. Backups can be made at various intervals. They may be full copies of all data stored in a given file system or database or *incremental*, containing only changes made to data since some previous backup copy was made. The period of time during which data must be inaccessible so that a backup copy can be started or completed is a variable at this level of availability.

RAID-protected storage. This option protects against disk drive failure. Again, variations exist, in terms of both RAID array *width* (number of disks in an array) and other parameters, such as redundancy of power supplies, cooling devices, controllers, host I/O bus interfaces, and paths between data and client.

Mirrored storage. Like RAID mirrored storage protects against disk failures; unlike RAID it protects against more than one simultaneous failureand also offers the unique ability to split a mirrored copy of data for backup or other purposes, thus further increasing application availability.

Clustered storage. Strictly speaking, clustering is an application availability enhancement capability. It is of little use, however, to fail applications over if a server fails if their storage cannot be failed over as well. Thus, storage devices that can be logically switched from one server to another enhance availability by protecting against application and server failures as well as storage failures.

Replicated storage. This option is similar to mirroring, but it offers the increased security of copying data across large distances in almost real time. This can keep data available (actually, restore data availability quickly) in the event of a disaster that might incapacitate an entire data center.

An important but subtle characteristic of storage availability quality of service is that the levels enumerated here are not mutually exclusive. For example, data may be replicated across long distances, but both source and targets for the replication may be mirrored or RAID arrays.

I/O Performance

Two similar progressions of quality of I/O performance service options can be outlined. There are two progressions because there are two fundamental I/O performance quality measures: *latency* (how fast an average request is satisfied) and *throughput* (how much data per unit time is transferred). While these measures correlate with each other (i.e., mechanisms that improve one tend to improve the other as well), they are not the same and deserve separate discussions.

I/O Throughput

As with other aspects of quality of service, several factors can affect I/O throughput:

Disk speed. The baseline for data transfer performance is the disk. Once a relatively straightforward arithmetic product of rotational speed and bit density, disk data transfer rates today can be affected by several factors. The two factors with the largest effect are rotational velocity and data location. Disks that rotate at 10,000 revolutions per minute are common today, with some 12,000 RPM and 15,000 RPM models also available. While direct comparisons with lower-speed disks are difficult, because speed and bit density tend to increase together, a 10,000-RPM disk can transfer data about 38 percent faster than a 7,200-RPM disk, and a 12,000-RPM disk can transfer data about 20 percent faster than a 10,000-RPM disk for a given bit density. Thus, for higher data transfer rates, disks with higher rotational speeds should be chosen. While this is almost an article of faith in large systems, for smaller systems with embedded disks or disk enclosures not engineered to dissipate the heat generated by high-speed disks, other techniques for enhancing data transfer performance may be more appropriate.

Data location. Today's disks use a *zoned recording* technique to increase storage capacity. Each recording zone is a group of adjacent tracks on which a fixed number of data blocks can be recorded. Since their circumference is larger, outer zones (tracks closer to the edge of a disk) can hold more data than inner zones (tracks closer to the disk's center). Since a disk rotates at constant speed, reading data from one track at a time, more data is transferred to or from an outer track in a single revolution than from an inner one. Thus, the layout of data on a disk can be important; good practice would be to locate data that must be transferred rapidly near the outer edge of a disk.

Disk cache. The management of disk cache can affect both read and write performance. Today's disk interfaces—ATA, SCSI, and Fibre Channel—can all transfer data faster than it can be read from or written to a disk surface. Data must therefore be buffered, whether it is being read or written. In the case of reading, data is held in cache until there is a relatively large amount available with which to schedule a bus transaction. For writing, data normally accumulates in the device cache because it is received from the host interface faster than the disk can move it onto disk media. Unless the data stream is long enough to overfill it, disk write cache functions as an elasticity buffer, absorbing momentary overloads while allowing data to be transferred to disk media at full speed.

Striped disks. Inevitably, it seems, applications outgrow their I/O power. With server processor speeds increasing even faster than disk data transfer rates, waiting for I/O requests to complete can become a significant part of application response time. The divide-and-conquer approach of disk striping can get more data transferred per unit time than an individual disk. The theory is that when an application reads or writes a very large block of data, the volume manager or RAID firmware divides the request into several smaller ones addressed to different disks. These disks all execute their assigned tasks concurrently and the application's request finishes sooner.

Striped disk arrays. Disk striping can be implemented either within a RAID subsystem or by a volume manager software component residing in one or more servers. One of the important benefits of server-based disk striping is that it can be used to stripe data across different types of disks, including the virtual disks presented by RAID controllers. Thus, performance increases can be compounded if server-based striping is used in conjunction with RAID subsystem-based striping.

Number of data paths. While today's I/O interconnects can comfortably carry the traffic generated by one of today's disks, the balance reverses quickly when data is striped across disks. Three or four high-performance disks or disk arrays transferring data at maximum speed can easily overwhelm a single Fibre Channel port's 100-megabyte-per-second data transfer capacity. This is another advantage of server-based striping, which can spread a striped array of physical or virtual disks across several separate paths between computer and data. Care with data path capacity must also be taken in complex fabrics consisting of multiple switches. If data on an array of disks from which high throughput is required is separated from its clients by switches connected by interswitch links (ISLs), care must be taken to ensure that sufficient interswitch bandwidth is configured to handle peak load.

Data path quality. Long cable runs, poor quality or mismatched link components, and careless installation can all affect the error rate of an interconnect that is fundamentally functional. High error rates mean lots of retries, which in turn mean less useful data transmitted on the interconnect. Large enterprises rapidly learn the value of expertise in the physical aspects of SAN configuration. It is not uncommon for enterprise SAN administrators to be skilled in physical link testing and diagnosis, cable installation, and determining the compatibility of components with each other.

The final factor in determining quality of data transfer service is the application itself. I/O subsystems can be configured to transfer data very fast, but they will fulfill their promise only if the applications that use them present them with a steady stream of requests to read or write a large amount of data.

The most basic way in which an application can increase data transfer performance is by requesting more data in each request. Since each I/O request incurs a roughly fixed overhead, the more data requested in each I/O, the more data is transferred for a given amount of overhead.

The second factor that affects data transfer performance is the rate at which an application makes I/O requests. If I/O requests are made faster than they can be satisfied, the I/O subsystem can use time during which data transfer is occurring to set up the next request. When this is done, data is more likely to reach the application in a continuous stream rather than in a series of bursts interrupted by delays caused, for example, by disk revolutions missed because no I/O request was outstanding.

File system and I/O subsystem strategies that make life easier for applications have evolved over the years. For reading, these strategies basically amount to anticipating application requests and *prereading*, or reading data ahead of the application requesting it, so that it can be delivered immediately when the application request is finally made. Anticipatory read-ahead strategies are found in disk drives, RAID subsystems, and file systems. They are used widely, because they deliver good read performance without requiring application modifications and the strategy they adopt entails little risk. (Preread data that is never requested must be discarded, so work has been done for no purpose, but there is no risk to data integrity.)

Similar strategies are used to accelerate the writing of large streams of data, with file systems, RAID subsystems, or disk drives caching data and writing it after or behind the application's request. In this case, performance is bounded by the size of the cache that holds data until it is written and the disparity between application write speed and the I/O system's ability to absorb data.

For example, if an application makes write requests that amount to 20 megabytes per second and a disk array can absorb data at 10 megabytes per second, 10 megabytes of cache are required for overflow for every second of the application's write stream. If the application writes 10-second streams (200 megabytes) separated by at least 10-second intervals, an I/O subsystem with 100 megabytes of cache will appear to perform at 20 megabytes per second. If the application writes data any faster than that, the cache will fill and apparent performance will be lower because some of the application's writes will have to wait for cache to be available.

The risks of write-behind, or, as it is often called, *write-back caching*, are greater than for read-ahead caching. The risk arises basically because in order to stimulate the application to make its next write request, the I/O subsystem signals that the previous request is complete as soon as it has cached the data from it. This is a risk to application and data integrity because once an application is informed that a write request has been completed, it may take action predicated on an assumption that the data it wrote is safely stored on nonvolatile (*persistent*) storage media. If its data is, in fact, held in a volatile cache, a power failure or other system fault could obliterate it, leading to inconsistent downstream results.

Volatile write-back cache has long been recognized as a weakness in I/O subsystems. Most RAID subsystems and operating system device drivers disable disk write caching for this reason. Similarly, file systems that use this technique make it clear that their semantics preserve the integrity of file system metadata, but not the data within files. The best solutions to the write-back caching problem are offered by RAID subsystems, most of which include specially designed cache that can be *flushed* (written to disk) or *held up* (powered continuously so that contents are retained) if something fails.

I/O Request Processing

Transaction processing is usually cited as the most frequently occurring application that generates heavy I/O request loads on a storage subsystem. Conventional transaction processing, exemplified by retail banking or point-of-sale data capture applications, has the general characteristic that, while I/O requests may be generated at a high rate, the tendency is for not much data to be requested. For example, an I/O request rate of 1,000 requests per second sounds high. If, however, each request reads or writes a 2-kilobyte database page, the 1,000 requests generate demand for only 2 megabytes per second of I/O, which, in principle, can easily be handled by a single instance of any I/O bus in use today.

Thus, high data transfer speeds tend not to be as important in transaction processing applications as they are in data mining, backup, and other data-intensive applications. What tends to be more important is the ability to execute small, independent I/O requests at a very high rate. Since each I/O request completely occupies a disk drive for the duration of its execution, the apparently simple way to configure a system to do lots of transaction processing I/O is to configure it with as many disks as possible. Assume, for the purposes of the example, that a disk can complete 100 single-page I/O requests per second to a random selection of disk block addresses. Presumably, 10 such disks should be able to deliver the required 1,000 requests per second. On the other hand, nothing in life is perfect and it's not good practice to design a system to operate at saturation with no margin for momentary peak loads, so a good configuration for delivering 1,000 I/O transactions per second might be 15 to 20 disks.

But things are not quite that simple. Not only must the system have the innate capability to deliver 1,000 completed I/O requests per second, the I/O load must be more or less evenly balanced across the disks. Every information services administrator has a tale of a system with one or two saturated disks that bottlenecked its performance while other disk resources sat idle or nearly so.

This is where data striping comes into transaction processing. Because of the perpendicular layout of data blocks striped across disks, discussed in Chapter 6, I/O requests that are uniformly distributed among the blocks of a disk tend to be uniformly distributed across an array of striped disks. Thus, maximum use is made of physical I/O resources.

Cache and I/O Request-Intensive Loads

Cache also figures heavily in delivering quality of I/O request service. In the case of requests for data that is widely distributed among a disk's or volume's blocks, however, read-ahead is not an effective strategy. Effective cache management strategies for I/O request-intensive loads focus on the assumption that if data has been used (read or written) recently, it is likely to be used again. Thus, cache managers retain cached data objects in cache until they are eventually pushed out by other, more recently accessed data objects.

Of course, this *least recently used* (LRU) cache management strategy is inherently flawed. Managing cache this way relies on the *absence* of events (cached data that is *not* referenced), detected by the occurrence of other unrelated events. Cache utilization could be more effective if the cache manager could somehow know that a data object that was read or written was or was not going to be read or written again in the near future. Hinting technologies have been proposed to improve cache management for these applications.

The basic concept of cache hints is that when an application makes an I/O request, it specifies whether it is likely to use the data again soon. The I/O subsystem (database manager, file system, volume manager, driver, host bus adapter, RAID controller, storage appliance, or disk drive) uses the hint to prioritize data objects for ejection from the cache. Using this scheme, objects that an application expects to reuse are likely to be retained and those not likely to be reused are discarded first. While this is still an imperfect scheme, it promises more effective cache utilization than blind least recently used scheduling. Its primary drawback is that it requires application awareness of the cache and is therefore unlikely to be implemented for any applications, with the exception of database managers.

One way to make hints about data reuse transparent to applications is to ask what is known about data at each stage of the I/O path. Thus, for example:

- A disk knows only that ranges of block addresses have been read or written. With no knowledge of the meaning of the data or metadata in those blocks, it is not in a good position to make cache retention decisions.

- A RAID controller or volume manager "knows" that ranges of virtual disk block addresses have been read or written. While not much is known about the application significance of data at this level, the RAID firmware or volume manager is aware of relationships between blocks in the same stripe of a RAID array or blocks on mirrored volumes that should be retained until volume operations are complete.

- A file system has very detailed knowledge of the significance of its metadata, and, in fact, most file systems cache metadata so that structural changes do not have undue impact on disk I/O.

- The point in the I/O path with perhaps the best application-independent awareness of data's significance is the database management system. Database managers know, for example, that totals records should remain in cache while detail records that contribute to the total are being processed. As another example, they know that if a record is read with an exclusive lock, it is highly likely to be modified and rewritten and so should remain in cache. Knowledge of more of data's semantics enables an I/O path component to make better caching decisions.

New Types of Transaction Processing

New applications are challenging the conventional assumption that transaction processing applications make a lot of I/O requests but don't transfer a lot of data. Chief among these are electronic mail and Web server applications, both of which handle substantial numbers of large, nontextual data objects. Not only do these applications and others like them need high transaction performance (rapid-fire accesses to randomly distributed data objects); they frequently need high data transfer performance as well—for example, to deliver graphical documents embedded in Web pages or electronic mail attachments to clients. These new applications make conventional storage configuration and management philosophies obsolete:

- For data transfer-intensive applications, configure the smallest number of devices that will do the job and as many paths through the SAN as needed to meet throughput requirements with a reasonable margin for handling peak loads.

- For I/O-intensive applications, configure enough devices to meet I/O request processing needs with a reasonable margin for handling peak loads and don't worry so much about data transfer paths.

Modern transactional applications often require *both* high data transfer capacity and high transaction processing capacity. They can no longer necessarily be categorized as data transfer intensive or I/O request intensive. They may shift dynamically from one behavior to the other, to a hybrid of both. Moreover, in a typical SAN, dynamically changing applications interact with each other, creating demands on I/O resources that aren't always easily understood.

The static online storage configurations of yesterday are thus no longer adequate. This creates a problem for administrators who configure storage for these new applications: There's no right answer to the optimal configuration. Ideally, SAN management for these changing I/O environments would be dynamic as well. Management tools that monitor I/O activity for an entire SAN, correlate with application activity, and either make recommendations to the system administrator or proactively implement online storage and SAN infrastructure configuration changes will ultimately be required.

Products that monitor I/O activity and recommend configuration changes based on observed patterns are available today. These products are excellent for assisting in the management of storage and data owned by a single server; however, they tend not to support multiple hosts or entire SAN fabrics independent of any single host's view.

SAN Management and Backup Cost

In Chapter 1, tape drive sharing was described as a major cost benefit enabled by SAN technology for several reasons:

- Any system tends to use its tape drives for a relatively small portion of the time. Most locally attached tape drives are idle most of the time.

- A SAN-attached tape drive can be accessed by any server on the SAN, so a SAN-based multihost system usually requires fewer tape drives than an otherwise equivalent system with locally attached online storage.

- A SAN-based multiserver system may make it easier to justify a robotic tape library by amortizing the library's cost across all the servers in the SAN.

- With SAN performance, tape drives can typically stream (transfer data continuously), shortening backup times, thereby simultaneously reducing both the number of tape drives required and improving the speed of backup jobs.

But, as Chapter 1 also points out, tape drives are inherently *single-stream* devices. When an application is using a tape drive—for example, to make a backup copy—no other applications can be permitted to access the drive for the duration of the backup operation.

In a perfectly managed SAN with no application malfunctions, an administrator could conceivably schedule operations so that only one application at a time used a tape drive. But this method of scheduling would be awkward and inflexible. Moreover, applications (and operating systems!) do not always perform flawlessly. A tape drive reservation mechanism that is both stronger and more amenable to automation is needed. Contemporary SAN management technology offers three such mechanisms:

- *SAN backup software.* Some vendors of SAN-aware backup applications offer tape sharing functionality embedded in their software. Software-based tape sharing is accomplished by distributed software components in each of the servers attached to a SAN, cooperating to ensure that only one of them at a time accesses a tape drive. Software tape sharing includes mechanisms by which applications can queue requests for tape drive access and for releasing tapes for general use when a server fails while it has a tape reserved for its exclusive use.

- *LUN masking.* Done by host bus adapters in cooperation with software in the server, LUN masking works by restricting the logical unit numbers (LUNs) for which operating system commands are accepted. By masking off the LUNs that represent tape drives in use by other servers, servers can cooperate in a scheme to reserve tape drives for exclusive use.

- *Zoning.* Done by the fabric in a Fibre Channel SAN, zoning has a similar effect to that of HBA-based LUN masking. A tape drive's port address is added to the fabric zone that contains the server that will control the backup operation and the online storage device that is the source for the data to be copied. If zones in the SAN of which other servers are part are configured so that the tape drive is not a part of them, those servers will experience no response to messages sent to the tape drive's port address.

Each of these techniques has its own advantages and drawbacks. For example, both SAN backup software and LUN masking are server-based solutions and therefore require operational servers to be fully functional. Tape sharing backup software tends to include built-in failover protocols, so that if a server fails while it has a tape drive reserved for its exclusive use, the drive is ultimately released. The weakness of these solutions is that, in both cases, failure of the tape sharing software leaves tape drives open to access by applications, even if other servers have nominally reserved them. Thus, while these solutions are adequate for most circumstances, they are more robust when augmented by other mechanisms that are independent of server operation.

Zoning is such a server-independent tape drive access control mechanism. If each of the servers in a SAN has a zone configured for backup, a SAN management component can allocate SAN-attached tape drives to a given server by moving them into its backup zone. As long as all the servers' backup zones are disjoint, no server can send any messages or data to a tape drive that is owned by another server. Effective use of zoning in this way requires cooperation between the backup software and the SAN infrastructure management facility provided by the switch or director vendor.

Backup software must manage application requests for tape drives across the SAN, maintaining queues of requests against which tape drives can be allocated as they become available. When a tape drive for which there is an outstanding request becomes available, the backup software issues the SAN management commands to add that drive's port address to the zone of the requesting server. Backup software also implements predefined SAN management policies such as media compatibility (e.g., refraining from allocating LTO tape drives to backup operations whose media of choice is DLT, limiting the number of tape drives that can be allocated to a single backup job, and so forth).

SAN Management and Backup Impact

Once the question of allocating SAN-attached tape drives to a server for backup is settled, the next task is to make the backup copy itself. Less obtrusive backups that complete in less time and with less impact on server and I/O resources are generally preferred by system administrators and application managers. Consistent backup copies of operational data (the only kind worth having) require that use of the file systems or databases to be backed up cease, at least momentarily. Then, either

- A full or incremental backup copy of actual operational data can be made while data remains idle.

- A *snapshot* or point-in-time frozen image of data can be made by one of several techniques and the backup copy made from the snapshot while processing of the operational data resumes.

Chapter 4 contains a thorough discussion of full and incremental backups, as well as split mirror and copy-on-write frozen image techniques, the uses for, and advantages and disadvantages of each. For the purposes of this chapter, we concern ourselves with the SAN management capabilities required to implement the various backup techniques.

As long as the server that executes a backup job is the same server on which applications that process the data run, SAN connectivity capabilities do not figure largely in backup. If the information processing department has designed its procedures to take advantage of a dedicated backup server to eliminate the load placed on application servers by backup processes, then SAN management comes into play. Figure 12.6 illustrates the dedicated backup server configuration.

In Figure 12.6, Server A processes data in a file system and Server B processes a database. When either is to be backed up, the respective application server sends a backup job request to the backup server shown in the center of the diagram. The backup server allocates the appropriate number of tape drives, takes over ownership of the file system or database to be backed up, and makes the copy.

The need for SAN manageability arises in the simple phrase "takes over ownership of the file system or database." To be sure, the SAN itself creates the data paths that

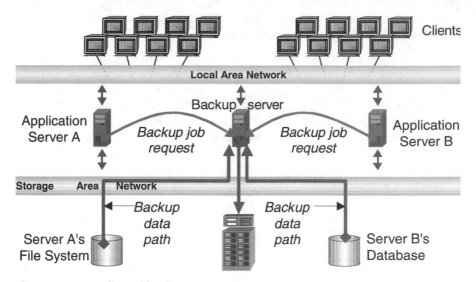

Figure 12.6 Dedicated backup server.

enable a backup server to take control of a file system or database. It is SAN management, however, that executes the policy directives to cause an orderly transition of ownership of the data objects to be backed up to the backup server.

As Chapter 8 discusses, all SAN-based distributed systems share storage and the data that resides on it in some sense (otherwise, why a SAN?). There are different levels of data sharing, however.

- If the frozen image from which the backup copy is to be made is a split mirror on separate physical or virtual disks from the operational data, all that is necessary is for ownership of that disk to be transferred from the application server to the backup server. This is the simplest kind of storage sharing, called *interval ownership* in Chapter 8. It can be accomplished by fabric-based zoning, tape virtualization servers, or under host software control.

- If the frozen image is a split mirror or snapshot, either of which resides in a volume occupying the same disks as the operational data, zoning cannot be used to effect the transfer of ownership. The disks that contain both operational data and the frozen image must remain under control of an application server so that operational data can be processed. If this is the case, *shareable volumes*, as described in Chapter 8, are required. That is, it must be possible for the volumes that contain both operational data and its frozen image to be mounted on (accessible by) both the application server and the backup server simultaneously. Since either a split mirror or a snapshot frozen image would appear to applications as a separate file system from the operational data file system, shareable file system technology is not required.

- A frozen image of operational data might also be a set of files within a file system or is part of a database that uses a file system for its underlying storage. If this is the case, then not only must the volumes containing the file system be shareable, but the file system itself must be shareable by the application and backup servers. For applications that create their own frozen images by closing and copying files and reopening the copies, sharing of individual files is not required. For databases that are embedded in file systems, files that contain database storage areas must be open simultaneously by both application and backup processes on their separate servers. To be useful in this case, a shareable file system must support simultaneous access to the same file by multiple applications running on multiple servers.

Thus, in order to utilize a dedicated backup server and realize the application server off-loading benefit that accrues from it, some kind of SAN-aware storage or data manager is required. If frozen data images can be confined to separate physical or virtual disks (storage entities that are seen through a single Fibre Channel port), then only interval ownership device sharing is required. If, the frozen images are more intimately intertwined operational data, then shareable volume, shareable file system, or shareable file techniques are necessary.

If the data to be backed up is stored in a database and database-aware backup is to be used (as opposed to backing up the files or file system containing the database storage areas), then the database management system itself partially manages the sharing. For example, the services of a shareable volume manager would be invoked if the online database management instance attempted to extend a container file while data records in it were being backed up. On the other hand, if an application attempted to modify a database record during the backup job, the database management system must recognize that the modified record is part of the backup set and make a before image copy of its contents before allowing an application to modify it.

SAN Management and Application Availability

In Chapter 1, enhanced application availability and scaling are described as two of the new information processing capabilities enabled by SAN technology. Both of these capabilities are delivered by clustering software, discussed in Chapter 8. Both capabilities require the cluster manager to manage SAN resources. Application availability is enhanced through failover, which requires synchronization of changes in SAN resource ownership with actions on applications. Application scaling requires that SAN-accessible data be shared concurrently by multiple servers. In both cases, the SAN management requirement is usually for *mechanisms*, APIs, or protocols that can be used by the cluster manager, rather than for higher-level capabilities invoked by administrators or policies. SAN management capabilities required for effective clustering include:

Protocols for heartbeating and messaging. Cluster manager instances run in each of the computers that make up a cluster. They must be able to intercommunicate reliably with low latency and system overhead. Additional semantics, such as same-order message delivery guarantees, may also be required. In principle, it might be possible to use normal LAN protocols for intercommunication among clustered servers. This is usually not done, however, because it carries undesirable latency and overhead and because it requires that networking services be completely operational in order for the clustering service to function. Heartbeat and messaging protocols may be carried on LAN connections (sometimes called *out-of-band*) or they may share the SAN interconnect with data access protocols (sometimes called (*in-band*).

I/O path and storage device accessibility management. Storage devices are among the critical resources required for applications to function. When an application or the server on which it is running fails and the cluster manager restarts it on an alternate server, ownership of the data and storage devices required by the application must move from the failed server to the failover server. Storage device ownership may be transferred by any of the mechanisms enumerated in the preceding section-zoning, LUN masking, LUN mapping, or software control. Whatever the mechanism for transferring storage device ownership, it must be accessible in the form of an API that a cluster agent can use to relinquish control of the resource (or to wrest control from an uncooperative failed server) and restart it on a failover server. The same is true of storage access paths. If application failover requires that an alternate path be used to access data, path management APIs are also required, so that cluster agents can execute any needed path management functions.

Data access management. Shared data clusters (clusters in which the same file systems or, in some implementations, even the same files, can be accessed simultaneously by multiple application instances operating on different servers) require intercommunication among the servers sharing data so that access requests can be coordinated. Coordination of shared data is done using a distributed lock manager, which passes messages among the servers that access shared file systems or databases. Cluster messaging protocols are often used for this purpose.

Long-distance data replication and global clustering. Data replication, discussed in Chapter 8, may be used to enable recovery of information processing capability after a disaster that incapacitates an entire data center. Data may be replicated either at the server level, using a MAN or WAN directly, or at the RAID subsystem level, using a SAN extended across a MAN or WAN. Whichever of these is used, SAN management facilities are required, for example, to configure and control replication or to switch applications from using primary data to using a replica. As with clustering within the data center, wide area clustering is most effective when it can be automated, with cluster state changes made in response to external events according to predefined policies. Since cluster state changes may involve reconfiguration of storage, SAN management APIs are required for automation.

Thus, SAN management functionality, usually in the form of APIs that can be invoked by cluster managers or agents in response to external events, is a necessity to achieve full benefit from a SAN.

SAN Management and Asset Utilization

The management capabilities available for a particular SAN have a powerful impact on how effectively the SAN's storage and infrastructure assets can be utilized. Asset utilization has at least three dimensions:

- *Asset tracking.* In an era when enterprises manage all their affairs electronically, it is not unusual for even a medium-size information processing organization to be responsible for hundreds of servers (and host bus adapters), dozens of Fibre Channel switches, RAID subsystems and software packages, and thousands of disk drives. Simply keeping track of what SAN assets an enterprise owns, where they are located, what state they are in, and how they are logically deployed is a formidable challenge. Information processing organizations need to keep track of their SAN assets in order to optimize deployment of storage capacity and I/O bandwidth and so that replenishment can be planned and carried out optimally.

- *Revision tracking.* Managing SAN assets is both more complex and more vital than conventional IT asset management because just about every component in a SAN is intelligent to some degree. Host bus adapters, switches and directors, RAID subsystems, disk and tape drives, operating system drivers, and applications all include software or firmware that must be upgraded periodically. Less frequent, but equally important, are hardware revisions. In a heterogeneous SAN, each component vendor is likely to have its own interoperability testing practices and its own compatibility matrix. Effective tracking of SAN assets includes tracking component revision levels and planning upgrades so as to avoid or minimize interoperability problems due to incompatible revisions.

- *Capacity planning.* Finally, with electronic business, planning for growth is both more difficult and more critical to enterprise success than with conventional business. We have asserted that it is difficult or even impossible to plan for IT growth in today's business environment and, in an overall sense, this is true. Unplanned storage and bandwidth requirements can pop up overnight due to external factors, such as competition, over which the enterprise has no control. What is also true is that, as time passes, applications' storage requirements exhibit patterns. Storage requirements might increase linearly because business increases or they might be cyclic, as with Web retail operations during Christmas season. Long-term storage trend analysis is more important than ever before, as administrators attempt to predict knowable requirements as best they can so that surprises have less impact on the enterprise as a whole.

SAN storage and I/O capacity planning tends to be more complex than with locally attached storage. A successful SAN is one in which asset utilization can be tracked and analyzed continuously so that trends can be discerned and asset growth and replenishment can be planned.

Thus, the ability for an administrator to know everything about the hardware and software assets that constitute his or her SAN can be crucial to success. Even with SANs of modest size, human-based *asset management by spreadsheet* is generally not a tractable solution. Automated tools for managing assets are required.

SAN Management Tools

Thus far, the storage and I/O configuration, performance and availability, and asset tracking aspects of SAN management have been discussed. In each case, it is clear that automated intelligence must be applied to the problems, if for no other reason than to manage the plethora of detail involved. An administrator attempting to manage a SAN without the assistance of comprehensive tools is all too prone to overlook some detail and leave a critical application without a storage growth path or exposed to a single interconnect link failure.

SAN management is an inherently more complex problem than management of the local I/O subsystem of a single server. For one thing, there are more interacting components, because instead of each server representing a separate management case, all servers, all storage, and the entire interconnect infrastructure must be considered as a whole. Universal interconnection also complicates management because storage is virtualized; a single physical asset, such as a disk drive or RAID subsystem, may form parts of several volumes that provide storage to several different servers. I/O activity is similarly complex. Each server and host bus adapter has data passing through it, as does each switch and each storage device. The storage capacity and I/O load at any point in a system may be attributable to several sources.

All this complexity suggests basic requirements for SAN management tools:

Discovery. SAN components are nontrivial to discover. There may be hundreds of them; they may occupy several widely separated computer rooms. Multiple paths between servers and switches fan out, creating complex interconnections, some of which can be zoned out. Some automated means of discovering what devices and servers are attached to a SAN and what paths interconnect them is needed.

Visualization. A typical enterprise SAN is considerably more complex than a single server's local I/O subsystem. It is difficult, if not impossible, to present a single visual image that represents a SAN adequately for management purposes. There are simply too many components and too many vantage points from which an administrator must view a SAN. Multiple views with zooming capability are required.

Interoperation. Since SANs are inherently multiplatform, with components supplied by different vendors, SAN management tools must be vendor and product aware and include databases or other ways of determining of *what works with what.*

Adaptability. When a vendor introduces a new component, it should be possible to integrate it into the SAN management infrastructure so that it can be tracked, configured, and monitored.

Automation. To the extent possible, SAN management tools should be policy based, performing routine operations automatically. With hundreds or even thousands of components in a SAN, administrator involvement in routine management must be by exception rather than by inspection. Event tracking as well as performance and availability monitoring and reporting should be automatic, with only exceptional combinations reported to human administrators for action. The human SAN administrator's principal tasks should be to set the overall policies according to which automated tools self-manage the SAN and to react to exceptional situations for which no policy exists.

Robustness. Quite simply, without SAN management tools, a SAN cannot be managed. The ability to manage a SAN must survive both component failures and site-incapacitating disasters. Thus, SAN management applications must be capable of running anywhere in the SAN, and SAN management databases must be replicated in widely separated locations for survivability.

Scalability. An enterprise's SANs may be distributed over a wide geographic area. It is impractical to expect administrators to travel to every server, infrastructure component, or storage device to perform operations on them. Some operations, such as adding disk drives or host bus adapters, are inherently physical. Most, however, can be performed remotely from a central management console. Central administration reduces the number of administrators required and increases administrative efficiency by reducing travel time. The quality of administrative service also tends to improve because, with a broader scope of operations, administrators tend to become more skilled at tasks and to acquire a broader picture of the enterprise's overall information processing operation.

Who's in Charge, Anyway? Organizing to Administer a Storage Network

In a typical information services organization, there are multiple administrative specialties:

System administration. System administrators manage application operating environments. A typical system administrator is responsible for one or more servers or clusters. System administration tasks typically include operating system installation and upgrade, system hardware configuration management, user account management, and fault and performance monitoring and management.

Network administration. Network administrators manage an enterprise's communications infrastructure. They are responsible for wiring, access points (hubs, switches, and routers), and public or private wide area network access. Network management tasks typically include network infrastructure design and deployment, wiring, access point installation and configuration, routing table definition, enabling and disabling local access ports, managing external wide area network services, and controlling user and system access to the enterprise network.

Database administration. Database administrators manage enterprise data from a logical abstraction standpoint. A typical database administrator is responsible for installation and configuration of database management software, negotiating and meeting multiple application and user data requirements by implementing appropriate database structures, monitoring and optimizing database performance, and managing database backups.

Application administration. As applications have become more standardized and the shift from in-house development to external acquisition has occurred, a few dominant applications have emerged. These in turn have spawned a class of administrators skilled in managing general accounting, human resources, customer relationship management, electronic mail, and other common enterprise applications. Philosophically very similar to database administrators, application administrators' responsibilities tend to include installation and upgrade of the application, data structure definition, performance monitoring and optimization, and problem management.

Of course, in smaller enterprises some or all of these roles may fall to an indispensable jack-of-all-trades. But as an enterprise grows, its data centers and applications increase in scope and complexity, and a staff of administrative specialists inevitably grows with it.

Aside from demonstrating that modern enterprise data centers are complex, constantly evolving organisms, this listing poses a bit of a conundrum for storage networking. When storage networks are installed, who should administer them?

- Surely not *system administrators*, whose responsibilities stop at the boundaries of their systems. Almost by definition, a storage network links the domains of several system administrators.

- Surely not *network administrators*, whose responsibilities normally do not extend to the devices connected to their networks. As far back as Chapter 1, we asserted that it makes no sense to think about a storage network infrastructure without thinking about the storage connected to it.

- Surely not *database* or *application administrators*, whose domains of responsibility are bounded by their particular databases or applications and don't encompass the entire enterprise. A major benefit of storage networking was to consolidate the physical storage resources used by all of these

Alas, the nature of storage networks is such that yet another administrative specialty seems to be indicated: In a sense, deployment of an enterprise storage network makes storage into an enterprise resource much in the same way that a network, database, or application is an enterprise resource.

A hypothetical storage administrator would be responsible for storage resources across the enterprise. System, database, and application administrators would negotiate storage and I/O requirements with the storage administrator, who would then be responsible for configuring and maintaining a storage network to meet them. The storage administrator would deliver an agreed-upon *quality of storage service* to each of these clients of the storage network. *Chapter 1* discusses quality of storage service metrics and how to deliver on them.

A Hidden Cost of SAN Deployment?

Apparently, then, part of the benefit of a storage network is offset by the need for additional administrators. While this may be literally true in a few borderline instances, it is more likely that installing a storage administrator along with a SAN will deliver both types of business benefit:

It reduces the cost of delivering a service. In this case, the service is system, database, or application administration. Today, all of these administrators are concerned to one degree or another with storage. Database and application administrators must make physically oriented decisions about where and on what kind of storage devices to locate database tables and application files. System administrators must be concerned with installing and configuring disk drives and RAID subsystems, allocating storage to I/O buses and host bus adapters, configuring server-based volumes, initializing and extending file systems, and so forth. The portion of their time that all of these administrators spend on these issues is consolidated in the storage administrator, thus making them more effective at their primary responsibilities.

It improves the quality of the service delivered. Simply put, the storage administrator is a storage professional—not a database or application professional or a system management professional. Ideally, storage administrators would be certified in their profession, according to one or more of the storage networking credentialing programs springing up around the industry as this book is written. Because the storage administrator deals only with storage, he or she should be more proficient at it than someone who deals with it occasionally in the course of conducting other duties.

The net result of appointing a storage administrator is actually likely to be a saving rather than a cost. The strong recommendation, therefore, is that when an enterprise begins to treat storage as an enterprise asset by installing a storage network, it should appoint a dedicated administrator to give it the care it deserves.

As with any well-run deployment of new technology, the key is to work through things in a methodical, planned manner, measure your success and failure as you go, and keep in mind the end goals at all times. Learning from your own successes and failures is a good lesson, but can be expensive. Learning from others who have been there before you or are going the same place as you can save you a lot of grief. A problem shared is a problem halved.

The State of SAN Management

As this book is written, SAN management is widely recognized among both users and vendors as a critical factor in advancing this technology. The development of effective SAN management tools and capabilities is proceeding apace on several fronts. The evolution of different facets of SAN management seems to have been occurring in four phases:

1. *Homogeneity.* Major system vendors were early to develop SAN management capabilities for their own product families. This makes sense from both opportunity and motivation standpoints. A vendor that supplies all the components in a SAN, including servers, infrastructure, and storage, is able to test all of those components as a system and to manage interoperability issues. When consumers forgo best-in-class purchasing and buy an entire SAN from one vendor, integration is usually a factor. A system vendor is *expected* to test its products exhaustively against each other and maintain coherent configuration control. Thus, the management capabilities that reach the market first tend to be system vendors' tools for the management of their own products.

2. *Affinity groupings.* Smaller system vendors, which may not have their own storage capabilities, are at a competitive disadvantage relative to larger vendors that are able to test and qualify entire SANs. In order for these vendors to succeed, however, SANs that include their products must be manageable. Groups of component vendors solve this problem by establishing *affinity groups* to advance their products to market parity with those of larger system vendors with more complete technology portfolios. Affinity groups develop what might be called

prestandards—common interfaces, protocols, or APIs that can be implemented or utilized by the members. For example, an HBA or switch vendor might develop an *element manager* for the component it supplies and integrate it into the affinity group's SAN management framework. These prestandards start the move to general interoperability in that they provide a level of interoperability between multiple vendors' products. Affinity group interoperability enables integrators to choose among several host bus adapters or switches, for example, when configuring solutions for customers.

3. *Standards.* Once a SAN technology has demonstrated that it is clearly going to catch on, independent component vendors begin to play an even larger role. Because of affinity group membership, vendors who sell only host bus adapters or switches, for example, can position their products as part of an integrated whole. Increasing comfort with the emerging technology emboldens end users to demand the ability to purchase best-in-class components from whichever vendors they choose. While most standardization activity begins as soon as it becomes clear that component vendors need to interoperate, it is only at this stage of market development that the motivation for standards with teeth comes into being. At this stage, vendors that have implemented management tools for their own components typically submit APIs or protocols developed in affinity groups to formal standardization bodies like ANSI and IETF.

4. *Interoperability.* A market of heterogeneous components that must interoperate in order to form a useful system reaches maturity when standards not only exist, but also are so mature that the need for case-by-case interoperability testing is minimal. Vendors' interoperability testing of components from different suppliers never entirely disappears. What does happen, however, is a shift from strict, inclusive supportability rules, in which vendors specify what interfacing components *do* work with their products, to more relaxed, broader guidelines that tend to specify known exceptions to interoperability.

As this book is written, the SAN industry is experiencing various phases of this four-stage evolution on different fronts. Basic protocol interoperation is in the late standards stage and approaching the interoperability stage desired by end users. Switch interoperability has made great strides recently and is squarely in the standards stage. Host bus adapter management has recently moved from an affinity group of vendors to a standardization body, so it is entering the standards stage. RAID subsystems, tape drives, media libraries, and applications, on the other hand, are in the homogeneous stage. Interoperability and heterogeneous management are clearly in the future for these components. Data interoperability across platforms is even further in the future; it is not clear at this point that it is even advantageous for different vendors' file systems to work together.

SAN Management and Standards

Like the rest of SAN technology, SAN management inherently relies on effective standards for interoperability. While accredited standards organizations have been able to take on standardization of SAN command and data protocols, the pressure to develop management standards rapidly has led to the creation of new organizations that claim responsibility for a sometimes bewildering variety of standardization activities. SAN management standardization is developed and promoted both by open industry associations and by *affinity groups* of interested companies.

Industry Association SAN Management Activities

Much of SAN management technology is based on the Simple Network Management Protocol (SNMP) administered by the Internet Engineering Task Force (IETF). SNMP is a mature standard that developed in response to the need to manage peer network elements. It is both general and simple, supporting the following:

- The extraction of information from the managed element (SNMP GET)
- The setting of parameters that control the managed element (SNMP SET)
- The processing of event signals emitted by the managed element (SNMP TRAP)

These operations are executed on structured data structures called *management information bases* (MIBs). When a group of interested parties perceives a need to manage a type of component, it typically drafts a MIB for the element and proposes it to the IETF. Over the years, MIBs for all significant network elements have been developed and many of the management applications in existence today work by GETting and SETting MIB parameters for the elements they manage and responding to TRAPs from those elements.

As SANs began to be deployed, vendors recognized that platform-independent management of SAN components would require the development of MIBs or something like them. EMC Corporation initiated the formation of an ad hoc organization of vendors whose main purpose was the development of MIBs for managing SAN components, particularly RAID subsystems. The Fibre Alliance organization works closely with other standards and industry organizations so that its work products are both broadly accepted and rigorous. As this book is written, Fibre Alliance MIBs have been further developed by working groups of the SNIA and submitted to the IETF for standardization.

Affinity Group SAN Management Activities

As Fibre Channel SAN technology began to be deployed, it became apparent that several of the management services that are common in peer networks would be required in order for SANs to fulfill the promise of the hardware technology. These services include device naming and discovery, time management, and zoning. The natural location for these services was within the SAN infrastructure—the one component that is guaranteed to be present in all SANs. All of the infrastructure vendors embarked on development of SAN management capabilities. Brocade Communications Corporation was the first to submit a management server specification for public standardization.

The X3T11 Fibre Channel Management Server proposed standard is based on this specification.

SAN configurations also represent the first time in the history of information technology when the server must be considered part of the network. Prior system configurations have been server-centric, meaning that only storage devices and paths need be discovered and allocated. With SANs, all components are peers from a management standpoint and servers must be discovered and managed as well.

The server's window on the SAN is the network interface card or host bus adapter. Recognizing this, a group of companies led by QLogic Corporation undertook an initiative in mid-2000 to create a common application programming interface by which management applications could interact with host bus adapters. The resulting *SAN/Device Management API* has been submitted to X3T11 for formal standardization.

SAN Management Challenges

Storage networking is a relatively new information processing technology and is still undergoing rapid development. While great progress has been made, challenges for developers remain, as this book is written. The challenges derive primarily from the complexity of the configurations enabled by SAN technology. With SAN technology, it is possible to create much larger, fully interconnected networks of storage devices and servers than has ever been possible before. Storage has become independent of the server, so the server is no longer the appropriate design center for the management of storage.

Today's principal challenges in SAN management are:

Security. To date, the majority of SANs have been installed in trusted environments, in which there is physical security. In many cases, SANs are installed within the computer room. In campus installations, many interconnect facilities are private or at least installed over trusted rights of way. As SAN installations spread over wider geographic areas, bridged over commercial communications facilities in many cases, this assumption no longer holds. As more storage across the enterprise is integrated into enterprise SANs, physical control of what is connected to the SAN will necessarily weaken and network-style authentication, authorization, and data security will become necessities.

Monitoring and analysis. The number and variety of devices that can be connected in a SAN are already beyond the capacity of unassisted management by humans. System administrators find themselves confronted with matrices consisting of dozens of servers connected to hundreds or even thousands of storage devices over multipath networks. Just managing logical connections is difficult to cope with. Managing for optimal performance and availability and proactively detecting and reacting to potential failures requires both monitoring and correlative analysis. Performance monitoring and fault detection tools exist for most major operating system platforms. But with SANs, the server's view is not the entire picture. Several servers may use the same physical path to access different logical devices. In large

SANs, interswitch links may be in the middle of several different server-to-storage device paths. Multiple servers' views of I/O performance will have to be correlated to provide an overall SAN-wide picture.

Intra-gration. Because SANs enable larger and more general configurations, it becomes difficult to correlate physical objects (disk and tape drives, RAID subsystems, switches, paths, and host bus adapters) with data abstractions. (file systems and database systems) for management purposes. At the same time it has become more necessary than ever before to deal with questions such as how important files or databases can be made to perform better or be better protected. The correlation between SAN components and data abstractions that are readily understood and dealt with by system administrators must come from the components that implement these functions. Similarly, seemingly disparate SAN events such as I/O error frequency and failure to meet application response time guarantees must be automatically correlated because the potential number and variety of such events are too great for an administrator to correlate manually. SAN software vendors must expose the properties of configurations enabled by their software (e.g., long-distance mirroring) to file systems and database management systems and must provide facilities by which events can be correlated to give administrators the complete SAN operational picture required for comprehensive management.

Inter-gration. Important as they are, SANs, alas, are not the only things in enterprise information processing environments that need to be managed. Computers themselves, applications, user profiles, network components and facilities, printers, and databases all need to be managed as well. All of these information processing facilities have their own management tools, most of which are integrated within enterprise system management frameworks such as Tivoli's Enterprise Console and Computer Associates' Unicenter. Some integration of SAN management tools with these enterprise management frameworks has occurred. Most enterprise system management frameworks are able to receive Simple Network Management Protocol (SNMP) *traps* or event report messages from SAN components, display them, correlate them with other system events, and issue alerts to a pager or email account or run scripts or command files. Several enterprise system management frameworks are able to launch SAN management tools in context, but there is as yet no comprehensive integration of SAN management tools with enterprise system management frameworks.

SAN architecture. Most SAN component vendors have recognized the importance of SAN manageability and acted upon it. Tools available from switch vendors make it possible to optimize a SAN from the switch point of view. Disjoint and overlapping zones can be created, redundant paths configured for performance and availability, and statistics collected. But little RAID subsystem or volume manager information is exposed through a typical switch management interface. From the RAID subsystem point of view, almost the reverse is true. Host bus adapter vendors provide APIs and management tools for managing the server's view of the SAN, but cannot see inside switches and RAID subsystems. Robotic media libraries also have their own management tools. None of these is correlated with the application view provided by clusters. In the coming years, complexity will drive SAN component and management tool vendors to work together to create a universal model for SANs, from which consistent and comprehensive management tools can be derived and from which persistent, transferable administrator skill sets can be learned.

Policy-based management. SANs' potential for physical and logical complexity simply makes it impossible for humans to manage SAN-based systems on a task basis. SAN management must evolve to permit administrators to set policies expressed in application or quality-of-service terms, which are implemented automatically by SAN management tool suites. Part of any SAN architecture must be a common expression of SAN management concepts in a way that allows them to be implemented by any tool suite that conforms to the architecture.

Heterogeneous data sharing. Although strictly speaking, it is an in-band function rather than a management feature, heterogeneous data sharing will enable new types of applications and pose new management challenges. Downtime windows will all but disappear, as applications are able to move from server to server without restarting, because their data never stops being accessible, even for an instant. Low-cost Windows servers will be deployed as engines for backup and other utility functions, not just for Windows applications, but for enterprise Unix platforms as well. These utility servers will have to be added to the SAN management environment, scheduled, and otherwise managed.

SAN Management Tomorrow: The Race to the Storage Dial Tone

Complex, global SANs are just beginning to be deployed and thus many of the issues mentioned in this chapter are really tomorrow's challenges rather than issues facing users of storage networking today. While the technologies to create global SANs exist, truly global SANs have not yet been widely deployed. As this book is written, the state of SAN deployment is more in the nature of SAN islands, which, if interconnected at all, are connected through servers using conventional wide area networking facilities and techniques, as Figure 12.7 illustrates.

Figure 12.7 illustrates a global network of data centers, each of which is equipped with a SAN. The SANs may be interconnected indirectly through the enterprise wide area messaging network (WAN). The interconnection is used for *replication*, which keeps widely separated copies of data in a state of near synchronization, while allowing for network overloads and link outages.

Where wide area SANs are deployed today, they tend to have a master/slave relationship, with data from a primary processing site being mirrored or replicated[2] directly to a secondary site over a point-to-point connection. Today, the functionality provided by these long-distance SANs is limited; therefore, managing them essentially consists of configuring for data replication and shifting operations from the primary data center to a secondary data center containing the replicated data. Figure 12.8 illustrates a typical wide area SAN replication configuration in use today.

[2] The distinction between mirroring and data replication is introduced in Chapter 2.

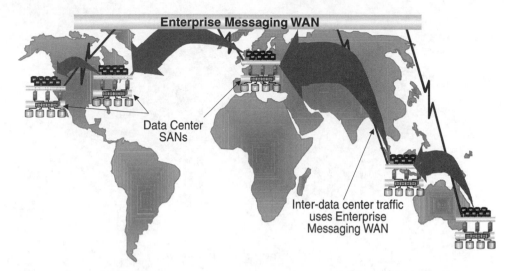

Figure 12.7   SAN islands.

In Figure 12.8, each data center SAN is connected to the SAN to the west of it through a wide area network link. RAID subsystems at each of the data centers are configured to replicate data across the private WAN. This form of replication, which is functionally identical to the server-based replication illustrated in Figure 12.7, can be used for disaster protection or for follow-the-sun processing, which steps both primary data and processing site from data center to data center as the business day progresses.

While the linked SANs illustrated in Figure 12.8 represent a major step forward, the potential for storage-centric computing created by high-speed global networking is even greater. Figure 12.9 illustrates a hypothetical SAN of the future. In Figure 12.9, an

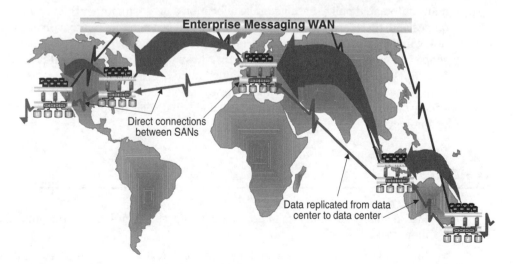

Figure 12.8   Wide area SANs: the first stage.

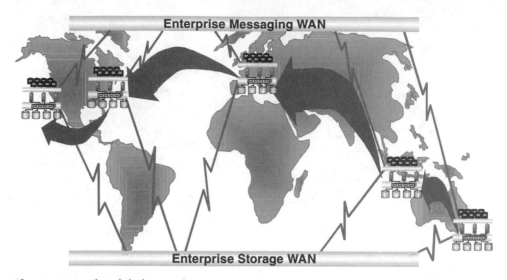

Figure 12.9 The global SAN of tomorrow.

enterprise backbone SAN links all of the enterprise's data center SANs to each other, much in the same way that the enterprise messaging backbone links its servers together.

With such configurations, the SAN applications and information processing functionality described in Chapter 2 can truly be deployed on a global scale. The nature of storage I/O is such that the distinction between synchronous mirroring and asynchronous data replication will be an enduring one and will figure in global SAN applications and functionality as they are deployed.

The type of global SAN illustrated in Figure 12.9 will enable SAN configurations connecting tens of thousands of servers and storage devices. The number of devices will make automated policy-based storage allocation a necessity rather than a luxury. Distances and, therefore, data propagation times will be such that relative physical location will become a factor in implementing storage allocation policies. In general, the scope and complexity of SANs such as that illustrated in Figure 12.9 will bring to the fore the SAN management challenges enumerated previously. Vendors are working both alone and in association to meet these challenges so that when global SANs are widely deployed, they will be manageable and will deliver the benefits enabled by the technology.

Summary

- SAN management consists of both network infrastructure and storage management tasks.
- Ideally, SAN management would deal with an integrated view of everything from applications and data to physical storage devices.

- Because they enable new types of functionality and new types of system configuration, SANs create the need for new types of management tasks such as discovery, namespace management, and zoning.

- Comprehensive SAN management can reduce storage cost through consolidation of online physical storage into fewer, larger units and through sharing of tape drives and media libraries. Management cost is also reduced by reducing the number of physical storage plants that must be managed.

- Fewer, larger storage units provide better, more predictable quality of online storage service. Tape sharing lowers the cost justification point for robotic media libraries, which improves quality of tape service by reducing the handling of media by humans.

- Managed SANs also improve application availability and scaling through clustering. Clustering services must have access to SAN management APIs so that failover and load balancing can be automated.

- Storage networking has accelerated the move toward quality of service-based storage management. Quality of service can be measured in terms of I/O throughput, responsiveness, and availability, either separately or together.

- SANs can reduce the impact of backup on application execution by allowing backup jobs to be run on dedicated backup servers. SAN management APIs are required so that ownership of storage devices and data can be transferred between application servers and backup servers.

- For maximum effectiveness, SAN management tools must deliver storage visualization, must interoperate, must be automated, must survive failures, and must be capable of centralized control of distributed SAN resources.

- Today, SAN management is available in a variety of forms, from strictly homogeneous solutions offered by system vendors to solutions of components offered by affinity groups of vendors who support each others' products. The industry is striving toward standards-based management of heterogeneous SANs. Several standards organizations and affinity groups are working on standardization of various aspects of SAN management.

- The state of SAN management today is barely adequate for small data center SANs. User acceptance is increasing the size and complexity of the average SAN, making more comprehensive SAN management capabilities a necessity. These capabilities include security, SAN-wide monitoring and analysis, and further integration of the components among themselves, as well as with SAN-aware applications.

Speculations on the Future of SANs

In this chapter we'll learn more about:

- What an enterprise storage network might look like in the year 2005.
- Some of the activities taking place in the industry and the changes they might lead to.

The Enterprise Data Wish List

Today, there is an impressive array of technology delivering an impressive set of data management capabilities to enterprises. Technology exists to allow an enterprise to do the following:

- Share a pool of online storage among multiple servers to reduce cost and improve responsiveness to unanticipated needs.
- Configure this pool of storage to have appropriate performance and availability characteristics as it is allocated to servers and applications.
- Back up data automatically across an entire enterprise with almost no application downtime.
- Share data among multiple servers simultaneously so that all applications operate from the same enterprise business information.
- Keep applications available full time to large and growing numbers of users using clustering technology to enable both failover and parallel operations.
- Replicate data across long distances for publication or consolidation and to protect an enterprise's ability to process data against disaster.
- Create coordinated global computing facilities that can hand off data and applications from site to site for business or disaster recovery reasons.

With this array of capabilities, it is almost tempting to ask what else is needed. What more can the storage networking industry segment produce that will bring additional benefits to users and IT administrators? Can storage networking contribute further than it already has to the enterprise bottom line? If today's capabilities aren't the ultimate in storage networking, what *would* an ideal storage network look like? The following sections paragraphs discuss storage network-related initiatives that are occurring in the industry and in the academic community. How these initiatives will affect the future is anyone's guess. What's certain is that, in the world of storage networking, this is only the beginning.

New Interconnects, New Dynamics

Today, the dominant SAN technology is Fibre Channel, and the dominant SAN device type is the block access storage device with the file system or database on the server side of the network. Other approaches are being developed, however, that challenge both the Fibre Channel and block mode SAN devices that dominate storage networking today.

Low-Latency NAS

One of the major reasons for adopting NAS devices for data center storage is simplicity of management. A considerable number of enterprise users accept the high I/O latency inherent in today's NAS technology as the trade-off for the reduced management cost that comes from making things simpler. NAS devices simplify data center management in three ways:

- *Heterogeneity*. NAS devices present files to any application server that implements one of the two dominant file access protocols: CIFS and NFS. The NAS device coordinates multiple servers' requests for data using file access semantics. NAS devices provide access to a single pool of data objects for servers of different types. NAS devices allow storage to be managed on a data center-wide basis, with little of the host-level complexity of SAN technology.

- *Flexibility*. For the ultimate in management simplicity, some vendors market self-contained NAS *appliances*, with few configuration options and correspondingly few management requirements. Enterprises with greater capacity or performance needs can invest in *NAS heads*, servers that perform NAS functions using various types of external storage devices. Some NAS heads allow users to configure their own storage devices. NAS devices can even be user-designed. Unix and Windows server operating systems can be configured to provide file services exclusively. NAS devices can be clustered for high-availability data access, and the entire gamut of storage of performance and storage availability features discussed in Chapter 6 are available.

- *Network properties*. NAS devices use TCP/IP network services to communicate with application clients. A NAS device may be grafted onto the enterprise LAN, or a parallel LAN may be constructed exclusively for data access. In either case, the same technologies and management skills that are required to administer the enterprise LAN are also useful for this type of storage network. With management cost becoming a larger and larger portion of information technology budgets, managing one network technology rather than two is a powerful argument in favor of the NAS approach.

Just about the only disadvantage of network-attached storage is the protocol overhead and the resulting data access latency and server loading. TCP/IP is an extremely flexible protocol, supporting any imaginable network topology and communication media. The price of this flexibility is high per-packet overhead, because, unlike Fibre Channel, TCP/IP is virtually always implemented in software. Each time a packet of data is received on a TCP/IP connection, software must analyze it to determine the meaning of its contents. In particular, data packets are not known to contain data until they are analyzed, so data cannot be transferred directly from host bus adapters or network interface cards into application buffers. Instead, when packet contents are analyzed and found to contain data, the data must be moved from kernel memory to application buffers.

Recently, two groups of NAS vendors have banded together to develop technologies for lower overhead access to data managed by NAS devices. One of these groups has proposed a new file access protocol called the *Direct Access File System*, or DAFS; the other is exploring low-latency access extensions to NFS, as this book is written. Both of these developments are closely related to the Virtual Interface Architecture (VIA), a proposed standard for a low-latency transport protocol that can be layered on any of several communication technologies.

The key properties of VIA are direct transmission of messages and large blocks of data between preallocated buffers in the application address spaces of two servers without traversing a software stack. Under the VIA protocol, pairs of cooperating processes running on different servers can send messages and large blocks of data directly to preallocated buffers in each others' memory spaces, bypassing TCP/IP or any other protocol stack. VIA provides low-latency intercommunication between applications without sacrificing data security during data transmission and reception.

One intuitively attractive use for this technology is direct connection between file access clients (redirectors) and file servers. Potentially, a file access protocol using VIA or a similar transport could have performance similar to that of block access SAN technology. If this proves to be true, the potential implications are profound. NAS devices using these protocols would offer all the management simplicity of today's NAS devices with data access performance and system loading comparable to that of SANs. Today, SAN-attached storage dominates the network storage market. A device offering NAS-style simplicity with SAN-style data access performance should be very attractive to many users and has the potential to change the way that enterprises think about data center storage.

A Single Enterprise Network Technology

Recently, most of the largest companies in network storage have banded together to develop protocols to support the connection of block access storage devices to TCP/IP networks. Multiple initiatives in this space go under different names, such as iSCSI, Storage over IP (SoIP), and ipStorage. In addition, protocols are being developed to run Fibre Channel protocols over TCI/IP (FCIP), and for encapsulating TCP/IP traffic over a Fibre Channel interconnect.

Using TCP/IP protocols and the underlying Ethernet interconnects to communicate between storage devices and computers has several apparent advantages:

Single network infrastructure. Organizations already maintain enterprise networks for application access and user intercommunication. Vendor relationships are established, and administrative skills and experience are in place. This contrasts with Fibre Channel infrastructure, which represents new capital equipment and administrative skill and training for most enterprises. With administrative cost rising as a percentage of overall IT budget, a common management skill set is a strong motivator.

Flexible network topologies. The TCP/IP protocol set has matured over a long period of time to handle the most complex networks that can be built. Routing, congestion control, and data security over insecure links are all solved problems in the TCP/IP space. Adopting TCP/IP as the storage I/O protocol would remove all architectural barriers to distributed system design. By contrast, Fibre Channel infrastructures are only now addressing some of the complex questions in network topology and security.

Network performance. Fibre Channel and Ethernet are taking different approaches to speed evolution. As this book is written, Fibre Channel is making a transition from 1-gigabit links to 2-gigabit links. By contrast, Ethernet's next transition, which has already begun to occur in development labs, is widely known to be from 1-gigabit links to 10-gigabit links. The Ethernet philosophy through the years has been one of infrequent but large (decimal order of magnitude) speed improvements that start as backbone interconnects and migrate outward to the edges of the network.

Network cost. Ethernet components are delivered to the market in very large quantities, which tends to drive prices down rather rapidly after a technology's introduction. The use of Ethernet as a storage hardware interconnect would only increase components, driving unit prices down further. This contrasts with Fibre Channel, most of whose manufacturing yield is delivered to the storage industry.

In fact, it is difficult to find a business or technology argument that does not favor Ethernet and TCP/IP as storage interconnects. The major counterarguments to Ethernet and TCP/IP reduce to software overhead and protocol maturity. The software overhead argument is largely focused on TCP/IP rather than Ethernet per se, and is articulated in the preceding section. It is clearly recognized as a valid concern by the ipStorage community and by ASIC vendors, several of which are developing ASICs that embed parts of TCP/IP protocol processing in silicon, as this book is written. Whether this will succeed in reducing TCP/IP processing overhead to Fibre Channel levels remains to be seen. If it fails, however, it will not be from want of having been attempted.

The protocol argument takes two forms. As was the case with Fibre Channel, the SCSI command and data transfer protocol has had to be mapped onto TCP/IP and Ethernet. Thus, while the underlying transport protocols are certainly mature, the functional or upper layer protocols are new inventions and will presumably take time to mature, as other protocols have before them. The second protocol argument is that the underlying Ethernet protocol is not designed for zero packet loss and that this will adversely affect its success as a storage I/O foundation. The counterargument is that the links used for storage I/O in actual practice will be of high quality, and actual lost packets will be rare. In addition, research and development is leading in the direction of zero-packet loss extensions for Ethernet links.

Whether one subscribes to these arguments or not, they are both temporary. If the investment stream in TCP/IP and Ethernet as a storage I/O interconnect is sustained—and there is every reason to believe that it will be based on the companies involved—the protocols will mature and any actual reliable transmission problems will be resolved. The advantages, on the other hand, are not time bounded. It is difficult to believe that Ethernet and TCP/IP do not have a significant place in the storage networks of the future.

Interestingly, the TCP/IP ASIC development spurred by the ipStorage community is equally applicable to DAFS. Lowering the processing overhead for the protocols underlying DAFS should do even more to improve performance and make consumers look even harder at taking the NAS approach to storage in the data center and across the enterprise.

Different Models, Different Capabilities

Not only are new interconnects and protocols being developed, new ways of storing, managing, and delivering data to applications are being researched. The limitations of network-accessible data storage today are primarily of four types:

- *Management automation.* Today's SAN hardware enables all of the capabilities enumerated in Chapter 2 To a large extent, the software to deliver them is falling into place in the market. What's missing is a means for administrators to manage the amounts of storage that are finding their way into data centers.

- *Availability.* RAID, mirroring, and data replication have brought protection against hardware and site failures to a high art. Even with all the progress described in Chapter 10, backup as a means of protecting against software bugs, procedural errors, and security breaches remains the weak link in the data availability chain.

- *Data over distance.* While file systems and database managers deliver very high integrity within a single system and even within a cluster, the ability to deliver data with equal integrity and performance to users and applications across the world, still lies in the future.

- *Functional partitioning.* Current models that partition data storage and I/O functionality have evolved from roots that are at least 15 years old. The roles of block access device (disk), file access device (file server or file system), and data object device (database management system) have not changed much during that time.

Much of the industrial and academic research and development occurring in network storage today is directed at extending capabilities in these four directions.

Automating Management: Virtualization and Quality of Storage Service

Today, the direction of network storage development appears to be the *virtualization* of storage on a data center-wide and later on a global basis. The goal is to enable administrators to manage storage independently of servers, whether or not the servers are cooperative with each other (as in a cluster).

Virtualization is being delivered in the forms of *in-band* and *out-of-band* appliances that deliver block access services (virtual disks) to application and database servers across a data center. Chapter 5 describes the architecture of these appliances.

In-band appliances are dedicated servers in the data path between storage devices and application servers. They fulfill a position similar to that of external RAID controllers in the storage I/O path. Out-of-band appliances maintain maps that describe virtual devices exported to servers. They send these maps to specialized driver components in application servers. These drivers use the maps to direct application I/O requests to the right physical resources to satisfy them.

Both of these types of appliances are being delivered to users today. Future appliances will abstract the storage they deliver to achieve the following goals:

- To allow the factoring of underlying physical properties such as the failure tolerance of LUNs exported by RAID subsystems can be factored into allocation decisions.

- To enable the quality of storage service agreements expressed in user-friendly terms to be negotiated with users, and to enable storage to be managed on that basis.

Availability: Abolishing Backup

As much as has been accomplished to mitigate the impact of backup on data and application availability (Chapter 10), this area remains a weak point in continuous availability. Today, recovery from hardware failures and site disasters has essentially been taken over by RAID, mirroring, and replication technologies. Backup is used primarily to protect against application and operational errors and security breaches that corrupt data, and as a mechanism to obtain copies of frozen images of data for archiving purposes. Backups based on frozen data images of either the split mirror or copy-on-write types fulfill the latter role.

Research and development is occurring in the other role of backup—providing the ability to roll back the clock, restoring data its state at a point in time before an error or security breach occurred. Developers are asking whether backup is the best possible mechanism for solving this problem using the base technologies that are available today. These researchers are restating the problem as providing the ability to turn back the clock on a collection of business data, restoring it to its state at any point in time in the recent past. Taking advantage of the low cost of physical storage and of the inexpensive processing power and bandwidth that is available for storage utility functions, developers are exploring the possibilities of replacing backup with a continuous timestamped log of changes, and restoring data to a point in time by rolling such a log backward.

This conceptually simple solution has many difficulties in detail to overcome. In the future, however, it is entirely possible that storage devices will be capable of rolling their contents backward through time to any point selected by an administrator.

Data over Distance:
Files across the Water

Chapter 9 discusses long-distance data replication and highlights some of the issues in maintaining higher degrees of consistency among data located at different sites. Volumes can be kept consistent to the block update level, files to a file update level, and databases to a transaction level, all based on a static primary-secondary relationship. In all of these models, the definitive copy of a set of data is held at the primary location, which changes infrequently, and only for reasons with far-reaching consequences, such as a site disaster that causes a secondary replica to be converted into a primary copy for application processing.

Research and development in this area is building on past academic research into federated file systems in which copies of data migrated to where they were used, and, in fact, if the primary locus of data utilization migrated to another location over time, the primary location of the definitive copy of data would eventually migrate to that location as well.

Today's distributed data management architectures are based heavily on hierarchical relationships between locations at which data is stored. The research and development community is exploring more organic *federated* relationships between data storage sites.—In a *federated* relationship, ownership of data objects automatically migrates to the locations where it makes most sense for them to be, constrained by the need to provide physical security, failure tolerance, and protection against procedural errors and security breaches.

New Partitionings: Using the
Intelligence in Storage Devices

Since the evolution of SCSI in the mid-1980s, the functional definition of a disk has been essentially constant. Minor changes were introduced when RAID subsystems implemented first-generation disk virtualization—perhaps the most important being the ability of a virtual disk to grow in capacity—but the basic model of a single vector of numbered blocks has remained the same.

Over that same period, processing power, I/O bandwidth, storage capacity, and connectivity have all increased by orders of magnitude and component cost has decreased equally fast. Researchers today are questioning whether the tried-and-true disk functional model is the most effective way to provide network storage services, given the capabilities of the components from which storage devices are built. This research and development is proceeding on several fronts in the general direction of *object-based storage devices* whose capabilities include the ability to manage their own capacity and export file-like objects to their clients.

The objective of object-based storage is to enable more dynamic networked computing and data access environments that scale over a wider range than today's data centers. The scaling improvements predicted for object-based storage result from two of their properties:

- They spread a large part of the processing done by file systems today (space allocation and management and I/O block mapping) across individual storage devices rather than concentrating it in a file system and volume manager as today's architectures do. Every time object-based storage capacity is added to a network, additional storage processing resources are added as well.

- They connect storage devices directly to storage clients, eliminating the inherent bottlenecks created by RAID controllers, file servers, and storage appliances. In a system with object-based storage, more processing power is attained by adding computers; more I/O is attained by adding object-based storage devices, and more network bandwidth is obtained by adding parallel mesh networks. The number of architectural bottlenecks has been reduced to a minimum.

Like other initiatives discussed in this section, there are many details to be worked out before object-based storage becomes a data center reality. For example, although the original concept was developed around disk drives, it appears today that RAID subsystems or in-band storage appliances will be the most effective platforms for early implementations. But, like the others as well, object-based storage may be a precursor of the way users will be buying their storage in the not-too-distant future.

In Closing . . .

Thus, our long journey through storage networking comes to an end. We hope we have provided a look into why executives and technicians alike should examine the concept of storage networks. We have described the benefits they can deliver to give an idea of what returns could reasonably be expected on a storage networking investment. We've discussed the technology that enables storage networks to deliver on their potential, particularly the software components that are revolutionizing the way people build and operate data centers. Finally, we have given some advice on the adoption and management of storage networks and, in this afterword, a glimpse at technology developments that may (or may not) lead to even farther-reaching change in the future.

It is the authors' belief that storage is by far the most dynamic segment of enterprise information technology. Part of our reason for writing this book has been to introduce this exciting area with its far-reaching potential for impacting the way enterprises conduct their business to practitioners in the industry and user community. We sincerely hope that this introduction has been useful, and we are looking forward to publishing the second edition of this book when some of the initiatives described in this afterword have come to fruition.

Richard Barker

Paul Massiglia

May 19, 2001

Storage Networking Organizations

his Appendix lists and describes the major principle industry associations and standards organizations that work on with storage networking.

In general, industry associations' members consist of companies and other interested parties whose joint purpose is to promote the technologies in which they are interested such as storage networking. Industry associations may develop and promote standards, undertake industrywide marketing activities, educate, and perform any other activities that help promote their technologies.

Standards organizations have a more narrowly defined role: to develop publicly available standards in enough detail for companies to use them as blueprints for product development. In the SAN space, standards are generally concerned with interfaces between pieces of equipment. The main goal of SAN standardization is to enable complementary equipment made by different vendors to interoperate. Standards organizations typically operate under very strict rules designed to give all organization members equal voices and at the same time to make progress as rapidly as the nature of the cooperative development process permits.

Industry Associations

The Storage Networking Industry Association (SNIA)

The Storage Networking Industry Association (www.snia.org) is an organization dedicated to the development of specifications (architectures, protocols, interfaces, and application program interfaces) that form the basis of common industry standards enabling compatibility among *storage networking* products. The SNIA is an international forum for the computer system industry of hardware and software developers, integrators, and IT professionals who evolve and promote storage networking technology and solutions.

The SNIA Mission

The SNIA mission is to ensure that storage networks become efficient, complete, and trusted solutions across the IT community. The SNIA is uniquely committed to delivering standards, architectures, education, and services to propel storage networking solutions into the broader market. Storage networking represents the next step of technological evolution for the networking and storage industries, and the SNIA is the point of cohesion for developers of storage and networking products, in addition to system integrators, application vendors, and service providers, as the systems' market embarks on the evolutionary journey called storage networking. The SNIA carries out the following functions:

- Provides an open forum for all storage networking vendors and integrators to work together

- Enables, supports, and drives product interoperability within storage networking

- Creates *meaningful* Technical Collateral (standards, widely adopted in products from our member companies)

- Provides an Open Technology Center, acting as a major resource for vendors and users to test and measure interoperability of products

- Produces compatibility tests for storage networking products that pass the compatibility test

- Provides a Storage Networking Web Resource Center

- Serves as *the* place where users, press, analysts, and developers go for information, guidance, and direction on storage networking decisions

- Offers the preeminent Storage Networking Conference serving the IT community and industry (called Storage Networking World)

- Strives to establish a common understanding with the IT community on the value of storage networking

The Importance of Open Standards

The SNIA works with standards bodies and vendors to create common storage networking standards. Without the common storage networking standards, the industry might fragment into incompatible product groups. The SNIA promotes standards for interoperability to a level that allows individual vendors to differentiate themselves in performance, reliability, functionality, and service. The SNIA working groups that create and promote these standards consist of top technical people from the association's membership.

Up-to-date details about the SNIA, along with information about membership, technology, and marketing activities can be found at www.snia.org/ on the Web. The SNIA is headquartered in the United States and has affiliate organizations in Europe and Japan.

The Fibre Channel Industry Association (FCIA)

The Fibre Channel Industry Association (www.fibrechannel.com) was formed through a merger of two former Fibre Channel-related industry associations, the Fibre Channel Association (FCA) and the Fibre Channel Community (FCC). The FCIA is organized as a mutual-benefit corporation whose purpose is to promote market adoption of Fibre Channel technologies. The FCIA develops test suites, hosts interoperability testing (plugfests), participates in industry conferences and trade shows, and provides information on Fibre Channel–related technologies, standards, and products to the general public. The FCIA is headquartered in the United States and has affiliate organizations in Europe and Japan.

Fibre Alliance (FA)

The Fibre Alliance (*www.fibrealliance.org*) is an industry consortium originally founded to develop and implement standard methods for managing heterogeneous Fibre Channel–based storage area networks. Fibre Alliance activities include the definition of Simple Network Management Protocol Management Information Bases (SNMP MIB) for storage network and device management. The Fibre Alliance works closely with the IETF (described later in this Appendix).

Infiniband Trade Association (IBTA)

The Infiniband Trade Association (http://infinibandta.org) is an industry consortium developing a new I/O specification for a channel-based switched fabric called *Infiniband.* The purpose of the fabric is to connect servers with storage and networking devices, as well as to other servers. In addition, Infiniband specifications define inter-server communications mechanisms to enable parallel clustering.

Jiro

Jiro (*www.jiro.org*) is an industry initiative formed by Sun Microsystems and developed under the Java Community Process (JCP). Jiro's goal is to enable the management of heterogeneous storage networks. The core technology in Jiro is defined in a specification entitled "Federated Management Architecture" available from Sun Microsystems Corporation.

Standards Organizations

The American National Standards Institute (ANSI)

The American National Standards Institute (*www.ansi.org*) is a coordinating organization for voluntary standards in the United States. The ANSI working committees most closely associated with storage networking are X3T10 (principally responsible for SCSI I/O interface standards) and X3T11 (principally responsible for Fibre Channel interface standards).

The X3T11 committee works on Fibre Channel standards (shown in the following table) of interest to SAN users and prospective users:

FC-AE	Developing reference system designs and implementation guides for the use of Fibre Channel in avionic, military, and real-time applications.
FC-AL-2	Developing a second-generation FC Arbitrated Loop definition, including the definition of new services for real-time applications.
FC-AL-3	Developing an FC-AL-3 standard. It is a requirement of this project that FC-AL-3 devices shall interoperate with devices operating in FC-AL-2 compliant mode. FC-AL-3 environments shall permit operation of FC-AL-2 devices. Included within the recommended scope of this project are (1) improved media access schemes and (2) other enhancements determined to be necessary by experience with existing implementations.
FC-AV	Developing definitions for the transport of ITU RBT-601 and ISO/IEC 3818 (including MPEG) protocols over FC; for supporting film formats and compression schemes, YUV and RGB formats, and so forth; and for synchronization of the FC segment with existing analog and digital segments.
FC-BB	Developing the mappings necessary to bridge between physically separate instances of the same network definition, including address mapping and translation, configuration discovery, management facilities, and mappings of FC Service definitions. Candidate network definitions include ATM and SDNET.
FC-FS	Consolidating the relevant sections (framing and signaling) from FC-PH, FC-PH-2, and FC-PH-3 and associated errata, annexes, and amendments into a single encompassing document. The project may also involve the deletion or obsolescing of outdated functions and features from those documents, the inclusion of additional link services, the inclusion of improvements and clarifications to the definitions of existing services as dictated by experience with existing implementations and other capabilities that will improve the performance of existing FC products and fit those products for new applications.
FC-GS-2	Developing a set of additional and enhanced service definitions that will be used to support the management and control of Fibre Channel configurations. Included within this scope are services such as distributed directory services, management services, security services, and an operations management service.

FC-GS-3   Developing a set of additional and enhanced services that will be used to support the management and control of Fibre Channel configurations. The scope of the project includes (1) Upper Layer Protocol Directory Services, (2) Management Services, (3) Time Services, (4) Other Services identified during the development of this standard. During the FC-GS-2 project, a number of additional services and extensions to the services in FC-GS-2 were identified, in many cases, as a direct result of bringing those services to the marketplace. These new services and extensions are addressed in FC-GS-3 and will increase the management and control capabilities for Fibre Channel configurations.

FC-MI   Making recommendations for interoperable device and switch practices in both fabric and loop environments (N_Ports, Private NL_Ports, and Public NL_Ports). The result will be a technical report covering (1) response to error conditions for loop and fabric-attached ports, (2) resource recovery in error situations for loop and fabric-attached ports, (3) discovery and address mapping, (4) global topology discovery encompassing connection points both within and outside the fabric, (5) any additional issues deemed important in creating interoperable loop and fabric-attached N_Ports and NL_Ports.

FC-SB-2   Developing a Fibre Channel Single-Byte Command Sets-2 (FC-SB-2) protocol mapping (FC-4 level) standard for the transport of the SBCON command protocol via Fibre Channel. The goal of FC-SB-2 is to provide improved functionality and data integrity, higher I/O throughput, efficient operation over greater distances, and increased I/O connectivity when compared with existing interface offerings such as SBCON and FC-SB.

FC-SL   Extending FC-AL to support isochronous and time-deterministic services, including QoS definitions and controls and methods of managing loop operational parameters.

FC-SW-2   Developing a Fibre Channel Second Generation Switch Fabric (FC-SW-2) standard. Included within the recommended scope of this project are extensions to the Inter-Switch Link definition to support (1) Unicast Path Selection; (2) coordination of the Common Service definitions being produced by Project 1134-D, Fibre Channel-Generic Services 2 (FC-GS-2); (3) models of flow control schemes defined by FC-PH-x; (4) Multicast Path Selection; and (5) other enhancements derived from experience with first-generation FC-SW implementations. Backward compatibility (with FC-SW) is a key goal.

FC-TAPE   Documenting a subset of existing Fibre Channel definitions to support streaming devices and medium changers, including support for additional functions defined in X3.269:1996 (FCP) and being defined in Project 1144-D, FCP-2. The project will focus on class 3 operation and private NL_Port configurations between SCSI initiators and targets. Support of streaming devices and medium changers over FC-AL using other FC classes of service or other configurations may be addressed in this project proposal if the specified target date can be met.

FC-VI   Developing a Fibre Channel-Virtual Interface Architecture (FC-VIA) mapping (FC-4) standard. The goal of FC-VIA is to provide a mapping between FC and VIA which fully exploits the potential of both. Included within the recommended scope of this project are the creation of mappings to Fibre

Channel for the transport of Virtual Interface Architecture and support for the full range of Fibre Channel topologies, including loops and fabrics, to enable scalable clustering solutions.

The Distributed Management Task Force (DMTF)

The Distributed Management Task Force (*www.dmtf.org*) works on management standards for computer system and enterprise environments. Standards for which DMTF is responsible include:

- WBEM, Web Based Enterprise Management, a set of technologies to enable the interoperable management of an enterprise. WBEM consists of CIM, an XML DTD defining the tags (XML encodings) to describe the CIM Schema and its data, and a set of HTTP operations for exchanging the XML-based information.

- CIM, Common Information Model, an object-oriented description of the entities and relationships in a business' management environment.

- DMI, Desktop Management Interface, an architecture and framework for laptop, desktop, and server management. It defines interfaces for management applications (MI, the management interface) and components (CI, the component interface) and a Service Layer that acts as a broker between them.

- DEN, Directory Enabled Networks, a mapping of the CIM schema to an LDAP Directory. DEN's goals are to provide a consistent and standard data model to describe a network, its elements, and its policies/rules.

- ARM, Application Response Measurement, originally an Open Group technical standard defining function calls for transaction monitoring. The ARM standard is advanced in both the Open Group and the Distributed Management Task Force. The DMTF has defined an object-oriented information model for describing "units of work" (i.e., transactions).

DMTF working groups of interest to storage networking users include:

- Applications—modeling the distribution of software
- Database—first modeling relational databases
- DMI—advancing the Desktop Management Interface APIs and data definitions
- Distributed Applications Performance (DAP)—defining ARM-related classes
- Management Services Definition—defining management service templates based on SLP (Service Locator Protocol)
- Events and Methods—CIM specification and schema changes
- LDAP mapping—of the CIM schema
- Mapping—CIM to/from DMI and SNMP
- Networks—modeling network endpoints, protocol constructs, and services
- Service and Policy—for policy-based management and storage of rules in a repository
- Support—defining help desk standards

- Systems and Devices—Managing the Core, System, Devices, and Physical Models
- User and Security—mapping from X.500 with security concepts
- WBEM Interoperability—defining the XML DTD and HTTP CIM operations

Storage Systems Standards Working Group (SSSWG)

The Storage Systems Standards Working Group (www.ssswg.org) is part of the Institute of Electrical and Electronics Engineers (IEEE). The SSSWG defines architectures and models of mass storage systems and also addresses tape driver and format issues.

The specific Project Authorization Requests within the SSSWG are as follows:

- 1244—Guide to Storage System Design.
- 1244.1—Media Management System (MMS) Architecture addressing the management of removable media. It defines the general schema for management, the expected components of the software system, and the data model.
- 1244.2—Session Security, Authentication, Initialization Protocol (SSAIP) of the MMS.
- 1244.3—Media Management Protocol (MMP) for both client and administrative applications. It defines the protocol for allocation/deallocation and mount/dismount of volumes, as well as for system administration.
- 1244.4—Drive Management Protocol (DMP) of the MMS. It specifies the protocol between the central management software and a program that manages a drive.
- 1244.5—Library Management Protocol (LMP) of the MMS. It specifies the protocol between the central management software and a program that manages an automated library or a vault.
- 1244.6—The Media Manager Interchange Protocol (MMIP) for the exchange of information between autonomous Media Managers.
- 1244.7—The Media Manager Control Interface Protocol (MMCIP) to interface the data management components of the MMS with existing library management systems.
- 1244.8—The C Language Procedural Interface facilitating the construction of the MMS's components.
- 1244.9—MMS User Mount Commands defining "command line interfaces" for mounting/unmounting and acquiring/releasing media.
- 1244.10—MMS Standard Administrative and Operational Commands defining "command line interfaces" for the administration and operation of an MMS.
- 1244.11—MOVER specifying a storage system data mover architecture and its interfaces, for use by the MMS. The goal is to allow the transfer of data between two endpoints in a distributed storage system.
- 1563.1—Recommended Practice for Portable Tape Driver Architecture providing a reference model for tape driver architectures.
- 1563.2—Common Tape Driver Semantics defining the operations and access semantics of tape drives, across various operating systems.

- 1563.3—Common Format For Data On Tape to define a self-identifying format and record structure for the storage of data and metadata on tapes.

The Internet Engineering Task Force (IETF) (http://www.ietf.org)

The Internet Engineering Task Force (www.ietf.org) is the standards body responsible for a wide variety of TCP/IP (Transmission Control Protocol/Internet Protocol) standards. Those of interest to users of storage networking include:

- SNMP, Simple Network Management Protocol: A protocol for monitoring and managing systems and devices in a network. The data being accessed is defined by a MIB (Management Information Base, also defined in the IETF). The functions supported by the protocol are the request and retrieval of MIB data, the setting or writing of data, and traps to signal the occurrence of events.
- IP over Fibre Channel
- Policy for QoS (quality of service)

NDMP

The Network Data Management Protocol (www.ndmp.org) from the Network Data Management Task Force is an open, standard protocol for network-based backup in a NAS environment. It allows a network backup application to control the retrieval of data from, and backup of, a server without third-party software. The control and data transfer components of the backup/restore are separated. The protocol is intended to support tape drives, but can be extended to address other devices and media in the future.

NSIC

The National Storage Industry Consortium (www.nsic.org) is a mutual-benefit corporation whose members have interest in digital information storage. NSIC interests include the following:

- Extremely High Density Recording (EHDR) for advances in hard disk drive technology
- Multiple Optical Recording Enhancements (MORE)
- Network-Attached Storage Devices (NASD) facilitating the access of storage devices via high-performance, scalable networks (for example, Fibre Channel)
- Tape for advances in magnetic tape recording

W3C

The Worldwide Web Consortium (www.w3c.org) is the standards body responsible for HTML (Hypertext Markup Language), XML (eXtensible Markup Language), and RDF (Resource Description Framework).

Dictionary of Storage Networking Terminology

In lieu of the author-created glossary that is typical for a book of this kind, we have included a transcription of the Storage Networking Industry Association (SNIA) Dictionary of Storage Networking Terminology. The SNIA has created and continues to maintain and enhance this dictionary in an effort to introduce uniform terminology to an industry that has grown rapidly from many independent creative sources.

While the authors have endeavored to conform to SNIA terminology throughout this book, the terms and definitions in this dictionary are an SNIA work product, and not that of the authors. By arrangement with the SNIA, the terms and definitions are reproduced without alteration. Cross-referenced terms that appear within definitions (and were originally hyperlinks in the Web document) appear in *italics* in this print version.

Printing a document such as this dictionary in a book effectively freezes it in time. The source document is continually updated by the SNIA. The reader is referred to the SNIA web pages, www.snia.org/dictionary, for the most up-to-date information.

The authors wish to express their gratitude to the SNIA for permission to reproduce this dictionary.

C ommon storage networking-related terms and the definitions applied to them by the Storage Networking Industry Association

The members of the Storage Networking Industry Association have collaborated to create this Dictionary of Storage and Storage Networking Terminology. The collaboration has been extensive, with many members making substantial contributions. There has also been extensive review and comment by the entire SNIA membership. This dictionary thus represents the storage networking industry's most comprehensive attempt to date to arrive at a common body of terminology for the technologies it represents. The reader should recognize that in this rapidly evolving field, new terminology is constantly being introduced, and common usage is shifting. The SNIA regards this dictionary as a living document, to be updated as necessary to reflect a consensus on common usage, and encourages readers to treat it in that spirit. Comments and suggestions for improvement are gratefully accepted at any time, with the understanding that any submission of comments or suggestions contributes them to SNIA; and SNIA will own all rights (including any copyright or intellectual property rights) in them. Comments and suggestions should be directed to *dictionary@SNIA.org*.

Most of the terms in this dictionary have meaning primarily in specific sub-contexts of storage networking, such as SCSI or Storage Systems. Wherever this is true, the primary context(s) for the term are noted between the term itself and its definition. Terms that do not have one or more contexts identified are generally applicable data processing industry terms.

The SNIA hereby grants permission for individuals to use this glossary for personal use only, and for corporations and other business entities to use this glossary for internal use only (including internal copying, distribution, and display) provided that:

1. Any definition reproduced must be reproduced in its entirety with no alteration, and,

2. Any document, printed or electronic, in which material from this glossary (or any portion hereof) is reproduced must acknowledge the SNIA copyright on that material, and must credit the SNIA for granting permission for its reuse.

8B/10B encoding CONTEXT [Fibre Channel]
An algorithm for encoding data for transmission in which each eight-bit *data byte* is converted to a 10-bit *transmission character.* Invented and patented by IBM Corporation, 8B/10B encoding is used in transmitting data on *Fibre Channel, ESCON,* and *Gigabit Ethernet.* 8B/10B encoding supports continuous transmission with a balanced number of ones and zeros in the code stream and detects single bit transmission errors.

access CONTEXT [Security]
The opportunity to make use of an information system resource.

access control CONTEXT [File System] [Security]
The granting or withholding of a service or access to a resource to a requestor based on the identity of the principal for which the requestor is acting.

access control list CONTEXT [File System] [Security]
A persistent list that enumerates the rights of principals (e.g., users and groups of users) to access resources. Often used in file system context to denote a persistent list maintained by a file system and defining user and group permissions for file and *directory* access.

access control mechanism CONTEXT [Security]
A security safeguard designed to detect and deny unauthorized access and permit authorized access in an information system.

access fairness CONTEXT [Fibre Channel]
A process by which nodes are guaranteed access to a Fibre Channel arbitrated loop independent of other nodes' activity.

access method CONTEXT [Fibre Channel] [Operating System]
1. The means used to access a physical transmission medium in order to transmit data.
2. (In IBM Corporation's OS/390 operating system and its precursors) A file organization method, such as sequential, random, indexed, etc., and the operating system software used to implement it.

access path CONTEXT [Storage System]
The combination of *host bus adapter, logical unit number,* route through the host-storage interconnect, controller, and logical unit used by a computer to communicate with a *storage device.* Some configurations support multiple access paths to a single device. *cf. multi-path I/O*

ACL CONTEXT [File System] [Security]
Acronym for *access control list.*

ACS   CONTEXT [Backup]
Acronym for *automated cartridge system*.

active   CONTEXT [Fibre Channel]
The state of a Fibre Channel *Sequence Initiator* between the start of transmission of the first data frame of a *sequence* and the completion of transmission of the last data frame in the sequence. Also, the state of a Fibre Channel *Sequence Recipient* between the start of reception of the first data frame of a *sequence* and the completion of reception of the last data frame in the sequence.

active-active (components, controllers)   CONTEXT [Storage System]
Synonym for *dual active* components or controllers.

active copper   CONTEXT [Fibre Channel]
A type of Fibre Channel physical connection that allows up to 30 meters of copper cable between adjacent devices..

active-passive (components, controllers)   CONTEXT [Storage System]
Synonym for *hot standby* components or controllers.

active component
A system component that requires electrical power to operate. In a storage subsystem, for example, active components might include power supplies, *storage devices*, fans, and controllers. By contrast, enclosures and canisters are not normally active components.

adapter
A hardware device that converts the timing and protocol of one bus or interface to another. Adapters are typically implemented as specialized hardware on system boards, or as add-in cards, to enable a computer system's processing hardware to access peripheral devices. An example adapter is a host Bus Adapter. Adapter is the preferred term in Fibre Channel contexts. *cf. adapter card, host bus adapter, network interface card, NIC*

adapter card
An *adapter* implemented as a printed circuit module.

adaptive array   CONTEXT [Storage System]
A *disk array* that is capable of changing its algorithm for virtual data address to physical data location mapping dynamically (i.e., while the array is operating). AutoRAID from Hewlett-Packard, which can change a given virtual disk representation from *mirrored* to *parity RAID*, is an adaptive array.

address   CONTEXT [Storage Device] [Storage System] [SCSI]
1. A fixed length bit pattern that uniquely identifies a block of data stored on a disk or tape. Typically treated as a number to which a mapping algorithm can be applied to determine the physical location of a block of data. Applying this mapping algorithm to disk block addresses yields the cylinder, head, and relative sector number at which data may be found. Tape block addresses typically refer to the relative position of a block of data in a single linear stream of blocks.
2. A fixed-length bit pattern that uniquely identifies a location (bit, byte, word, etc.) in a computer memory.
3. [SCSI] A byte whose value uniquely identifies a device connected to a SCSI bus for purposes of communication.

address identifier   CONTEXT [Fibre Channel]

An address value used to identify the source (*S ID*) or destination (*D ID*) of a frame. The *FC-SW* standard includes a table of special address identifier values and their meanings.

address resolution   CONTEXT [Network]

The process of determining a *MAC* address, given a more abstract *LAN* or *WAN* address.

Address Resolution Protocol   CONTEXT [Network]

1. Any protocol used to obtain a mapping from a higher layer address to a lower layer address. Abbreviated ARP. The acronym ARP is most often used to refer to the Ethernet Address Resolution Protocol (below).

2. The protocol used by an IP networking layer to map IP addresses to lower level hardware (i.e., MAC) addresses. There are four ARP messages for IP running over Ethernet: arp requests and replies and reverse arp request and replies.

addressing   CONTEXT [Storage System]

An algorithm by which areas of fixed disk, removable cartridge media, or computer system main memory are uniquely identified. *cf. block addressing, C-H-S addressing, explicit addressing, implicit addressing*

administration host   CONTEXT [Network]

A computer that manages one or more storage subsystems (e.g., *filers, disk array subsystems,* tape subsystems, etc.)

administrator

A person charged with the installation, *configuration*, and management of a computer system, network, *storage subsystem*, database, or application.

advanced encryption standard   CONTEXT [Security]

A cryptographic algorithm designated by *NIST* as a replacement for *DES*. Abbreviated AES. The actual algorithm selected is also known as Rijndael.

Advanced Intelligent Tape   CONTEXT [Storage Device]

A tape device and media technology introduced by Sony Corporation.

AES   CONTEXT [Security]

Acronym for *advanced encryption standard*.

agent

A program that performs one or more services (such as gathering information from the Internet), acting for or as a principal.

aggregation   CONTEXT [Network] [Storage System]

The combining of multiple similar and related objects or operations into a single one. Several disk or tape data streams are sometimes *aggregated* into a single stream for higher performance. Two or more disks can be *aggregated* into a single virtual disk for increased capacity. Two or more disks can be *aggregated* into a RAID array for high availability. Two or more I/O requests for adjacently located data can be *aggregated* into a single request to minimize request processing overhead and rotational latency. *cf. consolidation*

AH   CONTEXT [Security]

Acronym for *authentication header*

AIT   CONTEXT [Storage Device]

Acronym for *advanced intelligent tape*.

algorithmic mapping   CONTEXT [Storage System]

Use of an algorithm to translate from one data addressing domain to another. If a volume is algorithmically mapped, the physical location of a block of data may be calculated from its virtual volume address using known characteristics of the volume (e.g. stripe depth and number of member disks). *cf. dynamic mapping, tabular mapping*

alias   CONTEXT [Fibre Channel]

An alternate name for an entity that is more easily human-readable Aliases are sometimes used for grouping purposes. *cf. alias address identifier*

alias address identifier   CONTEXT [Fibre Channel]

One or more *address identifiers* which may be recognized by an *N Port* in addition to its N_Port Identifier. Alias address identifiers are used to form groups of N_Ports so that frames may be addressed to a group rather than to individual N_Ports. *cf. hunt group, multicast group*

AL_PA   CONTEXT [Fibre Channel]

Acronym for *Arbitrated Loop Physical Address*.

alternate client restore   CONTEXT [Backup]

The process of *restoring* files to a different client than the one from which they were *backed up*.

alternate path restore   CONTEXT [Backup]

The process of *restoring* files to a different *directory* than the one from which they were *backed up*.

always on   CONTEXT [General] [Fibre Channel]

1. The state of always having power applied (systems) or of being continually active (communication links).

2. [Fibre Channel] A state of always being powered on and/or continually active. In a Fibre Channel, *ESCON*, or *Gigabit Ethernet* context, "always on" describes the state of an operational link. It is constantly transmitting either *data frames*, *idles* or *fill words*. This can be contrasted with bursty transmissions and listening for a quiet line in Ethernet. For Fibre Channel management purposes being "always on" allows link level error detection on each transmitted word.

American National Standards Institute

A coordinating organization for voluntary standards in the United States. Often abbreviated ANSI. The ANSI working committees most closely aligned with storage networking interests are called X3T10 (principally responsible for SCSI I/O interface standards), and X3T11 (principally responsible for Fibre Channel interface standards).

ANSI

Acronym for *American National Standards Institute*.

ANSI T10

The *American National Standards Institute* T10 technical committee, the standards organization responsible for SCSI standards for communication between computers and storage subsystems and devices.

ANSI T11

The *American National Standards Institute* T11 technical committee, the standards organization responsible for Fibre Channel and certain other standards for moving electronic data into and out of computers and intelligent storage subsystems and devices.

ANSI X3T10

The *American National Standards Institute* committee responsible for standards for accessing and controlling I/O devices. ANSI X3T10 is responsible for the SCSI family of standards. Often shortened to *T10*.

ANSI X3T11

The *American National Standards Institute* committee responsible for standards for high performance I/O interfaces such as Fibre Channel and HIPPI. Often shortened to *T11*.

API

Acronym for *Application Programming Interface*.

appliance

An intelligent device programmed to perform a single well-defined function, such as providing file, Web, or print services. Appliances differ from general purpose computers in that their software is normally customized for the function they perform, pre-loaded by the vendor, and not alterable by the user. Appliances are generally considered to be capable of performing their specialized functions at lower cost and with higher reliability than general purpose servers. *cf. filer*

application I/O request
application read request
application write request   CONTEXT [Storage System]

I/O requests made by storage clients, as distinguished from member I/O requests made by a storage subsystem's own *control software*. SNIA publications do not generally distinguish between I/O requests made by the operating environment (e.g., for paging, swapping, and file system directory lookups, etc.) and those made by user applications.

application programming interface

An interface used by an application program to request services. Abbreviated API. The term API is usually used to denote interfaces between applications and the software components that comprise the operating environment (e.g., operating system, file system, volume manager, device drivers, etc.)

application response measurement

An *Open Group* technical standard defining function calls for transaction monitoring. The ARM standard is being advanced in both The Open Group and the *Distributed Management Task Force*. The latter organization has defined an object oriented information model for describing units of work (i.e., transactions).

application specific integrated circuit

An integrated circuit designed for a particular application, such as interfacing to a SCSI bus. Abbreviated ASIC.

arbitrated loop   CONTEXT [Fibre Channel]

1. A *Fibre Channel* interconnect topology in which each port is connected to the next, forming a loop. At any instant, only one port in a Fibre Channel Arbitrated Loop can transmit data. Before transmitting data, a port in a Fibre Channel Arbitrated Loop must participate with all

other ports in the loop in an arbitration to gain the right to transmit data. The arbitration logic is distributed among all of a loop's ports.

2. The version of the Fibre Channel protocol used with the arbitrated loop physical topology.

arbitrated loop physical address   CONTEXT [Fibre Channel]

An 8-bit value used to identify a participating device in an Arbitrated Loop.

arbitration

Any process by which a user of a shared resource negotiates with other users for the (usually temporary) right to use the resource. A port connected to a shared bus must win arbitration before it transmits data on the bus.

archive   CONTEXT [Backup]

A consistent copy of a collection of data, usually taken for the purpose of maintaining a long-term durable record of a business or application state. Archives are normally used for auditing or analysis rather than for application recovery. After files are archived, online copies of them are typically deleted, and must be restored by explicit action. *cf. <span CLASS="xref">backup</span>*

archiving   CONTEXT [Backup]

The act of creating an *archive*.

ARM

1. Acronym for *application response measurement*.

2. A common microprocessor architecture, as well as the name of the company that created the architecture.

ARP   CONTEXT [Network]

Acronym for *Address Resolution Protocol*.

array   CONTEXT [Storage System]

A *storage array*, i.e., a *disk array* or *tape array*.

array configuration   CONTEXT [Storage System]

1. Assignment of the disks and operating parameters for a disk array. Disk array configuration includes designating the array's member disks or extents and the order in which they are to be used, as well as setting parameters such as stripe depth, RAID model, cache allowance, spare disk assignments, etc. *cf. configuration, physical configuration.*

2. The arrangement of disks and operating parameters that results from such an assignment.

Association_Header   CONTEXT [Fibre Channel]

An optional header used to associate a Fibre Channel *exchange* with a process, system image, or multi-exchange I/O operation on an end system. May also be used as part of *Exchange Identifier* management.

ASIC

Acronym for *Application Specific Integrated Circuit*.

asymmetric cryptosystem   CONTEXT [Security]

A cryptographic algorithm in which different keys are used to encrypt and decrypt a single message or block of stored information. One of the keys is kept secret and referred to as a private key; the other key can be freely disclosed and is called a public key.

asynchronous I/O request   CONTEXT [Storage Device] [Storage System]
A request to perform an *asynchronous I/O operation.*

asynchronous I/O operation   CONTEXT [Storage Device] [Storage System]
An I/O operation whose initiator does not await its completion before proceeding with other work. Asynchronous I/O operations enable an initiator to have multiple concurrent I/O operations in progress.

Asynchronous Transfer Method   CONTEXT [Network]
A connection-oriented data communications technology based on switching 53 byte fixed-length units of data called *cells.* Abbreviated ATM. Each cell is dynamically routed. ATM transmission rates are multiples of 51.840 Mbits per second. In the United States, a public communications service called SONET uses ATM at transmission rates of 155, 622, 2048, and 9196 Mbits per second. These are called OC-3, OC-12, OC-48, and OC-192 respectively. A similar service called SDH is offered in Europe. ATM is also used as a LAN infrastructure, sometimes with different transmission rates and coding methods than are offered with SONET and SDH.

ATM   CONTEXT [Network]
Acronym for *Asynchronous Transfer Method.*

atomic operation
An indivisible operation that, from an external perspective, occurs either in its entirety or not at all. For example, database management systems that implement the concept of *business transactions* treat each business transaction as an atomic operation on the database. This means that either all of the database updates that comprise a transaction are performed or none of them are performed; it is never the case that some of them are performed and others not. RAID arrays must implement atomic write operations to properly reproduce single-disk semantics from the perspective of their clients. Atomic operations are required to ensure that component failures do not corrupt stored data.

attenuation
The power dissipation between an optical or electrical transmitter and a receiver. Expressed in units of decibels (dB).

audit trail   CONTEXT [Network] [Security]
A chronological record of system activities that enables the reconstruction and examination of a sequence of events and/or changes in an object. The term audit trail may apply to information in an information system, to message routing in a communications system, or to any transfer of sensitive material and/or information.

authentication   CONTEXT [Network]
The process of determining what principal a requestor or provider of services is or represents.

CONTEXT [Security]
A security measure designed to establish the validity of a transmission, message, or originator, or a means of verifying an individual's authorization to receive information.

authentication header   CONTEXT [Security]
A component of *IPsec* that permits the specification of various authentication mechanisms designed to provide connectionless integrity, data origin authentication, and an optional anti-replay service. Standardized by the *Internet Engineering Task Force.*

authorization   CONTEXT [Network]
The process of determining that a requestor is allowed to receive a service or perform an operation. *Access control* is an example of authorization.

CONTEXT [Security]

The limiting of usage of information system resources to authorized users, programs, processes or other systems. *Access control* is a specific type of authorization. Authorization is formally described as controlling usage by subjects of objects.

auto swap

Abbreviation for *automatic swap*. *cf. cold swap, hot swap, warm swap*

automated cartridge system   CONTEXT [Backup]

Synonym for *robot*.

automatic backup   CONTEXT [Backup]

A *backup* triggered by an event (e.g., a schedule point, or a threshold reached) rather than by human action.

automatic failover

Failover that occurs without human intervention.

automatic swap

The substitution of a replacement unit (*RU*) in a system for a defective one, where the substitution is performed by the system itself while it continues to perform its normal function (possibly at a reduced rate of performance). Automatic swaps are functional rather than physical substitutions, and do not require human intervention. Ultimately, however, defective components must be replaced in a physical hot, warm, or cold swap operation. *cf. cold swap, hot swap, warm swap, hot spare*

automatic switchover

Synonym for automatic *failover*.

availability

The amount of time that a system is available during those time periods when it is expected to be available. Availability is often measured as a percentage of an elapsed year. For example, 99.95% availability equates to 4.38 hours of downtime in a year (0.0005 * 365 * 24 = 4.38) for a system that is expected to be available all the time. *cf. data availability, high availability*

B_Port   CONTEXT [Fibre Channel]

A port on a Fibre Channel bridge device. *cf. E Port, F Port, FL Port, G Port, L Port, N Port, NL Port*

backing store

Non-volatile memory. The term *backing store* is often used to contrast with cache, which is a (usually) volatile random access memory used to speed up I/O operations. Data held in a volatile cache must be replicated in or saved to a non-volatile backing store so that it can survive a system crash or power failure.

backup   CONTEXT [Backup]

1. (noun) A collection of data stored on (usually removable) non-volatile storage media for purposes of recovery in case the original copy of data is lost or becomes inaccessible. Also called *backup copy*. To be useful for recovery, a backup must be made by copying the source data image when it is in a consistent state.

2. (noun) A process that creates a backup (definition 1).

3. (verb) The act of creating a backup. *cf. archive*

backup client   CONTEXT [Backup]
> A computer system containing online data to be backed up.

backup image   CONTEXT [Backup]
> The collection of data that constitutes a backup copy of a given set of online data.

backup manager   CONTEXT [Backup]
> An application program whose purpose is to schedule and manage *backup* operations.

backup policy   CONTEXT [Backup]
> An IT installation's rules for how and when backup should be performed. Backup policies specify information such as which files or directories are to be backed up, the schedule on which backups should occur, which devices and media are eligible to receive the backups, how many copies are to be made, and actions to be performed if a backup does not succeed.

backup window   CONTEXT [Backup]
> The period of time available for performing a *backup*. Backup windows are typically defined by operational necessity. For example, if data is used from 8AM until midnight, then the window between midnight and 8AM is available for making backup copies. For consistent backups, data may not be altered while the backup is occurring, so in some cases a backup window is an interval of time during which data and applications are unavailable.

bandwidth
> 1. The numerical difference between the upper and lower frequencies of a band of electromagnetic radiation.
> 2. Synonym for *data transfer capacity*.

basic input output system
> A relatively small program that resides in programmable, non-volatile memory on a personal computer and that is responsible for booting that computer and performing certain operating system independent I/O operations. Abbreviated BIOS. Standard BIOS interrupts are defined to allow access to the computer's disk, video and other hardware components (for example, INT13 for disk access).

baud   CONTEXT [Network]
> The maximum rate of signal state changes per second on a communications circuit. If each signal state change corresponds to a code bit, then the baud rate and the bit rate are the same. It is also possible for signal state changes to correspond to more than one code bit, so the baud rate may be lower than the code bit rate.

Bayonet Neil Councilman (connector)   CONTEXT [Network]
> A type of coaxial cable connector sometimes used in *Ethernet* applications. Abbreviated BNC. The specification for BNC connectors is contained in EIA/TIA 403-A and MIL-C-39012.

BB_buffer   CONTEXT [Fibre Channel]
> A buffer associated with *buffer to buffer flow control*.

BB_credit   CONTEXT [Fibre Channel]
> Buffer-to-buffer credit; used to determine how many frames can be sent to a recipient when *buffer to buffer flow control* is in use.

beginning running disparity   CONTEXT [Fibre Channel]
> The *running disparity* present at a transmitter or receiver when an ordered set is initiated.

BER   CONTEXT [Network] [Storage Device]
Acronym for *Bit Error Rate.*

Berkeley RAID Levels   CONTEXT [Storage System]
A family of disk array data protection and mapping techniques described by Garth Gibson, Randy Katz, and David Patterson in papers written while they were performing research into I/O subsystems at the University of California at Berkeley. There are six Berkeley RAID Levels, usually referred to by the names RAID Level 1, etc., through RAID Level 6. *cf. RAID 0, RAID 1, RAID 2, RAID 3, RAID 4, RAID 5, RAID 6.*

best effort (class of service)   CONTEXT [Fibre Channel] [Network]
A *class of service* which does not guarantee delivery of packets, *frames,* or *datagrams,* but for which the *network, fabric,* or *interconnect* makes every reasonable delivery effort.

big endian
A format for the storage and transmission of binary data in which the most significant bits are stored at the numerically lowest addresses, or are transmitted first on a serial link.

BIOS
Acronym for *basic input output system.*

bit error rate   CONTEXT [Network] [Storage Device]
The probability that a transmitted bit will be erroneously received. Abbreviated BER. The BER is measured by counting the number of bits in error at the output of a receiver and dividing by the total number of bits in the transmission. BER is typically expressed as a negative power of 10.

bit synchronization
The process by which the receiver of a serial communication establishes its clocking used to locate code bits in a received data stream.

black   CONTEXT [Security]
A designation applied to information systems in the context of security analysis, and to associated areas, circuits, components, and equipment, in which sensitive information is not processed.

blind mating
The ability of pairs of components to be connected without the electrical or optical connection points being visible. Blind mating is usually accomplished by mechanical guides (e.g., slots and rails) on the components.

block   CONTEXT [Fibre Channel] [Storage Device] [Storage System]
1. The unit in which data is stored and retrieved on disk and tape devices. Blocks are the atomic unit of data recognition (through a preamble and block header) and protection (through a *CRC* or *ECC*).
2. A unit of application data from a single *information category* that is transferred within a single *sequence.*

block addressing   CONTEXT [Storage Device] [Storage System]
An algorithm for uniquely identifying blocks of data stored on disk or tape media by number, and then translating these numbers into physical locations on the media. *cf. C-H-S addressing*

BNC   CONTEXT [Network]
Acronym for Bayonet Neil Councilman, a type of Coaxial Cable Connector.

Specifications for BNC style connectors are defined in EIA/TIA 403-A and MIL-C-39012.

boot
booting
bootstrapping

The loading of code from a disk or other storage device into a computer's memory. Bootstrapping is an appropriate term since a code load typically occurs in steps, starting with a very simple program (BIOS) that initializes the computer's hardware and reads a sequence of data blocks from a fixed location on a pre-determined disk, into a fixed memory location. The data thus read is the code for the next stage of bootstrapping—usually an operating system loader. The loader completes the hardware setup and results in an executing operating system, in memory.

bridge controller   CONTEXT [Storage System]

A storage controller that forms a bridge between two external I/O buses. Bridge controllers are commonly used to connect single-ended SCSI disks to differential SCSI or Fibre Channel host I/O buses.

broadcast   CONTEXT [Fibre Channel] [Network]

The simultaneous transmission of a message to all receivers (ports) connected to a communication facility. Broadcast can be contrasted with unicast (sending a message to a specific receiver) and multicast (sending a message to select subset of receivers). In a Fibre Channel context, broadcast specifically refers to the sending of a message to all *N Port*s connected to a *fabric. cf. multicast, unicast*

buffer

A solid state memory device or programming construct, used to hold data momentarily as it moves along an I/O path or between software components. Buffers allow devices to communicate using links with faster or slower data transfer speeds, allow devices with different native processing speeds to intercommunicate, and allow software components to intercommunicate, share data and coordinate their activities. *cf. cache*

buffer to buffer flow control   CONTEXT [Fibre Channel]

Flow control that occurs between two directly connected Fibre Channel ports, e.g., an *N Port* and its associated *F Port*. A port indicates the number of frames buffers that can be sent to it (its buffer credit), before the sender is required to stop transmitting and wait for the receipt of a "ready" indication. Buffer to buffer flow control is used only when an NL-Local port is logged into another NL-Local port, or when Nx ports are logged into Fx ports.

bypass circuit   CONTEXT [Fibre Channel]

A circuit that automatically removes a device from a data path (such as a Fibre Channel arbitrated loop) when valid signalling is lost.

byte   CONTEXT [Fibre Channel]

1. An eight-bit organizational unit for data.
2. The unit in which data is delivered to and by applications. In Fibre Channel, bytes are organized with the least significant bit denoted as bit 0 and most significant bit as bit 7. The most significant bit is shown on the left side in *FC-PH* documents, unless specifically indicated otherwise.

CA   CONTEXT [Security]

Acronym for *certification authority*

cable plant

All of an installation's passive communications elements (e.g., optical fibre, twisted pair, or coaxial cable, connectors, splices, etc.) between a transmitter and a receiver.

cache

A high speed memory or storage device used to reduce the effective time required to read data from or write data to a lower speed memory or device. *Read cache* holds data in anticipation that it will be requested by a client. *Write cache* holds data written by a client until it can be safely stored on more permanent storage media such as disk or tape. *cf. buffer, disk cache, write back cache, write through cache*

canister   CONTEXT [Storage System]

An enclosure for a single disk or tape. Canisters are usually designed to mount in *shelves*, which supply power, cooling, and I/O bus services to the devices. Canisters are used to minimize RF emissions and to simplify insertion and removal of devices in multi-device storage subsystems. *cf. shelf*

carousel   CONTEXT [Backup]

A media handling robot in which the media are stored in and selected from a rotating wheel.

carrier sense multiple access with collision detection   CONTEXT [Network]

A physical layer data transmission protocol used in Ethernet and fast Ethernet networks. Abbreviated CSMA/CD. *Carrier sense* refers to arbitration for a shared link. Unlike "always on" physical protocols, carrier sense protocols require a node wishing to transmit to wait for the absence of carrier (indicating that another node is transmitting) on the link. *Multiple access* refers to the party line nature of the link. A large number of nodes (up to 500 in the case of Ethernet) share access to a single link. Collision detection refers to the possibility that two nodes will simultaneously sense absence of carrier and begin to transmit, interfering with each other. Nodes are required to detect this interference, and cease transmitting. In the case of Ethernet, each node detecting a collision is required to wait for a random interval before attempting to transmit again.

cascading   CONTEXT [Fibre Channel]

The process of connecting two or more Fibre Channel *hubs* or *switches* together to increase the number of ports or extend distances.

catalog   CONTEXT [Backup] [File System]

1. [Backup] A stored list of backed up files and *directories* and the locations (media identifiers) of the backup copies. *Backup managers* use catalogs to determine what files must be backed up, and to determine which media must be mounted and read to perform a restore.
2. [File System] A persistent data structure used by some file systems to keep track of the files they manage.

CDR   CONTEXT [Fibre Channel]

Acronym for *Clock and Data Recovery*.

certification authority   CONTEXT [Security]

In a Public Key Infrastructure (PKI), the authority and organization responsible for issuing and revoking user certificates, and ensuring compliance with the PKI policies and procedures.

changed block

changed block point in time copy   CONTEXT [Storage System]

Any of a class of point in time copy implementations or the resulting copies in which the copy and its source share storage for portions (usually blocks) of the copy that are not subsequently modified (in the source, or in the copy if the copy is writeable). Storage is physically copied only as a consequence of modifications (to the source, or to the copy if the copy is writeable). A changed block copy occupies only the storage necessary to hold the blocks of storage that have been changed since the point in time at which the copy logically occurred.

channel

1. [storage] The electrical circuits that sense or cause the state changes in recording media and convert between those state changes and electrical signals that can be interpreted as data bits.

2. [I/O] Synonym for *I/O bus*. The term *channel* has other meanings in other branches of computer technology. The definitions given here are commonly used when discussing storage and networking. *cf. device channel, device I/O bus, I/O bus, host I/O bus*

character   CONTEXT [Fibre Channel]

1. In general computing usage, synonym for *byte*.

2. A 10-bit information unit transmitted and received by *FC-1*. *8B/10B encoding* provides the mapping between 8 bits of data and a 10 bit *transmission character*. Some transmission characters correspond to special codes and not all 10 bit sequences represent valid transmission characters.

character cell interface

Synonym for *command line interface*.

check data   CONTEXT [Storage System]

In a RAID array, data stored on member disks that can be used for *regenerating* any user data that becomes inaccessible.

checkpoint   CONTEXT [Backup] [File System]

1. The recorded state of an application at an instant of time, including data, in-memory variables, program counter, and all other context that would be required to resume application execution from the recorded state.

2. An activity of a file system (such as the High Performance File System, HPFS, or the Andrews File System, AFS) in which cached meta data (data about the structures of the file system) is periodically written to the file system's permanent store. This allows the file system to maintain consistency if an unexpected stop occurs.

chunk   CONTEXT [Storage System]
Synonym for *strip*.

chunk size   CONTEXT [Storage System]
Synonym for *stripe depth* and *strip size*.

C-H-S addressing   CONTEXT [Storage System]
Synonym for *cylinder-head-sector addressing*.

CIFS   CONTEXT [File System]
Acronym for *Common Internet File System*.

CIM   CONTEXT [Management] [Network]
Acronym for *Common Information Model*.

cipher   CONTEXT [Security]
Any cryptographic system in which arbitrary symbols or groups of symbols, represent units of plain text or in which units of plain text are rearranged, or both.

ciphertext   CONTEXT [Security]
Data that has been encrypted for security reasons. *cf. cleartext*

circuit   CONTEXT [Fibre Channel] [Network]
Synonym for *communication circuit*.

CKD (architecture)   CONTEXT [Storage System]
Synonym for *count-key-data* disk architecture.

Class 1   CONTEXT [Fibre Channel]
A connection-oriented class of communication service in which the entire bandwidth of the link between two ports is dedicated for communication between the ports and not used for other purposes. Also known as dedicated connection service. Class 1 service is not widely implemented. *cf. intermix*

Class 2   CONTEXT [Fibre Channel]
A connectionless Fibre Channel communication service which multiplexes frames from one or more *N Ports* or *NL Ports*. Class 2 frames are explicitly acknowledged by the receiver, and notification of delivery failure is provided. This *class of service* includes *end to end flow control*.

Class 3   CONTEXT [Fibre Channel]
A connectionless Fibre Channel communication service which multiplexes frames to or from one or more *N Ports* or *NL Ports*. Class 3 frames are *datagram*s, that is they are not explicitly acknowledged, and delivery is on a "best effort" basis.

Class 4   CONTEXT [Fibre Channel]
A connection-oriented class of communication service in which a fraction of the bandwidth of the link between two ports is dedicated for communication between the ports. The remaining bandwidth may be used for other purposes. Class 4 service supports bounds on the maximum time to deliver a frame from sender to receiver. Also known as fractional service. Class 4 service is not widely implemented.

Class 6   CONTEXT [Fibre Channel]
A connection-oriented class of communication service between two Fibre Channel ports that provides dedicated unidirectional connections for reliable *multicast*. Also known as unidirectional dedicated connection service. Class 6 service is not widely implemented.

classified information   CONTEXT [Security]
Information that an appropriate agency has determined to require protection against unauthorized disclosure and has caused to be marked to indicate its classified status.

class of service   CONTEXT [Networking] [Fibre Channel]
1. A mechanism for managing traffic in a network by specifying message or packet priority.
2. The characteristics and guarantees of the transport layer of a Fibre Channel circuit. Fibre Channel classes of service include: connection services (Classes 1), guaranteed frame delivery with end to end flow control (Class 2), packetized frame datagrams (Class 3), quality of service sub-channels (e.g., constant sub rate or constant latency) (Class 4). Different classes of service may simultaneously exist in a fabric. The form and reliability of delivery in Class 3 circuits may vary with the topology. Different classes of service may simultaneously exist in a fabric.
3. The identification and grouping of data packets based on a priority label (in the packet header) or via other mechanisms (such as "per hop behavior", defined by the IETF's Differentiated Services).

cleartext
Data that is not encrypted. *cf. ciphertext*

CLI

Acronym for *command line interface.*

client

1. An intelligent device or system that requests services from other intelligent devices, systems, or *appliance*s. *cf. server*

2. An asymmetric relationship with a second party (a *server*) in which the client initiates requests and the server responds to those requests.

client service request   CONTEXT [Fibre Channel]

A request issued by a client application to a well-known service. An example is a name service query.

cluster

A collection of computers that are interconnected (typically at high-speeds) for the purpose of improving reliability, availability, serviceability and/or performance (via load balancing). Often, clustered computers have access to a common pool of storage, and run special software to coordinate the component computers' activities.

CMIP   CONTEXT [Management] [Network]

Acronym for *Common Management Information Protocol.*

coaxial cable

An electrical transmission medium consisting of two concentric conductors separated by a dielectric material with the spacings and material arranged to give a specified electrical impedance. *cf. triaxial cable*

code balance   CONTEXT [Fibre Channel]

The number of 1 bits in a 10-bit transmitted data stream divided by 10 (e.g., 1110100011 has a code balance of 6/10 = 60%).

code bit   CONTEXT [Fibre Channel]

1. A bit (binary digit) of an encoded datum. Sequences of code bits make up symbols, each of which corresponds to a data element (word, byte, or other unit).

2. The smallest time period used by FC-0 for transmission on the media.

code byte   CONTEXT [Network]

A byte of an encoded datum. Sometimes called a symbol. Code bytes are the output of encoding or encryption processes. In communication theory contexts, a code byte is often referred to as a *code word. cf. data byte*

code violation   CONTEXT [Fibre Channel]

The error condition that occurs when a received *transmission character* cannot be decoded into a *valid data byte* or special code using the validity checking rules specified by the *transmission code.*

cold backup   CONTEXT [Backup]

Synonym for *offline backup. cf. hot backup, online backup*

cold swap

The substitution of a replacement unit (*RU*) in a system for a defective one, where external power must be removed from the system in order to perform the substitution. A cold swap is a physical substitution as well as a functional one. *cf. automatic swap, hot swap, warm swap*

comma character   CONTEXT [Fibre Channel]

1. Either of the seven bit sequences 0011111 or 1100000 in an encoded stream.
2. A special character containing a comma.

command line interface

A form of human interface to intelligent devices characterized by non-directive prompting and character string user input. Perceived by many users to be more difficult to comprehend and use than *graphical user interface*s (GUI).

Common Information Model   CONTEXT [Management] [Network]

An object oriented description of the entities and relationships in a business' management environment maintained by the *Distributed Management Task Force*. Abbreviated CIM. CIM is divided into a Core Model and Common Models. The Core Model addresses high-level concepts (such as systems and devices), as well as fundamental relationships (such as dependencies). The Common Models describe specific problem domains such as computer system, network, user or device management. The Common Models are subclasses of the Core Model and may also be subclasses of each other.

Common Internet File System   CONTEXT [Network]

A network file system access protocol originally designed and implemented by Microsoft Corporation under the name *Server Message Block* protocol, and primarily used by Windows clients to communicate file access requests to Windows servers. Abbreviated CIFS. Today, other implementations of the CIFS protocol allow other clients and servers to use it for intercommunication and interoperation with Microsoft operating systems.

Common Management Information Protocol   CONTEXT [Management] [Network]

A network management protocol built on the Open Systems Interconnection (OSI) communication model. Abbreviated CMIP. CMIP is more complete, and therefore larger than, SNMP.

communication circuit   CONTEXT [Fibre Channel] [Network]

1. A bidirectional path for message exchange within a Fibre Channel *fabric*.
2. In networking, a specific logical or physical path between two points over which communications occur.

communications security   CONTEXT [Network] [Security]

Protection of information while it's being transmitted, particularly via telecommunications. A particular focus of communications security is message authenticity. Communications security may include cryptography, transmission security, emission security, and physical security.

complex array   CONTEXT [Storage System]

A disk array whose *control software* protects and maps data according to more complex algorithms than those of the *Berkeley RAID Level*s. The most common complex arrays are multi-level *disk array*s, which perform more than one level of data address mapping, and *adaptive array*s, which are capable of changing data address mapping dynamically.

compression   CONTEXT [Backup] [File System] [Network] [Storage Device] [Storage System]

The process of encoding data to reduce its size. *Lossy* compression (i.e., compression using a technique in which a portion of the original information is lost) is acceptable for some forms of data (e.g., digital images) in some applications, but for most IT applications, *lossless* compression (i.e., compression using a technique that preserves the entire content of the original data, and from which the original data can be reconstructed exactly) is required.

computer security   CONTEXT [Security]

Measures and controls that ensure confidentiality, integrity, and availability of information system assets including hardware, software, firmware, and information being processed, stored, and communicated.

concatenation   CONTEXT [Network] [Storage System]

A logical joining of two series of data. Usually represented by the symbol "|". In data communications, two or more data are often concatenated to provide a unique name or reference (e.g., *S ID* | *X ID*). *Volume managers* concatenate disk address spaces to present a single larger address spaces.

concurrency

The property of overlapping in time. Usually refers to the execution of I/O operations or I/O requests.

concurrent
concurrent copy   CONTEXT [Storage System]

A hybrid point in time copy mechanism for which each copy is initially a changed block copy (i.e., shares unmodified storage with its source), but over time becomes a split mirror copy (i.e., does not share any storage with its source) without changing the point in time at which the copy logically occurred, independent of whether and where modifications to the source or the copy subsequently occur. A concurrent copy occupies at least the amount of storage required to hold changed blocks and grows to occupy as much storage as the copy source.

concurrent operations

Operations that overlap in time. The concept of concurrent I/O operations is central to the use of independent access arrays in throughput-intensive applications.

conditioning

The processing of a signal for the purpose of making it conform more closely to an ideal. *Power conditioning* is used to minimize voltage and frequency variations in an external power. Signal conditioning is used to reduce noise in logic or data signals.

confidentiality   CONTEXT [Security]

Encryption (in a security context).

configuration   CONTEXT [Storage System]

1. The process of installing or removing hardware or software components required for a system or subsystem to function.
2. Assignment of the operating parameters of a system, subsystem or device. Disk array configuration, for example, includes designating the array's member disks or extents, as well as parameters such as stripe depth, RAID model, cache allowance, etc.
3. The collection of a system's hardware and software components and operating parameters. *cf. array configuration, physical configuration.*

connection   CONTEXT [Fibre Channel]

Short form of *dedicated connection.*

connection initiator   CONTEXT [Fibre Channel]

An *N Port* which initiates a *Class 1* connection with a destination N_Port through a connect-request and receives a valid response from the destination N_Port to establish the connection.

connection recipient   CONTEXT [Fibre Channel]

An *N Port* which receives a *Class 1* connect-request from a *connection initiator* and accepts the connection request by transmitting a valid response.

connectionless buffer   CONTEXT [Fibre Channel]

A receive buffer used in a connectionless service and capable of receiving connectionless frames.

connectionless frame   CONTEXT [Fibre Channel]

A *frame* used in a connectionless service (i.e., *Class 1* frames with SOF(C1)., *Class 2*, and *Class 3* frames referred to individually or collectively)

connectionless integrity service   CONTEXT [Security]

A security service that provides data integrity service for an individual *IP datagram* by detecting modification of the datagram without regard to the ordering of the datagram in a stream of datagrams.

connectionless service   CONTEXT [Fibre Channel]

Communication between two *N Port*s or *NL Ports* without a dedicated connection.

console

1. A device for graphical or textual visual output from a computer system.

2. In systems, network and device management, an application that provides graphical and textual feedback regarding operation and status, and that may accept operator commands and input influencing operation and status. Sometimes called enterprise management console.

consolidation   CONTEXT [Storage System]

The process of accumulating the data for a number of sequential write requests in a cache, and performing a smaller number of larger write requests to achieve more efficient device utilization.

continuously increasing relative offset   CONTEXT [Fibre Channel]

A transmission control algorithm in which the frames containing the subblocks that comprise a block of information are transmitted strictly in the order of the subblocks. Continuously increasing relative offset simplifies reassembly and detection of lost frames relative to *random relative offset*.

control software   CONTEXT [Storage System]

A body of software that provides common control and management for one or more *disk arrays* or *tape arrays*. Control software presents the arrays of disks or tapes it controls to its operating environment as one or more *virtual disks* or *tapes*. Control software may execute in a disk controller or intelligent host bus adapter, or in a host computer. When it executes in a disk controller or adapter, control software is often referred to as *firmware*.

controller   CONTEXT [Storage System] [Management]

1. The control logic in a disk or tape that performs command decoding and execution, host data transfer, serialization and deserialization of data, error detection and correction, and overall management of device operations.

2. The control logic in a *storage subsystem* that performs command transformation and routing, aggregation (RAID, mirroring, striping, or other), high-level error recovery, and performance optimization for multiple storage devices.

3. A subclass of CIM_LogicalDevice. A CIM_Controller represents a device having a single protocol stack whose primary purpose is to communicate with, control, and reset connected

devices. There are many subclasses of CIM_Controller, addressing SCSI, PCI, USB, serial, parallel, and video controllers.

controller based array
controller based disk array   CONTEXT [Storage System]

A disk array whose *control software* executes in a disk subsystem controller. The member disks of a controller-based array are necessarily part of the same disk subsystem that includes the controller. *cf. host based array.*

controller cache   CONTEXT [Storage System]

A *cache* that resides within a controller and whose primary purpose is to improve disk or array I/O performance. *cf. cache, disk cache, host cache*

copy on write   CONTEXT [Storage System]

A technique for maintaining a point in time copy of a collection of data by copying only data which is modified after the instant of replicate initiation. The original source data is used to satisfy read requests for both the source data itself and for the unmodified portion of the point in time copy. *cf. pointer remapping*

copyback   CONTEXT [Storage System]

The replacement of a properly functioning array member by another disk, including copying of the member's contents to the replacing disk. Copyback, which is most often used to create or restore a particular physical configuration for an array (e.g., a particular arrangement of array members on device I/O buses), is accomplished without *reduction* of the array.

count-key-data   CONTEXT [Storage Device]

A disk data organization model in which the disk is assumed to consist of a fixed number of tracks, each having a maximum data capacity. Multiple records of varying length may be written on each track of a count-key-data disk, and the usable capacity of each track depends on the number of records written to it. Count-key-data (CKD) architecture derives its name from the record format, which consists of a field containing the number of bytes of data and a record address, an optional key field by which particular records can be easily recognized, and the data itself. Count-key-data is the storage architecture used by IBM Corporation's System 390 series of mainframe computer systems. *cf. fixed block architecture*

covert channel   CONTEXT [Security]

An unintended and/or unauthorized communications path that can be used to transfer information in a manner that violates a security policy.

credit   CONTEXT [Fibre Channel]

The number of receive buffers allocated to a transmitting *N Port, NL Port,* or *F Port.* The credit is the maximum number of outstanding frames that can be transmitted by that N_Port, NL_Port, or F_Port without causing a buffer overrun condition at the receiver.

CRC

Acronym for *cyclic redundancy check.*

CRU

Acronym for *Customer Replaceable Unit.*

cryptanalysis   CONTEXT [Security]

A set of operations performed in converting encrypted information to plain text without initial knowledge of the algorithm and/or key employed in the encryption.

cryptosystem   CONTEXT [Security]
A single means of encryption or decryption.

CSMA/CD
Acronym for *Carrier Sense Multiple Access with Collision Detection.*

cumulative incremental backup   CONTEXT [Backup]
A *backup* in which all data objects modified since the last *full backup* are copied. To restore data when cumulative incremental backups are in use, only the latest full backup and the latest cumulative incremental backup are required. *cf. differential incremental backup, full backup*

current running disparity   CONTEXT [Fibre Channel]
The running disparity present at a transmitter when the encoding of a *valid data byte* or special code is initiated, or at a receiver when the decoding of a *transmission character* is initiated.

customer replaceable unit
A unit, or component of a system that is designed to be replaced by "customers;" i.e., individuals who may not be trained as computer system service personnel. *cf. field replaceable unit*

cut through (switching)   CONTEXT [Fibre Channel]
A switching technique that allows a routing decision to be made and acted upon as soon as the destination address of a frame is received.

cyclic redundancy check
A scheme for checking the correctness of data that has been transmitted or stored and retrieved. Abbreviated CRC. A CRC consists of a fixed number of bits computed as a function of the data to be protected, and appended to the data. When the data is read or received, the function is recomputed, and the result is compared to that appended to the data. Cyclic redundancy checks differ from *error correcting code*s in that they can detect a wide range of errors, but are not capable of correcting them. *cf. error correcting code*

cylinder-head-sector addressing   CONTEXT [Storage Device]
A form of addressing data stored on a disk in which the cylinder, head/platter combination, and relative sector number on a track are specified. Abbreviated C-H-S addressing. *cf. block addressing*

D_ID   CONTEXT [Fibre Channel]
Acronym for *Destination Identifier. cf. S ID*

daemon   CONTEXT [Operating System]
A process that is always running on a computer system to service a particular set of requests. For example, in UNIX, lpd is a daemon that handles printing requests. Daemons are independent processes, and not part of an application program. Application requests may be serviced by a daemon.

data availability
The amount of time that a data is accessible by applications during those time periods when it is expected to be available. Data availability is often measured as a percentage of an elapsed year. For example, 99.95% availability equates to 4.38 hours of unavailability in a year (0.0005 * 365 * 24 = 4.38) for a set of data that is expected to be available all the time. *cf. availability, high availability*

data byte   CONTEXT [Network] [Storage Device] [Storage System]
A byte of user data as presented to a storage or communication facility. Data bytes are input to processes that encode for transmission or encrypt for privacy. *cf. code byte, data character.*

data character   CONTEXT [Fibre Channel] [Network]

Any *transmission character* associated by the *transmission code* with a *valid data byte*.

Data Encryption Standard   CONTEXT [Security]

A cryptographic data protection algorithm published by the National Institute of Standards and Technology in Federal Information Processing Standard (FIPS) Publication 46.

data frame   CONTEXT [Fibre Channel]

A *frame* containing information meant for *FC-4* (*ULP*) or the link application.

data manager   CONTEXT [File System]

A computer program whose primary purpose is to present a convenient view of data to applications, and map that view to an internal representation on a system, subsystem or device. File systems and database management systems are the most common forms of a data manager.

data model

A repository-specific representation of an *information model*. A database representation of the *CIM* schemas is an example of a data model.

data reliability

Expressed as *Mean Time to Data Loss* (*MTDL*). The length of the statically expected continuous span of time over which data stored by a population of identical disk subsystems can be correctly retrieved.

data stripe depth   CONTEXT [Storage System]

Synonym for *user data extent stripe depth*.

data striping   CONTEXT [Storage System]

A disk array data mapping technique in which fixed-length sequences of virtual disk data addresses are mapped to sequences of member disk addresses in a regular rotating pattern. Disk striping is commonly called RAID Level 0 or RAID 0 because of its similarity to common RAID data mapping techniques. It includes no data protection, however, so strictly speaking, the appellation RAID is a misnomer.

data transfer capacity

The maximum rate at which data can be transmitted. Bandwidth is sometimes expressed in terms of signaling capacity (e.g., SCSI), and sometimes in terms of data transmission capacity inclusive of protocol overhead (e.g., Fibre Channel). *cf. throughput, data transfer rate*

data transfer-intensive (application)

A characterization of applications. A data transfer-intensive application is an *I/O intensive* application which makes large *I/O request*s. Data transfer-intensive applications' I/O requests are usually *sequential*.

data transfer rate

The amount of data per unit time actually moved across an I/O bus in the course of executing an I/O load. The data transfer capacity of an I/O subsystem is an upper bound on its data transfer rate for any I/O load. For disk subsystem I/O, data transfer rate is usually expressed in MBytes/second (millions of bytes per second, where 1 million = 10^6). *cf. data transfer capacity*

database management system   CONTEXT [Database]

A set of computer programs with a user and/or programming interface that supports the definition of the format of a database, and the creation of and access to its data. A database management system removes the need for a user or program to manage low level database storage. It also provides security for and assures the integrity of the data it contains. Types of database management systems are relational (table-oriented) and object oriented. Abbreviated DBMS.

datagram   CONTEXT [Fibre Channel] [Network]
A message sent between two communicating entities for which no explicit link level acknowledgment is expected. Datagrams are often said to be sent on a "best efforts" basis.

DBMS   CONTEXT [Database]
Acronym for *database management system.*

decoding   CONTEXT [Fibre Channel]
Validity checking of received *transmission characters* and generation of *valid data byte*s and *special code*s from those characters.

decryption   CONTEXT [Security]
The operations performed in converting encrypted information to plain text with full knowledge of the algorithm and key(s) used to encrypt it. Decryption is the intended method for an authorized user to decrypt encrypted information.

dedicated connection   CONTEXT [Fibre Channel]
A communication circuit between two *N Ports* maintained by a Fibre Channel *fabric*. The port resources used by a dedicated connection cannot be used for other purposes during the life of the dedicated connection.

dedicated connection service   CONTEXT [Fibre Channel]
Synonym for *Class 1* service.

degraded mode   CONTEXT [Storage System]
Synonym for *reduced mode*. A mode of RAID array operation in which not all of the array's member disks are functioning, but the array as a whole is able to respond to application read and write requests to its virtual disks.

degaussing   CONTEXT [Security]
A procedure that reduces magnetic flux to virtual zero by applying a reverse magnetizing field. Also called demagnetizing. Degaussing is used to ensure that no residual signal remains on magnetic media from which previously stored information could be recovered.

delimiter   CONTEXT [Fibre Channel]
An *ordered set* used to indicate a *frame* boundary.

DEN   CONTEXT [Network]
Acronym for *Directory Enabled Network.*

denial of service   CONTEXT [Security]
Result of any action or series of actions that prevents any part of an information system from functioning.

DES   CONTEXT [Security]
Acronym for *Data Encryption Standard*

Desktop Management Interface   CONTEXT [Management] [Network]
A former name for the *Distributed Management Task Force* (DMTF).

destination identifier   CONTEXT [Fibre Channel]

> An address contained in a Fibre Channel frame that identifies the destination of the frame.

destination N_Port   CONTEXT [Fibre Channel]

> The *N Port* to which a *frame* is addressed.

device   CONTEXT [Management] [Storage System]

> 1. Synonym for *storage device.*
> 2. CIM_LogicalDevice is an object that abstracts the configuration and operational aspects of hardware. Subclasses of CIM_LogicalDevice include low-level sensors, processors, storage devices and printer hardware.

device bus
device I/O bus   CONTEXT [Storage System]

> An *I/O bus* used to connect storage devices to a *host bus adapter* or *intelligent controller.* Device I/O bus is the preferred term.

device channel   CONTEXT [Storage System]

> A *channel* used to connect storage devices to a host I/O bus adapter or intelligent controller. The preferred term is *device I/O bus.*

device fanout   CONTEXT [Storage System]

> The ability of a storage controller to connect host computers to multiple storage devices using a single host I/O bus address. Device fanout allows computer systems to connect to substantially more storage devices than could be connected directly.

DHCP   CONTEXT [Network]

> Acronym for *dynamic host control protocol.*

differential incremental backup   CONTEXT [Backup]

> A *backup* in which data objects modified since the last *full backup* or *incremental backup* are copied. To restore data when differential incremental backups are in use, the newest full backup and all differential backups newer than the newest full backup are required. *cf. cumulative incremental backup, full backup*

differential (signaling)   CONTEXT [SCSI]

> A SCSI electrical signaling technique in which each control and data signal is represented by a voltage differential between two signal lines. Differential signaling can be used over longer distances than the alternative *single ended* signaling. *cf. single ended* (signaling)

differentiated services   CONTEXT [Management]

> A protocol defined by the *IETF* for managing network traffic based on the type of packet or message being transmitted. Abbreviated DiffServ. DiffServ rules define how a packet flows through a network based on a 6 bit field (the Differentiated Services Code Point) in the IP header. The Differentiated Services Code Point specifies the "per hop behavior" (bandwidth, queuing and forward/drop status) for the packet or message.

DiffServ   CONTEXT [Management]

> Abbreviation for *Differentiated Services.*

digest   CONTEXT [Security]

> A computationally efficient function mapping binary strings of arbitrary length to binary strings of some fixed length.

Digital Linear Tape   CONTEXT [Backup]

A family of tape device and media technologies developed by Quantum Corporation.

digital signature   CONTEXT [Security]

A cryptographic process used to assure information authenticity, integrity, and *nonrepudiation*. Generally refers to assurances that can be externally verified by entities not in possession of the key used to sign the information. For example a *secure hash* of the information encrypted with the originator's private key when an asymmetric cryptosystem is used. Some algorithms that are used in digital signatures cannot be used to encrypt data. (e.g., *DSA*).

directory   CONTEXT [File System] [Management] [Network]

1. A mechanism for organizing information.

2. A file or other persistent data structure in a file system that contains information about other files. Directories are usually organized hierarchically (i.e., a directory may contain both information about files and other directories), and are used to organize collections of files for application or human convenience.

3. An *LDAP*-based repository consisting of class definitions and instances of those classes. An example of an enterprise-wide LDAP directory is Microsoft's Active Directory (AD) or Novell's NetWare Directory Service (NDS).

directory enabled network   CONTEXT [Management] [Network]

An industry initiative, now part of the *DMTF*'s mission, to map the *CIM* schema to an *LDAP* Directory. Abbreviated DEN. DEN's goals are to provide a consistent and standard data model to describe a network, its elements and its policies/rules. Policies are defined to provide *quality of service* or to manage to a specified *class of service*.

directory tree   CONTEXT [File System]

A collective term for a *directory*, all of its files, and the directory trees of each of its subdirectories.

discard policy   CONTEXT [Fibre Channel]

An error handling policy that allows an *N Port* or *NL Port* to discard data frames received following detection of a missing frame in a *sequence*.

disconnection   CONTEXT [Fibre Channel]

The process of removing a *dedicated connection* between two *N Port*s.

disk
disk drive   CONTEXT [Storage Device]

A non-volatile, randomly addressable, re-writable data storage device. This definition includes both rotating magnetic and optical disks and *solid-state disks*, or non-volatile electronic storage elements. It does not include specialized devices such as *write-once-read-many* (*WORM*) optical disks, nor does it include so-called *RAM disks* implemented using software to control a dedicated portion of a host computer's volatile random access memory.

disk array   CONTEXT [Storage System]

A set of disks from one or more commonly accessible *disk subsystem*s, combined with a body of *control software*. The control software presents the disks' storage capacity to hosts as one or more *virtual disk*s. Control software is often called firmware or microcode when it runs in a disk controller. Control software that runs in a host computer is usually called a volume manager.

disk array subsystem   CONTEXT [Storage System]

A *disk subsystem* which includes *control software* with the capability to organize its disks as *disk array*s.

disk block   CONTEXT [Storage Device] [Storage System]

The unit in which data is stored and retrieved on a *fixed block architecture* disk. Disk blocks are of fixed usable size (with the most common being 512 bytes), and are usually numbered consecutively. Disk blocks are also the unit of on-disk protection against errors; whatever mechanism a disk employs to protect against data errors (e.g., *ECC*) protects individual blocks of data. *cf. sector*

disk cache

1. A *cache* that resides within a disk.

2. A cache that resides in a controller or host whose primary purpose is to improve disk or array I/O performance. *cf. cache, controller cache, host cache*

disk image backup   CONTEXT [Backup] [Windows]

A backup consisting of a copy of each of the blocks comprising a disk's usable storage area. A disk image backup incorporates no information about the objects contained on the disk, and hence cannot be used for individual object restoration.

disk shadowing   CONTEXT [Storage System]

Synonym for *mirroring*.

disk striping   CONTEXT [Storage System]

Synonym for *data striping*.

disk subsystem   CONTEXT [Storage System]

A *storage subsystem* that supports only disk devices.

disk scrubbing   CONTEXT [Storage System]

A function which reads all of the *user data* and *check data* blocks in a *RAID array* and relocates them if *media defects* are found. Disk scrubbing can have a noticeable negative effect on application performance.

disparity   CONTEXT [Fibre Channel]

The difference between the number of ones and the number of zeros in a *transmission character*.

Distributed Management Task Force   CONTEXT [Management]

An industry organization that develops management standards for computer system and enterprise environments. DMTF standards include WBEM, *CIM, DMI, DEN* and *ARM*. Abbreviated DMTF. The DMTF has a Web site at www.dmtf.org.

DLT   CONTEXT [Storage Device]

Acronym for *Digital Linear Tape*.

DMI

Acronym for *Desktop Management Interface*.

DMTF   CONTEXT [Management]

Acronym for *Distributed Management Task Force*.

DNS   CONTEXT [Network]

Acronym for *Domain Name Service*.

document type definition   CONTEXT [Network]

In *XML*, a specification of the permissible tags or "markup codes" in a document, and their meanings. Tags are delimited by the characters, "<" and ">". Abbreviated DTD. When a DTD is available for a document, a universal reader (program) can parse the document and display or print it.

domain

1. A shared user authorization database which contains users, groups, and their security policies.
2. A set of interconnected network elements and addresses that are administered together and that may communicate.

domain controller   CONTEXT [Windows]

A Windows NT or Windows 2000 server that contains a copy of a user account database. A Windows domain may contain both a primary and a backup domain controller.

Domain Name Service   CONTEXT [Network]

A computer program that converts between *IP* addresses and symbolic names for *nodes* on a network in a standard way. Abbreviated DNS. Most operating systems include a version of Domain Name Service.

DoS   CONTEXT [Security]

Acronym for *denial of service*

double buffering

A technique often used to maximize data transfer rate by constantly keeping two I/O requests for consecutively addressed data outstanding. A software component begins a double-buffered I/O stream by making two I/O requests in rapid sequence. Thereafter, each time an I/O request completes, another is immediately made, leaving two outstanding. If a disk subsystem can process requests fast enough, double buffering allows data to be transferred at a disk or disk array's *full volume transfer rate.*

drive letter   CONTEXT [Windows]

A single letter of the alphabet by which applications and users identify a partition of physical or virtual disk to the Windows operating system. The number of letters in the alphabet limits the number of disks that can be referenced.

driver
driver software

Synonyms for *I/O driver.*

DSA   CONTEXT [Security]

Acronym for a specific algorithm proposed by NIST in 1991 for use in digital signatures.

DTD

Acronym for *Document Type Definition.*

dual active (components)

A pair of components, such as the controllers in a failure tolerant storage subsystem that share a task or class of tasks when both are functioning normally. When one of the components fails, the other takes on the entire task. Dual active controllers are connected to the same set of storage devices, improve both I/O performance and failure tolerance compared to a single controller. Dual active components are also called *active-active* components.

duplicate   CONTEXT [Backup]

1. (noun) A general term for a copy of a collection of data, including point in time copies.
2. (verb) The action of making a duplicate as defined above. *cf. replicate, snapshot*
3. Any *redundant* component in a system.

dynamic host control protocol   CONTEXT [Network]

An Internet protocol that allows *nodes* to dynamically acquire ("lease") network addresses for periods of time rather than having to pre-configure them. Abbreviated DHCP. DHCP greatly simplifies the administration of large networks, and networks in which nodes frequently join and depart.

dynamic mapping   CONTEXT [Storage System]

A form of *mapping* in which the correspondence between addresses in the two address spaces can change over time. *cf. algorithmic mapping, tabular mapping*

E_Port   CONTEXT [Fibre Channel]

An expansion port on a Fibre Channel switch. E_Ports are used to link multiple Fibre Channel switches together into a *fabric*. *cf. F Port, FL Port, G Port, L Port, N Port, NL Port*

EBU   CONTEXT [Standards]

Acronym for *European Broadcast Union*.

ECC

Acronym for *error correcting code*.

EE_buffer   CONTEXT [Fibre Channel]

A buffer associated with *end-to-end flow control*.

EE_credit   CONTEXT [Fibre Channel]

A credit scheme used to manage *end-to-end flow control* during the exchange of frames between two communicating devices.

electronic storage element   CONTEXT [Storage Device]

Synonym for *solid state disk*.

embedded controller
embedded storage controller   CONTEXT [Storage System]

An intelligent storage controller that mounts in a host computer's housing and attaches directly to a host's internal I/O bus. Embedded controllers obviate the need for *host bus adapter*s and external host I/O buses. Embedded storage controllers differ from host bus adapters in that they provide functions beyond I/O bus protocol conversion (e.g., RAID).

Encapsulating Security Payload   CONTEXT [Security]

A component of IPsec that permits the specification of various confidentiality mechanisms.

encoding   CONTEXT [Fibre Channel]

Generation of *transmission character*s from *valid data byte*s and *special code*s.

encryption   CONTEXT [Security]

The conversion of plaintext to encrypted text with the intent that it only be accessible to authorized users who have the appropriate decryption key.

end-to-end encryption   CONTEXT [Security]

Encryption of information at its origin and decryption at its intended destination without intermediate decryption.

end to end flow control   CONTEXT [Fibre Channel] [Network]

1. Control of message flow between the two end parties to a communication on a network.
2. Flow control that occurs between two connected Fibre Channel N-Ports.

enterprise resource management   CONTEXT [Management] [Network]

Software that manages all aspects of an organization's assets, systems, services and functions.

The management of a set of resources in the wider perspective of an organization's entire business. Managing in an enterprise context requires that entities be named uniquely and locatable within the enterprise, that heterogeneity of platforms and services may be assumed, and that the dynamic nature of the environment is taken into account.

Enterprise Systems Connection   CONTEXT [Storage System]

A 200 Mbps serial I/O bus used on IBM Corporation's Enterprise System 9000 data center computers. Abbreviated ESCON. Similar to Fibre Channel in many respects, ESCON is based on redundant switches to which computers and storage subsystems connect using serial optical connections.

entry port
exit port   CONTEXT [Backup]

A port in a media library through which media can be inserted or removed without exposing internal library components. Also called exit port.

EOF

Acronym for *end of frame.*

ERM

Acronym for *Enterprise Resource Management.*

error correcting code

A scheme for checking the correctness of data that has been stored and retrieved, and correcting it if necessary. Abbreviated ECC. An ECC consists of a number of bits computed as a function of the data to be protected, and appended to the data. When the data and ECC are read, the function is recomputed, the result is compared to the ECC appended to the data, and correction is performed if necessary. Error correcting codes differ from *cyclic redundancy check*s in that the latter can detect errors, but are not generally capable of correcting them. *cf. cyclic redundancy check*

ESCON   CONTEXT [Storage System]

Acronym for *Enterprise Systems Connection.*

ESP   CONTEXT [Security]

Acronym for *Encapsulating Security Payload*

ESRM

Acronym for *Enterprise Storage Resource Management.*

Ethernet   CONTEXT [Network]

The predominant local area networking technology, based on packetized transmissions between physical *port*s over a variety of electrical and optical *media*. Ethernet can transport any of several upper layer protocols, the most popular of which is *TCP/IP*. Ethernet standards are maintained by the IEEE 802.3 committee. The unqualified term Ethernet usually refers to 10 Mbps transmission on multi-point copper. Fast Ethernet is used to denote 100 Mbps transmission, also on multipoint copper facilities. Ethernet and Fast Ethernet both use *CSMA/CD* physical signaling. Gigabit Ethernet (abbreviated GBE) transmits at 1250 Mega*baud* (1Gbit of data per second) using *8b/10b encoding* with constant transmission detection.

Ethernet adapter   CONTEXT [Network]

An *adapter* that connects an intelligent device to an *Ethernet* network. Usually called an Ethernet network interface card, or Ethernet NIC. *cf. NIC*

European Broadcast Union   CONTEXT [Standards]

A European-based television (Video) standardization group coordinated with SMPTE and loosely affiliated with FC-AV. Abbreviated EBU.

EVSN   CONTEXT [Backup]

Acronym for *External Volume Serial Number*.

exchange   CONTEXT [Fibre Channel]

A set of one or more non-concurrent related *sequence*s passing between a pair of Fibre Channel *port*s. An exchange encapsulates a "conversation" such as a SCSI task or an IP exchange. Exchanges may be bidirectional and may be short or long lived. The parties to an exchange are identified by an Originator Exchange_Identifier (OX_ID) and a Responder Exchange_Identifier (RX_ID).

Exchange_Identifier   CONTEXT [Fibre Channel]

A generic term denoting either an *Originator Exchange Identifier* (OX_ID) or a *Responder Exchange Identifier* (RX_ID).

exchange status block   CONTEXT [Fibre Channel]

A data structure which contains the state of an *exchange*. An originator *N Port* or *NL Port* has an *Originator* Exchange Status Block and a Responder N_Port or NL_Port has a *Responder* Exchange Status Block for each concurrently active exchange.

exclusive connection   CONTEXT [Fibre Channel]

A Class 1 *dedicated connection* without *intermix*.

exit port   CONTEXT [Backup]

A port in a media library through which media can be inserted or removed without exposing internal library components. *cf. entry port*

expansion card
expansion module

A collective term for optional adapters in the form of printed circuit modules that can be added to intelligent devices. Expansion cards include *host bus adapters*, *network interface cards*, as well as NVRAM, console, and other special purpose adapters.

expansion slot

A mounting and internal bus attachment device within an intelligent device into which *expansion cards* are inserted.

explicit addressing   CONTEXT [Storage Device] [Storage System]

A form of *addressing* used with disks in which the data's address is explicitly specified in the access request. *cf. implicit addressing*

export (verb)

1. Synonym for *present*. To cause to appear or make available. Disk array *control software* exports virtual disks to its host environment. In file systems, a directory may be exported or made available for access by remote clients.

2. To move objects, such as data, from within a system to a location outside the system, usually requiring a transformation during the move.

eXtensible Markup Language

A universal format for structured documents and data on the World Wide Web. Abbreviated XML. The World Wide Web Consortium is responsible for the XML specification. *cf. http://www.w3.org/XML/.*

extent   CONTEXT [Storage Device] [Storage System]

1. A set of consecutively addressed *FBA* disk blocks that is allocated to consecutive addresses of a single file.

2. A set of consecutively located tracks on a CKD disk that is allocated to a single file.

3. A set of consecutively addressed disk blocks that is part of a single virtual disk-to-member disk array mapping. A single disk may be organized into multiple extents of different sizes, and may have multiple (possibly) non-adjacent extents that are part of the same virtual disk-to-member disk array mapping. This type of extent is sometimes called a *logical disk*.

4. A subclass or instance of the CIM_StorageExtent object. *CIM* models both removable and nonremovable types of storage media.

external controller
external disk controller
external storage controller   CONTEXT [Storage System]

An intelligent storage controller that mounts outside its host computer's enclosure and attaches to hosts via external I/O buses. External storage controllers usually mount in the enclosure containing the disks they control.

external volume serial number   CONTEXT [Backup]

A humanly readable volume serial number on a removable media or cartridge. Abbreviated EVSN. *cf. label*

eye

The region of an *eye diagram* that does not occur for correctly formed pulses. This is in the center of the eye diagram and distinguishes presence of signal (region above the eye) from absence of signal (region below the eye).

eye diagram

A diagram used to specify optical or electrical pulse characteristics for transmitters. The horizontal axis represents normalized time from pulse start and the vertical axis represents normalized amplitude. *cf. eye opening*

eye opening

The time interval across the *eye*, measured at a 50% normalized eye amplitude, which is error free to the specified *BER*.

F_Port   CONTEXT [Fibre Channel]

1. A *port* that is part of a Fibre Channel *fabric*. An F_Port on a Fibre Channel fabric connects to a node's *N_Port*. F_Ports are frame routing ports, and are insensitive to higher level protocols. *cf. E_Port, FL_Port, G_Port, L_Port, N_Port, NL_Port*

2. The Link_Control_Facility within a fabric which attaches to an N_Port through a link. An N_Port uses a well-known address (hex 'FFFFFE') to address the F_Port attached to it.

F_Port name   CONTEXT [Fibre Channel]

A *Name Identifier* associated with an *F_Port*.

fabric   CONTEXT [Fibre Channel]

A Fibre Channel switch or two or more Fibre Channel *switch*es interconnected in such a way that data can be physically transmitted between any two N_Ports on any of the switches. The switches comprising a Fibre Channel fabric are capable of routing frames using only the *D_ID* in a *FC-2* frame header.

fabric login   CONTEXT [Fibre Channel]

> The process by which a Fibre Channel node establishes a logical connection to a fabric switch.

Fabric Name   CONTEXT [Fibre Channel]

> A *Name Identifier* associated with a *fabric*.

failback

> The restoration of a failed system component's share of a load to a replacement component. For example, when a failed controller in a redundant configuration is replaced, the devices that were originally controlled by the failed controller are usually *failed back* to the replacement controller to restore the I/O balance, and to restore failure tolerance. Similarly, when a defective fan or power supply is replaced, its load, previously borne by a redundant component can be *failed back* to the replacement part.

failed over

> A mode of operation for failure tolerant systems in which a component has failed and its function has been assumed by a redundant component. A system that protects against single failures operating in failed over mode is not failure tolerant, since failure of the redundant component may render the system unable to function. Some systems (e.g., clusters) are able to tolerate more than one failure; these remain failure tolerant until no redundant component is available to protect against further failures.

failover

> The automatic *substitution* of a functionally equivalent system component for a failed one. The term failover is most often applied to intelligent controllers connected to the same storage devices and host computers. If one of the controllers fails, failover occurs, and the survivor takes over its I/O load.

failure tolerance

> The ability of a system to continue to perform its function (possibly at a reduced performance level) when one or more of its components has failed. Failure tolerance in disk subsystems is often achieved by including *redundant* instances of components whose failure would make the system inoperable, coupled with facilities that allow the redundant components to assume the function of failed ones.

fanout   CONTEXT [Storage System]

> Synonym for *device fanout*.

fast SCSI   CONTEXT [SCSI]

> A form of SCSI that provides 10 *megatransfer*s per second. Wide fast SCSI has a 16-bit data path, and transfers 20 MBytes per second. Narrow fast SCSI transfers 10 MBytes per second. *cf. wide SCSI, Ultra SCSI, Ultra2 SCSI, Ultra3 SCSI*.

fault tolerance

> Synonym for *failure tolerance*.

FBA   CONTEXT [Storage Device]

> Acronym for *Fixed Block Architecture*.

FC-PH   CONTEXT [Fibre Channel]

> The Fibre Channel physical standard, consisting of *FC-0*, *FC-1*, and *FC-2*.

FC-0   CONTEXT [Fibre Channel]

> The Fibre Channel protocol level that encompasses the physical characteristics of the interface and data transmission media. Specified in *FC-PH*.

FC-1   CONTEXT [Fibre Channel]
The Fibre Channel protocol level that encompasses *8B/10B encoding*, and transmission protocol. Specified in *FC-PH*.

FC-2   CONTEXT [Fibre Channel]
The Fibre Channel protocol level that encompasses signaling protocol rules and the organization of data into *frame*s, *sequence*s, and *exchange*s. Specified in *FC-PH*.

FC-3   CONTEXT [Fibre Channel]
The Fibre Channel protocol level that encompasses common services between *FC-2* and *FC-4*. FC-3 contains no services in most implementations.

FC-4   CONTEXT [Fibre Channel]
The Fibre Channel protocol level that encompasses the mapping of upper layer protocols (ULP) such as IP and SCSI to lower protocol layers (*FC-0* through *FC-3*). For example, the mapping of SCSI commands is an *FC-4* ULP that defines the control interface between computers and storage.

FC-AE   CONTEXT [Fibre Channel]
Acronym for *Fibre Channel Avionics Environment*.

FC-AL   CONTEXT [Fibre Channel]
Acronym for *Fibre Channel Arbitrated Loop*.

FC-AV   CONTEXT [Fibre Channel]
Acronym for *Fibre Channel Audio Video*.

FC-GS2   CONTEXT [Fibre Channel]
Acronym for *Fibre Channel Generic Services*.

FC-SB
FC-SB2   CONTEXT [Fibre Channel]
Acronym for *Fibre Channel Single Byte* (command set).

FC-SW
FC-SW2   CONTEXT [Fibre Channel]
Acronym for *Fibre Channel Switched* (fabric interconnect).

FC-VI   CONTEXT [Fibre Channel]
Acronym for *Fibre Channel Virtual Interface*.

FCA   CONTEXT [Fibre Channel]
Acronym for *Fibre Channel Association*.

FCP   CONTEXT [Fibre Channel]
Acronym for *Fibre Channel Protocol*.

FCSI   CONTEXT [Fibre Channel]
Acronym for *Fibre Channel Systems Initiative*.

FDDI   CONTEXT [Network]
Acronym for *Fiber Distributed Data Interface*.

FDDI adapter   CONTEXT [Network]
An *adapter* that connects an intelligent device to an *FDDI* network. Both *FDDI-fiber* adapters that connect to optical fiber FDDI networks, and *FDDI-TP* adapters that connect to twisted

copper pair FDDI networks exist. Although network interface cards are usually referred to as NICs rather than as adapters, the term *FDDI adapter* is more common than FDDI NIC. *cf. adapter, NIC*

Federal Information Processing Standard   CONTEXT [Security]

Standards (and guidelines) produced by NIST for government-wide use in the specification and procurement of Federal computer systems.

Federated Management Architecture Specification   CONTEXT [Management] [Network]

A specification from Sun Microsystems Computer Corporation that defines a set of Java APIs for heterogeneous storage resource and storage network management. This specification is a central technology of *JIRO*.

Fibre   CONTEXT [Fibre Channel]

1. A general term used to cover all transmission media specified in *FC-PH*.
2. The *X3T11* standardization committee's preferred spelling of the name of *Fibre Channel* technology.

Fibre Channel   CONTEXT [Fibre Channel]

A set of standards for a serial I/O bus capable of transferring data between two *port*s at up to 100 MBytes/second, with standards proposals to go to higher speeds. Fibre Channel supports point to point, *arbitrated loop*, and switched topologies. Fibre Channel was completely developed through industry cooperation, unlike SCSI, which was developed by a vendor and submitted for standardization after the fact.

Fibre Channel Association   CONTEXT [Fibre Channel]

A former trade association incorporated 1993 to promote Fibre Channel technology in the market. Abbreviated FCA. Separate FCA Europe and FCA Japan organizations also exist. In 1999, FCA merged with *FCLC* to form the *FCIA*.

Fibre Channel Avionics Environment   CONTEXT [Fibre Channel]

A technical committee and industry group whose goal is to standardize Fibre Channel for avionics, defense, and other mobile applications.

Fibre Channel Arbitrated Loop   CONTEXT [Fibre Channel]

A form of Fibre Channel *network* in which up to 126 *node*s are connected in a loop topology, with each node's *L Port* transmitter connecting to the L_Port receiver of the node to its logical right. Nodes connected to a Fibre Channel Arbitrated Loop arbitrate for the single transmission that can occur on the loop at any instant using a Fibre Channel Arbitrated Loop protocol that is different from Fibre Channel switched and point to point protocols. An arbitrated loop may be private (no fabric connection) or public (attached to a fabric by an FL_Port).

Fibre Channel Community
Fibre Channel Loop Community

A former trade association incorporated 1995 to promote *Fibre Channel Arbitrated Loop* technology for storage applications. Abbreviated FCLC. Name changed to Fibre Channel Community in 1997 to reflect changing goals and interests of the organization. In 1999, FCLC merged with *FCA* to form the *FCIA*.

Fibre Channel Generic Services   CONTEXT [Fibre Channel]

An ANSI standard that specifies several Fibre Channel services such as the Name Server, Management Server, Time Server and others. Abbreviated FC-GS-2.

Fibre Channel Industry Association   CONTEXT [Fibre Channel]

The industry association resulting from the 1999 merger of the *Fibre Channel Association* and the *Fibre Channel Community*.

Fibre Channel Name   CONTEXT [Fibre Channel]

A *Name Identifier* that is unique in the context of Fibre Channel. Essentially unused; most Fibre Channel name identifiers are *World Wide Names* that are unique across heterogeneous networks.

Fibre Channel Protocol   CONTEXT [Fibre Channel]

The serial SCSI command protocol used on Fibre Channel networks. Abbreviated FCP. FCP standardization is the responsibility of the *X3T10* committee.

Fibre Channel Service Protocol   CONTEXT [Fibre Channel]

A *FC-4* protocol that defines all services independently of topology or fabric type.

Fibre Channel Single Byte (command set)   CONTEXT [Fibre Channel]

The industry standard command protocol for *ESCON* over Fibre Channel. Abbreviated FC-SB. A second version is known as FC-SB2.

Fibre Channel Switched (fabric interconnect)   CONTEXT [Fibre Channel]

The standard governing the form of Fibre Channel *network* in which *node*s are connected to a fabric topology implemented by one or more switches. Abbreviated FC-SW. Each FC-SW node's *N Port* connects to an *F Port* on a *switch*. Pairs of nodes connected to a FC-SW network can communicate concurrently. *cf. fabric, Fibre Channel Arbitrated Loop*

Fibre Channel Systems Initiative   CONTEXT [Fibre Channel]

An industry association sponsored by Hewlett-Packard, IBM and SUN with the goals of creating Fibre Channel profiles and promoting use of Fibre Channel for computer systems applications. Abbreviated FCSI. FCSI was formed in 1993, and dissolved in 1995.

Fibre Channel Virtual Interface   CONTEXT [Fibre Channel]

A proposed standard for application-level distributed interprocess communication based on Intel Corporation's V1.0 Virtual Interface (VI) Architecture; formerly known as VIA. Abbreviated FC-VI.

Fibre Connect   CONTEXT [Fibre Channel]

IBM Corporation's implementation of *ESCON* over Fibre Channel. Abbreviated FICON. Later standardized as *Fibre Channel Single Byte* Command Set.

Fibre Distributed Data Interface   CONTEXT [Network]

An ANSI standard for a *token ring* Metropolitan Area Networks (MANs), based on the use of optical fiber cable to transmit data at a rate of 100 Mbits/second. Both optical fiber and twisted copper pair variations of the FDDI physical standard exist. FDDI is a completely separate set of standards from Fibre Channel. The two are not directly interoperable.

FICON   CONTEXT [Fibre Channel]

Acronym for *Fibre Connect.*

field replaceable unit

A unit, or component of a system that is designed to be replaced "in the field;" i.e., without returning the system to a factory or repair depot. Field replaceable units may either be customer-replaceable, or their replacement may require trained service personnel. *cf. customer replaceable unit*

file   CONTEXT [File System]

An abstract data object made up of (a.) an ordered sequence of data bytes stored on a disk or tape, (b.) a symbolic name by which the object can be uniquely identified, and (c.) a set of properties, such as ownership and access permissions that allow the object to be managed by a *file system* or *backup manager.* Unlike the permanent address spaces of storage media, files may be created and deleted, and in most file systems, may expand or contract in size during their lifetimes.

file server   CONTEXT [File System]

A computer whose primary purpose is to serve files to clients. A file server may be a general purpose computer that is capable of hosting additional applications or a special purpose computer capable only of serving files. *cf. filer*

file system   CONTEXT [File System]

A software component that imposes structure on the address space of one or more physical or virtual disks so that applications may deal more conveniently with abstract named data objects of variable size (*files*). File systems are often supplied as operating system components, but are implemented and marketed as independent software comonents.

filer   CONTEXT [File System]

An intelligent network node whose hardware and software are designed to provide file services to client computers. Filers are pre-programmed by their vendors to provide file services, and are not normally user programmable. *cf. appliance, file server*

firmware

Low-level software for booting and operating an intelligent device. Firmware generally resides in read-only memory (ROM) on the device

fill byte
fill word   CONTEXT [Fibre Channel]

A *transmission word* that is an *idle* or an ARBx primitive signal. Fill words are transmitted between *frames, primitive signals,* and *primitive sequences* to keep a fibre channel network active.

FIPS   CONTEXT [Security]

Acronym for *Federal Information Processing Standard*

fixed block architecture

A model of disks in which storage space is organized as linear, dense address spaces of blocks of a fixed size. Abbreviated FBA. Fixed block architecture is the disk model on which *SCSI* is predicated. *cf. count-key-data.*

FL_Port   CONTEXT [Fibre Channel]

A *port* that is part of a Fibre Channel *fabric.* An FL_Port on a Fibre Channel fabric connects to an arbitrated loop. Nodes on the loop use *NL Port*s to connect to the loop. NL_Ports give nodes on a loop access to nodes on the fabric to which the loop's FL_Port is attached. *cf. E Port, F Port, G Port, L Port, N Port, NL Port*

FLOGI   CONTEXT [Fibre Channel]

Acronym for *fabric login.*

formatting   CONTEXT [Storage Device] [Storage System]

The preparation of a disk for use by writing required information on the media. Disk controllers format disks by writing block header and trailer information for every block on the disk. Host software components such as *volume managers* and *file systems* format disks by writing the initial structural information required for the volume or file system to be populated with data and managed.

frame   CONTEXT [Fibre Channel]
> An ordered vector of *words* that is the basic unit of data transmission in a Fibre Channel network. A Fibre Channel frame consists of a Start of Frame Word (SoF) (40 bits); a Frame Header (8 Words or 320 bits); data (0 to 524 Words or 0 to 2192 ten bit encoded bytes; a *CRC* (One Word or 40 bits); and an End of Frame (EoF) (40 bits). *cf. data frame*

frame content   CONTEXT [Fibre Channel]
> The information contained in a *frame* between its Start-of-Frame and End-of-Frame delimiters, excluding the delimiters.

FRU
> Acronym for field *Field Replaceable Unit.*

FSP   CONTEXT [Fibre Channel]
> Acronym for *Fibre Channel Service Protocol.*

full backup   CONTEXT [Backup]
> A *backup* in which all of a defined set of data objects are copied, regardless of whether they have been modified since the last backup. A full backup is the basis from which incremental backups are taken. *cf. cumulative incremental backup, differential incremental backup*

full duplex
> Concurrent transmission and reception of data on a single link.

full volume transfer rate
> The average rate at which a single disk transfers a large amount of data (e.g., more than one *cylinder*) in response to one I/O request. The full-volume data transfer rate accounts for any delays (e.g., due to inter-sector gaps, inter-track switching time and seeks between adjacent cylinders) that may occur during the course of a large data transfer. Full volume transfer rate may differ depending on whether data is being read or written. If this is true, it is appropriate to speak of full-volume read rate or full-volume write rate. Also known as *spiral data transfer rate.*

G_Port   CONTEXT [Fibre Channel]
> A port on a Fibre Channel switch that can function either as an F_Port or as an E_Port. The functionality of a G_Port is determined during port login. A G_Port functions as an F_Port when connected to a N_Port, and as an E_Port when connected to an E_Port. *cf. E Port, F Port, FL Port, L Port, N Port, NL Port*

GBE   CONTEXT [Network]
> Acronym for *Gigabit Ethernet.*

Gb
Gbit
gigabit
> 1. Shorthand for 1,000,000,000 (10^9) bits. Storage Networking Industry Association publications typically use the term Gbit to refer to 10^9 bits, rather than 1,073,741,824 (2^{30}) bits.
>
> 2. For Fibre Channel, 1,062,500,000 bits per second

GB
GByte
> Synonym for gigabyte. Shorthand for 1,000,000,000 (10^9) bytes. The Storage Networking Industry Association uses GByte to refer to 10^9 bytes, as is common in I/O-related applications rather than the 1,073,741,824 (2^{30}) convention sometimes used in describing computer system random access memory.

GBIC   CONTEXT [Fibre Channel]
Acronym for *gigabit interface converter*

geometry
The mathematical description of the layout of blocks on a disk. The primary aspects of a disk's geometry are the number of recording bands and the number of tracks and blocks per track in each, the number of data tracks per cylinder, and the number and layout of spare blocks reserved to compensate for media defects.

gigabaud link module   CONTEXT [Fibre Channel]
A transceiver that converts between electrical signals used by host bus adapters (and similar Fibre Channel devices) and either electrical or optical signals suitable for transmission. Abbreviated GLM. Gigabaud link modules allow designers to design one type of device and adapt it for either copper or optical applications. Gigabaud link modules are used less often than gigabit interface converters because they cannot be *hot swapped*. *cf. gigabit interface converter*

gigabit
Synonym for *Gbit*.

Gigabit Ethernet   CONTEXT [Network]
A group of *Ethernet* standards in which data is transmitted at 1Gbit per second. Gigabit Ethernet carries data at 1250 Mega*baud* using an adaptation of the Fibre Channel Physical Layer (*8b/10b encoding*); Abbreviated GBE. GBE standards are handled by IEEE 802.3z.

gigabit interface converter   CONTEXT [Fibre Channel]
A transceiver that converts between electrical signals used by host bus adapters (and similar Fibre Channel and Ethernet devices) and either electrical or optical signals suitable for transmission. Abbreviated GBIC. Gigabit interface converters allow designers to design one type of device and adapt it for either copper or optical applications. Unlike *gigabaud link modules* (GLMs), GBICs can be *hot swapped,* and are therefore gradually supplanting the former type of transceiver. *cf. gigabaud link module*

gigabyte
Synonym for *GByte*.

Gigabyte System Network
1. A common name for the HIPPI-6400 standard for 800 MByte per second links.
2. A network of devices that implement the HIPPI-6400 standard.

GLM   CONTEXT [Fibre Channel]
Acronym for *gigabaud link module.*

graphical user interface
A form of user interface to intelligent devices characterized by pictorial displays and highly structured, forms oriented input. Valued for perceived ease of use compared with *character cell interface.*

group
A collection of computer user identifiers used as a convenience in assigning resource access rights or operational privileges.

GSN
Acronym for *Gigabyte System Network.*

GUI

Acronym for *Graphical User Interface*.

hacker   CONTEXT [Security]

An unauthorized user who attempts to gain and/or succeeds in gaining access to an information system.

hard zone   CONTEXT [Fibre Channel]

A zone consisting of *zone members* which are permitted to communicate with one another via the *fabric*. Hard zones are enforced by fabric switches, which prohibit communication among members not in the same zone. Well-known addresses are implicitly included in every zone.

HBA

Acronym for *Host Bus Adapter*.

hierarchical storage management   CONTEXT [Backup]

The automated migration of data objects among storage devices, usually based on inactivity. Abbreviated HSM. Hierarchical storage management is based on the concept of a cost-performance storage hierarchy. By accepting lower access performance (higher access times), one can store objects less expensively. By automatically moving less frequently accessed objects to lower levels in the hierarchy, higher cost storage is freed for more active objects, and a better overall cost:performance ratio is achieved.

high availability

The ability of a system to perform its function continuously (without interruption) for a significantly longer period of time than the reliabilities of its individual components would suggest. High availability is most often achieved through *failure tolerance*. High availability is not an easily quantifiable term. Both the bounds of a system that is called highly available and the degree to which its availability is extraordinary must be clearly understood on a case-by-case basis.

High Performance Parallel Interface

An *ANSI* standard for an 800 Mbit/second I/O interface primarily used in supercomputer networks. Abbreviated *HIPPI*. The subsequent 6400 Mbit per second I/O interface standard, HIPPI-6400, is more commonly referred to as the *Gigabyte System Network* (GSN) standard.

high speed serial direct connect   CONTEXT [Fibre Channel]

A form factor that allows quick connect/disconnect for Fibre Channel copper interfaces.

HIPPI

Acronym for *High Performance Parallel Interface*.

host

A *host computer*.

host adapter

Synonym for *host bus adapter*.

host based array
host based disk array   CONTEXT [Storage System]

Synonym for *volume*. A disk array whose *control software* executes in one or more host computers rather than in a disk controller. The member disks of a host-based array may be part of different disk subsystems. *cf. controller based array, volume.*

host bus

Synonym for *host I/O bus*.

host bus adapter

An *I/O adapter* that connects a *host I/O bus* to a computer's memory system. Abbreviated HBA. Host bus adapter is the preferred term in SCSI contexts. *Adapter* and *NIC* are the preferred terms in Fibre Channel contexts. The term NIC is used in networking contexts such as *Ethernet* and *token ring*. *cf. adapter, host adapter, I/O adapter, network interface card, NIC.*

host cache CONTEXT [Storage]

A *cache* that resides within a host computer whose primary purpose is to improve disk or array I/O performance. Host cache may be associated with a file system or database, in which case, the data items stored in the cache are file or database entities. Alternatively, host cache may be associated with the device driver stack, in which case the cached data items are sequences of disk blocks. *cf. cache, controller cache, disk cache*

host computer

Any computer system to which disks, disk subsystems, or file servers are attached and accessible for data storage and I/O. Mainframes, servers, workstations and personal computers, as well as multiprocessors and clustered computer complexes, are all referred to as host computers in SNIA publications.

host environment

A storage subsystem's *host computer* or host computers, inclusive of operating system and other required software instance(s). The term host environment is used in preference to host computer to emphasize that multiple host computers are being discussed, or to emphasize the importance of the operating system or other software in the discussion.

host I/O bus CONTEXT [Storage System]

An *I/O bus* used to connect a host computer's host bus adapter to storage subsystems or storage devices. *cf. device I/O bus, I/O bus, channel*

hot backup CONTEXT [Backup]

Synonym for *online backup*. *cf. cold backup, offline backup*

hot disk

A disk whose capacity to execute I/O requests is saturated by the aggregate I/O load directed to it from one or more applications.

hot file

A frequently accessed file. Hot files are generally the root cause of *hot disk*s, although this is not always the case. A hot disk can also be caused by operating environment I/O, such as paging or swapping.

hot spare (disk)

A disk being used as a *hot standby* component.

hot standby (component, controller)

A redundant component in a failure tolerant storage subsystem that is powered and ready to operate, but which does not operate as long as a companion primary component is functioning. Hot standby components increase storage subsystem availability by allowing systems to continue to function when a component such as a controller fails. When the term hot standby is used to denote a disk, it specifically means a disk that is spinning and ready to be written to, for example, as the target of a *rebuilding* operation.

hot swap

The substitution of a replacement unit (*RU*) in a system for a defective unit, where the substitution can be performed while the system is performing its normal functioning normally. Hot swaps are physical operations typically performed by humans—*cf. automatic swap, cold swap, warm swap.*

hot swap adapter

An *adapter* that can be *hot swap*ped into or out of an intelligent device. Some adapters that are called hot swap adapters should more properly be termed *warm swap adapters*, because the function they perform is interrupted while the substitution occurs.

HSM   CONTEXT [Backup]

Acronym for *hierarchical storage management.*

HSSDC   CONTEXT [Fibre Channel]

Acronym for *High Speed Serial Direct Connect.*

HTML

Acronym for *HyperText Markup Language.*

HTTP

Acronym for *HyperText Transfer Protocol.*

hub

A communications infrastructure device to which nodes on a multi-point bus or loop are physically connected. Commonly used in Ethernet and Fibre Channel networks to improve the manageability of physical cables. Hubs maintain the logical loop topology of the network of which they are a part, while creating a "hub and spoke" physical star layout. Unlike *switches*, hubs do not aggregate bandwidth. Hubs typically support the addition or removal of nodes from the bus while it is operating.

hub port   CONTEXT [Fibre Channel]

A *port* on a Fibre Channel *hub* whose function is to pass data transmitted on the physical loop to the next port on the hub. Hub ports include loop healing port bypass functions. Some hubs have additional management functionality. There is no definition of a hub port in any Fibre Channel standard.

hunt group   CONTEXT [Fibre Channel]

A set of associated *N Ports* in a single node attached to the same fabric. A hunt group is assigned a special alias address identifier that enables a switch to route any frames containing the identifier to be routed to any available *N Port* in the group. *FC-PH* does not presently specify how a hunt group can be realized.

HyperText Markup Language

The set of tags or "markup" codes that describe how a document is displayed by a Web browser. Tags are delimited by the characters, "<" and ">". For example, the markup code "<p>" indicates that a new paragraph is beginning, while "</p>" indicates that the current paragraph is ending.

Hypertext Transfer Protocol

An application level protocol, usually run over TCP/IP, that enables the exchange of files via the World Wide Web.

ICMP

Acronym for *Internet Control Message Protocol.*

idempotency

A property of operations on data. An idempotent operation is one that has the same result no matter how many times it is performed on the same data. Writing a block of data to a disk is an idempotent operation, whereas writing a block of data to a tape is not, because writing a block of data twice to the same tape results in two adjacent copies of the block.

idle
idle word CONTEXT [Fibre Channel]

An ordered set of four *transmission characters* normally transmitted between *frame*s to indicate that a fibre channel network is idle.

IETF CONTEXT [Network] [Standards]
Acronym for *Internet Engineering Task Force.*

ignored (field) CONTEXT [Fibre Channel]
A field that is not interpreted by its receiver.

IKE CONTEXT [Network] [Security]
Acronym for *Internet Key Exchange*

implicit addressing CONTEXT [Storage Device]

A form of *addressing* usually used with tapes in which the data's address is inferred from the form of the the access request. Tape requests do not include an explicit block number, but instead specify the *next* or *previous* block from the current tape position, from which the block number must be inferred by device firmware. *cf. explicit addressing*

in-band (transmission) CONTEXT [Fibre Channel]

Transmission of a protocol other than the primary data protocol over the same medium as the primary data protocol. Management protocols are a common example of in-band transmission.

incremental backup CONTEXT [Backup]

A collective term for cumulative incremental backups and differential incremental backups. Any backup in which only data objects modified since the time of some previous backup are copied. *cf. cumulative incremental backup, differential incremental backup, full backup*

independent access array

A disk array whose data mapping is such that different member disks can execute multiple application I/O requests concurrently. *cf. parallel access array*

infinite buffer CONTEXT [Fibre Channel]

A term indicating that at the *FC-2* level, the amount of buffering available at the Sequence Recipient is assumed to be unlimited. Buffer overrun must be prevented by each ULP by choosing an appropriate amount of buffering per *sequence* based on its *maximum transfer unit* size.

information category CONTEXT [Fibre Channel]

A frame header field indicating the category to which the frame payload belongs (e.g., Solicited Data, Unsolicited Data, Solicited Control and Unsolicited Control).

information model

A repository-independent definition of entities (i.e., objects) and the relationships and interactions between these entities. For example, the *CIM* schemas are an example of an information model. An information model differs from a *data model* which is a repository-specific.

information technology

All aspects of information creation, access, use, storage, transport and management. The term information technology addresses all aspects of computer and storage systems, networks, users and software in an enterprise. Abbreviated IT.

information unit   CONTEXT [Fibre Channel]

> A related collection of data specified by *FC-4* to be transferred as a single *FC-2* sequence.

information system   CONTEXT [Security]

> The entire infrastructure, organization, personnel and components for the collection, processing, storage, transmission, display, dissemination and disposition of information.

inherent cost

> The cost of a system expressed in terms of the number and type of components it contains. The concept of inherent cost allows technology-based comparisons of disk subsystem alternatives by expressing cost in terms of number of disks, ports, modules, fans, power supplies, cabinets, etc. Because it is inexpensively reproducible, software is generally assumed to have negligible inherent cost.

initial relative offset   CONTEXT [Fibre Channel]

> The *relative offset* of the *block* or sub-block transmitted by the first *frame* in a sequence. The initial relative offset is specified by an *upper level protocol* and need not be zero.

initialization   CONTEXT [Fibre Channel]

> 1. The startup and initial configuration of a device, system, piece of software or network.
> 2. For *FC-1*, the period beginning with power on and continuing until the transmitter and receiver at that level become operational.

initiator

> The system component that originates an I/O command over an I/O bus or network. *I/O adapter*s, network interface cards, and intelligent controller device I/O bus control ASICs are typical initiators. *cf. LUN, originator, target, target ID*

inode   CONTEXT [File System]

> A *persistent* data structure in a UNIX or UNIX-like file system that describes the location of some or all of the disk blocks allocated to the file.

instantiation

> The creation of an instance of a class or object oriented abstraction.

intelligent controller   CONTEXT [Storage System]

> A storage controller that includes a processor or sequencer programmed to enable it to handle a substantial portion of I/O request processing autonomously.

intelligent device

> A computer, storage controller, *storage device*, or *appliance*.

Intelligent Peripheral Interface   CONTEXT [Network]

> A high-performance standards-based I/O interconnect. Abbreviated IPI.

intercabinet   CONTEXT [Fibre Channel]

> A specification for Fibre Channel copper cabling that allows up to 30m distance between two enclosures that contain devices with Fibre Channel ports.

interconnect

> A physical facility by which system elements are connected together and through which they can communicate with each other. *I/O bus*es, and *network*s are both interconnects.

interface connector   CONTEXT [Fibre Channel]

An optical or electrical connector which connects the *media* to the Fibre Channel transmitter or receiver. An interface connector consists of both a receptacle and a plug.

intermix   CONTEXT [Fibre Channel]

A Fibre Channel class of service that provides a full bandwidth dedicated *Class 1* connection, but allows connectionless *Class 2* and *Class 3* traffic to share the link during intervals when bandwidth is unused.

International Standards Organization   CONTEXT [Standards]

The international standards body. Abbreviated ISO. ISO-published standards have the status of international treaties.

Internet Control Message Protocol   CONTEXT [Network]

A control protocol strongly related to *IP* and *TCP*, and used to convey a variety of control and error indications.

Internet Engineering Task Force   CONTEXT [Network] [Security] [Standards]

A large open international community of network designers, operators, vendors, and researchers concerned with evolution and smooth operation of the Internet, and responsbile for producing *RFCs*. The standards body responsible for Internet standards, including *SNMP*, *TCP/IP* and policy for QoS. Abbreviated IETF. The IETF has a Web site at www.ietf.org.

Internet Key Exchange   CONTEXT [Network] [Security]

A protocol used to obtain authenticated keying material. Standardized by the Internet Engineering Task Force and described in RFC 2409.

Internet Protocol   CONTEXT [Network]

A protocol that provides connectionless best effort delivery of *datagrams* across heterogeneous physical networks. Abbreviated IP. *cf. TCP, UDP*

interrupt

A hardware or software signal that causes a computer to stop executing its instruction stream and switch to another stream. Software interrupts are triggered by application or other programs. Hardware interrupts are caused by external events, to notify software so it can deal with the events. The ticking of a clock, completion or reception of a transmission on an I/O bus or network, application attempts to execute invalid instructions or reference data for which they do not have access rights, and failure of some aspect of the computer hardware itself are all common causes of hardware interrupts.

interrupt switch

A human-activated switch present on some intelligent devices that is used to generate *interrupts*. Usually used for debugging purposes.

intracabinet   CONTEXT [Fibre Channel]

A Fibre Channel specification for copper cabling that allows up to 13m total cable length within a single enclosure that may contain multiple devices.

I/O

Acronym for input/output. The process of moving data between a computer system's main memory and an external device or interface such as a storage device, display, printer, or network connected to other computer systems. I/O is a collective term for *reading*, or moving data into a computer system's memory, and *writing*, or moving data from a computer system's memory to another location.

I/O adapter

1. An adapter that converts between the timing and protocol requirements of an intelligent device's memory bus and those of an I/O bus or network. In the context of storage subsystems, I/O adapters are contrasted with embedded *storage controllers*, which not only adapt between buses, but also perform transformations such as device fan-out, data caching, and RAID.

2. Synonym for *host bus adapter*.

I/O bus

Any path used to transfer data and control information between components of an I/O subsystem. An I/O bus consists of wiring (either cable or backplane), connectors, and all associated electrical drivers, receivers, transducers, and other required electronic components. I/O buses are typically optimized for the transfer of data, and tend to support more restricted configurations than *network*s. In this book, an I/O bus that connects a host computer's *host bus adapter* to intelligent storage controllers or devices is called a *host I/O bus*. An I/O bus that connects storage controllers or host I/O bus adapters to devices is called a *device I/O bus. cf. channel, device channel, device I/O bus, host I/O bus, network*

I/O bottleneck

Any resource in the I/O path (e.g., device driver, host bus adapter, I/O bus, intelligent controller, or disk) whose performance limits the performance of a storage subsystem as a whole.

I/O driver

A host computer software component (usually part of an operating system) whose function is to control the operation of peripheral controllers or adapters attached to the host computer. I/O drivers manage communication and data transfer between applications and I/O devices, using *host bus adapter*s as agents. In some cases, drivers participate in data transfer, although this is rare with disk and tape drivers, since most host bus adapters and controllers contain specialized hardware to perform data transfers.

I/O intensity

A characterization of applications. An I/O-intensive application is one whose performance depends strongly on the performance of the I/O subsystem that provides its I/O services. I/O intensive applications may be data transfer intensive or I/O request intensive.

I/O load

A sequence of I/O requests made to an I/O subsystem. The requests that comprise an I/O load include both user I/O and host overhead I/O, such as swapping, paging, and file system activity.

I/O load balancing

Synonym for *load balancing*.

I/O operation

A read, write, or control function performed to, from or within a computer system. For example I/O operations are requested by *control software* in order to satisfy application *I/O request*s made to virtual disks. *cf. I/O request*

I/O request

A request by an application to read or write a specified amount of data. In the context of real and virtual disks, I/O requests specify the transfer of a number of blocks of data between consecutive disk block addresses and contiguous memory locations. *cf. I/O operation*

I/O subsystem   CONTEXT [Storage System]

A collective term for the set of devices and software components that operate together to provide data transfer services. A *storage subsystem* is one type of I/O subsystem.

IP   CONTEXT [Network]
Acronym for *Internet Protocol.*

IPI
Acronym for *Intelligent Peripheral Interface.*

IPsec   CONTEXT [Network] [Security]
Acronym for *IP Security*

IP Security   CONTEXT [Network] [Security]
A suite of cryptographic algorithms, protocols and procedures used to provide communication security for IP-based communications. Standardized by the Internet Engineering Task Force.

ISO   CONTEXT [Standards]
Acronym for *International Standards Organization.*

IT
Acronym for *Information Technology.*

Java
An object oriented computer programming language that is similar to but simpler than C++. Java was created by Sun Microsystems Computer Corporation.

JBOD   CONTEXT [Storage Device] [Storage System]
Acronym for "Just a Bunch Of Disks." Originally used to mean a collection of disks without the coordinated control provided by *control software;* today the term JBOD most often refers to a cabinet of disks whether or not RAID functionality is present. *cf. disk array*

Jini
An architecture and supporting services for publishing and discovering devices and services on a network. Jini was created by Sun Microsystems Computer Corporation.

Jiro
A Sun Microsystems Computer Corporation initiative, developed using the Java Community Process. Jiro's goal is to enable the management of heterogeneous storage networks. The core technology in Jiro is defined in the *Federated Management Architecture Specification.*

jitter   CONTEXT [Fibre Channel]
Deviation in timing that a bit stream encounters as it traverses a physical medium.

K28.5   CONTEXT [Fibre Channel]
A special 10-bit character used to indicate the beginning of a Fibre Channel command.

KB
KByte
Synonyms for *kilobyte.*

key   CONTEXT [Security]
Usually a sequence of random or pseudorandom bits used to direct cryptographic operations and/or for producing other keys. The same plaintext encrypted with different keys yields different ciphertexts, each of which requires a different key for decryption. In a *symmetric cryptosystem* the encryption and decryption keys are the same. In an *asymmetric cryptosystem* the encryption and decryption keys are different.

key exchange   CONTEXT [Security]

A cryptographic protocol and procedure in which two communicating entities determine a shared key in a fashion such that a third party who reads all of their communication cannot effectively determine the value of the key. A common approach to key exchange requires such a third party to compute a discrete logarithm over a large field in order to determine the key value and relies on the computational intractability of the discrete logarithm problem for suitably selected large fields for its security.

key management   CONTEXT [Security]

The supervision and control of the process by which keys are generated, stored, protected, transferred, loaded, used, revoked and destroyed.

key pair   CONTEXT [Security]

A *public key* and its corresponding *private key* as used in public key cryptography (i.e., asymmetric cryptosystem).

keying material   CONTEXT [Security]

A key or authentication information in physical or magnetic form.

kilobyte

1. 1,000 (10^3) bytes of data. (Common storage industry usage).
2. 1,024 (2^10) bytes of data. (Common usage in software contexts).

Which is meant is typically clear from the context in which the term is used.

L_Port   CONTEXT [Fibre Channel]

A *port* used to connect a *node* to a Fibre Channel *arbitrated loop*. *cf. E Port, F Port, FL Port, G Port, N Port, NL Port*

label   CONTEXT [Backup]

An identifier associated with a removable media or cartridge. Labels may be humanly readable, machine readable, or both. *cf. external volume serial number, media ID*

LAN   CONTEXT [Network]

Acronym for *Local Area Network*.

LANE   CONTEXT [Network]

Acronym for *Local Area Network Emulation*.

LAN-free backup

A disk backup methodology in which a SAN appliance performs the actual backup I/O operations, thus freeing the LAN server to perform I/O operations on behalf of LAN clients. Differentiated from *serverless backup* by the requirement of an additional SAN appliance to perform the backup I/O operations.

large read request
large write request
large I/O request

An I/O request that specifies the transfer of a large amount of data. 'Large' obviously depends on the context, but typically refers to requests for 64 KBytes or more of *cf. small I/O request*

latency

1. Synonym for I/O request execution time, the time between the making of an I/O request and completion of the request's execution.
2. Short for rotational latency, the time between the completion of a seek and the instant of arrival of the first block of data to be transferred at the disk's read/write head.

latent fault

A failure of a system component that has not been recognized because the failed aspect of the component has not been exercised since the occurrence of the failure. A field-developed media defect on a disk surface is a latent fault until an attempt is made to read the data in a block that spans the defect.

LBA

Acronym for *logical block address.*

LDAP

Acronym for *Lightweight Directory Access Protocol.*

LDM

Acronym for *Logical Disk Manager.*

LED

Acronym for *Light Emitting Diode.*

library   CONTEXT [Backup]

A robotic media handler capable of storing multiple pieces of removable media and loading and unloading them from one or more drives in arbitrary order.

light emitting diode

A multimode light source based on inexpensive optical diodes. Abbreviated LED. Available in a variety of wavelengths; 1300 nanometer wavelength is typical for data communications. The practical transfer rate limit for LEDs is 266 Mbps.

Lightweight Directory Access Protocol

An IETF protocol for creating, accessing and removing objects and data from a directory. It provides the ability to search, compare, add, delete and modify directory objects, as well as modifying the names of these objects. It also supports *bind, unbind* and *abandon* (cancel) operations for a session. LDAP got its name from its goal of being a simpler form of DAP (Directory Access Protocol), from the X.500 set of standards.

link   CONTEXT [General] [Fibre Channel]

1. A physical connection (electrical or optical) between two nodes of a network.
2. [Fibre Channel] Two unidirectional fibres transmitting in opposite directions and their associated transmitters and receivers.
3. [Fibre Channel] The full-duplex *FC-0* level association between *FC-1* entities in directly attached *port*s.
4. [Fibre Channel] The point to point physical connection from one element of a Fibre Channel fabric to the next

LIP   CONTEXT [Fibre Channel]

Acronym for *loop initialization primitive.*

LISM   CONTEXT [Fibre Channel]
Acronym for loop initialization select master.

load balancing
The adjustment of system and/or application components and data so that application I/O or computational demands are spread as evenly as possible across a system's physical resources. I/O load balancing may be done manually (by a human) or automatically (by some means that does not require human intervention). *cf. I/O load optimization, load sharing*

load optimization
The manipulation of an I/O load in such a way that performance is optimal by some objective metric. Load optimization may be achieved by *load balancing* across several components, or by other means, such as request reordering or interleaved execution. *cf. load balancing, load sharing*

load sharing
The division of an I/O load or task among several storage subsystem components, without any attempt to equalize each component's share of the work. Each affected component bears a percentage of a shared load. When a storage subsystem is load sharing, it is possible for some of the sharing components to be operating at full capacity, to the point of actually limiting performance, while others are underutilized. *cf. I/O load balancing, load optimization*

local area network   CONTEXT [Network]
A communications infrastructure designed to use dedicated wiring over a limited distance (typically a diameter of less than five kilometers) to connect a large number of intercommunicating nodes. *Ethernet* and *token ring* are the two most popular LAN technologies. *cf. wide area network*

local area network emulation
A collection of protocols and services that combine to create an emulated *local area network* using *ATM* as the underlying network. Abbreviated LANE. Local area network emulation enables intelligent devices with ATM connections to communicate with remote LAN-connected devices as if they were directly connected to the LAN.

local F_Port   CONTEXT [Fibre Channel]
The *F Port* to which a particular *N Port* is directly attached by a *link*.

logical block   CONTEXT [Storage Device] [Storage System]
A block of data stored on a disk or tape, and associated with an *address* for purposes of retrieval or overwriting. The term logical block is typically used to refer to the host's view of data addressing on a physical device. Within a storage device, there is often a further conversion between the logical blocks presented to hosts and the physical media locations at which the corresponding data is stored. *cf. physical block, virtual block*

logical block address   CONTEXT [Storage Device] [Storage System]
The *address* of a logical block. Logical block addresses are typically used in hosts' I/O commands. The SCSI disk command protocol, for example, uses logical block addresses.

logical disk   CONTEXT [Storage System]
A set of consecutively addressed FBA disk blocks that is part of a single virtual disk to physical disk mapping. Logical disks are used in some array implementations as constituents of logical volumes or *partitions*. Logical disks are normally not visible to the host environment, except during array configuration operations. *cf. extent, virtual disk*

logical disk manager   CONTEXT [Windows]
A name for the volume management *control software* in the Windows NT operating system.

logical unit   CONTEXT [SCSI]
The entity within a SCSI target that executes I/O commands. SCSI I/O commands are sent to a target and executed by a logical unit within that target. A SCSI physical disk typically has a single logical unit. Tape drives and array controllers may incorporate multiple logical units to which I/O commands can be addressed. Each logical unit exported by an array controller corresponds to a virtual disk. *cf. LUN, target, target ID*

logical unit number   CONTEXT [SCSI]
The SCSI identifier of a logical unit within a *target*.

logical volume   CONTEXT [Storage System]
A virtual disk made up of *logical disk*s. Also called a *virtual disk*, or *volume set*.

login server   CONTEXT [Fibre Channel]
An intelligent entity within a Fibre Channel fabric that receives and executes fabric login requests.

long wavelength laser   CONTEXT [Fibre Channel]
A laser with a wavelength 1300 nm or longer; usually 1300 or 1550 nanometers; widely used in the telecommunications industry.

Loop Initialization   CONTEXT [Fibre Channel]
The protocol by which a *Fibre Channel Arbitrated Loop* network initializes upon power up or recovers after a failure or other unexpected condition. Usually abbreviated LIP. During a LIP, the nodes present on the arbitrated loop identify themselves and acquire addresses on the loop for communication. No data can be transferred on an arbitrated loop until a LIP is complete.

loop initialization primitive   CONTEXT [Fibre Channel]
A Fiber Channel primitive used to (1.) initiate a procedure that results in unique addressing for all nodes, (2.) indicate a loop failure, or (3.) reset a specific node.

loop initialization select master   CONTEXT [Fibre Channel]
The process by which a temporary Fibre Channel arbitrated loop master is determined during *loop initialization*. Abbreviated LISM.

loopback   CONTEXT [Fibre Channel]
An *FC-1* operational mode in which information passed to the FC-1 transmitter is shunted directly to the FC-1 receiver. When a Fibre Channel interface is in loopback mode, the loopback signal overrides any external signal detected by the receiver.

loop port state machine   CONTEXT [Fibre Channel]
Logic that monitors and performs the tasks required for initialization and access to a Fibre Channel arbitrated loop.

LWL   CONTEXT [Fibre Channel]
Acronym for *Long Wavelength Laser*.

LUN   CONTEXT [SCSI]
Acronym for *Logical Unit Number*.

MAC   CONTEXT [Network]
Acronym for *Media Access Control*.

magnetic remanence   CONTEXT [Security]

A magnetic representation of residual information remaining on a magnetic medium after the medium has been *degaussed.*

MAN

Acronym for *Metropolitan Area Network.*

Managed Object Format   CONTEXT [Management]

The syntax and formal description of the objects and associations in the *CIM* schemas. Abbreviated as MOF. MOF can also be translated to *XML* using a *Document Type Definition* published by the *DMTF.*

Management Information Base   CONTEXT [Management]

A specification that defines a set of management variables for a network *node* that can be read (and possibly written) using the *SNMP* protocol. Abbreviated MIB.

The specification and formal description of a set of objects and variables that can be read and possibly written using the *SNMP* protocol. Abbreviated MIB. Various standard MIBs are defined by the *IETF.*

mandatory (provision)   CONTEXT [Standards]

A provision in a standard which must be supported in order for an implementation of the standard to be compliant.

mapping   CONTEXT [Storage System]

Conversion between two data addressing spaces. For example, mapping refers to the conversion between physical disk block addresses and the block addresses of the virtual disks presented to operating environments by *control software.*

mapping boundary   CONTEXT [Storage System]

A virtual disk block address of some significance to a disk array's mapping algorithms. The first and last blocks of a user data space strip or check data strip are mapping boundaries.

maximum transfer unit   CONTEXT [Network]

The largest amount of data that is permissible to transmit as one unit according to a protocol specification. Abbreviated MTU. The Ethernet MTU is 1536 eight bit bytes. The Fibre Channel MTU is 2112 eight bit bytes.

MB
MByte

Shorthand for *megabyte.*

Mb
Mbit

Shorthand for *megabit.*

MBps

Acronym for megabytes per second. A measure of *bandwidth* or data transfer rate.

Mbps

Acronym for megabits per second. A measure of *bandwidth* or data transfer rate.

MD5   CONTEXT [Security]

A specific *message-digest algorithm* producing a 128-bit *digest* which is used as authentication data by an authentication service.

mean time between failures
> The average time from start of use to first failure in a large population of identical systems, components, or devices. Abbreviated MTBF.

mean time to (loss of) data availability
> The average time from startup until a component failure causes a loss of timely user data access in a large population of storage devices. Loss of availability does not necessarily imply loss of data; for some classes of failures (e.g., failure of non-redundant intelligent storage controllers), data remains intact, and can again be accessed after the failed component is replaced.

mean time to data loss
> The average time from startup until a component failure causes a permanent loss of user data in a large population of storage devices. Mean time to data loss is similar to MTBF for disks and tapes, but is likely to differ in RAID arrays, where redundancy can protect against data loss due to component failures.

mean time to repair
> The average time between a failure and completion of repair in a large population of identical systems, components, or devices. Mean time to repair comprises all elements of repair time, from the occurrence of the failure to restoration of complete functionality of the failed component. This includes time to notice and respond to the failure, time to repair or replace the failed component, and time to make the replaced component fully operational. In mirrored and RAID arrays, for example, the mean time to repair a disk failure includes the time required to reconstruct user data and check data from the failed disk on the replacement disk. Abbreviated MTTR.

meaningful (control field)   CONTEXT [Standards]
> In a standard, a control field or bit that must be correctly interpreted by a receiver. Control fields are either meaningful or "not meaningful", in which case they must be ignored.

media

> 1. The material in a storage device on which data is recorded.
>
> 2. A physical link on which data is transmitted between two points.

media access control   CONTEXT [Network]
> Algorithms that control access to physical media, especially in shared media networks.

media ID   CONTEXT [Backup]
> An machine readable identifier written on a piece of removable media that remains constant throughout the media's life. *cf. external volume serial number, label*

media manager   CONTEXT [Backup]
> A backup software component responsible for tracking the location, contents, and state of removable storage media.

media robot   CONTEXT [Backup]
> Synonym for *robotic media handler*.

media stacker   CONTEXT [Backup]
> A *robotic media handler* in which media must be moved sequentially by the robot. Usually services a single drive. A stacker may be able to load media into a drive in arbitrary order, but must cycle through media in sequence to do so.

megabaud

> One million *baud* (elements of transmitted information) per second, including data, signalling, overhead.

megabit

> 1,000,000 (10^6) bits. The SNIA uses the 10^6 convention commonly found in data transfer-related literature rather than the 1,048,576 (2^20) convention common in computer system random access memory and software literature.

megabyte

> 1,000,000 (10^6) bytes. The SNIA uses the 10^6 convention commonly found in storage and data transfer-related literature rather than the 1,048,576 (2^20) convention common in computer system random access memory and software literature.

megatransfer   CONTEXT [SCSI]

> The transfer of one million data units per second. Used to describe the characteristics of parallel I/O buses like SCSI, for which the data transfer rate depends upon the amount of data transferred in each data cycle. *cf. SCSI, fast SCSI, Ultra SCSI, Ultra2 SCSI, wide SCSI*

member
member disk   CONTEXT [Storage System]

> A disk that is in use as a member of a disk array.

message-digest algorithm   CONTEXT [Security]

> An algorithm which produces a *secure hash*

metadata   CONTEXT [File System] [Storage System]

> Data that describes data. In disk arrays, metadata consists of items such as array membership, member extent sizes and locations, descriptions of logical disks and partitions, and array state information. In file systems, metadata includes file names, file properties and security information, and lists of block addresses at which each file's data is stored.

metropolitan area network   CONTEXT [Network]

> A network that connects nodes distributed over a metropolitan (city-wide) area as opposed to a local area (campus) or wide area (national or global). Abbreviated MAN. From a storage perspective, MANs are of interest because there are MANs over which block storage protocols (e.g., ESCON, Fibre Channel) can be carried natively, whereas most WANs that extend beyond a single metropolitan area do not currently support such protocols.

MIB   CONTEXT [Management]

> Acronym for *Management Information Base.*

MIME   CONTEXT [Network]

> Acronym for *Multipurpose Internet Mail Extensions.*

mirroring   CONTEXT [Storage System]

> A form of storage array in which two or more identical copies of data are maintained on separate media. Also known as *RAID Level 1*, disk shadowing, real-time copy, and t1 copy.

mirrors
mirrored disks   CONTEXT [Storage System]

> The disks of a *mirrored array.*

mirrored array   CONTEXT [Storage System]

> Common term for a disk array that implements RAID Level 1, or *mirroring* to protecting data against loss due to disk or device I/O bus failure.

MLS   CONTEXT [Security]

> Acronym for *multilevel security*

modeling language

> A language for describing the concepts of an *information* or *data model*. One of the most popular modeling languages in use today is UML (*Unified Modeling Language*). The essence of modeling languages is that they be capable of conveying the model concepts.

MOF   CONTEXT [Management]

> Acronym for *Managed Object Format*.

monitor (program)

> A program that executes in an *operating environment* and keeps track of system resource utilization. Monitors typically record CPU utilization, I/O request rates, data transfer rates, RAM utilization, and similar statistics. A monitor program, which may be an integral part of an operating system, a separate software product, or a part of a related component, such as a database management system, is a necessary prerequisite to manual I/O load balancing.

mount

> In the *Network File System* (NFS), a protocol and set of procedures to specify a remote host and file system or directory to be accessed. Also specified is the location of the accessed directories in the local file hierarchy.

MTBF

> Acronym for *Mean Time Between Failures*.

MTDA

> Acronym for *Mean Time until (Loss of) Data Availability*.

MTDL

> Acronym for *Mean Time to Data Loss*.

MTTR

> Acronym for *Mean Time To Repair*.

MTU   CONTEXT [Network]

> Acronym for *Maximum Transfer Unit*.

multicast   CONTEXT [Fibre Channel] [Network]

> The simultaneous transmission of a message to a subset of more than one of the ports connected to a communication facility. In a Fibre Channel context, multi-cast specifically refers to the sending of a message to multiple *N Ports* connected to a *fabric*.

multicast group   CONTEXT [Fibre Channel] [Network]

> A set of ports associated with an address or identifier that serves as the destination for multicast *packets* or *frames* that are to be delivered to all ports in the set.

multi-level disk array   CONTEXT [Storage System]

> A disk array with two levels of data mapping. The virtual disks created by one mapping level become the members of the second level. The most frequently encountered multi-level disk

arrays use mirroring at the first level, and stripe data across the resulting mirrored arrays at the second level.

multilevel security   CONTEXT [Security]

Allows users and resources of different sensitivity levels to access a system concurrently, while ensuring that only information for which the user or resource has *authorization* is made available. Requires a formal computer security policy model which assigns specific access characteristics to both *subjects* and *objects*.

multimode (fiber optic cable)   CONTEXT [Fibre Channel] [Network]

A fiber optic cabling specification that allows up to 500 meter distances between devices.

multi-threaded

Having multiple concurrent or pseudo-concurrent execution sequences. Used to describe processes in computer systems. Multi-threaded processes are one means by which I/O request-intensive applications can make maximum use of disk arrays to increase I/O performance.

multi-path I/O   CONTEXT [Storage System]

The facility for a host to direct I/O requests to a *storage device* on more than one *access path*. Multi-path I/O requires that devices be uniquely identifiable by some means other than by bus address.

Multipurpose Internet Mail Extensions   CONTEXT [Network]

A specification that defines the mechanisms for specifying and describing the format of Internet message bodies. An HTTP response containing a MIME Content-Type header allows the HTTP client to invoke the appropriate application for processing the received data.

N_Port   CONTEXT [Fibre Channel]

A *port* that connects a *node* to a *fabric* or to another node. Nodes' N_Ports connect to fabrics' F_Ports or to other nodes' N_Ports. N_Ports handle creation, detection, and flow of message units to and from the connected systems. N_Ports are end points in point to point links. *cf. E Port, F Port, FL Port, G Port, L Port, NL Port*

N_Port Name   CONTEXT [Fibre Channel]

A *Name Identifier* associated with an *N Port*.

NAA   CONTEXT [Network] [Standards]

Acronym for *Network Address Authority*.

Name_Identifier   CONTEXT [Fibre Channel]

A 64 bit identifier, consisting of a 60 bit value concatenated with a 4 bit Network_Address_Authority_Identifier. Name_Identifiers identify Fibre Channel entities such as *N Port, node, F Port,* or *fabric*.

name server   CONTEXT [Fibre Channel] [Network]

An intelligent entity in a network that translates between symbolic node names and network addresses. In a Fibre Channel network, a name server translates between *world wide name*s and fabric addresses.

naming

The mapping of address space to a set of objects. Naming is typically used either for human convenience (e.g., symbolic names attached to files or storage devices), or to establish a level of independence between two system components (e.g., identification of files by inode names or identification of computers by IP addresses).

namespace   CONTEXT [File System] [Management]

1. The set of valid names recognized by a file system. One of the four basic functions of file systems is maintenance of a namespace so that invalid and duplicate names do not occur.

2. In *XML*, a document at a specific Web address (URL) that lists the names of data elements and attributes that are used in other XML files.

3. In *CIM* and *WBEM*, a collection of object definitions and instances that are logically consistent.

NAS   CONTEXT [Network] [Storage System]
Acronym for *network attached storage*.

National Committee Information Technology Standards   CONTEXT [Standards]
A committee of *ANSI* that serves as the governing body of *X3T11* and other standards organizations.

National Institute of Standards and Technology   CONTEXT [Security]
A non-regulatory federal agency within the U.S. Commerce Department's Technology Administration. NIST's mission is to develop and promote measurement, standards, and technology to enhance productivity, facilitate trade, and improve the quality of life. Specifically, the Computer Security Division within NIST's Information Technology Laboratory managed the Advanced Encryption Standard (AES) program.

NCITS   CONTEXT [Standards]
Acronym for *National Committee Information Technology Standards*.

NDMP   CONTEXT [Management] [Network]
Acronym for *Network Data Management Protocol*.

network   CONTEXT [Network]
An *interconnect* that enables communication among a collection of attached *node*s. A network consists of optical or electrical transmission media, infrastructure in the form of *hub*s and/or *switch*es, and *protocol*s that make message sequences meaningful. In comparison to *I/O buses*, networks are typically characterized by large numbers of nodes that act as peers, large inter-node separation, and flexible configurability. *cf. channel, I/O bus, local area network, storage area network*

network adapter   CONTEXT [Network]
An *adapter* that connects an intelligent device to a network. Usually called a network interface card, or Ethernet NIC. *cf. Ethernet adapter, NIC*

Network Address Authority (identifier)   CONTEXT [Fibre Channel]
A four bit identifier defined in *FC-PH* to denote a *network address authority* (i.e., an organization such as *CCITT* or *IEEE* that administers network addresses).

network attached storage   CONTEXT [Network] [Storage System]

1. A term used to refer to *storage elements* that connect to a network and provide file access services to computer systems. Abbreviated NAS. A NAS Storage Element consists of an engine, which implements the file services, and one or more devices, on which data is stored. NAS elements may be attached to any type of network. When attached to *SAN*s, NAS elements may be considered to be members of the SAS class of storage elements.

2. A class of systems that provide file services to host computers. A host system that uses network attached storage uses a *file system device driver* to access data using file access protocols such as *NFS* or *CIFS*. *NAS* systems interpret these commands and perform the internal file and device I/O operations necessary to execute them. *cf. storage area network*

Network Data Management Protocol   CONTEXT [Backup]

A communications protocol that allows intelligent devices on which data is stored, robotic library devices, and backup applications to intercommunicate for the purpose of performing backups. Abbreviated NDMP.

An open standard protocol for network-based backup of *NAS* devices. Abbreviated NDMP. NDMP allows a network backup application to control the retrieval of data from, and backup of, a server without third-party software. The control and data transfer components of backup and restore are separated. NDMP is intended to support tape drives, but can be extended to address other devices and media in the future. The Network Data Management Task Force has a Web site at http://www.ndmp.org.

Network File System (protocol)   CONTEXT [File System]

A distributed *file system* and its associated network protocol originally developed by Sun Microsystem Computer Corporation and commonly implemented in UNIX systems, although most other computer systems have implemented NFS clients and/or servers. Abbreviated NFS. The *IETF* is responsible for the NFS standard.

network interface card   CONTEXT [Network]

An *I/O adapter* that connects a computer or other type of node to a network. Abbreviated NIC. A NIC is usually a circuit module; however, the term is sometimes used to denote an ASIC or set of ASICs on a computer *system board* that perform the network I/O adapter function. The term NIC is universally used in Ethernet and *token ring* contexts. In Fibre Channel contexts, the terms adapter and NIC are used in preference to host bus adapter. *cf. adapter, host bus adapter, I/O adapter*

NFS   CONTEXT [File System] [Storage System]
Acronym for *Network File System.*

NIC   CONTEXT [Network]
Acronym for *Network Interface Card.*

NIST   CONTEXT [Security]
Acronym for *National Institute of Standards and Technology*

NL_Port   CONTEXT [Fibre Channel]

A *port* specific to *Fibre Channel Arbitrated Loop.* An NL_Port has the same functional, logical, and message handling capability as an *N Port*, but connects to an arbitrated loop rather than to a fabric. Some implementations can function either as N_Ports or as NL_Ports depending on the network to which they are connected. An NL_Port must replicate frames and pass them on when in passive loop mode. *cf. E Port, F Port, FL Port, G Port, N Port*

node   CONTEXT [Network] [Storage System]

An addressable entity connected to an I/O bus or network. Used primarily to refer to computers, storage devices, and storage subsystems. The component of a node that connects to the bus or network is a *port.*

node name

A *Name Identifier* associated with a *node.*

normal operation
normal mode

A state of a system in which the system is functioning within its prescribed operational bounds. For example, when a disk array subsystem is operating in normal mode, all disks are up, no extraordinary actions (e.g., reconstruction) are being performed, and environmental conditions are within operational range. Sometimes called optimal mode.

non-linear mapping   CONTEXT [Storage System]

Any form of *tabular mapping* in which there is not a fixed size correspondence between the two mapped address spaces. Non-linear mapping is required in disk arrays that compress data, since the space required to store a given range of virtual blocks depends on the degree to which the contents of those blocks can be compressed, and therefore changes as block contents change. *cf. algorithmic mapping, dynamic mapping, tabular mapping*

non-OFC (laser)   CONTEXT [Fibre Channel]

A laser transceiver whose lower-intensity output does not require special OFC mechanisms.

non-repeating ordered set   CONTEXT [Fibre Channel]

An *ordered set* passed by *FC-2* to *FC-1* for transmission which has non-idempotent semantics, i.e., it cannot be retransmitted.

nonrepudiation   CONTEXT [Security]

Assurance that a *subject* cannot later deny having performed some action. For communication, this may involve providing the sender of data with proof of delivery and the recipient with proof of the sender's identity, so neither can later deny having participated in the communication. *Digital signatures* are often used as a non-repudiation mechanism for stored information in combination with timestamps.

non-transparent failover

A *failover* from one component of a redundant system to another that is visible to the external environment. For example, a controller failover in a redundant disk subsystem is non-transparent if the surviving controller exports the other's virtual disks at different host I/O bus addresses or on a different host I/O bus. *cf. transparent failover*

Non-Uniform Memory Architecture

A computer architecture that enables memory to be shared by multiple processors, with different processors having different access speeds to different parts of the memory. Abbreviated NUMA.

non-volatile random access memory

Computer system random access memory that has been made impervious to data loss due to power failure through the use of *UPS*, batteries, or implementation technology such as *flash memory*. Abbreviated NVRAM.

non-volatility

A property of data. Non-volatility refers to the property that data will be preserved, even if certain environmental conditions are not met. Used to describe data stored on disks or tapes. If electrical power to these devices is cut, data stored on them is nonetheless preserved.

not operational (receiver or transmitter)   CONTEXT [Fibre Channel]

A receiver or transmitter that is not capable of receiving or transmitting an encoded bit stream based on rules defined by *FC-PH* for error control. For example, *FC-1* is not operational during initialization.

NUMA

Acronym for *Non-Uniform Memory Architecture*.

NVRAM

Acronym for *Non-Volatile Random Access Memory*.

NVRAM cache

A quantity of *NVRAM* used as a cache. NVRAM cache is particularly useful in RAID array subsystems, *filer*s, database servers, and other intelligent devices that must keep track of the state of multi-step I/O operations even if power fails during the execution of the steps.

NVRAM card

A printed circuit module containing *NVRAM*.

object   CONTEXT [Security]

In the context of access control, an entity to which access is controlled and/or usage of which is restricted to authorized subjects. Information system resources are often examples of objects.

object oriented (methodology)

A methodology for decomposing an entity or problem by its key abstractions, versus by its procedures or steps. The key abstractions become classes in an *information* or *data model*, and embody well-defined behaviors called *methods*, with a unique set of data attributes. Instances of a class are called objects. Abbreviated OO.

OC-n   CONTEXT [Network]

A data rate that is a multiple of the fundamental *SONET* rate of 51.84 Mbits/sec. OC-3 (155 Mbits/sec), OC-12 (622 Mbits/sec), OC-48 (2488 Mbits/sec), and OC-192 (9953 Mbits/sec) are currently in common use. *cf. Asynchronous Transfer Method*

OFC   CONTEXT [Fibre Channel]

Acronym for *Open Fibre Control*.

offline backup   CONTEXT [Backup]

A *backup* created while the source data is not in use. Off-line backups provide internally consistent *Dictionary C.html - Term checkpoint* images of source data. *cf. online backup*

online backup   CONTEXT [Backup]

A *backup* created while the source data is in use by applications. If source data is being modified by applications during an online backup, the backup is not guaranteed to be an internally consistent image of application data as of some point in time *Dictionary C.html - Term checkpoint*. *Snapshot*s of on-line data initiated while applications are in a quiescent state are sometimes used as backup source data to overcome this limitation. *cf. offline backup*

OO

Acronym for *object oriented*.

open   CONTEXT [General] [Fibre Channel]

1. [General] Any system or aspect of a system whose function is governed by a readily accessible standard rather than by a privately owned specification.
2. [Fibre Channel] A period of time that begins when a *sequence* or *exchange* is initiated and ends when the sequence or exchange is normally or abnormally terminated.
3. [General] Not electrically terminated, as an unplugged cable.

open fibre control

A safety interlock system that limits the optical power level on an open optical fibre cable.

Open Group, the

A cross-industry consortium for open systems standards and their certification. Unix, management and security standards are developed within the Open Group. The Open Group's Web site is at www.opengroup.org.

open interconnect

Synonym for *standard interconnect*.

operating environment

A collective term for the hardware architecture and operating system of a computer system.

operation   CONTEXT [Fibre Channel]

An *FC-2* construct that encapsulates one or more possibly concurrent *exchanges* into a single abstraction for higher level protocols.

Operation_Associator   CONTEXT [Fibre Channel]

A value used in the Association_Header to identify a specific operation within a node and correlate communicating processes related to that operation. The Operation_Associator is a handle by which an operation within a given node is referred to by another communicating Node. Operation_Associator is a generic reference to Originator Operation_Associator and Responder Operation_Associator.

operational (state)   CONTEXT [Fibre Channel]

The state of a receiver or transmitter that is capable of receiving or transmitting an encoded bit stream based on the rules defined by *FC-PH* for error control. Those receivers capable of accepting signals from transmitters requiring laser safety procedures are not considered operational after power on until a signal of a duration longer than that associated with laser safety procedures is present at the fibre attached to the receiver.

optical fall time

The time interval required for the falling edge of an optical pulse to transition between specified percentages of the signal amplitude. For lasers the transitions are measured between the 80% and 20% points. For LED media the specification points are 90% and 10%.

optional (characteristic)   CONTEXT [Standards]

Characteristics of a standard that are specified by the standard but not required for compliance. If an optional characteristic of a standard is implemented, it must be implemented as defined in the standard.

ordered set   CONTEXT [Fibre Channel]

A *transmission word* (sequence of four 10-bit code bytes) with a *special character* in its first (leftmost) position and data characters in the remaining three positions. An ordered set is represented by the combination of special codes and data bytes which, when encoded, result in the generation of the transmission characters specified for the ordered set. Ordered sets are used for low-level Fibre Channel link functions such as frame demarcation, signaling between the ends of a link, initialization after power on, and some basic recovery actions.

originator   CONTEXT [Fibre Channel]

The party initiating an *exchange*.

Originator Exchange_Identifier   CONTEXT [Fibre Channel]

An identifier assigned by an *originator* to identify an *exchange*. Abbreviated OX_ID. An OX_ID is meaningful only to its originator.

overwrite procedure   CONTEXT [Security]

The process of writing patterns of data on top of the data stored on a magnetic medium for the purpose of obliterating the data.

out-of-band (transmission)   CONTEXT [Fibre Channel]
Transmission of management information for Fibre Channel components outside of the Fibre Channel network, typically over Ethernet.

OX_ID   CONTEXT [Fibre Channel]
Acronym for *Originator Exchange Identifier.*

panic
A colloquial term describing a software program's reaction to an incomprehensible state. In an operating system context, a panic is usually a system call or unexpected state that causes the system to abruptly stop executing so as to eliminate the possibility that the cause of the panic will cause further damage to the system, applications, or data.

parallel access array   CONTEXT [Storage System]
A disk array model in which data transfer and data protection algorithms assume that all member disks operate in unison, with each participating in the execution of every application I/O request. A parallel access array is only capable of executing one I/O request at a time. True parallel access would require that an array's disks be rotationally synchronized. In actual practice, arrays approximate parallel access behavior. Ideal *RAID Level 2* and *RAID Level 3* arrays are parallel access arrays. *cf. independent access array*

parallel (transmission)
Simultaneous transmission of multiple data bits over multiple physical lines.

parity disk   CONTEXT [Storage System]
In a RAID Level 3 or 4 array, the single disk on which the parity *check data* is stored.

parity RAID   CONTEXT [Storage System]
A collective term used to refer to *Berkeley RAID Levels* 3, 4, and 5.

parity RAID array   CONTEXT [Storage System]
A *RAID array* whose data protection mechanism is one of *Berkeley RAID Levels* 3, 4, or 5.

partition   CONTEXT [Storage System]
1. A subdivision of the capacity of a physical or virtual disk. Partitions are consecutively numbered ranges of blocks that are recognized by MS-DOS, Windows, and most UNIX operating systems.
2. Synonym for the type of *extent* used to configure arrays.
3. A contiguously addressed range of logical blocks on a physical media that is identifiable by an operating system via the partition's type and subtype fields. A partition's type and subtype fields are recorded on the physical media and hence make the partition self-identifying.

partitioning   **CONTEXT [Storage System]**
Presentation of the usable storage capacity of a disk or array to an operating environment in the form of several virtual disks whose aggregate capacity approximates that of the underlying physical or virtual disk. Partitioning is common in MS-DOS, Windows, and UNIX environments. Partitioning is useful with hosts which cannot support the full capacity of a large disk or array as one device. It can also be useful administratively, for example, to create hard subdivisions of a large virtual disk.

passive copper   CONTEXT [Fibre Channel]
A low-cost Fibre Channel connection that allows up to 13 meter copper cable lengths.

passphrase   CONTEXT [Security]

A sequence of characters longer than the acceptable length of a password that is transformed by a password system into a virtual password of acceptable length.

password   CONTEXT [Security]

A protected private alphanumeric string used to authenticate an identity or to authorize access to data.

path

1. The *access path* from a host computer to a storage device.
2. The combination of device address and file system directory elements used to locate a file within a file system.
3. Any route through an interconnect that allows two devices to communicate.
4. A sequence of computer instructions that performs a given function, such as I/O request execution.

path length   CONTEXT [General] [Backup] [File System]

1. [General] The number of instructions (a rough measure of the amount of time) required by a computer to perform a specific activity, such as I/O request execution.
2. [Backup] [File System] The number of characters in a *path name*.

path name   CONTEXT [File System]

The complete list of nested sub-directories through which a file is reached.

payload   CONTEXT [Fibre Channel] [Network]

Contents of the data field of a communications frame or packet. In Fibre Channel, the payload excludes *optional header*s and *fill byte*s, if they are present.

PB

Acronym for petabyte (10^{15} bytes).

PBC   CONTEXT [Fibre Channel]

Acronym for *Port Bypass Circuit*.

PCI

Acronym for *Peripheral Component Interconnect*.

PDC   CONTEXT [Windows]

Acronym for *Primary Domain Controller*.

pcnfsd

A *daemon* that permits personal computers to access file systems accessed through the *NFS* protocol.

penetration   CONTEXT [Security]

An unauthorized bypassing of the security mechanisms of a system.

Peripheral Component Interconnect

A bus for connecting interface modules to a computer system. Abbreviated PCI. Variations of PCI support 32 and 64 bit parallel data transfers at 33 and 66 MHz cycle times. A 133 MHz PCIX has been proposed by Compaq, HP, and IBM.

persistence

Synonym for non-volatility. Usually used to distinguish between data and *metadata* held in *DRAM*, which is lost when electrical power is lost, and data held on *non-volatile* storage (disk, tape, battery-backed DRAM, etc.) that survives, or *persists* across power outages.

physical configuration

The installation, removal, or re-installation of disks, cables, HBAs, and other components required for a system or subsystem to function. Physical configuration is typically understood to include address assignments, such as PCI slot number, SCSI target ID, Logical Unit Number, etc. *cf. array configuration, configuration*

physical block   CONTEXT [Storage Device]

A physical area on a recording media at which data is stored. Distinguished from the *logical* and *virtual block* views typically presented to the operating environment by storage devices.

physical block address

The address of a *physical block*. A number that can be algorithmically converted to a physical location on storage media.

physical disk   CONTEXT [Storage System] [Operating System]

1. [Storage System] A disk. Used to emphasize a contrast with *virtual disk*s.
2. [Operating System] A host operating system's view of an online storage device.

physical extent   CONTEXT [Storage System]

A number of consecutively addressed blocks on a physical disk. Physical extents are created by *control software* as building blocks from which redundancy groups and volume sets are created. Called p_extent by *ANSI*.

physical extent block number   CONTEXT [Storage System]

The relative position of a block within a *physical extent*. Physical extent block numbers are used to develop higher-level constructs in RAID array striped data mapping, not for application or data addressing.

PKI   CONTEXT [Security]

Acronym for *public key infrastructure*

plaintext   CONTEXT [Security]

Unencrypted information.

PLDA   CONTEXT [Fibre Channel]

Acronym for *Private Loop Direct Attach.*

PLOGI   CONTEXT [Fibre Channel]

Acronym for *port login.*

point in time copy   CONTEXT [Backup]

A fully usable copy of a defined collection of data that contains an image of the data as it appeared at a single point in time. The copy is considered to have logically occurred at that point in time, but implementations may perform part or all of the copy at other times (e.g., via database log replay or rollback) as long as the result is a consistent copy of the data as it appeared at that point in time. Implementations may restrict point in time copies to be read-only or may permit subsequent writes to the copy. Three important classes of point in time copies are *split mirror*, *changed block*, and *concurrent*. *Pointer remapping* and *copy on write* are implementation techniques often used for the latter two classes. *cf. snapshot*

pointer copy   CONTEXT [Backup]

A *point in time copy* made using the *pointer remapping* technique.

pointer remapping   CONTEXT [Backup]

A technique for maintaining a point in time copy in which pointers to all of the source data and copy data are maintained. When data is overwritten, a new location is chosen for the updated data, and the pointer for that data is remapped to point to it. If the copy is read-only, pointers to its data are never modified. *cf. copy on write*

policy processor

In an intelligent device, the processor that schedules the overall activities. Policy processors are usually augmented by additional processors, state machines, or sequencers that perform the lower-level functions required to implement overall policy.

port

1. An *I/O adapter* used to connect an *intelligent device* (node) to an I/O bus or network.

2. [storage subsystems] Synonym for the head end of a device *I/O bus* containing the arbitration logic.

Port_ID   CONTEXT [Fibre Channel]

A unique 24-bit address assigned to an *N Port*. There may be at most 2^24 or 16.7 million N_Ports in a single Fibre Channel fabric. There may be at most 127 *NL Ports* in a single loop. For point to point (N_Port to N_Port) connection, there are only 2. In some implementations, a device's Port_ID is derived from its *World Wide Name*. In other cases Port_ID's are permanently assigned in association with specific physical ports. Port_ID's may or may not survive a *Loop Initialization Process* or in the case of a switched fabric, a reconfiguration of the Fibre Channel switch.

port bypass circuit   CONTEXT [Fibre Channel]

A circuit that automatically opens and closes a Fibre Channel arbitrated loop so that nodes can be added to or removed from the loop with minimal disruption of operations. Port bypass circuits are typically found in Fibre Channel hubs and disk enclosures.

port login   CONTEXT [Fibre Channel]

The port-to-port login process by which Fibre Channel initiators establish sessions with targets.

port name   CONTEXT [Fibre Channel]

A unique 64-bit indentifier assigned to a Fibre Channel port.

POST

Acronym for *Power On Self Test.*

power conditioning

The regulation of power supplied to a system so that acceptable ranges of voltage and frequency are maintained. Power conditioning is sometimes done by a storage subsystem, but may also be an environmental requirement.

power on self test

A set of internally stored diagnostic programs run by intelligent devices when powered on. Abbreviated POST. These diagnostic programs verify the basic integrity of hardware before software is permitted to run on it.

present (verb)

To cause to appear or to make available. For example, RAID *control software* and *volume managers present* virtual disks to host environments. Synonym for *export.*

primary domain controller   CONTEXT [Windows]

A domain controller that has been assigned as or has negotiated to become the primary authentication server for the domain of which it is a part.

primitive sequence   CONTEXT [Fibre Channel]

An *ordered set* transmitted repeatedly and continuously until a specified response is received.

primitive signal   CONTEXT [Fibre Channel]

An *ordered set* with a special meaning such as an *idle* or Receiver_Ready (R_RDY).

private key   CONTEXT [Security]

A key which is used in a *symmetric cryptosystem* in both encryption and decryption processes, or in an *asymmetric cryptosystem* for one, but not both, of those processes. A private key must remain confidential to the using party if communication security is to be maintained.

private key cryptography   CONTEXT [Security]

An encryption methodology in which the encryptor and decryptor use the same key, which must be kept secret. cf. *symmetric cryptosystem*

private loop   CONTEXT [Fibre Channel]

A Fibre Channel arbitrated loop with no fabric attachment.

private loop device   CONTEXT [Fibre Channel]

A Fibre Channel arbitrated loop device that does not support fabric login.

process policy   CONTEXT [Fibre Channel]

An error handling policy that allows an *N Port* to continue processing data frames following detection of one or more missing frames in a *sequence.*

Process_Associator   CONTEXT [Fibre Channel]

A value in the Association_Header that identifies a process or a group of processes within a *node.* Communicating processes in different nodes use Process_Associators to address each other. Originating processes have Originator Process_Associators; responding processes have Responder Process_Associators.

profile   CONTEXT [Standards]

A proper subset of a standard that supports interoperability across a set of products or in a specific application. Profiles exist for *FCP* (*FCSI* and *PLDA*), *IP,* and other areas. A profile is a vertical slice through a standard containing physical, logical and behavioral elements required for interoperability.

proprietary interconnect
proprietary I/O bus   CONTEXT [Storage System]

An I/O bus (either a host I/O bus or a device I/O bus) whose transmission characteristics and protocols are the intellectual property of a single vendor, and which require the permission of that vendor to be implemented in the products of other vendors. *cf. open interconnect*

protected space
protected space extent

The storage space available for application data in a *physical extent* that belongs to a *redundancy group.*

protocol   CONTEXT [Fibre Channel] [Network] [SCSI]

A set of rules for using an interconnect or network so that information conveyed on the interconnect can be correctly interpreted by all parties to the communication. Protocols include such aspects of communication as data representation, data item ordering, message formats, message and response sequencing rules, block data transmission conventions, timing requirements, and so forth.

public key   CONTEXT [Security]

A key which is used in an *asymmetric cryptosystem* for either the encryption or decryption process where the *private key* is not used, and which can be shared amongst a group of users without impacting the security of the cryptosystem.

public key cryptography   CONTEXT [Security]

An encryption system using a linked pair of keys. What one key of the pair encrypts, the other decrypts. Either key can be used for encryption and decryption. *cf. asymmetric cryptosystem.*

public key infrastructure   CONTEXT [Security]

A framework established to issue, maintain, and revoke public key certificates accommodating a variety of security technologies.

public loop   CONTEXT [Fibre Channel]

A Fibre Channel arbitrated loop with an attachment to a fabric.

public loop device   CONTEXT [Fibre Channel]

A Fibre Channel arbitrated loop device that supports fabric login and services.

pull technology

The transmission of information in response to a request for that information. An example of a pull technology is polling. *cf. push technology*

push technology

The transmission of information from a source or initiator without the source being requested to send that information. An example of a push technology is an *SNMP trap. cf. pull technology*

PVC   CONTEXT [Fibre Channel]

QoS

Acronym for *quality of service.*

quiesce (verb)   CONTEXT [Backup]

To bring a device or an application to a state in which (a.) it is able to operate, (b.) all of its data is consistent and stored on non-volatile storage, and (c.) processing has been suspended and there are no tasks in progress (i.e., all application tasks have either been completed or not started).

quiescent state   CONTEXT [Backup]

An application or device state in which (a.) the application or device is able to operate, (b.) all of its data is consistent and stored on non-volatile storage, and (c.) processing has been suspended and there are no tasks in progress (i.e., all tasks have either been completed or not started).

quality of service   CONTEXT [Management]

A technique for managing computer system resources such as bandwidth by specifying user visible parameters such as message delivery time. Policy rules are used to describe the operation of network elements to make these guarantees. Relevant standards for QoS in the *IETF* are the RSVP (Resource Reservation Protocol) and COPS (Common Open Policy Service) protocols. RSVP allows for the reservation of bandwidth in advance, while COPS allows routers and switches to obtain policy rules from a server.

RAID   CONTEXT [Storage System]

1. An acronym for *Redundant Array of Independent Disks*, a family of techniques for managing multiple disks to deliver desirable cost, data availability, and performance characteristics to host environments.
2. A *Redundant Array of Independent Disks*.
3. A phrase adopted from the 1988 SIGMOD paper *A Case for Redundant Arrays of Inexpensive Disks*.

RAID 0

RAID Level 0   CONTEXT [Storage System]

Synonym for *data striping*.

RAID 1

RAID Level 1   CONTEXT [Storage System]

Synonym for *mirroring*.

RAID 2

RAID Level 2   CONTEXT [Storage System]

A form of *RAID* in which a Hamming code computed on stripes of data on some of an array's disks is stored on the remaining disks and serves as check data.

RAID 3

RAID Level 3   CONTEXT [Storage System]

A form of *parity RAID* in which all disks are assumed to be rotationally synchronized, and in which the *data stripe* size is no larger than the *exported* block size.

RAID 4

RAID Level 4   CONTEXT [Storage System]

A form of *parity RAID* in which the disks operate independently, the data strip size is no smaller than the *exported* block size, and all parity check data is stored on one disk.

RAID 5

RAID Level 5   CONTEXT [Storage System]

A form of *parity RAID* in which the disks operate independently, the data strip size is no smaller than the *exported* block size, and parity check data is distributed across the array's disks.

RAID 6

RAID Level 6   CONTEXT [Storage System]

Any form of RAID that can continue to execute read and write requests to all of an array's virtual disks in the presence of two concurrent disk failures. Both dual check data computations (parity and Reed Solomon) and orthogonal dual parity check data have been proposed for RAID Level 6.

RAID Advisory Board   CONTEXT [Storage System]

An organization of suppliers and users of storage subsystems and related products whose goal is to foster the understanding of storage subsystem technology among users, and to promote all aspects of storage technology in the market.

RAID array   CONTEXT [Storage System]

Acronym for *Redundant Array of Independent Disks*.

RAMdisk   CONTEXT [Storage Device]

A quantity of host system random access memory (RAM) managed by software and presented to applications as a high-performance disk. RAMdisks generally emulate disk I/O functional characteristics, but unless augmented by special hardware to make their contents non-volatile, they cannot tolerate loss of power without losing data. *cf. solid state disk*

random I/O
random I/O load
random reads
random writes   CONTEXT [Storage System]

Any I/O load whose consecutively issued read and/or write requests do not specify adjacently located data. The term random I/O is commonly used to denote any I/O load that is not sequential, whether or not the distribution of data locations is indeed random. Random I/O is characteristic of I/O request-intensive applications. *cf. sequential I/O*

random relative offset   CONTEXT [Fibre Channel]

A transmission control algorithm in which the *frames* containing the subblocks that comprise a block of information may be transmitted in any order. This complicates reassembly and detection of lost frames by comparison with *continuously increasing offset*.

rank   CONTEXT [Storage System]

1. A set of physical disk positions in an enclosure, usually denoting the disks that are or can be members of a single *array*.

2. The set of corresponding target identifiers on all of a controller's device I/O buses. Like the preceding definition, the disks identified as a rank by this definition usually are or can be members of a single array.

3. Synonym for a stripe in a redundancy group. Because of the diversity of meanings attached to this term by disk subsystem developers, SNIA publications make minimal use of it.

RAS

1. Acronym for Reliability, Availability, and Serviceability.

2. Acronym for Remote Access Server (Windows NT dialup networking server).

raw partition

A disk *partition* not managed by a *volume manager*. The term raw partition is frequently encountered when discussing database systems because some database system vendors recommend volumes or files for underlying database storage, while others recommend direct storage on raw partitions.

raw partition backup   CONTEXT [Backup]

A bit-by-bit copy of a *partition* image. A raw partition backup incorporates no information about the objects contained on the partition, and hence cannot be used for individual object restoration. *cf. disk image backup*

read/write head   CONTEXT [Storage Device]

The magnetic or optical recording device in a disk. Read/write heads are used both to write data by altering the recording media's state, and to read data by sensing the alterations. Disks typically have read/write heads, unlike tapes, in which reading and writing are often done using separate heads.

real time copy   CONTEXT [Storage System]

Synonym for *mirroring*.

rebuild
rebuilding   CONTEXT [Storage System]

The *regeneration* and writing onto one or more replacement disks of all of the user data and check data from a failed disk in a mirrored or RAID array. In most arrays, a rebuild can occur while applications are accessing data on the array's virtual disks.

receiver   CONTEXT [Fibre Channel]

1. An interconnect or network device that includes a detector and signal processing electronics.

2. The portion of a Link_Control_Facility dedicated to receiving an encoded bit stream, converting the stream into transmission characters, and decoding the characters using the rules specified by *FC-PH*.

3. A circuit that converts an optical or electrical media signal to a (possibly retimed) electrical serial logic signal.

receptacle

The stationary (female) half of the interface connector on a *transmitter* or *receiver*.

reconstruction   CONTEXT [Storage System]

Synonym for *rebuilding*.

recorded volume serial number   CONTEXT [Backup]

Synonym for *media ID*. Abbreviated RVSN.

recovery   CONTEXT [Backup]

The recreation of a past operational state of an entire application or computing environment. Recovery is required after an application or computing environment has been destroyed or otherwise rendered unusable. It may include *restoration* of application data, if that data had been destroyed as well. *cf. restoration*

red   CONTEXT [Security]

In the context of security analysis, a designation applied to information systems and associated areas, circuits, components, and equipment in which sensitive information is being processed.

red/black concept   CONTEXT [Security]

The separation of electrical and electronic circuits, components, equipment, and systems that handle sensitive information (red) in electrical form, from those that handle on information that is not sensitive (black) in the same form.

reduced mode   CONTEXT [Storage System]

Synonym for *degraded mode*.

reduction   CONTEXT [Storage System]

The removal of a member disk from a RAID array, placing the array in *degraded mode*. Reduction most often occurs because of member disk failure; however, some RAID implementations allow reduction for system management purposes.

redundancy

The inclusion of extra components of a given type in a system (beyond those required by the system to carry out its function) for the purpose of enabling continued operation in the event of a component failure.

redundancy group   CONTEXT [Management] [Storage System]

1. A collection of extents organized by for the purpose of providing data protection. Within a redundancy group, a single type of data protection is employed. All of the usable storage capacity in a redundancy group is protected by check data stored within the group, and no usable storage external to a redundancy group is protected by check data within it.

2. A class defined in the CIM schema (CIM_RedundancyGroup) consisting of a collection of objects in which redundancy is provided. Three subclasses of CIM_RedundancyGroup are defined as (1.) CIM_SpareGroup for sparing and failover, (2.) CIM_ExtraCapacityGroup for

load sharing or load balancing, and (3.) CIM_StorageRedundancyGroup to describe the redundancy algorithm in use.

redundancy group stripe   CONTEXT [Storage System]

A set of sequences of correspondingly numbered physical extent blocks in each of the physical extents comprising a redundancy group. The check data blocks in a redundancy group stripe protect the protected space in that stripe.

redundancy group stripe depth   CONTEXT [Storage System]

The number of consecutively numbered physical extent blocks in one physical extent of a redundancy group stripe. In the conventional striped data mapping model, redundancy group stripe depth is the same for all stripes in a redundancy group.

redundant (components)

Components of a system that have the capability to substitute for each other when necessary, as, for example, when one of the components fails, so that the system can continue to perform its function. In storage subsystems, power distribution units, power supplies, cooling devices, and controllers are often configured to be redundant. The disks comprising a *mirror set* are redundant. A *parity RAID array*'s member disks are redundant, since surviving disks can collectively replace the function of a failed disk.

redundant (configuration, system)

A system or configuration of a system in which failure tolerance is achieved by the presence of redundant instances of all components that are critical to the system's operation.

Redundant Array of Independent Disks   CONTEXT [Storage System]

A *disk array* in which part of the physical storage capacity is used to store redundant information about user data stored on the remainder of the storage capacity. The redundant information enables *regeneration* of user data in the event that one of the array's *member disk*s or the access path to it fails.

Although it does not conform to this definition, disk striping is often referred to as RAID (*RAID Level 0*).

regeneration   CONTEXT [Storage System]

Recreation of user data from a failed disk in a RAID array using check data and user data from surviving members. Regeneration may also be used to recover data from an unrecoverable media error. Data in a *parity RAID* array is regenerated by computing the exclusive OR of the contents of corresponding blocks from the array's remaining disks. Data in a RAID Level 6 array is regenerated by choosing the more convenient of two parity algorithms and executing it.

registered state change notification   CONTEXT [Fibre Channel]

A Fibre Channel switch function that allows notification to registered nodes if a change occurs to other specified nodes.

rekeying   CONTEXT [Security]

The process of changing the key used for an ongoing communication session.

relative offset   CONTEXT [Fibre Channel]

A displacement, expressed in bytes, used to divide a quantity of data into blocks and subblocks for transmission in separate frames. Relative offsets are used to reassemble data at the receiver and verify that all data has arrived.

relative offset space   CONTEXT [Fibre Channel]

A numerical range defined by a sending upper level protocol for an *information category*. The range starts at zero, representing the upper level–defined origin, and extends to a highest value. *Relative offset* values are required to lie within the appropriate relative offset space.

removable media storage device
> A storage device designed so that its storage media can be readily removed and inserted. Tapes, CDROMs, and optical disks are removable media devices.

repeater   CONTEXT [Fibre Channel]
> A circuit that uses a clock recovered from an incoming signal to generate an outbound signal.

repeating ordered set   CONTEXT [Fibre Channel]
> An ordered set issued by *FC-2* to *FC-1* for repeated transmission until a subsequent transmission request is issued by FC-2.

replacement disk   CONTEXT [Storage System]
> A disk available for use as or used to replace a failed member disk in a RAID array.

replacement unit
> A component or collection of components in a system which are always replaced (*swapped*) as a unit when any part of the collection fails. Abbreviated RU. Replacement units may be *field replaceable*, or they may require that the system of which they are part be returned to a factory or repair depot for replacement. Field replaceable units may be *customer replaceable*, or their replacement may require trained service personnel. Typical replacement units in a disk subsystem include disks, controller logic boards, power supplies, cooling devices, and cables. Replacement units may be *cold, warm,* or *hot swappable*.

replay attack   CONTEXT [Security]
> An attack in which a valid data transmission is maliciously or fraudulently repeated, either by the originator or by an adversary who intercepts the data and retransmits it.

replica   CONTEXT [Backup]
> A general term for a copy of a collection of data. *cf. duplicate, point in time copy, snapshot*

replicate   CONTEXT [Backup]
> 1. (noun) A general term for a copy of a collection of data. *cf. duplicate, point in time copy, snapshot*
> 2. (verb) The action of making a replicate as defined above.
>
> A characterization of applications. Also known as *throughput-intensive*. A request-intensive application is an I/O-intensive application whose I/O load consists primarily of large numbers of I/O requests for relatively small amounts of data. Request-intensive applications are typically characterized by random *I/O load*s.

Request for Comment   CONTEXT [Security]
> Internet-related specifications, including standards, experimental definitions, informational documents, and best practice definitions, produced by the *IETF.*

request intensive (application)
reserved (field)   CONTEXT [Fibre Channel]
> 1. In a standard, a field in a data structure set aside for future definition. Some standards prescribe implementation behavior with respect to reserved fields (e.g., originators of data structures containing reserved fields must zero fill them; consumers of data structures containing reserved fields must ignore them, etc.); others do not.
> 2. A field filled with binary zeros by a source *N Port* and ignored by a destination N_Port. Each bit in a reserved field is denoted by "r" in the Fibre Channel standards. Future enhancements to *FC-PH* may define usages for reserved fields. Implementations should not check or interpret reserved fields. Violation of this guideline may result in loss of compatibility with future implementations which comply with future enhancements to FC-PH.

responder   CONTEXT [Fibre Channel]

Synonym for *target*. Used only in Fibre Channel contexts.

Responder Exchange_Identifier   CONTEXT [Fibre Channel]

An identifier assigned by a *responder* to identify an *exchange*. Abbreviated RX_ID. An RX_ID is meaningful only to the responder that originates it.

restoration   CONTEXT [Backup]

The copying of a *backup* to on-line storage for application use. Restoration normally occurs after part or all of an application's data has been destroyed or become inaccessible. *cf. recovery*

retention period   CONTEXT [Backup] [File System]

1. [Backup] The length of time that a *backup image* should be kept.
2. [File System] In some file systems, such as that shipped with IBM Corporation's OS/390 operating system, a property of a file that can be used to implement backup and data migration policies.

retimer   CONTEXT [Fibre Channel]

A circuit that uses a clock independent of the incoming signal to generate an outbound signal.

return loss   CONTEXT [Fibre Channel]

The ratio of the strength of a returned signal to that of the incident signal that caused it. In electrical circuits, return loss is caused by impedance discontinuities. Optical return loss is caused by index of refraction differences.

RFC   CONTEXT [Security]

Acronym for *Request for Comment*

robot
robotic media handler   CONTEXT [Backup]

A mechanical handler capable of storing multiple pieces of removable media and loading and unloading them from one or more drives in arbitrary order in response to electronic commands. *cf. library*

rotational latency   CONTEXT [Storage Device]

The interval between the end of a disk seek and the time at which the starting block address specified in the I/O request passes the disk head. Exact rotational latencies for specific sequences of I/O operations can only be obtained by detailed disk drive simulation or measurement. The simplifying assumption that on average, requests wait for half a disk revolution time of rotational latency works well in practice. Half of a disk revolution time is therefore defined to be the average rotational latency.

row   CONTEXT [Storage System]

The set of blocks with corresponding physical extent block addresses in each of an array's member physical extents. The concept of rows is useful for locking the minimal amount of data during a RAID array update so as to maximize the potential for parallel execution.

RSA   CONTEXT [Security]

Acronym for both a *public key* algorithm and a corporation in the business of algorithm design, derived from the names of the founders (Rivest, Shamir & Adelman).

RSCN   CONTEXT [Fibre Channel]

Acronym for *registered state change notification*.

RU

Acronym for *replaceable unit. cf. CRU, FRU*

run length

The number of consecutive identical bits in a transmitted signal. For example, the pattern 0011111010 has run lengths of 2, 5, 1, 1, and 1.

running disparity   CONTEXT [Fibre Channel]

The cumulative *disparity* (positive or negative) of all previously issued *transmission characters.*

RVSN   CONTEXT [Backup]

Acronym for *recorded volume serial number.*

symmetric cryptosystem   CONTEXT [Security]

A cryptographic algorithm in which the same key is used to encrypt and decrypt a single message or block of stored information. Keys used in a symmetric cryptosystem must be kept secret.

S_ID   CONTEXT [Fibre Channel]

Acronym for *Source Identifier.*

S_Port   CONTEXT [Fibre Channel]

A logical port inside a *switch* addressable by external *N Port*s for service functions. An S_Port may be an implicit switch port or a separate entity such as a *name server* connected to and controlled by the switch. S_Ports have well known port names to facilitate early discovery by N_Ports.

SAN   CONTEXT [Fibre Channel] [Network] [Storage System]

1. Acronym for *storage area network.* (This is the normal usage in *SNIA* documents.)
2. Acronym for Server Area Network which connects one or more servers.
3. Acronym for System Area Network for an interconnected set of system elements.

SAN attached storage

A term used to refer to storage elements that connect directly to a *storage area network* and provide file, database, block, or other types of data access services to computer systems. Abbreviated SAS. SAS elements that provide file access services are commonly called Network Attached Storage, or NAS devices. *cf. NAS*

SAS

Acronym for *SAN attached storage.*

saturated disk

A disk whose instantaneous I/O load is as great as or greater than its capability to satisfy the requests comprising the load. Mathematically, a saturated disk's I/O queue eventually becomes indefinitely long. In practice, however, user reaction or other system factors generally reduce the rate of new request arrival for a saturated disk.

scale (verb)

In computer systems, to grow or support growth in such a way that all capabilities of the system remain in constant ratio to each other. For example, a storage subsystem whose data transfer capacity increases by the addition of buses as its storage capacity increases by the addition of disks is said to scale.

schema

> A collection of *information models* or *data models*.

script

> 1. A parameterized list of primitive I/O bus operations intended to be executed in sequence. Often used with respect to *ports*, most of which are able to execute scripts of I/O commands autonomously (without policy processor assistance).
>
> 2. A sequence of instructions intended to be parsed and carried out by another program. Perl, VBScript, JavaScript, and Tcl are all scripting languages.

SCSI   CONTEXT [SCSI]

> Acronym for *Small Computer System Interface*.

SCSI adapter   CONTEXT [SCSI]

> An *adapter* that connects an *intelligent device* to a *SCSI bus*. *cf. HBA, host bus adapter*

SCSI address   CONTEXT [SCSI]

> The full address used by a computer to communicate with a SCSI device, including an adapter number (required with computers configured with multiple SCSI adapters), and the *target ID* of the device. SCSI addresses do not include logical unit number, because those are not used for communication.

SCSI bus   CONTEXT [SCSI]

> Any parallel (multi-signal) I/O bus that implements some version of the ANSI SCSI standard. A wide SCSI bus may connect up to 16 *initiator*s and *target*s. A narrow SCSI bus may connect up to eight initiators and targets. *cf. initiator, target*

SCSI Enclosure Services   CONTEXT [SCSI]

> An *ANSI X3T10* standard for management of environmental factors such as temperature, power, voltage, etc. Abbreviated SES.

SCSI Parallel Interface   CONTEXT [SCSI]

> The family of SCSI standards that define the characteristics of the parallel version of the SCSI interface. Abbreviated SPI. Several versions of SPI, known as SPI, SPI2, SPI3, etc., have been developed. Each version provides for greater performance and functionality than preceding ones.

SCSI Trade Association

> A trade association incorporated in 1996 to promote all forms of SCSI technology in the market. Abbreviated STA.

SDH   CONTEXT [Network]

> Acronym for *Synchronous Digital Hierarchy*.

sector   CONTEXT [Storage Device]

> The unit in which data is physically stored and protected against errors on a *fixed block architecture* disk. A sector typically consists of a synchronization pattern, a header field containing the block's address, data, a checksum or error correcting code, and a trailer. Adjacent sectors are often separated by information used to assist in track centering. Most often, each sector holds a *block* of data. *cf. disk block*

secure hash   CONTEXT [Security]

> An algorithm that generates a digest from its input (e.g., a message). The digest has the properties that different inputs are extraordinarily unlikely to have the same fingerprint, small changes

in its input lead to large changes in its output, and it is computationally intractable to generate an input that has the same fingerprint as a given input.

Secure Sockets Layer.   CONTEXT [Security]

A suite of cyrptographic algorithms, protocols and procedures used to provide security for communications used to access the World Wide Web. The characters "https:" at the front of a URL cause SSL to be used to enhance *communication security*. More recent versions of SSL are known as TLS (Transport Level Security) and are standardized by the Internet Engineering Task Force (IETF)

SEQ_ID
Sequence Identifier   CONTEXT [Fibre Channel]

A number transmitted with each *data frame* in a sequence that identifies the frame as part of the sequence.

sequence   CONTEXT [Fibre Channel]

A set of Fibre Channel *data frame*s with a common Sequence_ID (SEQ_ID), corresponding to one message element, block, or Information Unit. Sequences are transmitted from initiator to recipient, with an acknowledgment, if applicable, transmitted from recipient to initiator. *cf. Sequence Initiator, Sequence Recipient*

sequence initiative   CONTEXT [Fibre Channel]

A Fibre Channel protocol feature that designates which end of an exchange has authority to send the next sequence.

Sequence Initiator   CONTEXT [Fibre Channel]

An *N Port* which initiates a *sequence* and transmits data frames to a destination N_Port. *cf. Sequence Recipient*

Sequence Recipient   CONTEXT [Fibre Channel]

An *N Port* or *NL Port* which receives Data frames from a *Sequence Initiator* and, if applicable, transmits responses (*Link Control frames*) to the Sequence Initiator.

Sequence Status Block   CONTEXT [Fibre Channel]

A data structure which tracks the state of a *sequence*. Both *Sequence Initiators* and *Sequence Recipients* have Sequence Status Blocks for each active sequence.

sequential I/O
sequential I/O load
sequential reads
sequential writes

An I/O load consisting of consecutively issued read or write requests to adjacently located data. Sequential I/O is characteristic of *data transfer intensive* applications. *cf. random I/O*

SERDES

Acronym for *Serializer Deserializer*.

serial (transmission)   CONTEXT [Fibre Channel]

The transmission of data bits one at a time over a single link.

serial adapter

An *adapter* that connects an intelligent device to an RS232 or RS425 serial communications link. Serial adapters are sometimes used by storage subsystems, filers, and other intelligent devices to connect to serial consoles for management purposes. *cf. adapter, host adapter*

serial console

A real or emulated communication terminal used by humans to manage an intelligent device. Serial consoles connect to the devices' serial *adapter*s.

serial SCSI   CONTEXT [SCSI]

Any implementation of SCSI that uses serial data transmission (as opposed to multi-conductor *parallel* buses). Optical and electrical Fibre Channel, SSA, and IEEE 1394 are examples of serial SCSI implementations.

serializer deserializer

A mechanism for converting data from parallel to serial form and from serial to parallel form.

server

1. An intelligent device, usually a computer, that provides services to other intelligent devices, usually other computers or *appliance*s. *cf. client*

2. An asymmetric relationship with a second party (a *client*) in which the client initiates requests and the server responds to those requests.

serverless backup

A disk backup methodology in which either the disk being backed up or the tape device receiving the backup manages and performs actual backup I/O operations. Server-free backup frees the LAN server to perform I/O operations on behalf of LAN clients and reduces the number of trips the backup data takes through processor memory. Differentiated from *LAN-free backup* in that no additional SAN appliance is required to offload backup I/O operations from the LAN server.

Server Message Block (protocol)   CONTEXT [Network]

A network file system access protocol designed and implemented by Microsoft Corporation and used by Windows clients to communicate file access requests to Windows servers. Abbreviated SMB. Current versions of the SMB protocol are usually referred to as CIFS, the *Common Internet File System*.

service level agreement

An agreement between a service provider, such as an IT department, an internet services provider, or an intelligent device acting as a server, and a service consumer. A service level agreement defines parameters for measuring the service, and states quantitative values for those parameters. Abbreviated SLA.

SES   CONTEXT [SCSI] [Standards]

1. Acronym for *SCSI Enclosure Services*.

2. Acronym for *Solution Exchange Standard*.

share   CONTEXT [File System]

A resource such as data or a printer device made available for use by users on other computer systems. For example, a printer or a collection of files stored in a single directory tree on a file server may be made available as a share. CIFS clients, which include most networked personal computers, typically map a share to a drive letter.

shielded enclosure   CONTEXT [Security]

A room or container designed to attenuate electromagnetic radiation.

shelf   CONTEXT [Storage System]

A modular enclosure for storage devices (disks and tapes). Storage shelves usually contain power supplies and cooling devices, and have pre-wired backplanes that carry power and I/O bus signals to the devices mounted in them. *cf. canister*

SIA

1. Acronym for Semiconductor Industries Association.

2. Acronym for SCSI Industry Association.

simple name server   CONTEXT [Fibre Channel] [Network]

A service provided by a Fibre Channel switch that simplifies discovery of devices attached to the fabric.

SID

Acronym for *Security Identifier.*

Simple Network Management Protocol   CONTEXT [Network] [Standards]

An *IETF* protocol for monitoring and managing systems and devices in a network. The data being monitored and managed is defined by a *MIB*. The functions supported by the protocol are the request and retrieval of data, the setting or writing of data, and *traps* that signal the occurrence of events.

single (component) configuration

A configuration in which the referenced component is not redundant. *cf. redundant (component)*

single ended (signaling)   CONTEXT [SCSI]

An electrical signaling technique in which all control and data signals are represented by a voltage difference from a common ground. *cf. differential*

single mode (fiber optic cable)   CONTEXT [Fibre Channel] [Network]

A fiber optic cabling specification that provides for up to 10 kilometer distance between devices.

single point of failure

One component or path in a system, the failure of which would make the system inoperable. Abbreviated SPOF.

SIS   CONTEXT [Management] [Standards]

Acronym for *Service Incident Standard.*

SLA

Acronym for *Service Level Agreement.*

Small Computer Storage Interface (SCSI)   CONTEXT [SCSI]

A collection of ANSI standards and proposed standards which define I/O buses primarily intended for connecting storage subsystems or devices to hosts through *host bus adapter*s. Originally intended primarily for use with small (desktop and desk-side workstation) computers, SCSI has been extended to serve most computing needs, and is arguably the most widely implemented I/O bus in use today.

small read request
small write request
small I/O request

An I/O, read, or write request that specifies the transfer of a relatively small amount of data. 'Small' usually depends on the context, but most often refers to 8 KBytes or fewer. *cf. large I/O request*

SMB   CONTEXT [File System] [Network]

Acronym for *Server Message Block.*

SMI   CONTEXT [Fibre Channel] [Management] [Network]
Acronym for *Structure of Management Information.*

SMPTE   CONTEXT [Standards]
Acronym for *Society of Motion Picture and Television Engineers.*

snapshot   CONTEXT [Backup] [Storage System]
1. A fully usable copy of a defined collection of data that contains an image of the data as it appeared at the point in time at which the copy was initiated. A snapshot may be either a *duplicate* or a *replicate* of the data it represents.
2. The CIM_Snapshot class. An optional construct that can be used to represent a storage extent that contains either a full copy of another storage extent or the changes to that extent (in the case of a delta before or delta after copy). A CIM snapshot is not equivalent to a volume or file-based snapshot, or a point in time copy. It represents storage used to hold a copied image of an extent, or to hold changes to an extent.

SNIA   CONTEXT [Network] [Standards] [Storage System]
Acronym for *Storage Networking Industry Association.*

sniffer   CONTEXT [Security]
A software tool for auditing and identifying network traffic packets.

SNMP   CONTEXT [Network] [Management]
Acronym for *Simple Network Management Protocol.*

SNS   CONTEXT [Network]
Acronym for *Simple Name Server.*

Society of Motion Picture and Television Engineers   CONTEXT [Standards]
An indistry association whose goal is to standardize television and motion picture industry information interchange protocols.

soft zone   CONTEXT [Fibre Channel]
A zone consisting of zone members that are permitted to communicate with each other via the fabric.

Soft zones are typically implemented through a combination of *name server* and Fibre Channel protocol—when a port contacts the name server, the name server returns information only about Fibre Channel ports in the same zone(s) as the requesting port. This prevents ports outside the zone(s) from being discovered and hence the Fibre Channel protocol will not attempt to communicate with such ports. In contrast to *hard zones*, soft zones are not enforced by hardware; e.g., a frame that is erroneously addressed to a port that should not receive it will nonetheless be delivered. Well known addresses {link} are implicitly included in every zone. cf. *zone, hard zone*

SOF   CONTEXT [Fibre Channel]
Acronym for *start of frame.*

solicited control   CONTEXT [Fibre Channel]
An *information category* indicated in a Fibre Channel frame header.

solicited data   CONTEXT [Fibre Channel]
An *information category* indicated in a Fibre Channel frame header.

solid state disk   CONTEXT [Storage Device]
A *disk* whose storage capability is provided by solid-state random access memory rather than magnetic or optical media. A solid state disk generally offers very high access performance com-

pared to that of rotating magnetic disks, because it eliminates mechanical seek and rotation time. It may also offer very high data transfer capacity. Cost per byte of storage, however, is typically quite high, and volumetric density is lower. A solid state disk includes some mechanism such as battery backup or magnetic backing store that allows its operating environment to treat it as non-volatile storage. *cf. RAMdisk*

Solution Exchange Standard   CONTEXT [Management]

A *DMTF* standard that defines the exchange of support or help desk information.

Service Incident Standard   CONTEXT [Management]

A *DMTF* standard that defines how a support or help desk incident is processed.

SONET   CONTEXT [Network]

Acronym for *Synchronous Optical Network*.

Source Identifier   CONTEXT [Fibre Channel]

A number in a Fibre Channel *frame* that identifies the source of the frame. Abbreviated S_ID. *cf. D_ID*

source N_Port   CONTEXT [Fibre Channel]

The *N Port* from which a frame is transmitted.

spare (disk, extent)   CONTEXT [Storage System]

An object reserved for the purpose of substitution for a like object in case of that object's failure.

special character   CONTEXT [Fibre Channel]

Any *transmission character* that is valid in the *transmission code* but does not correspond to a *valid data byte*. Special characters are used to denote special functions.

special code   CONTEXT [Fibre Channel]

A code which, when encoded using the rules specified by the *transmission code*, results in a special character. Special codes are typically associated with control signals related to protocol management (e.g., *K28.5*).

SPI

Acronym for *SCSI Parallel Interface*.

spiral data transfer rate

Synonym for *full volume transfer rate*.

split I/O request

1. An I/O request to a virtual disk which requires two or more I/O operations to satisfy, because the virtual data addresses in the request map to more than one extent on one or more disks.

2. An application I/O request that is divided into two or more sub-requests by a file system or other operating system component because the amount of data requested is too large for the operating environment to handle as a unit.

split mirror
split mirror copy
split mirror point in time copy   CONTEXT [Storage System]

Any of a class of *point in time copy* implementations or the resulting copies in which the storage for the copy is synchronized to the source of the copy and then split. A split mirror copy occupies as much storage as the source of the copy.

SPOF
> Acronym for *Single Point of Failure.*

spoofing   CONTEXT [Security]
> Unauthorized use of legitimate indentification and authentication data to mimic a subject different from the attacker. Impersonating, masquerading, piggybacking, and mimicking are forms of spoofing.

SR   CONTEXT [Fibre Channel]
> Acronym for *Sequence Recipient.*

SRM   CONTEXT [Management]
> Acronym for *storage resource management.*

STA
> Acronym for *SCSI Trade Association.*

stand alone drive   CONTEXT [Backup]
> A removable media drive that is not associated with a media stacker or robot.

standard interconnect   CONTEXT [Standards]
> An I/O or network interconnect whose specifications are readily available to the public, and which can therefore easily be implemented in a vendor's products without license or royalty payments. Also called open interconnect.

star
> A physical network configuration in which every node is connected directly to, and only to, a central point. All communications pass through the central point, which may be a *hub* or a *switch.*

start of frame   CONTEXT [Fibre Channel]
> A group of ordered sets that delineate the beginning of a frame.

storage area network   CONTEXT [Fibre Channel] [Network] [Storage System]
> 1. A network whose primary purpose is the transfer of data between computer systems and storage elements and among storage elements. Abbreviated SAN. A SAN consists of a communication infrastructure, which provides physical connections, and a management layer, which organizes the connections, storage elements, and computer systems so that data transfer is secure and robust. The term SAN is usually (but not necessarily) identified with block I/O services rather than file access services.
> 2. A storage system consisting of storage elements, storage devices, computer systems, and/or appliances, plus all control software, communicating over a network.
>
> Note: The SNIA definition specifically does not identify the term SAN with Fibre Channel technology. When the term SAN is used in connection with Fibre Channel technology, use of a qualified phrase such as "Fibre Channel SAN" is encouraged. According to this definition an Ethernet-based network whose primary purpose is to provide access to storage elements would be considered a SAN. SANs are sometimes also used for system interconnection in clusters.

storage array   CONTEXT [Storage System]
> A collection of disks or tapes from one or more commonly accessible storage subsystems, combined with a body of *control software.*

storage controller   CONTEXT [Storage System]
> An *intelligent controller* to which storage devices are attached.

storage device   CONTEXT [Storage Device]

A collective term for *disks*, *tapes*, *disk arrays*, *tape arrays*, and any other mechanisms capable of non-volatile data storage. This definition is specifically intended to exclude aggregating *storage elements* such as RAID array subsystems, robotic tape libraries, filers, and file servers.

storage domain   CONTEXT [Storage System]

A collection of storage resources and supporting software and interfaces that are managed as a unit.

storage element

Any device designed and built primarily for the purpose of persistent data storage and delivery. This definition is specifically intended to encompass disk drives, tape drives, RAID array subsystems, robotic tape libraries, filers, file servers, and any other types of *storage devices*.

storage extent

A CIM object called CIM_StorageExtent. A storage extent instance may represent either removable or nonremovable media. *cf. extent*

storage networking

The practice of creating, installing, administering, or using networks whose primary purpose is the transfer of data between computer systems and storage elements and among storage elements.

Storage Networking Industry Association   CONTEXT [Network] [Standards] [Storage System]

An association of producers and consumers of storage networking products whose goal is to further storage networking technology and applications.

storage resource management   CONTEXT [Management]

Management of physical and logical storage resources, including storage elements, storage devices, appliances, virtual devices, disk volume, and file resources.

storage subsystem   CONTEXT [Storage System]

An integrated collection of (a.) storage controllers and/or *host bus adapters*, (b.) storage devices such as disks, CDROMs, tapes, media loaders, and robots, and (c.) any required *control software* that provides storage services to one or more computers.

storage volume

In CIM, a StorageVolume is a subclass of CIM_StorageExtent and represents an object presented to an operating system (for example by a hardware RAID cabinet), to a file system (for example, by a software volume manager) or to another entity. Storage volumes do NOT participate in CIM_StorageRedundancyGroups. They are directly realized in hardware or are the end result of assembling and building on lower level extents.

store and forward (switching)   CONTEXT [Fibre Channel] [Network]

A switching technique that requires buffering an entire frame before a routing decision is made.

streamed sequence   CONTEXT [Fibre Channel]

A new *sequence* initiated by a *Sequence Initiator* in any class of service for an *exchange* while it already has sequences open for that exchange.

strip   CONTEXT [Storage System]

A number of consecutively addressed blocks in a single *extent*. A disk array's uses strips to map virtual disk block addresses to member disk block addresses. Also known as *stripe element*.

strip size   CONTEXT [Storage System]
>   Synonym for *stripe depth*.

stripe   CONTEXT [Storage System]
>   The set of *strip*s at corresponding locations of each member extent of a disk array which uses striped data mapping. The strips in a stripe are associated with each other in a way (e.g., relative extent block addresses) that allows membership in the stripe to be quickly and uniquely determined by a computational algorithm. Parity RAID uses uses stripes to map virtual disk block addresses to member extent block addresses.

stripe depth   CONTEXT [Storage System]
>   The number of blocks in a strip in a disk array which uses striped data mapping. Also, the number of consecutively addressed virtual disk blocks mapped to consecutively addressed blocks on a single member extent of a disk array.

stripe element   CONTEXT [Storage System]
>   Synonym for *strip*.

stripe size   CONTEXT [Storage System]
>   The number of blocks in a *stripe*. A striped array's stripe size is the stripe depth multiplied by the number of member extents. A parity RAID array's stripe size is the stripe depth multiplied by one less than the number of member extents.

striped array
striped disk array   CONTEXT [Storage System]
>   A disk array with striped data mapping but no redundancy for failure protection. Striped arrays are usually used to improve I/O performance on data that is of low value or easily replaced.

stripeset   CONTEXT [Storage System]
>   Synonym for *striped array*.

striping   CONTEXT [Storage System]
>   1. Short for *data striping*; also known as RAID Level 0 or RAID 0. A mapping technique in which fixed-size consecutive ranges of virtual disk data addresses are mapped to successive array members in a cyclic pattern.
>   2. A network technique for aggregating the bandwidth of several links between the same pair of nodes. A single data stream can be spread across the links for higher aggregate bandwidth. Sometimes called port aggregation.

Structure of Management Information   CONTEXT [Fibre Channel] [Management] [Network]
>   A notation for setting or retrieving management variables over SNMP.

SSL   CONTEXT [Security]
>   Acronym for *Secure Sockets Layer*.

subdirectory   CONTEXT [File System]
>   A directory in a hierarchical directory tree whose parent is a directory.

subject   CONTEXT [Security]
>   In the context of access control or authorization, an entity whose access or usage is controlled. Users are examples of subjects.

substitution
>   The assumption of a component's function in a system by a functionally equivalent component.

SVC   CONTEXT [Network]
Acronym for *Switched Virtual Circuit*.

swap
swapping
The installation of a replacement unit in place of a defective unit in a system. *Units* are any parts of a system which may either field replaceable (FRUs) by a vendor service representative or consumer replaceable (CRUs).

A physical swap operation may be *cold, warm,* or *hot,* depending on the state in which the disk subsystem must be in order to perform it. A functional swap operation may be an *auto swap* or it may require human intervention.

switch   CONTEXT [Fibre Channel] [Network]
A network infrastructure component to which multiple nodes attach. Unlike *hubs*, switches typically have internal bandwidth that is a multiple of link bandwidth, and the ability to rapidly switch node connections from one to another. A typical switch can accommodate several simultaneous full link bandwidth transmissions between different pairs of nodes. *cf. hub*

switch-back
Synonym for *failback*.

switch-over
Synonym for *failover*.

switched over (system)
Synonym for *failed over*.

Synchronous Digital Hierarchy   CONTEXT [Network]
An *ISO* standard with 155, 622, 2048, and 9953 Mbps serial data rates in steps of 4. A common worldwide telecommunications methodology. SDH uses a light scrambling of data to remove only the lowest frequency elements with the goal of achieving maximum digital bandwidth use.

synchronization   CONTEXT [Fibre Channel]
1. A receiver's identification of a *transmission word* boundary.
2. The act of aligning or making two entities be equivalent at a specified point in time.

synchronous operations
Operations which have a fixed time relationship to each other. Most commonly used to denote I/O operations which occur in time sequence, i.e., a successor operation does not occur until its predecessor is complete.

Synchronous Optical Network   CONTEXT [Network]
A standard for optical network elements. Abbreviated SONET. SONET provides modular building blocks, fixed overheads, integrated operations channels, and flexible payload mappings. Basic SONET provides a bandwidth of 51.840 megabits/second. This is known as OC-1. Higher bandwidths that are n times the basic rate are available (known as OC-n). OC-3, OC-12, OC-48, and OC-192 are currently in common use.

system board
A printed circuit module containing mounting devices for processor(s), memory, and adapter cards, and implementing basic computer functions such as memory access, processor and I/O bus clocking, and human interface device attachment.

system disk

> The disk on which a computer system's operating software is stored. The system disk is usually the disk from which the operating system is *bootstrapped* (initially loaded into memory). The system disk frequently contains the computer system's swap and/or page files as well. It may also contain libraries of common software shared among several applications.

system under test

> An entity being tested to verify functional behavior or determine performance characteristics. Distinguished from *test system*.

T1 copy   CONTEXT [Storage System]
> Synonym for *mirroring*.

T10   CONTEXT [SCSI]
> The ANSI T10 technical committee, the standards organization responsible for SCSI standards for communication between computers and storage subsystems and devices.

T11   CONTEXT [Fibre Channel]
> The ANSI T11 technical committee, the standards organization responsible for Fibre Channel and certain other standards for moving electronic data into and out of computers and intelligent storage subsystems and devices.

tabular mapping   CONTEXT [Storage System]
> A form of *mapping* in which a lookup table contains the correspondence between the two address spaces being mapped to each other. If a mapping between two address spaces is tabular, there is no mathematical formula that will convert addresses in one space to addresses in the other. *cf. algorithmic mapping, dynamic mapping*

tape
tape drive
tape transport   CONTEXT [Storage Device]
> A storage device that writes data sequentially in the order in which it is delivered, and reads data in the order in which it is stored on the media. Unlike disks, tapes use *implicit data addressing*. *cf. disk*

tape array   CONTEXT [Storage System]
> A collection of tapes from one or more commonly accessible storage subsystems, combined with a body of *control software*.

target   CONTEXT [SCSI]
> The system component that receives a SCSI I/O command command. *cf. initiator, LUN, target ID*

target ID   CONTEXT [SCSI]
> The *SCSI* bus address of a target device or controller.

TByte

> Shorthand for *terabyte*.

TCO

> Acronym for *Total Cost of Ownership*.

TCP   CONTEXT [Network]
> Acronym for *Transmission Control Protocol. cf. IP*

TCP/IP   CONTEXT [Network]
Shorthand for the suite of protocols that includes *TCP, IP, UDP,* and *ICMP.* This is the basic set of communication protocols used on the Internet.

tenancy   CONTEXT [Fibre Channel]
The possession of a Fibre Channel arbitrated loop by a device to conduct a transaction.

terabyte
Shorthand for 1,000,000,000,000 ($10^{\wedge}12$) bytes. SNIA publications typically use the $10^{\wedge}12$ convention commonly found in I/O literature rather than the 1,099,5111,627,776 ($2^{\wedge}40$) convention sometimes used when discussing random access memory.

test system
A collection of equipment used to perform a test. In functional and performance testing, it is generally important to clearly define the test system, and distinguish it from the *system under test.*

third party copy   CONTEXT [Backup] [Management]
A protocol for performing tape backups using minimal server resources by copying data directly from the source device (disk or array) to the target device (tape transport) without passing through a server.

threat   CONTEXT [Security]
Any circumstance or event with the potential to harm an information system through unauthorized access, destruction, disclosure, modification of data, and/or denial of service.

throughput
The number of I/O requests satisfied per unit time. Expressed in I/O requests/second, where a *request* is an application request to a storage subsystem to perform a read or write operation.

throughput-intensive (application)
A *request intensive* application.

time server
An intelligent entity in a network that enables all nodes in the network to maintain a common time base within close tolerances.

TNC   CONTEXT [Network]
Acronym for Threaded Neil Councilman, a type of Coaxial Cable Connector.

Specifications for TNC style connectors are defined in MIL-C-39012 and MIL-C-23329.

token ring (network)   CONTEXT [Network]
1. A network in which each node's transmitter is connected to the receiver of the node to its logical right, forming a continuous ring. Nodes on a token ring network gain the right to transmit data by retaining a token (a specific unique message) when they receive it. When a node holding the token has transmitted its allotment of data, it forwards the token to the next node in the ring.
2. A LAN protocol for token ring networks governed by IEEE Standard 802.3 that operates at speeds of 4 Mbits/second and 16 Mbits/second.

topology
The logical layout of the components of a computer system or network and their interconnections. Topology deals with questions of what components are directly connected to other compo-

nents from the standpoint of being able to communicate. It does not deal with questions of physical location of components or interconnecting cables.

total cost of ownership

The comprehensive cost of a particular capability such as data processing, storage access, file services, etc. Abbreviated TCO, total cost of ownership includes acquisition, environment, operations, management, service, upgrade, loss of service, and residual value. *cf. inherent cost*

TPC　CONTEXT [Backup] [Management]

Acronym for *third party copy*.

transceiver　CONTEXT [Fibre Channel]

A transmitter and receiver combined in one package.

transmission character　CONTEXT [Fibre Channel]

Any encoded character (valid or invalid) transmitted across a physical interface specified by FC-0. Valid transmission characters are specified by the transmission code and include data characters and special characters.

transmission code　CONTEXT [Fibre Channel]

A means of encoding data to enhance its transmission characteristics. The transmission code specified by *FC-PH* is byte-oriented, with both *valid data byte*s and *special code*s encoded into 10-bit *transmission characters*.

Transmission Control Protocol

The Internet connection oriented network transport protocol. Abbreviated TCP. TCP provides a reliable delivery service.

transmission word　CONTEXT [Fibre Channel]

A string of four contiguous *transmission characters* aligned on boundaries that are zero modulo 4 from a previously received or transmitted special character. *FC-1* transmission and reception operates in transmission word units.

transmitter　CONTEXT [Fibre Channel]

1. The portion of a Link_Control_Facility that converts valid data bytes and special codes into transmission characters using the rules specified by the transmission code, converting these transmission characters into a bit stream, and transmitting this bit stream on an optical or electrical transmission medium.

2. An electronic circuit that converts an electrical logic signal to a signal suitable for an optical or electrical communications media.

transparent failover

A *failover* from one component of a system to another that is transparent to the external operating environment. Often used to refer to paired disk controllers, one of which exports the other's virtual disks at the same host bus addresses after a failure. *cf. non-transparent failover*

trap　CONTEXT [Management]

A type of *SNMP* message used to signal that an event has occurred.

triaxial cable

An electrical transmission medium consisting of three concentric conductors separated by a dielectric material with the spacings and material arranged to give a specified electrical impedance. *cf. coaxial cable*

trojan horse   CONTEXT [Security]

A computer program containing hidden code that allows the unauthorized collection, falsification, or destruction of information.

tunneling   CONTEXT [Security]

A technology that enables one network protocol to send its data via another network protocol's connections. Tunneling works by encapsulating the first network protocol within packets carried by the second protocol. A tunnel may also encapsulate a protocol within itself (e.g., an IPsec gateway operates in this fashion, encapsulating IP in IP and inserting additional IPsec information between the two IP headers).

UDP   CONTEXT [Network]

Acronym for *User Datagram Protocol.*

ULP   CONTEXT [Fibre Channel]

Acronym for *Upper Layer Protocol.*

Ultra SCSI   CONTEXT [SCSI]

A form of SCSI capable of 20 *megatransfer*s per second. *Single ended* Ultra SCSI supports bus lengths of up to 1.5 meters. *Differential* Ultra SCSI supports bus lengths of up to 25 meters. Ultra SCSI specifications define both narrow (8 data bits) and wide (16 data bits) buses. A narrow Ultra SCSI bus transfers data at a maximum of 20 MBytes per second. A wide Ultra SCSI bus transfers data at a maximum of 40 MBytes per second.

Ultra2 SCSI   CONTEXT [SCSI]

A form of SCSI capable of 40 *megatransfer*s per second. There is no *single ended* Ultra2 SCSI specification. Low voltage *differential* (LVD) Ultra2 SCSI supports bus lengths of up to 12 meters. High voltage differential Ultra2 SCSI supports bus lengths of up to 25 meters. Ultra2 SCSI specifications define both narrow (8 data bits) and wide (16 data bits) buses. A narrow Ultra SCSI bus transfers data at a maximum of 40 MBytes per second. A wide Ultra2 SCSI bus transfers data at a maximum of 80 MBytes per second.

Ultra3 SCSI   CONTEXT [SCSI]

A form of SCSI capable of 80 *megatransfer*s per second. There is no *single ended* Ultra3 SCSI specification. Low voltage *differential* (LVD) Ultra2 SCSI supports bus lengths of up to 12 meters. There is no high voltage differential Ultra3 SCSI specification. Ultra3 SCSI specifications only define wide (16 data bits) buses. A wide Ultra3 SCSI bus transfers data at a maximum of 160 MBytes per second.

UML   CONTEXT [Management]

Acronym for *Unified Modeling Language.*

unauthorized disclosure   CONTEXT [Security]

The exposure of information to individuals not authorized to receive or access it.

unclassified   CONTEXT [Security]

Information that is not designated as *classified.*

unicast   CONTEXT [Network]

The transmission of a message to single receivers. Unicast can be contrasted with broadcast (sending a message to all receivers on a network) and multicast (sending a message to a select subset of receivers).

Unicode

A standard for a 16-bit character set (each character has a 16-bit number associated with it). Unicode allows for up to 2^16, or 65,536 characters, each of which may have a unique representation. It accommodates several non-English characters and symbols, and is therefore an aid to development of products with multilingual user interfaces. Unicode was designed and is maintained by the non-profit industry consortium, Unicode Inc.

uninterruptible power source

A source of electrical power that is not affected by outages in a building's external power source. Abbreviated UPS. UPSs may generate their own power using gasoline generators, or they may consist of large banks of batteries. UPSs are typically installed to prevent service outages due to external power grid failure in computer applications deemed by their owners to be "mission critical."

Unified Modeling Language   CONTEXT [Management]

A visual approach that uses a variety of diagrams (such as use case, class, interaction, state, activity, and others) to specify the objects of a model and their relationships. Abbreviated UML. Various tools exist for turning UML diagrams into program code.

unsolicited control   CONTEXT [Fibre Channel]

An *information category* indicated in a Fibre Channel *frame* header.

unsolicited data   CONTEXT [Fibre Channel]

An *information category* indicated in a Fibre Channel *frame* header.

upper layer protocol   CONTEXT [Fibre Channel]

A *protocol* used on a Fibre Channel network at or above the *FC-4* level. Abbreviated ULP. *SCSI* and *IP* are examples of ULPs.

UPS

Acronym for *Uninterruptible Power Source.*

usable capacity   CONTEXT [Storage Device] [Storage System]

The storage capacity in a disk or disk array that is available for storing user data. Usable capacity of a disk is the total formatted capacity of a disk minus the capacity reserved for media defect compensation and *metadata*. Usable capacity of a disk array is the sum of the usable capacities of the array's member disks minus the capacity required for *check data* and metadata.

user data extent   CONTEXT [Storage System]

The protected space in one or more contiguously located redundancy group stripes in a single redundancy group. In RAID arrays, collections of user data extents comprise the *virtual disks* or *volume sets* presented to the operating environment.

user data extent stripe depth   CONTEXT [Storage System]

The number of consecutive blocks of protected space in a single user data extent that are mapped to consecutive virtual disk block addresses. In principle, each user data extent that is part of a virtual disk may have a different user data extent stripe depth. User data extent stripe depth may differ from the redundancy group stripe depth of the protected space extent in which it resides.

User Datagram Protocol   CONTEXT [Network]

An Internet protocol that provides connectionless *datagram* delivery service to applications. Abbreviated UDP. UDP over *IP* adds the ability to address multiple endpoints within a single network node to IP.

user identification number

A unique number that identifies an individual to a computer system. Abbreviated UID. UIDs are the result of *authentication* processes that use account names, passwords, and possibly other data to verify that a user is actually who she represents herself to be. UIDs are input to *authorization* processes that grant or deny access to resources based on the identification of the requesting user.

valid data byte   CONTEXT [Fibre Channel]

A string of eight contiguous bits within *FC-1* which represents a value between 0 and 255.

valid frame   CONTEXT [Fibre Channel]

A received frame containing a valid Start_of_Frame (SOF), a valid End_of_Frame (EOF), valid data characters, and proper Cyclic Redundancy Check (CRC) of the Frame Header and Data Field.

validity control bit   CONTEXT [Fibre Channel]

A control bit that indicates whether a field is valid. If a validity control bit indicates that a field is invalid, the value in the field is treated as invalid.

VBA   CONTEXT [Storage System]

Acronym for virtual *Virtual Block Address*.

VCI

Acronym for *Virtual Channel Identifier*.

VCSEL   CONTEXT [Fibre Channel]

Acronym for *Vertical Cavity Surface Emitting Laser*.

vendor unique   CONTEXT [Standards]

Aspects of a standard (e.g., functions, codes, etc.) not defined by the standard, but explicitly reserved for private usage between parties using the standard. Different implementations of a standard may assign different meanings to vendor unique aspects of the standard.

verify
verification   CONTEXT [Backup]

The object-by-object comparison of the contents of a *backup image* with the online data objects from which it was made.

versioning   CONTEXT [Backup]

The maintenance of multiple *point-in-time copies* of a collection of data. Versioning is used to minimize recovery time by increasing the number of intermediate checkpoints from which an application can be restarted.

Vertical Cavity Surface Emitting Laser   CONTEXT [Fibre Channel]

A surface emitting laser source fabricated on a planar wafer with emission perpendicular to the wafer.

VI
VIA

Acronyms for *Virtual Interface Architecture*.

virtual block   CONTEXT [Storage System]

A block in the address space presented by a *virtual disk*. Virtual blocks are the atomic units in which a virtual disk's storage capacity is typically presented by RAID arrays to their operating environments.

virtual block address   CONTEXT [Storage System]

The *address* of a virtual block. Virtual block addresses are typically used in hosts' I/O commands addressed to the virtual disks instantiated by RAID arrays. SCSI disk commands addressed to RAID arrays are actually using virtual block addresses in their logical block address fields.

virtual channel identifier   CONTEXT [Network]

A unique numerical tag contained in an *ATM* cell header. Abbreviated VCI. A VCI identifies an ATM virtual channel over which the cell containing it is to travel.

virtual circuit   CONTEXT [Fibre Channel]

1. A set of state information shared by two communicating nodes that is independent of the particular path taken by any particular transmission.

2. A unidirectional path between two communicating N_Ports. Fibre Channel virtual circuits may be limited to a fraction of the bandwidth available on the physical link.

virtual device   CONTEXT [Storage System]

A device presented to an operating environment by *control software* or by a *volume manager*. From an application standpoint, a virtual device is equivalent to a physical one. In some implementations, virtual devices may differ from physical ones at the operating system level (e.g., booting from a host based disk array may not be possible).

virtual disk   CONTEXT [Storage System]

A set of disk blocks presented to an *operating environment* as a range of consecutively numbered logical blocks with disk-like storage and I/O semantics. The virtual disk is the disk array object that most closely resembles a physical disk from the operating environment's viewpoint. *cf. logical disk*

Virtual Interface Architecture

An *API* specification for direct communication among distributed applications developed by Intel, Compaq, and Microsoft. Abbreviated VIA. VIA reduces interprocess communication *latency* by obviating the need for applications to use processor interrupt or operating system paths to intercommunicate, while maintaining security on the communications path. VIA is interconnect neutral. *cf. Fibre Channel Virtual Interface*

virtual path identifier   CONTEXT [Network]

An eight-bit field in an *ATM* cell header that denotes the cell over which the cell should be routed.

virtual tape   CONTEXT [Storage System]

A *virtual device* with the characteristics of a *tape*.

virus   CONTEXT [Security]

A type of programmed threat. A code fragment (not an independent program) that replicates by attaching to another program, and either damaging information directly or causing *denial of service*.

volatility

A property of data. Volatility refers to the certainty that data will be obliterated if certain environmental conditions are not met. For example, data held in DRAM is volatile, since if electrical power to DRAM is cut, the data in it is obliterated. *cf. non-volatility, persistence*

volume   CONTEXT [Storage System]

1. Synonym for *virtual disk*. Used to denote virtual disks created by *volume manager* control software.

2. A piece of *removable media* that has been prepared for use by a *backup manager* (e.g., by the writing of a *media ID*).

volume group   CONTEXT [Backup]

A collection of *removable media* that reside in a single location, for example in a single robot or group of interconnected robots.

volume manager   CONTEXT [Storage System]

Common term for host-based *control software.*

volume pool   CONTEXT [Backup]

A logical collection of removable media designated for a given purpose, for example, for holding the copies of a single repetitive backup job, or for backing up data from a given client or set of clients. A volume pool is an administrative entity, whereas a volume group is a physical one.

volume set   CONTEXT [Storage System]

Synonym for *virtual disk.*

VPI

Acronym for *Virtual Path Identifier.*

vulnerability   CONTEXT [Security]

A weakness in an information system, system security procedures, internal controls, or implementation that could be exploited.

WAN   CONTEXT [Network]

Acronym for wide *Wide Area Network.*

warm spare (disk)   CONTEXT [Storage System]

A spare to which power is applied, and which is not operating, but which is otherwise usable as a hot spare.

warm swap

The substitution of a replacement unit (*RU*) in a system for a defective one, where in order to perform the substitution, the system must be stopped (caused to cease performing its function), but power need not be removed. Warm swaps are manual (performed by humans) physical operations. *cf. automatic swap, cold swap, hot swap*

Wave Division Multiplexing

The splitting of light into a series of "colors" from a few (sparse) to many with a narrow wavelength separation (Dense WDM) for the purpose of carrying simultaneous traffic over the same physical fiber (9 micron usually). Each "color" is a separate data stream.

WBEM   CONTEXT [Management]

Acronym for *Web Based Enterprise Management.*

WDM   CONTEXT [Windows]

Acronym for *Wave Division Multiplexing.*

Acronym for *Windows Driver Model.*

Web Based Enterprise Management   CONTEXT [Management]

Web-Based Enterprise Management is an initiative in the *DMTF.* Abbreviated WBEM. It is a set of technologies that enables interoperable management of an enterprise. WBEM consists of *CIM,* an *XML* DTD defining the tags (XML encodings) to describe the CIM Schema and its data, and a set of *HTTP* operations for exchanging the XML-based information. CIM joins the XML data description language and HTTP transport protocol with an underlying information model, CIM, to create a conceptual view of the enterprise.

well-known address   CONTEXT [Fibre Channel]

An *address identifier* used to access a service provided by a Fibre Channel fabric. A well-known address is not subject to zone restrictions; i.e., a well-known address is always accessible, irrespective of the current active *zone set.*

wide SCSI   CONTEXT [SCSI]

Any form of SCSI using a 16-bit data path. In a wide SCSI implementation, the data transfer rate in MBytes per second is twice the number of *megatransfer*s per second because each transfer cycle transfers two bytes. *cf. fast SCSI, Ultra SCSI, Ultra2 SCSI, Ultra3 SCSI*

wide area network   CONTEXT [Network]

A a communications network that is geographically dispersed and that includes telecommunications links.

Windows Driver Model   CONTEXT [Windows]

A Microsoft specification for device drivers to operate in both the Windows NT and Windows 95/98 operating systems.

Windows Internet Naming Service   CONTEXT [Windows]

A facility of the Windows NT operating system that translates between IP addresses and symbolic names for network nodes and resources.

Windows Management Instrumentation   CONTEXT [Windows]

The name of the Microsoft framework that supports *CIM* and *WBEM.* A set of Windows NT operating system facilities that enable operating system components to provide management information to management agents.

WINS   CONTEXT [Windows]

Acronym for *Windows Internet Naming Service.*

WMI   CONTEXT [Windows]

Acronym for *Windows Management Instrumentation.*

word   CONTEXT [General] [Fibre Channel]

1. An addressable unit of data in computer memory. Typically defined to be 16 consecutively addressed bits. Most processor architectures include arithmetic and logical instructions that operate on words.

2. [Fibre Channel] The smallest Fibre Channel data element consisting of 40 serial bits representing either a flag (K28.5) plus three encoded data bytes (ten encoded bits each) or four ten bit encoded data bytes.

3. [Fibre Channel] A string of four contiguous bytes occurring on boundaries that are zero modulo four from a specified reference. *cf. transmission word*

workgroup

A group of UNIX or Windows computer system users, usually with a common mission or project, that is created for administrative simplicity.

world wide name   CONTEXT [Fibre Channel]

1. A 64-bit unsigned *Name Identifier* which is worldwide unique. *cf. Fibre Channel Name*

2. A unique 48 or 64 bit number assigned by a recognized naming authority (often via block assignment to a manufacturer) that identifies a connection or a set of connections to the network. Abbreviated WWN. A WWN is assigned for the life of a connection (device). Most networking technologies (e.g., Ethernet, FDDI, etc.) use a world wide name convention.

worm   CONTEXT [Security]

An independent program that replicates from computer to computer across network connections, often clogging networks and computer systems as it spreads.

write hole   CONTEXT [Storage System]

A potential data corruption problem for parity RAID technology resulting from an array failure while application I/O is outstanding, followed by an unrelated member disk failure (some time after the array has been returned to service). Data corruption can occur if member data and parity become inconsistent due to the array failure, resulting in a false regeneration when data from the failed member disk is subsequently requested by an application. Parity RAID implementations typically include mechanisms to eliminate the possibility of write holes.

write back cache

A caching technique in which the completion of a write request is signaled as soon as the data is in cache, and actual writing to non-volatile media occurs at a later time. Write back cache includes an inherent risk that an application will take some action predicated on the write completion signal, and a system failure before the data is written to non-volatile media will cause media contents to be inconsistent with that subsequent action. For this reason, good write back cache implementations include mechanisms to preserve cache contents across system failures (including power failures) and to flush the cache at system restart time. *cf. write through cache*

write penalty

Low apparent application write performance to independent access RAID arrays' virtual disks. The write penalty is inherent in independent access RAID data protection techniques, which require multiple member I/O requests for each application write request, and ranges from minimal (mirrored arrays) to substantial (RAID Levels 5 and 6). Many RAID array designs include features such as write-back cache specifically to minimize the write penalty.

write through cache

A caching technique in which the completion of a write request is not signaled until data is safely stored on non-volatile media. Write performance with a write through cache is approximately that of a non-cached system, but if the data written is also held in cache, subsequent read performance may be dramatically improved. *cf. write back cache*

WWN   CONTEXT [Fibre Channel]

Acronym for *World Wide Name*.

X_ID   CONTEXT [Fibre Channel]

Acronym for *Exchange Identifier*.

X3T10   CONTEXT [SCSI]

The ANSI X3T10 technical committee, the standards organization responsible for SCSI standards for communication between computers and storage subsystems and devices.

X3T11   CONTEXT [Fibre Channel]

The ANSI X3T11 technical committee, the standards organization responsible for Fibre Channel and certain other standards for moving electronic data in and out of computers.

XML

Acronym for *eXtensible Markup Language*.

zero filling   CONTEXT [Security]

The process of filling unused storage locations in an information system with the representation of the character denoting "0."

zeroization   CONTEXT [Security]

The process of removing or eliminating the key from a cryptographic program or device.

zone   CONTEXT [Fibre Channel]

A collection of Fibre Channel N_Ports and/or NL_Ports (i.e., device ports) that are permitted to communicate with each other via the fabric. Any two N_Ports and/or NL_Ports that are not members of at least one common zone are not permitted to communicate via the fabric. Zone membership may be specified by: 1) port location on a switch (i.e., Domain_ID and port number); or, 2) the device's N_Port_Name; or, 3) the device's address identifier; or, 4) the device's Node_Name. *Well known addresses* are implicitly included in every zone.

zone set   CONTEXT [Fibre Channel]

A set of zone definitions for a fabric. Zones in a zone set may overlap (i.e., a port may be a member of more than one zone). Fabric management may support switching between zone sets to enforce different access restrictions (e.g., at different times of day).

Zoning   CONTEXT [Fibre Channel]

A method of subdividing a *storage area network* into disjoint *zones*, or subsets of nodes on the network. Storage area network nodes outside a zone are invisible to nodes within the zone. Moreover, with switched *SAN*s, traffic within each zone may be physically isolated from traffic outside the zone.

New Terms Adopted September 2001

block virtualization

The act of applying *virtualization* to one or more block based (storage) services for the purpose of providing a new aggregated, higher level, richer, simpler, secure etc. block service to clients. *cf. file virtualization*

Block virtualization functions can be nested.

A disk drive, RAID system or volume manager all perform some form of block address to (different) block address mapping or aggregation.

file system virtualization

1. The act of aggregating multiple file systems into one large virtual file system. Uses access data objects through the virtual file system; they are unaware of the underlying partitioning.

2. The act of providing additional new or different functionality, e.g., a different file access protocol, on top of one or more existing file systems.

file virtualization

1. The use of *virtualization* to present several underlying file or directory objects as one single composite file.

2. The use of virtualization to provide HSM-like properties in a storage system.

3. The use of virtualization to present an integrated file interface when file data and metadata are managed separately in the storage system. *cf. block virtualization*

host-based virtualization
server-based virtualization

Virtualization implemented in a host computer rather than in a storage subsystem or storage appliance.

Virtualization can be implemented either in host computers, in storage subsystems or storage appliances, or in a specific virtualization appliance in the storage interconnect fabric.

in-band virtualization

Virtualization functions or services that are in the data path. In a system that implements in-band virtualization, virtualization services such as address mapping are performed by the same functional components used to read or write data. *cf. out-of-band virtualization*

infrastructure-based virtualization

Virtualization implemented in the storage fabric, in separate devices designed for the purpose, or in network devices. Examples are separate devices or additional functions in existing devices that aggregate multiple individual file system applications or block storage subsystems into one such virtual service, functions providing transparent block or file system mirroring functions, or functions that provide new security or management services.

out-of-band virtualization

Virtualization functions or services that are not in the data path. Examples are functions related to meta data, the management of data or storage, security management, backup of data, etc.

storage device virtualization

Virtualization of storage devices such as disk, tape drive, RAID shelves, etc.

storage sub-system virtualization

The implementation of *virtualization* in a storage subsystem.

storage virtualization

1. The act of abstracting, hiding, or isolating the internal function of a storage (sub) system or service from applications, computer servers or general network resources for the purpose of enabling application and network independent management of storage or data.

2. The application of *virtualization* to storage services or devices for the purpose of aggregating, hiding complexity or adding new capabilities to lower level storage resources.

Storage can be virtualized simultaneously in multiple layers of a system, for instance to create HSM-like systems.

tape virtualization
tape drive virtualization
tape library virtualization

The act of creating abstracted tape devices by applying *virtualization* to tape drives or tape libraries.

virtualization

The act of integrating one or more (back end) services or functions with additional (front end) functionality for the purpose of providing useful abstractions. Typically virtualization hides some of the back end complexity, or adds and integrates new functionality with existing back end services.

Examples of virtualization are the aggregation of multiple instances of a service into one virtualized service, or to add security to an otherwise insecure service.

Virtualization can be nested or applied to multiple layers of a system.

NOTES

symmetric virtualization

Synonym for in-band virtualization. In-band virtualization is the preferred term.

asymmetric virtualization

Synonym for out-of-band virtualization. Out-of-band virtualization is the preferred term.

Index